THE KUBERNETES WORKSHOP

Learn how to build and run highly scalable workloads on Kubernetes

Zachary Arnold, Sahil Dua, Wei Huang, Faisal Masood, Melony Qin, and Mohammed Abu Taleb

THE KUBERNETES WORKSHOP

Authors: Zachary Arnold, Sahil Dua, Wei Huang, Faisal Masood, Melony Qin, and Mohammed Abu Taleb

Reviewers: Cory Cordell, Simon Krenger, Alok Malakar, and Craig Newton

Managing Editors: Prachi Jain, Clara Joseph, and Aniket Shedge

Acquisitions Editors: Royluis Rodrigues, Kunal Sawant, Sneha Shinde, Archie Vankar, and Alicia Wooding

Production Editor: Salma Patel

First published: September 2020

Production reference: 2020321

ISBN: 978-1-83882-075-6

Published by Packt Publishing Ltd.

Livery Place, 35 Livery Street

Birmingham B3 2PB, UK

WHY LEARN WITH A PACKT WORKSHOP?

LEARN BY DOING

Packt Workshops are built around the idea that the best way to learn something new is by getting hands-on experience. We know that learning a language or technology isn't just an academic pursuit. It's a journey towards the effective use of a new tool—whether that's to kickstart your career, automate repetitive tasks, or just build some cool stuff.

That's why Workshops are designed to get you writing code from the very beginning. You'll start fairly small—learning how to implement some basic functionality—but once you've completed that, you'll have the confidence and understanding to move onto something slightly more advanced.

As you work through each chapter, you'll build your understanding in a coherent, logical way, adding new skills to your toolkit and working on increasingly complex and challenging problems.

CONTEXT IS KEY

All new concepts are introduced in the context of realistic use-cases, and then demonstrated practically with guided exercises. At the end of each chapter, you'll find an activity that challenges you to draw together what you've learned and apply your new skills to solve a problem or build something new.

We believe this is the most effective way of building your understanding and confidence. Experiencing real applications of the code will help you get used to the syntax and see how the tools and techniques are applied in real projects.

BUILD REAL-WORLD UNDERSTANDING

Of course, you do need some theory. But unlike many tutorials, which force you to wade through pages and pages of dry technical explanations and assume too much prior knowledge, Workshops only tell you what you actually need to know to be able to get started making things. Explanations are clear, simple, and to-the-point. So you don't need to worry about how everything works under the hood; you can just get on and use it.

Written by industry professionals, you'll see how concepts are relevant to real-world work, helping to get you beyond "Hello, world!" and build relevant, productive skills. Whether you're studying web development, data science, or a core programming language, you'll start to think like a problem solver and build your understanding and confidence through contextual, targeted practice.

ENJOY THE JOURNEY

Learning something new is a journey from where you are now to where you want to be, and this Workshop is just a vehicle to get you there. We hope that you find it to be a productive and enjoyable learning experience.

Packt has a wide range of different Workshops available, covering the following topic areas:

- Programming languages
- Web development
- Data science, machine learning, and artificial intelligence
- Containers

Once you've worked your way through this Workshop, why not continue your journey with another? You can find the full range online at http://packt.live/2MNkuyl.

If you could leave us a review while you're there, that would be great. We value all feedback. It helps us to continually improve and make better books for our readers, and also helps prospective customers make an informed decision about their purchase.

Thank you,
The Packt Workshop Team

Table of Contents

Chapter 2: An Overview of Kubernetes 55

Chapter 3: kubectl – Kubernetes Command Center 111

Chapter 4: How to Communicate with Kubernetes (API Server) 135

Chapter 7: Kubernetes Controllers 277

Chapter 9: Storing and Reading Data on Disk 347

Chapter 12: Your Application and HA 451

Chapter 13: Runtime and Network Security in Kubernetes 485

Chapter 14: Running Stateful Components in Kubernetes 515

Chapter 15: Monitoring and Autoscaling in Kubernetes 545

Chapter 17: Advanced Scheduling in Kubernetes 623

Chapter 18: Upgrading Your Cluster without Downtime 665

Chapter 19: Custom Resource Definitions in Kubernetes 697

PREFACE

ABOUT THE BOOK

Thanks to its extensive support for managing hundreds of containers that run cloud-native applications, Kubernetes is the most popular open source container orchestration platform that makes cluster management easy. This workshop adopts a practical approach to get you acquainted with the Kubernetes environment and its applications.

Starting with an introduction to the fundamentals of Kubernetes, you'll install and set up your Kubernetes environment. You'll understand how to write YAML files and deploy your first simple web application container using Pod. You'll then assign human-friendly names to Pods, explore various Kubernetes entities and functions, and discover when to use them. As you work through the chapters, this Kubernetes book will show you how you can make full-scale use of Kubernetes by applying a variety of techniques for designing components and deploying clusters. You'll also get to grips with security policies for limiting access to certain functions inside the cluster. Toward the end of the book, you'll get a rundown of Kubernetes advanced features for building your own controller and upgrading to a Kubernetes cluster without downtime.

By the end of this workshop, you'll be able to manage containers and run cloud-based applications efficiently using Kubernetes.

AUDIENCE

Whether you are new to the world of web programming or are an experienced developer or software engineer looking to use Kubernetes for managing and scaling containerized applications, you'll find this workshop useful. A basic understanding of Docker and containerization is necessary to make the most of this book.

ABOUT THE CHAPTERS

Chapter 1, Introduction to Kubernetes and Containers, begins with containerization technologies as well as various underlying Linux technologies that enable containerization. The chapter ends by introducing Kubernetes into the picture, while laying out the advantages it brings to the table.

Chapter 2, An Overview of Kubernetes, gives you your first hands-on introduction to Kubernetes and provides an overview of the architecture of Kubernetes.

Chapter 3, kubectl – Kubernetes Command Center, lays out the various ways of using kubectl while underlining the principle of declarative management.

Chapter 4, How to Communicate with Kubernetes (API Server), dives into the details of the Kubernetes API server and the various ways of communicating with it.

Chapter 5, Pods, introduces the basic Kubernetes object used to deploy any application.

Chapter 6, Labels and Annotations, covers the basic mechanism used in Kubernetes to group, classify, and link different objects.

Chapter 7, Kubernetes Controllers, introduces various Kubernetes controllers, such as Deployments and StatefulSets, among others, which are some of the key enablers of the declarative management approach.

Chapter 8, Service Discovery, describes how you can make different Kubernetes objects discoverable within the cluster as well as from outside the cluster.

Chapter 9, Storing and Reading Data on Disk, explains the various data storage abstractions offered by Kubernetes to enable applications to read and store data on disks.

Chapter 10, ConfigMaps and Secrets, teaches you how to decouple application configuration data from the application itself, while looking at the advantages of taking this approach.

Chapter 11, Build Your Own HA Cluster, walks you through setting up your own highly available, multi-node Kubernetes cluster on the **Amazon Web Services** (**AWS**) platform.

Chapter 12, Your Application and HA, lays out some concepts behind continuous integration using Kubernetes and demonstrates a few of them using a highly available, multi-node, managed Kubernetes cluster running on **Amazon Elastic Kubernetes Service**.

Chapter 13, Runtime and Network Security in Kubernetes, gives you an overview of the ways in which your application and cluster can be attacked, before covering the access control and security features offered by Kubernetes.

Chapter 14, Running Stateful Components in Kubernetes, teaches you how to properly use different Kubernetes abstractions to reliably deploy stateful applications.

Chapter 15, Monitoring and Autoscaling in Kubernetes, covers the ways in which you can monitor different Kubernetes objects and then use that information to scale the capacity of your cluster.

Chapter 16, Kubernetes Admission Controllers, describes how Kubernetes allows us to extend the functionalities provided by the API server to implement custom policies before a request is accepted by the API server.

Chapter 17, Advanced Scheduling in Kubernetes, describes how the scheduler places pods on the Kubernetes cluster. You will use advanced features to influence scheduler placement decisions for the pods.

Chapter 18, Upgrading Your Cluster without Downtime, teaches you how you can upgrade your Kubernetes platform to a newer version without suffering any downtime for your platform or application.

Chapter 19, Custom Resource Definitions in Kubernetes, shows you one of the main ways in which to extend the functionalities provided by Kubernetes. You will see how custom resources allow you to implement concepts specific to your own domain on your cluster.

> **NOTE**
>
> The solution to the activities presented in the chapters can be found at this address: https://packt.live/304PEoD.

CONVENTIONS

Code words in text, database table names, folder names, filenames, file extensions, pathnames, dummy URLs, and user input are shown as follows: "Create a file named **sample-pod.yaml** in your current working directory."

A block of code, a terminal command, or text to create a YAML file is set as follows:

```
kubectl -n webhooks create secret tls webhook-server-tls \
--cert "tls.crt" \
--key "tls.key"
```

New important words are shown like this: "Kubernetes provides this capability via **Admission Controllers**."

Key parts of code snippets are highlighted as follows:

```
kind: Pod
metadata:
  name: infra-libraries-application-staging
  namespace: metadata-activity
  labels:
    environment: staging
    team: infra-libraries
  annotations:
      team-link: "https://jira-link/team-link-2"
spec:
  containers:
```

Words that you see on the screen, for example, in menus or dialog boxes, appear in the text like this: "On the left sidebar, click on **`Configuration`** and then on **`Data Sources`**."

Long code snippets are truncated and the corresponding names of the code files on GitHub are placed at the top of the truncated code. The permalinks to the entire code are placed below the code snippet. It should look as follows:

`mutatingcontroller.go`

```
//create the response with patch bytes
var admissionResponse *v1beta1.AdmissionResponse
admissionResponse = &v1beta1.AdmissionResponse {
    allowed: true,
    Patch:   patchBytes,
    PatchType: func() *v1beta1.PatchType {
        pt := v1beta1.PatchTypeJSONPatch
        return &pt
    }(),
}
```

`The complete code for this example can be found at` https://packt.live/35ieNiX.

SETTING UP YOUR ENVIRONMENT

Before we explore the book in detail, we need to set up specific software and tools. In the following section, we shall see how to do that.

HARDWARE REQUIREMENTS

You need at least a dual core CPU with virtualization support, 4 GB of memory, and 20 GB of free disk space.

OPERATING SYSTEM REQUIREMENTS

Our recommended operating system is Ubuntu 20.04 LTS or macOS 10.15. If you are using Windows, you can dual boot Ubuntu. We have provided the instructions for that at the end of this section.

VIRTUALIZATION

You need to have virtualization features enabled on your hardware as well as your operating system.

In Linux, you can run the following command to check whether virtualization is enabled:

```
grep -E --color 'vmx|svm' /proc/cpuinfo
```

You should get a non-empty response to this command. If you get an empty response, then you don't have virtualization enabled.

In macOS, run the following command:

```
sysctl -a | grep -E --color 'machdep.cpu.features|VMX'
```

If virtualization is enabled, you should be able to see **VMX** in your output.

> **NOTE**
>
> You will not be able to follow the instructions in the book if your host environment is virtualized, since Minikube (by default) runs all Kubernetes components in a virtual machine, which will not work if the host environment itself is virtualized. It is possible to use Minikube without a hypervisor, but your results may sometimes be different compared to our demonstrations in this book. Therefore, our recommendation is that one of the recommended operating systems is directly installed on your machine.

INSTALLATION AND SETUP

This section lists installation instructions for all the software that you will need for this book. Since we are recommending Ubuntu, we will use the APT package manager to install most of the required software in Ubuntu.

For macOS, we recommend that you use Homebrew for convenience. You can install it by running this script in your terminal:

```
/bin/bash -c "$(curl -fsSL https://raw.githubusercontent.com/Homebrew/
install/master/install.sh)"
```

The terminal output for this script will show you what changes will be applied and then ask for your confirmation. Once confirmed, the installation can be completed.

UPDATING YOUR PACKAGE LISTS

Before you use APT to install any packages in Ubuntu, make sure that your package lists are up to date. Use the following command:

```
sudo apt update
```

Furthermore, you may choose to upgrade any upgradable packages on your machine by using the following command:

```
sudo apt upgrade
```

Similarly, in the case of macOS, update the package lists for Homebrew using the following command:

```
brew update
```

INSTALLING GIT

The code bundle for this workshop is available on our GitHub repository. You can use Git to clone the repository to get all the code files.

Use the following command to install Git on Ubuntu:

```
sudo apt install git-all
```

If you use Xcode on macOS, it is likely that you may already have Git installed. You can check that by running this command:

```
git --version
```

If you get a **`Command not found`** error, then you don't have it installed. You can install it via Homebrew using this command:

```
brew install git
```

JQ

jq is a JSON parser that is useful for extracting any information from API responses in JSON format. You can install it using the following command on Ubuntu:

```
sudo apt install jq
```

You can use the following command for installation on macOS:

```
brew install jq
```

TREE

Tree is a package that will allow you to see the directory structure in the terminal. You can install it using the following command on Ubuntu:

```
sudo apt install tree
```

You can use the following command for installation on macOS:

```
brew install tree
```

THE AWS CLI

The AWS command line tool is a CLI tool that you can use from your terminal to manage your AWS resources. You can install it using the installation instructions at this URL: https://docs.aws.amazon.com/cli/latest/userguide/install-cliv2.html.

MINIKUBE AND KUBECTL

Minikube allows us to create a single-node Kubernetes cluster for learning and testing purposes. kubectl is a command line interface tool that allows us to communicate with our cluster. You will find detailed installation instructions for these tools in *Chapter 2, An Overview of Kubernetes*.

Even if you have Minikube installed already, we recommend that you work with the version that is specified in *Chapter 2, An Overview of Kubernetes*, in order to guarantee the reproducibility of all instructions in this book.

Minikube requires you to have a hypervisor installed. We will go with VirtualBox.

VIRTUALBOX

VirtualBox is an open source hypervisor that can be used by Minikube to virtualize a node for our cluster. Use the following command to install VirtualBox on Ubuntu:

```
sudo apt install virtualbox
```

For installation on macOS, first get the appropriate file from this link:

https://www.virtualbox.org/wiki/Downloads.

Then, follow the installation instructions mentioned here:

https://www.virtualbox.org/manual/ch02.html#installation-mac.

DOCKER

Docker is the default containerization engine used by Kubernetes. You will learn more about Docker in *Chapter 1, Introduction to Kubernetes and Containers*.

To install Docker, follow the installation instructions at this link:

https://docs.docker.com/engine/install/.

To install Docker in Mac, following the installation instructions at the following link:

https://docs.docker.com/docker-for-mac/install/.

To install Docker in Ubuntu, following the installation instructions at the following link:

https://docs.docker.com/engine/install/ubuntu/.

GO

Go is a programming language that is used to build the applications demonstrated in this book. Also, Kubernetes is written in Go. To install Go on your machine, use the following command for Ubuntu:

```
sudo apt install golang-go
```

For installation on macOS, use the following instructions:

1. Use the following command to install Go:

```
brew install golang
```

> **NOTE**
>
> The code is tested with Go versions 1.13 and 1.14. Please make sure that you have these versions although the code is expected to work for all 1.x versions.

2. Now, we need to set a few environment variables. Use the following commands:

```
mkdir - p $HOME/go
export GOPATH=$HOME/go
export GOROOT="$(brew --prefix golang)/libexec"
export PATH="$PATH:${GOPATH}/bin:${GOROOT}/bin"
```

KOPS

kops is a command line interface tool that allows you to set up a Kubernetes cluster on AWS. The actual process of installing Kubernetes using kops is covered in *Chapter 11, Build Your Own HA Cluster*. To ensure the reproducibility of the instructions given in this book, we recommend that you install kops version 1.15.1.

For installation on Ubuntu, follow these steps:

1. Download the binary for kops version 1.15.1 using the following command:

```
curl -LO https://github.com/kubernetes/kops/releases/download/1.15.0/
kops-linux-amd64
```

2. Now, make the binary executable using the following command:

```
chmod +x kops-linux-amd64
```

3. Add the executable to your path:

```
sudo mv kops-linux-amd64 /usr/local/bin/kops
```

4. Check whether kops has been successfully installed by running the following command:

```
kops version
```

If kops has been successfully installed, you should get a response stating the version as 1.15.0.

For installation on macOS, follow these steps:

1. Download the binary for kops version 1.15.1 using the following command:

```
curl -LO https://github.com/kubernetes/kops/releases/download/1.15.0/
kops-darwin-amd64
```

2. Now, make the binary executable using the following command:

```
chmod +x kops-darwin-amd64
```

3. Add the executable to your path:

```
sudo mv kops-darwin-amd64 /usr/local/bin/kops
```

4. Check whether kops has been successfully installed by running the following command:

```
kops version
```

If kops has been successfully installed, you should get a response stating the version as 1.15.0.

DUAL-BOOTING UBUNTU FOR WINDOWS USERS

In this section, you will find instructions on how to dual-boot Ubuntu if you are running Windows.

> **NOTE**
>
> Before installing any operating system, it is highly recommended that you back up your system state as well as all of your data.

RESIZING PARTITIONS

If you have Windows set up on your machine, it is most likely that your hard disk is completely utilized – that is, all of the available space is partitioned and formatted. We need to have some unallocated space on the hard disk. Hence, we will resize a partition with plenty of free space to make space for our Ubuntu partitions:

1. Open the Computer Management utility. Press **`Win + R`** and enter **`compmgmt.msc`**:

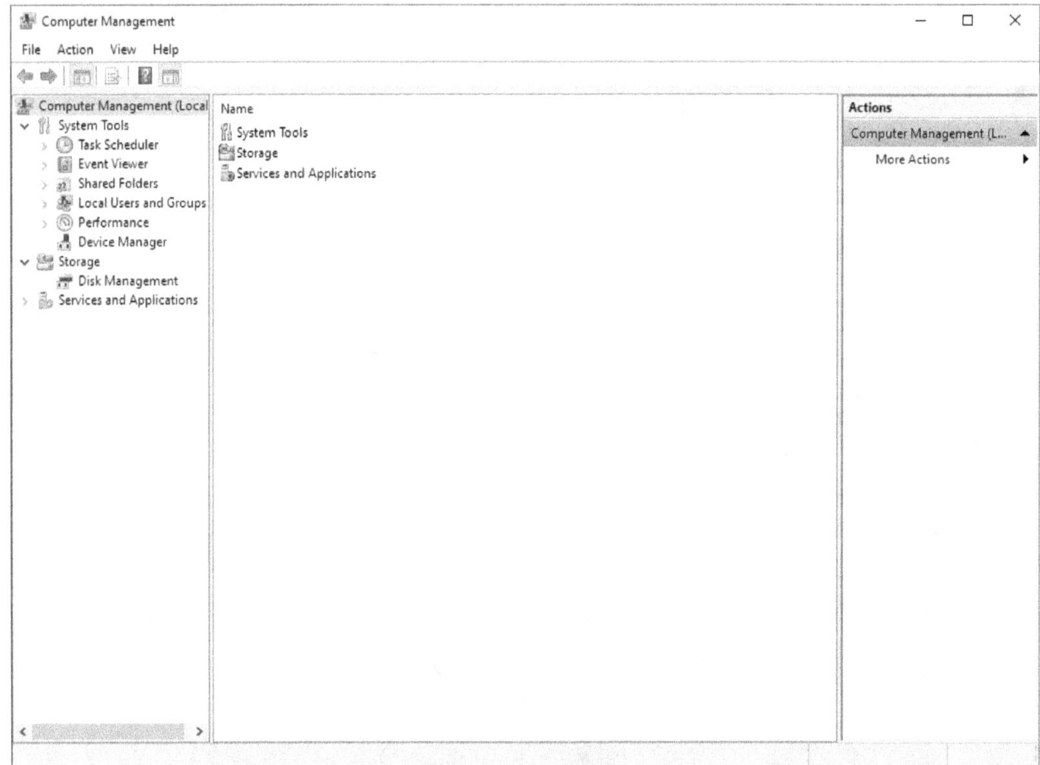

Figure 0.1: The Computer Management utility on Windows

2. In the left side pane, go to the **`Storage > Disk Management`** option as shown here:

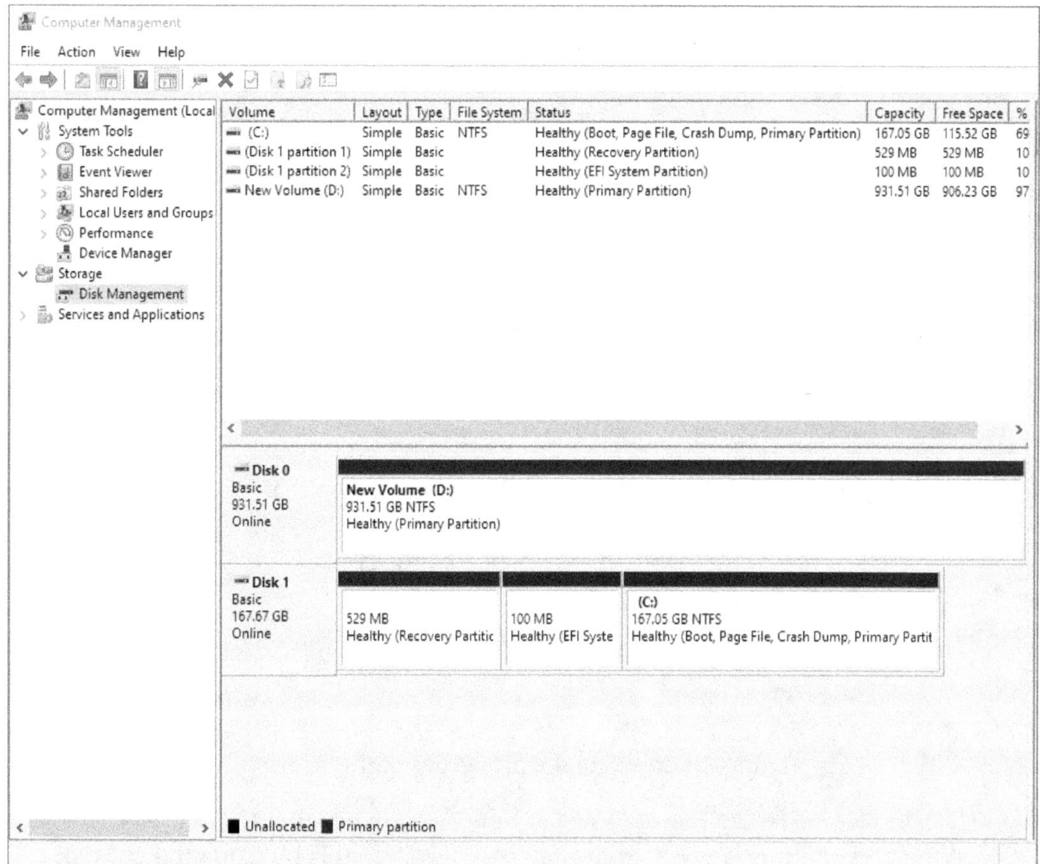

Figure 0.2: Disk Management

You will see a summary of all your partitions in the lower half of the screen. You can also see the drive letters associated with all of the partitions and information about the Windows boot drive. If you have a partition that has plenty of free space (20 GB +) and is neither the boot drive (`C:`), nor the recovery partition, nor the EFI system partition, this will be the ideal option to choose. If there's no such partition, then you can resize the `C:` drive.

3. In this example, we will choose the **`D:`** drive. You can right-click on any partition and open **`Properties`** to check the free space available:

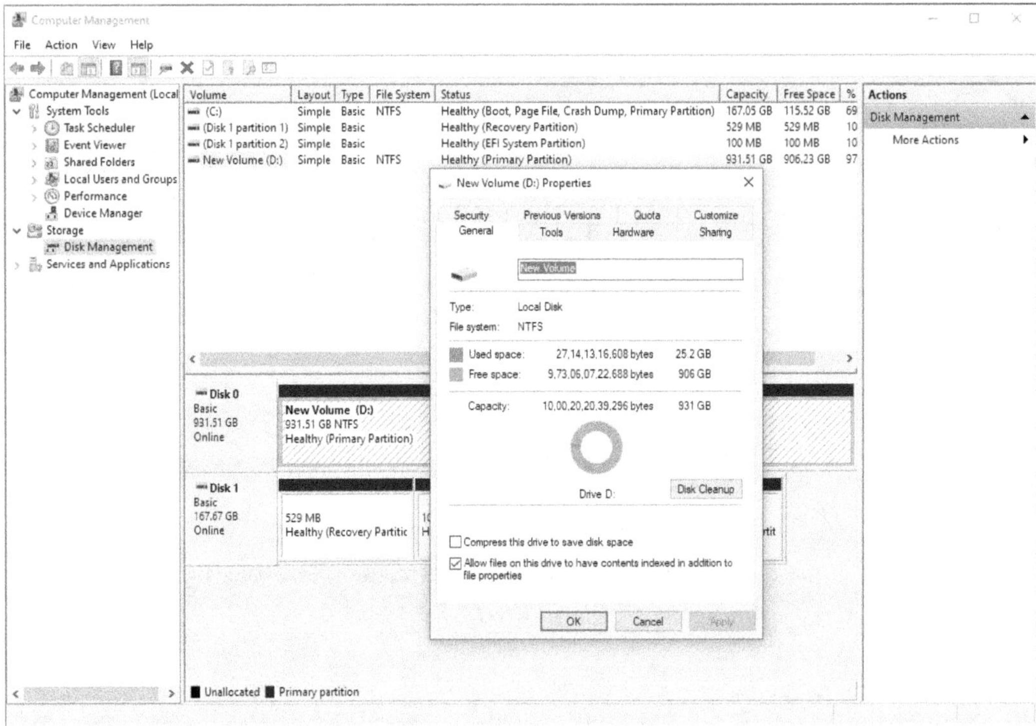

Figure 0.3: Checking the properties of the D: drive

Now, before we resize the partition, we need to ensure that there are no errors on the filesystem or any hardware faults. We will do this by using the **chkdsk** utility on Windows.

4. Open Command Prompt by pressing **`Win + R`** and entering **`cmd.exe`**. Now, run the following command:

```
chkdsk D: /f
```

Replace the drive letter with the one that you want to use. You should see a response similar to the following:

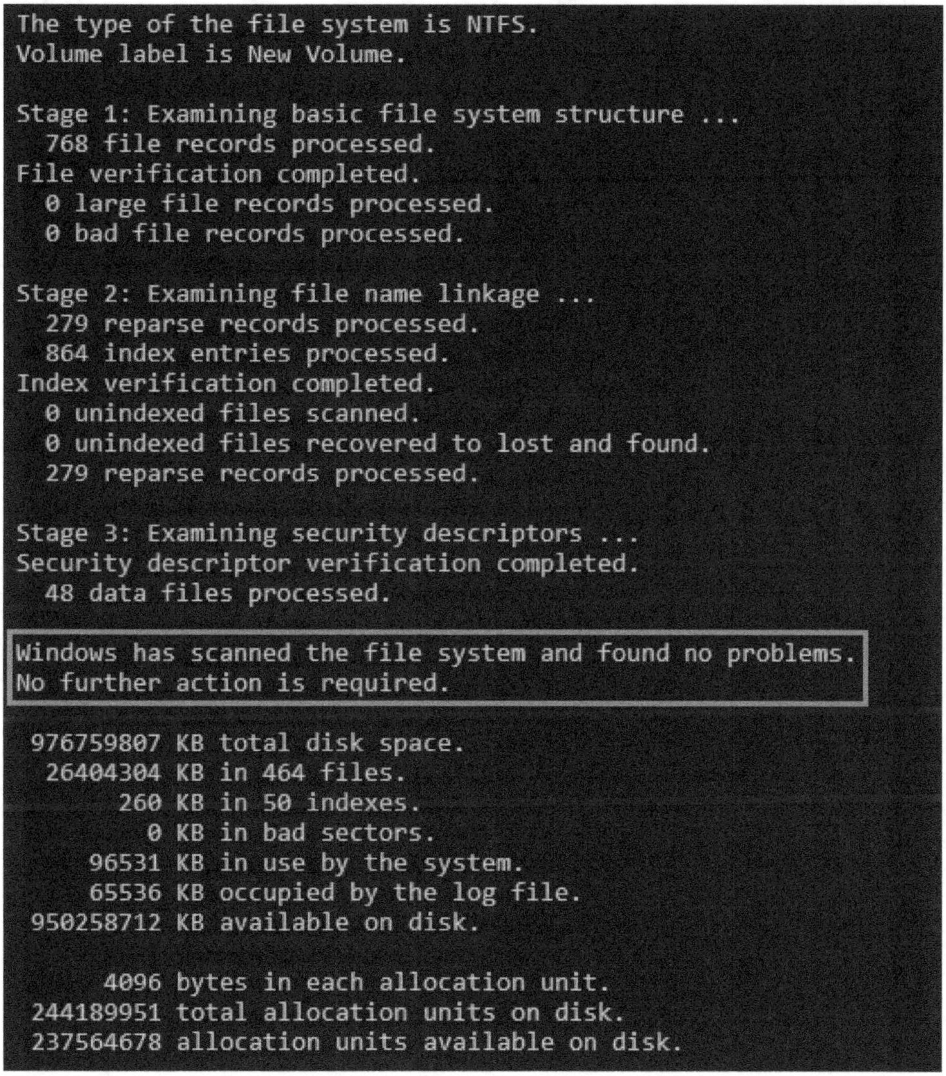

```
The type of the file system is NTFS.
Volume label is New Volume.

Stage 1: Examining basic file system structure ...
  768 file records processed.
File verification completed.
  0 large file records processed.
  0 bad file records processed.

Stage 2: Examining file name linkage ...
  279 reparse records processed.
  864 index entries processed.
Index verification completed.
  0 unindexed files scanned.
  0 unindexed files recovered to lost and found.
  279 reparse records processed.

Stage 3: Examining security descriptors ...
Security descriptor verification completed.
  48 data files processed.

Windows has scanned the file system and found no problems.
No further action is required.

 976759807 KB total disk space.
  26404304 KB in 464 files.
       260 KB in 50 indexes.
         0 KB in bad sectors.
     96531 KB in use by the system.
     65536 KB occupied by the log file.
 950258712 KB available on disk.

      4096 bytes in each allocation unit.
 244189951 total allocation units on disk.
 237564678 allocation units available on disk.
```

Figure 0.4: Scanning a drive for any filesystem errors

Note that in this screenshot, Windows reports that it has scanned the filesystem and found no problems. If any problems are encountered for your case, you should get them fixed first to prevent the loss of data.

5. Now, come back to the **Computer Management** window, right-click on the desired drive, and then click on **Shrink Volume**, as shown here:

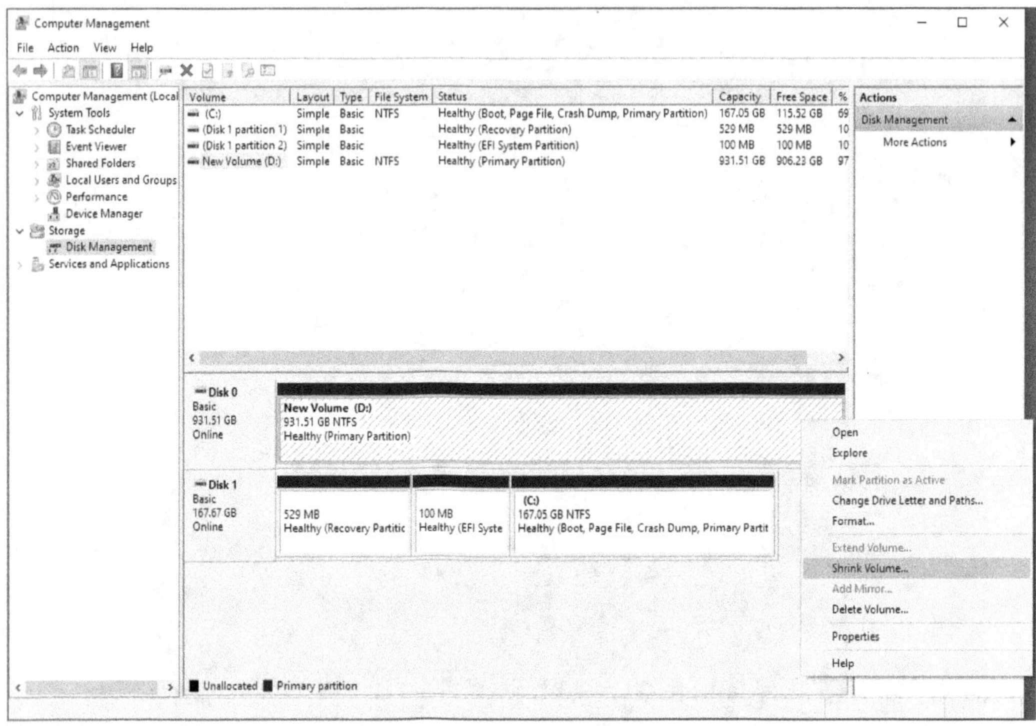

Figure 0.5: Opening the Shrink Volume dialog box

6. In the prompt window, enter the amount of space you want to clear in the only field that you can edit. In this example, we are clearing approximately 25 GB of disk space by shrinking our **D:** drive:

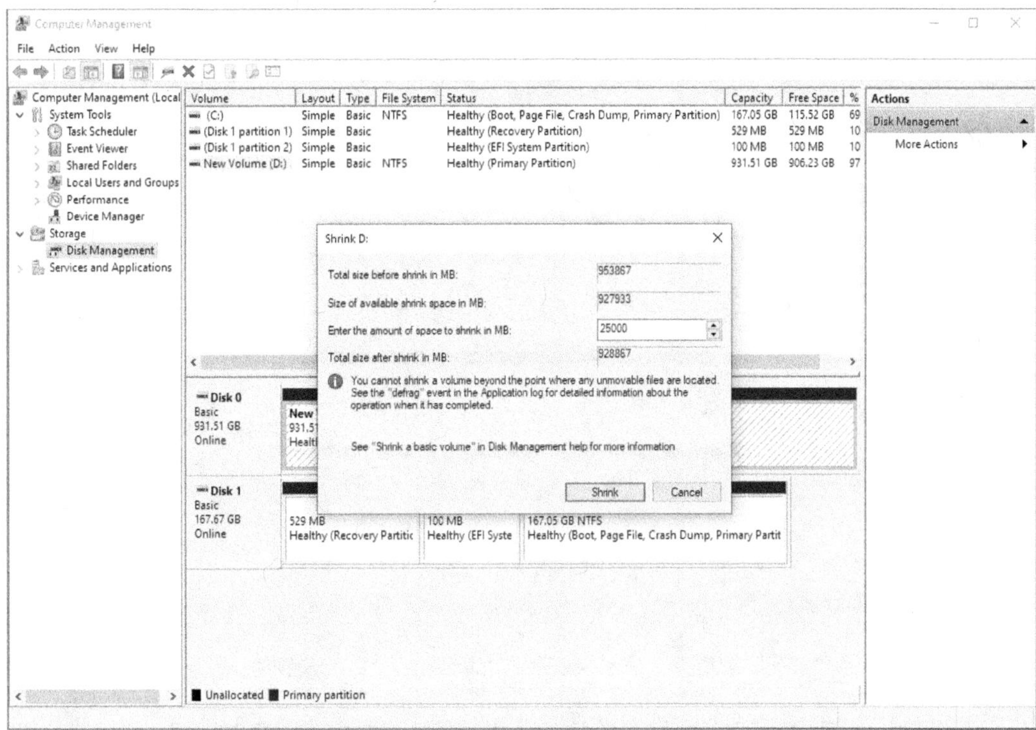

Figure 0.6: Clearing 25 GB by shrinking the existing volume

7. After you shrink your drive, you should be able to see unallocated space on your drive, as seen here:

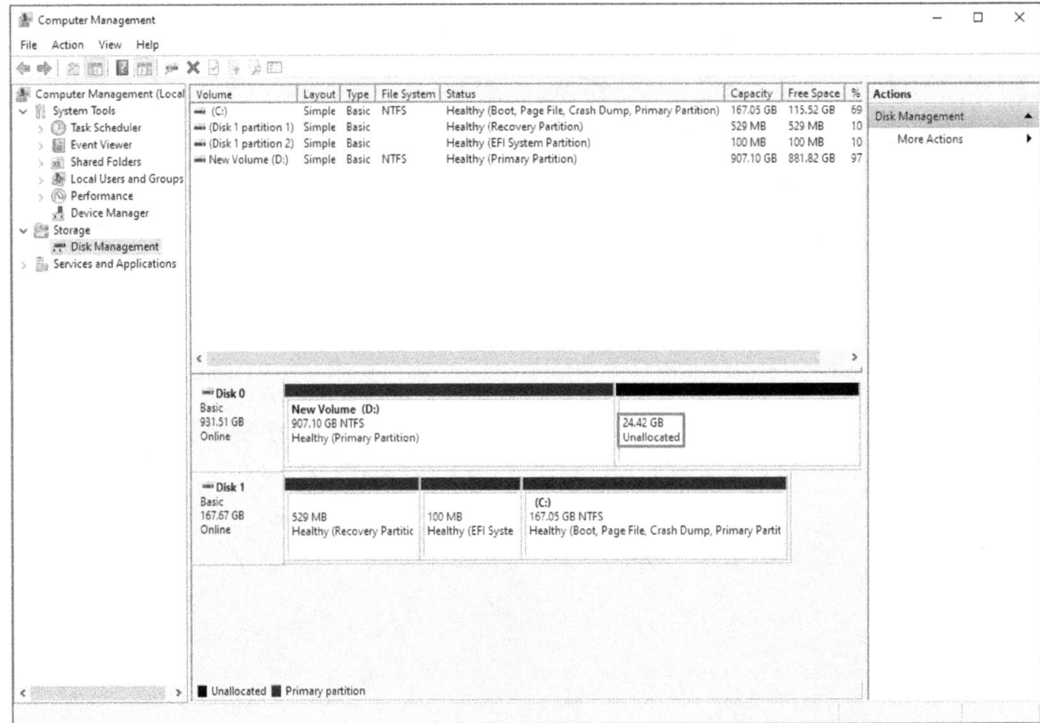

Figure 0.7: Unallocated space after shrinking the volume

Now we are ready to install Ubuntu. But first, we need to download it and create a bootable USB, which is one of the most convenient installation media.

CREATING A BOOTABLE USB DRIVE TO INSTALL UBUNTU

You will need a flash drive with a minimum capacity of 4 GB. Note that all the data on this will be erased:

1. Download the ISO image for Ubuntu Desktop from this link: https://releases.ubuntu.com/20.04/.

2. Next, we need to burn the ISO image to a USB flash disk and create a bootable USB drive. There are many tools available for this, and you can use any of them. In this example, we are using Rufus, which is free and open source. You can get it from this link: https://www.fosshub.com/Rufus.html.

3. Once you have installed Rufus, plug in your USB flash disk and open Rufus. Ensure that the proper **`Device`** option is selected, as shown in the following screenshot.
4. Press the **`SELECT`** button under **`Boot selection`** and then open the Ubuntu 18.04 image that you have downloaded.
5. The choice for **`Partition scheme`** will depend on how your BIOS and your disk drive are configured. **`GPT`** will be the best option for most modern systems, while **`MBR`** will be compatible with older systems:

Figure 0.8: Configurations for Rufus

6. You may leave all other options on default, and then press **START**. After completion, close Rufus. You now have a bootable USB drive ready to install Ubuntu.

INSTALLING UBUNTU

Now, we will use the bootable USB drive to install Ubuntu:

1. To install Ubuntu, boot using the bootable installation media that we just created. In most cases, you should be able to do that by simply having the USB drive plugged in while starting up your machine. If you don't automatically boot into the Ubuntu setup, go into your BIOS settings and ensure that your USB device is at the highest boot priority and that Secure Boot is turned off. The instructions for entering the BIOS setup are usually displayed on the splash screen (the screen with your PC manufacturer logo when you start up your computer) that is displayed during POST checks. You may also have the option to enter a boot menu while starting up. Usually, you have to hold down **Delete**, **F1**, **F2**, **F12**, or some other key while your PC boots up. It depends on your motherboard's BIOS.

   You should see a screen with a **Try Ubuntu** or **Install Ubuntu** option. If you don't see this screen, and instead you see a shell with a message that begins with **Minimal BASH Like Line Editing is Supported...**, then it is likely that there may have been some data corruption while downloading the ISO file or creating your bootable USB drive. Check the integrity of the downloaded ISO file by calculating the **MD5**, **SHA1**, or **SHA256** hash of your downloaded file and comparing it to the ones you can find in the files named **MD5SUMS**, **SHA1SUMS**, or **SHA256SUMS** on the Ubuntu download page mentioned earlier. Then, repeat the steps in the previous section to reformat and recreate the bootable USB drive.

   If you have set the highest boot priority to the correct USB device in the BIOS and you are still unable to boot using your USB device (your system may just ignore it and boot into Windows instead), then there are two most likely issues:

   - The USB drive was not properly configured to be recognized as a bootable device or the GRUB bootloader was not properly set up. Verifying the integrity of your downloaded image and recreating the bootable USB drive should fix this in most cases.

   - You have chosen the wrong **Partition scheme** option for your system configuration. Try the other one and recreate the USB drive.

2. Once you boot your machine using the USB drive, select **`Install Ubuntu`**.
3. Choose the language that you want and then press **`Continue`**.
4. On the next screen, choose the appropriate keyboard layout and continue to the next screen.
5. On the next screen, select **`Normal installation`**.

   Check the **`Download updates while installing Ubuntu`** and **`Install third-party software for graphics and Wi-Fi hardware and additional media formats`** options.

   Then, continue to the next screen.
6. On the next screen, select **`Install Ubuntu alongside Windows Boot Manager`**, and then click **`Install now`**. You will see a prompt describing the changes that Ubuntu will make to your system, such as the new partitions that will be created. Confirm the changes and proceed to the next screen.
7. On the next screen, choose your region and press **`Continue`**.
8. On the next screen, set your name (optional), username, computer name, and password, and then press **`Continue`**.

   The installation should now begin. It will take a while depending on your system configurations. Once the installation is complete, you will be prompted to restart your computer. Unplug your USB drive, and then click **`Restart Now`**.

   If you forget to remove your USB drive, you may boot back into the Ubuntu installation. In that case, just exit the setup. If a live instance of Ubuntu has been started up, restart your machine. Remember to remove the USB drive this time.

   If, after restarting, you boot directly into Windows with no option to choose the operating system, the likely issue is that the GRUB bootloader installed by Ubuntu has not taken precedence over the Windows bootloader. In some systems, the precedence/priority for bootloaders on your hard disk is set in the BIOS. You will need to explore your BIOS settings menu to find the appropriate setting. It may be named something similar to **`UEFI Hard Disk Drive Priorities`**. Ensure that **`GRUB/Ubuntu`** is set to the highest priority.

OTHER REQUIREMENTS

Docker Hub account: You can create a free Docker account at this link: https://hub.docker.com/.

AWS account: You will need your own AWS account and some basic knowledge about using AWS. You can create an account here: https://aws.amazon.com/.

> **NOTE**
>
> The requirements of the exercises and activities in this book go beyond the AWS free tier, so you should be aware that you will incur bills for the use of the cloud service. You can use the pricing information available here: https://aws.amazon.com/pricing/.

ACCESSING THE CODE FILES

You can find the complete code files of this book at https://packt.live/3bE3zWY.

After installing Git, you can clone the repository using the following command:

```
git clone https://github.com/PacktWorkshops/Kubernetes-Workshop
cd Kubernetes-Workshop
```

If you have any issues or questions about installation, please email us at **workshops@packt.com**.

1

INTRODUCTION TO KUBERNETES AND CONTAINERS

OVERVIEW

The chapter begins by describing the evolution of software development and delivery, beginning with running software on bare-metal machines, through to the modern approach of containerization. We will also take a look at the underlying Linux technologies that enable containerization. By the end of the chapter, you will be able to run a basic Docker container from an image. You will also be able to package a custom application to make your own Docker image. Next, we will take a look at how we can control the resource limits and group for a container. Finally, the end of the chapter describes why we need to have a tool such as Kubernetes, along with a short introduction to its strengths.

INTRODUCTION

About a decade ago, there was a lot of discussion over software development paradigms such as service-oriented architecture, agile development, and software design patterns. In hindsight, those were all great ideas, but only a few of them were practically adopted a decade ago.

One of the major reasons for the lack of adoption of these paradigms is that the underlying infrastructure couldn't offer the resources or capabilities for abstracting fine-grained software components and managing an optimal software development life cycle. Hence, a lot of duplicated efforts were still required for resolving some common issues of software development such as managing software dependencies and consistent environments, software testing, packaging, upgrading, and scaling.

In recent years, with Docker at the forefront, containerization technology has provided a new encapsulation mechanism that allows you to bundle your application, its runtime, and its dependencies, and also brings in a new angle to view the development of software. By using containerization technology, the underlying infrastructure gets abstracted away so that applications can be seamlessly moved among heterogeneous environments. However, along with the rising volume of containers, you may need orchestration tools to help you to manage their interactions with each other as well as to optimize the utilization of the underlying hardware.

That's where Kubernetes comes into play. Kubernetes provides a variety of options to automate deployment, scaling, and the management of containerized applications. It has seen explosive adoption in recent years and has become the de-facto standard in the container orchestration field.

As this is the first chapter of this book, we will start with a brief history of software development over the past few decades, and then illustrate the origins of containers and Kubernetes. We will focus on explaining what problems they can solve, and **three key reasons** why their adoption has seen a considerable rise in recent years.

THE EVOLUTION OF SOFTWARE DEVELOPMENT

Along with the evolution of virtualization technology, it's common for companies to use **virtual machines** (**VMs**) to manage their software products, either in the public cloud or an on-premises environment. This brings huge benefits such as automatic machine provisioning, better hardware resource utilization, resource abstraction, and more. More critically, for the first time, it employs the separation of computing, network, and storage resources to unleash the power of software development from the tediousness of hardware management. Virtualization also brings in the ability to manipulate the underlying infrastructure programmatically. So, from a system administrator and developer's perspective, they can better streamline the workflow of software maintenance and development. This is a big move in the history of software development.

However, in the past decade, the scope and life cycle of software development have changed vastly. Earlier, it was not uncommon for software to be developed in big monolithic chunks with a slow-release cycle. Nowadays, to catch up with the rapid changes of business requirements, a piece of software may need to be broken down into individual fine-grained subcomponents, and each component may need to have its release cycle so that it can be released as often as possible to get feedback from the market earlier. Moreover, we may want each component to be scalable and cost-effective.

So, how does this impact application development and deployment? In comparison to the bare-metal era, adopting VMs doesn't help much since VMs don't change the granularity of how different components are managed; the entire software is still deployed on a single machine, only it is a virtual one instead of a physical one. Making a number of interdependent components work together is still not an easy task.

A straightforward idea here is to add an abstraction layer to connect the machines with the applications running on them. This is so that application developers would only need to focus on the business logic to build the applications. Some examples of this are **Google App Engine** (**GAE**) and Cloud Foundry.

The **first issue** with these solutions is the lack of consistent development experience among different environments. Developers develop and test applications on their machines with their local dependencies (both at the programming language and operating system level); while in a production environment, the application has to rely on another set of dependencies underneath. And we still haven't talked about the software components that need the cooperation of different developers in different teams.

The **second issue** is that the hard boundary between applications and the underlying infrastructure would limit the applications from being highly performant, especially if the application is sensitive to the storage, compute, or network resources. For instance, you may want the application to be deployed across multiple availability zones (isolated geographic locations within data centers where cloud resources are managed), or you may want some applications to coexist, or not to coexist, with other particular applications. Alternatively, you may want some applications to adhere to particular hardware (for example, solid-state drives). In such cases, it becomes hard to focus on the functionality of the app without exposing the topological characteristics of the infrastructure to upper applications.

In fact, in the life cycle of software development, there is no clear boundary between the infrastructure and applications. What we want to achieve is to manage the applications automatically, while making optimal use of the infrastructure.

So, how could we achieve this? Docker (which we will introduce later in this chapter) solves the **first issue** by leveraging Linux containerization technologies to encapsulate the application and its dependencies. It also introduces the concept of Docker images to make the software aspect of the application runtime environment lightweight, reproducible, and portable.

The **second issue** is more complicated. That's where Kubernetes comes in. Kubernetes leverages a battle-tested design rationale called the Declarative API to abstract the infrastructure as well as each phase of application delivery such as deployment, upgrades, redundancy, scaling, and more. It also offers a series of building blocks for users to choose, orchestrate, and compose into the eventual application. We will gradually move on to study Kubernetes, which is the core of this book, toward the end of this chapter.

> **NOTE**
>
> If not specified particularly, the term "container" might be used interchangeably with "Linux container" throughout this book.

VIRTUAL MACHINES VERSUS CONTAINERS

A **virtual machine** (**VM**), as the name implies, aims to emulate a physical computer system. Technically, VMs are provisioned by a hypervisor, and the hypervisor runs on the host OS. The following diagram illustrates this concept:

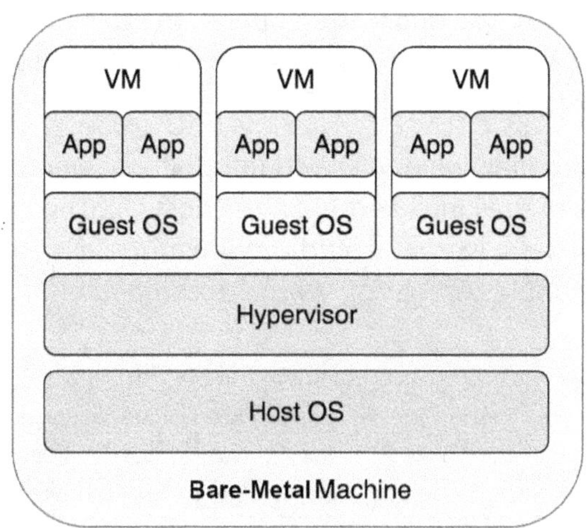

Figure 1.1: Running applications on VMs

Here, the VMs have full OS stacks, and the OS running on the VM (called the **`Guest OS`**) must rely on the underlying hypervisor to function. The applications and operating system reside and run inside the VM. Their operations go through the guest OS's kernel and are then translated to the system calls by the hypervisor, which are eventually executed on the host OS.

Containers, on the other hand, don't need a hypervisor underneath. By leveraging some Linux containerization technologies such as namespaces and cgroups (which we will revisit later), each container runs independently on the host OS. The following diagram illustrates containerization, taking Docker containers as an example:

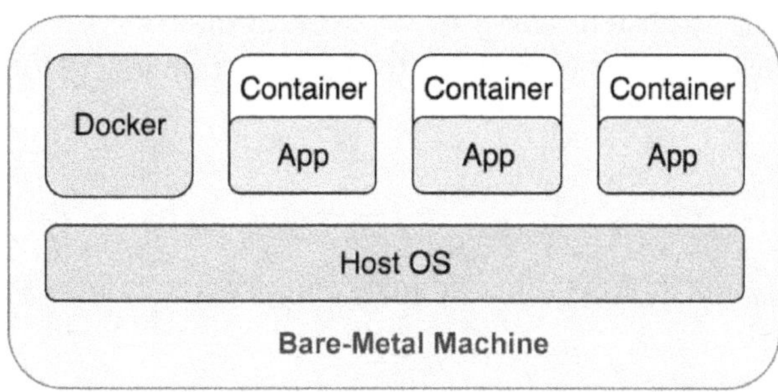

Figure 1.2: Running applications in containers

It's worth mentioning that we put Docker beside the containers instead of between the containers and the host OS. That's because, technically, it's not necessary to have Docker Engine hosting those containers. Docker Engine plays more of a manager role to manage the life cycle of the containers. It is also inappropriate to liken Docker Engine to the hypervisor because once a container is up and running, we don't need an extra layer to "translate" the application operations to be understandable by the host OS. From *Figure 1.2*, you can also tell that applications inside the containers are essentially running directly on the host OS.

When we spin up a container, we don't need to bring up an entire OS; instead, it leverages the features of the Linux kernel on the host OS. Therefore, containers start up faster, function with less overhead, and require much less space compared to VMs. The following is a table comparing VMs with containers:

Virtual Machines	**Containers**
Heavy on resource requirements	Light on resource requirements
Startup time in minutes	Startup time in milliseconds
Image is hard to make, reuse, and update	Image is easy to make, reuse, and update
Each VM runs its own OS	Containers share the host OS kernel
Extra resource overhead due to the translation by the hypervisor	Almost-native performance
Hardware-level virtualization	OS-level virtualization
Fully isolated	Process-level isolated

Figure 1.3: Comparison of VMs and Containers

Looking at this comparison, it seems that containers win in all aspects except for isolation. The Linux container technologies that are leveraged by the containers are not new. The key Linux kernel features, namespace, and cgroup (which we will study later in this chapter) have existed for more than a decade. There were some older container implementations such as LXC and Cloud Foundry Warden before the emergence of Docker. Now, an interesting question is: given that container technology has so many benefits, why has it been adopted in recent years instead of a decade ago? We will find some answers to this question in the following sections.

DOCKER BASICS

Until now, we have seen the different advantages that containerization provides as opposed to running applications on a VM. Docker is the most commonly used containerization technology by a wide margin. In this section, we will start with some Docker basics and perform some exercises to get you first-hand experience of working with Docker.

> **NOTE**
>
> Apart from Docker, there are other container managers such as containerd and podman. They behave differently in terms of features and user experiences, for example, containerd and podman are claimed to be more lightweight than Docker, and better fit than Kubernetes. However, they are all **Open Container Initiatives** (**OCI**) compliant to guarantee the container images are compatible.

Although Docker can be installed on any OS, you should be aware that, on Windows and macOS, it actually creates a Linux VM (or uses equivalent virtualization technology such as HyperKit in macOS) and embeds Docker into the VM. In this chapter, we will use Ubuntu 18.04 LTS as the OS and the Docker Community Edition 18.09.7.

Before you proceed, please ensure that Docker is installed as per the instructions in the *Preface*. You can confirm whether Docker is installed by querying the version of Docker using the following command:

```
docker --version
```

You should see the following output:

```
Docker version 18.09.7, build 2d0083d
```

> **NOTE**
>
> All the commands in the following sections are executed as **`root`**. Enter **`sudo -s`** in the terminal, followed by the admin password when prompted, to get root access.

WHAT'S BEHIND DOCKER RUN?

After Docker is installed, running a containerized application is quite simple. For demonstration purposes, we will use the Nginx web server as an example application. We can simply run the following command to start up the Nginx server:

```
docker run -d nginx
```

You should see the similar result:

```
Unable to find image 'nginx:latest' locally
latest: Pulling from library/nginx
8d691f585fa8: Pull complete
5b07f4e08ad0: Pull complete
abc291867bca: Pull complete
Digest: sha256:922c815aa4df050d4df476e92daed4231f466acc8ee90e0e774951b0fd7195a4
Status: Downloaded newer image for nginx:latest
96c374000f6f84aec7367b4e50939d257a83c746c0ca3436b2349047cafab7c0
```

Figure 1.4: Starting up Nginx

This command involves several actions, described as follows:

1. **`docker run`** tells Docker Engine to run an application.
2. The **`-d`** parameter (short for **`--detach`**) forces the application to run in the background so that you won't see the output of the application in the terminal. Instead, you have to run **`docker logs <container ID>`** to implicitly get the output.

> **NOTE**
>
> The "detached" mode usually implies that the application is a long-running service.

3. The last parameter, **`nginx`**, indicates the image name on which the application is based. The image encapsulates the Nginx program as well as its dependencies.

The output logs explain a brief workflow: first, it tried to fetch the **nginx** image locally, which failed, so it retrieved the image from a public image repository (Docker Hub, which we will revisit later). Once the image is downloaded locally, it uses that image to start an instance, and then outputs an ID (in the preceding example, this is **96c374**...), identifying the running instance. As you can observe, this is a hexadecimal string, and you can use the beginning four or more unique characters in practice to refer to any instance. You should see that even the terminal outputs of the **docker** commands truncate the ID.

The running instance can be verified using the following command:

```
docker ps
```

You should see the following result:

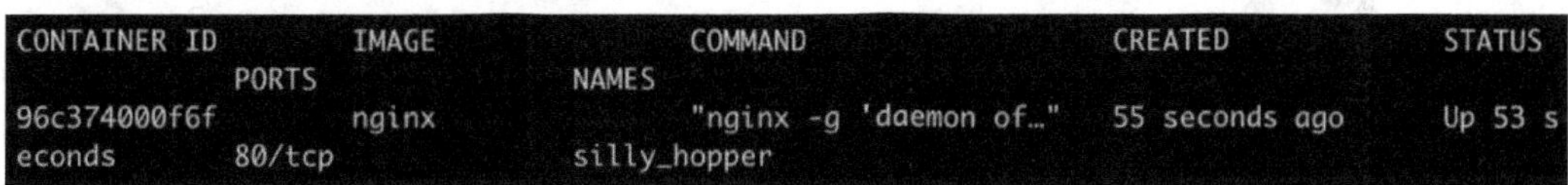

Figure 1.5: Getting a list of all the running Docker containers

The **docker ps** command lists all the running containers. In the preceding example, there is only one container running, which is **nginx**. Unlike a typical Nginx distribution that runs natively on a physical machine or VM, the **nginx** container functions in an isolated manner. The **nginx** container does not, by default, expose its service on host ports. Instead, it serves at the port of its container, which is an isolated entity. We can get to the **nginx** service by calling on port **80** of the container IP.

First, let's get the container IP by running the following command:

```
docker inspect --format '{{.NetworkSettings.IPAddress}}' <Container ID or NAME>
```

You should see the following output (it may vary depending on your local environment):

```
172.17.0.2
```

As you can see, in this case, the **nginx** container has an IP address of **172.17.0.2**. Let's check whether Nginx responds by accessing this IP on port **80**:

```
curl <container IP>:80
```

You should see the following output:

```
<!DOCTYPE html>
<html>
<head>
<title>Welcome to nginx!</title>
<style>
    body {
        width: 35em;
        margin: 0 auto;
        font-family: Tahoma, Verdana, Arial, sans-serif;
    }
</style>
</head>
<body>
<h1>Welcome to nginx!</h1>
<p>If you see this page, the nginx web server is successfully installed and
working. Further configuration is required.</p>

<p>For online documentation and support please refer to
<a href="http://nginx.org/">nginx.org</a>.<br/>
Commercial support is available at
<a href="http://nginx.com/">nginx.com</a>.</p>

<p><em>Thank you for using nginx.</em></p>
</body>
</html>
```

Figure 1.6: Response of the Nginx container

As you can see in *Figure 1.6*, we get a response, which is displayed in the terminal as the source HTML of the default home page.

Usually, we don't rely on the internal IP to access the service. A more practical way is to expose the service on some port of the host. To map the host port **8080** to the container port **80**, use the following command:

```
docker run -p 8080:80 -d nginx
```

You should see a similar response:

```
39bf70d02dcc5f038f62c276ada1675c25a06dd5fb772c5caa19f02edbb0622a
```

The **-p 8080:80** parameter tells Docker Engine to start the container and map the traffic on port 8080 of the host to the inside container at port **80**. Now, if we try to access the **localhost** on port **8080**, we will be able to access the containerized **nginx** service. Let's try it out:

```
curl localhost:8080
```

You should see the same output as in *Figure 1.6*.

Nginx is an example of a type of workload that doesn't have a fixed termination time, that is, it does not just show output and then terminates. This is also known as a **long-running service**. The other type of workload, which just runs to completion and exits, is called a **short-time service**, or simply a **job**. For containers running jobs, we can omit the **-d** parameter. Here is an example of a job:

```
docker run hello-world
```

You should see the following response:

```
Unable to find image 'hello-world:latest' locally
latest: Pulling from library/hello-world
1b930d010525: Pull complete
Digest: sha256:c3b4ada4687bbaa170745b3e4dd8ac3f194ca95b2d0518b417fb47e5879d9b5f
Status: Downloaded newer image for hello-world:latest

Hello from Docker!
This message shows that your installation appears to be working correctly.

To generate this message, Docker took the following steps:
 1. The Docker client contacted the Docker daemon.
 2. The Docker daemon pulled the "hello-world" image from the Docker Hub.
    (amd64)
 3. The Docker daemon created a new container from that image which runs the
    executable that produces the output you are currently reading.
 4. The Docker daemon streamed that output to the Docker client, which sent it
    to your terminal.

To try something more ambitious, you can run an Ubuntu container with:
 $ docker run -it ubuntu bash

Share images, automate workflows, and more with a free Docker ID:
 https://hub.docker.com/

For more examples and ideas, visit:
 https://docs.docker.com/get-started/
```

Figure 1.7: Running the hello-world image

Now, if you run **docker ps**, which is intended to list running containers, it doesn't show the **hello-world** container. This is as expected since the container has finished its job (that is, printing out the response text that we saw in the previous screenshot) and exited. To be able to find the exited container, you can run the same command with the **-a** flag, which will show all the containers:

```
docker ps -a
```

You should see the following output:

```
CONTAINER ID        IMAGE               COMMAND                  CREATED             STATUS
                    PORTS                  NAMES
286bc0c92b3a        hello-world         "/hello"                 5 minutes ago       Exited
(0) 5 minutes ago                          trusting_hawking
39bf70d02dcc        nginx               "nginx -g 'daemon of…"   6 minutes ago       Up 6 mi
nutes               0.0.0.0:8080->80/tcp   optimistic_jackson
96c374000f6f        nginx               "nginx -g 'daemon of…"   16 hours ago        Up 16 h
ours                80/tcp                 silly_hopper
```

Figure 1.8: Checking our exited container

For a container that has stopped, you can delete it using **docker rm <container ID>**, or rerun it with **docker run <container ID>**. Alternatively, if you rerun the **docker run hello-world**, it will again bring up a new container with a new ID and exit after it finishes its job. You can try this out yourself as follows:

```
docker run hello-world
docker ps -a
```

You should see the following output:

```
CONTAINER ID        IMAGE               COMMAND                  CREATED             STATUS
                    PORTS                  NAMES
43c01e2055cf        hello-world         "/hello"                 3 seconds ago       Exited
(0) 2 seconds ago                          nervous_dhawan
286bc0c92b3a        hello-world         "/hello"                 6 minutes ago       Exited
(0) 6 minutes ago                          trusting_hawking
39bf70d02dcc        nginx               "nginx -g 'daemon of…"   7 minutes ago       Up 7 mi
nutes               0.0.0.0:8080->80/tcp   optimistic_jackson
96c374000f6f        nginx               "nginx -g 'daemon of…"   16 hours ago        Up 16 h
ours                80/tcp                 silly_hopper
```

Figure 1.9: Checking multiple exited containers

Thus, you can see that running multiple containers based on the same underlying image is pretty straightforward.

By now, you should have a very basic understanding of how a container is launched, and how to check its status.

DOCKERFILES AND DOCKER IMAGES

In the VM era, there was no standard or unified way to abstract and pack various kinds of applications. The traditional way was to use a tool, such as Ansible, to manage the installation and update the processes for each application. This is still used nowadays, but it involves lots of manual operations and is error-prone due to inconsistencies between different environments. From a developer's perspective, applications are developed on local machines, which are vastly different from the staging and eventual production environment.

So, how does Docker resolve these issues? The innovation it brings is called **`Dockerfile`** and Docker image. A **`Dockerfile`** is a text file that abstracts a series of instructions to build a reproducible environment including the application itself as well as all of its dependencies.

By using the **`docker build`** command, Docker uses the **`Dockerfile`** to generate a standardized entity called a Docker image, which you can run on almost any OS. By leveraging Docker images, developers can develop and test applications in the same environment as the production one, because the dependencies are abstracted and bundled within the same image. Let's take a step back and look at the **`nginx`** application we started earlier. Use the following command to list all the locally downloaded images:

```
docker images
```

You should see the following list:

```
REPOSITORY          TAG                 IMAGE ID            CREATED             SIZE
nginx               latest              540a289bab6c        3 weeks ago         126MB
hello-world         latest              fce289e99eb9        10 months ago       1.84kB
```

Figure 1.10: Getting a list of images

Unlike VM images, Docker images only bundle the necessary files such as application binaries, dependencies, and the Linux root filesystem. Internally, a Docker image is separated into different layers, with each layer being stacked on top of another one. In this way, upgrading the application only requires an update to the relevant layers. This reduces both the image footprint as well as the upgrade time.

The following figure shows the hierarchical layers of a hypothetical Docker image that is built from the base OS layer (Ubuntu), the Java web application runtime layer (Tomcat), and the topmost user application layer:

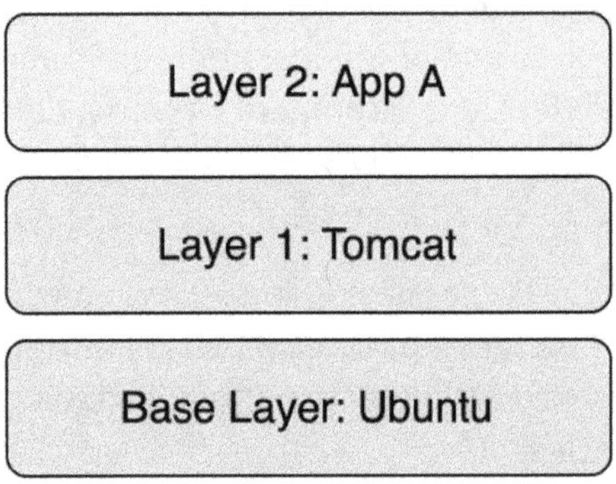

Figure 1.11: An example of stacked layers in a container

Note that it is common practice to use the images of a popular OS as a starting point for building Docker images (as you will see in the following exercise) since it conveniently includes the various components required to develop an application. In the preceding hypothetical container, the application would use Tomcat as well as some dependencies included in Ubuntu in order to function properly. This is the only reason that Ubuntu is included as the base layer. If we wanted, we could bundle the required dependencies without including the entire Ubuntu base image. So, don't confuse this with the case of a VM, where including a guest OS is necessary.

Let's take a look at how we can build our own Docker image for an application in the following exercise.

EXERCISE 1.01: CREATING A DOCKER IMAGE AND UPLOADING IT TO DOCKER HUB

In this exercise, we will build a Docker image for a simple application written in Go.

We're going to use Go in this exercise so that the source code and its language dependencies can be compiled into a single executable binary. However, you're free to use any programming language you prefer; just remember to bundle the language runtime dependencies if you're going to use Java, Python, Node.js, or any other language:

1. For this exercise, we will create a file named **Dockerfile**. Note that this filename has no extension. You can use your preferred text editor to create this file with the following content:

```
FROM alpine:3.10

COPY k8s-for-beginners /

CMD ["/k8s-for-beginners"]
```

> **NOTE**
>
> From the terminal, whenever you create a file using any simple text editor such as vim or nano or using the **cat** command, it will be created in the current working directory in any Linux distro or even macOS. The default working directory when you open the terminal is **/home/**. If you prefer to use a different directory, please take that into account when following any of the exercise steps throughout this book.

The first line specifies which base image to use as the foundation. This example uses Alpine, a popular base image that takes only about 5 MB and is based on Alpine Linux. The second line copies a file called **k8s-for-beginners** from the directory where the **Dockerfile** is located to the root folder of the image. In this example, we will build a tiny web server and compile it to a binary with the name **k8s-for-beginners**, which will be placed in the same directory as the **Dockerfile**. The third line specifies the default startup command. In this case, we just start our sample web server.

2. Next, let's build our sample web server. Create a file named **main.go** with the following content:

```
package main

import (
        "fmt"
        "log"
        "net/http"
)

func main() {
        http.HandleFunc("/", handler)
        log.Fatal(http.ListenAndServe("0.0.0.0:8080", nil))
}

func handler(w http.ResponseWriter, r *http.Request) {
        log.Printf("Ping from %s", r.RemoteAddr)
        fmt.Fprintln(w, "Hello Kubernetes Beginners!")
}
```

   As you can observe from **func main()**, this application serves as a web server that accepts an incoming HTTP request at port 8080 on the root path and responds with the message **Hello Kubernetes Beginners**.

3. To verify this program works, you can just run **go run main.go**, and then open **http://localhost:8080** on the browser. You're expected to get the "**Hello Kubernetes Beginners!**" output.

4. Use **go build** to compile runtime dependencies along with the source code into one executable binary. Run the following command in the terminal:

```
CGO_ENABLED=0 GOOS=linux GOARCH=amd64 go build -o k8s-for-beginners
```

> **NOTE**
>
> Unlike *step 3*, the arguments **GOOS=linux GOARCH=amd64** tell the Go compiler to compile the program on a specific platform, which turns out to be compatible with the Linux distro we are going to build this problem into. **CGO_ENABLED=0** is aimed to generate a statically linked binary so that it can work with some minimum-tailored image (For example, alpine).

5. Now, check whether the **k8s-for-beginners** file is created:

```
ls
```

You should see the following response:

```
Dockerfile k8s-for-beginners  main.go
```

6. Now we have both the **Dockerfile** and the runnable binary. Build the Docker image by using the following command:

```
docker build -t k8s-for-beginners:v0.0.1 .
```

Don't miss the dot (**.**) at the end of this command. You should see the following response:

```
Sending build context to Docker daemon  5.863MB
Step 1/3 : FROM alpine:3.10
3.10: Pulling from library/alpine
89d9c30c1d48: Pull complete
Digest: sha256:c19173c5ada610a5989151111163d28a67368362762534d8a8121ce95cf2bd5a
Status: Downloaded newer image for alpine:3.10
 ---> 965ea09ff2eb
Step 2/3 : COPY k8s-for-beginners /
 ---> 6b859897a4e9
Step 3/3 : CMD ["/k8s-for-beginners"]
 ---> Running in 5b6edafbb116
Removing intermediate container 5b6edafbb116
 ---> 59261c473efe
Successfully built 59261c473efe
Successfully tagged k8s-for-beginners:v0.0.1
```

Figure 1.12: Output of docker build command

There are two parameters in the command that we used: **-t k8s-for-beginners:v0.0.1** provides a tag on the image with format **<imagename:version>**, while **.** (the dot at the end of the command) denotes the path to look for the **Dockerfile**. In this case, **.** refers to the current working directory.

> **NOTE**
>
> If you clone the GitHub repository for this chapter, you will find that we have provided a copy of the **Dockerfile** in each directory so that you can conveniently run the **docker build** command by navigating to the directory.

7. Now, we have the **`k8s-for-beginners:v0.0.1`** image available locally. You can confirm that by running the following command:

```
docker images
```

You should see the following response:

```
REPOSITORY          TAG       IMAGE ID       CREATED              SIZE
k8s-for-beginners   v0.0.1    59261c473efe   About a minute ago   11.4MB
nginx               latest    540a289bab6c   3 weeks ago          126MB
alpine              3.10      965ea09ff2eb   3 weeks ago          5.55MB
hello-world         latest    fce289e99eb9   10 months ago        1.84kB
```

Figure 1.13: Verifying whether our Docker image has been created

An interesting thing to observe is that the image merely consumes 11.4 MB, which includes both the Linux system files and our application. A tip here is to only include necessary files in the Docker image to make it compact so that it is easy to distribute and manage.

Now that we have built our image, we will run it in a container in the next exercise. Another thing to note is that, currently, this image resides on our local machine, and we can build a container using it only on our machine. However, the advantage of packaging an application with its dependencies is that it can be easily run on different machines. To easily facilitate that, we can upload our images to online Docker image repositories such as Docker Hub (https://hub.docker.com/).

> **NOTE:**
>
> In addition to Docker Hub, there are other public image repositories such as quay.io, gcr.io, and more. You can refer to the documentation of the respective repository to configure it properly in your Docker client.

EXERCISE 1.02: RUNNING YOUR FIRST APPLICATION IN DOCKER

In *Exercise 1.01, Creating a Docker Image and Uploading it to Docker Hub*, we packaged the web application into a Docker image. In this exercise, we will run it and push it to Docker Hub:

1. First, we should clean up any leftover containers from the previous exercise by running the following command in the terminal:

```
docker rm -f $(docker ps -aq)
```

You should see the following response:

```
43c01e2055cf
286bc0c92b3a
39bf70d02dcc
96c374000f6f
```

We have seen that **docker ps -a** returns the information of all the containers. The extra **q** in the **-aq** flag means "quiet" and the flag will only display numeric IDs. These IDs will be passed to **docker rm -f**, and, therefore, all the containers will be removed forcefully.

2. Run the following command to start the webserver:

```
docker run -p 8080:8080 -d k8s-for-beginners:v0.0.1
```

You should see the following response:

```
9869e9b4ab1f3d5f7b2451a7086644c1cd7393ac9d78b6b4c1bef6d423fd25ac
```

As you can see in the preceding command, we are mapping the internal port **8080** of the container to the host machine's port **8080**. The **8080:8080** parameter preceded by **-p** maps port **8080** of the container to port **8080** on the host machine. The **-d** parameter indicates the detached mode. By default, Docker checks the local registry first. So, in this case, the local Docker image will be used for launching the container.

3. Now, let us check whether it works as expected by sending an HTTP request to **localhost** at port **8080**:

```
curl localhost:8080
```

The **curl** command checks for a response from the stated address. You should see the following response:

```
Hello Kubernetes Beginners!
```

4. We can also observe the logs of the running container by using the following commands:

```
docker logs <container ID>
```

You should see the following logs:

```
2019/11/18  05:19:41 Ping from 172.17.0.1:41416
```

> **NOTE**
>
> Before running the following commands, you should register for a Docker Hub account and have your username and password ready.

5. Finally, we need to log in to Docker Hub, and then push the local image to the remote Docker Hub registry. Use the following command:

```
docker login
```

Now enter the username and password to your Docker Hub account when prompted. You should see the following response:

```
Login with your Docker ID to push and pull images from Docker Hub. If you don't have a Docke
r ID, head over to https://hub.docker.com to create one.
Username: hweicdl
Password:
WARNING! Your password will be stored unencrypted in /root/.docker/config.json.
Configure a credential helper to remove this warning. See
https://docs.docker.com/engine/reference/commandline/login/#credentials-store

Login Succeeded
```

Figure 1.14: Logging in to Docker Hub

6. Next, we will push the local image, **k8s-for-beginners:v0.0.1**, to the remote Docker Hub registry. Run the following command:

```
docker push k8s-for-beginners:v0.0.1
```

You should see the following response:

```
The push refers to repository [docker.io/library/k8s-for-beginners]
5b751225b338: Preparing
77cae8ab23bf: Preparing
denied: requested access to the resource is denied
```

Figure 1.15: Failing to push the image to Docker Hub

But wait, why does it say, "**requested access to the resource is denied**"? That is because the parameter followed by the **docker push** must comply with a **<username/imagename:version>** naming convention. In the previous exercise, we specified a local image tag, **k8s-for-beginners:v0.0.1**, without a username. In the **docker push** command, if no username is specified, it will try to push to the repository with the default username, **library**, which also hosts some well-known libraries such as Ubuntu, nginx, and more.

7. To push our local image to our own user, we need to give a compliant name for the local image by running **docker tag <imagename:version> <username/imagename:version>**, as shown in the following command:

```
docker tag k8s-for-beginners:v0.0.1 <your_DockerHub_username>/
k8s-for-beginners:v0.0.1
```

8. You can verify that the image has been properly tagged using the following command:

```
docker images
```

You should see the following output:

```
REPOSITORY                   TAG       IMAGE ID       CREATED          SIZE
hweicdl/k8s-for-beginners    v0.0.1    59261c473efe   15 minutes ago   11.4
MB
k8s-for-beginners            v0.0.1    59261c473efe   15 minutes ago   11.4
MB
nginx                        latest    540a289bab6c   3 weeks ago      126M
B
alpine                       3.10      965ea09ff2eb   3 weeks ago      5.55
MB
hello-world                  latest    fce289e99eb9   10 months ago    1.84
kB
```

Figure 1.16: Checking the tagged Docker image

After tagging it properly, you can tell that the new image actually has the same **IMAGE ID** as the old one, which implies they're the same image.

9. Now that we have the image tagged appropriately, we're ready to push this image to Docker Hub by running the following command:

```
docker push <your_username>/k8s-for-beginners:v0.0.1
```

You should see a response similar to this:

```
The push refers to repository [docker.io/hweicdl/k8s-for-beginners]
5b751225b338: Pushed
77cae8ab23bf: Pushed
v0.0.1: digest: sha256:5dbf6d7cc759c163fc239e033a44f3cc88eebaa58e8ed4fe26cd7d0574b911d6 size
: 739
```

Figure 1.17: Image successfully pushed to Docker Hub

10. The image will be live after a short time on Docker Hub. You can verify it by replacing the **<username>** with your username in the following link: **https://hub.docker.com/repository/docker/<username>/k8s-for-beginners/tags**.

You should be able to see some information regarding your image, similar to the following image:

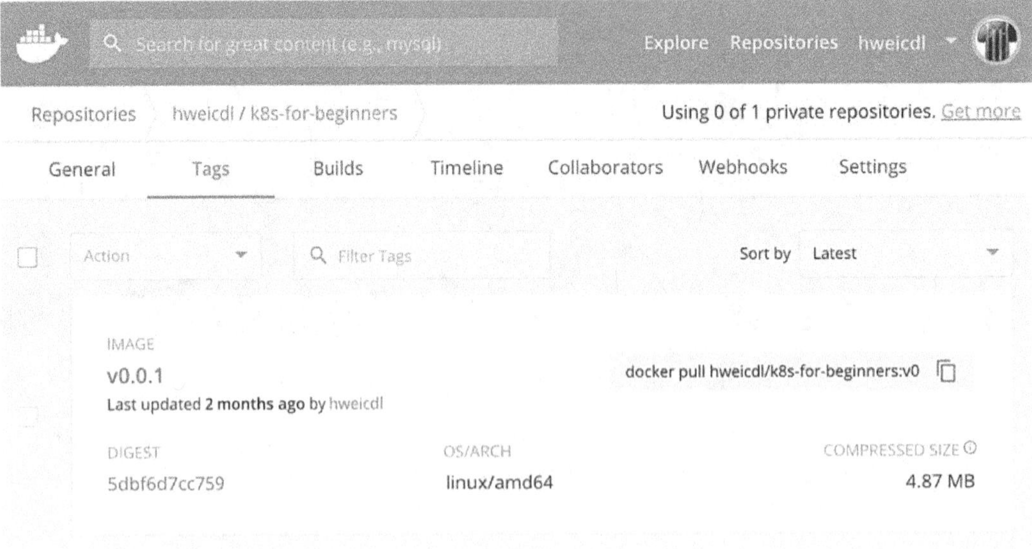

Figure 1.18: The Docker Hub page for our image

Now our Docker image is publicly accessible for anyone to use, just like the **nginx** image we used at the beginning of this chapter.

In this section, we learned how to build Docker images and push them to Docker Hub. Although it looks inconspicuous, it is the first time we have a unified mechanism to manage the applications, along with their dependencies, consistently across all environments. Docker images and their underlying layered filesystem are also the **primary reason** why container technology has been widely adopted in recent years, as opposed to a decade ago.

In the next section, we will dive a little deeper into Docker to see how it leverages Linux container technologies.

The Essence of Linux Container Technology

All things look elegant and straightforward from the outside. But what's the magic working underneath to make a container so powerful? In this section, we will try to open the hood to take a look inside. Let us take a look at a few Linux technologies that lay the foundation for containers.

Namespace

The first key technology relied upon by containers is called a **Linux namespace**. When a Linux system starts up, it creates a default namespace (the `root` namespace). Then, by default, the processes created later join the same namespace, and, hence, they can interact with each other boundlessly. For example, two processes are able to view the files in the same folder, and also interact through the `localhost` network. This sounds pretty straightforward, but technically it's all credited to the `root` namespace, which connects all the processes.

To support advanced use cases, Linux offers the namespace API to enable different processes being grouped into different namespaces so that only the processes that belong to the same namespace can be aware of each other. In other words, different groups of processes are isolated. This also explains why we mentioned earlier that the isolation of Docker is process-level. The following is a list of the types of namespaces supported in the Linux kernel:

- Mount namespaces
- **PID** (**Process ID**) namespaces
- Network namespaces
- **IPC** (**Inter-Process Communication**) namespaces
- **UTS** (**Unix Time-sharing System**) namespaces

- User namespaces (since Linux kernel 3.8)
- Cgroup namespaces (since Linux kernel 4.6)
- Time namespaces (to be implemented in a future version of the Linux kernel)

For the sake of brevity, we will choose two easy ones (UTS and PID) and use concrete examples to explain how they're reflected in Docker later.

> **NOTE**
>
> If you are running macOS, some of the following commands will need to be used differently, since we are exploring Linux features. Docker on macOS runs inside a Linux VM using HyperKit. So, you need to open another terminal session and log into the VM:
>
> **`screen ~/Library/Containers/com.docker.docker/Data/vms/0/tty`**
>
> After this command, you may see an empty screen. Press *Enter*, and you should have root access to the VM that is running Docker. To exit the session, you can press *Ctrl* + *A* + *K*, and then press *Y* when asked for confirmation for killing the window.
>
> We recommend that you use a different terminal window to access the Linux VM. We will mention which commands need to be run in this terminal session if you are using macOS. If you are using any Linux OS, you can ignore this and simply run all the commands in the same terminal session, unless mentioned otherwise in the instructions.

Once a Docker container is created, Docker creates and associates a number of namespaces with the container. For example, let's take a look at the sample container we created in the previous section. Let's use the following command:

```
docker inspect --format '{{.State.Pid}}' <container ID>
```

The preceding command checks the PID of the container running on the host OS. You should see a response similar to the following:

```
5897
```

In this example, the PID is **5897**, as you can see in the preceding response. Now, run this command in the Linux VM:

```
ps -ef | grep k8s-for-beginners
```

This should give an output similar to this:

```
root      5897  5879  0 05:19 ?        00:00:00 /k8s-for-beginners
root      6097  2212  0 06:09 pts/0    00:00:00 grep --color=auto k8s-for-beginners
```

Figure 1.19: Checking the PID of our process

The **ps -ef** command lists all the running processes on the host OS, and **| grep k8s-for-beginners** then filters this list to display the processes that have **k8s-for-beginners** in their name. We can see that the process also has the PID **5897**, which is consistent with the first command. This reveals an important fact that a container is nothing but a particular process running directly on the host OS.

Next, run this command:

```
ls -l /proc/<PID>/ns
```

For macOS, run this command in the VM terminal. You should see the following output:

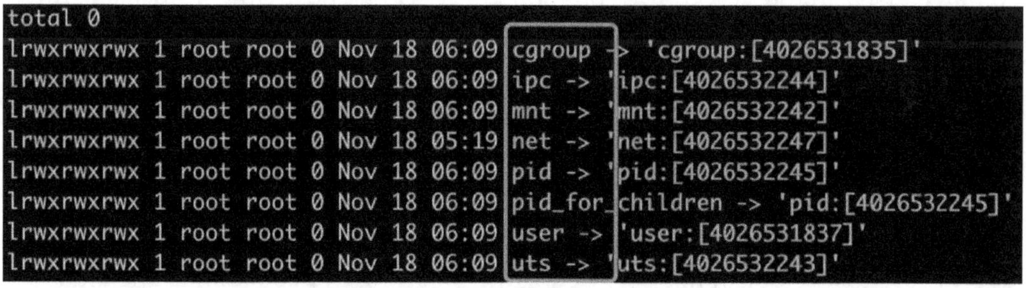

```
total 0
lrwxrwxrwx 1 root root 0 Nov 18 06:09 cgroup -> 'cgroup:[4026531835]'
lrwxrwxrwx 1 root root 0 Nov 18 06:09 ipc -> 'ipc:[4026532244]'
lrwxrwxrwx 1 root root 0 Nov 18 06:09 mnt -> 'mnt:[4026532242]'
lrwxrwxrwx 1 root root 0 Nov 18 05:19 net -> 'net:[4026532247]'
lrwxrwxrwx 1 root root 0 Nov 18 06:09 pid -> 'pid:[4026532245]'
lrwxrwxrwx 1 root root 0 Nov 18 06:09 pid_for_children -> 'pid:[4026532245]'
lrwxrwxrwx 1 root root 0 Nov 18 06:09 user -> 'user:[4026531837]'
lrwxrwxrwx 1 root root 0 Nov 18 06:09 uts -> 'uts:[4026532243]'
```

Figure 1.20: Listing the different namespaces created for our container

This command checks the **/proc** folder (which is a Linux pseudo-filesystem) to list all the namespaces created along with the start of the container. The result shows some well-known namespaces (take a look at the highlighted rectangle) such as **uts**, **pid**, **net**, and more. Let's take a closer look at them.

The **uts** namespace is created to enable the container to have its hostname instead of the host's hostname. By default, a container is assigned its container ID as the hostname, and it can be changed using the **-h** parameter while running a container, as shown here:

```
docker run -h k8s-for-beginners -d packtworkshops/the-kubernetes-
workshop:k8s-for-beginners
```

This should give the following response:

```
df6a15a8e2481ec3e46dedf7850cb1fbef6efafcacc3c8a048752da24ad793dc
```

Using the returned container ID, we can enter the container and check its hostname using the following two commands one after the other:

```
docker exec -it <container ID> sh
hostname
```

You should see the following response:

```
k8s-for-beginners
```

The **docker exec** command tries to enter into the container and execute the **sh** command to launch the shell inside the container. And once we're inside the container, we run the **hostname** command to check the hostname from inside the container. From the output, we can tell that the **-h** parameter is in effect because we can see **k8s-for-beginners** as the hostname.

In addition to the **uts** namespace, the container is also isolated in its own **PID** namespace, so it can only view the processes launched by itself, and the launching process (specified by **CMD** or **ENTRYPOINT** in the **Dockerfile** that we created in *Exercise 1.01, Creating a Docker Image and Uploading it to Docker Hub*) is assigned **PID 1**. Let's take a look at this by entering the following two commands one after the other:

```
docker exec -it <container ID> sh
ps
```

You should see the following response:

```
PID   USER     TIME  COMMAND
    1 root      0:00 /k8s-for-beginners
   28 root      0:00 sh
   33 root      0:00 ps
```

Figure 1.21: The list of processes inside our container

Docker provides the **--pid** option for a container to join another container's PID namespace.

In addition to the **uts** and **pid** namespaces, there are some other namespaces that Docker leverages. We will examine the network namespace ("**net**" in *Figure 1.20*) in the next exercise.

EXERCISE 1.03: JOINING A CONTAINER TO THE NETWORK NAMESPACE OF ANOTHER CONTAINER

In this exercise, we will recreate the **k8s-for-beginners** container without host mapping, and then create another container to join its network namespace:

1. As with the previous exercise, remove all the existing containers by running the following command:

```
docker rm -f $(docker ps -aq)
```

   You should see an output similar to this:

```
43c01e2055cf
286bc0c92b3a
39bf70d02dcc
96c374000f6f
```

2. Now, begin by running our container using the following command:

```
docker run -d packtworkshops/the-kubernetes-workshop:k8s-for-beginners
```

   You should see the following response:

```
33003ddffdf4d85c5f77f2cae2528cb2035d37f0a7b7b46947206ca104bbbaa5
```

3. Next, we will get the list of running containers so that we can see the container ID:

```
docker ps
```

You should see the following response:

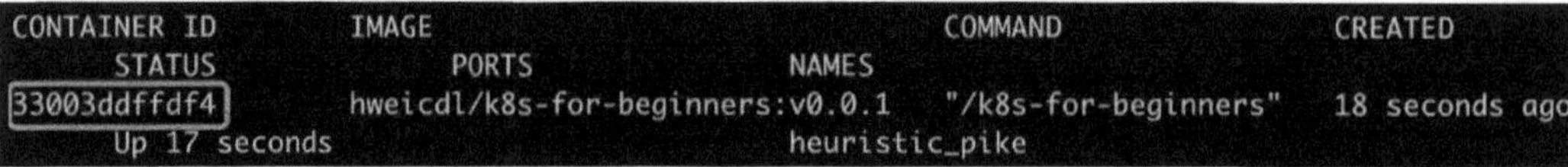
CONTAINER ID IMAGE COMMAND CREATED
STATUS PORTS NAMES
33003ddffdf4 hweicdl/k8s-for-beginners:v0.0.1 "/k8s-for-beginners" 18 seconds ago
Up 17 seconds heuristic_pike

Figure 1.22: Getting a list of all of the running containers

4. Now, we will run an image called **`netshoot`** in the same network namespace as the container that we created in *step 1*, by using the **`--net`** parameter:

```
docker run -it --net container:<container ID> nicolaka/netshoot
```

Use the container ID of our previous container that we obtained in the previous step. You should see a response that is similar to the following:

```
Unable to find image 'nicolaka/netshoot:latest' locally
latest: Pulling from nicolaka/netshoot
e7c96db7181b: Pull complete
e8ad7601444c: Pull complete
1c3e3a777e70: Pull complete
916dd651caf3: Pull complete
4375fed2538e: Pull complete
8631605717d0: Pull complete
dd4fb07f87c6: Pull complete
Digest: sha256:8b020dc72d8ef07663e44c449f1294fc47c81a10ef5303dc8c2d9635e8ca22b1
Status: Downloaded newer image for nicolaka/netshoot:latest
                    dP            dP                             dP
                    88            88                             88
88d888b. .d8888b. d8888P .d8888b. 88d888b. .d8888b. .d8888b. d8888P
88'  `88 88ooood8   88   Y8ooooo. 88'  `88 88'  `88 88'  `88   88
88    88 88.  ...   88         88 88    88 88.  .88 88.  .88   88
dP    dP `88888P'   dP   `88888P' dP    dP `88888P' `88888P'   dP

Welcome to Netshoot! (github.com/nicolaka/netshoot)

root @ /
 [1]
```

Figure 1.23: Starting up the netshoot container

`nicolaka/netshoot` is a tiny image packaged with some commonly used network libraries such as **`iproute2`**, **`curl`**, and more.

5. Now, let's run the **curl** command inside **netshoot** to check whether we are able to access the **k8s-for-beginners** container:

```
curl localhost:8080
```

You should see the following response:

```
Hello Kubernetes Beginners!
```

The preceding example proves that the **netshoot** container was created by joining the network namespace of **k8s-for-beginners**; otherwise, accessing port **8080** on **localhost** wouldn't have got us a response.

6. This can also be verified by double-checking the network namespace IDs of the two containers, which we will do in the following steps.

To confirm our result, let us first open another terminal without exiting the **netshoot** container. Get the list of containers to ensure both containers are running:

```
docker ps
```

You should see a response as follows:

```
CONTAINER ID        IMAGE                              COMMAND                  CREATED
      STATUS              PORTS               NAMES
61d0fa62bc49        nicolaka/netshoot                  "/bin/bash -l"           38 minutes ago
      Up 38 minutes                           naughty_visvesvaraya
33003ddffdf4        hweicdl/k8s-for-beginners:v0.0.1   "/k8s-for-beginners"     About an hour
ago   Up About an hour                        heuristic_pike
```

Figure 1.24: Checking whether both of the k8s-for-beginners and netshoot containers are online

7. Next, get the PID of the **k8s-for-beginners** container:

```
docker inspect --format '{{.State.Pid}}' <container ID>
```

You should see the following response:

```
7311
```

As you can see, the PID for this example is **7311**.

8. Now get the pseudo-filesystem of the process using the preceding PID:

   ```
   ls -l /proc/<PID>/ns/net
   ```

   If you are using macOS, run this command on the Linux VM in another terminal session. Use the PID you obtained in the previous step in this command. You should see the following response:

   ```
   lrwxrwxrwx 1 root root 0 Nov 19 08:11 /proc/7311/ns/net ->
   'net:[4026532247]'
   ```

9. Similarly, get the PID of the **netshoot** container using the following command:

   ```
   docker inspect --format '{{.State.Pid}}' <container ID>
   ```

   Use the appropriate container ID from *step 6* in this command. You should see the following response:

   ```
   8143
   ```

   As you can see, the PID of the **netshoot** container is **8143**.

10. Next, we can get its pseudo-filesystem using its PID or by using this command:

    ```
    ls -l /proc/<PID>/ns/net
    ```

    If you are using macOS, run this command on the Linux VM in another session. Use the PID from the previous step in this command. You should see the following response:

    ```
    lrwxrwxrwx 1 root root 0 Nov 19 09:15 /proc/8143/ns/net ->
    'net:[4026532247]'
    ```

    As you can observe from the outputs of *step 8* and *step 10*, the two containers share the same network namespace (**4026532247**).

11. As a final cleanup step, let's remove all of the containers:

    ```
    docker rm -f $(docker ps -aq)
    ```

    You should see a response similar to the following:

    ```
    61d0fa62bc49
    33003ddffdf4
    ```

12. What if you want to join a container to the host's root namespace? Well, **--net host** is a good way of achieving that. To demonstrate this, we will start a container using the same image, but with the **--net host** parameter:

```
docker run --net host -d packtworkshops/the-kubernetes-workshop:k8s-for-beginners
```

    You should see the following response:

```
8bf56ca0c3dc69f09487be759f051574f291c77717b0f8bb5e1760c8e20aebd0
```

13. Now, list all of the running containers:

```
docker ps
```

    You should see the following response:

```
CONTAINER ID        IMAGE                                COMMAND                 CREATED
     STATUS              PORTS               NAMES
8bf56ca0c3dc        hweicdl/k8s-for-beginners:v0.0.1    "/k8s-for-beginners"   27 seconds ago
     Up 26 seconds                           gifted_cori
```

Figure 1.25: Listing all the containers

14. Get the PID of the running container using the following command:

```
docker inspect --format '{{.State.Pid}}' <container ID>
```

    Use the appropriate container ID in this command. You should see the following response:

```
8380
```

15. Find the network namespace ID by looking up the PID:

```
ls -l /proc/<PID>/ns/net
```

    If you are using macOS, run this command on the Linux VM. Use the appropriate PID in this command. You should see the following response:

```
lrwxrwxrwx 1 root root 0 Nov 19 09:20 /proc/8380/ns/net ->
'net:[4026531993]'
```

    You may be confused by the **4026531993** namespace. By giving the **--net host** parameter, shouldn't Docker bypass the creation of a new namespace? The answer to this is that it's not a new namespace; in fact, it's the aforementioned Linux root namespace. We will confirm this in the next step.

16. Get the namespace of PID **1** of the host OS:

```
ls -l /proc/1/ns/net
```

If you are using macOS, run this command on the Linux VM. You should see the following response:

```
lrwxrwxrwx 1 root root 0 Nov 19 09:20 /proc/1/ns/net ->
'net:[4026531993]'
```

As you can see in this output, this namespace of the host is the same as that of the container we saw in *step 15*.

From this exercise, we can get an impression of how a container is isolated into different namespaces, and also which Docker parameter can be used to relate it with other namespaces.

CGROUPS

By default, no matter which namespace a container joins, it can use all of the available resources of the host. That is, for sure, not what we want when we are running multiple containers on a system; otherwise, a few containers may hog the resources shared among all the containers.

To address this, the **cgroups** (short for **Control Groups**) feature was introduced in Linux kernel version 2.6.24 onward to limit the resource usage of processes. Using this feature, a system administrator can control the most important resources, such as memory, CPU, disk space, and network bandwidth.

In Ubuntu 18.04 LTS, a series of cgroups under path **`/sys/fs/cgroup/<cgroup type>`** are created by default.

> **NOTE**
>
> You can run **`mount -t cgroup`** in order to view all the cgroups in Ubuntu; though, we are leaving them out of the scope of this book since they are not very relevant to us.

Right now, we don't quite care about the system processes and their cgroups; we just want to focus on how Docker is related in the whole cgroups picture. Docker has its cgroups folders under the path **/sys/fs/cgroup/<resource kind>/docker**. Use the **find** command to retrieve the list:

```
find /sys/fs/cgroup/* -name docker -type d
```

If you are using macOS, run this command on the Linux VM in another session. You should see the following results:

```
/sys/fs/cgroup/blkio/docker
/sys/fs/cgroup/cpu,cpuacct/docker
/sys/fs/cgroup/cpuset/docker
/sys/fs/cgroup/devices/docker
/sys/fs/cgroup/freezer/docker
/sys/fs/cgroup/hugetlb/docker
/sys/fs/cgroup/memory/docker
/sys/fs/cgroup/net_cls,net_prio/docker
/sys/fs/cgroup/perf_event/docker
/sys/fs/cgroup/pids/docker
/sys/fs/cgroup/systemd/docker
```

Figure 1.26: Getting all the cgroups related to Docker

Each folder is read as a control group, and the folders are hierarchical, meaning that each cgroup has a parent from which it inherits properties, all the way up to the root cgroup, which is created at the system start.

To illustrate how a cgroup works in Docker, we will use the **memory** cgroup, highlighted in *Figure 1.26* as an example.

But first, let's remove all existing containers using the following command:

```
docker rm -f $(docker ps -aq)
```

You should see a response similar to the following:

```
61d0fa62bc49
```

Let's confirm that by using the following command:

```
docker ps
```

You should see an empty list as follows:

```
CONTAINER ID        IMAGE           COMMAND                 CREATED               STATUS
         PORTS              NAMES
```

Let's see whether there is a **cgroup** memory folder:

```
find /sys/fs/cgroup/memory/docker/* -type d
```

If you are using macOS, run this command on the Linux VM. You should then see the following response:

```
root@ubuntu: ~# find /sys/fs/cgroup/memory/docker/* -type d
```

No folders show up. Now, let's run a container:

```
docker run -d packtworkshops/the-kubernetes-workshop:k8s-for-beginners
```

You should see the output similar to the following:

```
8fe77332244b2ebecbda27a4496268264218c4e59614d59b5849a22b12941e1
```

Check the **cgroup** folder again:

```
find /sys/fs/cgroup/memory/docker/* -type d
```

If you are using macOS, run this command on the Linux VM. You should see this response:

```
/sys/fs/cgroup/memory/
docker/8fe77332244b2ebecbda27a4496268264218c4e59614d59b5849a22b12941e1
```

By now, you can see that once we create a container, Docker creates its cgroup folder under a specific resource kind (in our example, it's memory). Now, let's take a look at which files are created in this folder:

```
ls /sys/fs/cgroup/memory/
docker/8fe77332244b2ebecbd8a2704496268264218c4e59614d59b5849022b12941e1
```

If you are using macOS, run this command on the Linux VM. Please use the appropriate path that you obtained from the previous screenshot for your instance. You should see the following list of files:

```
59b5849a22b12941e1
cgroup.clone_children                  memory.limit_in_bytes
cgroup.event_control                   memory.max_usage_in_bytes
cgroup.procs                           memory.move_charge_at_immigrate
memory.failcnt                         memory.numa_stat
memory.force_empty                     memory.oom_control
memory.kmem.failcnt                    memory.pressure_level
memory.kmem.limit_in_bytes             memory.soft_limit_in_bytes
memory.kmem.max_usage_in_bytes         memory.stat
memory.kmem.slabinfo                   memory.swappiness
memory.kmem.tcp.failcnt                memory.usage_in_bytes
memory.kmem.tcp.limit_in_bytes         memory.use_hierarchy
memory.kmem.tcp.max_usage_in_bytes     notify_on_release
memory.kmem.tcp.usage_in_bytes         tasks
memory.kmem.usage_in_bytes
```

Figure 1.27: Exploring memory cgroups created by Docker

We won't go through every setting here. The setting we're interested in is **`memory.limit_in_bytes`**, as highlighted previously, which denotes how much memory the container can use. Let's see what value is written in this file:

```
cat /sys/fs/cgroup/memory/
docker/8fe77332244b2ebecbd8a2704496268264218c4e59614d59b5849022b12941e1/
memory.limit_in_bytes
```

If you are using macOS, run this command on the Linux VM. You should see the following response:

```
9223372036854771712
```

The value **`9223372036854771712`** is the largest positive signed integer ($2^{63} - 1$) in a 64-bit system, which means unlimited memory can be used by this container.

To discover how Docker deals with the containers that overuse claimed memory, we're going to show you another program that consumes a certain amount of RAM. The following is a Golang program used to consume 50 MB of RAM incrementally and then hold the entire program (sleep for 1 hour) so as to not exit:

```
package main

import (
        "fmt"
        "strings"
        "time"
)

func main() {
        var longStrs []string
        times := 50
        for i := 1; i <= times; i++ {
                fmt.Printf("===============%d===============\n", i)
                // each time we build a long string to consume 1MB
                    (1000000 * 1byte) RAM
                longStrs = append(longStrs, buildString(1000000,
                    byte(i)))
        }
        // hold the application to exit in 1 hour
        time.Sleep(3600 * time.Second)
}

// buildString build a long string with a length of `n`.
func buildString(n int, b byte) string {
        var builder strings.Builder
        builder.Grow(n)
        for i := 0; i < n; i++ {
                builder.WriteByte(b)
        }
        return builder.String()
}
```

You may try building an image using this code, as shown in *Exercise 1.01*, *Creating a Docker Image and Uploading it to Docker Hub*. This code will be used in place of the code provided in *step 2* of that exercise, and then you can tag the image with **<username>/memconsumer**. Now, we can test resource limitations. Let's use the Docker image and run it with the **--memory** (or **-m**) flag to instruct Docker that we only want to use a certain amount of RAM.

If you are using Ubuntu or any other Debian-based Linux, to continue with the chapter, you may need to manually enable cgroup memory and swap capabilities if you see the following warning message when running this command:

```
docker info > /dev/null
```

This is the warning message that you may see:

```
WARNING: No swap limit support
```

The steps to enable cgroup memory and swap capabilities are as follows:

> **NOTE**
>
> The following three steps are not applicable if you are using macOS.

1. Edit the **/etc/default/grub** file (you may need root privileges for this). Add or edit the **GRUB_CMDLINE_LINUX** line to add the following two key-value pairs:

   ```
   GRUB_CMDLINE_LINUX="cgroup_enable=memory swapaccount=1"
   ```

2. Run **update-grub** using root privileges.
3. Reboot the machine.

Next, we should be able to limit the container memory usage to 100 MB by running the following command:

```
docker run --name memconsumer -d --memory=100m --memory-swap=100m
packtworkshops/the-kubernetes-workshop:memconsumer
```

> **NOTE**
>
> This command pulls the image that we have provided for this demonstration. If you have built your image, you can use that by using **<your_username>/<tag_name>** in the preceding command.

You should see the following response:

```
WARNING: Your kernel does not support swap limit capabilities or the
cgroup is not mounted. Memory limited without swap.
366bd13714cadb099c7ef6056e3b72853735473938b2e633a5cdbf9e94273143
```

This command disables usage on the swap memory (since we specify the same value on **--memory** and **--memory-swap**) so as to gauge the consumption of memory easily.

Let's check the status of our container:

```
docker ps
```

You should see the following response:

```
CONTAINER ID        IMAGE                           COMMAND             CREATED             STAT
US                  PORTS               NAMES
366bd13714ca        hweicdl/memconsumer:v0.0.1      "/main"             35 seconds ago      Up 3
4 seconds                               memconsumer
```

Figure 1.28: Getting the list of containers

Now, let's confirm the restrictions placed on the container by reading the **cgroup** file for the container:

```
cat /sys/fs/cgroup/memory/
docker/366bd13714cadb099c7ef6056e3b7285373547e9e8b2e633a5cdbf9e94273143/
memory.limit_in_bytes
```

If you are using macOS, run this command on the Linux VM. Please use the appropriate path in this command. You should see the following response:

```
104857600
```

The container is launched with a request of 100 MB of RAM, and it runs without any problem since it internally only consumes 50 MB of RAM. From the cgroup setting, you can observe that the value has been updated to **104857600**, which is exactly 100 MB.

But what if the container requests less than 50 MB, while the program running in it requires more than 50 MB? How will Docker and Linux respond to that? Let's take a look.

First, let's remove any running containers:

```
docker rm -f $(docker ps -aq)
```

You should see the following response:

```
366bd13714ca
```

Next, we're going to run the container again, but we will request only 20 MB of memory:

```
docker run --name memconsumer -d --memory=20m --memory-swap=20m
packtworkshops/the-kubernetes-workshop:memconsumer
```

You should see this response:

```
298541bc46855a749f9f8944860a73f3f4f2799ebda7969a5eada60e3809539bab
```

Now, let's check the status of our container:

```
docker ps
```

You should see an empty list like this:

```
CONTAINER ID        IMAGE           COMMAND           CREATED             STATUS
        PORTS               NAMES
```

As you can see, we cannot see our container. Let's list all kinds of containers:

```
docker ps -a
```

You should see the following output:

```
CONTAINER ID        IMAGE                           COMMAND             CREATED             STA
TUS                           PORTS                  NAMES
298541bc4685        hweicdl/memconsumer:v0.0.1    "/memconsumer"      About a minute ago    Exi
ted (137) About a minute ago                       memconsumer
```

Figure 1.29: Getting a list of all containers

We found our container. It has been forcibly killed. It can be verified by checking the container logs:

```
docker logs memconsumer
```

You should see the following output:

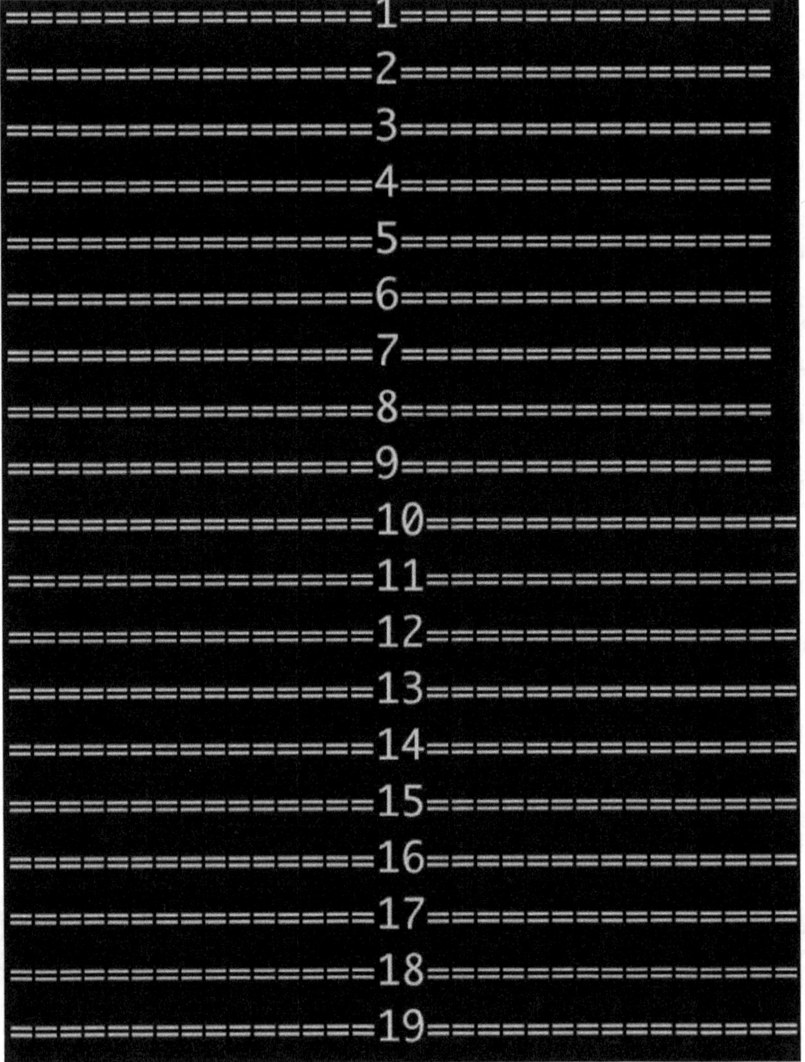

Figure 1.30: The logs of our terminated container

The container tried to increase the memory consumed by 1 MB each time, and when it came to the memory limit (20 MB), it was killed.

From the preceding examples, we have seen how Docker exposes flags to end-users, and how those flags interact with underlying Linux cgroups to limit resource usage.

CONTAINERIZATION: THE MINDSET CHANGE

In the previous sections, we looked at the anatomy of Linux namespaces and cgroups. We explained that a container is essentially a process running natively on the host OS. It is a special process with additional limitations such as OS-level isolation from other processes and the control of resource quotas.

Since Docker 1.11, **containerd** has been adopted as the default container runtime, instead of directly using Docker Daemon (**`dockerd`**) to manage containers. Let's take a look at this runtime. First, restart our container normally:

```
docker run -d packtworkshops/the-kubernetes-workshop:k8s-for-beginners
```

You should see the following response:

```
c7ee681ff8f73fa58cf0b37bc5ce08306913f27c5733c725f7fe97717025625d
```

We can use **`ps -aef --forest`** to list all of the running processes in a hierarchy, and then use **`| grep containerd`** to filter the output by the **`containerd`** keyword. Finally, we can use **`-A 1`** to output one extra line (using **`-A 1`**) so that at least one running container shows up:

```
ps -aef --forest | grep containerd -A 1
```

If you are using macOS, run this command on the Linux VM without the **`--forest`** flag. You should see the following response:

```
root      1037     1  0 05:51 ?        00:00:00 /usr/bin/containerd
root     19374  1037  0 05:54 ?        00:00:00  \_ containerd-shim -namespace moby -workdir /var/lib
/containerd/io.containerd.runtime.v1.linux/moby/c7ee681ff8f73fa58cf0b37bc5ce08306913f27c5733c725f7fe9
7717025625d -address /run/containerd/containerd.sock -containerd-binary /usr/bin/containerd -runtime-
root /var/run/docker/runtime-runc
root     19394 19374  1 05:54 ?        00:00:00      \_ /k8s-for-beginners
--
root     19455 19121  0 05:54 pts/0    00:00:00                          \_ grep containerd -A 1
root      1073     1  0 05:51 ?        00:00:00 /usr/bin/python3 /usr/share/unattended-upgrades/unatt
ended-upgrade-shutdown --wait-for-signal
--
root     19145     1  0 05:54 ?        00:00:00 /usr/bin/dockerd -H fd:// --containerd=/run/container
d/containerd.sock
```

Figure 1.31: Getting processes related to containerd

In the output, we can see that **`containerd`** (PID **`1037`**) acts as the top parent process, and it manages **`containerd-shim`** (PID **`19374`**), and **`containerd-shim`** manages most of the child processes of **`k8s-for-beginners`** (PID **`19394`**), which is the container we started.

Keeping the core idea of a container in mind can help you while migrating any VM-based applications to container-based ones. Basically, there are two patterns to deploy applications in containers:

SEVERAL APPLICATIONS IN ONE CONTAINER

This kind of implementation requires a supervisor application to launch and hold the container. And then, we can put applications into the container as child processes of the supervisor. The supervisor has several variants:

- A customized wrapper script: This needs complicated scripting to control the failures of managed applications.
- A third-party tool such as supervisord or systemd: Upon application failures, the supervisor is responsible for getting it restarted.

ONE APPLICATION IN ONE CONTAINER

This kind of implementation does not require any supervisor as in the previous case. In fact, the life cycle of the application is tied to the life cycle of the container.

A COMPARISON OF THESE APPROACHES

By deploying several applications in a single container, we are essentially treating a container as a VM. This *container as a lightweight VM* approach was once used as a promotion slogan of container technologies. However, as explained, they vary in a lot of aspects. Of course, this way can save the migration efforts from the VM-based development/deployment model to the containers, but it also introduces several drawbacks in the following aspects:

- **Application life cycle control**: Looking from the outside, the container is exposed as one state, as it is essentially a single host process. The life cycles of the internal applications are managed by the "supervisor", and, therefore, cannot be observed from the outside. So, looking from the outside, you may observe that a container stays healthy, but some applications inside it may be restarting persistently. It may keep restarting due to a fatal error in one of its internal applications, which you may not be able to point out.
- **Version upgrade**: If you want to upgrade any one of the different applications in a container, you may have to pull down the entire container. This causes unnecessary downtime for the other applications in that container, which don't need a version upgrade. Thus, if the applications require components that are developed by different teams, their release cycles have to be tightly coupled.

- **Horizontal scaling**: If only one application needs to be scaled out, you have no option but to scale out the whole container, which will also replicate all the other applications. This leads to a waste of resources on the applications that don't need scaling.
- **Operational concerns**: Checking the logs of the applications becomes more challenging as the standard output (**`stdout`**) and error (**`stderr`**) of the container don't represent the logs of the applications inside containers. You have to make an extra effort to manage those logs, such as installing additional monitoring tools to diagnose the health of each application.

Technically, having multiple applications in a single container works, and it doesn't require many mindset changes from a VM perspective. However, when we adopt the container technology to enjoy its benefits, we need to make a trade-off between migration conveniences and long-term maintainability.

The second way (that is, having one application in one container) enables a container to automatically manage the life cycle of the only application present inside it. In this way, we can unify container management by leveraging native Linux capabilities, such as getting an application status by checking the container state and fetching application logs from the **`stdout/stderr`** of the container. This enables you to manage each application in its own release cycle.

However, this is not an easy task. It requires you to rethink the relationship and dependencies of different components so as to break the monolithic applications into microservices. This may require a certain amount of refactoring of the architectural design to include both source code and delivery pipeline changes.

To summarize, adopting container technology is a break-up-and-reorganize journey. It not only takes time for the technology to mature but also, more importantly, it requires changes in people's mindsets. Only with this mindset change can you restructure the applications as well as the underlying infrastructure to unleash the value of containers and enjoy their real benefits. It's the **second reason** that container technologies only started to rise in recent years instead of a decade ago.

THE NEED FOR CONTAINER ORCHESTRATION

The **k8s-for-beginners** container we built in *Exercise 1.01, Creating a Docker Image and Uploading it to Docker Hub*, is nothing but a simple demonstration. In the case of a serious workload deployed in a production environment, and to enable hundreds of thousands of containers running in a cluster, we have many more things to consider. We need a system to manage the following problems:

CONTAINER INTERACTIONS

As an example, suppose that we are going to build a web app with a frontend container displaying information and accepting user requests, and a backend container serving as a datastore that interacts with the frontend container. The first challenge is to figure out how to specify the address of the backend container to the frontend container. It is not a good idea to hardcode the IP, as the container IP is not static. In a distributed system, it is not uncommon for containers or machines to fail due to unexpected issues. So, the link between any two containers must be discoverable and effective across all the machines. On the other hand, the second challenge is that we may want to limit which containers (for example, the backend container) can be visited by which kind of containers (for example, its corresponding frontend ones).

NETWORK AND STORAGE

All the examples that we gave in the previous sections used containers running on the same machine. This is pretty straightforward, as the underlying Linux namespaces and cgroup technologies were designed to work within the same OS entity. If we want to run thousands of containers in a production environment, which is pretty common, we have to resolve the network connectivity issue to ensure that different containers across different machines are able to connect with each other. On the other hand, local or temporary on-disk storage doesn't always work for all workloads. Applications may need the data to be stored remotely and be available to be mounted at will to any machine in the cluster the container is run on, no matter if the container is starting up for the first time or restarting after a failure.

RESOURCE MANAGEMENT AND SCHEDULING

We have seen that a container leverages Linux cgroups to manage its resource usage. To be a modern resource manager, it needs to build an easy-to-use resource model to abstract resources such as CPU, RAM, disk, and GPU. We need to manage a number of containers efficiently, and to provision and free up resources in time so as to achieve high cluster utilization.

Scheduling involves assigning an appropriate machine in the cluster for each of our workloads to run on. We will take a closer look at scheduling as we proceed further in this book. To ensure that each container has the best machine to run, the scheduler (a Kubernetes component that takes care of scheduling) needs to have a global view of the distribution of all containers across the different machines in the cluster. Additionally, in large data centers, the containers would need to be distributed based on the physical locations of the machines or the availability zones of the cloud services. For example, if all containers supporting a service are allocated to the same physical machine, and that machine happens to fail, the service will experience a period of outage regardless of how many replicas of the containers you had deployed.

FAILOVER AND RECOVERY

Application or machine errors are quite common in a distributed system. Therefore, we must consider container and machine failures. When containers encounter fatal errors and exit, they should be able to be restarted on the same or another suitable machine that is available. We should be able to detect machine faults or network partitions so as to reschedule the containers from problematic machines to healthy ones. Moreover, the reconciliation process should be autonomous, to make sure the application is always running in its desired state.

SCALABILITY

As demand increases, you may want to scale up an application. Take a web frontend application as an example. We may need to run several replicas of it and use a load balancer to distribute the incoming traffic evenly among the many replicas of containers supporting the service. To walk one step further, depending on the volume of incoming requests, you may want the application to be scaled dynamically, either horizontally (by having more or fewer replicas), or vertically (by allocating more or fewer resources). This takes the difficulty of system design to another level.

Service Exposure

Suppose we've tackled all the challenges mentioned previously; that's to say, all things are working great within the cluster. Well, here comes another challenge: how can the applications be accessed externally? On one hand, the external endpoint needs to be associated with the underlying on-premises or cloud environment so that it can leverage the infrastructure's API to make itself always accessible. On the other hand, to keep the internal network traffic always going through, the external endpoint needs to be associated with internal backing replicas dynamically – any unhealthy replicas need to be taken out and backfilled automatically to ensure that the application remains online. Moreover, L4 (TCP/UDP) and L7 (HTTP, HTTPS) traffic has different characteristics in terms of packets, and, therefore, needs to be treated in slightly different ways to ensure efficiency. For example, the HTTP header information can be used to reuse the same public IP to serve multiple backend applications.

Delivery Pipeline

From a system administrator's point of view, a healthy cluster must be monitorable, operable, and autonomous in responding to failures. This requires the applications deployed on to the cluster to follow a standardized and configurable delivery pipeline so that it can be managed well at different phases, as well as in different environments.

An individual container is typically used only for completing a single functionality, which is not enough. We need to provide several building blocks to connect the containers all together to accomplish a complicated task.

Orchestrator: Putting All the Things Together

We don't mean to overwhelm you, but the aforementioned problems are very serious, and they arise as a result of the large number of containers that need to be automatically managed. Compared to the VM era, containers do open another door for application management in a large, distributed cluster. However, this also takes container and cluster management challenges to another level. In order to connect the containers to each other to accomplish the desired functionality in a scalable, high-performant, and self-recovering manner, we need a well-designed container orchestrator. Otherwise, we would not be able to migrate our applications from VMs to containers. It's the **third reason** why containerization technologies began to be adopted on a large scale in recent years, particularly upon the emergence of Kubernetes – which is the de facto container orchestrator nowadays.

WELCOME TO THE KUBERNETES WORLD

Unlike typical software that usually evolves piece by piece, Kubernetes got a kick-start as it was designed based on years of experience on Google's internal large-scale cluster management software such as Borg and Omega. That's to say, Kubernetes was born equipped with lots of best practices in the container orchestration and management field. Since day one, the team behind it understood the real pain points and came up with proper designs for tackling them. Concepts such as pods, one IP per pod, declarative APIs, and controller patterns, among others that were first introduced by Kubernetes, seemed to be a bit "impracticable", and some people at that time might have questioned their real value. However, 5 years later, those design rationales remain unchanged and have proven to be the key differentiators from other software.

Kubernetes resolves all the challenges mentioned in the previous section. Some of the well-known features that Kubernetes provides are:

- **Native support for application life cycle management**

  This includes built-in support for application replicating, autoscaling, rollout, and rollback. You can describe the desired state of your application (for example, how many replicas, which image version, and so on), and Kubernetes will automatically reconcile the real state to meet its desired state. Moreover, when it comes to rollout and rollback, Kubernetes ensures that the old replicas are replaced by new ones gradually to avoid downtime of the application.

- **Built-in health-checking support**

  By implementing some "health check" hooks, you can define when the containers can be viewed as ready, alive, or failed. Kubernetes will only start directing traffic to a container when it's healthy as well as ready. It will also restart the unhealthy containers automatically.

- **Service discovery and load balancing**

  Kubernetes provides internal load balancing between different replicas of a workload. Since containers can fail occasionally, Kubernetes doesn't use an IP for direct access. Instead, it uses an internal DNS and exposes each service with a DNS record for communication within a cluster.

- **Configuration management**

  Kubernetes uses labels to describe the machines and workloads. They're respected by Kubernetes' components to manage containers and dependencies in a loosely coupled and flexible fashion. Moreover, the simple but powerful labels can be used to achieve advanced scheduling features (for example, taint/toleration and affinity/anti-affinity).

  In terms of security, Kubernetes provides the Secret API to allow you to store and manage sensitive information. This can help application developers to associate the credentials with your applications securely. From a system administrator's point of view, Kubernetes also provides varied options for managing authentication and authorization.

  Moreover, some options such as ConfigMaps aim to provide fine-grained mechanics to build a flexible application delivery pipeline.

- **Network and storage abstraction**

  Kubernetes initiates the standards to abstract the network and storage specifications, which are known as the CNI (Container Network Interface) and CSI (Container Storage Interface). Each network and storage provider follows the interface and provides its implementation. This mechanism decouples the interface between Kubernetes and heterogeneous providers. With that, end users can use standard Kubernetes APIs to orchestrate their workloads in a portable manner.

Under the hood, there are some key concepts supporting the previously mentioned features, and, more critically, Kubernetes provides different extension mechanics for end-users to build customized clusters or even their own platform:

- **The Declarative API**

  The Declarative API is a way to describe what you want to be done. Under this contract, we just specify the desired final state rather than describing the steps to get there.

  The declarative model is widely used in Kubernetes. It not only enables Kubernetes' core features to function in a fault-tolerant way but also serves as a golden rule to build Kubernetes extension solutions.

- **Concise Kubernetes core**

  It is common for a software project to grow bigger over time, especially for famous open source software such as Kubernetes. More and more companies are getting involved in the development of Kubernetes. But fortunately, since day one, the forerunners of Kubernetes set some baselines to keep Kubernetes' core neat and concise. For example, instead of binding to a particular container runtime (for example, Docker or Containerd), Kubernetes defines an interface (**CRI** or the **container runtime interface**) to be technology-agnostic so that users can choose which runtime to use. Also, by defining the **CNI** (**Container Network Interface**), it delegates the pod and host's network routing implementation to different projects such as Calico and Weave Net. In this way, Kubernetes is able to keep its core manageable, and also encourage more vendors to join, so the end-users can have more choices to avoid vendor lock-ins.

- **Configurable, pluggable, and extensible design**

  All Kubernetes' components provide configuration files and flags for users to customize the functionalities. And each core component is implemented strictly to adhere to the public Kubernetes API; for advanced users, you can choose to implement a part of or the entire component yourself to fulfill a special requirement, as long as it is subject to the API. Moreover, Kubernetes provides a series of extension points to extend Kubernetes' features, as well as building your platform.

In the course of this book, we will walk you through the high-level Kubernetes architecture, its core concepts, best practices, and examples to help you master the essentials of Kubernetes, so that you can build your applications on Kubernetes, and also extend Kubernetes to accomplish complex requirements.

ACTIVITY 1.01: CREATING A SIMPLE PAGE COUNT APPLICATION

In this activity, we will create a simple web application that counts the number of visitors. We will containerize this application, push it to a Docker image registry, and then run the containerized application.

A PageView Web App

We will first build a simple web application to show the pageviews of a particular web page:

1. Use your favorite programming language to write an HTTP server to listen on port **8080** at the root path (**/**). Once it receives a request, it adds **1** to its internal variable and responds with the message **Hello, you're visitor #i**, where **i** is the accumulated number. You should be able to run this application on your local development environment.

> **NOTE**
>
> In case you need help with the code, we have provided a sample piece of code written in Go, which is also used for the solution to this activity. You can get this from the following link: https://packt.live/2DcCQUH.

2. Compose a **Dockerfile** to build the HTTP server and package it along with its dependencies into a Docker image. Set the startup command in the last line to run the HTTP server.

3. Build the **Dockerfile** and push the image to a public Docker images registry (for example, https://hub.docker.com/).

4. Test your Docker images by launching a Docker container. You should use either Docker port mapping or an internal container IP to access the HTTP server.

You can test whether your application is working by repeatedly accessing it using the **curl** command as follows:

```
root@ubuntu:~# curl localhost: 8080
Hello, you're visitor #1.
root@ubuntu:~# curl localhost: 8080
Hello, you're visitor #2.
root@ubuntu:~# curl localhost: 8080
Hello, you're visitor #3.
```

Bonus Objective

Until now, we have implemented the basics of Docker that we have learned in this chapter. However, we can demonstrate the need to link different containers by extending this activity.

For an application, usually, we need multiple containers to focus on different functionalities and then connect them together as a fully functional application. Later on, in this book, you will learn how to do this using Kubernetes; however, for now, let's connect the containers directly.

We can enhance this application by attaching a backend datastore to it. This will allow it to persist its state even after the container is terminated, that is, it will retain the number of visitors. If the container is restarted, it will continue the count instead of resetting it. Here are some guidelines for building on top of the application that you have built so far.

A Backend Datastore

We may lose the pageview number when the container dies, so we need to persist it into a backend datastore:

1. Run one of the three well-known datastores: Redis, MySQL, or MongoDB within a container.

> **NOTE**
>
> The solution to this activity can be found at the following address: https://packt.live/304PEoD. We have implemented Redis for our datastore.

You can find more details about the usage of the Redis container at this link: https://hub.docker.com/_/redis.

If you wish to use MySQL, you can find details about its usage at this link: https://hub.docker.com/_/mysql.

If you wish to use MongoDB, you can find details about its usage at this link: https://hub.docker.com/_/mongo.

2. You may need to run the container using the **--name db** flag to make it discoverable. If you are using Redis, the command should look like this:

```
docker run --name db -d redis
```

Modifying the Web App to Connect to a Backend Datastore

1. Every time a request comes in, you should modify the logic to read the pageview number from the backend, then add **1** to its internal variable, and respond with a message of **Hello, you're visitor #i**, where **i** is the accumulated number. At the same time, store the added pageview number in the datastore. You may need to use the datastore's specific SDK **Software Development Kit (SDK)** to connect to the datastore. You can put the connection URL as **db:<db port>** for now.

> **NOTE**
>
> You may use the source code from the following link: https://packt.live/3lBwOhJ.
>
> If you are using the code from this link, ensure that you modify it to map to the exposed port on your datastore.

2. Rebuild the web app with a new image version.
3. Run the web app container using the **--link db:db** flag.
4. Verify that the pageview number is returned properly.
5. Kill the web app container and restart it to see whether the pageview number gets restored properly.

Once you have created the application successfully, test it by accessing it repeatedly. You should see it working as follows:

```
root@ubuntu:~# curl localhost: 8080
Hello, you're visitor #1.
root@ubuntu:~# curl localhost: 8080
Hello, you're visitor #2.
root@ubuntu:~# curl localhost: 8080
Hello, you're visitor #3.
```

Then, kill the container and restart it. Now, try accessing it. The state of the application should be persisted, that is, the count must continue from where it was before you restarted the container. You should see a result as follows:

```
root@ubuntu:~# curl localhost: 8080
Hello, you're visitor #4.
```

> **NOTE**
>
> The solution to this activity can be found at the following address: https://packt.live/304PEoD.

SUMMARY

In this chapter, we walked you through a brief history of software development and explained some of the challenges in the VM era. With the emergence of Docker, containerization technologies open a new gate in terms of resolving the problems that existed with earlier methods of software development.

We walked you through the basics of Docker and detailed the underlying features of Linux such as namespaces and cgroups, which enable containerization. We then brought up the concept of container orchestration and illustrated the problems it aims to solve. Finally, we gave a very brief overview of some of the key features and methodologies of Kubernetes.

In the next chapter, we will dive a little deeper and take a look at Kubernetes' architecture to understand how it works.

2

AN OVERVIEW OF KUBERNETES

OVERVIEW

In this chapter, we will have our first hands-on introduction to Kubernetes. This chapter will give you a brief overview of the different components of Kubernetes and how they work together. We will also try our hand at working with some fundamental Kubernetes components.

By the end of this chapter, you will have a single-node Minikube environment set up where you can run many of the exercises and activities in this book. You will be able to understand the high-level architecture of Kubernetes and identify the roles of the different components. You will also learn the basics required to migrate containerized applications to a Kubernetes environment.

INTRODUCTION

We ended the previous chapter by providing a brief and abstract introduction to Kubernetes, as well as some of its advantages. In this chapter, we will provide you with a much more concrete high-level understanding of how Kubernetes works. First, we will walk you through how to install Minikube, which is a handy tool that creates a single-node cluster and provides a convenient learning environment for Kubernetes. Then, we will take a 10,000-foot overview of all the components, including their responsibilities and how they interact with each other. After that, we will migrate the Docker application that we built in the previous chapter to Kubernetes and illustrate how it can enjoy the benefits afforded by Kubernetes, such as creating multiple replicas, and version updates. Finally, we will explain how the application responds to external and internal traffic.

Having an overview of Kubernetes is important before we dive deeper into the different aspects of it so that when we learn more specifics about the different aspects, you will have an idea of where they fit in the big picture. Also, when we go even further and explore how to use Kubernetes to deploy applications in a production environment, you will have an idea of how everything is taken care of in the background. This will also help you with optimization and troubleshooting.

SETTING UP KUBERNETES

Had you asked the question, "*How do you easily install Kubernetes?*" three years ago, it would have been hard to give a compelling answer. Embarrassing, but true. Kubernetes is a sophisticated system, and getting it installed and managing it well isn't an easy task.

However, as the Kubernetes community has expanded and matured, more and more user-friendly tools have emerged. As of today, based on your requirements, there are a lot of options to choose from:

- If you are using physical (bare-metal) servers or **virtual machines** (**VMs**), Kubeadm is a good fit.
- If you're running on cloud environments, Kops and Kubespray can ease Kubernetes installation, as well as integration with the cloud providers. In fact, we will teach you how to deploy Kubernetes on AWS using Kops in *Chapter 11, Build Your Own HA Cluster*, and we will take another look at the various options we can use to set up Kubernetes.

- If you want to drop the burden of managing the Kubernetes control plane (which we will learn about later in this chapter), almost all cloud providers have their Kubernetes managed services, such as **Google Kubernetes Engine** (**GKE**), **Amazon Elastic Kubernetes Service** (**EKS**), **Azure Kubernetes Service** (**AKS**), and **IBM Kubernetes Service** (**IKS**).
- If you just want a playground to study Kubernetes in, Minikube and Kind can help you spin up a Kubernetes cluster in minutes.

We will use Minikube extensively throughout this book as a convenient learning environment. But before we proceed to the installation process, let's take a closer look at Minikube itself.

AN OVERVIEW OF MINIKUBE

Minikube is a tool that can be used to set up a single-node cluster, and it provides handy commands and parameters to configure the cluster. It primarily aims to provide a local testing environment. It packs a VM containing all the core components of Kubernetes that get installed onto your host machine, all at once. This allows it to support any operating system, as long as there is a virtualization tool (also known as a Hypervisor) pre-installed. The following are the most common Hypervisors supported by Minikube:

- VirtualBox (works for all operating systems)
- KVM (Linux-specific)
- Hyperkit (macOS-specific)
- Hyper-V (Windows-specific)

Regarding the required hardware resources, the minimum requirement is 2 GB RAM and any dual-core CPU that supports virtualization (Intel VT or AMD-V), but you will, of course, need a more powerful machine if you are trying out heavier workloads.

Just like any other modern software, Kubernetes provides a handy command-line client called kubectl that allows users to interact with the cluster conveniently. In the next exercise, we will set up Minikube and use some basic kubectl commands. We will go into more detail about kubectl in the next chapter.

EXERCISE 2.01: GETTING STARTED WITH MINIKUBE AND KUBERNETES CLUSTERS

In this exercise, we will use Ubuntu 20.04 as the base operating system to install Minikube, using which we can start a single-node Kubernetes cluster easily. Once the Kubernetes cluster has been set up, you should be able to check its status and use **kubectl** to interact with it:

> **NOTE**
>
> Since this exercise deals with software installations, you will need to be logged in as root/superuser. A simple way to switch to being a root user is to run the following command: **sudo su -**.
>
> In *step 9* of this exercise, we will create a regular user and then switch back to it.

1. First, ensure that VirtualBox is installed. You can confirm this by using the following command:

```
which VirtualBox
```

You should see the following output:

```
/usr/bin/VirtualBox
```

If VirtualBox has been successfully installed, the **which** command should show the path of the executable, as shown in the preceding screenshot. If not, then please ensure that you have installed VirtualBox as per the instructions provided in the *Preface*.

2. Download the Minikube standalone binary by using the following command:

```
curl -Lo minikube https://github.com/kubernetes/minikube/releases/
download/<version>/minikube-<ostype-arch> && chmod +x minikube
```

In this command, **<version>** should be replaced with a specific version, such as **v1.5.2** (which is the version we will use in this chapter) or the **latest**. Depending on your host operating system, **<ostype-arch>** should be replaced with **linux-amd64** (for Ubuntu) or **darwin-amd64** (for macOS).

> **NOTE**
>
> To ensure compatibility with the commands provided in this book, we recommend that you install Minikube version **v1.5.2**.

You should see the following output:

```
  % Total    % Received % Xferd  Average Speed   Time    Time     Time  Current
                                 Dload  Upload   Total   Spent    Left  Speed
100   610    0   610    0     0    997      0 --:--:-- --:--:-- --:--:--   996
100 46.3M  100 46.3M    0     0  5135k      0  0:00:09  0:00:09 --:--:-- 5730k
```

Figure 2.1: Downloading the Minikube binary

The preceding command contains two parts: the first command, **curl**, downloads the Minikube binary, while the second command, **chmod**, changes the permission to make it executable.

3. Move the binary into the system path (in the example, it's **/usr/local/bin**) so that we can directly run Minikube, regardless of which directory the command is run in:

```
mv minikube /usr/local/bin
```

When executed successfully, the move (**mv**) command does not give a response in the terminal.

4. After running the move command, we need to confirm that the Minikube executable is now in the correct location:

```
which minikube
```

You should see the following output:

```
/usr/local/bin/minikube
```

> **NOTE**
>
> If the **which minikube** command doesn't give you the expected result, you may need to explicitly add **/usr/local/bin** to your system path by running **export PATH=$PATH:/usr/local/bin**.

5. You can check the version of Minikube using the following command:

```
minikube version
```

You should see the following output:

```
minikube version: v1.5.2
commit: 792dbf92a1de583fcee76f8791cff12e0c9440ad-dirty
```

6. Now, let's download kubectl version **v1.16.2** (so that it's compatible with the version of Kubernetes that our setup of Minikube will create later) and make it executable by using the following command:

```
curl -LO https://storage.googleapis.com/kubernetes-release/release/
v1.16.2/bin/<ostype>/amd64/kubectl && chmod +x kubectl
```

As mentioned earlier, **<ostype>** should be replaced with **linux** (for Ubuntu) or **darwin** (for macOS).

You should see the following output:

```
  % Total    % Received % Xferd  Average Speed   Time    Time     Time  Current
                                 Dload  Upload   Total   Spent    Left  Speed
100 44.5M  100 44.5M    0     0  7232k      0  0:00:06  0:00:06 --:--:-- 8551k
```

Figure 2.2: Downloading the kubectl binary

7. Then, move it to the system path, just like we did for the executable of Minikube earlier:

```
mv kubectl /usr/local/bin
```

8. Now, let's check whether the executable for kubectl is at the correct path:

```
which kubectl
```

You should see the following response:

```
/usr/local/bin/kubectl
```

9. Since we are currently logged in as the **root** user, let's create a regular user called **k8suser** by running the following command:

```
useradd k8suser
```

Enter your desired password when you are prompted for it. You will also be prompted to enter other details, such as your full name. You may choose to skip those details by simply pressing *Enter*. You should see an output similar to the following:

```
Adding user `k8suser' ...
Adding new group `k8suser' (1000) ...
Adding new user `k8suser' (1000) with group `k8suser' ...
Creating home directory `/home/k8suser' ...
Copying files from `/etc/skel' ...
Enter new UNIX password:
Retype new UNIX password:
passwd: password updated successfully
Changing the user information for k8suser
Enter the new value, or press ENTER for the default
        Full Name []:
        Room Number []:
        Work Phone []:
        Home Phone []:
        Other []:
Is the information correct? [Y/n] Y
```

Figure 2.3: Creating a new Linux user

Enter **Y** and hit *Enter* to confirm the final prompt for creating a user, as shown at the end of the previous screenshot.

10. Now, switch user from **root** to **k8suser**:

```
su - k8suser
```

You should see the following output:

```
root@ubuntu:~# su - k8suser
k8suser@ubuntu:~$
```

11. Now, we can create a Kubernetes cluster using **minikube start**:

```
minikube start --kubernetes-version=v1.16.2
```

> **NOTE**
>
> If you want to manage multiple clusters, Minikube provides a **--profile <profile name>** parameter to each cluster.

It will take a few minutes to download the VM images and get everything set up. After Minikube has started up successfully, you should see a response that looks similar to the following:

```
minikube v1.5.2 on Ubuntu 18.04
Automatically selected the 'virtualbox' driver (alternates: [none])
Downloading VM boot image ...
> minikube-v1.5.1.iso.sha256: 65 B / 65 B [-------------] 100.00% ? p/s 0s
> minikube-v1.5.1.iso: 143.76 MiB / 143.76 MiB [-] 100.00% 59.85 MiB p/s 3s
Creating virtualbox VM (CPUs=2, Memory=2000MB, Disk=20000MB) ...
Preparing Kubernetes v1.16.2 on Docker '18.09.9' ...
Downloading kubeadm v1.16.2
Downloading kubelet v1.16.2
Pulling images ...
Launching Kubernetes ...
Waiting for: apiserver
Done! kubectl is now configured to use "minikube"
```

Figure 2.4: Minikube first startup

As we mentioned earlier, Minikube starts up a VM instance with all the components of Kubernetes inside it. By default, it uses VirtualBox, and you can use the **--vm-driver** flag to specify a particular hypervisor driver (such as **hyperkit** for macOS). Minikube also provides the **--kubernetes-version** flag so you can specify the Kubernetes version you want to use. If not specified, it will use the latest version that was available when the Minikube release was finalized. In this chapter, to ensure compatibility of the Kubernetes version with the kubectl version, we have specified Kubernetes version **v1.16.2** explicitly.

The following commands should help establish that the Kubernetes cluster that was started by Minikube is running properly.

12. Use the following command to get the basic status of the various components of the cluster:

```
minikube status
```

You should see the following response:

```
host: Running
kubelet: Running
apiserver: Running
kubeconfig: Configured
```

13. Now, let's look at the version of the kubectl client and Kubernetes server:

```
kubectl version --short
```

You should see the following response:

```
Client Version: v1.16.2
Server Version: v1.16.2
```

14. Let's learn how many machines comprise the cluster and get some basic information about them:

```
kubectl get node
```

You should see a response similar to the following:

```
NAME          STATUS          ROLES          AGE          VERSION
minikube      Ready           master         2m41s        v1.16.2
```

After finishing this exercise, you should have Minikube set up with a single-node Kubernetes cluster. In the next section, we will enter the Minikube VM to take a look at how the cluster is composed and the various components of Kubernetes that make it work.

KUBERNETES COMPONENTS OVERVIEW

By completing the previous exercise, you have a single-node Kubernetes cluster up and running. Before playing your first concert, let's hold on a second and pull the curtains aside to take a look backstage to see how Kubernetes is architected behind the scenes, and then check how Minikube glues its various components together inside its VM.

Kubernetes has several core components that make the wheels of the machine turn. They are as follows:

- API server
- etcd
- Controller manager
- Scheduler
- Kubelet

These components are critical for the functioning of a Kubernetes cluster.

Besides these core components, you would deploy your applications in containers, which are bundled together as pods. We will learn more about pods in *Chapter 5, Pods*. These pods, and several other resources, are defined by something called API objects.

An **API object** describes how a certain resource should be honored in Kubernetes. We usually define API objects using a human-readable manifest file, and then use a tool (such as kubectl) to parse it and hand it over to a Kubernetes API server. Kubernetes then tries to create the resource specified in the object and match its state to the desired state in the object definition, as mentioned in the manifest file. Next, we will walk you through how these components are organized and behave in a single-node cluster created by Minikube.

Minikube provides a command called **`minikube ssh`** that's used to gain SSH access from the host machine (in our machine, it's the physical machine running Ubuntu 20.04) to the **`minikube`** virtual machine, which serves as the sole node in our Kubernetes cluster. Let's see how that works:

```
minikube ssh
```

You will see the following output:

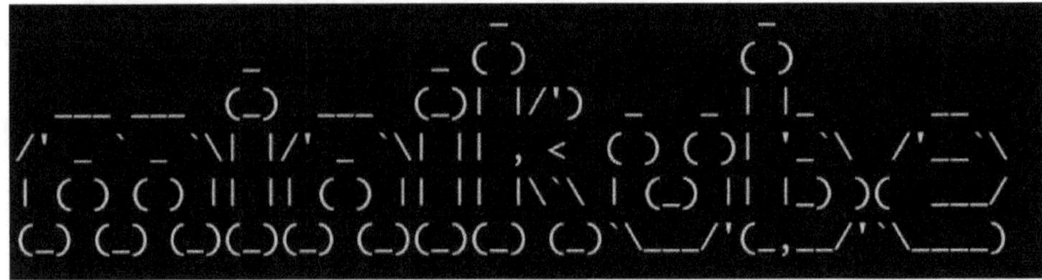

Figure 2.5: Accessing the Minikube VM via SSH

> **NOTE**
>
> All the commands that will be shown later in this section are presumed to have been run inside the Minikube VM, after running **`minikube ssh`**.

Container technology brings the convenience of encapsulating your application. Minikube is no exception - it leverages containers to glue the Kubernetes components together. In the Minikube VM, Docker is pre-installed so that it can manage the core Kubernetes components. You can take a look at this by running **`docker ps`**; however, the result may be overwhelming as it includes all the running containers - both the core Kubernetes components and add-ons, as well as all the columns - which will output a very large table.

To simplify the output and make it easier to read, we will pipe the output from **`docker ps`** into two other Bash commands:

1. **`grep -v pause`**: This will filter the results by not displaying the "sandbox" containers.

   Without **`grep -v pause`**, you would find that each container is "paired" with a "sandbox" container (in Kubernetes, it's implemented as a **`pause`** image). This is because, as mentioned in the previous chapter, Linux containers can be associated (or isolated) by joining the same (or different) Linux namespace. In Kubernetes, a "sandbox" container is used to bootstrap a Linux namespace, and then the containers that run the real application are able to join that namespace. Finer details about how all this works under the hood have been left out of scope for the sake of brevity.

   > **NOTE**
   >
   > If not specified explicitly, the term "namespace" is used interchangeably with "Kubernetes namespace" across this book. In terms of "Linux namespace", "Linux" would not be omitted to avoid confusion.

2. **`awk '{print $NF}'`**: This will only print the last column with a container name.

   Thus, the final command is as follows:

```
docker ps | grep -v pause | awk '{print $NF}'
```

You should see the following output:

```
NAMES
k8s_coredns_coredns-5644d7b6d9-ptps6_kube-system_cd40b8e7-b86e-4451-b4d2-3b364b69574e_0
k8s_coredns_coredns-5644d7b6d9-5sz8f_kube-system_10985af6-c3bf-4eeb-9929-013dfdd20811_0
k8s_storage-provisioner_storage-provisioner_kube-system_c846ce4e-f65e-4f69-a855-f295ef722c
aa_0
k8s_kube-proxy_kube-proxy-dzn4n_kube-system_3d2eb82c-39f6-4162-90f2-b2a549a90792_0
k8s_kube-addon-manager_kube-addon-manager-minikube_kube-system_c3e29047da86ce6690916750ab6
9c40b_0
k8s_kube-apiserver_kube-apiserver-minikube_kube-system_ea167c1941ae64c8329acadaee8ceb69_0
k8s_etcd_etcd-minikube_kube-system_130dcd7636e79f6a2565de2a48e48a38_0
k8s_kube-controller-manager_kube-controller-manager-minikube_kube-system_67888a6f41348f1a4
1e319a7f77279a2_0
k8s_kube-scheduler_kube-scheduler-minikube_kube-system_74dea8da17aa6241e5e4f7b2ba4e1d8e_0
```

Figure 2.6: Getting the list of containers by running the Minikube VM

The highlighted containers shown in the preceding screenshot are basically the core components of Kubernetes. We'll discuss each of these in detail in the following sections.

ETCD

A distributed system may face various kinds of failures (network, storage, and so on) at any moment. To ensure it still works properly when failures arise, critical cluster metadata and state must be stored in a reliable way.

Kubernetes abstracts the cluster metadata and state as a series of API objects. For example, the node API object represents a Kubernetes worker node's specification, as well as its latest status.

Kubernetes uses **etcd** as the backend key-value database to persist the API objects during the life cycle of a Kubernetes cluster. It is important to note that nothing (internal cluster resources or external clients) is allowed to talk to etcd without going through the API server. Any updates to or requests from etcd are made only via calls to the API server.

In practice, etcd is usually deployed with multiple instances to ensure the data is persisted in a secure and fault-tolerant manner.

API SERVER

The API server allows standard APIs to access Kubernetes API objects. It is the only component that talks to backend storage (etcd).

Additionally, by leveraging the fact that it is the single point of contact for communicating to etcd, it provides a convenient interface for clients to "watch" any API objects that they may be interested in. Once the API object has been created, updated, or deleted, the client that is "watching" will get instant notifications so they can act upon those changes. The "watching" client is also known as the "controller", which has become a very popular entity that's used in both built-in Kubernetes objects and Kubernetes extensions.

> **NOTE**
>
> You will learn more about the API server in *Chapter 4, How to Communicate with Kubernetes (API Server)*, and about controllers in *Chapter 7, Kubernetes Controllers*.

SCHEDULER

The scheduler is responsible for distributing the incoming workloads to the most suitable node. The decision regarding distribution is made by the scheduler's understanding of the whole cluster, as well as a series of scheduling algorithms.

> **NOTE**
>
> You will learn more about the scheduler in *Chapter 17, Advanced Scheduling in Kubernetes*.

CONTROLLER MANAGER

As we mentioned earlier in the *API Server* subsection, the API server exposes ways to "watch" almost any API object and notify the watchers about the changes in the API objects being watched.

It works pretty much like a Publisher-Subscriber pattern. The controller manager acts as a typical subscriber and watches the only API objects that it is interested in, and then attempts to make appropriate changes to move the current state toward the desired state described in the object.

For example, if it gets an update from the API server saying that an application claims two replicas, but right now there is only one living in the cluster, it will create the second one to make the application adhere to its desired replica number. The reconciliation process keeps running across the controller manager's life cycle to ensure that all applications stay in their expected state.

The controller manager aggregates various kinds of controllers to honor the semantics of API objects, such as Deployments and Services, which we will introduce later in this chapter.

WHERE IS THE KUBELET?

Note that etcd, the API server, the scheduler, and the controller manager comprise the control plane of Kubernetes. A machine that runs these components is called a master node. The kubelet, on the other hand, is deployed on each worker machine.

In our single-node Minikube cluster, the kubelet is deployed on the same node that carries the control plane components. However, in most production environments, it is not deployed on any of the master nodes. We will learn more about production environments when we deploy a multi-node cluster in *Chapter 11, Build Your Own HA Cluster*.

The kubelet primarily aims at talking to the underlying container runtime (for example, Docker, containerd, or cri-o) to bring up the containers and ensure that the containers are running as expected. Also, it's responsible for sending the status update back to the API server.

However, as shown in the preceding screenshot, the **`docker ps`** command doesn't show anything named **`kubelet`**. To start, stop, or restart any software and make it auto-restart upon failure, usually, we need a tool to manage its life cycle. In Linux, systemd has that responsibility. In Minikube, the kubelet is managed by systemd and runs as a native binary instead of a Docker container. We can run the following command to check its status:

```
systemctl status kubelet
```

You should see an output similar to the following:

```
• kubelet.service - kubelet: The Kubernetes Node Agent
   Loaded: loaded (/usr/lib/systemd/system/kubelet.service; disabled; vendor preset: enabl
ed)
  Drop-In: /etc/systemd/system/kubelet.service.d
           └─10-kubeadm.conf
   Active: active (running) since Wed 2019-11-27 01:04:43 UTC; 1 day 4h ago
     Docs: http://kubernetes.io/docs/
 Main PID: 3298 (kubelet)
    Tasks: 19 (limit: 2161)
   Memory: 39.3M
   CGroup: /system.slice/kubelet.service
           └─3298 /var/lib/minikube/binaries/v1.16.2/kubelet --authorization-mode=Webhook...
```

Figure 2.7: Status of kubelet

By default, the kubelet has the configuration for **`staticPodPath`** in its config file (which is stored at **`/var/lib/kubelet/config.yaml`**). kubelet is instructed to continuously watch the changes in files under that path, and each file under that path represents a Kubernetes component. Let's understand what this means by first finding **`staticPodPath`** in the kubelet's **`config`** file:

```
grep "staticPodPath" /var/lib/kubelet/config.yaml
```

You should see the following output:

```
staticPodPath: /etc/kubernetes/manifests
```

Now, let's see the contents of this path:

```
ls /etc/kubernetes/manifests
```

You should see the following output:

```
addon-manager.yaml.tmpl kube-apiserver.yaml       kube-scheduler.yaml
etcd.yaml               kube-controller-manager.yaml
```

As shown in the list of files, the core components of Kubernetes are defined by objects that have a definition specified in YAML files. In the Minikube environment, in addition to managing the user-created pods, the kubelet also serves as a systemd equivalent in order to manage the life cycle of Kubernetes system-level components, such as the API server, the scheduler, the controller manager, and other add-ons. Once any of these YAML files is changed, the kubelet auto-detects that and updates the state of the cluster so that it matches the desired state defined in the updated YAML configuration.

We will stop here without diving deeper into the design of Minikube. In addition to "static components", the kubelet is also the manager of "regular applications" to ensure that they're running as expected on the node and evicts pods according to the API specification or upon resource shortage.

KUBE-PROXY

kube-proxy appears in the output of the `docker ps` command, but it was not present at `/etc/kubernetes/manifests` when we explored that directory in the previous subsection. This implies its role – it's positioned more as an add-on component instead of a core one.

kube-proxy is designed as a distributed network router that runs on every node. Its ultimate goal is to ensure that inbound traffic to a **Service** (this is an API object that we will introduce later) endpoint can be routed properly. Moreover, if multiple containers are serving one application, it is able to balance the traffic in a round-robin manner by leveraging the underlying Linux iptables/IPVS technology.

There are also some other add-ons such as CoreDNS, though we will skip those so that we can focus on the core components and get a high-level picture.

> **NOTE**
>
> Sometimes, kube-proxy and CoreDNS are also considered core components of a Kubernetes installation. To some extent, that's technically true as they're mandatory in most cases; otherwise, the Service API object won't work. However, in this book, we're leaning more toward categorizing them as "add-ons" as they focus on the implementation of one particular Kubernetes API resource instead of general workflow. Also, kube-proxy and CoreDNS are defined in `addon-manager.yaml.tmpl` instead of being portrayed on the same level as the other core Kubernetes components.

KUBERNETES ARCHITECTURE

In the previous section, we gained a first impression of the core Kubernetes components: etcd, the API server, the scheduler, the controller manager, and the kubelet. These components, plus other add-ons, comprise the Kubernetes architecture, which can be seen in the following diagram:

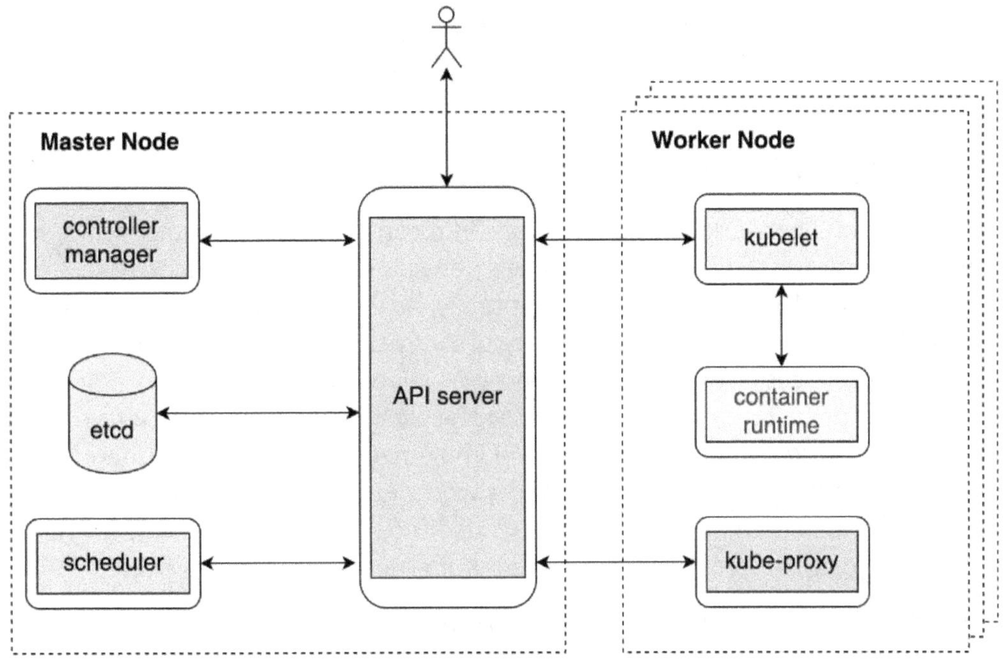

Figure 2.8: Kubernetes architecture

At this point, we won't look at each component in too much detail. However, at a high-level view, it's critical to understand how the components communicate with each other and why they're designed in that way.

The first thing to understand is which components the API server can interact with. From the preceding diagram, we can easily tell that the API server can talk to almost every other component (except the container runtime, which is handled by the kubelet) and that it also serves to interact with end-users directly. This design makes the API server act as the "heart" of Kubernetes. Additionally, the API server also scrutinizes incoming requests and writes API objects into the backend storage (etcd). This, in other words, makes the API server the throttle of security control measures such as authentication, authorization, and auditing.

The second thing to understand is how the different Kubernetes components (except for the API server) interact with each other. It turns out that there is no explicit connection among them – the controller manager doesn't talk to the scheduler, nor does the kubelet talk to kube-proxy.

You read that right – they do need to work in coordination with each other to accomplish many functionalities, but they never directly talk to each other. Instead, they communicate implicitly via the API server. More precisely, they communicate by watching, creating, updating, or deleting corresponding API objects. This is also known as the controller/operator pattern.

CONTAINER NETWORK INTERFACE

There are several networking aspects to take into consideration, such as how a pod communicates with its host machine's network interface, how a node communicates with other nodes, and, eventually, how a pod communicates with any pod across different nodes. As the network infrastructure differs vastly in the cloud or on-premises environments, Kubernetes chooses to solve those problems by defining a specification called the **Container Network Interface** (**CNI**). Different CNI providers can follow the same interface and implement their logic that adheres to the Kubernetes standards to ensure that the whole Kubernetes network works. We will revisit the idea of the CNI in *Chapter 11, Build Your Own HA Cluster*. For now, let's return to our discussion of how the different Kubernetes components work.

Later in this chapter, *Exercise 2.05, How Kubernetes Manages a Pod's Life Cycle*, will help you consolidate your understanding of this and clarify a few things, such as how the different Kubernetes components operate synchronously or asynchronously to ensure a typical Kubernetes workflow, and what would happen if one or more of these components malfunctions. The exercise will help you better understand the overall Kubernetes architecture. But before that, let's introduce our containerized application from the previous chapter to the Kubernetes world and explore a few benefits of Kubernetes.

MIGRATING CONTAINERIZED APPLICATION TO KUBERNETES

In the previous chapter, we built a simple HTTP server called **`k8s-for-beginners`**, and it runs as a Docker container. It works perfectly for a sample application. However, what if you have to manage thousands of containers, and coordinate and schedule them properly? How can you upgrade a service without downtime? How do you keep a service healthy upon unexpected failure? These problems exceed the abilities of a system that simply uses containers alone. What we need is a platform that can orchestrate, as well as manage, our containers.

We have told you that Kubernetes is the solution that we need. Next, we will walk you through a series of exercises regarding how to orchestrate and run containers in Kubernetes using a Kubernetes native approach.

POD SPECIFICATION

A straightforward thought is that we wish to see what the equivalent API call or command to run a container in Kubernetes is. As explained in *Chapter 1, Introduction to Kubernetes and Containers*, a container can join another container's namespace so that they can access each other's resources (for example, network, storage, and so on) without additional overhead. In the real world, some applications may need several containers working closely, either in parallel or in a particular order (the output of one will be processed by another). Also, some generic containers (for example, logging agent, network throttling agent, and so on) may need to work closely with their target containers.

Since an application may often need several containers, a container is not the minimum operational unit in Kubernetes; instead, it introduces a concept called **pods** to bundle one or multiple containers. Kubernetes provides a series of specifications to describe how this pod is supposed to be, including several specifics such as images, resource requests, startup commands, and more. To send this pod spec to Kubernetes, particularly to the Kubernetes API server, we're going to use kubectl.

> **NOTE**
>
> We will learn more about pods in *Chapter 5*, *Pods*, but we will use them in this chapter for the purpose of simple demonstrations. You can refer to the complete list of available pod specifications at this link: https://godoc.org/k8s.io/api/core/v1#PodSpec.

Next, let's learn how to run a single container in Kubernetes by composing the pod spec file (also called the specification, manifest, config, or configuration file). In Kubernetes, you can use YAML or JSON to write this specification file, though YAML is commonly used since it is more human-readable and editable.

Consider the following YAML spec for a very simple pod:

```
kind: Pod
apiVersion: v1
metadata:
  name: k8s-for-beginners
spec:
  containers:
  - name: k8s-for-beginners
    image: packtworkshops/the-kubernetes-workshop:k8s-for-beginners
```

Let's go through the different fields briefly:

- **kind** tells Kubernetes which type of object you want to create. Here, we are creating a **Pod**. In later chapters, you will see many other kinds, such as Deployment, StatefulSet, ConfigMap, and so on.
- **apiVersion** specifies a particular version of an API object. Different versions may behave a bit differently.
- **metadata** includes some attributes that can be used to uniquely identify the pod, such as name and namespace. If we don't specify a namespace, it goes in the **default** namespace.
- **spec** contains a series of fields describing the pod. In this example, there is one container that has its image URL and name specified.

Pods are one of the simplest Kubernetes objects to deploy, so we will use them to learn how to deploy objects using YAML manifests in the following exercise.

APPLYING A YAML MANIFEST

Once we have a YAML manifest ready, we can use **kubectl apply -f <yaml file>** or **kubectl create -f <yaml file>** to instruct the API server to persist the API resources defined in this manifest. When you create a pod from scratch for the first time, it doesn't make much difference which of the two commands you use. However, we may often need to modify the YAML (let's say, for example, if we want to upgrade the image version) and reapply it. If we use the **kubectl create** command, we have to delete and recreate it. However, with the **kubectl apply** command, we can rerun the same command and the delta change will be calculated and applied automatically by Kubernetes.

This is very convenient from an operational point of view. For example, if we use some form of automation, it is much simpler to repeat the same command. So, we will use **kubectl apply** across the following exercise, regardless of whether it's the first time it's being applied or not.

> **NOTE**
>
> A detailed on kubectl can be obtained in *Chapter 4, How to Communicate with Kubernetes (API Server).*

EXERCISE 2.02: RUNNING A POD IN KUBERNETES

In the previous exercise, we started up Minikube and looked at the various Kubernetes components running as pods. Now, in this exercise, we shall deploy our pod. Follow these steps to complete this exercise:

> **NOTE**
>
> If you have been trying out the commands from the *Kubernetes Components Overview* section, don't forget to leave the SSH session by using the **exit** command before beginning this exercise. Unless otherwise specified, all commands using **kubectl** should run on the host machine and not inside the Minikube VM.

1. In Kubernetes, we use a spec file to describe an API object such as a pod. As mentioned earlier, we will stick to YAML as it is more human-readable and editable friendly. Create a file named **k8s-for-beginners-pod.yaml** (using any text editor of your choice) with the following content:

```
kind: Pod
apiVersion: v1
metadata:
  name: k8s-for-beginners
spec:
  containers:
  - name: k8s-for-beginners
    image: packtworkshops/the-kubernetes-workshop:k8s-for-
      beginners
```

> **NOTE**
>
> Please replace the image path in the last line of the preceding YAML file with the path to your image that you created in the previous chapter.

2. On the host machine, run the following command to create this pod:

```
kubectl apply -f k8s-for-beginners-pod.yaml
```

   You should see the following output:

```
pod/k8s-for-beginners created
```

3. Now, we can use the following command to check the pod's status:

```
kubectl get pod
```

   You should see the following response:

```
NAME                 READY    STATUS     RESTARTS    AGE
k8s-for-beginners    1/1      Running    0           7s
```

   By default, **kubectl get pod** will list all the pods using a table format. In the preceding output, we can see the **k8s-for-beginners** pod is running properly and that it has one container that is ready (**1/1**). Moreover, kubectl provides an additional flag called **-o** so we can adjust the output format. For example, **-o yaml** or **-o json** will return the full output of the pod API object in YAML or JSON format, respectively, as it's stored version in Kubernetes' backend storage (etcd).

4. You can use the following command to get more information about the pod:

```
kubectl get pod -o wide
```

   You should see the following output:

```
NAME                READY   STATUS    RESTARTS   AGE   IP           NODE       NOMINATED N
ODE   READINESS GATES
k8s-for-beginners   1/1     Running   0          57s   172.17.0.4   minikube   <none>
      <none>
```

Figure 2.9: Getting more information about pods

   As you can see, the output is still in the table format and we get additional information such as **IP** (the internal pod IP) and **NODE** (which node the pod is running on).

5. You can get the list of nodes in our cluster by running the following command:

```
kubectl get node
```

You should see the following response:

```
NAME          STATUS      ROLES       AGE       VERSION
minikube      Ready       master      30h       v1.16.2
```

6. The IP listed in *Figure 2.9* refers to the internal IP Kubernetes assigned for this pod, and it's used for pod-to-pod communication, not for routing external traffic to pods. Hence, if you try to access this IP from outside the cluster, you will get nothing. You can try that using the following command from the host machine, which will fail:

```
curl 172.17.0.4:8080
```

> **NOTE**
>
> Remember to change **`172.17.0.4`** to the value you get for your environment in *step 4*, as seen in *Figure 2.9*.

The **`curl`** command will just hang and return nothing, as shown here:

```
k8suser@ubuntu:~$ curl 172.17.0.4:8080
^C
```

You will need to press *Ctrl* + *C* to abort it.

7. In most cases, end-users don't need to interact with the internal pod IP. However, just for observation purposes, let's SSH into the Minikube VM:

```
minikube ssh
```

You will see the following response in the terminal:

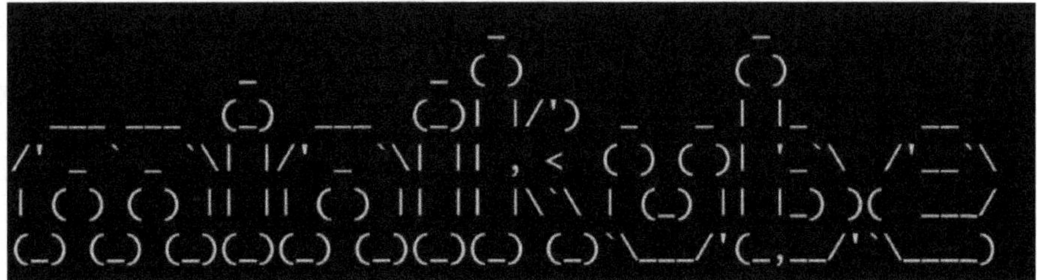

Figure 2.10: Accessing the Minikube VM via SSH

8. Now, try calling the IP from inside the Minikube VM to verify that it works:

```
curl 172.17.0.4:8080
```

You should get a successful response:

```
Hello Kubernetes Beginners!
```

With this, we have successfully deployed our application in a pod on the Kubernetes cluster. We can confirm that it is working since we get a response when we call the application from inside the cluster. Now, you may end the Minikube SSH session using the **`exit`** command.

SERVICE SPECIFICATION

The last part of the previous section proves that network communication works great among different components inside the cluster. But in the real world, you would not expect users of your application to gain SSH access into your cluster to use your applications. So, you would want your application to be accessed externally.

To facilitate just that, Kubernetes provides a concept called a **Service** to abstract the network access to your application's pods. A Service acts as a network proxy to accept network traffic from external users and then distributes it to internal pods. However, there should be a way to describe the association rule between the Service and the corresponding pods. Kubernetes uses labels, which are defined in the pod definitions, and label selectors, which are defined in the Service definition, to describe this relationship.

> **NOTE**
>
> You will learn more about labels and label selectors in *Chapter 6*, *Labels and Annotations*.

Let's consider the following sample spec for a Service:

```
kind: Service
apiVersion: v1
metadata:
  name: k8s-for-beginners
spec:
  selector:
    tier: frontend
```

```
  type: NodePort
  ports:
  - port: 80
    targetPort: 8080
```

Similar to a pod spec, here, we define **kind** and **apiVersion**, while **name** is defined under the **metadata** field. Under the **spec** field, there are several critical fields to take note of:

- **selector** defines the labels to be selected to match a relationship with the corresponding pods, which, as you will see in the following exercise, are supposed to be labeled properly.
- **type** defines the type of Service. If not specified, the default type is **ClusterIP**, which means it's only used within the cluster, that is, internally. Here, we specify it as **NodePort**. This means the Service will expose a port in each node of the cluster and associate the port with the corresponding pods. Another well-known type is called **LoadBalancer**, which is typically not implemented in a vanilla Kubernetes offering. Instead, Kubernetes delegates the implementation to each cloud provider, such as GKE, EKS, and so on.
- **ports** include a series of **port** fields, each with a **targetPort** field. The **targetPort** field is the actual port that's exposed by the destination pod.

  Thus, the Service can be accessed internally via **<service ip>:<port>**. Now, for example, if you have an NGINX pod running internally and listening on port 8080, then you should define **targetPort** as **8080**. You can specify any arbitrary number for the **port** field, such as **80** in this case. Kubernetes will set up and maintain the mapping between **<service IP>:<port>** and **<pod IP>:<targetPort>**. In the following exercise, we will learn how to access the Service from outside the cluster and bring external traffic inside the cluster via the Service.

In the following exercise, we will define Service manifests and create them using **kubectl apply** commands. You will learn that the common pattern for resolving problems in Kubernetes is to find out the proper API objects, then compose the detailed specs using YAML manifests, and finally create the objects to bring them into effect.

EXERCISE 2.03: ACCESSING A POD VIA A SERVICE

In the previous exercise, we observed that an internal pod IP doesn't work for anyone outside the cluster. In this exercise, we will create Services that will act as connectors to map the external requests to the destination pods so that we can access the pods externally without entering the cluster. Follow these steps to complete this exercise:

1. Firstly, let's tweak the pod spec from *Exercise 2.02, Running a Pod in Kubernetes*, to apply some labels. Modify the contents of the **k8s-for-beginners-pod1.yaml** file, as follows:

```
kind: Pod
apiVersion: v1
metadata:
  name: k8s-for-beginners
  labels:
    tier: frontend
spec:
  containers:
  - name: k8s-for-beginners
    image: packtworkshops/the-kubernetes-workshop:k8s-for-
      beginners
```

   Here, we added a label pair, **tier: frontend**, under the **labels** field.

2. Because the pod name remains the same, let's rerun the **apply** command so that Kubernetes knows that we're trying to update the pod's spec, instead of creating a new pod:

```
kubectl apply -f k8s-for-beginners-pod1.yaml
```

   You should see the following response:

```
pod/k8s-for-beginners configured
```

   Behind the scenes, for the **kubectl apply** command, kubectl generates the difference of the specified YAML and the stored version in the Kubernetes server-side storage (that is, etcd). If the request is valid (that is, we have not made any errors in the specification format or the command), kubectl will send an HTTP patch to the Kubernetes API server. Hence, only the delta changes will be applied. If you look at the message that's returned, you'll see it says **pod/k8s-for-beginners configured** instead of **created**, so we can be sure it's applying the delta changes and not creating a new pod.

3. You can use the following command to explicitly display the labels that have been applied to existing pods:

```
kubectl get pod --show-labels
```

You should see the following response:

```
NAME                READY  STATUS    RESTARTS   AGE   LABELS
k8s-for-beginners 1/1    Running   0          16m   tier=frontend
```

Now that the pod has the **tier: frontend** attribute, we're ready to create a Service and link it to the pods.

4. Create a file named **k8s-for-beginners-svc.yaml** with the following content:

```
kind: Service
apiVersion: v1
metadata:
  name: k8s-for-beginners
spec:
  selector:
    tier: frontend
  type: NodePort
  ports:
  - port: 80
    targetPort: 8080
```

5. Now, let's create the Service using the following command:

```
kubectl apply -f k8s-for-beginners-svc.yaml
```

You should see the following response:

```
service/k8s-for-beginners created
```

6. Use the **get** command to return the list of created Services and confirm whether our Service is online:

```
kubectl get service
```

You should see the following response:

NAME	TYPE	CLUSTER-IP	EXTERNAL-IP	PORT(S)	AGE
k8s-for-beginners	NodePort	10.109.16.179	<none>	80:32571/TCP	17s
kubernetes	ClusterIP	10.96.0.1	<none>	443/TCP	31h

Figure 2.11: Getting the list of Services

So, you may have noticed that the **`PORT(S)`** column outputs **`80:32571/TCP`**. Port **`32571`** is an auto-generated port that's exposed on every node, which is done intentionally so that external users can access it. Now, before moving on to the next step, exit the SSH session.

7. Now, we have the "external port" as **`32571`**, but we still need to find the external IP. Minikube provides a utility we can use to easily access the **`k8s-for-beginners`** Service:

```
minikube service k8s-for-beginners
```

You should see a response that looks similar to the following:

NAMESPACE	NAME	TARGET PORT	URL
default	k8s-for-beginners		http://192.168.99.100:32571

Figure 2.12: Getting the URL and port to access the NodePort Service

Depending on your environment, this may also automatically open a browser web page so you can access the Service. From the URL, you will be able to see that the Service port is **`32571`**. The external IP is actually the IP of the Minikube VM.

8. You can also access our application from outside the cluster via the command line:

```
curl http://192.168.99.100:32571
```

You should see the following response:

```
Hello Kubernetes Beginners!
```

As a summary, in this exercise, we created a **NodePort** Service to enable external users to access the internal pods without entering the cluster. Under the hood, there are several layers of traffic transitions that make this happen:

- The first layer is from the external user to the machine IP at the auto-generated random port (3XXXX).
- The second layer is from the random port (3XXXX) to the Service IP (10.X.X.X) at port **80**.
- The third layer is from the Service IP (10.X.X.X) ultimately to the pod IP at port **8080**.

The following is a diagram illustrating these interactions:

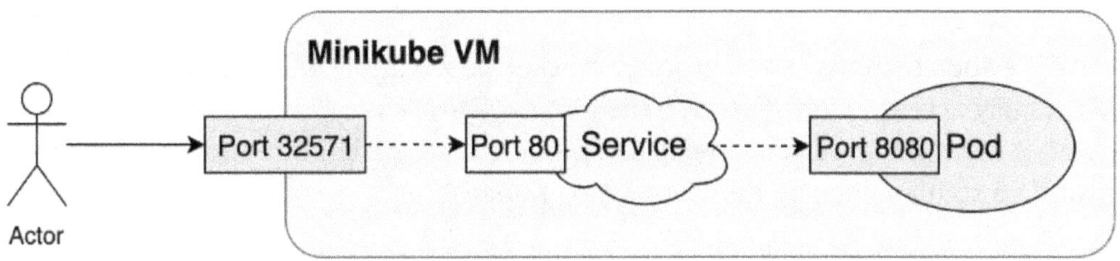

Figure 2.13: Routing traffic from a user outside the cluster to the pod running our application

SERVICES AND PODS

In *step 3* of the previous exercise, you may have noticed that the Service tries to match pods by labels (the **selector** field under the **spec** section) instead of using a fixed pod name or something similar. From a pod's perspective, it doesn't need to know which Service is bringing traffic to it. (In some rare cases, it can even be mapped to multiple Services; that is, multiple Services may be sending traffic to a pod.)

This label-based matching mechanism is widely used in Kubernetes. It enables the API objects to be loosely coupled at runtime. For example, you can specify **tier: frontend** as the label selector, which will, in turn, be associated with the pods that are labeled as **tier: frontend**.

Due to this, by the time the Service is created, it doesn't matter if the backing pods exist or not. It's totally acceptable for backing pods to be created later, and after they are created, the Service object will become associated with the correct pods. Internally, the whole mapping logic is implemented by the service controller, which is part of the controller manager component. It's also possible that a Service may have two matching pods at a time, and later a third pod is created with matching labels, or one of the existing pods gets deleted. In either case, the service controller can detect such changes and ensure that users can always access their application via the Service endpoint.

It's a very commonly used pattern in Kubernetes to orchestrate your application using different kinds of API objects and then glue them together by using labels or other loosely coupled conventions. It's also the key part of container orchestration.

DELIVERING KUBERNETES-NATIVE APPLICATIONS

In the previous sections, we migrated a Docker-based application to Kubernetes and successfully accessed it from inside the Minikube VM, as well as externally. Now, let's see what other benefits Kubernetes can provide if we design our application from the ground up so that it can be deployed using Kubernetes.

Along with the increasing usage of your application, it may be common to run several replicas of certain pods to serve a business functionality. In this case, grouping different containers in a pod alone is not sufficient. We need to go ahead and create groups of pods that are working together. Kubernetes provides several abstractions for groups of pods, such as Deployments, DaemonSets, Jobs, CronJobs, and so on. Just like the Service object, these objects can also be created by using a spec that's been defined in a YAML file.

To start understanding the benefits of Kubernetes, let's use a Deployment to demonstrate how to replicate (scale up/down) an application in multiple pods.

Abstracting groups of pods using Kubernetes gives us the following advantages:

- **Creating replicas of pods for redundancy**: This is the main advantage of abstractions of groups of pods such as Deployments. A Deployment can create several pods with the given spec. A Deployment will automatically ensure that the pods that it creates are online, and it will automatically replace any pods that fail.

- **Easy upgrades and rollbacks**: Kubernetes provides different strategies that you can use to upgrade your applications, as well as rolling versions back. This is important because in modern software development, the software is often developed iteratively, and updates are released frequently. An upgrade can change anything in the Deployment specification. It can be an update of labels or any other field(s), an image version upgrade, an update on its embedded containers, and so on.

Let's take a look at some notable aspects of the spec of a sample Deployment:

k8s-for-beginners-deploy.yaml

```
apiVersion: apps/v1
kind: Deployment
metadata:
  name: k8s-for-beginners
spec:
  replicas: 3
  selector:
    matchLabels:
      tier: frontend
  template:
    metadata:
      labels:
        tier: frontend
    spec:
      containers:
      - name: k8s-for-beginners
        image: packtworkshops/the-kubernetes-workshop:k8s-for-
          beginners
```

In addition to wrapping the pod spec as a "template", a Deployment must also specify its kind (`Deployment`), as well as the API version (`apps/v1`).

> **NOTE**
>
> For some historical reason, the spec name `apiVersion` is still being used. But technically speaking, it literally means `apiGroupVersion`. In the preceding Deployment example, it belongs to the `apps` group and is version `v1`.

In the Deployment spec, the **replicas** field instructs Kubernetes to start three pods using the pod spec defined in the **template** field. The **selector** field plays the same role as we saw in the case of the Service – it aims to associate the Deployment object with specific pods in a loosely coupled manner. This is particularly useful if you want to bring any preexisting pods under the management of your new Deployment.

The replica number defined in a Deployment or other similar API object represents the desired state of how many pods are supposed to be running continuously. If some of these pods fail for some unexpected reason, Kubernetes will automatically detect that and create a corresponding number of pods to take their place. We will explore that in the following exercise.

We'll see a Deployment in action in the following exercise.

EXERCISE 2.04: SCALING A KUBERNETES APPLICATION

In Kubernetes, it's easy to increase the number of replicas running the application by updating the **replicas** field of a Deployment spec. In this exercise, we'll experiment with how to scale a Kubernetes application up and down. Follow these steps to complete this exercise:

1. Create a file named **k8s-for-beginners-deploy.yaml** using the content shown here:

```
apiVersion: apps/v1
kind: Deployment
metadata:
  name: k8s-for-beginners
spec:
  replicas: 3
  selector:
    matchLabels:
      tier: frontend
  template:
    metadata:
      labels:
        tier: frontend
    spec:
      containers:
      - name: k8s-for-beginners
        image: packtworkshops/the-kubernetes-workshop:k8s-for-
          beginners
```

If you take a closer look, you'll see that this Deployment spec is largely based on the pod spec from earlier exercises (**k8s-for-beginners-pod1.yaml**), which you can see under the **template** field.

2. Next, we can use kubectl to create the Deployment:

```
kubectl apply -f k8s-for-beginners-deploy.yaml
```

You should see the following output:

```
deployment.apps/k8s-for-beginners created
```

3. Given that the Deployment has been created successfully, we can use the following command to show all the Deployment's statuses, such as their names, running pods, and so on:

```
kubectl get deploy
```

You should get the following response:

```
NAME                 READY   UP-TO-DATE   AVAILABLE   AGE
k8s-for-beginners    3/3     3            3           41s
```

> **NOTE**
>
> As shown in the previous command, we are using **deploy** instead of **deployment**. Both of these will work and **deploy** is an allowed short name for **deployment**. You can find a quick list of some commonly used short names at this link: https://kubernetes.io/docs/reference/kubectl/overview/#resource-types.
>
> You can also view the short names by running **kubectl api-resources**, without specifying the resource type.

4. A pod called **k8s-for-beginners** exists that we created in the previous exercise. To ensure that we see only the pods being managed by the Deployment, let's delete the older pod:

```
kubectl delete pod k8s-for-beginners
```

You should see the following response:

```
pod "k8s-for-beginners" deleted
```

5. Now, get a list of all the pods:

```
kubectl get pod
```

You should see the following response:

```
NAME                                 READY   STATUS    RESTARTS   AGE
k8s-for-beginners-66644bb776-7j9mw   1/1     Running   0          106s
k8s-for-beginners-66644bb776-dzf9j   1/1     Running   0          106s
k8s-for-beginners-66644bb776-fg8s5   1/1     Running   0          106s
```

Figure 2.14: Getting the list of pods

The Deployment has created three pods, and their labels (specified in the **labels** field in *step 1*) happen to match the Service we created in the previous section. So, what will happen if we try to access the Service? Will the network traffic going to the Service be smartly routed to the new three pods? Let's test this out.

6. To see how the traffic is distributed to the three pods, we can simulate a number of consecutive requests to the Service endpoint by running the **curl** command inside a Bash **for** loop, as follows:

```
for i in $(seq 1 30); do curl <minikube vm ip>:<service node port>;
done
```

> **NOTE**
>
> In this command, use the same IP and port that you used in the previous exercise if you are running the same instance of Minikube. If you have restarted Minikube or have made any other changes, please get the proper IP of your Minikube cluster by following *step 9* of the previous exercise.

Once you've run the command with the proper IP and port, you should see the following output:

```
Hello Kubernetes Beginners!
Hello Kubernetes Beginners!
Hello Kubernetes Beginners!
Hello Kubernetes Beginners!
Hello Kubernetes Beginners!
Hello Kubernetes Beginners!
Hello Kubernetes Beginners!
Hello Kubernetes Beginners!
Hello Kubernetes Beginners!
Hello Kubernetes Beginners!
Hello Kubernetes Beginners!
Hello Kubernetes Beginners!
Hello Kubernetes Beginners!
Hello Kubernetes Beginners!
Hello Kubernetes Beginners!
```

Figure 2.15: Repeatedly accessing our application

From the output, we can tell that all 30 requests get the expected response.

7. You can run **`kubectl logs <pod name>`** to check the log of each pod. Let's go one step further and figure out the exact number of requests each pod has responded to, which might help us find out whether the traffic was evenly distributed. To do that, we can pipe the logs of each pod into the **`wc`** command to get the number of lines:

```
kubectl logs <pod name> | wc -l
```

Run the preceding command three times, copying the pod name you obtained, as shown in *Figure 2.16*:

```
k8suser@ubuntu:~$ kubectl logs k8s-for-beginners-66644bb776-7j9mw | wc -l
9
k8suser@ubuntu:~$ kubectl logs k8s-for-beginners-66644bb776-dzf9j | wc -l
10
k8suser@ubuntu:~$ kubectl logs k8s-for-beginners-66644bb776-fg8s5 | wc -l
11
```

Figure 2.16: Getting the logs of each of the three pod replicas running our application

The result shows that the three pods handled **9**, **10**, and **11** requests, respectively. Due to the small sample size, the distribution is not absolutely even (that is, **10** for each), but it is sufficient to indicate the default round-robin distribution strategy used by a Service.

> **NOTE**
>
> You can read more about how kube-proxy leverages iptables to perform the internal load balancing by looking at the official documentation: https://kubernetes.io/docs/concepts/services-networking/service/#proxy-mode-iptables.

8. Next, let's learn how to scale up a Deployment. There are two ways of accomplishing this: one way is to modify the Deployment's YAML config, where we can set the value of **replicas** to another number (such as **5**), while the other way is to use the **kubectl scale** command, as follows:

```
kubectl scale deploy k8s-for-beginners --replicas=5
```

You should see the following response:

```
deployment.apps/k8s-for-beginners scaled
```

9. Let's verify whether there are five pods running:

```
kubectl get pod
```

You should see a response similar to the following:

```
NAME                                 READY   STATUS    RESTARTS   AGE
k8s-for-beginners-66644bb776-7j9mw   1/1     Running   0          16m
k8s-for-beginners-66644bb776-cdlgh   1/1     Running   0          69s
k8s-for-beginners-66644bb776-dzf9j   1/1     Running   0          16m
k8s-for-beginners-66644bb776-fg8s5   1/1     Running   0          16m
k8s-for-beginners-66644bb776-jhb5x   1/1     Running   0          69s
```

Figure 2.17: Getting the list of pods

The output shows that the existing three pods are kept and that two new pods are created.

10. Similarly, you can specify replicas that are smaller than the current number. In our example, let's say that we want to shrink the replica's number to **2**. The command for this would look as follows:

```
kubectl scale deploy k8s-for-beginners --replicas=2
```

You should see the following response:

```
deployment.apps/k8s-for-beginners scaled
```

11. Now, let's verify the number of pods:

```
kubectl get pod
```

You should see a response similar to the following:

```
NAME                                  READY   STATUS    RESTARTS   AGE
k8s-for-beginners-66644bb776-7j9mw    1/1     Running   0          18m
k8s-for-beginners-66644bb776-dzf9j    1/1     Running   0          18m
```

Figure 2.18: Getting the list of pods

As shown in the preceding screenshot, there are two pods, and they are both running as expected. Thus, in Kubernetes' terms, we can say, "the Deployment is in its desired state".

12. We can run the following command to verify this:

```
kubectl get deploy
```

You should see the following response:

```
NAME                  READY    UP-TO-DATE    AVAILABLE    AGE
k8s-for-beginners     2/2      2             2            19m
```

13. Now, let's see what happens if we delete one of the two pods:

```
kubectl delete pod <pod name>
```

You should get the following response:

```
pod "k8s-for-beginners-66644bb776-7j9mw" deleted
```

14. Check the status of the pods to see what has happened:

```
kubectl get pod
```

You should see the following response:

```
NAME                                 READY   STATUS    RESTARTS   AGE
k8s-for-beginners-66644bb776-dzf9j   1/1     Running   0          20m
k8s-for-beginners-66644bb776-pwsjn   1/1     Running   0          22s
```

Figure 2.19: Getting the list of pods

We can see that there are still two pods. From the output, it's worth noting that the first pod name is the same as the second pod in *Figure 2.18* (this is the one that was not deleted), but that the highlighted pod name is different from any of the pods in *Figure 2.18*. This indicates that the highlighted one is the pod that was newly created to replace the deleted one. The Deployment created a new pod so that the number of running pods satisfies the desired state of the Deployment.

In this exercise, we have learned how to scale a deployment up and down. You can scale other similar Kubernetes objects, such as DaemonSets and StatefulSets, in the same way. Also, for such objects, Kubernetes will try to auto-recover the failed pods.

POD LIFE CYCLE AND KUBERNETES COMPONENTS

The previous sections in this chapter briefly described the Kubernetes components and how they work internally with each other. On the other hand, we also demonstrated how to use some Kubernetes API objects (Pods, Services, and Deployments) to compose your applications.

But how is a Kubernetes API object managed by different Kubernetes components? Let's consider a pod as an example. Its life cycle can be illustrated as follows:

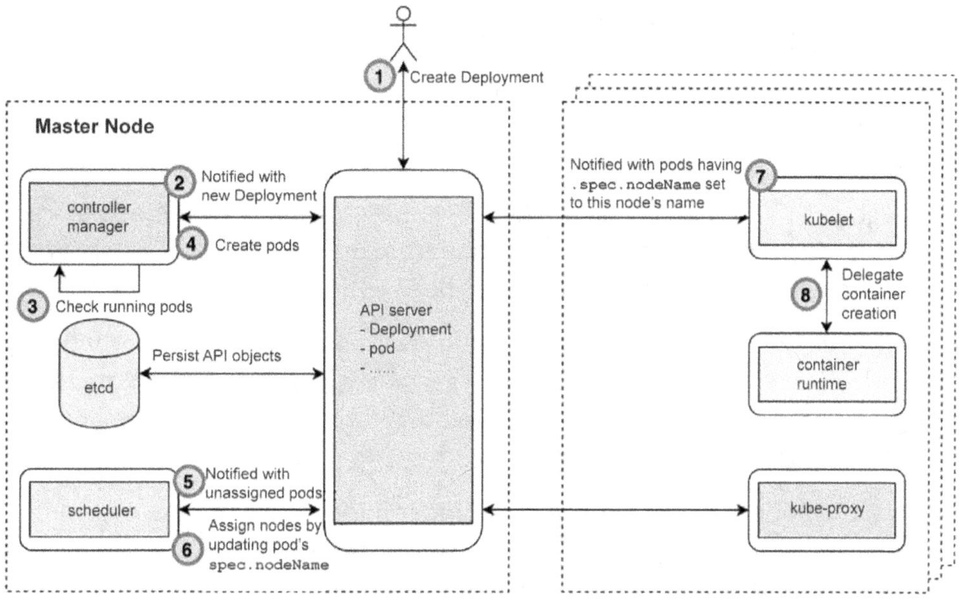

Figure 2.20: The process behind the creation of a pod

This entire process can be broken down as follows:

1. A user starts to deploy an application by sending a Deployment YAML manifest to the Kubernetes API server. The API server verifies the request and checks whether it's valid. If it is, it persists the Deployment API object to its backend datastore (etcd).

> **NOTE**
>
> For any step that evolves by modifying API objects, interactions have to happen between etcd and the API server, so we don't list the interactions as extra steps explicitly.

2. By now, the pod hasn't been created yet. The controller manager gets a notification from the API server that a Deployment has been created.

3. Then, the controller manager checks whether the desired number of replica pods are running already.

4. If there are not enough pods running, it creates the appropriate number of pods. The creation of pods is accomplished by sending a request with the pod spec to the API server. It's quite similar to how a user would apply the Deployment YAML, but with the major difference being that this happens inside the controller manager in a programmatic manner.

5. Although pods have been created, they're nothing but some API objects stored in etcd. Now, the scheduler gets a notification from the API server saying that new pods have been created and no node has been assigned for them to run.

6. The scheduler checks the resource usage, as well as existing pods allocation, and then calculates the node that fits best for each new pod. At the end of this step, the scheduler sends an update request to the API server by setting the pod's **nodeName** spec to the chosen node.

7. By now, the pods have been assigned a proper node to run on. However, no physical containers are running. In other words, the application doesn't work yet. Each kubelet (running on different worker nodes) gets notifications, indicating that some pods are expected to be run. Each kubelet will then check whether the pods to be run have been assigned the node that a kubelet is running on.

8. Once the kubelet determines that a pod is supposed to be on its node, it calls the underlying container runtime (Docker, containerd, or cri-o, for instance) to spin up the containers on the host. Once the containers are up, the kubelet is responsible for reporting its status back to the API server.

With this basic flow in mind, you should now have a vague understanding of the answers to the following questions:

- Who is in charge of pod creation? What's the state of the pod upon creation?
- Who is responsible for placing a pod? What's the state of the pod after placement?
- Who brings up the concrete containers?
- Who is in charge of the overall message delivery process to ensure that all components work together?

In the following exercise, we will use a series of concrete experiments to help you solidify this understanding. This will allow you to see how things work in practice.

EXERCISE 2.05: HOW KUBERNETES MANAGES A POD'S LIFE CYCLE

As a Kubernetes cluster comprises multiple components, and each component works simultaneously, it's usually difficult to know what's exactly happening in each phase of a pod's life cycle. To solve this problem, we will use a film editing technique to "play the whole life cycle in slow motion", so as to observe each phase. We will turn off the master plane components and then attempt to create a pod. Then, we will respond to the errors that we see, and slowly bring each component online, one by one. This will allow us to slow down and examine each stage of the process of pod creation step-by-step. Follow these steps to complete this exercise:

1. First, let's delete the Deployment and Service we created earlier by using the following command:

   ```
   kubectl delete deploy k8s-for-beginners && kubectl delete service
   k8s-for-beginners
   ```

   You should see the following response:

   ```
   deployment.apps "k8s-for-beginners" deleted
   service "k8s-for-beginners" deleted
   ```

2. Prepare two terminal sessions: one (host terminal) to run commands on your host machine and another (Minikube terminal) to pass commands inside the Minikube VM via SSH. Thus, your Minikube session will be initiated like this:

   ```
   minikube ssh
   ```

   You will see the following output:

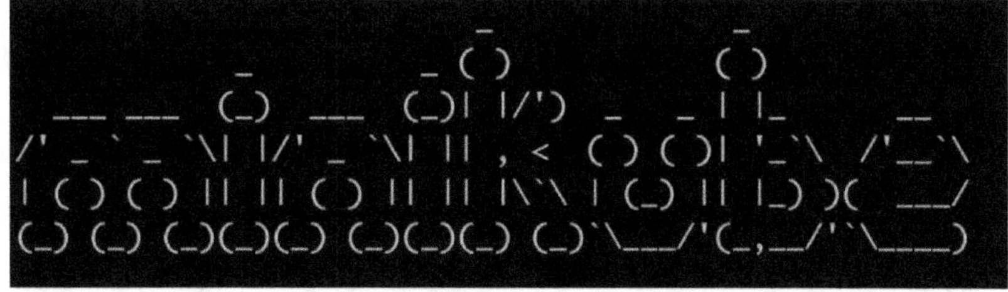

Figure 2.21: Accessing the Minikube VM via SSH

> **NOTE**
>
> All **kubectl** commands are expected to be run in the host terminal session, while all **docker** commands are to be run in the Minikube terminal session.

3. In the Minikube session, clean up all stopped Docker containers:

```
docker rm $(docker ps -a -q)
```

You should see the following output:

```
4e4d85467928
3f450986aa45
ce9fadaaae1c
Error response from daemon: You cannot remove a running container 75439759292b1ccabd
64321d50961eab65fe2dc0a7a8a65631d583aad6ee4627. Stop the container before attempting
 removal or force remove
Error response from daemon: You cannot remove a running container e6a70641b409ffa75c
a2ecd978acd5c000c760d7d2b847f8584c89518cd32bd0. Stop the container before attempting
 removal or force remove
```

Figure 2.22: Cleaning up all stopped Docker containers

You may see some error messages such as "You cannot remove a running container ...". This is because the preceding **docker rm** command runs against all containers (**docker ps -a -q**), but it won't stop any running containers.

4. In the Minikube session, stop the kubelet by running the following command:

```
sudo systemctl stop kubelet
```

This command does not show any response upon successful execution.

> **NOTE**
>
> Later in this exercise, we will manually stop and start other Kubernetes components, such as the API server, that are managed by the kubelet in a Minikube environment. Hence, it's required that you stop the kubelet first in this exercise; otherwise, the kubelet will automatically restart its managed components.
>
> Note that in typical production environments, unlike Minikube, it's not necessary to run the kubelet on the master node to manage the master plane components; the kubelet is only a mandatory component on worker nodes.

5. After 30 seconds, check the cluster's status by running the following command in your host terminal session:

```
kubectl get node
```

You should see the following response:

```
NAME        STATUS     ROLES    AGE    VERSION
minikube    NotReady   master   32h    v1.16.2
```

It's expected that the status of the **minikube** node is changed to **NotReady** because the kubelet has been stopped.

6. In your Minikube session, stop **kube-scheduler**, **kube-controller-manager**, and **kube-apiserver**. As we saw earlier, all of these are running as Docker containers. Hence, you can use the following commands, one after the other:

```
docker stop $(docker ps | grep kube-scheduler | grep -v pause | awk
'{print $1}')

docker stop $(docker ps | grep kube-controller-manager | grep -v
pause | awk '{print $1}')

docker stop $(docker ps | grep kube-apiserver | grep -v pause | awk
'{print $1}')
```

You should see the following responses:

```
$ docker stop $(docker ps | grep kube-scheduler | grep -v pause | awk '{print $1}')
11d8a27e3ee0
$ docker stop $(docker ps | grep kube-controller-manager | grep -v pause | awk '{print $1}
')
35facb013c8f
$ docker stop $(docker ps | grep kube-apiserver | grep -v pause | awk '{print $1}')
9e1cf098b67c
```

Figure 2.23: Stopping the containers running Kubernetes components

As we explained in the *Kubernetes Components Overview* section, the **grep -v pause | awk '{print $1}'** command can fetch the exact container ID (**$1** = the first column) of the required Docker containers. Then, the **docker pause** command can pause that running Docker container.

Now, the three major Kubernetes components have been stopped.

7. Now, you need to create a Deployment spec on your host machine. Create a file named **k8s-for-beginners-deploy2.yaml** with the following content:

```
apiVersion: apps/v1
kind: Deployment
metadata:
  name: k8s-for-beginners
spec:
  replicas: 1
  selector:
    matchLabels:
      tier: frontend
  template:
    metadata:
      labels:
        tier: frontend
    spec:
      containers:
      - name: k8s-for-beginners
        image: packtworkshops/the-kubernetes-workshop:k8s-for-
          beginners
```

8. Try to create the Deployment by running the following command on your host session:

```
kubectl apply -f k8s-for-beginners-deploy2.yaml
```

You should see a response similar to this:

```
error: unable to recognize "k8s-for-beginners-deploy2.yaml": Get https://192.168.99.100:84
43/api?timeout=32s: dial tcp 192.168.99.100:8443: connect: connection refused
```

Figure 2.24: Trying to create a new Deployment

Unsurprisingly, we got a network timeout error since we intentionally stopped the Kubernetes API server. If the API server is down, you cannot run any **kubectl** commands or use any equivalent tools (such as Kubernetes Dashboard) that rely on API requests:

```
The connection to the server 192.168.99.100:8443 was refused - did
you specify the right host or port?
```

9. Let's see what happens if we restart the API server and try to create the Deployment once more. Restart the API server container by running the following command in your Minikube session:

```
docker start $(docker ps -a | grep kube-apiserver | grep -v pause |
awk '{print $1}')
```

   This command tries to find the container ID of the stopped container carrying the API server, and then it starts it. You should get a response like this:

```
9e1cf098b67c
```

10. Wait for 10 seconds. Then, check whether the API server is online. You can run any simple kubectl command for this. Let's try getting the list of nodes by running the following command in the host session:

```
kubectl get node
```

   You should see the following response:

```
NAME        STATUS      ROLES     AGE     VERSION
minikube    NotReady    master    32h     v1.16.2
```

   As you can see, we are able to get a response without errors.

11. Let's try to create the Deployment again:

```
kubectl apply -f k8s-for-beginners-deploy2.yaml
```

   You should see the following response:

```
deployment.apps/k8s-for-beginners created
```

12. Let's check whether the Deployment has been created successfully by running the following command:

```
kubectl get deploy
```

   You should see the following response:

```
NAME                READY    UP-TO-DATE    AVAILABLE    AGE
k8s-for-beginners   0/1      0             0            113s
```

   From the preceding screenshot, there seems to be something wrong as in the **`READY`** column, we can see **`0/1`**, which indicates that there are 0 pods associated with this Deployment, while the desired number is 1 (which we specified in the **`replicas`** field in the Deployment spec).

13. Let's check that all the pods that are online:

```
kubectl get pod
```

You should get a response similar to the following:

```
No resources found in default namespace.
```

We can see that our pod has not been created. This is because the Kubernetes API server only creates the API objects; the implementation of any API object is carried out by other components. For example, in the case of Deployment, it's **kube-controller-manager** that creates the corresponding pod(s).

14. Now, let's restart the **kube-controller-manager**. Run the following command in your Minikube session:

```
docker start $(docker ps -a | grep kube-controller-manager | grep -v
pause | awk '{print $1}')
```

You should see a response similar to the following:

```
35facb013c8f
```

15. After waiting for a few seconds, check the status of the Deployment by running the following command in the host session:

```
kubectl get deploy
```

You should see the following response:

```
NAME                READY     UP-TO-DATE    AVAILABLE    AGE
k8s-for-beginners   0/1       1             0            5m24s
```

As we can see, the pod that we are looking for is still not online.

16. Now, check the status of the pod:

```
kubectl get pod
```

You should see the following response:

```
NAME                                  READY   STATUS    RESTARTS   AGE
k8s-for-beginners-66644bb776-kvwfr    0/1     Pending   0          51s
```

Figure 2.25: Getting the list of pods

The output is different from the one in *step 15*, as in this case, one pod was created by **kube-controller-manager**. However, we can see **Pending** under the **STATUS** column. This is because assigning a pod to a suitable node is not the responsibility of **kube-controller-manager**; it's the responsibility of **kube-scheduler**.

17. Before starting **kube-scheduler**, let's take a look at some additional information about the pod:

```
kubectl get pod -o wide
```

You should see the following response:

```
NAME                                 READY   STATUS    RESTARTS   AGE    IP       NODE
 NOMINATED NODE   READINESS GATES
k8s-for-beginners-66644bb776-kvwfr   0/1     Pending   0          104s   <none>   <none>
 <none>           <none>
```

Figure 2.26: Getting more information about the pod

The highlighted **NODE** column indicates that no node has been assigned to this pod. This proves that the scheduler is not working properly, which we know because we took it offline. If the scheduler were to be online, this response would indicate that there is no place to land this pod.

> **NOTE**
>
> You will learn a lot more about pod scheduling in *Chapter 17*, *Advanced Scheduling in Kubernetes*.

18. Let's restart **kube-scheduler** by running the following command in the Minikube session:

```
docker start $(docker ps -a | grep kube-scheduler | grep -v pause |
awk '{print $1}')
```

You should see a response similar to the following:

```
11d8a27e3ee0
```

19. We can verify that **kube-scheduler** is working by running the following command in the host session:

```
kubectl describe pod k8s-for-beginners-66644bb776-kvwfr
```

Please get the pod name from the response you get at *step 17*, as seen in *Figure 2.26*. You should see the following output:

```
Name:           k8s-for-beginners-66644bb776-kvwfr
Namespace:      default
Priority:       0
Node:           <none>
```

We are truncating the output screenshots for a better presentation. Please take a look at the following excerpt, highlighting the **Events** section:

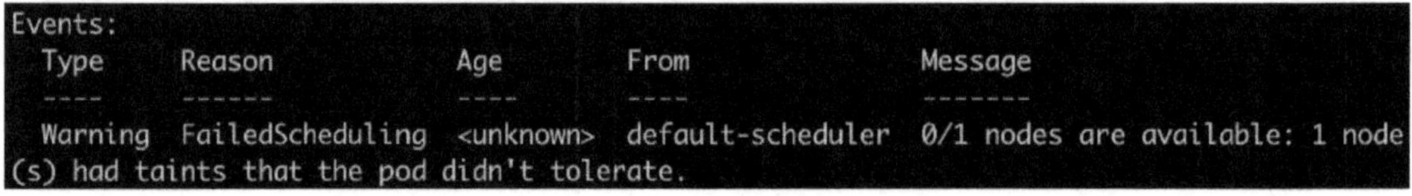

```
Events:
  Type     Reason            Age        From               Message
  ----     ------            ----       ----               -------
  Warning  FailedScheduling  <unknown>  default-scheduler  0/1 nodes are available: 1 node
(s) had taints that the pod didn't tolerate.
```

Figure 2.27: Examining the events reported by the pod

In the **Events** section, we can see that the **kube-scheduler** has tried scheduling, but it reports that there is no node available. Why is that?

This is because, earlier, we stopped the kubelet, and the Minikube environment is a single-node cluster, so there is no available node(s) with a functioning kubelet for the pod to be placed.

20. Let's restart the kubelet by running the following command in the Minikube session:

```
sudo systemctl start kubelet
```

This should not give any response in the terminal upon successful execution.

21. In the host terminal, verify the status of the Deployment by running the following command in the host session:

```
kubectl get deploy
```

You should see the following response:

```
NAME                READY   UP-TO-DATE   AVAILABLE   AGE
k8s-for-beginners   1/1     1            1           11m
```

Now, everything looks healthy as the Deployment shows **1/1** under the **READY** column, which means that the pod is online.

22. Similarly, verify the status of the pod:

```
kubectl get pod -o wide
```

You should get an output similar to the following:

```
NAME                                READY   STATUS    RESTARTS   AGE     IP           NOD
E        NOMINATED NODE   READINESS GATES
k8s-for-beginners-66644bb776-kvwfr   1/1     Running   0          6m48s   172.17.0.4   min
ikube    <none>           <none>
```

Figure 2.28: Getting more information about the pod

We can see **Running** under **STATUS** and that it's been assigned to the **minikube** node.

In this exercise, we traced each phase of a pod's life cycle by breaking the Kubernetes components and then recovering them one by one. Now, based on the observations we made about this exercise; we have better clarity regarding the answers to the questions that were raised before this exercise:

- **Steps 12 – 16**: We saw that in the case of a Deployment, a controller manager is responsible for requesting the creation of pods.
- **Steps 17 – 19**: The scheduler is responsible for choosing a node to place in the pod. It assigns the node by setting a pod's **nodeName** spec to the desired node. Associating a pod to a node, at this moment, merely happened at the level of the API object.
- **Steps 20 – 22**: The kubelet actually brings up the containers to get our pod running.

Throughout a pod's life cycle, Kubernetes components cooperate by updating a pod's spec properly. The API server serves as the key component that accepts pod update requests, as well as to report pod changes to interested parties.

In the following activity, we will bring together the skills we learned in the chapter to find out how we can migrate from a container-based environment to a Kubernetes environment in order to run our application.

ACTIVITY 2.01: RUNNING THE PAGEVIEW APP IN KUBERNETES

In *Activity 1.01, Creating a Simple Page Count Application*, in the previous chapter, we built a web application called Pageview and connected it to a Redis backend datastore. So, here is a question: without making any changes to the source code, can we migrate the Docker-based application to Kubernetes and enjoy Kubernetes' benefits immediately? Try it out in this activity with the guidelines given.

This activity is divided into two parts: in the first part, we will create a simple pod with our application that is exposed to traffic outside the cluster by a Service and connected to a Redis datastore running as another pod. In the second part, we will scale the application to three replicas.

Connecting the Pageview App to a Redis Datastore Using a Service

Similar to the **--link** option in Docker, Kubernetes provides a Service that serves as an abstraction layer to expose one application (let's say, a series of pods tagged with the same set of labels) that can be accessed internally or externally. For example, as we discussed in this chapter, a frontend app can be exposed via a **NodePort** Service so that it can be accessed by external users. In addition to that, in this activity, we need to define an internal Service in order to expose the backend application to the frontend application. Follow these steps:

1. In *Activity 1.01, Creating a Simple Page Count Application*, we built two Docker images – one for the frontend Pageview web app and another for the backend Redis datastore. You can use the skills we learned in this chapter to migrate them into Kubernetes YAMLs.

2. Two pods (each managed by a Deployment) for the application is not enough. We also have to create the Service YAML to link them together.

   Ensure that the **targetPort** field in the manifest is consistent with the exposed port that was defined in the Redis image, which was **6379** in this case. In terms of the **port** field, theoretically, it can be any port, as long as it's consistent with the one specified in the Pageview application.

   The other thing worth mentioning here is the **name** field of the pod for Redis datastore. It's the symbol that's used in the source code of the Pageview app to reference the Redis datastore.

   Now, you should have three YAMLs – two pods and a Service. Apply them using **kubectl -f <yaml file name>**, and then use **kubectl get deploy,service** to ensure that they're created successfully.

3. At this stage, the Pageview app should function well since it's connected to the Redis app via the Service. However, the Service only works as the internal connector to ensure they can talk to each other inside the cluster.

   To access the Pageview app externally, we need to define a **`NodePort`** Service. Unlike the internal Service, we need to explicitly specify the **`type`** as **`NodePort`**.

4. Apply the external Service YAML using **`kubectl -f <yaml file name>`**.

5. Run **`minikube service <external service name>`** to fetch the Service URL.

6. Access the URL multiple times to ensure that the Pageview number gets increased by one each time.

With that, we have successfully run the Pageview application in Kubernetes. But what if the Pageview app is down? Although Kubernetes can create a replacement pod automatically, there is still downtime between when the failure is detected and when the new pod is ready.

A common solution is to increase the replica number of the application so that the whole application is available as long as there is at least one replica running.

Running the Pageview App in Multiple Replicas

The Pageview app can certainly work with a single replica. However, in a production environment, high availability is essential and is achieved by maintaining multiple replicas across nodes to avoid single points of failure. (This will be covered in detail in upcoming chapters.)

In Kubernetes, to ensure the high availability of an application, we can simply increase the replica number. Follow these steps to do so:

1. Modify the Pageview YAML to change **`replicas`** to **3**.

2. Apply these changes by running **`kubectl apply -f <pageview app yaml>`**.

3. By running **`kubectl get pod`**, you should be able to see three Pageview pods running.

4. Access the URL shown in the output of the **`minikube service`** command multiple times.

   Check the logs of each pod to see whether the requests are handled evenly among the three pods.

5. Now, let's verify the high availability of the Pageview app. Terminate any arbitrary pods continuously while keeping one healthy pod. You can achieve this manually or automatically by writing a script. Alternatively, you can open another terminal and check whether the Pageview app is always accessible.

If you opt for writing scripts to terminate the pods, you will see results similar to the following:

```
Keeping Pod k8s-pageview-74bb5d4dfd-2c8qz running
Killing Pod k8s-pageview-74bb5d4dfd-2xklc
pod "k8s-pageview-74bb5d4dfd-2xklc" deleted
Killing Pod k8s-pageview-74bb5d4dfd-f2r9g
pod "k8s-pageview-74bb5d4dfd-f2r9g" deleted
Keeping Pod k8s-pageview-74bb5d4dfd-2c8qz running
Killing Pod k8s-pageview-74bb5d4dfd-qnmf2
pod "k8s-pageview-74bb5d4dfd-qnmf2" deleted
Killing Pod k8s-pageview-74bb5d4dfd-vjqht
pod "k8s-pageview-74bb5d4dfd-vjqht" deleted
Keeping Pod k8s-pageview-74bb5d4dfd-2c8qz running
Killing Pod k8s-pageview-74bb5d4dfd-c86dh
pod "k8s-pageview-74bb5d4dfd-c86dh" deleted
Killing Pod k8s-pageview-74bb5d4dfd-zl7bq
pod "k8s-pageview-74bb5d4dfd-zl7bq" deleted
Keeping Pod k8s-pageview-74bb5d4dfd-2c8qz running
Killing Pod k8s-pageview-74bb5d4dfd-pr9gh
pod "k8s-pageview-74bb5d4dfd-pr9gh" deleted
Killing Pod k8s-pageview-74bb5d4dfd-twd4z
pod "k8s-pageview-74bb5d4dfd-twd4z" deleted
Keeping Pod k8s-pageview-74bb5d4dfd-2c8qz running
Killing Pod k8s-pageview-74bb5d4dfd-mrbgt
pod "k8s-pageview-74bb5d4dfd-mrbgt" deleted
Killing Pod k8s-pageview-74bb5d4dfd-rpgzz
pod "k8s-pageview-74bb5d4dfd-rpgzz" deleted
```

Figure 2.29: Killing pods via a script

Assuming that you take a similar approach and write a script to check whether the application is online, you should see an output similar to the following:

```
Hello, you're the visitor #29.
Hello, you're the visitor #30.
Hello, you're the visitor #31.
Hello, you're the visitor #32.
Hello, you're the visitor #33.
Hello, you're the visitor #34.
Hello, you're the visitor #35.
Hello, you're the visitor #36.
Hello, you're the visitor #37.
Hello, you're the visitor #38.
Hello, you're the visitor #39.
Hello, you're the visitor #40.
Hello, you're the visitor #41.
Hello, you're the visitor #42.
Hello, you're the visitor #43.
Hello, you're the visitor #44.
Hello, you're the visitor #45.
Hello, you're the visitor #46.
Hello, you're the visitor #47.
Hello, you're the visitor #48.
```

Figure 2.30: Repeatedly accessing the application via the script

NOTE

The solution to this activity can be found at the following address: https://packt.live/304PEoD.

A GLIMPSE INTO THE ADVANTAGES OF KUBERNETES FOR MULTI-NODE CLUSTERS

You can only truly appreciate the advantages of Kubernetes after seeing it in the context of a multi-node cluster. This chapter, like many of the other chapters in this book, uses a single-node cluster (Minikube environment) to demonstrate the features that Kubernetes provides. However, in a real-world production environment, Kubernetes is deployed with multiple workers and master nodes. Only then can you ensure that a fault in a single node won't impact the general availability of the application. And reliability is just one of the many benefits that a multi-node Kubernetes cluster can bring to us.

But wait – isn't it true that we can implement applications and deploy them in a highly available manner *without using Kubernetes*? That's true, but that usually comes with a lot of management hassle, both in terms of managing the application as well as the infrastructure. For example, during the initial Deployment, you may have to intervene manually to ensure that all redundant containers are not running on the same machine. In the case of a node failure, you will have to not only ensure that a new replica is respawned properly but to guarantee high availability, you also need to ensure that the new one doesn't land on the nodes that are already running existing replicas. This can be achieved either by using a DevOps tool or injecting logic on the application side. However, either way is very complex. Kubernetes provides a unified platform that we can use to wire apps to proper nodes by describing the high availability features we want using Kubernetes primitives (API objects). This pattern frees the minds of application developers, as they only need to consider how to build their applications. Features that are required for high availability, such as failure detection and recovery, are taken care of by Kubernetes under the hood.

SUMMARY

In this chapter, we used Minikube to provision a single-node Kubernetes cluster and gave a high-level overview of Kubernetes' core components, as well as its key design rationale. After that, we migrated an existing Docker container to Kubernetes and explored some basic Kubernetes API objects, such as pods, Services, and Deployments. Lastly, we intentionally broke a Kubernetes cluster and restored it one component at a time, which allowed us to understand how the different Kubernetes components work together to get a pod up and running on a node.

Throughout this chapter, we have used kubectl to manage our cluster. We provided a quick introduction to this tool, but in the following chapter, we will take a closer look at this powerful tool and explore the various ways in which we can use it.

3

KUBECTL – KUBERNETES COMMAND CENTER

OVERVIEW

In this chapter, we will demystify some common kubectl commands and see how we can use kubectl to control our Kubernetes cluster. We will begin this chapter by taking a brief look at what the end-to-end process looks like when using kubectl commands to communicate with a Kubernetes cluster. Then, we will set up a few shortcuts and autocompletion for the Bash terminal. We will begin with the basics of using kubectl by learning how to create, delete, and manage Kubernetes objects. We will learn about the two approaches to managing resources in Kubernetes - declarative and imperative - with exercises. By the end of this chapter, you will also have learned how to update a live application running on your Kubernetes cluster in real-time using kubectl.

INTRODUCTION

In *Chapter 1, Introduction to Kubernetes and Containers*, we saw that Kubernetes is a portable and highly extensible open-source container orchestration tool. It provides very powerful capabilities that can be used to manage containerized workloads at scale. In the previous chapter, you got the big picture of how the different components of Kubernetes work together to achieve the desired goals. We also demonstrated some basic usage of kubectl in *Chapter 2, An Overview of Kubernetes*. In this chapter, we will take a closer look at this utility and look at how we can make use of its potential.

To reiterate, kubectl is a command-line utility for interacting with Kubernetes clusters and performing various operations. There are two ways to use kubectl while managing your cluster - imperative management, which focuses on commands rather than the YAML manifests to achieve the desired state, and declarative management, which focuses on creating and updating YAML manifest files. kubectl can support both these management techniques to manage Kubernetes API objects (also called Kubernetes API primitives). In the previous chapter, we saw how the various components constantly try to change the state of the cluster from the actual state to the desired state. This can be achieved by using kubectl commands or YAML manifests.

kubectl allows you to send commands to Kubernetes clusters. The **`kubectl`** command can be used to deploy applications, inspect, and manage Kubernetes objects, or troubleshoot and view logs. Interestingly, even though kubectl is the standard tool for controlling and communicating with a Kubernetes cluster, it doesn't come with Kubernetes. So, even if you are running kubectl on any of the nodes of your cluster, you need to install the kubectl binary separately, which we did in *Exercise 2.01, Getting Started with Minikube and Kubernetes Clusters*, in the previous chapter.

This chapter will walk you through the behind-the-scenes functionality of kubectl and provide more insights into how to use kubectl commands to interact with some commonly used Kubernetes objects. We will learn how to set up some shortcuts for kubectl. We will walk you through not only creating new objects with kubectl but also making changes to a live Deployment in Kubernetes. But before that, let's take a peek behind the curtains and get an idea of exactly how kubectl communicates with Kubernetes.

HOW KUBECTL COMMUNICATES WITH KUBERNETES

As we saw in the previous chapter, the API server manages communications between the end-user and Kubernetes, and it also acts as an API gateway to the cluster. To achieve this, it implements the RESTful API over the HTTP and HTTPS protocols to perform CRUD operations to populate and modify Kubernetes API objects such as pods, services, and more based upon the instructions sent by a user via kubectl. These instructions can be in various forms. For example, to retrieve information for pods running in the cluster, we would use the **`kubectl get pods`** command, while to create a new pod, we would use the **`kubectl run`** command.

First, let's take a look at what happens behind the scenes when you run a **`kubectl`** command. Take a look at the following illustration, which provides an overview of the process, and then we will take a closer look at the different details of the process:

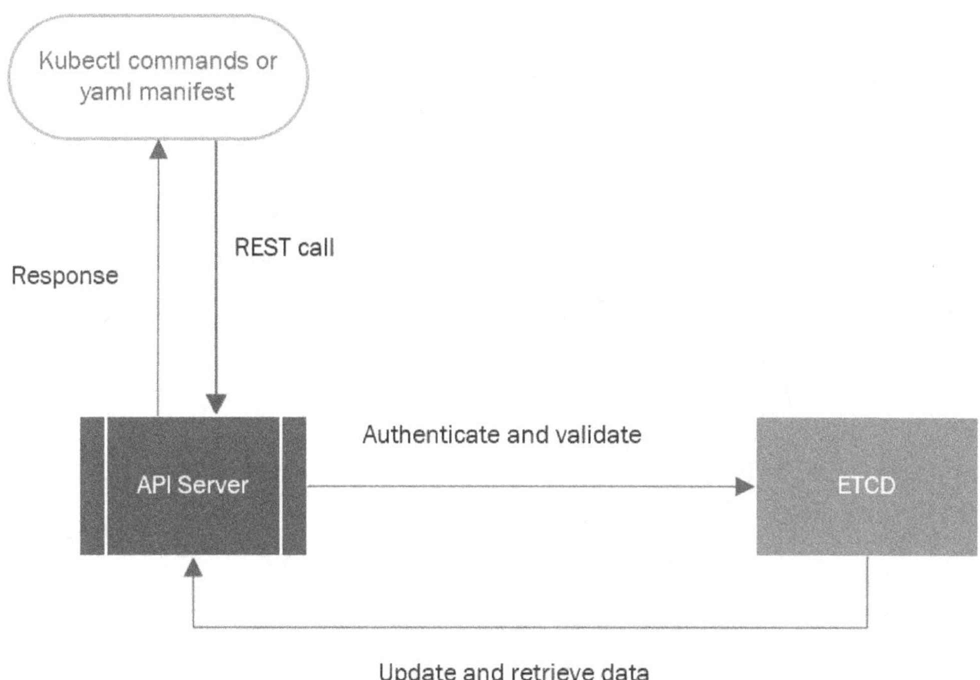

Figure 3.1: A representative flowchart for the kubectl utility

A kubectl command is translated into an API call, which is then sent to the API server. The API server then authenticates and validates the requests. Once the authentication and validation stages have been successful, the API server retrieves and updates data in **`etcd`** and responds with the requested information.

SETTING UP ENVIRONMENTS WITH AUTOCOMPLETION AND SHORTCUTS

In most Linux environments, you can set up autocompletion for kubectl commands before you start working with the instructions mentioned in this chapter. Learning how autocompletion and shortcuts work in Linux environments will be significantly helpful for those who are interested in getting certifications such as **Certified Kubernetes Administrator** (**CKA**) and **Certified Kubernetes Application Developer** (**CKAD**), which are conferred by the Linux Foundation. We'll learn how to set up autocompletion in the following exercise.

EXERCISE 3.01: SETTING UP AUTOCOMPLETION

In this exercise, we will show you how to set up autocompletion and an alias for kubectl commands in Bash. This is a useful feature that will help you save time and avoid typos. Perform the following steps to complete this exercise:

1. We will need the **`bash-completion`** package, so install it if it is not already installed. You can go to the GitHub repository to get installation instructions for various platforms, at https://github.com/scop/bash-completion. If you are running Ubuntu 20.04, you can install it via the APT package manager using the following command:

```
sudo apt-get install bash-completion
```

2. You can use the following command to set up autocomplete in Bash:

```
source <(kubectl completion bash)
```

> **NOTE**
>
> This command, as well as the subsequent commands in this exercise, will not show any responses in the terminal upon successful execution.

3. If you want to make autocomplete persistent in your Bash shell, you can use the following command, which will write **kubectl** autocomplete to the **.bashrc** file in your current user directory:

```
echo "source <(kubectl completion bash)" >> ~/.bashrc
```

4. You can also set up an alias for your **kubectl** commands by using the **alias** keyword, as follows:

```
alias k=kubectl
```

5. Similarly, if you want to set up an alias for some specific commands, you can use commands similar to the following:

```
alias kcdp='kubectl describe po'
alias kcds='kubectl describe svc'
alias kcdd='kubectl describe deploy'
```

6. Finally, you can use the following command to set up the completion of **kubectl** commands when you press *Tab*:

```
complete -F __start_kubectl k
```

> **NOTE**
>
> You can also to set up autocomplete in **zsh** (an alternative to the Bash shell) by using the following commands:
>
> **source <(kubectl completion zsh)**
>
> **echo "if [$commands[kubectl]]; then source <(kubectl completion zsh); fi" >> ~/.zshrc**

By the end of this exercise, you will have an autocomplete set up for your Bash shell. You can also use aliases such as **k** instead of **kubectl** in your commands. However, to avoid confusion and maintain a standardized structure, we will use the full commands throughout this book.

SETTING UP THE KUBECONFIG CONFIGURATION FILE

In most enterprise environments, there is generally more than one Kubernetes cluster, depending on the strategy of the organization. An administrator, developer, or any other role dealing with Kubernetes clusters would need to interact with several of those clusters and switch between them to perform different operations on different clusters.

A configuration file makes things a lot easier. You can use this file to store information about different clusters, users, namespaces, and authentication mechanisms. Such configuration files are referred to as **kubeconfig** files. Note that kubeconfig is a generic way to refer to kubectl configuration files and that it is not the name of the **`config`** file. kubectl uses such files to store the information needed for us to choose a cluster and communicate with its API server.

By default, kubectl looks for the file in the **`$HOME/.kube`** directory. In most scenarios, you can specify a **`KUBECONFIG`** environment variable or use the **`--kubeconfig`** flag to specify the kubeconfig files. Those files are usually saved in **`$HOME/.kube/config`**.

> **NOTE**
>
> You can find out more about how to configure access to multiple clusters by setting up the **`KUBECONFIG`** environment variable and the **`--kubeconfig`** flag at https://kubernetes.io/docs/tasks/access-application-cluster/configure-access-multiple-clusters/#set-the-kubeconfig-environment-variable.

Security contexts are used to define the privilege and access control settings for the pods. We will revisit the idea of access control and security in *Chapter 13, Runtime and Network Security in Kubernetes*.

Let's take a look at the kubeconfig file to understand how this works. You can view the kubeconfig file using the following command:

```
kubectl config view
```

Alternatively, you can also use the following command:

```
cat $HOME/.kube/config
```

You should get an output similar to the following:

```
apiVersion: v1
clusters:
- cluster:
    certificate-authority: /home/testcloudadmin/.minikube/ca.crt
    server: https://192.168.99.100:8443
  name: minikube
contexts:
- context:
    cluster: minikube
    user: minikube
  name: minikube
current-context: minikube
kind: Config
preferences: {}
users:
- name: minikube
  user:
    client-certificate: /home/testcloudadmin/.minikube/client.crt
    client-key: /home/testcloudadmin/.minikube/client.key
```

Figure 3.2: The output of kubectl config view command

A **context** is a set of information that you need to access a cluster. It contains the name of the cluster, the user, and the namespace. The **current-context** field in *Figure 3.2* shows the current context that you are working with. If you want to switch the current context, you can use the following command:

```
kubectl config use-context <the cluster you want to switch to>
```

For example, if we wanted to switch to a context named **minikube**, we would use the following command:

```
kubectl config use-context minikube
```

This would give an output similar to the following:

```
Switched to context "minikube".
```

Common kubectl Commands

As previously described, kubectl is a CLI tool that is used to communicate with the Kubernetes API server. kubectl has a lot of useful commands for working with Kubernetes. In this section, we're going to walk you through some commonly used kubectl commands and shortcuts that are used to manage Kubernetes objects.

Frequently Used kubectl Commands to Create, Manage, and Delete Kubernetes Objects

There are several simple kubectl commands that you will use almost all the time. In this section, we will take a look at some of the basic kubectl commands:

- **get <object>**: You can use this command to get the list of the desired types of objects. Using **all** instead of specifying an object type will get the list of all kinds of objects. By default, this will get the list of specified object types in the default namespace. You can use the **-n** flag to get objects from a specific namespace; for example, **kubectl get pod -n mynamespace**.
- **describe <object-type> <object-name>**: You can use this command to check all the relevant information of a specific object; for example, **kubectl describe pod mypod**.
- **logs <object-name>**: You can use this command to check all the relevant logs of a specific object to find out what happened when that object was created; for example, **kubectl logs mypod**.
- **edit <object-type> <object-name>**: You can use this command to edit a specific object; for example, **kubectl edit pod mypod**.
- **delete <object-type> <object-name>**: You can use this command to delete a specific object; for example, **kubectl delete pod mypod**.
- **create <filename.yaml>**: You can use this command to create a bunch of Kubernetes objects that have been defined in the YAML manifest file; for example, **kubectl create -f your_spec.yaml**.
- **apply <filename.yaml>**: You can use this command to create or update a bunch of Kubernetes objects that have been defined in the YAML manifest file; for example, **kubectl apply -f your_spec.yaml**.

WALKTHROUGH OF SOME SIMPLE KUBECTL COMMANDS

In this section, we're going to walk you through some of the commonly used kubectl commands. This section is mostly for demonstration purposes, so you may not see the exact output that you see in these images. However, this section will help you understand how these commands are used. You will use most of them extensively in later exercises, as well as throughout this book. Let's take a look:

- If you want to display nodes, use the following command:

```
kubectl get nodes
```

  You will see an output similar to the following:

```
NAME                         STATUS   ROLES   AGE   VERSION
aks-nodepool1-29936823-0     Ready    agent   34d   v1.13.12
virtual-node-aci-linux       Ready    agent   8d    v1.14.3-vk-azure-aci-v1.1.0.1
```

Figure 3.3: The output of kubectl get nodes command

  Since we set up aliases in *Exercise 3.01*, *Setting up Autocompletion*, you can also get the same result using the following command:

```
k get no
```

- If you want to display all current namespaces, you can use the following command:

```
kubectl get namespaces
```

  You should see an output similar to the following:

```
NAME               STATUS      AGE
default            Active      7m5s
kube-node-lease    Active      7m14s
kube-public        Active      7m14s
kube-system        Active      7m15s
```

  You can also get the same result using the following shortened command:

```
k get ns
```

- If you want to check the version of **`kubectl`**, you can use the following command:

```
kubectl version
```

You will see an output similar to the following:

```
Client version: version.Info{Major:"1",
Minor:"17", GitVersion:"v1.17.2, GitCommit:
59603c6e503c87169aea6106f57b9f242f64df89", GitTreeState:"clean",
BuildDate:"2020-01-21T22:17:28Z, GoVersion:"go1.13.5", Compiler:"gc",
Platform:"linux/amd64}
Server version: version.Info{Major:"1",
Minor:"17", GitVersion:"v1.17.2, GitCommit:
59603c6e503c87169aea6106f57b9f242f64df89", GitTreeState:"clean",
BuildDate:"2020-01-18T23:22:30Z, GoVersion:"go1.13.5", Compiler:"gc",
Platform:"linux/amd64}
```

- If you want to see some information regarding your current Kubernetes cluster, you can use the following command:

```
kubectl cluster-info
```

You should see an output similar to the following:

```
Kubernetes master is running at https://192.168.99.100:8443
KubeDNS is running at https://192.168.99.100:8443/api/v1/namespaces/kube-system/services/kube-dns:dns/proxy

To further debug and diagnose cluster problems, use 'kubectl cluster-info dump'.
```

Figure 3.4: The output of kubectl cluster-info command

Before we move on further with the demonstrations, we will mention a few commands that you can use to create a sample application, which we have already provided in the GitHub repository for this chapter. Use the following command to fetch the YAML specification for all the objects required to run the application:

```
curl https://raw.githubusercontent.com/PacktWorkshops/Kubernetes-Workshop/master/Chapter03/Activity03.01/sample-application.yaml --output sample-application.yaml
```

Now, you can deploy the **sample-application.yaml** file using the following command:

```
kubectl apply -f sample-application.yaml
```

If you can see the following output, this means that the sample application has been successfully created in your Kubernetes cluster:

```
deployment.apps/redis-back created
service/redis-back created
deployment.apps/melonvote-front created
service/melonvote-front created
```

Now that you have deployed the provided application, if you try any of the commands shown later in this section, you will see the various objects, events, and so on related to this application. Note that your output may not exactly match the images shown here:

- You can use the following command to get everything in your cluster under the **default** namespace:

```
kubectl get all
```

This will give an output similar to the following:

```
NAME                                      READY   STATUS    RESTARTS   AGE
pod/aci-helloworld-8875447cd-lhc6j        1/1     Running   0          28d
pod/melonvote-front-56687f5fdd-5rksw      1/1     Running   0          7d6h
pod/redis-back-559c848b4c-s94x9           1/1     Running   0          7d6h

NAME                      TYPE           CLUSTER-IP     EXTERNAL-IP    PORT(S)        AGE
service/kubernetes        ClusterIP      10.0.0.1       <none>         443/TCP        34d
service/melonvote-front   LoadBalancer   10.0.243.12    40.68.95.73    80:32651/TCP   7d6h
service/redis-back        ClusterIP      10.0.133.234   <none>         6379/TCP       7d6h

NAME                                 READY   UP-TO-DATE   AVAILABLE   AGE
deployment.apps/aci-helloworld       1/1     1            1           34d
deployment.apps/melonvote-front      1/1     1            1           7d6h
deployment.apps/redis-back           1/1     1            1           7d6h

NAME                                          DESIRED   CURRENT   READY   AGE
replicaset.apps/aci-helloworld-8875447cd      1         1         1       34d
replicaset.apps/melonvote-front-56687f5fdd    1         1         1       7d6h
replicaset.apps/melonvote-front-85c8b7cf8d    0         0         0       7d6h
replicaset.apps/redis-back-559c848b4c         1         1         1       7d6h

NAME                                                         REFERENCE                    TARGETS              MINPODS   MAXPODS   REPLI
CAS   AGE
horizontalpodautoscaler.autoscaling/keda-hpa-melonkedaaf   Deployment/melonkedaaf   <unknown>/5 (avg)   1         100       0
      34d
```

Figure 3.5: The output of kubectl get all command

- Events describe what has happened so far in the Kubernetes cluster, and you can use events to get a better insight into your cluster and aid in any troubleshooting efforts. To list all the events in the default namespace, use the following command:

```
kubectl get events
```

This will give an output similar to the following:

LAST SEEN	TYPE	REASON	KIND	MESSAGE
14s	Warning	FailedGetScale	HorizontalPodAutoscaler	deployments/scale.apps "melonkedaaf" not found

Figure 3.6: The output of kubectl get events command

- A service is an abstraction that's used to expose an application to the end-user. You will learn more about services in *Chapter 8*, *Service Discovery*. You can use the following command to list all services:

```
kubectl get services
```

This will give an output similar to the following:

```
NAME              TYPE           CLUSTER-IP     EXTERNAL-IP   PORT(S)        AGE
kubernetes        ClusterIP      10.0.0.1       <none>        443/TCP        34d
melonvote-front   LoadBalancer   10.0.243.12    40.68.95.73   80:32651/TCP   7d6h
redis-back        ClusterIP      10.0.133.234   <none>        6379/TCP       7d6h
```

Figure 3.7: The output of kubectl get services command

You can get the same result using the following shortened command:

```
k get svc
```

- A Deployment is an API object that allows us to easily manage and update pods. You will learn more about Deployments in *Chapter 7*, *Kubernetes Controllers*. You can get the list of Deployments using the following command:

```
kubectl get deployments
```

This should give a response similar to the following:

```
NAME              READY   UP-TO-DATE   AVAILABLE   AGE
aci-helloworld    1/1     1            1           34d
melonvote-front   1/1     1            1           7d6h
redis-back        1/1     1            1           7d6h
```

You can also get the same result using the following shortened version of the command:

```
k get deploy
```

SOME USEFUL FLAGS FOR THE GET COMMAND

As you have seen, the **get** command is a pretty standard command that is used when we need to get the list of objects in our cluster. It also has several useful flags. Let's take a look at a few of them here:

- If you want to list a particular type of resource from all your namespaces, you can add the **--all-namespaces** flag in the command. For example, if we want to list all Deployments from all namespaces, we can use the following command:

```
kubectl get deployments --all-namespaces
```

This will give an output similar to this:

```
NAMESPACE     NAME                                      READY   UP-TO-DATE   AVAILABLE   AGE
default       aci-helloworld                            1/1     1            1           34d
default       melonvote-front                           1/1     1            1           7d6h
default       redis-back                                1/1     1            1           7d6h
keda          keda                                      1/1     1            1           34d
keda          osiris-osiris-edge-activator              1/1     1            1           34d
keda          osiris-osiris-edge-endpoints-controller   1/1     1            1           34d
keda          osiris-osiris-edge-endpoints-hijacker     1/1     1            1           34d
keda          osiris-osiris-edge-proxy-injector         1/1     1            1           34d
keda          osiris-osiris-edge-zeroscaler             1/1     1            1           34d
kube-system   aci-connector-linux                       1/1     1            1           34d
kube-system   coredns                                   5/5     5            5           34d
kube-system   coredns-autoscaler                        1/1     1            1           34d
kube-system   kubernetes-dashboard                      1/1     1            1           34d
kube-system   metrics-server                            1/1     1            1           34d
kube-system   tunnelfront                               1/1     1            1           34d
```

Figure 3.8: The output of kubectl get deployments under all namespaces

You can also see that there is an additional column on the left-hand side that specifies the namespaces of the respective Deployments.

- If you want to list a specific type of resource from a specific namespace, you can use the **-n** flag. Here, the **-n** flag stands for **namespace**. For example, if you want to list all Deployments in a namespace called **keda**, the following command would be used:

```
kubectl get deployments -n keda
```

This command would show an output similar to the following:

```
NAME                                      READY   UP-TO-DATE   AVAILABLE   AGE
keda                                      1/1     1            1           34d
osiris-osiris-edge-activator              1/1     1            1           34d
osiris-osiris-edge-endpoints-controller   1/1     1            1           34d
osiris-osiris-edge-endpoints-hijacker     1/1     1            1           34d
osiris-osiris-edge-proxy-injector         1/1     1            1           34d
osiris-osiris-edge-zeroscaler             1/1     1            1           34d
```

Figure 3.9: The output of kubectl get deployments under the keda namespace

- You can add the **--show-labels** flag to display the labels of the objects in the list. For example, if you wanted to get the list of all the pods in the **default** namespace, along with their labels, you would use the following command:

```
kubectl get pods --show-labels
```

This command should give an output similar to the following:

```
NAME                                READY   STATUS    RESTARTS   AGE    LABELS
aci-helloworld-8875447cd-lhc6j      1/1     Running   0          28d    app=aci-helloworld,pod-template-hash=8875447cd
melonvote-front-56687f5fdd-5rksw    1/1     Running   0          7d6h   app=melonvote-front,pod-template-hash=56687f5fdd
redis-back-559c848b4c-s94x9         1/1     Running   0          7d6h   app=redis-back,pod-template-hash=559c848b4c
```

Figure 3.10: The output of kubectl get pods with all labels

There is an additional column on the right-hand side that specifies the labels of the pods.

- You can use the **-o wide** flag to display more information about objects. Here, the **-o** flag stands for **output**. Let's look at a simple example of how to use this flag:

```
kubectl get pods -o wide
```

This will give an output similar to the following:

```
NAME                                READY   STATUS    RESTARTS   AGE    IP            NODE                          NOMINATED NODE
READINESS GATES
aci-helloworld-8875447cd-lhc6j      1/1     Running   0          28d    10.241.0.5    virtual-node-aci-linux        <none>
<none>
melonvote-front-56687f5fdd-5rksw    1/1     Running   0          7d6h   10.240.0.6    aks-nodepool1-29936823-0      <none>
<none>
redis-back-559c848b4c-s94x9         1/1     Running   0          7d6h   10.240.0.28   aks-nodepool1-29936823-0      <none>
<none>
```

Figure 3.11: The output of kubectl get pods with additional information

You can also see there are additional columns on the right-hand side that specify which nodes the pods are running on, as well as the internal IP addresses of the node. You can find more ways to use the **-o** flag at https://kubernetes.io/docs/reference/kubectl/overview/#output-options.

> **NOTE**
>
> We will limit this section to commands that are commonly used to limit the scope of this chapter. You can find a lot more kubectl commands at https://kubernetes.io/docs/reference/generated/kubectl/kubectl-commands.

POPULATING DEPLOYMENTS IN KUBERNETES

As we mentioned earlier, Deployment is a convenient way to manage and update pods. Defining a Deployment in Kubernetes is an effective and efficient way to provide declarative updates for the application running in your cluster.

You can create a Deployment by using kubectl imperative commands or by using declarative YAML manifest files. In the following exercise, we're going to deploy an application (we will go with Nginx for this exercise) in Kubernetes and learn how to interact with Deployments using kubectl commands, as well as how to modify the YAML manifest file.

EXERCISE 3.02: CREATING A DEPLOYMENT

There are two ways to create a Deployment in Kubernetes - using the **kubectl create/run** command and creating a manifest file in YAML format and then using the **kubectl apply** command. We can achieve the same goal with those two options. Let's try both and then compare them:

1. Create a Deployment using the following command directly:

```
kubectl create deployment kubeserve --image=nginx:1.7.8
```

   You can expect an output similar to the following:

```
deployment.apps/kubeserve created
```

> **NOTE**
>
> You can also create a Deployment using the **kubectl run** command. To achieve the same results here, you could use the following commands:
>
> **kubectl run nginx --image=nginx:1.7.8**
>
> **kubectl run nginx --image=nginx:1.7.8 --replicas=3**

2. You can also create a Deployment by defining the YAML manifest file for your Deployment. Use your preferred text editor to create a file named **sample-deployment.yaml** with the following content:

```
apiVersion: apps/v1
kind: Deployment
metadata:
  name: kubeserve
  labels:
    app: kubeserve
spec:
  replicas : 3
  selector:
```

```
    matchLabels:
      app: kubeserve
  template:
    metadata:
      labels:
        app: kubeserve
    spec:
      containers:
      - name: nginx
        image: nginx
        ports:
        - containerPort: 80
```

In this YAML definition, the **replicas** field defines the number of replica pods in this Deployment.

3. Use the following command to apply the configuration you've defined in the YAML manifest file:

```
kubectl apply -f sample-deployment.yaml
```

The sample output will look as follows:

```
kubectl apply -f sample-deployment.yaml
```

4. Use the following command to check the Deployments that currently exist in the **default** namespace:

```
kubectl get deployments
```

The output will look as follows:

```
NAME              READY    UP-TO-DATE    AVAILABLE    AGE
aci-helloworld    1/1      1             1            27d
kubeserve         3/3      3             3            26m
```

In this exercise, we have seen the differences in using the different approaches to create a Deployment. The **kubectl create** command is widely used for testing. For most enterprise solutions where modern DevOps approaches are implemented, it makes more sense to use YAML definitions to conveniently define configurations, and then track them with source control tools such as Git. When your organization integrates YAML definitions with DevOps tools, it makes the solution more manageable and traceable.

Now that we have seen how to create a Deployment, in the next exercise, we will learn how to modify or update a Deployment that is already running. This is something that you will need to do quite often as the software is updated to new versions, bugs are identified and fixed, the demands on your application change, or your organization moves on to completely new solutions. We will also learn how to roll back a Deployment to an earlier version, which is something that you will want to do if an update does not lead to the expected outcome.

EXERCISE 3.03: UPDATING A DEPLOYMENT

In this exercise, we will update the application that we deployed in the previous exercise to a more recent version and demonstrate how we can roll back the Deployment to a previous version if necessary.

Similar to the two approaches that we saw for creating a Deployment, there are two ways to update an application as well – using the **kubectl set image** command and updating the YAML manifest file and then using the **kubectl apply** command. These steps will guide you through both approaches:

1. First, let's get the details of the current Deployment using the following command:

```
kubectl describe deploy kubeserve
```

   You'll get an output similar to the following:

```
Containers:
  nginx:
    Container ID:   docker://ac74053b0beff086fc1232a6212787c6845630536a65bee4b47e11653f7256af
    Image:          nginx:1.7.8
    Image ID:       docker-pullable://nginx@sha256:2c390758c6a4660d93467ce5e70e8d08d6e401f748bffba7885ce160ca7e481d
    Port:           <none>
    Host Port:      <none>
    State:          Running
      Started:      Sun, 16 Feb 2020 12:01:36 +0000
    Ready:          True
    Restart Count:  0
    Environment:    <none>
    Mounts:
      /var/run/secrets/kubernetes.io/serviceaccount from default-token-46457 (ro)
```

Figure 3.12: Describing the kubeserve Deployment

2. You can update the image using the following command:

```
kubectl set image deployment/kubeserve nginx=nginx:1.9.1 --record
```

   The **image** subcommand indicates that we want to update the **image** field of the object, as defined in the YAML manifest that we saw in *Step 2* of the previous exercise.

Then, we specify the object in the **<object-type>/<object name>** format.

The next part, **nginx=nginx:1.9.1**, tells Kubernetes to look for the specific image tagged as **1.9.1** in the Docker Hub repository of NGINX. You can check out the available tags at https://hub.docker.com/_/nginx?tab=tags.

The **--record** flag is very helpful when you want to save the updates that have been made by your **kubectl** commands to the current resource.

By applying this, you'll get an output similar to the following:

```
deployment.extensions/kubeserve image updated
```

3. Now, let's get the details of the Deployment using the following command:

```
kubectl describe deploy kubeserve
```

You should see the following output:

```
Containers:
  nginx:
    Container ID:   docker://d2093551244d220d7c6acbf823abbcd0e142f8b37579af38ddb8acf2e4897036
    Image:          nginx:1.9.1
    Image ID:       docker-pullable://nginx@sha256:2f68b99bc0d6d25d0c56876b924ec20418544ff28e1fb89a4c27679a40da811b
    Port:           <none>
    Host Port:      <none>
    State:          Running
      Started:      Sun, 16 Feb 2020 12:07:31 +0000
    Ready:          True
    Restart Count:  0
    Environment:    <none>
    Mounts:
      /var/run/secrets/kubernetes.io/serviceaccount from default-token-46457 (ro)
```

Figure 3.13: Using the kubectl describe command to check the image version in the container

In the preceding screenshot, you can see that the image has been successfully updated to version **1.9.1**.

Another way to achieve the same result is to modify the YAML file and then use the **kubectl apply** command. We will use the same YAML file that we created in the previous exercise. If you do not have the YAML file for an object, you can export the YAML manifest using the following command:

```
kubectl get deploy kubeserve -o yaml > kubeserve-spec.yaml
```

This command will output a file named **kubeserve-spec.yaml** with the manifest that is in effect in the cluster. Then, you can use vim, nano, or any other text editor to edit it and then apply the edited **kubeserve-spec.yaml** manifest using the **kubectl apply** command, as shown in the previous exercise, with the addition of the **--record** flag.

4. If you want to perform a rollback, you can use the following command:

```
kubectl rollout undo deployments kubeserve
```

You'll see an output similar to the following:

```
deployment.extensions/kubeserve rolled back
```

5. You can use the **kubectl rollout history** command to check all the revisions for a specific Deployment, as shown here:

```
kubectl rollout history deployment kubeserve
```

You'll see an output similar to the following:

```
deployment.extensions/kubeserve
REVISION  CHANGE-CAUSE
1         <none>
3         kubectl set image deployment/kubeserve nginx=nginx:1.91 --record=true
4         <none>
```

Figure 3.14: The output of the kubectl rollout history command

6. You can also use the following command to check the details of a specific revision:

```
kubectl rollout history deployment kubeserve --revision=3
```

The output for this command will be as follows:

```
deployment.extensions/kubeserve with revision #3
Pod Template:
  Labels:       app=kubeserve
        pod-template-hash=6995cffd5f
  Annotations:  kubernetes.io/change-cause: kubectl set image deployment/kubeserve nginx=nginx:1.91 --record=true
  Containers:
   nginx:
    Image:      nginx:1.91
    Port:       80/TCP
    Host Port:  0/TCP
    Environment:        <none>
    Mounts:     <none>
  Volumes:      <none>
```

Figure 3.15: Checking the details of revision 3

7. You can roll back a Deployment to a specific revision by specifying the **--to-revision** flag:

```
kubectl rollout undo deployments kubeserve --to-revision=3
```

You'll see an output similar to the following:

```
deployment.extensions/kubeserve rolled back
```

In this exercise, we have learned how to update an already existing Deployment, as well as how to roll back a Deployment to its earlier specs.

Deployments allow us to define a desired state for the replica pod in a declarative way. We will revisit how Deployment works and discover more about it in *Chapter 7, Kubernetes Controllers*. If you delete the individual pod replica intentionally or if the pod fails for any reason, since we define a Deployment with a set number of replicas, the Deployment will keep recreating the pod as many times as you delete it. This is what we call *auto-healing*. Therefore, you need to delete the Deployment itself, which will also delete all the pods managed by it. We will learn how to do that in the following exercise.

EXERCISE 3.04: DELETING A DEPLOYMENT

In this exercise, we will delete the Deployment we created in the previous exercise:

1. Get a list of existing Deployments using the following command:

```
kubectl get deployment
```

You can expect an output similar to the following:

```
NAME              READY    UP-TO-DATE    AVAILABLE    AGE
aci-helloworld    1/1      1             1            27d
kubeserve         3/3      3             3            26m
melonkedaaf       0/0      0             0            26d
```

2. Let's say that, for the purpose of this exercise, we want to delete the **kubeserve** Deployment that we created in the previous exercise. Use the following command to delete the Deployment:

```
kubectl delete deployment kubeserve
```

The sample output will be similar to the following:

```
deployment.extensions "kubeserve" deleted
```

3. Get the list of Deployments to check and make sure that the target Deployment has been deleted successfully:

```
kubectl get deployment
```

You should see an output similar to the following:

```
NAME              READY    UP-TO-DATE    AVAILABLE    AGE
aci-helloworld    1/1      1             1            27d
kubeserve         0/0      0             0            26d
```

You can use the **kubectl delete** command to delete any other object as well. However, as we mentioned earlier, in cases such as pods managed by Deployments, it is pointless to delete individual pods as the Deployment will just recreate them, so you need to delete the Deployment.

ACTIVITY 3.01: EDITING A LIVE DEPLOYMENT FOR A REAL-LIFE APPLICATION

Imagine that you are a SysOps engineer who has been asked to manage a cluster and deploy a web application. You have deployed it to your Kubernetes cluster and made it available to the public. You have been monitoring this application ever since it was deployed successfully, and you've detected that the web application has been experiencing throttling issues during peak times. Based on your monitoring, the solution that you want to implement is to assign more memory and CPU to this application. Therefore, you need to edit the Deployment so that you can allocate enough CPU and memory resources to run the application and test this application at the end. You need to demonstrate that your web application is up and running and that it can be accessed through a public IP address via a browser of your choice.

To simulate this scenario, we're going to deploy a sample application in a Kubernetes cluster and show you how to edit a live Deployment. Editing a live Deployment is something that you will need to do when fixing issues or for testing purposes.

You can use the following command to get the YAML manifest file that you're going to use in this activity:

```
curl https://raw.githubusercontent.com/PacktWorkshops/Kubernetes-
Workshop/master/Chapter03/Activity03.01/sample-application.yaml --output
sample-application.yaml
```

This manifest file defines all the different objects that are required to run the application, as well as the application itself.

> **NOTE**
>
> This manifest has been adapted from an open-source sample provided by Microsoft Azure, available at https://github.com/Azure-Samples/azure-voting-app-redis.

Perform the following steps to complete this activity:

1. First, deploy the target web application using the **kubectl apply** command and the provided YAML definition file.
2. Get the IP address of the service that exposes your application. For this simple scenario, this will be similar to *Exercise 2.03, Accessing a Pod via a Service*, from the previous chapter. Later chapters will explain how to work with ingress controllers and create ingress resources to expose the frontend applications.
3. Use the **kubectl edit** command to edit the live deployment. You will need to edit the deployment named **melonvote-front**. The following are the fields that you need to modify to satisfy the requirements of this scenario. You can simply double these values:

   a) **resources.limits.cpu**: This is the resource limit for CPU usage.

   b) **resources.limits.memory**: This is the resource limit for memory usage.

   c) **resources.requests.cpu**: This is the minimum CPU usage requested to get your application up and running.

   d) **resources.requests.memory**: This is the minimum memory usage requested to get your application up and running.

By the end of this activity, you will be able to see the UI of the application that you deployed with Kubernetes:

Figure 3.16: Expected output of the activity

> **NOTE**
>
> The solution to this activity can be found at the following address: https://packt.live/304PEoD.

SUMMARY

This chapter demystified how kubectl allows us to control our Kubernetes cluster using API calls. First, we learned how to set up an environment for kubectl commands and looked at a number of shortcuts. Furthermore, we covered how to create, edit, and delete a Kubernetes object using kubectl commands and looked at a Deployment as an example. Finally, we deployed a real-life application and showed you how to edit a live Deployment. Every example in this chapter has been applied in a general context; however, we believe that the skills developed in this chapter can help you resolve specific problems that you might encounter in a professional environment.

In the next chapter, you'll explore the other side of this bridge and dive deeper into how the API server works. You will also take a closer look at REST API requests and how the API server deals with them.

4

HOW TO COMMUNICATE WITH KUBERNETES (API SERVER)

OVERVIEW

In this chapter, we will build a foundational understanding of the Kubernetes API server and the various ways of interacting with it. We will learn how kubectl and other HTTP clients communicate with the Kubernetes API server. We will use some practical demonstrations to trace these communications and see the details of HTTP requests. Then, we will also see how we can look up the API details so that you can write your own API request from scratch. By the end of this chapter, you will be able to create API objects by directly communicating with the API server using any HTTP client, such as curl, to make RESTful API calls to the API server.

INTRODUCTION

As you will recall from *Chapter 2, An Overview of Kubernetes*, the API server acts as the central hub that communicates with all the different components in Kubernetes. In the previous chapter, we took a look at how we can use kubectl to instruct the API server to do various things.

In this chapter, we will take a further look into the components that make up the API server. As the API server is at the center of our entire Kubernetes system, it is important to learn how to effectively communicate with the API server itself and how API requests are processed. We will also look at various API concepts, such as resources, API groups, and API versions, which will help you understand the HTTP requests and responses that are made to the API server. Finally, we will interact with the Kubernetes API using multiple REST clients to achieve many of the same results we did in the previous chapter using the kubectl command-line tool.

THE KUBERNETES API SERVER

In Kubernetes, all communications and operations between the control plane components and external clients, such as kubectl, are translated into **RESTful API** calls that are handled by the API server. Effectively, the API server is a RESTful web application that processes RESTful API calls over HTTP to store and update API objects in the etcd datastore.

The API server is also a frontend component that acts as a gateway to and from the outside world, which is accessed by all clients, such as the kubectl command-line tool. Even the cluster components in the control plane interact with each other only through the API server. Additionally, it is the only component that interacts directly with the etcd datastore. Since the API server is the only way for clients to access the cluster, it must be properly configured to be accessible by clients. You will usually see the API server implemented as **`kube-apiserver`**.

> **NOTE**
>
> We will explain the RESTful API in more detail in the *The Kubernetes API* section later in this chapter.

Now, let's recall how the API server looks in our Minikube cluster by running the following command:

```
kubectl get pods -n kube-system
```

You should see the following response:

```
NAME                                READY   STATUS    RESTARTS   AGE
coredns-5644d7b6d9-gxrgx            1/1     Running   0          8m27s
coredns-5644d7b6d9-tv4g7            1/1     Running   0          8m27s
etcd-minikube                       1/1     Running   0          7m27s
kube-addon-manager-minikube         1/1     Running   0          8m30s
kube-apiserver-minikube             1/1     Running   0          7m40s
kube-controller-manager-minikube    1/1     Running   0          7m30s
kube-proxy-hgwpr                    1/1     Running   0          8m27s
kube-scheduler-minikube             1/1     Running   0          7m19s
storage-provisioner                 1/1     Running   1          8m27s
```

Figure 4.1: Observing how the API server is implemented in Minikube

As we saw in previous chapters, in the Minikube environment, the API server is referred to as **`kube-apiserver-minikube`** in the **`kube-system`** namespace. As you can see in the preceding screenshot, we have a single instance of the API server: **`kube-apiserver-minikube`**.

The API server is stateless (that is, its behavior will be consistent regardless of the state of the cluster) and is designed to scale horizontally. Usually, for the high availability of clusters, it is recommended to have at least three instances to handle the load and fault tolerance better.

KUBERNETES HTTP REQUEST FLOW

As we learned in earlier chapters, when we run any **`kubectl`** command, the command is translated into an HTTP API request in JSON format and is sent to the API server. Then, the API server returns a response to the client, along with any requested information. The following diagram shows the API request life cycle and what happens inside the API server when it receives a request:

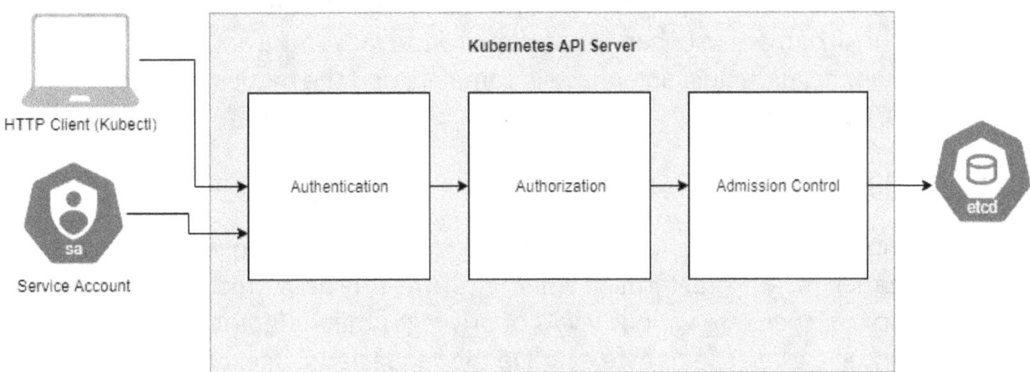

Figure 4.2: API server HTTP request flow

As you can see in the preceding figure, the HTTP request goes through the authentication, authorization, and admission control stages. We will take a look at each of these in the following subtopics.

AUTHENTICATION

In Kubernetes, every API call needs to authenticate with the API server, regardless of whether it comes from outside the cluster, such as those made by kubectl, or a process inside the cluster, such as those made by kubelet.

When an HTTP request is sent to the API server, the API server needs to authenticate the client sending this request. The HTTP request will contain the information required for authentication, such as the username, user ID, and group. The authentication method will be determined by either the header or the certificate of the request. To deal with these different methods, the API server has different authentication plugins, such as ServiceAccount tokens, which are used to authenticate ServiceAccounts, and at least one other method to authenticate users, such as X.509 client certificates.

> **NOTE**
>
> The cluster administrator usually defines authentication plugins during cluster creation. You can learn more about the various authentication strategies and authentication plugins at https://kubernetes.io/docs/reference/access-authn-authz/authentication/.
>
> We will take a look at the implementation of certificate-based authentication in *Chapter 11*, *Build Your Own HA Cluster*.

The API server will call those plugins one by one until one of them authenticates the request. If all of them fail, then the authentication fails. If the authentication succeeds, then the authentication phase is complete and the request proceeds to the authorization phase.

AUTHORIZATION

After authentication is successful, the attributes from the HTTP request are sent to the authorization plugin to determine whether the user is permitted to perform the requested action. There are various levels of privileges that different users may have; for example, can a given user create a pod in the requested namespace? Can the user delete a Deployment? These kinds of decisions are made in the authorization phase.

Consider an example where you have two users. A user called **ReadOnlyUser** (just a hypothetical name) should be allowed to list pods in the `default` namespace only, and **ClusterAdmin** (another hypothetical name) should be able to perform all tasks across all namespaces:

User	Privileges	Namespace
ClusterAdmin	Can perform all tasks	All namespaces
ReadOnlyUser	Can read pod status	default

Figure 4.3: Privileges for our two users

To understand this better, take a look at the following demonstration:

> **NOTE**
>
> We will not dive into too much detail about how to create users as this will be discussed in *Chapter 13, Runtime and Network Security in Kubernetes*. For this demonstration, the users, along with their permissions, are already set up, and the limitation of their privileges is demonstrated by switching contexts.

```
abutaleb@AbuTalebPC:~$ kubectl config use-context ReadOnlyUser
Switched to context "ReadOnlyUser".
abutaleb@AbuTalebPC:~$
abutaleb@AbuTalebPC:~$
abutaleb@AbuTalebPC:~$ kubectl get pods -n default
NAME                         READY   STATUS    RESTARTS   AGE
mynginx-8668b9977f-mgcq6     1/1     Running   0          11m
abutaleb@AbuTalebPC:~$
abutaleb@AbuTalebPC:~$
abutaleb@AbuTalebPC:~$ kubectl delete pod mynginx-8668b9977f-mgcq6
Error from server (Forbidden): pods "mynginx-8668b9977f-mgcq6" is forbidden:
 User "system:serviceaccount:default:readonlysa" cannot delete resource "pod
s" in API group "" in the namespace "default"
abutaleb@AbuTalebPC:~$
abutaleb@AbuTalebPC:~$
abutaleb@AbuTalebPC:~$ kubectl get pods --all-namespaces
Error from server (Forbidden): pods is forbidden: User "system:serviceaccoun
t:default:readonlysa" cannot list resource "pods" in API group "" at the clu
ster scope
abutaleb@AbuTalebPC:~$
```

Figure 4.4: Demonstrating different user privileges

Notice, from the preceding screenshot, that the **ReadOnlyUser** can only **list** pods in the default namespace, but when trying to perform other tasks, such as deleting a pod in the **default** namespace or listing pods in other namespaces, the user will get a **Forbidden** error. This **Forbidden** error is returned by the authorization plugin.

kubectl provides a tool that you can call by using **kubectl auth can-i** to check whether an action is allowed for the current user.

Let's consider the following examples in the context of the previous demonstration. Let's say that the **ReadOnlyUser** runs the following commands:

```
kubectl auth can-i get pods --all-namespaces
kubectl auth can-i get pods -n default
```

The user should see the following responses:

```
abutaleb@AbuTalebPC:~$ kubectl auth can-i get pods --all-namespaces
no
abutaleb@AbuTalebPC:~$ kubectl auth can-i get pods -n default
yes
```

Figure 4.5: Checking privileges for ReadOnlyUser

Now, after switching context, let's say that the **ClusterAdmin** user runs the following commands:

```
kubectl auth can-i delete pods
kubectl auth can-i get pods
kubectl auth can-i get pods --all-namespaces
```

The user should see the following response:

```
abutaleb@AbuTalebPC:~$ kubectl auth can-i delete pods
yes
abutaleb@AbuTalebPC:~$ kubectl auth can-i get pods
yes
abutaleb@AbuTalebPC:~$ kubectl auth can-i get pods --all-namespaces
yes
```

Figure 4.6: Checking privileges for ClusterAdmin

Unlike authentication phase modules, authorization modules are checked in sequence. If multiple authorization modules are configured, and if any authorizer approves or denies a request, that decision is immediately returned, and no other authorizer will be contacted.

ADMISSION CONTROL

After the request is authenticated and authorized, it goes to the admission control modules. These modules can modify or reject requests. If the request is only trying to perform a READ operation, it bypasses this stage; but if it is trying to create, modify, or delete, it will be sent to the admission controller plugins. Kubernetes comes with a set of predefined admission controllers, although you can define custom admission controllers as well.

These plugins may modify the incoming object, in some cases to apply system-configured defaults or even to deny the request. Like authorization modules, if any admission controller module rejects the request, then the request is dropped and it will not process further.

Some examples are as follows:

- If we configure a custom rule that every object should have a label (which you will learn how to do in *Chapter 16, Kubernetes Admission Controllers*), then any request to create an object without a label will be rejected by the admission controllers.
- When you delete a namespace, it goes to the **Terminating** state, where Kubernetes will try to evict all the resources in it before deleting it. So, we cannot create any new objects in this namespace. **`NamespaceLifecycle`** is what prevents that.
- When a client tries to create a resource in a namespace that does not exist, the **`NamespaceExists`** admission controller rejects the request.

Out of the different modules included in Kubernetes, not all of the admission control modules are enabled by default, and the default modules usually change based on the Kubernetes version. Providers of cloud-based Kubernetes solutions, such as **Amazon Web Services** (**AWS**), Google, and Azure, control which plugins can be enabled by default. Cluster administrators can also decide which modules to enable or disable when initializing the API server. By using the **`--enable-admission-plugins`** flag, administrators can control which modules should be enabled other than the default ones. On the other hand, the **`--disable-admission-plugins`** flag controls which modules from the default modules should be disabled.

> **NOTE**
>
> You will learn more about admission controllers, including creating custom ones, in *Chapter 16, Kubernetes Admission Controllers*.

As you will recall from *Chapter 2, An Overview of Kubernetes*, when we created a cluster using the **`minikube start`** command, Minikube enabled several modules for us by default. Let's take a closer look at that in the next exercise in which we will not only view the different API modules enabled for us by default but also start Minikube with a custom set of modules.

EXERCISE 4.01: STARTING MINIKUBE WITH A CUSTOM SET OF MODULES

In this exercise, we will take a look at how to view the different API modules enabled for our instance of Minikube, and then restart Minikube using a custom set of API modules:

1. If Minikube is not already running on your machine, start it up by using the following command:

   ```
   minikube start
   ```

   You should see the following response:

```
   Deleting "minikube" in virtualbox ...
   The "minikube" cluster has been deleted.
   Successfully deleted profile "minikube"
AbuTalebMBP:~ mohammed$ minikube start
   minikube v1.5.2 on Darwin 10.14.6
   Automatically selected the 'virtualbox' driver
   Creating virtualbox VM (CPUs=2, Memory=2000MB, Disk=20000MB) ...
   Preparing Kubernetes v1.16.2 on Docker '18.09.9' ...
   Pulling images ...
   Launching Kubernetes ...
   Waiting for: apiserver
   Done! kubectl is now configured to use "minikube"
```

Figure 4.7: Starting up Minikube

2. Now, let's see which modules are enabled by default. Use the following command:

```
kubectl describe pod kube-apiserver-minikube -n kube-system | grep
enable-admission-plugins
```

You should see the following response:

```
    --enable-admission-plugins=NamespaceLifecycle,LimitRanger,ServiceAccount,D
efaultStorageClass,DefaultTolerationSeconds,NodeRestriction,MutatingAdmissionWeb
hook,ValidatingAdmissionWebhook,ResourceQuota
```

Figure 4.8: Default modules enabled in Minikube

As you can observe from the preceding output, Minikube has enabled the following modules for us: **NamespaceLifecycle**, **LimitRanger**, **ServiceAccount**, **DefaultStorageClass**, **DefaultTolerationSeconds**, **NodeRestriction**, **MutatingAdmissionWebhook**, **ValidatingAdmissionWebhook**, and **ResourceQuota**.

> **NOTE**
>
> To know more about modules, please refer the following link: https://kubernetes.io/docs/reference/access-authn-authz/admission-controllers/

3. Another way to check the modules is to view the API server manifest by running the following command:

```
kubectl exec -it kube-apiserver-minikube -n kube-system -- kube-
apiserver -h | grep "enable-admission-plugins" | grep -vi deprecated
```

> **NOTE**
>
> We used **grep -vi deprecated** because there is another flag, **--admission-control**, that we are discarding from the output, as this flag will be deprecated in future versions.

kubectl has the **exec** command, which allows us to execute a command to our running pods. This command will execute **kube-apiserver -h** inside our **kube-apiserver-minikube** pod and return the output to our shell:

```
      --enable-admission-plugins strings        admission plugins that should be
enabled in addition to default enabled ones (NamespaceLifecycle, LimitRanger, Se
rviceAccount, TaintNodesByCondition, Priority, DefaultTolerationSeconds, Default
StorageClass, StorageObjectInUseProtection, PersistentVolumeClaimResize, Mutatin
gAdmissionWebhook, ValidatingAdmissionWebhook, RuntimeClass, ResourceQuota). Com
ma-delimited list of admission plugins: AlwaysAdmit, AlwaysDeny, AlwaysPullImage
s, DefaultStorageClass, DefaultTolerationSeconds, DenyEscalatingExec, DenyExecOn
Privileged, EventRateLimit, ExtendedResourceToleration, ImagePolicyWebhook, Limi
tPodHardAntiAffinityTopology, LimitRanger, MutatingAdmissionWebhook, NamespaceAu
toProvision, NamespaceExists, NamespaceLifecycle, NodeRestriction, OwnerReferenc
esPermissionEnforcement, PersistentVolumeClaimResize, PersistentVolumeLabel, Pod
NodeSelector, PodPreset, PodSecurityPolicy, PodTolerationRestriction, Priority,
ResourceQuota, RuntimeClass, SecurityContextDeny, ServiceAccount, StorageObjectI
nUseProtection, TaintNodesByCondition, ValidatingAdmissionWebhook. The order of
plugins in this flag does not matter.
```

Figure 4.9: Checking the modules enabled by default in Minikube

4. Now, we will start Minikube with our desired configuration. Use the following command:

```
minikube start --extra-config=apiserver.enable-admission-plugins="Limi
tRanger,NamespaceExists,NamespaceLifecycle,ResourceQuota,ServiceAccou
nt,DefaultStorageClass,MutatingAdmissionWebhook"
```

As you can see here, the **minikube start** command has the **--extra-config** configurator flag, which allows us to pass additional configurations to our cluster installation. In our case, we can use the **--extra-config** flag, along with **--enable-admission-plugins**, and specify the plugins we need to enable. Our command should produce this output:

```
😄  minikube v1.5.2 on Darwin 10.15.1
💡  Tip: Use 'minikube start -p <name>' to create a new cluster, or 'minikube de
lete' to delete this one.
🏃  Using the running virtualbox "minikube" VM ...
⌛  Waiting for the host to be provisioned ...
🐳  Preparing Kubernetes v1.16.2 on Docker '18.09.9' ...
    ▪ apiserver.enable-admission-plugins=LimitRanger,NamespaceExists,NamespaceLi
fecycle,ResourceQuota,ServiceAccount,DefaultStorageClass,MutatingAdmissionWebhoo
k
🔄  Relaunching Kubernetes using kubeadm ...
⌛  Waiting for: apiserver
🏄  Done! kubectl is now configured to use "minikube"
```

Figure 4.10: Restarting Minikube with a custom set of modules

5. Now, let's compare this instance of Minikube with our earlier one. Use the following command:

```
kubectl describe pod kube-apiserver-minikube -n kube-system | grep
enable-admission-plugins
```

You should see the following response:

```
    --enable-admission-plugins=LimitRanger,NamespaceExists,NamespaceLifecycle,
ResourceQuota,ServiceAccount,DefaultStorageClass,MutatingAdmissionWebhook
```

Figure 4.11: Checking a custom set of modules for Minikube

If you compare the set of modules seen here to the ones in *Figure 4.7*, you will notice that only the specified plugins were enabled; while the **DefaultTolerationSeconds**, **NodeRestriction**, and **ValidatingAdmissionWebhook** modules are no longer enabled.

> **NOTE**
>
> You can revert to the default configurations in Minikube by running **minikube start** again.

VALIDATION

After letting the request pass through all three stages, the API server then validates the object—that is, it checks whether the object specification, which is carried in JSON format in the response body, meets the required format and standard.

After successful validation, the API server stores the object in the etcd datastore and returns a response to the client. After that, as you learned in *Chapter 2, An Overview of Kubernetes*, other components, such as the scheduler and the controller manager, take over to find a suitable node and actually implement the object on your cluster.

THE KUBERNETES API

The Kubernetes API uses JSON over HTTP for its requests and responses. It follows the REST architectural style. You can use the Kubernetes API to read and write Kubernetes resource objects.

> **NOTE**
>
> For more details about the RESTful API, please refer to https://restfulapi.net/.

Kubernetes API allows clients to create, update, delete, or read a description of an object via standard HTTP methods (or HTTP verbs), such as the examples in the following table:

HTTP Verbs	Usage	Example URL path
POST	Creates new resources, such as a new pod	/api/v1/namespaces/{namespace}/pods
PUT	Replaces or updates an existing resource; for example, replaces the status of the specified Deployment	/apis/apps/v1/namespaces/{namespace}/deployments/{name}/status
GET	Retrieves the details of a resource; for example, reading a specified Service	/api/v1/namespaces/{namespace}/services/{name}
PATCH	Partially updates existing resources; for example, updating the image for a pod	/api/v1/namespaces/{namespace}/pods/{name}
DELETE	Deletes resources, such as deleting a pod	/api/v1/namespaces/{namespace}/pods/{name}

Figure 4.12: HTTP verbs and their usage

In the context of Kubernetes API calls, it is helpful to understand how these HTTP methods map to API request verbs. So, let's take a look at which verbs are sent through which methods:

- **`GET`**: **`get`**, **`list`**, and **`watch`**

  Some example kubectl commands are **`kubectl get pod`**, **`kubectl describe pod <pod-name>`**, and **`kubectl get pod -w`**.

- **POST**: **create**

  An example kubectl command is **kubectl create -f <filename.yaml>**.

- **PATCH**: **patch**

  An example kubectl command is **kubectl set image deployment/kubeserve nginx=nginx:1.9.1**.

- **DELETE**: **delete**

  An example kubectl command is **kubectl delete pod <pod-name>**.

- **PUT**: **update**

  An example kubectl command is **kubectl apply -f <filename.yaml>**.

> **NOTE**
>
> If you have not encountered these commands yet, you will in the upcoming chapters. Feel free to refer back to this chapter or the following Kubernetes documentation to find out how each API request works for any command: https://kubernetes.io/docs/reference/kubernetes-api/.

As mentioned earlier, these API calls carry JSON data, and all of them have a JSON schema identified by the **Kind** and **apiVersion** fields. **Kind** is a string that identifies the type of JSON schema that an object should have, and **apiVersion** is a string that identifies the version of the JSON schema the object should have. The next exercise should give you a better idea about this.

You can refer to the Kubernetes API reference documentation to see the different HTTP methods in action, at https://kubernetes.io/docs/reference/kubernetes-api/.

For example, if you need to create a Deployment in a specific namespace, under **WORKLOADS APIS**, you can navigate to **Deployment v1 apps** > **Write Operations** > **Create**. You will see the HTTP request and different examples using **kubectl** or **curl**. The following page from the API reference docs should give you an idea of how to use this reference:

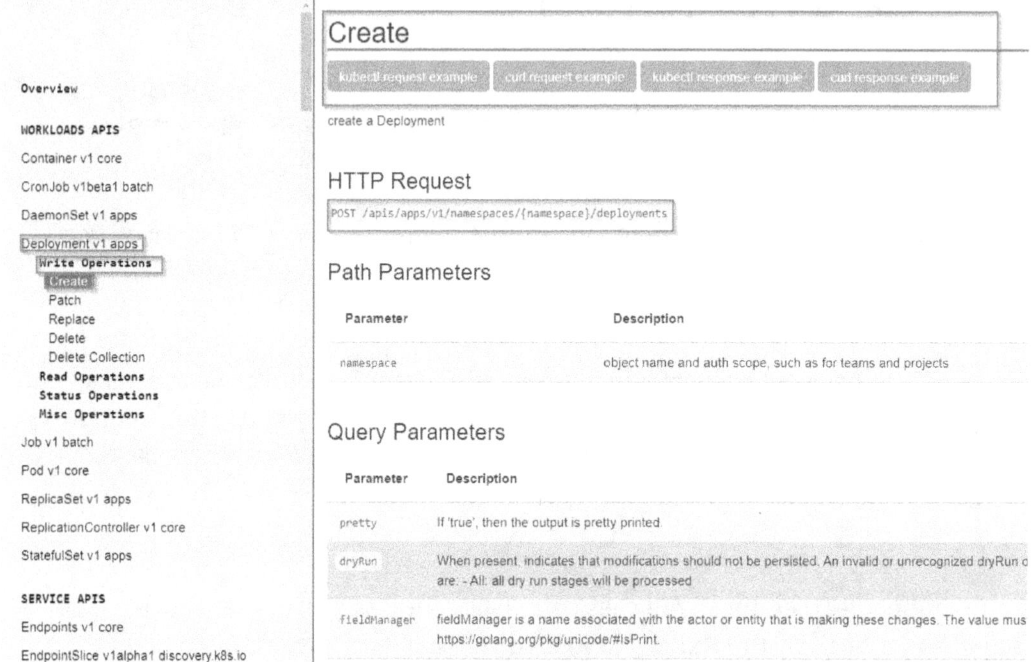

Figure 4.13: HTTP request for the kubectl create command

You will need to keep the version of your API server in mind when you refer to the previously mentioned documentation. You can find your Kubernetes API server version by running **kubectl version --short** command and looking for **Server Version**. For example, if your Kubernetes API server version is running version 1.14, you should navigate to the Kubernetes version 1.14 reference documentation (https://v1-14.docs.kubernetes.io/docs/reference/generated/kubernetes-api/v1.14/) to look up the relevant API information.

The best way to understand this is by tracing a **kubectl** command. Let's do exactly that in the following section.

TRACING KUBECTL HTTP REQUESTS

Let's try tracing the HTTP requests that kubectl sends to the API server to better understand them. Before we begin, let's get all the pods in the **kube-system** namespace by using the following command:

```
kubectl get pods -n kube-system
```

This command should display the output in a table view, as you can see in the following screenshot:

NAME	READY	STATUS	RESTARTS	AGE
coredns-5644d7b6d9-292kd	1/1	Running	0	6m20s
coredns-5644d7b6d9-2lg9r	1/1	Running	0	6m20s
etcd-minikube	1/1	Running	0	5m16s
kube-addon-manager-minikube	1/1	Running	0	6m28s
kube-apiserver-minikube	1/1	Running	0	3m
kube-controller-manager-minikube	1/1	Running	0	3m
kube-proxy-cpbjg	1/1	Running	0	6m21s
kube-scheduler-minikube	1/1	Running	0	5m7s
storage-provisioner	1/1	Running	0	6m19s

Figure 4.14: Getting the list of pods in the kube-system namespace

Behind the scenes, since kubectl is a REST client, it invokes an HTTP **GET** request to the API server endpoint and requests information from **/api/v1/namespaces/kube-system/pods**.

We can enable verbose output by adding **--v=8** to our **kubectl** command. **v** indicates the verbosity of the command. The higher the number, the more details we get in the response. This number can range from **0** to **10**. Let's see the output with verbosity of **8**:

```
kubectl get pods -n kube-system --v=8
```

This should give output as follows:

```
I1123 15:04:42.086493    5477 loader.go:375] Config loaded from file:  /Users/mohammed/.kube/config
I1123 15:04:42.096144    5477 round_trippers.go:420] GET https://192.168.99.110:8443/api/v1/namespaces/kube-system/pods?limit=500
I1123 15:04:42.096166    5477 round_trippers.go:427] Request Headers:
I1123 15:04:42.096175    5477 round_trippers.go:431]     Accept: application/json;as=Table;v=v1beta1;g=meta.k8s.io, application/j
son
I1123 15:04:42.096181    5477 round_trippers.go:431]     User-Agent: kubectl/v1.16.3 (darwin/amd64) kubernetes/b3cbbae
I1123 15:04:42.107066    5477 round_trippers.go:446] Response Status: 200 OK in 10 milliseconds
I1123 15:04:42.107092    5477 round_trippers.go:449] Response Headers:
I1123 15:04:42.107115    5477 round_trippers.go:452]     Cache-Control: no-cache, private
I1123 15:04:42.107128    5477 round_trippers.go:452]     Content-Type: application/json
I1123 15:04:42.107145    5477 round_trippers.go:452]     Date: Sat, 23 Nov 2019 13:04:42 GMT
I1123 15:04:42.107397    5477 request.go:968] Response Body: {"kind":"Table","apiVersion":"meta.k8s.io/v1beta1","metadata":{"self
Link":"/api/v1/namespaces/kube-system/pods","resourceVersion":"1051"},"columnDefinitions":[{"name":"Name","type":"string","format
":"name","description":"Name must be unique within a namespace. Is required when creating resources, although some resources may
allow a client to request the generation of an appropriate name automatically. Name is primarily intended for creation idempotenc
e and configuration definition. Cannot be updated. More info: http://kubernetes.io/docs/user-guide/identifiers#names","priority":
0},{"name":"Ready","type":"string","format":"","description":"The aggregate readiness state of this pod for accepting traffic.","
priority":0},{"name":"Status","type":"string","format":"","description":"The aggregate status of the containers in this pod.","pr
iority":0},{"name":"Restarts","type":"integer","format":"","description":"The number of times the containers in this pod have bee
n restarted.","priority":0},{"name":"Age","type":"str [truncated 9336 chars]
NAME                               READY   STATUS    RESTARTS   AGE
coredns-5644d7b6d9-292kd           1/1     Running   0          8m25s
coredns-5644d7b6d9-2lg9r           1/1     Running   0          8m25s
etcd-minikube                      1/1     Running   0          7m21s
kube-addon-manager-minikube        1/1     Running   0          8m33s
kube-apiserver-minikube            1/1     Running   0          5m5s
kube-controller-manager-minikube   1/1     Running   0          5m5s
kube-proxy-cpbjg                   1/1     Running   0          8m26s
kube-scheduler-minikube            1/1     Running   0          7m12s
storage-provisioner                1/1     Running   0          8m24s
```

Figure 4.15: Output of a get pods command with a verbosity of 8

Let's examine the preceding output bit by bit to get a better understanding of it:

- The first part of the output is as follows:

```
42.086493    5477 loader.go:375] Config loaded from file:  /Users/mohammed/.kube/config
```

Figure 4.16: Part of the output indicating the loading of the config file

  From this, we can see that kubectl loaded the configuration from our kubeconfig file, which has the API server endpoint, port, and credentials, such as the certificate or the authentication token.

- This is the next part of the output:

```
5477 round_trippers.go:420] GET https://192.168.99.110:8443/api/v1/namespaces/kube-system/pods?limit=500
```

Figure 4.17: Part of the output indicating the HTTP GET request

In this, you can see the **HTTP GET** request mentioned as **GET https://192.168.99.100:8443/api/v1/namespaces/kube-system/pods?limit=500**. This line contains the operation that we need to perform against the API server, and **/api/v1/namespaces/kube-system/pods** is the API path. You can also see **limit=500** at the end of the URL path, which is the chunk size; kubectl fetches a large number of resources in chunks to improve latency. We will see some examples relating to retrieving large results sets in chunks later in this chapter.

- The next part of the output is as follows:

```
5477 round_trippers.go:427] Request Headers:
5477 round_trippers.go:431]     Accept: application/json;as=Table;v=v1beta1;g=meta.k8s.io, application/json
5477 round_trippers.go:431]     User-Agent: kubectl/v1.16.3 (darwin/amd64) kubernetes/b3cbbae
```

Figure 4.18: Part of the output indicating request headers

As you can see in this part of the output, **Request Headers** describes the resource to be fetched or the client requesting the resource. In our example, the output has two parts for content negotiation:

a) **Accept**: This is used by HTTP clients to tell the server what content types they'll accept. In our example, we can see that kubectl informed the API server about the **application/json** content type. If this does not exist in the request header, the server will return the default preconfigured representation type, which is the same as **application/json** for the Kubernetes API as it uses the JSON schema. We can also see that it is requesting the output as a table view, which is indicated by **as=Table** in this line.

b) **User-Agent**: This header contains information about the client that is requesting this information. In this case, we can see that kubectl is providing information about itself.

- Let's examine the next part:

```
5477 round_trippers.go:446] Response Status: 200 OK in 10 milliseconds
```

Figure 4.19: Part of the output indicating the response status

Here, we can see that the API server returns the **200 OK** HTTP status code, which indicates that the request has been processed successfully on the API server. We can also see the time taken to process this request, which is 10 milliseconds.

- Let's look at the next part:

```
5477 round_trippers.go:449] Response Headers:
5477 round_trippers.go:452]     Cache-Control: no-cache, private
5477 round_trippers.go:452]     Content-Type: application/json
5477 round_trippers.go:452]     Date: Sat, 23 Nov 2019 13:04:42 GMT
```

Figure 4.20: Part of the output indicating the response headers

As you can see, this part shows the **Response Headers**, which include details such as the date and time of the request, in our example.

- Now, let's come to the main response sent by the API server:

```
I1123 15:04:42.107397    5477 request.go:968] Response Body: {"kind":"Table","apiVersion":"meta.k8s.io/v1beta1","meta
data":{"selfLink":"/api/v1/namespaces/kube-system/pods","resourceVersion":"1051"},"columnDefinitions":[{"name":"Name"
,"type":"string","format":"name","description":"Name must be unique within a namespace. Is required when creating res
ources, although some resources may allow a client to request the generation of an appropriate name automatically. Na
me is primarily intended for creation idempotence and configuration definition. Cannot be updated. More info: http://
kubernetes.io/docs/user-guide/identifiers#names","priority":0},{"name":"Ready","type":"string","format":"","descripti
on":"The aggregate readiness state of this pod for accepting traffic.","priority":0},{"name":"Status","type":"string"
,"format":"","description":"The aggregate status of the containers in this pod.","priority":0},{"name":"Restarts","ty
pe":"integer","format":"","description":"The number of times the containers in this pod have been restarted.","priori
ty":0},{"name":"Age","type":"str [truncated 9336 chars]
```

Figure 4.21: Part of the output indicating the response body

The **Response Body** contains the resource data that was requested by the client. In our case, this is information about the pods in the **kube-system** namespace. Here, this information is in raw JSON format before kubectl can present it as a neat table. However, the highlighted section at the end of the previous screenshot shows that the response body does not have all the JSON output that we requested; part of the **Response Body** is truncated. This is because **--v=8** displays the HTTP request content with truncation of the response content.

To see the full response body, you can run the same command with **--v=10**, which does not truncate the output at all. The command would look like as follows:

```
kubectl get pods -n kube-system --v=10
```

We will not examine the command with **--v=10** verbosity for the sake of brevity.

- Now, we come to the final part of the output that we are examining:

```
NAME                                 READY   STATUS    RESTARTS   AGE
coredns-5644d7b6d9-292kd             1/1     Running   0          8m25s
coredns-5644d7b6d9-2lg9r             1/1     Running   0          8m25s
etcd-minikube                        1/1     Running   0          7m21s
kube-addon-manager-minikube          1/1     Running   0          8m33s
kube-apiserver-minikube              1/1     Running   0          5m5s
kube-controller-manager-minikube     1/1     Running   0          5m5s
kube-proxy-cpbjg                     1/1     Running   0          8m26s
kube-scheduler-minikube              1/1     Running   0          7m12s
storage-provisioner                  1/1     Running   0          8m24s
```

Figure 4.22: Part of the output indicating the final result

This is the final output as a table, which is what was requested. kubectl has taken the raw JSON data and formatted it as a neat table for us.

> **NOTE**
>
> You can learn more about kubectl verbosity and debugging flags at https://kubernetes.io/docs/reference/kubectl/cheatsheet/#kubectl-output-verbosity-and-debugging.

API RESOURCE TYPE

In the previous section, we saw that the HTTP URL was made up of an API resource, API group, and API version. Now, let's learn about the resource type defined in the URL, such as pods, namespaces, and services. In JSON form, this is called `Kind`:

- **Collection of resource**: This represents a collection of instances for a resource type, such as all pods in all namespaces. In a URL, this would be as follows:

```
GET /api/v1/pods
```

- **Single resource**: This represents a single instance of a resource type, such as retrieving details of a specific pod in a given namespace. The URL for this case would be as follows:

```
GET /api/v1/namespaces/{namespace}/pods/{name}
```

Now that we have learned about various aspects of a request made to the API server, let's learn about the scope of API resources in the next section.

SCOPE OF API RESOURCES

All resource types can either be cluster-scoped resources or namespace-scoped resources. The scope of a resource affects the access of that resource and how that resource is managed. Let's look at the differences between namespace and cluster scope.

NAMESPACE-SCOPED RESOURCES

As we saw in *Chapter 2, An Overview of Kubernetes*, Kubernetes makes use of Linux namespaces to organize most Kubernetes resources. Resources in the same namespace share the same control access policies and authorization checks. When a namespace is deleted, all resources in that namespace are also deleted.

Let's see what forms the request paths for interacting with namespace-scoped resources take:

- Return the information about a specific pod in a namespace:

  ```
  GET /api/v1/namespaces/{my-namespace}/pods/{pod-name}
  ```

- Return the information about a collection of all Deployments in a namespace:

  ```
  GET /apis/apps/v1/namespaces/{my-namespace}/deployments
  ```

- Return the information about all instances of the resource type (in this case, services) across all namespaces:

  ```
  GET /api/v1/services
  ```

  Notice that when we are looking for information against all namespaces, it will not have **namespace** in the URL.

You can get a full list of namespace-scoped API resources by using the following command:

```
kubectl api-resources --namespaced=true
```

You should see a response similar to this:

```
NAME                        SHORTNAMES   APIGROUP                       NAMESPACED   KIND
bindings                                                                true         Binding
configmaps                  cm                                          true         ConfigMap
endpoints                   ep                                          true         Endpoints
events                      ev                                          true         Event
limitranges                 limits                                      true         LimitRange
persistentvolumeclaims      pvc                                         true         PersistentVolumeClaim
pods                        po                                          true         Pod
podtemplates                                                            true         PodTemplate
replicationcontrollers      rc                                          true         ReplicationController
resourcequotas              quota                                       true         ResourceQuota
secrets                                                                 true         Secret
serviceaccounts             sa                                          true         ServiceAccount
services                    svc                                         true         Service
controllerrevisions                      apps                           true         ControllerRevision
daemonsets                  ds           apps                           true         DaemonSet
deployments                 deploy       apps                           true         Deployment
replicasets                 rs           apps                           true         ReplicaSet
statefulsets                sts          apps                           true         StatefulSet
localsubjectaccessreviews                authorization.k8s.io           true         LocalSubjectAccessRevie
horizontalpodautoscalers    hpa          autoscaling                    true         HorizontalPodAutoscaler
cronjobs                    cj           batch                          true         CronJob
jobs                                     batch                          true         Job
leases                                   coordination.k8s.io            true         Lease
events                      ev           events.k8s.io                  true         Event
ingresses                   ing          extensions                     true         Ingress
ingresses                   ing          networking.k8s.io              true         Ingress
networkpolicies             netpol       networking.k8s.io              true         NetworkPolicy
poddisruptionbudgets        pdb          policy                         true         PodDisruptionBudget
rolebindings                             rbac.authorization.k8s.io      true         RoleBinding
roles                                    rbac.authorization.k8s.io      true         Role
```

Figure 4.23: Listing out all the namespace-scoped resources

CLUSTER-SCOPED RESOURCES

Most Kubernetes resources are namespace-scoped, but the namespace resource itself is not namespace-scoped. Resources that are not scoped within namespaces are cluster-scoped. Other examples of cluster-scoped resources are nodes. Since a node is cluster-scoped, you can deploy a pod on the desired node regardless of what namespace you want the pod to be in, and a node can host different pods from different namespaces.

Let's see how the request paths for interacting with cluster-scoped resources look:

- Return the information about a specific node in the cluster:

```
GET /api/v1/nodes/{node-name}
```

- Return the information of all instances of the resource type (in this case, nodes) in the cluster:

```
GET /api/v1/nodes
```

- You can get a full list of cluster-scoped API resources by using the following command:

```
kubectl api-resources --namespaced=false
```

You should see an output similar to this:

```
NAME                              SHORTNAMES   APIGROUP                       NAMESPACED   KIND
componentstatuses                 cs                                          false        ComponentStatus
namespaces                        ns                                          false        Namespace
nodes                             no                                          false        Node
persistentvolumes                 pv                                          false        PersistentVolume
mutatingwebhookconfigurations                  admissionregistration.k8s.io   false        MutatingWebhookC
onfiguration
validatingwebhookconfigurations                admissionregistration.k8s.io   false        ValidatingWebhoo
kConfiguration
customresourcedefinitions         crd,crds     apiextensions.k8s.io           false        CustomResourceDe
finition
apiservices                                    apiregistration.k8s.io         false        APIService
tokenreviews                                   authentication.k8s.io          false        TokenReview
selfsubjectaccessreviews                       authorization.k8s.io           false        SelfSubjectAcces
sReview
selfsubjectrulesreviews                        authorization.k8s.io           false        SelfSubjectRules
Review
subjectaccessreviews                           authorization.k8s.io           false        SubjectAccessRev
iew
certificatesigningrequests        csr          certificates.k8s.io            false        CertificateSigni
ngRequest
runtimeclasses                                 node.k8s.io                    false        RuntimeClass
podsecuritypolicies               psp          policy                         false        PodSecurityPolic
y
clusterrolebindings                            rbac.authorization.k8s.io      false        ClusterRoleBindi
ng
clusterroles                                   rbac.authorization.k8s.io      false        ClusterRole
priorityclasses                   pc           scheduling.k8s.io              false        PriorityClass
csidrivers                                     storage.k8s.io                 false        CSIDriver
csinodes                                       storage.k8s.io                 false        CSINode
storageclasses                    sc           storage.k8s.io                 false        StorageClass
volumeattachments                              storage.k8s.io                 false        VolumeAttachment
```

Figure 4.24: Listing out all cluster-scoped resources

API GROUPS

An API group is a collection of resources that are logically related to each other. For example, Deployments, ReplicaSets, and DaemonSets all belong to the apps API group: **apps/v1**.

> **NOTE**
>
> You will learn about Deployments, ReplicaSets, and DaemonSets in detail in *Chapter 7*, *Kubernetes Controllers*. In fact, this chapter will talk about many API resources that you will encounter in later chapters.

The **--api-group** flag can be used to scope the output to a specific API group, as we will see in the following sections. Let's take a closer look at the various API groups in the following sections.

CORE GROUP

This is also called the legacy group. It contains objects such as pods, services, nodes, and namespaces. The URL path for these is **/api/v1**, and nothing other than the version is specified in the **apiVersion** field. For example, consider the following screenshot where we are getting information about a pod:

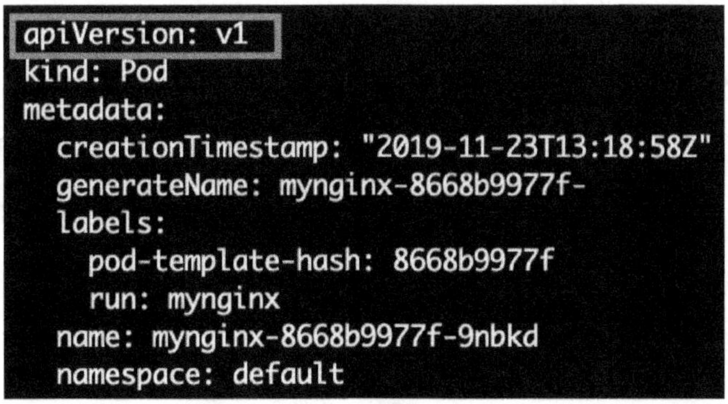

```
apiVersion: v1
kind: Pod
metadata:
  creationTimestamp: "2019-11-23T13:18:58Z"
  generateName: mynginx-8668b9977f-
  labels:
    pod-template-hash: 8668b9977f
    run: mynginx
  name: mynginx-8668b9977f-9nbkd
  namespace: default
```

Figure 4.25: API group of a pod

As you can see here, the **apiVersion: v1** field indicates that this resource belongs to the core group.

Resources showing a blank entry in the **kubectl api-resources** command output are part of the core group. You can also specify an empty argument flag (**--api-group=''**) to only display the core group resources, as follows:

```
kubectl api-resources --api-group=''
```

You should see an output as follows:

```
NAME                     SHORTNAMES   APIGROUP   NAMESPACED   KIND
bindings                                         true         Binding
componentstatuses        cs                      false        ComponentStatus
configmaps               cm                      true         ConfigMap
endpoints                ep                      true         Endpoints
events                   ev                      true         Event
limitranges              limits                  true         LimitRange
namespaces               ns                      false        Namespace
nodes                    no                      false        Node
persistentvolumeclaims   pvc                     true         PersistentVolumeClaim
persistentvolumes        pv                      false        PersistentVolume
pods                     po                      true         Pod
podtemplates                                     true         PodTemplate
replicationcontrollers   rc                      true         ReplicationController
resourcequotas           quota                   true         ResourceQuota
secrets                                          true         Secret
serviceaccounts          sa                      true         ServiceAccount
services                 svc                     true         Service
```

Figure 4.26: Listing out the resources in the core API group

NAMED GROUP

This group includes objects for whom the request URL is in the **/apis/$NAME/$VERSION** format. Unlike the core group, named groups contain the group name in the URL. For example, let's consider the following screenshot where we have information about a Deployment:

```
apiVersion: apps/v1
kind: Deployment
metadata:
  annotations:
    deployment.kubernetes.io/revision: "1"
  creationTimestamp: "2019-11-23T13:18:58Z"
  generation: 1
  labels:
    run: mynginx
  name: mynginx
  namespace: default
  resourceVersion: "2127"
  selfLink: /apis/apps/v1/namespaces/default/deployments/mynginx
  uid: ebaec8b8-ca0c-48e8-bf62-3b98a1a85a29
spec:
  progressDeadlineSeconds: 600
  replicas: 1
  revisionHistoryLimit: 10
```

Figure 4.27: The API group of a Deployment

As you can see, the highlighted field showing **apiVersion: apps/v1** indicates that this resource belongs to the **apps** API group.

You can also specify the **--api-group='<NamedGroup Name>'** flag to display the resources in that specified named group. For example, let's list out the resources under the **apps** API group by using the following command:

```
kubectl api-resources --api-group='apps'
```

This should give the following response:

```
NAME                   SHORTNAMES   APIGROUP   NAMESPACED   KIND
controllerrevisions                 apps       true         ControllerRevision
daemonsets             ds           apps       true         DaemonSet
deployments            deploy       apps       true         Deployment
replicasets            rs           apps       true         ReplicaSet
statefulsets           sts          apps       true         StatefulSet
```

Figure 4.28: Listing out the resources in the apps API group

All of these resources in the preceding screenshot are clubbed together because they are part of the **apps** named group, which we specified in our query command.

As another example, let's look at the **rbac.authorization.k8s.io API group**, which has resources to determine authorization policies. We can look at the resources in that group by using the following command:

```
kubectl api-resources --api-group='rbac.authorization.k8s.io'
```

You should see the following response:

```
NAME                  SHORTNAMES   APIGROUP                    NAMESPACED   KIND
clusterrolebindings                rbac.authorization.k8s.io   false        ClusterRoleBinding
clusterroles                       rbac.authorization.k8s.io   false        ClusterRole
rolebindings                       rbac.authorization.k8s.io   true         RoleBinding
roles                              rbac.authorization.k8s.io   true         Role
```

Figure 4.29: Listing out the resources in the rbac.authorization.k8s.io API group

SYSTEM-WIDE

This group consists of system-wide API endpoints, such as **/version**, **/healthz**, **/logs**, and **/metrics**. For example, let's consider the output of the following command:

```
kubectl version --short --v=6
```

This should give an output similar to this:

```
I1123 15:25:14.635404    7930 loader.go:375] Config loaded from file:  /Users/mohammed/.kube/config
I1123 15:25:14.653550    7930 round_trippers.go:443] GET https://192.168.99.110:8443/version?timeout=32s 20
0 OK in 14 milliseconds
Client Version: v1.16.3
Server Version: v1.16.2
```

Figure 4.30: Request URL for the kubectl version command

As you can see in this screenshot, when you run **kubectl --version**, this goes to the **/version special entity**, as seen in the **GET** request URL.

API VERSIONS

In the Kubernetes API, there is the concept of API versioning; that is, the Kubernetes API supports multiple versions of a type of resource. These different versions may act differently. Each one has a different API path, such as **`/api/v1`** or **`/apis/extensions/v1beta1`**.

The different API versions differ in terms of stability and support:

- **Alpha**: This version is indicated by **`alpha`** in the **`apiVersion`** field—for example, **`/apis/batch/v1alpha1`**. The alpha version of resources is disabled by default as it is not intended for production clusters but can be used by early adopters and developers who are willing to provide feedback and suggestions and report bugs. Also, support for alpha resources may be dropped without notice by the time the final stable version of Kubernetes is finalized.
- **Beta**: This version is indicated by **`beta`** in the **`apiVersion`** field—for example, **`/apis/certificates.k8s.io/v1beta1`**. The beta version of resources is enabled by default, and the code behind it is well tested. However, using it is recommended for scenarios that are not business-critical because it is possible that changes in subsequent releases may reduce incompatibilities; that is, some features may not be supported for a long time.
- **Stable**: For these versions, the **`apiVersion`** field just contains the version number without any mention of **`alpha`** or **`beta`**—for example, **`/apis/networking.k8s.io/v1`**. The Stable version of resources is supported for many subsequent versions releases of Kubernetes. So, this version of API resources is recommended for any critical use cases.

You can get a complete list of the API versions enabled in your cluster by using the following command:

```
kubectl api-versions
```

You should see a response similar to this:

```
admissionregistration.k8s.io/v1
admissionregistration.k8s.io/v1beta1
apiextensions.k8s.io/v1
apiextensions.k8s.io/v1beta1
apiregistration.k8s.io/v1
apiregistration.k8s.io/v1beta1
apps/v1
authentication.k8s.io/v1
authentication.k8s.io/v1beta1
authorization.k8s.io/v1
authorization.k8s.io/v1beta1
autoscaling/v1
autoscaling/v2beta1
autoscaling/v2beta2
batch/v1
batch/v1beta1
certificates.k8s.io/v1beta1
coordination.k8s.io/v1
coordination.k8s.io/v1beta1
events.k8s.io/v1beta1
extensions/v1beta1
networking.k8s.io/v1
networking.k8s.io/v1beta1
node.k8s.io/v1beta1
policy/v1beta1
rbac.authorization.k8s.io/v1
rbac.authorization.k8s.io/v1beta1
scheduling.k8s.io/v1
scheduling.k8s.io/v1beta1
storage.k8s.io/v1
storage.k8s.io/v1beta1
v1
```

Figure 4.31: List of enabled versions of API resources

An interesting thing that you may observe in this screenshot is that some API resources, such as **autoscaling**, have multiple versions; for example, for **autoscaling**, there is **v1beta1**, **v1beta2**, and **v1**. So, what is the difference between them and which one should you use?

Let's again consider the example of **autoscaling**. This feature allows you to scale the number of pods in a replication controller, such as Deployments, ReplicaSets, or StatefulSets, based on specific metrics. For example, you can autoscale the number of pods from 3 to 10 if the average CPU load exceeds 50%.

In this case, the difference in the versions is that of feature support. The Stable release for autoscaling is **autoscaling/v1**, which only supports scaling the number of pods based on the average CPU metric. The beta release for autoscaling, which is **autoscaling/v2beta1**, supports scaling based on CPU and memory utilization. The newer version in the beta release, which is **autoscaling/v2beta2**, supports scaling the number of pods based on custom metrics in addition to CPU and memory. However, since the beta release is still not meant to be used for business-critical scenarios when you create an autoscaling resource, it will use the **autoscaling/v1** version. However, you can still use other versions to use additional features by specifying the beta version in the YAML file until the required features are added to the stable release.

All of this information can seem overwhelming. However, Kubernetes provides ways to access all the information you need to navigate your way around the API resources. You can use kubectl to access the Kubernetes docs and get the necessary information about the various API resources. Let's see how that works in the following exercise.

EXERCISE 4.02: GETTING INFORMATION ABOUT API RESOURCES

Let's say that we want to create an ingress object. For the purposes of this exercise, you don't need to know much about ingress; we will learn about it in the upcoming chapters.

We will use kubectl to get more information about the Ingress API resource, determine which API versions are available, and find out which groups it belongs to. If you recall from previous sections, we need this information for the **apiVersion** field of our YAML manifest. Then, we also get the information required for the other fields of our manifest file:

1. Let's first ask our cluster for all the available API resources that match the **ingresses** keyword:

   ```
   kubectl api-resources | grep ingresses
   ```

   This command will filter the list of all the API resources by the **ingresses** keyword. You should get the following output:

   ```
   ingresses     ing     extensions            true         Ingress
   ingresses     ing     networking.k8s.io     true         Ingress
   ```

We can see that we have ingress resources on two different API groups—**extensions** and **networking.k8s.io**.

2. We have also seen how we can get API resources belonging to specific groups. Let's check the API groups that we saw in the previous step:

```
kubectl api-resources --api-group="extensions"
```

You should get the following output:

```
NAME        SHORTNAMES    APIGROUP      NAMESPACED      KIND
ingresses   ing           extensions    true            Ingress
```

Now, let's check the other group:

```
kubectl api-resources --api-group="networking.k8s.io"
```

You should see the following output:

```
NAME               SHORTNAMES   APIGROUP            NAMESPACED   KIND
ingresses          ing          networking.k8s.io   true         Ingress
networkpolicies    netpol       networking.k8s.io   true         NetworkPolicy
```

Figure 4.32: Listing out the resources in the networking.k8s.io API group

However, if we were to use an ingress resource, we still don't know whether we should use the one from the **extensions** group or the **networking.k8s.io** group. In the next step, we will get some more information that will help us decide that.

3. Use the following command to get more information:

```
kubectl explain ingress
```

You should get this response:

```
KIND:     Ingress
VERSION:  extensions/v1beta1

DESCRIPTION:
     Ingress is a collection of rules that allow inbound connections to reach
     the endpoints defined by a backend. An Ingress can be configured to give
     services externally-reachable urls, load balance traffic, terminate SSL,
     offer name based virtual hosting etc. DEPRECATED - This group version of
     Ingress is deprecated by networking.k8s.io/v1beta1 Ingress. See the release
     notes for more information.

FIELDS:
   apiVersion   <string>
     APIVersion defines the versioned schema of this representation of an
     object. Servers should convert recognized schemas to the latest internal
     value, and may reject unrecognized values. More info:
     https://git.k8s.io/community/contributors/devel/sig-architecture/api-conventions
```

Figure 4.33: Getting details of the ingress resource from the extensions API group

As you can see, the **kubectl explain** command describes the API resource, as well as the details about the fields associated with it. We can also see that ingress uses the **extensions/v1beta1** API version, but if we read the **DESCRIPTION**, it mentions that this group version of ingress is deprecated by **networking.k8s.io/v1beta1**. Deprecated means that the standard is in the process of being phased out, and even though it is currently supported, it is not recommended for use.

> **NOTE**
>
> If you compare this to the different versions of **autoscaling** that we saw just before this exercise, you may think that the logical upgrade path from **v1beta** would be **v2beta**, and that would totally make sense. However, the ingress resource was moved from the **extensions** group to the **networking.k8s.io** group, and so this bucks the naming trend.

4. It is not a good idea to use a deprecated version, so let's say that you want to use the **networking.k8s.io/v1beta1** version instead. However, we need to get more information about it first. We can add a flag to the **kubectl explain** command to get information about a specific version of an API resource, as follows:

```
kubectl explain ingress --api-version=networking.k8s.io/v1beta1
```

You should see this response:

```
KIND:     Ingress
VERSION:  networking.k8s.io/v1beta1

DESCRIPTION:
     Ingress is a collection of rules that allow inbound connections to reach
     the endpoints defined by a backend. An Ingress can be configured to give
     services externally-reachable urls, load balance traffic, terminate SSL,
     offer name based virtual hosting etc.
```

Figure 4.34: Getting details of the ingress resource from the networking.k8s.io API group

5. We can also filter the output of the **kubectl explain** command by using the **JSONPath** identifier. This allows us to get information about the various fields that we need to specify while defining the YAML manifest. So, for example, if we would like to see the **spec** fields for Ingress, the command will be as follows:

```
kubectl explain ingress.spec --api-version=networking.k8s.io/v1beta1
```

This should give a response as follows:

```
KIND:     Ingress
VERSION:  networking.k8s.io/v1beta1

RESOURCE: spec <Object>

DESCRIPTION:
     Spec is the desired state of the Ingress. More info:
     https://git.k8s.io/community/contributors/devel/sig-architecture/api-
s.md#spec-and-status

     IngressSpec describes the Ingress the user wishes to exist.

FIELDS:
   backend      <Object>
     A default backend capable of servicing requests that don't match any
     At least one of 'backend' or 'rules' must be specified. This field i
     optional to allow the loadbalancer controller or defaulting logic to
     specify a global default.

   rules        <[]Object>
     A list of host rules used to configure the Ingress. If unspecified,
     rule matches, all traffic is sent to the default backend.

   tls  <[]Object>
     TLS configuration. Currently the Ingress only supports a single TLS
     443. If multiple members of this list specify different hosts, they
     multiplexed on the same port according to the hostname specified thr
     the SNI TLS extension, if the ingress controller fulfilling the ingr
     supports SNI.
```

Figure 4.35: Filtering the output of the kubectl explain command to get the spec fields of ingress

6. We can dive deeper to get more details about the nested fields. For example, if you wanted to get more details about the **backend** field of ingress, we can specify **ingress.spec.backend** to get the required information:

```
kubectl explain ingress.spec.backend --api-version=networking.k8s.io/
v1beta1
```

This will give the following output:

```
KIND:     Ingress
VERSION:  networking.k8s.io/v1beta1

RESOURCE: backend <Object>

DESCRIPTION:
     A default backend capable of servicing requests that don't match any rule.
     At least one of 'backend' or 'rules' must be specified. This field is
     optional to allow the loadbalancer controller or defaulting logic to
     specify a global default.

     IngressBackend describes all endpoints for a given service and port.

FIELDS:
   serviceName  <string> -required-
     Specifies the name of the referenced service.

   servicePort  <string> -required-
     Specifies the port of the referenced service.
```

Figure 4.36: Filtering the output of the kubectl explain command to get the spec.backend field of ingress

Similarly, we can repeat this for any field that you need information about, which is handy for building or modifying a YAML manifest. So, we have seen that the **kubectl explain** command is very useful when you are looking for more details and documentation about an API resource. It is also very useful when creating or modifying objects using YAML manifest files.

HOW TO ENABLE/DISABLE API RESOURCES, GROUPS, OR VERSIONS

In a typical cluster, not all API groups are enabled by default. It depends on the cluster use case as determined by the administrators. For example, some Kubernetes cloud providers disable resources that use the alpha level for stability and security reasons. However, those can still be enabled on the API server by using the **--runtime-config** flag, which accepts comma-separated lists.

To be able to create any resource, the group and version should be enabled in the cluster. For example, when you try to create a **CronJob** that uses **apiVersion: batch/v2alpha1** in its manifest file, if the group/version is not enabled, you will get an error similar to the following:

```
No matches for kind "CronJob" in version "batch/v2alpha1".
```

To enable **batch/v2alpha1**, you will need to set **--runtime-config=batch/v2alpha1** on the API server. This can be done either during the creation of the cluster or by updating the **/etc/kubernetes/manifests/kube-apiserver.yaml** manifest file. The flag also supports disabling an API group or version by setting a **false** value to the specific version—for example, **--runtime-config=batch/v1=false**.

--runtime-config also supports the **api/all** special key, which is used to control all API versions. For example, to turn off all API versions except **v1**, you can pass the **--runtime-config=api/all=false,api/v1=true** flag. Let's try our own hands-on example of creating and disabling API groups and versions in the following exercise.

EXERCISE 4.03: ENABLING AND DISABLING API GROUPS AND VERSIONS ON A MINIKUBE CLUSTER

In this exercise, we will create specific API versions while starting up Minikube, disable certain API versions in our running cluster, and then enable/disable resources in an entire API group:

1. Start Minikube with the flag shown in the following command:

   ```
   minikube start --extra-config=apiserver.runtime-config=batch/v2alpha1
   ```

   You should see the following response:

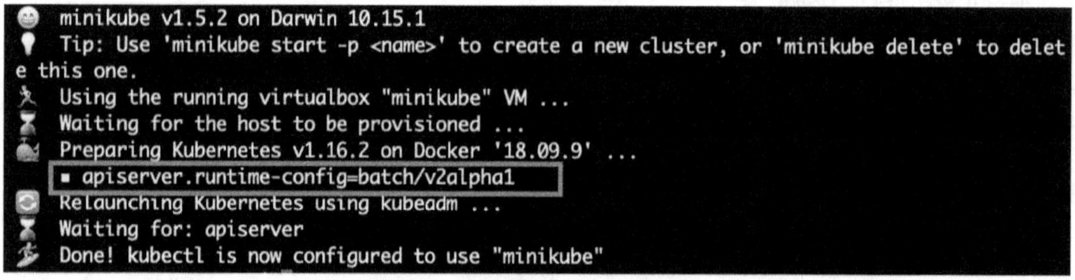

```
minikube v1.5.2 on Darwin 10.15.1
Tip: Use 'minikube start -p <name>' to create a new cluster, or 'minikube delete' to delet
e this one.
Using the running virtualbox "minikube" VM ...
Waiting for the host to be provisioned ...
Preparing Kubernetes v1.16.2 on Docker '18.09.9' ...
 ▪ apiserver.runtime-config=batch/v2alpha1
Relaunching Kubernetes using kubeadm ...
Waiting for: apiserver
Done! kubectl is now configured to use "minikube"
```

Figure 4.37: Starting up Minikube with an additional API resource group

> **NOTE**
>
> You can refer to the **minikube start** documentation for further details about the **--extra-config** flag, at https://minikube.sigs.k8s.io/docs/handbook/config/.

2. You can confirm it is enabled by checking the details about the **kube-apiserver-minikube** pod. Use the **describe pod** command and filter the results by the **runtime** keyword:

```
kubectl describe pod kube-apiserver-minikube -n kube-system | grep
runtime
```

   You should see the following response:

```
--runtime-config=batch/v2alpha1
```

3. Another way to confirm this is by looking at the enabled API versions by using the following command:

```
kubectl api-versions | grep batch/v2alpha1
```

   You should see the following response:

```
batch/v2alpha1
```

4. Now, let's create a resource called a **CronJob**, which uses **batch/v2alpha1** to confirm that our API server accepts the API. Create a file named **sample-cronjob.yaml** with the following contents:

```
apiVersion: batch/v2alpha1
kind: CronJob
metadata:
  name: hello
spec:
  schedule: "*/1 * * * *"
  jobTemplate:
    spec:
      template:
        spec:
          containers:
          - name: hello
            image: busybox
```

```
            args:
            - /bin/sh
            - -c
            - date; echo Hello from the Kubernetes cluster
          restartPolicy: OnFailure
```

5. Now, create a **CronJob** by using this YAML file:

```
kubectl create -f sample-cronjob.yaml
```

You should see the following output:

```
cronjob.batch/hello created
```

As you can see, the API server accepted our YAML file and the **CronJob** is created successfully.

6. Now, let's disable **batch/v2alpha1** on our cluster. To do that, we need to access the Minikube virtual machine (VM) using SSH, as demonstrated in previous chapters:

```
minikube ssh
```

You should see this response:

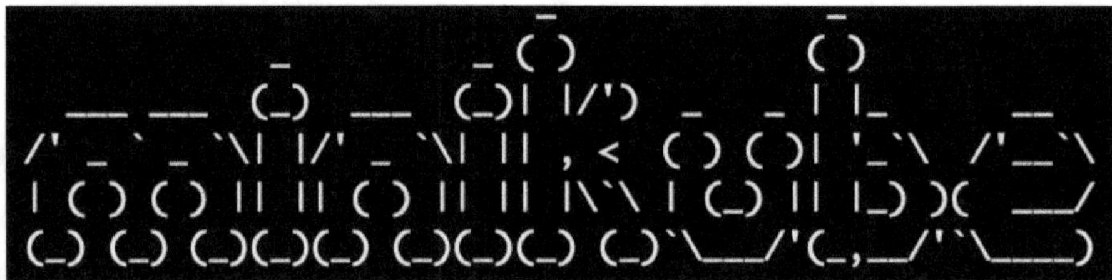

Figure 4.38: Accessing the Minikube VM via SSH

7. Open the API server manifest file. This is the template Kubernetes uses for the API server pods. We will use vi to modify this file, although you can use any text editor of your preference:

```
sudo vi /etc/kubernetes/manifests/kube-apiserver.yaml
```

You should see a response like the following:

```
apiVersion: v1
kind: Pod
metadata:
  creationTimestamp: null
  labels:
    component: kube-apiserver
    tier: control-plane
  name: kube-apiserver
  namespace: kube-system
spec:
  containers:
  - command:
    - kube-apiserver
    - --advertise-address=10.210.254.205
    - --allow-privileged=true
    - --authorization-mode=Node,RBAC
    - --client-ca-file=/var/lib/minikube/certs/ca.crt
    - --enable-admission-plugins=NamespaceLifecycle,LimitRar
    - --enable-bootstrap-token-auth=true
    - --etcd-cafile=/var/lib/minikube/certs/etcd/ca.crt
    - --etcd-certfile=/var/lib/minikube/certs/apiserver-etcc
    - --etcd-keyfile=/var/lib/minikube/certs/apiserver-etcd-
    - --etcd-servers=https://127.0.0.1:2379
    - --insecure-port=0
    - --kubelet-client-certificate=/var/lib/minikube/certs/a
    - --kubelet-client-key=/var/lib/minikube/certs/apiserver
    - --kubelet-preferred-address-types=InternalIP,ExternalI
    - --proxy-client-cert-file=/var/lib/minikube/certs/front
    - --proxy-client-key-file=/var/lib/minikube/certs/front-
    - --requestheader-allowed-names=front-proxy-client
    - --requestheader-client-ca-file=/var/lib/minikube/certs
    - --requestheader-extra-headers-prefix=X-Remote-Extra-
    - --requestheader-group-headers=X-Remote-Group
    - --requestheader-username-headers=X-Remote-User
    - --runtime-config=batch/v2alpha1
    - --secure-port=8443
```

Figure 4.39: The API server spec file

Look for the line that contains **`--runtime-config=batch/v2alpha1`** and change it to **`--runtime-config=batch/v2alpha1=false`**. Then, save the modified file.

8. End the SSH session by using the following command:

```
exit
```

9. For the changes in the API server manifest to take effect, we need to restart the API server and the controller manager. Since these are deployed as stateless pods, we can simply delete them and they will automatically get deployed again. First, let's delete the API server by running this command:

   ```
   kubectl delete pods -n kube-system -l component=kube-apiserver
   ```

   You should see this output:

   ```
   pod "kube-apiserver-minikube" deleted
   ```

   Now, let's delete the controller manager:

   ```
   kubectl delete pods -n kube-system -l component=kube-controller-
   manager
   ```

   You should see this output:

   ```
   pod "kube-controller-manager-minikube" deleted
   ```

   Note that for both of these commands, we did not delete the pods by their names. The **-l** flag looks for labels. These commands deleted all the pods in the **kube-system** namespace that had labels that match the ones specified after the **-l** flag.

10. We can confirm that **batch/v2alpha1** is no longer shown in API versions by using the following command:

    ```
    kubectl api-versions | grep batch/v2alpha1
    ```

    This command will not give you any response, indicating that we have disabled **batch/v2alpha1**.

So, we have seen how we can enable or disable a specific group or version of API resources. But this is still a broad approach. What if you wanted to disable a specific API resource?

For our example, let's say that you want to disable ingress. We saw in the previous exercise that we have ingresses in the **extensions** as well as **networking.k8s.io** API groups. If you are targeting a specific API resource, you need to specify its group and version. Let's say that you want to disable ingress from the **extensions** group because it is deprecated. In this group, we have just one version of ingresses, which is **v1beta**, as you can observe from *Figure 4.33*.

To achieve this, all we have to do is modify the **`--runtime-config`** flag to specify the resource that we want. So, if we wanted to disable ingress from the **`extensions`** group, the flag would be as follows:

```
--runtime-config=extensions/v1beta1/ingresses=false
```

To disable the resource, we can use this flag when starting up Minikube, as shown in *step 1* of this exercise, or we can add this line to the API server's manifest file, as shown in *step 7* of this exercise. Recall from this exercise that if we instead want to enable the resource, we just need to remove the **`=false`** part from the end of this flag.

INTERACTING WITH CLUSTERS USING THE KUBERNETES API

Up until now, we've been using the Kubernetes kubectl command-line tool, which made interacting with our cluster quite convenient. It does that by extracting the API server address and authentication information from the client kubeconfig file, which is located in **`~/.kube/config`** by default, as we saw in the previous chapter. In this section, we will look at the different ways to directly access the API server with HTTP clients such as curl.

There are two possible ways to directly access the API server via the REST API—by using kubectl in proxy mode or by providing the location and authentication credentials directly to the HTTP client. We will explore both methods to understand the pros and cons of each one.

ACCESSING THE KUBERNETES API SERVER USING KUBECTL AS A PROXY

kubectl has a great feature called **kubectl proxy**, which is the recommended approach for interacting with the API server. This is recommended because it is easier to use and provides a more secure way of doing so because it verifies the identity of the API server by using a self-signed certificate, which prevents **man-in-the-middle (MITM)** attacks.

kubectl proxy routes the requests from our HTTP client to the API server while taking care of authentication by itself. Authentication is also handled by using the current configuration in our kubeconfig file.

In order to demonstrate how to use kubectl proxy, let's first create an NGINX Deployment with two replicas in the default namespace and view it using **`kubectl get pods`**:

```
kubectl create deployment mynginx --image=nginx:latest
```

This should give an output like the following:

```
deployment.apps/mynginx created
```

Now, we can scale our Deployment to two replicas with the following command:

```
kubectl scale deployment mynginx --replicas=2
```

You should see an output similar to this:

```
deployment.apps/mynginx scaled
```

Let's now check whether the pods are up and running:

```
kubectl get pods
```

This gives an output similar to the following:

```
NAME                          READY     STATUS     RESTARTS    AGE
mynginx-565f67b548-gk5n2      1/1       Running    0           2m30s
mynginx-565f67b548-q6slz      1/1       Running    0           2m30s
```

To start a proxy to the API server, run the **kubectl proxy** command:

```
kubectl proxy
```

This should give output as follows:

```
Starting to serve on 127.0.0.1:8001
```

Note from the preceding screenshot that the local proxy connection is running on **127.0.0.1:8001**, which is the default. We can also specify a custom port by adding the **--port=<YourCustomPort>** flag, while adding an **&** (ampersand) sign at the end of our command to allow the proxy to run in the terminal background so that we can continue working in the same terminal window. So, the command would look like this:

```
kubectl proxy --port=8080 &
```

This should give the following response:

```
[1] 48285
AbuTalebMBP:~ mohammed$ Starting to serve on 127.0.0.1:8080
```

The proxy is run as a background job, and in the preceding screenshot, **[1]** indicates the job number and **48285** indicates its process ID. To exit a proxy running in the background, you can run **fg** to bring the job back to the foreground:

```
fg
```

This will show the following response:

```
kubectl proxy --port=8080
^C
```

After getting the proxy to the foreground, we can simply use *Ctrl* + *C* to exit it (if there's no other job running).

> **NOTE**
>
> If you are not familiar with job control, you can learn about it at https://www.gnu.org/software/bash/manual/html_node/Job-Control-Basics.html.

We can now start exploring the API using curl:

```
curl http://127.0.0.1:8080/apis
```

Recall that even though we are mostly using YAML for convenience, the data is stored in etcd in JSON format. You will see a long response that begins something like this:


```
{
  "kind": "APIGroupList",
  "apiVersion": "v1",
  "groups": [
    {
      "name": "apiregistration.k8s.io",
      "versions": [
        {
          "groupVersion": "apiregistration.k8s.io/v1",
          "version": "v1"
        },
        {
          "groupVersion": "apiregistration.k8s.io/v1beta1",
          "version": "v1beta1"
        }
      ],
      "preferredVersion": {
        "groupVersion": "apiregistration.k8s.io/v1",
        "version": "v1"
      }
    },
    {
      "name": "extensions",
      "versions": [
```


Figure 4.40: The response from the API server

But how do we find the exact path to query the Deployment we created earlier? Also, how do we query the pods created by that Deployment?

You can start by asking yourself a few questions:

- What are the API version and API group used by Deployments?

  In *Figure 4.27*, we saw that the Deployments are in **apps/v1**, so we can start by adding that to the path:

```
curl http://127.0.0.1:8080/apis/apps/v1
```

- Is it a namespace-scoped resource or a cluster-scoped resource? If it is a namespace-scoped resource, what is the name of the namespace?

  We also saw in the scope of the API resources section that Deployments are namespace-scoped resources. When we created the Deployment, since we did not specify a different namespace, it went to the **default** namespace. So, in addition to the **apiVersion** field, we would need to add **namespaces/default/deployments** to our path:

```
curl http://127.0.0.1:8080/apis/apps/v1/namespaces/default/
deployments
```

  This will return a large output with the JSON data that is stored on this path. This is the part of the response that gives us the information that we need:


```
{
  "kind": "DeploymentList",
  "apiVersion": "apps/v1",
  "metadata": {
    "selfLink": "/apis/apps/v1/namespaces/default/deploym
ents",
    "resourceVersion": "131356"
  },
  "items": [
    {
      "metadata": {
        "name": "mynginx",
        "namespace": "default",
        "selfLink": "/apis/apps/v1/namespaces/default/dep
loyments/mynginx",
        "uid": "90935fea-80a6-4d77-8340-65e2a445d057",
```


Figure 4.41: Getting information about all the Deployments using curl

As you can see in this output, this lists all the Deployments in the **default** namespace. You can infer that from **"kind": "DeploymentList"**. Also, note that the response is in JSON format and is not neatly presented as a table.

Now, we can specify a specific Deployment by adding it to our path:

```
curl http://127.0.0.1:8080/apis/apps/v1/namespaces/default/deployments/
mynginx
```

You should see this response:

```
{
  "kind": "Deployment",
  "apiVersion": "apps/v1",
  "metadata": {
    "name": "mynginx",
    "namespace": "default",
    "selfLink": "/apis/apps/v1/namespaces/default/deploym
ents/mynginx",
    "uid": "90935fea-80a6-4d77-8340-65e2a445d057",
    "resourceVersion": "129928",
    "generation": 2,
```

Figure 4.42: Getting information about our NGINX Deployment using curl

You can use this method with any other resource as well.

CREATING OBJECTS USING CURL

When you use any HTTP client, such as curl, to send requests to the API server to create objects, you need to change three things:

1. Change the **HTTP** request method to **POST**. By default, curl will use the **GET** method. To create objects, we need to use the **POST** method, as we learned in *The Kubernetes API* section. You can change this using the **-X** flag.

2. Change the HTTP request header. We need to modify the header to inform the API server what the intention of the request is. We can modify the header using the **-H** flag. In this case, we need to set the header to **'Content-Type: application/yaml'**.

3. Include the spec of the object to be created. As you learned in the previous two chapters, each API resource is persisted in the etcd as an API object, which is defined by a YAML spec/manifest file. To create an object, you need to use the **`--data`** flag to pass the YAML manifest to the API server so that it can persist it in etcd as an object.

So, the curl command, which we will implement in the following exercise, will look something like this:

```
curl -X POST <URL-path> -H 'Content-Type: application/yaml' --data <spec/
manifest>
```

At times, you will have the manifest files handy. However, that may not always be the case. Also, we have not yet seen what manifests for namespaces look like.

Let's consider a case where we want to create a namespace. Usually, you would create a namespace as follows:

```
kubectl create namespace my-namespace
```

This will give the following response:

```
namespace/my-namespace created
```

Here, you can see that we created a namespace called **`my-namespace`**. However, for passing the request without using kubectl, we need the spec used to define a namespace. We can get that by using the **`--dry-run=client`** and **`-o`** flags:

```
kubectl create namespace my-second-namespace --dry-run=client -o yaml
```

This will give the following response:

```
apiVersion: v1
kind: Namespace
metadata:
  creationTimestamp: null
  name: my-second-namespace
spec: {}
status: {}
```

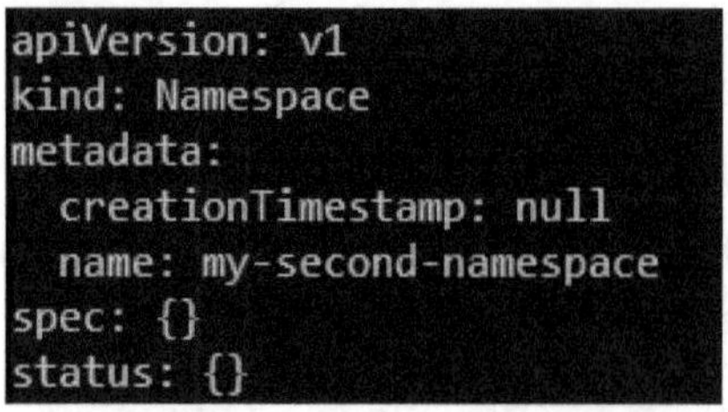

Figure 4.43: Getting the spec for a namespace using dry-run

When you run a **kubectl** command with the **--dry-run=client** flag, the API server takes it through all the stages of a normal command, except that it does not persist the changes into etcd. So, the command is authenticated, authorized, and validated, but changes are not permanent. This is a great way to test whether a certain command works, and also to get the manifest that the API server would have created for this command, as you can see in the previous screenshot. Let's see how to put this in practice and use curl to create a Deployment.

EXERCISE 4.04: CREATING AND VERIFYING A DEPLOYMENT USING KUBECTL PROXY AND CURL

For this exercise, we will create an NGINX Deployment called **nginx-example** with three replicas in a namespace called **example**. We will do this by sending our requests to the API server with curl via kubectl proxy:

1. First, let's start our proxy:

```
kubectl proxy &
```

   This should give the following response:

```
[1] 50034
AbuTalebMBP:~ mohammed$ Starting to serve on 127.0.0.1:8080
```

   The proxy started as a background job and is listening on the localhost at port **8001**.

2. Since the **example** namespace does not exist, we should create that namespace before creating the Deployment. As we learned in the previous section, we need to get the spec that should be used to create the namespace. Let's use the following command:

```
kubectl create namespace example --dry-run -o yaml
```

> **NOTE**
>
> For Kubernetes versions 1.18+, please use **--dry-run=client**.

This will give the following output:

```
apiVersion: v1
kind: Namespace
metadata:
  creationTimestamp: null
  name: example
spec: {}
status: {}
```

Figure 4.44: Getting the spec required for our namespace

Now, we have the spec required for creating the namespace.

3. Now, we need to send a request to the API server using curl. Namespaces belong to the core group and hence the path will be **/api/v1/namespaces**. The final **curl** command to create the namespace after adding all required parameters should look like the following:

```
curl -X POST http://127.0.0.1:8001/api/v1/namespaces -H 'Content-
    Type: application/yaml' --data "
apiVersion: v1
kind: Namespace
metadata:
  creationTimestamp: null
  name: example
spec: {}
status: {}
"
```

> **NOTE**
>
> You can discover the required path for any resource, as shown in the previous exercise. In this command, the double-quotes (") after **--data** allow you to enter multi-line input in Bash, which is delimited by another double-quote at the end. So, you can copy the output from the previous step here before the delimiter.

Now, if everything was correct in our command, you should get a response like the following:


```
{
  "kind": "Namespace",
  "apiVersion": "v1",
  "metadata": {
    "name": "example",
    "selfLink": "/api/v1/namespaces/example",
    "uid": "003a5217-9836-4525-af13-80e6f8c97022",
    "resourceVersion": "3448348",
    "creationTimestamp": "2020-05-02T18:14:37Z"
  },
  "spec": {
    "finalizers": [
      "kubernetes"
    ]
  },
  "status": {
    "phase": "Active"
  }
```


Figure 4.45: Using curl to send a request to create a namespace

4. The same procedure applies to Deployment. So, first, let's use the **`kubectl create`** command with **`--dry-run=client`** to get an idea of how our YAML data looks:

```
kubectl create deployment nginx-example -n example
--image=nginx:latest --dry-run -o yaml
```

> **NOTE**
>
> For Kubernetes versions 1.18+, please use **`--dry-run=client`**.

You should get the following response:

```
apiVersion: apps/v1
kind: Deployment
metadata:
  creationTimestamp: null
  labels:
    app: nginx-example
  name: nginx-example
  namespace: example
spec:
  replicas: 1
  selector:
    matchLabels:
      app: nginx-example
  strategy: {}
  template:
    metadata:
      creationTimestamp: null
      labels:
        app: nginx-example
    spec:
      containers:
      - image: nginx:latest
        name: nginx
        resources: {}
status: {}
```

Figure 4.46: Using curl to send a request to create a Deployment

> **NOTE**
>
> Notice that the namespace will not show if you are using the **`--dry-run=client`** flag because we need to specify it in our API path.

5. Now, the command for creating the Deployment will be constructed similarly to the command for creating the namespace. Note that the namespace is specified in the API path:

```
curl -X POST http://127.0.0.1:8001/apis/apps/v1/namespaces/example/
    deployments -H 'Content-Type: application/yaml' --data "
apiVersion: apps/v1
kind: Deployment
metadata:
  creationTimestamp: null
  labels:
    run: nginx-example
  name: nginx-example
spec:
  replicas: 3
  selector:
    matchLabels:
      run: nginx-example
  strategy: {}
  template:
    metadata:
      creationTimestamp: null
      labels:
        run: nginx-example
    spec:
      containers:
      - image: nginx:latest
        name: nginx-example
        resources: {}
status: {}
"
```

If everything is correct, you should get a response like the following from the API server:


```
{
  "kind": "Deployment",
  "apiVersion": "apps/v1",
  "metadata": {
    "name": "nginx-example",
    "namespace": "example",
    "selfLink": "/apis/apps/v1/namespaces/example/deployments
/nginx-example",
    "uid": "1b45af44-60fc-4391-b04c-4c61f6877d88",
    "resourceVersion": "3448599",
    "generation": 1,
    "creationTimestamp": "2020-05-02T18:17:42Z",
    "labels": {
      "run": "nginx-example"
    }
  },
  "spec": {
    "replicas": 3,
    "selector": {
      "matchLabels": {
        "run": "nginx-example"
      }
    },
    "template": {
      "metadata": {
        "creationTimestamp": null,
        "labels": {
          "run": "nginx-example"
        }
      },
      "spec": {
        "containers": [
          {
            "name": "nginx-example",
            "image": "nginx:latest",
            "resources": {

            },
            "terminationMessagePath": "/dev/termination-log",
            "terminationMessagePolicy": "File",
```


Figure 4.47: Response from API server after creating a Deployment

Note that the kubectl proxy process is still running in the background. If you are done with interacting with the API server using kubectl proxy, then you may want to stop the proxy from running in the background. To do that, run the **fg** command to bring the kubectl proxy process to the foreground and then press *Ctrl* + *C*.

So, we have seen how we can interact with the API server using kubectl proxy, and by using curl, we have been able to create an NGINX Deployment in a new namespace.

DIRECT ACCESS TO THE KUBERNETES API USING AUTHENTICATION CREDENTIALS

Instead of using kubectl in proxy mode, we can provide the location and credentials directly to the HTTP client. This approach can be used if you are using a client that may get confused by proxies, but it is less secure than using the kubectl proxy due to the risk of MITM attacks. To mitigate this risk, it is recommended that you import the root certificate and verify the identity of the API server when using this method.

When thinking about accessing the cluster using credentials, we need to understand how authentication is configured and what authentication plugins are enabled in our cluster. Several authentication plugins can be used, which allow different ways of authenticating with the server:

- Client certificates
- ServiceAccount bearer tokens
- Authenticating proxy
- HTTP basic auth

> **NOTE**
>
> Note that the preceding list includes only some of the authentication plugins. You can learn more about authentication at https://kubernetes.io/docs/reference/access-authn-authz/authentication/.

Let's check what authentication plugins are enabled in our cluster by looking at the API server running process using the following command and looking at the flags passed to the API server:

```
kubectl exec -it kube-apiserver-minikube -n kube-system -- /bin/sh -c
"apt update ; apt -y install procps ; ps aux | grep kube-apiserver"
```

This command will first install/update **procps** (a tool used to inspect processes) within the API server, which is running as a pod on our Minikube server. Then, it will get the list of processes and filter it by using the **kube-apiserver** keyword. You will get a long output, but here is the part that we are interested in:

```
:31 kube-apiserver --advertise-address=192.168.0.105 --allow-
privileged=true --authorization-mode=Node,RBAC --client-ca-fi
le=/var/lib/minikube/certs/ca.crt --enable-admission-plugins=
NamespaceLifecycle,LimitRanger,ServiceAccount,DefaultStorageC
lass,DefaultTolerationSeconds,NodeRestriction,MutatingAdmissi
onWebhook,ValidatingAdmissionWebhook,ResourceQuota --enable-b
ootstrap-token-auth=true --etcd-cafile=/var/lib/minikube/cert
s/etcd/ca.crt --etcd-certfile=/var/lib/minikube/certs/apiserv
er-etcd-client.crt --etcd-keyfile=/var/lib/minikube/certs/api
server-etcd-client.key --etcd-servers=https://127.0.0.1:2379
--insecure-port=0 --kubelet-client-certificate=/var/lib/minik
ube/certs/apiserver-kubelet-client.crt --kubelet-client-key=/
var/lib/minikube/certs/apiserver-kubelet-client.key --kubelet
-preferred-address-types=InternalIP,ExternalIP,Hostname --pro
xy-client-cert-file=/var/lib/minikube/certs/front-proxy-clien
t.crt --proxy-client-key-file=/var/lib/minikube/certs/front-p
roxy-client.key --requestheader-allowed-names=front-proxy-cli
ent --requestheader-client-ca-file=/var/lib/minikube/certs/fr
ont-proxy-ca.crt --requestheader-extra-headers-prefix=X-Remot
e-Extra- --requestheader-group-headers=X-Remote-Group --reque
stheader-username-headers=X-Remote-User --secure-port=8443 --
service-account-key-file=/var/lib/minikube/certs/sa.pub --ser
vice-cluster-ip-range=10.96.0.0/12 --tls-cert-file=/var/lib/m
inikube/certs/apiserver.crt --tls-private-key-file=/var/lib/m
inikube/certs/apiserver.key
```

Figure 4.48: Getting the details flags passed to the API server

The following two flags from this screenshot tell us some important information:

- **--client-ca-file=/var/lib/minikube/certs/ca.crt**
- **--service-account-key-file=/var/lib/minikube/certs/sa.pub**

These flags tell us that we have two different authentication plugins configured—X.509 client certificates (based on the first flag) and ServiceAccount tokens (based on the second flag). We will now learn how to use both of these authentication methods for communicating with the API server.

METHOD 1: USING CLIENT CERTIFICATE AUTHENTICATION

X.509 certificates are used for authenticating external requests, which is the current configuration in our kubeconfig file. The **--client-ca-file=/var/lib/minikube/certs/ca.crt** flag indicates the certificate authority that is used to validate client certificates, which will authenticate with the API server. An X.509 certificate defines a subject, which is what identifies a user in Kubernetes. For example, the X.509 certificate used for SSL by https://www.google.com/ has a subject containing the following information:

```
Common Name = www.google.com
Organization = Google LLC
Locality = Mountain View
State = California
Country = US
```

When an X.509 certificate is used for authenticating a Kubernetes user, the **Common Name** of the subject is used as the username for the user, and the **Organization** field is used as the group membership of that user.

Kubernetes uses a TLS protocol for all of its API calls as a security measure. The HTTP client that we have been using so far, curl, can work with TLS. Earlier, kubectl proxy took care of communicating over TLS for us, but if we want to do it directly using curl, we need to add three more details to all of our API calls:

- **--cert**: The client certificate path
- **--key**: The private key path
- **--cacert**: The certificate authority path

So, if we combine them, the command syntax should look as follows:

```
curl --cert <ClientCertificate> --key <PrivateKey> --cacert
<CertificateAuthority> https://<APIServerAddress:port>/api
```

In this section, we will not create these certificates, but instead, we will be using the certificates that were created when we bootstrapped our cluster using Minikube. All the relevant information can be taken from our kubeconfig file, which was prepared by Minikube when we initialized the cluster. Let's see that file:

```
kubectl config view
```

You should get the following response:

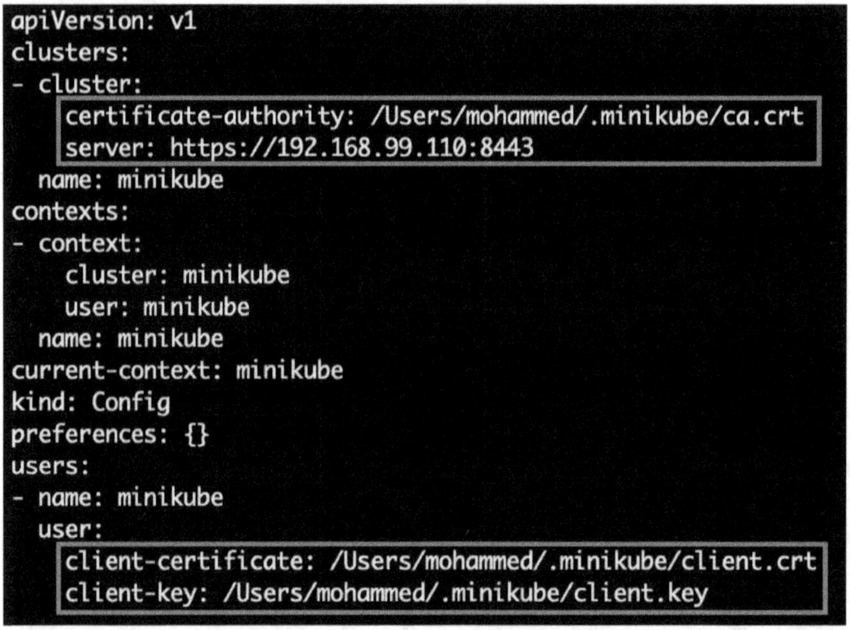

```
apiVersion: v1
clusters:
- cluster:
    certificate-authority: /Users/mohammed/.minikube/ca.crt
    server: https://192.168.99.110:8443
  name: minikube
contexts:
- context:
    cluster: minikube
    user: minikube
  name: minikube
current-context: minikube
kind: Config
preferences: {}
users:
- name: minikube
  user:
    client-certificate: /Users/mohammed/.minikube/client.crt
    client-key: /Users/mohammed/.minikube/client.key
```

Figure 4.49: The API server IP and authentication certificates in kubeconfig

The final command should look like the following: you can see that we can explore the API:

```
curl --cert ~/.minikube/client.crt --key ~/.minikube/client.key --cacert
~/.minikube/ca.crt https://192.168.99.110:8443/api
```

You should get the following response:

```
{
  "kind": "APIVersions",
  "versions": [
    "v1"
  ],
  "serverAddressByClientCIDRs": [
    {
      "clientCIDR": "0.0.0.0/0",
      "serverAddress": "192.168.99.110:8443"
    }
  ]
}
```

Figure 4.50: Response from API server

So, we can see that the API server is responding to our calls. You can use this method to achieve everything that we have done in the previous section using kubectl proxy.

METHOD 2: USING A SERVICEACCOUNT BEARER TOKEN

Service accounts are meant to authenticate processes running within the cluster, such as pods, to allow internal communication with the API server. They use signed bearer **JSON Web Tokens** (**JWTs**) to authenticate with the API server. These tokens are stored in Kubernetes objects called **Secrets**, which are a type of entities used to store sensitive information, such as the aforementioned authentication tokens. The information stored inside a Secret is Base64-encoded.

So, each ServiceAccount has a corresponding secret associated with it. When a pod uses a ServiceAccount to authenticate with the API server, the secret is mounted on the pod and the bearer token is decoded and then mounted at the following location inside a pod: **`/run/secrets/kubernetes.io/serviceaccount`**. This can then be used by any process in the pod to authenticate with the API server. Authentication by use of ServiceAccounts is enabled by a built-in module known as an admission controller, which is enabled by default.

However, ServiceAccounts alone are not sufficient; once authenticated, Kubernetes also needs to permit any actions for that ServiceAccount (which is the authorization phase). This is managed by **Role-Based Access Control** (**RBAC**) policies. In Kubernetes, you can define certain **Roles**, and then use **RoleBinding** to *bind* those Roles to certain users or ServiceAccounts.

A Role defines what actions (API verbs) are allowed and which API groups and resources can be accessed. A RoleBinding defines which user or ServiceAccount can assume that Role. A ClusterRole is similar to a Role, except that a Role is namespace-scoped, while a ClusterRole is a cluster-scoped policy. The same distinction is true for RoleBinding and ClusterRoleBinding.

> **NOTE**
>
> You will learn more about secrets in *Chapter 10, ConfigMaps and Secrets*; more on RBAC in *Chapter 13, Runtime and Network Security in Kubernetes*; and admission controllers in *Chapter 16, Kubernetes Admission Controllers*.

Every namespace contains a ServiceAccount called **default**. We can see that by using the following command:

```
kubectl get serviceaccounts --all-namespaces
```

You should see the following response:

```
NAMESPACE          NAME                                   SECRETS   AGE
default            default                                1         10h
example            default                                1         9h
kube-node-lease    default                                1         10h
kube-public        default                                1         10h
kube-system        attachdetach-controller                1         10h
kube-system        bootstrap-signer                       1         10h
kube-system        certificate-controller                 1         10h
kube-system        clusterrole-aggregation-controller     1         10h
kube-system        coredns                                1         10h
kube-system        cronjob-controller                     1         10h
kube-system        daemon-set-controller                  1         10h
kube-system        default                                1         10h
kube-system        deployment-controller                  1         10h
```

Figure 4.51: Examining default ServiceAccounts for each namespace

As mentioned earlier, a ServiceAccount is associated with a secret that contains the CA certificate of the API server and a bearer token. We can view the ServiceAccount-associated secret in the **default** namespace, as follows:

```
kubectl get secrets
```

You should get the following response:

```
NAME                  TYPE                                  DATA   AGE
default-token-wtkk5   kubernetes.io/service-account-token   3      10h
```

We can see that we have a secret named **`default-token-wtkk5`** (where **`wtkk5`** is a random string) in our default namespace. We can view the content of the Secret resource by using the following command:

```
kubectl get secrets default-token-wtkk5 -o yaml
```

This command will get the object definition as it is stored in etcd and display it in YAML format so that it is easy to read. This will produce an output as follows:


```
apiVersion: v1
data:
  ca.crt: LS0tLS1CRUdJTiBDRVJUSUZJQ0FURS0tLS0tCk1JSUM1ekNDQWMrZ0F3SUJBZ01C
QVRBTkJna3Foa2lHOXcwQkFRc0ZBREFWTVJNd0VRWURWUVFERXdwdGFXNXAKYTNWaVpVTkJNQj
RYRFRFNU1URXhOVEUzTURreU0xb1hEVEk1TVRFeE16RTNNRGt5TTFvd0ZURVRNQkVHQTFVRQpB
eE1LYldsdWFXdDFZbVZEUVRDQ0FTSXdEUVlKS29aSWh2Y05BUUVCQlFBRGdnRVBBRENDQVFvQ2
dnRUJBT05XCk9CR2VaS1ZQVk81eWUzRXBZbE5kTVhNV2VDQWF4Rnl6MkZIYm8yT2xKN055Uzhp
RmIvQlR0Z29tancyWG5LQ0cKdXNWS0k1d1lRRklJYUFtY1doZnBXU21WM0Z2N0xEWEFJRXg4N0
MwQTM1YnMvN2EwcTY2cURCKzJCU1ZMSTlGaQptTFlnWk1IcklNMDBmV2NlT29nZW1CUi9DRHVR
T3ZmOXJLQzBXYkswckJ3Mm4weE1mMmpGZFBhb3dHelo4MmloClNMVks3RDJ3akN0NWVoMTNVMk
1QZldUb0hDVWhiV2RnL2t0UVpGQ29ZK05hWHdEeUZZTlFoUWZUeHdVNmk0NFYKRDdrUFBkK0dX
aDk2cS9SUDRIK3h4NGE4NmdpdGJMSjBGbnJXY25TdzdjNmxZN0kzVTJzVFZDNXk4Qk5ZT01GNQ
pGeW9WY25vSmNOYnFRakJuSTFrQ0F3RUFBYU5DTUVBd0RnWURWUjBQQVFIL0JBUURBZ0trTUIw
R0ExVWRKUVFXCk1CUUdDQ3NHQVFVRkJ3TUNCZ2dyQmdFRkJRY0RBVEFQQmdOVkhSTUJBZjhFQl
RBREFRSC9NQTBHQ1NxR1NJYjMKRFFFQkN3VUFBNE1CQVFCN3lZTm5MazdraXB5enAzUnFvQ21Z
SWhtRUMxN2RmN3VJbU11UnJPcXlNUFhJb1VVOQpzcnFMb3ExUEZSSzFsZ1JIMm1KY0RBYk9SYm
xYcytkTGY2T3ljSmNzcXhkdnNhQU83Nk0wUkI1Z0YyQzVUTjBOCjJlSm82UjRaTjZxUDJORm9E
MFNYRkgyYUgydkpnRFVERHNCL0RTVzVHOUpiZTZ6SmlpMkFmWncydjdjT1E2RlEKTitQUVRSOV
F5TStwaW9rN0dvc0x0RDhOMGRIWmZvUVlTVy94ak5abncVElmYjgwRXIxb2RIREw0N2pVdnZP
bApXcWgyYjNzd25ja1dWWUJpVzk2RVRpek9wSnMyazM2QjhGeGVHMG83L1lWaVZ0eC9qQjRLLy
toWi85c3QxUGR4Cm1aZXNCTzlCYmdNci9ROXY4QUZXWFJMM1d0VWIvWVN3cHZ6UwotLS0tLUVO
RCBDRVJUSUZJQ0FURS0tLS0tCg==
  namespace: ZGVmYXVsdA==
  token: ZXlKaGJHY2lPaUpTVXpJMU5pSXNJbXRwWkNJNklqZENZamcyYlU5VWJWSnNUa3RwV
Uc4emJrOVdVMHd0VmswM055MHdZalJOVVdGUlRGSmZaVEZXUTNNaWZRLmV5SnBjM01pT2lKcmR
XSmxjbTVsZEdWekwzTmxjblpwWTJWaFkyTnZkVzUwSW13aWEzVmlaWEp1WlhSbGN5NXBieTl6W
lhKMmFXTmxZV05qYjNWdWRDOXVZVzFsYzNCaFkyVWlPaUprWldaaGRXeDBJaXdpYTNWaVpYSnV
aWFJsY3k1cGJ5OXpaWEoyYVdObFlXTmpiM1Z1ZEM5elpXTnlaWFF1Ym1GdFpTSTZJbVJsWm1GM
WJIUXRkRzlyWlc0dGQzUnJhelZpTENKcmRXSmxjbTVsZEdWekxtbHZMM05sY25acFkyVmhZMk5
2ZFc1MEwzTmxjblpwWTJWaFkyTnZkVzUwTFhOaGJXVWlPaUprWldaaGRXeDBJaXdpYTNWaVpYSn
lib1VYWWlhNdWFXOHZjM1Z5ZG1salpXRmpZMjkxYm5RdmMyVnlkbWxqWlMxaFkyTnZkVzUwTG5
WcFpDSTZJbUkwTURRMlpHSTJMVFZpTlRVdE5EZzNNeTA1WmpOakxUTTJOV0UwTkdWaFpqWTFNU
01zSW5OMVlpSTZJbk41YzNSbGJUcHpaWEoyYVdObFlXTmpiM1Z1ZERwa1pXWmhkV3gwT21SbFp
tRjFiSFFpZlEucmptYzR2cEFtYW4waHpKSmltMUNiNXpwbGV6MHlSQjR3TFRqakdsNE8zVlVxe
U5KVkdOZHdqYWptMS0zQTRHTm5Id1hQZHB2b3hVS2F4RUUzaC1HQ1htZ1pIS2NGekI3ZzhSTmI
wbVBROV8zLUFKWmhkQUNFM1c5a01lRVhFIcGRhU1BZVWxxeUI4MzRlZ1lIVTA4Y3RQVkFicXJvL
XRjWmEyMG9iWkppb2plTlRuUUdCNWY2Mm0wSWcxTXFYczRnd3A0MWpqd3ZQajRPZTVjaFpmMnB
```


Figure 4.52: Displaying the information stored in a secret

Note from the preceding secret that **namespace**, **token**, and the CA certificate of the API server (ca.crt) are Base64-encoded. You can decode it using **base64 --decode** in your Linux terminal, as follows:

```
echo "<copied_value>" | base64 --decode
```

Copy and paste the value from **ca.crt** or **token** in the preceding command. This will output the decoded value, which you can then write to a file or a variable for later use. However, in this demonstration, we will show another method to get the values.

Let's take a peek into one of our pods:

```
kubectl exec -it <pod-name> -- /bin/bash
```

This command enters the pod and then runs a Bash shell on it. Then, once we have the shell running inside a pod, we can explore the various mount points available in the pod:

```
df -h
```

This will give an output similar to the following:

```
Filesystem      Size  Used Avail Use% Mounted on
overlay          17G  2.0G   15G  13% /
tmpfs            64M     0   64M   0% /dev
tmpfs           970M     0  970M   0% /sys/fs/cgroup
/dev/sda1        17G  2.0G   15G  13% /etc/hosts
shm              64M     0   64M   0% /dev/shm
tmpfs           970M   12K  970M   1% /run/secrets/kubernetes.io/serviceaccount
tmpfs           970M     0  970M   0% /proc/acpi
tmpfs           970M     0  970M   0% /proc/scsi
tmpfs           970M     0  970M   0% /sys/firmware
```

Figure 4.53: The mount point for the bearer token

The mount point can be explored further:

```
ls /var/run/secrets/kubernetes.io/serviceaccount
```

You should see an output similar to the following:

```
ca.crt  namespace  token
```

As you can see here, the mount point contains the API server CA certificate, the namespace this secret belongs to, and the JWT bearer token. If you are trying these commands on your terminal, you can exit the pod's shell by entering an **exit**.

If we try to access the API server using curl from inside the pod, we would need to provide the CA path and the token. Let's try to list all the pods in the pod's namespace by accessing the API server from inside a pod.

We can create a new Deployment and start a Bash terminal with the following procedure:

```
kubectl run my-bash --rm --restart=Never -it --image=ubuntu -- bash
```

This may take a few seconds to start up, and then you will get a response similar to this:

```
If you don't see a command prompt, try pressing enter.
root@my-bash: /#
```

This will start up a Deployment running Ubuntu and immediately take us inside the pod and open up the Bash shell. The **--rm** flag in this command will delete the pod after all the processes inside the pod are terminated—that is, after we leave the pod using the **exit** command. But for now, let's install curl:

```
apt update && apt -y install curl
```

This should produce a response similar to this:

```
Get:1 http://security.ubuntu.com/ubuntu bionic-security InRelease
88.7 kB]
Get:2 http://archive.ubuntu.com/ubuntu bionic InRelease [242 kB]
Get:3 http://security.ubuntu.com/ubuntu bionic-security/restricted
amd64 Packages [23.7 kB]
Get:4 http://archive.ubuntu.com/ubuntu bionic-updates InRelease [8
.7 kB]
Get:5 http://archive.ubuntu.com/ubuntu bionic-backports InRelease
```

Figure 4.54: Installing curl

Now that we have installed curl, let's try to list the pods using curl by accessing the API path:

```
curl https://kubernetes/api/v1/namespaces/$NAMESPACE/pods
```

You should see the following response:

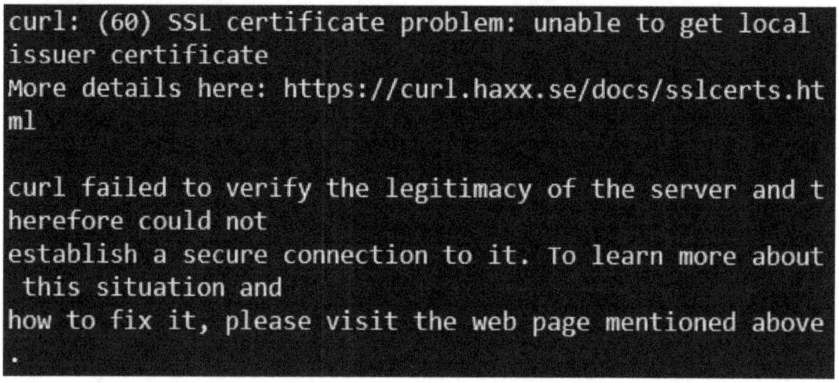

```
curl: (60) SSL certificate problem: unable to get local
issuer certificate
More details here: https://curl.haxx.se/docs/sslcerts.ht
ml

curl failed to verify the legitimacy of the server and t
herefore could not
establish a secure connection to it. To learn more about
 this situation and
how to fix it, please visit the web page mentioned above
.
```

Figure 4.55: Trying to access the API without TLS

Notice that the command has failed. This happened since Kubernetes forces all communication to use TLS, which usually rejects insecure connections (without any authentication tokens). Let's add the **--insecure** flag, which will allow an insecure connection with curl, and observe the results:

```
curl --insecure https://kubernetes/api/v1/namespaces/$NAMESPACE/pods
```

You should get a response as follows:

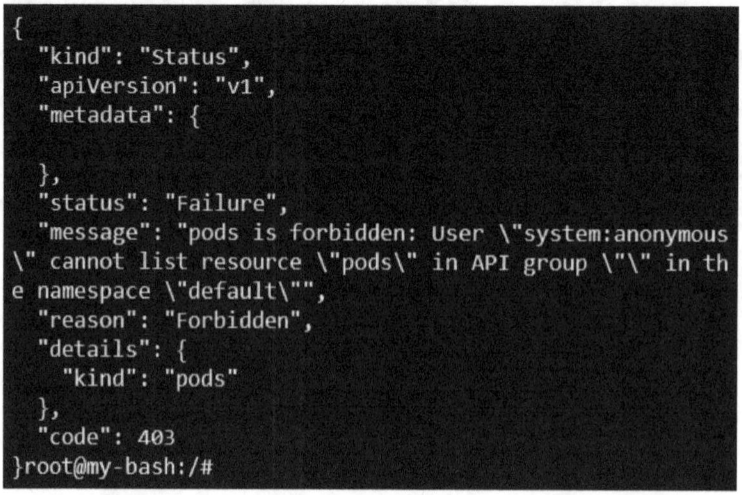

```
{
  "kind": "Status",
  "apiVersion": "v1",
  "metadata": {

  },
  "status": "Failure",
  "message": "pods is forbidden: User \"system:anonymous
\" cannot list resource \"pods\" in API group \"\" in th
e namespace \"default\"",
  "reason": "Forbidden",
  "details": {
    "kind": "pods"
  },
  "code": 403
}root@my-bash:/#
```


Figure 4.56: Anonymous request to the API server

We can see that we were able to reach the server using an insecure connection. However, the API server treated our request as anonymous since there was no identity provided to our command.

Now, to make commands easier, we can add the namespace, CA certificate (**ca.crt**), and the token to variables so that the API server knows the identity of the service account generating the API request:

```
CACERT=/run/secrets/kubernetes.io/serviceaccount/ca.crt

TOKEN=$(cat /run/secrets/kubernetes.io/serviceaccount/token)

NAMESPACE=$(cat /run/secrets/kubernetes.io/serviceaccount/namespace)
```

Note that here we can use the values directly as they are in plaintext (not encoded) when looking from inside a pod, compared to having to decode them from a Secret. Now, we have all the parameters ready. When using bearer token authentication, the client should send this token in the header of the request, which is the authorization header. This should look like this: **Authorization: Bearer <token>**. Since we have added the token into a variable, we can simply use that. Let's run the **curl** command to see whether we can list the pods using the identity of the ServiceAccount:

```
curl --cacert $CACERT -H "Authorization: Bearer $TOKEN" https://
kubernetes/api/v1/namespaces/$NAMESPACE/pods
```

You should get the following response:

```
{
  "kind": "Status",
  "apiVersion": "v1",
  "metadata": {

  },
  "status": "Failure",
  "message": "pods is forbidden: User \"system:serviceaccount:default:default\" cannot
 list resource \"pods\" in API group \"\" in the namespace \"default\"",
  "reason": "Forbidden",
  "details": {
    "kind": "pods"
  },
  "code": 403
```

Figure 4.57: Request to the API server using the default ServiceAccount

Notice that we were able to reach the API server, and the API server verified the **"system:serviceaccount:default:default"** identity, which is represented in this format: **system:<resource_type>:<namespace>:<resource_name>** However, we still got a **Forbidden** error because ServiceAccounts do not have any permissions by default. We need to manually assign permissions to our default ServiceAccount in order to be able to list pods. This can be done by creating a RoleBinding and linking it to the **view** ClusterRole.

Open another terminal window, ensuring that you don't close the terminal session running the **my-bash** pod (because the pod will be deleted and you will lose your progress if you close it). Now, in the second terminal session, you can run the following command to create a **rolebinding defaultSA**-view to attach the **view** ClusterRole to the ServiceAccount:

```
kubectl create rolebinding defaultSA-view \
  --clusterrole=view \
  --serviceaccount=default:default \
  --namespace=default
```

> **NOTE**
>
> The view ClusterRole should already exist for your Kubernetes cluster, as it is one of the default ClusterRoles available for use.

As you might recall from the previous chapter, this is an imperative approach to creating resources; you will learn how to create manifests for RBAC policies in *Chapter 13, Runtime and Network Security in Kubernetes*. Note that we have to specify the ServiceAccount as **<namespace>:<ServiceAccountName>**, and we have a **--namespace** flag since a RoleBinding can only apply to the ServiceAccounts within that namespace. You should get the following response:

```
rolebinding.rbac.authorization.k8s.io/defaultSA-view created
```

Now, go back to the terminal window where we accessed the **my-bash** pod. With the necessary permissions set, let's try our curl command again:

```
curl --cacert $CACERT -H "Authorization: Bearer $TOKEN" https://
kubernetes/api/v1/namespaces/$NAMESPACE/pods
```

You should get the following response:

```
{
  "kind": "PodList",
  "apiVersion": "v1",
  "metadata": {
    "selfLink": "/api/v1/namespaces/default/pods",
    "resourceVersion": "56216"
  },
  "items": [
    {
      "metadata": {
        "name": "curlexample-6fdd4f7cdf-942hz",
        "generateName": "curlexample-6fdd4f7cdf-",
        "namespace": "default",
        "selfLink": "/api/v1/namespaces/default/pods/cur
lexample-6fdd4f7cdf-942hz",
        "uid": "3af8ba5d-c83e-4336-be76-ffef0bcbdcd6",
        "resourceVersion": "55857",
        "creationTimestamp": "2019-11-27T23:04:26Z",
        "labels": {
          "pod-template-hash": "6fdd4f7cdf",
```

Figure 4.58: Successful response from the API server

Our ServiceAccount can now authenticate with the API server, and it is authorized to list pods in the default namespace.

It is also valid to use ServiceAccount bearer tokens outside the cluster. You may want to use tokens instead of certificates as an identity for long-standing jobs since the token does not expire as long as the ServiceAccount exists, whereas a certificate has an expiry date set by the certificate-issuing authority. An example of this is CI/CD pipelines, where external services commonly use ServiceAccount bearer tokens for authentication.

ACTIVITY 4.01: CREATING A DEPLOYMENT USING A SERVICEACCOUNT IDENTITY

In this activity, we will bring together all that we have learned in this chapter. We will be using various operations on our cluster and using different methods to access the API server.

Perform the following operations using kubectl:

1. Create a new namespace called **`activity-example`**.
2. Create a new ServiceAccount called **`activity-sa`**.

3. Create a new RoleBinding called **activity-sa-clusteradmin** to attach the **activity-sa** ServiceAccount to the **cluster-admin** ClusterRole (which exists by default). This step is to ensure that our ServiceAccount has the necessary permissions to interact with the API server as a cluster admin.

Perform the following operations using curl with bearer tokens for authentication:

1. Create a new NGINX Deployment with the identity of the **activity-sa** ServiceAccount.

2. List the pods in your Deployment. Once you use curl to check the Deployment, if you have successfully gone through the previous steps, you should get a response that looks something like this:


```
{
  "kind": "PodList",
  "apiVersion": "v1",
  "metadata": {
    "selfLink": "/api/v1/namespaces/activity-example/pods",
    "resourceVersion": "53388"
  },
  "items": [
    {
      "metadata": {
        "name": "activity-nginx-84d75f9495-pgf64",
        "generateName": "activity-nginx-84d75f9495-",
        "namespace": "activity-example",
        "selfLink": "/api/v1/namespaces/activity-example/pod
s/activity-nginx-84d75f9495-pgf64",
        "uid": "d57dfbb7-a437-4366-8cdc-2dc24adef0d3",
        "resourceVersion": "53001",
        "creationTimestamp": "2019-12-03T21:13:58Z",
        "labels": {
          "pod-template-hash": "84d75f9495",
          "run": "activity-nginx"
        },
        "ownerReferences": [
          {
            "apiVersion": "apps/v1",
            "kind": "ReplicaSet",
```


Figure 4.59: Expected response when checking the Deployment

3. Finally, delete the namespace with all associated resources. When using curl to delete a namespace, you should see a response with **phase** set to **terminating** for the **status** field of the namespace resource, as in the following screenshot:

```
"status": {
  "phase": "Terminating"
```

> **NOTE**
>
> The solution to this activity can be found at the following address: https://packt.live/304PEoD.

SUMMARY

In this chapter, we took a closer look at the Kubernetes API server, the way that Kubernetes uses the RESTful API, and how API resources are defined. We learned that all commands from the kubectl command-line utility are translated into RESTful HTTP API calls and are sent to the API server. We learned that API calls go through multiple stages, including authentication, authorization, and admission control. We also had a closer look at each stage and some of the modules involved.

Then, we learned about some API resources, how they are categorized as namespace-scoped or cluster-scoped resources, and their API group and API version. We then learned how we can use this information to build an API path for interacting with the Kubernetes API.

We also applied what we learned by making an API call directly to the API server, using the curl HTTP client to interact with objects by using different authentication methods, such as ServiceAccounts and an X.509 certificate.

In the next few chapters, we will inspect most of the commonly used API objects more closely, mainly focusing on the different functionalities offered by these objects to enable us to deploy and maintain our application in a Kubernetes cluster. We will begin this series of chapters by taking a look at the basic unit of deployment in Kubernetes (pods) in the next chapter.

5

PODS

OVERVIEW

This chapter introduces the concept of pods and teaches how to properly configure and deploy them. We will begin by creating a simple pod with your application container running in it. We will explain what the different aspects of pod configuration mean and decide which configuration to use based on your application or use case. You will be able to define resource allocation requirements and limits for pods. We will then move on to see how we can debug the pod, check the logs, and make changes to it when needed. Some more useful tools for managing faults in pods, such as liveness and readiness probes and restart policies, are also covered in this chapter.

INTRODUCTION

In the previous chapter, we learned how to use kubectl to interact with the Kubernetes API. In this chapter and the upcoming chapters, we will use that knowledge to interact with the API to create various types of Kubernetes objects.

In a Kubernetes system, many entities represent the state of the cluster and what the cluster's workload looks like. These entities are known as Kubernetes objects. Kubernetes objects describe various things, for example, what containers will be running in the cluster, what resources they will be using, how those containers will interact with each other, and how they will be exposed to the outer world.

A pod is the basic building block of Kubernetes, and it can be described as the basic unit of deployment. Just like we define a process as a program in execution, we can define a pod as a running process in the Kubernetes world. Pods are the smallest unit of replication in Kubernetes. A pod can have any number of containers running in it. A pod is basically a wrapper around containers running on a node. Using pods instead of individual containers has a few benefits. For example, containers in a pod have shared volumes, Linux namespaces, and cgroups. Each pod has a unique IP address and the port space is shared by all the containers in that pod. This means that different containers inside a pod can communicate with each other using their corresponding ports on localhost.

Ideally, we should use multiple containers in a pod only when we want them to be managed and located together in the Kubernetes cluster. For example, we may have a container running our application and another container that fetches logs from the application container and forwards them to some central storage. In this case, we would want both of our containers to stay together, to share the same IP so that they can communicate over localhost, and to share the same storage so that the second container can read the logs our application container is generating.

In this chapter, we will cover what a pod is, how it works, and how to define its pod spec, which describes the state of a pod. We will go through different phases of the life cycle of a pod and learn how to control the pods using health checks or probes. Let's begin by learning how a pod is configured.

POD CONFIGURATION

In order to be able to successfully configure a pod, we must first be able to read and understand a pod configuration file. Here is an example pod configuration file:

```
apiVersion: v1

kind: Pod

metadata:
  name: pod-name

spec:
  containers:
  - name: container1-name
    image: container1-image
  - name: container2-name
    image: container2-image
```

We can break down the configuration of a pod into four main components:

- **apiVersion**: Version of the Kubernetes API we are going to use.
- **kind**: The kind of Kubernetes object we are trying to create, which is a **Pod** in this case.
- **metadata**: Metadata or information that uniquely identifies the object we're creating.
- **spec**: Specification of our pod, such as container name, image name, volumes, and resource requests.

apiVersion, **kind**, and **metadata** apply to all types of Kubernetes objects and are required fields. **spec** is also a required field; however, its layout is different for different types of objects.

The following exercise demonstrates how to use such a pod configuration file to create a simple pod.

EXERCISE 5.01: CREATING A POD WITH A SINGLE CONTAINER

In this exercise, we aim to create our first simple pod that runs a single container. To complete this exercise, perform the following steps:

1. Create a file called **single-container-pod.yaml** with the following contents:

```
apiVersion: v1
kind: Pod
metadata:
  name: first-pod
spec:
  containers:
  - name: my-first-container
    image: nginx
```

2. Run the following command in Terminal to create a pod with the preceding configuration:

```
kubectl create -f single-container-pod.yaml
```

You should see the following response:

```
pod/first-pod created
```

The output indicates that the pod has been created.

3. Verify that the pod was created by getting the list of all the pods using this command:

```
kubectl get pods
```

You should see the following response:

```
NAME        READY     STATUS     RESTARTS     AGE
first-pod   1/1       Running    0            5m44s
```

4. Now that we have created our first pod, let's look into it in more detail. To do that, we can describe the pod we just created using the following command in Terminal:

```
kubectl describe pod first-pod
```

You should see the following output:

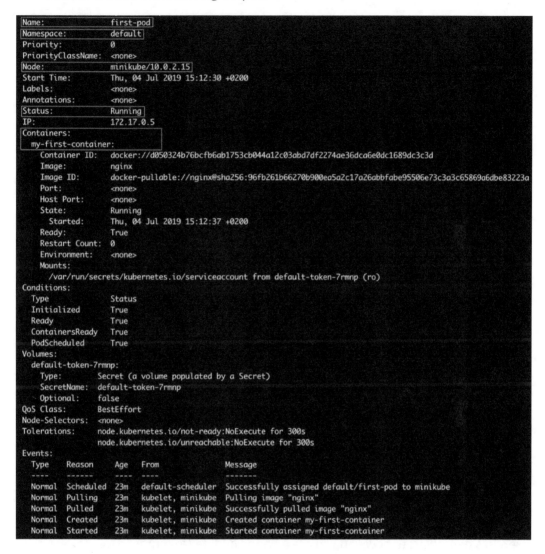

```
Name:               first-pod
Namespace:          default
Priority:           0
PriorityClassName:  <none>
Node:               minikube/10.0.2.15
Start Time:         Thu, 04 Jul 2019 15:12:30 +0200
Labels:             <none>
Annotations:        <none>
Status:             Running
IP:                 172.17.0.5
Containers:
  my-first-container:
    Container ID:   docker://d050324b76bcfb6ab1753cb044a12c03abd7df2274ae36dca6e0dc1689dc3c3d
    Image:          nginx
    Image ID:       docker-pullable://nginx@sha256:96fb261b66270b900ea5a2c17a26abbfabe95506e73c3a3c65869a6dbe83223a
    Port:           <none>
    Host Port:      <none>
    State:          Running
      Started:      Thu, 04 Jul 2019 15:12:37 +0200
    Ready:          True
    Restart Count:  0
    Environment:    <none>
    Mounts:
      /var/run/secrets/kubernetes.io/serviceaccount from default-token-7rmnp (ro)
Conditions:
  Type              Status
  Initialized       True
  Ready             True
  ContainersReady   True
  PodScheduled      True
Volumes:
  default-token-7rmnp:
    Type:        Secret (a volume populated by a Secret)
    SecretName:  default-token-7rmnp
    Optional:    false
QoS Class:       BestEffort
Node-Selectors:  <none>
Tolerations:     node.kubernetes.io/not-ready:NoExecute for 300s
                 node.kubernetes.io/unreachable:NoExecute for 300s
Events:
  Type    Reason     Age   From               Message
  ----    ------     ----  ----               -------
  Normal  Scheduled  23m   default-scheduler  Successfully assigned default/first-pod to minikube
  Normal  Pulling    23m   kubelet, minikube  Pulling image "nginx"
  Normal  Pulled     23m   kubelet, minikube  Successfully pulled image "nginx"
  Normal  Created    23m   kubelet, minikube  Created container my-first-container
  Normal  Started    23m   kubelet, minikube  Started container my-first-container
```

Figure 5.1: Describing first-pod

The output shows various details about the pod we just created. In the following sections, we shall go through the highlighted sections of the preceding output to find out more about the pod that's running.

NAME

This field states the name of the pod, and it is also sometimes referred to as the pod ID. Pod names are unique in a particular namespace. A pod name can be a maximum of 253 characters long. The characters allowed in a pod name are numerals (0-9), lowercase letters (a-z), hyphens (-), and dots (.).

Consider the second line in the output shown in *Figure 5.1*:

```
Name: first-pod
```

It is the same as the one we mentioned in our YAML configuration.

NAMESPACE

Kubernetes supports namespaces to create multiple virtual clusters within the same physical cluster. We may need to use namespaces if we want to provide separate environments to our different teams working on the same cluster. Namespaces also help in scoping the object names. For example, you cannot have two pods with the same name within the same namespace. However, it's possible to have two pods with the same name in two different namespaces. Now, consider the second line in the output shown in *Figure 5.1*:

```
Namespace: default
```

We can either temporarily change the namespace of the request by passing the **--namespace** argument for a particular kubectl command, or we can update the kubectl config to change the namespace for all subsequent kubectl commands. To create a new namespace, we can use the following command:

```
kubectl create namespaces <namespace-name>
```

There are two ways to create pods in different namespaces – by using a CLI command, or by specifying the namespace in the pod configuration. The following exercises demonstrate how you can create pods in different namespaces to reap the benefits of namespaces that were mentioned earlier.

EXERCISE 5.02: CREATING A POD IN A DIFFERENT NAMESPACE BY SPECIFYING THE NAMESPACE IN THE CLI

In this exercise, we will create a pod in a namespace other than **default**. We will do that using the same pod configuration from *Exercise 5.01, Creating a Pod with a Single Container*, by specifying the namespace in the command argument. Follow these steps to complete the exercise:

1. Run the following command to view all the available namespaces in our Kubernetes cluster:

   ```
   kubectl get namespaces
   ```

   You should see the following list of namespaces:

   ```
   NAME              STATUS    AGE
   default           Active    16d
   kube-node-lease   Active    16d
   kube-public       Active    16d
   kube-system       Active    16d
   ```

   The output shows all the namespaces in our Kubernetes cluster. The **default** namespace is, as the word implies, the default namespace for all Kubernetes objects created without any namespace.

2. Run the following command to create the pod with the **single-container-pod.yaml** pod configuration but in a different namespace:

   ```
   kubectl --namespace kube-public create -f single-container-pod.yaml
   ```

   You should see the following response:

   ```
   pod/first-pod created
   ```

   > **NOTE**
   >
   > If you create a pod in a particular namespace, you can only view it by switching to that namespace.

3. Verify that the pod was created in the **kube-public** namespace:

```
kubectl --namespace kube-public get pods
```

You should see the following response:

```
NAME          READY     STATUS     RESTARTS    AGE
first-pod     1/1       Running    0           8s
```

The output here shows that we have successfully created the pod in the **kube-public** namespace.

The next exercise demonstrates how to create a pod in different namespace based on a YAML file.

EXERCISE 5.03: CREATING A POD IN A DIFFERENT NAMESPACE BY SPECIFYING THE NAMESPACE IN THE POD CONFIGURATION YAML FILE

In this exercise, we shall add a line to the YAML configuration file to specify that all pods created using this file use a specified namespace.

1. Run the following command to view all the available namespaces in our Kubernetes cluster:

```
kubectl get namespaces
```

You should see the following list of namespaces:

```
NAME              STATUS    AGE
default           Active    16d
kube-node-lease   Active    16d
kube-public       Active    16d
kube-system       Active    16d
```

2. Next, create a file named **single-container-pod-with-namespace.yaml** with the following configuration:

```
apiVersion: v1
kind: Pod
metadata:
  name: first-pod-with-namespace
  namespace: kube-public
spec:
```

```
  containers:
  - name: my-first-container
    image: nginx
```

3. Run the following command to create a pod with the **single-container-pod-with-namespace.yaml** pod configuration:

```
kubectl create -f single-container-pod-with-namespace.yaml
```

You should see the following response:

```
pod/first-pod-with-namespace created
```

4. Verify that the pod was created in the **kube-public** namespace:

```
kubectl --namespace kube-public get pods
```

You should see the following list of pods:

```
NAME                         READY    STATUS      RESTARTS    AGE
first-pod                    1/1      Running     0           5m2s
first-pod-with-namespace     1/1      Running     0           46s
```

The output shows that the new pod we created occupies the **kube-public** namespace. Any other pods created using the **single-container-pod-with-namespace.yaml** pod configuration will occupy the same namespace.

In the following exercise, we shall change the default kubectl namespace so that all pods without a defined namespace take our newly defined namespace instead of **default**.

EXERCISE 5.04: CHANGING THE NAMESPACE FOR ALL SUBSEQUENT KUBECTL COMMANDS

In this exercise, we will change the namespace for all subsequent kubectl commands from **default** to **kube-public**.

1. Run the following command to view all the available namespaces in our Kubernetes cluster:

```
kubectl get namespaces
```

You should see the following list of namespaces:

```
NAME               STATUS      AGE
default            Active      16d
kube-node-lease    Active      16d
kube-public        Active      16d
kube-system        Active      16d
```

2. Run the following command to change the namespace for all subsequent requests by modifying the current context:

```
kubectl config set-context $(kubectl config current-context)
--namespace kube-public
```

   You should see the following response:

```
Context "minikube" modified.
```

3. Run the following command to list all the pods in the **kube-public** namespace without using the **namespace** argument:

```
kubectl get pods
```

   You should see the following list of pods:

```
NAME                        READY     STATUS      RESTARTS    AGE
first-pod                   1/1       Running     0           48m
first-pod-with-namespace    1/1       Running     0           44m
```

   The output shows that the preceding command lists all the pods that we have created in the **kube-public** namespace. We saw in *Exercise 5.01*, *Creating a Pod with a Single Container*, that the **kubectl get pods** command shows pods in the default namespace. But here, we get results from the **kube-public** namespace instead.

4. In this step, we will undo the changes so that it doesn't affect the upcoming exercises in this chapter. We will change the default namespace to **default** again to avoid any confusion:

```
kubectl config set-context $(kubectl config current-context)
--namespace default
```

   You should see the following response:

```
Context "minikube" modified.
```

In this exercise, we have seen how to change and reset the default namespace of the context.

NODE

As you have learned in earlier chapters, nodes are the various machines running in our cluster. This field reflects the node in the Kubernetes cluster where this pod was running. Knowing what node a pod is running on can help us with debugging issues with that pod. Observe the sixth line of the output shown in *Figure 5.1*:

```
Node: minikube/10.0.2.15
```

We can list all the nodes in our Kubernetes cluster by running the following command:

```
kubectl get nodes
```

You should see the following response:

```
NAME        STATUS    ROLES     AGE       VERSION
minikube    Ready     <none>    16d       v1.14.3
```

In this case, there's only one node in our cluster because we are using Minikube for these exercises:

```
apiVersion: v1
kind: Pod
metadata:
  name: firstpod
spec:
  nodeName: my-favorite-node # run this pod on a specific node
  containers:
  - name: my-first-pod
    image: nginx
```

If we have more than one node in our cluster, we can configure our pod to run on a particular node by adding the following **nodeName** field to the configuration, as seen in the sixth line in the previous spec.

> **NOTE**
>
> In a production environment, **nodeName** is typically not used for assigning a certain pod to run on the desired node. In the next chapter, we will learn about **nodeSelector**, which is a better way to control which node the pod gets assigned to.

STATUS

This field tells us the status of the pod so that we can take appropriate action, such as starting or stopping a pod as required. While this demonstration shows one of the ways to get the status of the pod, in actual practice, you would want to automate actions based on the pod status. Consider the tenth line of the output shown in *Figure 5.1*:

```
Status: Running
```

This states that the current status of the pod is **Running**. This field reflects which phase of its life cycle a pod is in. We will talk about various phases of a pod's life cycle in the next section of this chapter.

CONTAINERS

Earlier in this chapter, we saw that we can bundle various containers inside a pod. This field lists all the containers that we have created in this pod. Consider the output field from line 12 onwards in *Figure 5.1*:

Containers:
my-first-container:
Container ID: docker://d050324b76bcfb6ab1753cb044a12c03abd7df2274ae36dca6e0dc1689dc3c3d
Image: nginx
Image ID: docker-pullable://nginx@sha256:96fb261b66270b900ea5a2c17a26abbfabe95506e73c3a3c65869a6dbe83223a
Port: <none>
Host Port: <none>
State: Running
Started: Thu, 04 Jul 2019 15:12:37 +0200
Ready: True
Restart Count: 0
Environment: <none>
Mounts:
/var/run/secrets/kubernetes.io/serviceaccount from default-token-7rmnp (ro)

Figure 5.2: Containers field from the describe command

We have only one in this case. We can see that the name and the image of the container are the same as we specified in the YAML configuration. The following is a list of the other fields that we can set:

- **`Image`**: Name of the Docker image
- **`Args`**: The arguments to the entry point for the container
- **`Command`**: The command to run on the container once it starts
- **`Ports`**: A list of ports to expose from the container

- **`Env`**: A list of environment variables to be set in the container
- **`resources`**: The resource requirements of the container

In the following exercise, we shall create a container using a simple command.

EXERCISE 5.05: USING CLI COMMANDS TO CREATE A POD RUNNING A CONTAINER

In this exercise, we will create a pod that will run a container by running a command.

1. First, let's create a file named **`pod-with-container-command.yaml`** with the following pod configuration:

   ```
   apiVersion: v1
   kind: Pod
   metadata:
     name: command-pod
   spec:
     containers:
     - name: container-with-command
       image: ubuntu
       command:
       - /bin/bash
       - -ec
       - while :; do echo '.'; sleep 5; done
   ```

2. Run the following command to create the pod using the configuration defined in the **`pod-with-container-command.yaml`** file:

   ```
   kubectl create -f pod-with-container-command.yaml
   ```

   You should see the following response:

   ```
   pod/command-pod created
   ```

   The YAML file we created in the previous step instructs the pod to start a container with an Ubuntu image and run the following command:

   ```
   /bin/bash -ec "while :; do echo '.'; sleep 5; done"
   ```

   This command should print a dot (**`.`**) character on a new line every 5 seconds.

3. Let's check the logs of this pod to verify that it's doing what it's expected to do. To check the logs of a pod, we can use the **`kubectl logs`** command:

   ```
   kubectl logs command-pod -f
   ```

You should see the following response:

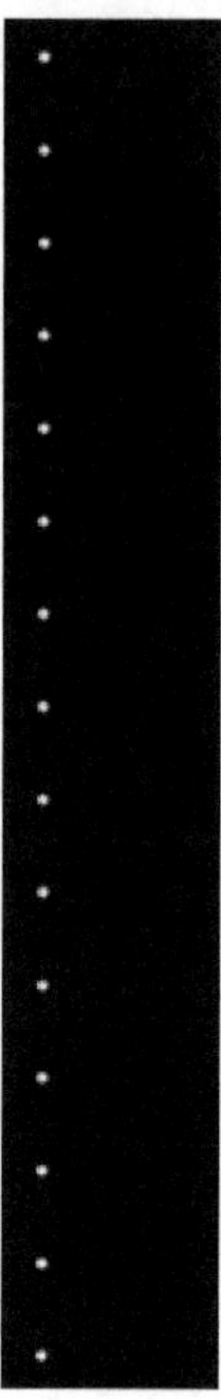

Figure 5.3: Following logs for command-pod

In the log, which keeps updating periodically, we see a dot (`.`) character printed on a new line every 5 seconds. Thus, we have successfully created the desired container.

> **NOTE**
>
> The `-f` flag is to follow the logs on the container. That is, the log keeps updating in real-time. If we skip that flag, we will see the logs without following them.

In the next exercise, we shall run a container that opens up a port, which is something that you would have to do regularly to make the container accessible to the rest of your cluster or the internet.

EXERCISE 5.06: CREATING A POD RUNNING A CONTAINER THAT EXPOSES A PORT

In this exercise, we will create a pod that runs a container that will expose a port that we can access from outside the pod.

1. First, let's create a file named **pod-with-exposed-port.yaml** with the following pod configuration:

```
apiVersion: v1
kind: Pod
metadata:
  name: port-exposed-pod
spec:
  containers:
    - name: container-with-exposed-port
      image: nginx
      ports:
        - containerPort: 80
```

2. Run the following command to create the pod using the **pod-with-exposed-port.yaml** file:

```
kubectl create -f pod-with-exposed-port.yaml
```

   You should see the following response:

```
pod/port-exposed-pod created
```

   This pod should create a container and expose its port **80**. We have configured the pod to run a container with an **nginx** image, which is a popular web server.

3. Next, we will forward port **80** from the pod to localhost:

```
sudo kubectl port-forward pod/port-exposed-pod 80
```

   You should see the following response:

```
Forwarding from 127.0.0.1:80 -> 80
Forwarding from [::1] -> 80
```

This will expose port **80** from the pod to localhost port **80**.

> **NOTE**
>
> We will need to keep this command running in one terminal.

4. Now, we can simply enter either `http://localhost` or `http://127.0.0.1` in the address bar of the browser.

5. Alternatively, we can run the following command and see the HTML source code of the default index page in the response:

```
curl 127.0.0.1
```

You should see the following output:

```
<!DOCTYPE html>
<html>
<head>
<title>Welcome to nginx!</title>
<style>
    body {
        width: 35em;
        margin: 0 auto;
        font-family: Tahoma, Verdana, Arial, sans-serif;
    }
</style>
</head>
<body>
<h1>Welcome to nginx!</h1>
<p>If you see this page, the nginx web server is successfully installed and
working. Further configuration is required.</p>

<p>For online documentation and support please refer to
<a href="http://nginx.org/">nginx.org</a>.<br/>
Commercial support is available at
<a href="http://nginx.com/">nginx.com</a>.</p>

<p><em>Thank you for using nginx.</em></p>
</body>
</html>
```

Figure 5.4: Getting the HTML source using curl

6. Next, let's verify that the pod is actually receiving the request by checking the logs using the **kubectl logs** command:

```
kubectl logs port-exposed-pod
```

You should see the following response:

```
127.0.0.1 - - [04/Jul/2019:15:37:48 +0000] "GET / HTTP/1.1" 200 612 "-" "Mozilla/5.0 (Macintosh; Inte
l Mac OS X 10_14_4) AppleWebKit/537.36 (KHTML, like Gecko) Chrome/75.0.3770.100 Safari/537.36" "-"
```

Figure 5.5: Checking the logs for the nginx pod

The log shows that our container that is running an **nginx** image is receiving our HTTP request to localhost and responding as expected.

We can also define the minimum and maximum resource allocation for our containers. This is useful for managing the resources used by our deployments. This can be achieved using the following two fields in the YAML configuration file:

- **limits**: Describes the maximum amount of resources allowed for this container.
- **requests**: Describes the minimum amount of resources required for this container.

We can use these fields to define the minimum and maximum memory and CPU resources for our containers. The CPU resource is measured in CPU units. 1 CPU unit means that the container has access to 1 logical CPU core.

In the next exercise, we shall create a container with defined resource requirements.

EXERCISE 5.07: CREATING A POD RUNNING A CONTAINER WITH RESOURCE REQUIREMENTS

In this exercise, we will create a pod with a container that has resource requirements. First of all, let's see how we can configure the container's resource requirements:

1. Create a file named **pod-with-resource-requirements.yaml** with a pod configuration that specifies both **limits** and **requests** for memory and CPU resources, as shown here:

```
apiVersion: v1
kind: Pod
metadata:
  name: resource-requirements-pod
spec:
  containers:
    - name: container-with-resource-requirements
      image: nginx
      resources:
        limits:
          memory: "128M"
          cpu: "1"
        requests:
          memory: "64M"
          cpu: "0.5"
```

   In this YAML file, we define the minimum memory requirement for the container to be 64 MB and the maximum memory that the container can occupy to be 128 MB. If the container tries to allocate more than 128 MB of memory, it will be killed with a status of **OOMKilled**.

   The minimum CPU requirement for CPU is 0.5 (which can also be understood as 500 milli-CPUs and can be written as **500m** instead of **0.5**) and the container will only be allowed to use a maximum of 1 CPU unit.

2. Next, we will create the pod that uses this YAML configuration with the **kubectl create** command:

```
kubectl create -f pod-with-resource-requirements.yaml
```

   You should see the following response:

```
pod/resource-requirements-pod created
```

3. Next, let's make sure the pod is created with the correct resource requirements. Check the pod definitions using the **describe** command:

```
kubectl describe pod resource-requirements-pod
```

You should see the following output:

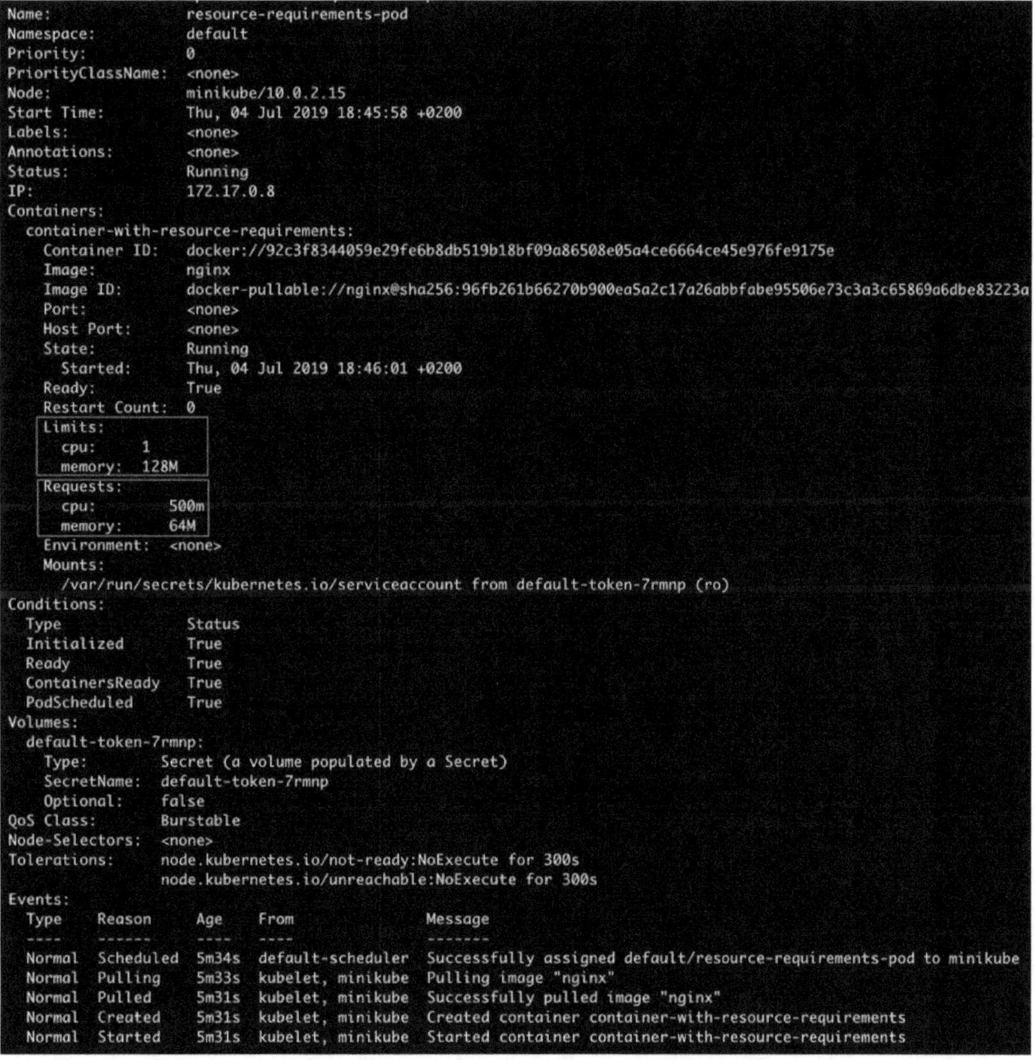

Figure 5.6: Describing resource-requirements-pod

The highlighted fields in the output show that the pod has been assigned the **limits** and **requests** sections that we stated in the YAML file.

What happens if we define unrealistic resource requirements for our pod? Let's explore that in the following exercise.

EXERCISE 5.08: CREATING A POD WITH RESOURCE REQUESTS THAT CAN'T BE MET BY ANY OF THE NODES

In this exercise, we will create a pod with large resource requests that are too big for the nodes in the cluster and see what happens.

1. Create a file named **pod-with-huge-resource-requirements.yaml** with the following pod configuration:

```
apiVersion: v1
kind: Pod
metadata:
  name: huge-resource-requirements-pod
spec:
  containers:
    - name: container-with-huge-resource-requirements
      image: nginx
      resources:
        limits:
          memory: "128G"
          cpu: "1000"
        requests:
          memory: "64G"
          cpu: "500"
```

   In this YAML file, we define the minimum requirement to be 64 GB of memory and 500 CPU cores. It is unlikely that the machine that you are running this exercise on would meet those requirements.

2. Next, we will create the pod that uses this YAML configuration with the **kubectl create** command:

```
kubectl create -f pod-with-huge-resource-requirements.yaml
```

You should see the following response:

```
pod/huge-resource-requirements-pod created
```

3. Now, let's see what's going on with our pod. Get its status using the **kubectl get** command:

```
kubectl get pod huge-resource-requirements-pod
```

You should see the following response:

```
NAME                             READY   STATUS    RESTARTS   AGE
huge-resource-requirements-pod   0/1     Pending   0          55s
```

Figure 5.7: Getting the status of huge-resource-requirements-pod

We see that the pod has been in the **Pending** state for almost a minute. That's unusual!

4. Let's dig deeper and describe the pod using the following command:

```
kubectl describe pod huge-resource-requirements-pod
```

You should see the following output:

```
Name:               huge-resource-requirements-pod
Namespace:          default
Priority:           0
PriorityClassName:  <none>
Node:               <none>
Labels:             <none>
Annotations:        <none>
Status:             Pending
IP:
Containers:
  container-with-huge-resource-requirements:
    Image:      nginx
    Port:       <none>
    Host Port:  <none>
    Limits:
      cpu:     1k
      memory:  128G
    Requests:
      cpu:        500
      memory:     64G
    Environment:  <none>
    Mounts:
      /var/run/secrets/kubernetes.io/serviceaccount from default-token-7rmnp (ro)
Conditions:
  Type           Status
  PodScheduled   False
Volumes:
  default-token-7rmnp:
    Type:        Secret (a volume populated by a Secret)
    SecretName:  default-token-7rmnp
    Optional:    false
QoS Class:       Burstable
Node-Selectors:  <none>
Tolerations:     node.kubernetes.io/not-ready:NoExecute for 300s
                 node.kubernetes.io/unreachable:NoExecute for 300s
Events:
  Type     Reason            Age                 From               Message
  ----     ------            ----                ----               -------
  Warning  FailedScheduling  67s (x4 over 2m18s)  default-scheduler  0/1 nodes are available:
1 Insufficient cpu, 1 Insufficient memory.
```

Figure 5.8: Describing huge-resource-requirements-pod

Let's focus on the last line of the output. We can clearly see that there's a warning stating that the Kubernetes controller couldn't find any nodes that satisfy the CPU and memory requirements of the pod. Hence, the pod scheduling has failed.

To summarize, pod scheduling works on the basis of resource requirements. A pod will only be scheduled on a node that satisfies all its resource requirements. If we do not specify a resource (memory or CPU) limit, there's no upper bound on the number of resources a pod can use.

This poses the risk of one bad pod consuming too much CPU or allocating too much memory that impacts the other pods running in the same namespace/cluster. Hence, it's a good idea to add resource requests and limits to the pod configuration in a production environment.

As mentioned earlier in the chapter, a pod can run more than one container. In the following exercise, we will create a pod with more than one container.

EXERCISE 5.09: CREATING A POD WITH MULTIPLE CONTAINERS RUNNING INSIDE IT

In this exercise, we will create a pod with multiple containers. For that, we can use the configuration that we used in the previous section, with the only difference being that the **containers** field will now contain more than one container spec. Follow these steps to complete the exercise:

1. Create a file named **multiple-container-pod.yaml** with the following pod configuration:

```
apiVersion: v1
kind: Pod
metadata:
  name: multi-container-pod
spec:
  containers:
    - name: first-container
      image: nginx
    - name: second-container
      image: ubuntu
      command:
        - /bin/bash
        - -ec
        - while :; do echo '.'; sleep 5; done
```

2. Next, we will create a pod that uses the preceding YAML configuration with the **kubectl create** command:

```
kubectl create -f multiple-container-pod.yaml
```

   You should see the following response:

```
pod/multi-container-pod created
```

3. Next, we will describe the pod and see what containers it is running:

```
kubectl describe pod multi-container-pod
```

You should see the following output:

```
Name:               multi-container-pod
Namespace:          default
Priority:           0
PriorityClassName:  <none>
Node:               minikube/10.0.2.15
Start Time:         Thu, 04 Jul 2019 18:58:17 +0200
Labels:             <none>
Annotations:        <none>
Status:             Running
IP:                 172.17.0.9
Containers:
  first-container:
    Container ID:   docker://79cf12f74a2d46a270adbcf453582706baf68d1b8d17a2e154c4201cce45c327
    Image:          nginx
    Image ID:       docker-pullable://nginx@sha256:96fb261b66270b900ea5a2c17a26abbfabe95506e73c3a3c65869a6dbe83223a
    Port:           <none>
    Host Port:      <none>
    State:          Running
      Started:      Thu, 04 Jul 2019 18:58:21 +0200
    Ready:          True
    Restart Count:  0
    Environment:    <none>
    Mounts:
      /var/run/secrets/kubernetes.io/serviceaccount from default-token-7rmnp (ro)
  second-container:
    Container ID:  docker://4ffa27ee3bb68ced739e05556267bcf3ab684dc04cdea736a2413406b72f76a5
    Image:         ubuntu
    Image ID:      docker-pullable://ubuntu@sha256:9b1702dcfe32c873a770a32cfd306dd7fc1c4fd134adfb783db68defc8894b3c
    Port:          <none>
    Host Port:     <none>
    Command:
      /bin/bash
      -ec
      while :; do echo '.'; sleep 5; done
    State:          Running
      Started:      Thu, 04 Jul 2019 18:58:23 +0200
    Ready:          True
    Restart Count:  0
    Environment:    <none>
    Mounts:
      /var/run/secrets/kubernetes.io/serviceaccount from default-token-7rmnp (ro)
Conditions:
  Type              Status
  Initialized       True
  Ready             True
  ContainersReady   True
  PodScheduled      True
Volumes:
  default-token-7rmnp:
    Type:        Secret (a volume populated by a Secret)
    SecretName:  default-token-7rmnp
    Optional:    false
QoS Class:       BestEffort
Node-Selectors:  <none>
Tolerations:     node.kubernetes.io/not-ready:NoExecute for 300s
                 node.kubernetes.io/unreachable:NoExecute for 300s
```

Figure 5.9: Describing multi-container-pod

As can be seen from the preceding output, we have two containers running in a single pod. Now, we need to make sure we can access the logs from either container.

We can specify the container name to get the logs for a particular container running in a pod, as shown here:

```
kubectl logs <pod-name> <container-name>
```

For example, to see the logs for a second container that is printing out dots on a new line every 5 seconds, use this command:

```
kubectl logs multi-container-pod second-container -f
```

You should see the following response:

Figure 5.10: The logs for second-container inside multi-container-pod

The output we see here is similar to *Exercise 5.05, Using CLI Commands to Create a Pod Running a Container*, as we have essentially used a similar container as we defined there.

Thus, we have created a pod with multiple containers and accessed the logs of the desired container.

LIFE CYCLE OF A POD

Now that we know how to run a pod and how to configure it for our use cases, in this section, we will talk about the life cycle of a pod to understand how it works in more detail.

PHASES OF A POD

Every pod has a pod status that tells us what stage of its life cycle a pod is in. We can see the pod status by running the **kubectl get** command:

```
kubectl get pod
```

You will see the following response:

```
NAME          READY        STATUS         RESTARTS        AGE
first-pod     1/1          Running        0               5m44s
```

For our first pod, named **first-pod**, we see that the pod is in the **Running** state.

Let's see what the different states that a pod can have in its life cycle are:

- **Pending**: This means that the pod has been submitted to the cluster, but the controller hasn't created all its containers yet. It may be downloading images or waiting for the pod to be scheduled on one of the cluster nodes.
- **Running**: This state means that the pod has been assigned to one of the cluster nodes and at least one of the containers is either running or is in the process of starting up.
- **Succeeded**: This state means that the pod has run, and all of its containers have been terminated with success.
- **Failed**: This state means the pod has run and at least one of the containers has terminated with a non-zero exit code, that is, it has failed to execute its commands.
- **Unknown**: This means that the state of the pod could not be found. This may be because of the inability of the controller to connect with the node that the pod was assigned to.

> **NOTE**
>
> The **get pod** command cannot get evicted or deleted pods. To do that, you can use the **--show-all** flag, but it has been deprecated since Kubernetes v1.15.

PROBES/HEALTH CHECKS

A probe is a health check that can be configured to check the health of the containers running in a pod. A probe can be used to determine whether a container is running or ready to receive requests. A probe may return the following results:

- **Success**: The container passed the health check.
- **Failure**: The container failed the health check.
- **Unknown**: The health check failed for unknown reasons.

TYPES OF PROBES

The following types of probes are available for us to use.

LIVENESS PROBE

This is a health check that's used to determine whether a particular container is running or not. If a container fails the liveness probe, the controller will try to restart the pod on the same node according to the restart policy configured for the pod.

It's a good idea to specify a liveness probe when we want the container to be terminated and restarted when a particular check fails.

READINESS PROBE

This is a health check that's used to determine whether a particular container is ready to receive requests or not. How we define the readiness of a container depends largely on the application running inside the container.

For example, for a container serving a web application, readiness may mean that the container has loaded all static assets, established a connection with the database, started the webserver, and opened a specific port on the host to start serving requests. On the other hand, for a container serving some data, the readiness probe should succeed only when it has loaded all the data from disk and is ready to start serving the requests for that data.

If a container fails its readiness probe, the Kubernetes controller will ensure that the pod doesn't receive any requests. If a container specifies a readiness probe, its default state will be **Failure** until the readiness probe succeeds. The container will start receiving requests only after the readiness probe returns with the **Success** state. If no readiness probe is configured, the container will start receiving requests as soon as it starts.

CONFIGURATION OF PROBES

There are a bunch of generic fields we can use to configure the probes:

Field Name	Default	Minimum	Description
`initialDelaySeconds`	-	-	Number of seconds that the controller will wait before launching the probes.
`timeoutSeconds`	1	1	Number of seconds after which a probe (health check) will time out.
`periodSeconds`	10	1	Number of seconds after which the probe will be repeated periodically.
`successThreshold`	1	1	Minimum consecutive number of times a probe should succeed before it is considered successful.
`failureThreshold`	3	1	Maximum consecutive number of times a probe will be allowed to fail before the probe is considered to have failed. Once a pod fails a probe `failureThreshold` number of times, the controller will give up on it and take action depending on whether it is a liveness or readiness probe.

Figure 5.11: Table showing configuration fields for probes

IMPLEMENTATION OF PROBES

Probes (liveness or readiness) can be implemented by passing a command to the container, getting it to fetch some resources, or trying to connect to it, as we shall see in this section. We can use different implementations for liveness and readiness probes within the same container.

COMMAND PROBE

In the command implementation of a probe, the controller will get the container to execute the specified command in order to perform the probe on the container. For this implementation, we use the **`command`** field. This field specifies the command to execute in order to perform the probe on the container. It can either be a string or an array.

The following example shows how liveness and readiness probe configuration can be used in the container spec:

```
livenessProbe:
  exec:
    command:
    - cat
    - /tmp/health
  initialDelaySeconds:
  periodSeconds: 15
  failureThreshold: 3

readinessProbe:
  exec:
    command:
    - cat
    - /tmp/health
  initialDelaySeconds:
  periodSeconds: 15
```

HTTP REQUEST PROBE

In this type of probe, the controller will send a GET HTTP request to the given address (host and port) to perform the probe on the container. It's possible to set the custom HTTP headers to be sent in the probe request.

We can set the following fields to configure an HTTP request probe:

- **host**: Hostname to which the request will be made. It defaults to the pod IP address.
- **path**: Path to make the request to.
- **port**: Name or number of the port to make the request to.
- **httpHeaders**: Custom headers to be set in the request.
- **scheme**: Scheme to use while making the request. The default value is HTTP.

Here's an example of an HTTP request probe for liveness and readiness:

```
livenessProbe:
  httpGet:
    path: /health-check
    port: 8080
  initialDelaySeconds: 10
  periodSeconds: 20

readinessProbe:
  httpGet:
    path: /health-check
    port: 8080
  initialDelaySeconds: 5
  periodSeconds: 10
```

TCP SOCKET PROBE

In this implementation of a probe, the controller will try to establish a connection on the given host and the specified port number. We can use the following two fields for this probe:

- **`host`**: Hostname to which the connection will be established. It defaults to the pod IP address.
- **`port`**: Name or number of the port to connect to.

Here's an example of a TCP socket probe:

```
livenessProbe:
  tcpSocket:
    port: 8080
  initialDelaySeconds: 10
  periodSeconds: 20

readinessProbe:
  tcpSocket:
    port:8080
  initialDelaySeconds: 5
  periodSeconds: 10
```

RESTART POLICY

We can specify **restartPolicy** in the pod specification to instruct the controller about the conditions required to restart the pod. The default value of **restartPolicy** is **Always**. It can take the following values:

- **Always**: Always restart the pod when it terminates.
- **OnFailure**: Restart the pod only when it terminates with failure.
- **Never**: Never restart the pod after it terminates.

If we want the pod to crash and restart when it has some issues or becomes unhealthy, we should set the restart policy to either **Always** or **OnFailure**.

In the following exercise, we shall create a liveness probe with the command implementation.

EXERCISE 5.10: CREATING A POD RUNNING A CONTAINER WITH A LIVENESS PROBE AND NO RESTART POLICY

In this exercise, we will create a pod with a liveness probe and no restart policy. Not specifying a restart policy for a pod means that the default policy of **Always** will be used.

1. Create **liveness-probe.yaml** with the following pod configuration:

```
apiVersion: v1
kind: Pod
metadata:
  name: liveness-probe
spec:
  containers:
    - name: ubuntu-container
      image: ubuntu
      command:
        - /bin/bash
        - -ec
        - touch /tmp/live; sleep 30; rm /tmp/live; sleep 600
      livenessProbe:
        exec:
```

```
        command:
          - cat
          - /tmp/live
      initialDelaySeconds: 5
      periodSeconds: 5
```

This pod configuration means that there will be a container created from an Ubuntu image and the following command will be run once it starts:

```
/bin/bash -ec "touch /tmp/live; sleep 30; rm /tmp/live; sleep 600"
```

The preceding command creates an empty file at path **/tmp/live**, sleeps for 30 seconds, deletes the **/tmp/live** file, and then sleeps for 10 minutes before terminating with success.

Next, we have a liveness probe that executes the following command every 5 seconds with an initial delay of 5 seconds:

```
cat /tmp/live
```

2. Run the following command to create the pod using **liveness-probe.yaml**:

```
kubectl create -f liveness-probe.yaml
```

3. When the container starts, the liveness probe will succeed because the command will execute successfully. Now, let's wait for at least 30 seconds and run the **describe** command:

```
kubectl describe pod liveness-probe
```

You should see the following output:

```
Name:                liveness-probe
Namespace:           default
Priority:            0
PriorityClassName:   <none>
Node:                minikube/10.0.2.15
Start Time:          Thu, 04 Jul 2019 19:18:02 +0200
Labels:              <none>
Annotations:         <none>
Status:              Running
IP:                  172.17.0.8
Containers:
  ubuntu-container:
    Container ID:  docker://48c9d901474a25835f00fb5a9e2e2ed38823f12ba24691b7b3383b0d392f016a
    Image:         ubuntu
    Image ID:      docker-pullable://ubuntu@sha256:9b1702dcfe32c873a770a32cfd306dd7fc1c4fd134adfb783db68defc8894b3c
    Port:          <none>
    Host Port:     <none>
    Command:
      /bin/bash
      -ec
      touch /tmp/ready; sleep 30; rm /tmp/ready; sleep 600
    State:          Running
      Started:      Thu, 04 Jul 2019 19:18:05 +0200
    Ready:          True
    Restart Count:  0
    Liveness:       exec [cat /tmp/ready] delay=5s timeout=1s period=5s #success=1 #failure=3
    Environment:    <none>
    Mounts:
      /var/run/secrets/kubernetes.io/serviceaccount from default-token-7rmnp (ro)
Conditions:
  Type              Status
  Initialized       True
  Ready             True
  ContainersReady   True
  PodScheduled      True
Volumes:
  default-token-7rmnp:
    Type:        Secret (a volume populated by a Secret)
    SecretName:  default-token-7rmnp
    Optional:    false
QoS Class:       BestEffort
Node-Selectors:  <none>
Tolerations:     node.kubernetes.io/not-ready:NoExecute for 300s
                 node.kubernetes.io/unreachable:NoExecute for 300s
Events:
  Type     Reason     Age  From               Message
  ----     ------     ---- ----               -------
  Normal   Scheduled  35s  default-scheduler  Successfully assigned default/liveness-probe to minikube
  Normal   Pulling    34s  kubelet, minikube  Pulling image "ubuntu"
  Normal   Pulled     32s  kubelet, minikube  Successfully pulled image "ubuntu"
  Normal   Created    32s  kubelet, minikube  Created container ubuntu-container
  Normal   Started    32s  kubelet, minikube  Started container ubuntu-container
  Warning  Unhealthy  0s   kubelet, minikube  Liveness probe failed: cat: /tmp/ready: No such file or directory
```

Figure 5.12: Describing liveness-probe: first failure

In the last line, which is highlighted, we can see that the liveness probe has failed for the first time.

4. Let's wait for a few more seconds until the probe has failed three times and run the same command again:

```
kubectl describe pod liveness-probe
```

You should see the following output:

```
Name:               liveness-probe
Namespace:          default
Priority:           0
PriorityClassName:  <none>
Node:               minikube/10.0.2.15
Start Time:         Thu, 04 Jul 2019 19:18:02 +0200
Labels:             <none>
Annotations:        <none>
Status:             Running
IP:                 172.17.0.8
Containers:
  ubuntu-container:
    Container ID:  docker://48c9d901474a25835f00fb5a9e2e2ed38823f12ba24691b7b3383b0d392f016a
    Image:         ubuntu
    Image ID:      docker-pullable://ubuntu@sha256:9b1702dcfe32c873a770a32cfd306dd7fc1c4fd134adfb783db68defc8894b3c
    Port:          <none>
    Host Port:     <none>
    Command:
      /bin/bash
      -ec
      touch /tmp/ready; sleep 30; rm /tmp/ready; sleep 600
    State:          Running
      Started:      Thu, 04 Jul 2019 19:18:05 +0200
    Ready:          True
    Restart Count:  0
    Liveness:       exec [cat /tmp/ready] delay=5s timeout=1s period=5s #success=1 #failure=3
    Environment:    <none>
    Mounts:
      /var/run/secrets/kubernetes.io/serviceaccount from default-token-7rmnp (ro)
Conditions:
  Type              Status
  Initialized       True
  Ready             True
  ContainersReady   True
  PodScheduled      True
Volumes:
  default-token-7rmnp:
    Type:        Secret (a volume populated by a Secret)
    SecretName:  default-token-7rmnp
    Optional:    false
QoS Class:       BestEffort
Node-Selectors:  <none>
Tolerations:     node.kubernetes.io/not-ready:NoExecute for 300s
                 node.kubernetes.io/unreachable:NoExecute for 300s
Events:
  Type     Reason     Age               From               Message
  ----     ------     ----              ----               -------
  Normal   Scheduled  50s               default-scheduler  Successfully assigned default/liveness-probe to minikube
  Normal   Pulling    49s               kubelet, minikube  Pulling image "ubuntu"
  Normal   Pulled     47s               kubelet, minikube  Successfully pulled image "ubuntu"
  Normal   Created    47s               kubelet, minikube  Created container ubuntu-container
  Normal   Started    47s               kubelet, minikube  Started container ubuntu-container
  Warning  Unhealthy  5s (x3 over 15s)  kubelet, minikube  Liveness probe failed: cat: /tmp/ready: No such file or directory
  Normal   Killing    5s                kubelet, minikube  Container ubuntu-container failed liveness probe, will be restarted
```

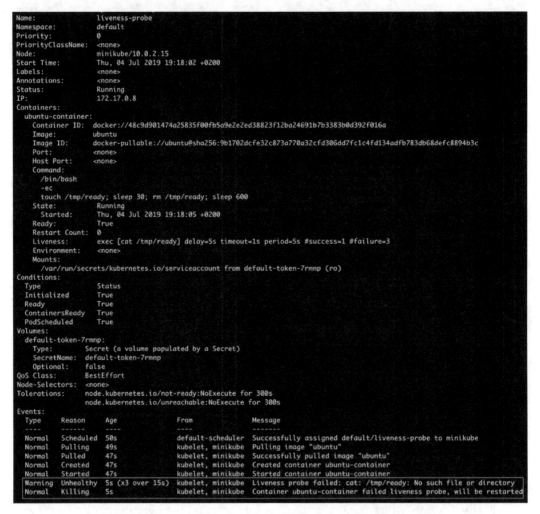

Figure 5.13: Describing liveness-probe: after three failures

The last two highlighted lines in the output tell us that the liveness probe has failed three times. And now, the pod will be killed and restarted.

5. Next, we will verify that the pod has been restarted at least once using the following command:

```
kubectl get pod liveness-probe
```

You should see the following response:

```
NAME              READY    STATUS     RESTARTS   AGE
liveness-probe    1/1      Running    1          89s
```

This output shows that the pod has been restarted upon failing the liveness probe.

Let's now take a look at what happens if we set the restart policy to **Never**.

EXERCISE 5.11: CREATING A POD RUNNING A CONTAINER WITH A LIVENESS PROBE AND A RESTART POLICY

In this exercise, we will use the same pod configuration from the last exercise, the only difference being that the **restartPolicy** field will be set to **Never**. Follow these steps to complete the activity:

1. Create **liveness-probe-with-restart-policy.yaml** with the following pod configuration:

```
apiVersion: v1
kind: Pod
metadata:
  name: liveness-probe-never-restart
spec:
  restartPolicy: Never
  containers:
    - name: ubuntu-container
      image: ubuntu
      command:
        - /bin/bash
        - -ec
        - touch /tmp/ready; sleep 30; rm /tmp/ready; sleep 600
      livenessProbe:
        exec:
          command:
            - cat
            - /tmp/ready
        initialDelaySeconds: 5
        periodSeconds: 5
```

2. Run the following command to create the pod using **`liveness-probe.yaml`**:

```
kubectl create -f liveness-probe-with-restart-policy.yaml
```

You should see the following response:

```
pod/liveness-probe-never-restart created
```

3. Let's wait for around one minute and run the **`describe`** command:

```
kubectl describe pod liveness-probe-never-restart
```

You should see the following output:

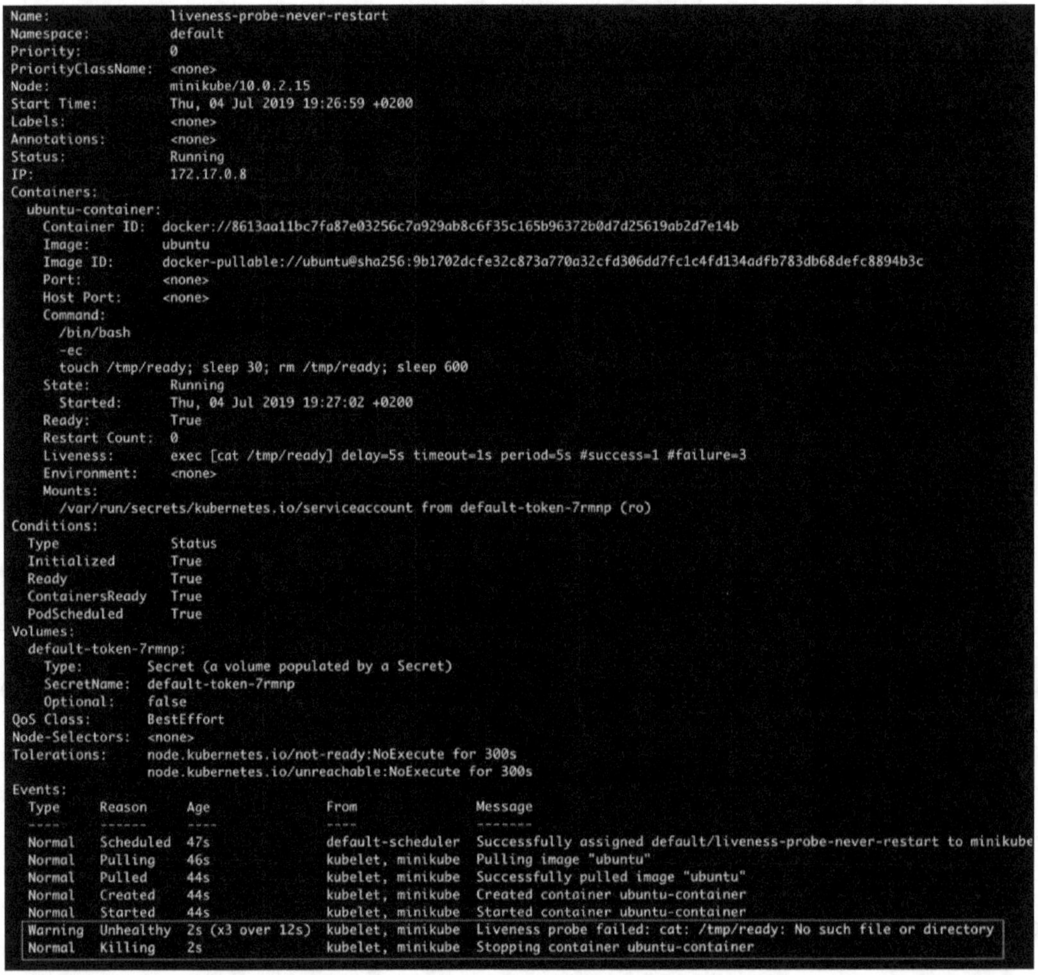

```
Name:               liveness-probe-never-restart
Namespace:          default
Priority:           0
PriorityClassName:  <none>
Node:               minikube/10.0.2.15
Start Time:         Thu, 04 Jul 2019 19:26:59 +0200
Labels:             <none>
Annotations:        <none>
Status:             Running
IP:                 172.17.0.8
Containers:
  ubuntu-container:
    Container ID:  docker://8613aa11bc7fa87e03256c7a929ab8c6f35c165b96372b0d7d25619ab2d7e14b
    Image:         ubuntu
    Image ID:      docker-pullable://ubuntu@sha256:9b1702dcfe32c873a770a32cfd306dd7fc1c4fd134adfb783db68defc8894b3c
    Port:          <none>
    Host Port:     <none>
    Command:
      /bin/bash
      -ec
      touch /tmp/ready; sleep 30; rm /tmp/ready; sleep 600
    State:          Running
      Started:      Thu, 04 Jul 2019 19:27:02 +0200
    Ready:          True
    Restart Count:  0
    Liveness:       exec [cat /tmp/ready] delay=5s timeout=1s period=5s #success=1 #failure=3
    Environment:    <none>
    Mounts:
      /var/run/secrets/kubernetes.io/serviceaccount from default-token-7rmnp (ro)
Conditions:
  Type              Status
  Initialized       True
  Ready             True
  ContainersReady   True
  PodScheduled      True
Volumes:
  default-token-7rmnp:
    Type:        Secret (a volume populated by a Secret)
    SecretName:  default-token-7rmnp
    Optional:    false
QoS Class:       BestEffort
Node-Selectors:  <none>
Tolerations:     node.kubernetes.io/not-ready:NoExecute for 300s
                 node.kubernetes.io/unreachable:NoExecute for 300s
Events:
  Type     Reason     Age                From               Message
  ----     ------     ----               ----               -------
  Normal   Scheduled  47s                default-scheduler  Successfully assigned default/liveness-probe-never-restart to minikube
  Normal   Pulling    46s                kubelet, minikube  Pulling image "ubuntu"
  Normal   Pulled     44s                kubelet, minikube  Successfully pulled image "ubuntu"
  Normal   Created    44s                kubelet, minikube  Created container ubuntu-container
  Normal   Started    44s                kubelet, minikube  Started container ubuntu-container
  Warning  Unhealthy  2s (x3 over 12s)   kubelet, minikube  Liveness probe failed: cat: /tmp/ready: No such file or directory
  Normal   Killing    2s                 kubelet, minikube  Stopping container ubuntu-container
```

Figure 5.14: Describing liveness-probe-never-restart

As we can see, in the last two highlighted lines, the controller will only kill the container and will never attempt to restart it, respecting the restart policy specified in the pod specification.

In the following exercise, we shall take a look at the implementation of a readiness probe.

EXERCISE 5.12: CREATING A POD RUNNING A CONTAINER WITH A READINESS PROBE

In this exercise, we will create a pod with a container that has a readiness probe.

1. Create a file named **readiness-probe.yaml** with the following pod configuration:

```
apiVersion: v1
kind: Pod
metadata:
  name: readiness-probe
spec:
  containers:
    - name: ubuntu-container
      image: ubuntu
      command:
        - /bin/bash
        - -ec
        - sleep 30; touch /tmp/ready; sleep 600
      readinessProbe:
        exec:
          command:
            - cat
            - /tmp/ready
        initialDelaySeconds: 10
        periodSeconds: 5
```

The preceding pod configuration specifies that there will be a container created from an Ubuntu image and the following command will be run once it starts:

```
/bin/bash -ec "sleep 30; touch /tmp/ready; sleep 600"
```

The preceding command sleeps for 30 seconds, creates an empty file at **/tmp/ready**, and then sleeps for 10 minutes before terminating with success.

Next, we have a readiness probe that executes the following command every 5 seconds with an initial delay of 10 seconds:

```
cat /tmp/ready
```

2. Run the following command to create the pod using **readiness-probe.yaml**:

```
kubectl create -f readiness-probe.yaml
```

You should see the following response:

```
pod/readiness-probe created
```

When the container starts, the default value of the readiness probe will be **Failure**. It will wait for 10 seconds before executing the probe for the first time.

3. Let's check the state of the pod:

```
kubectl get pod readiness-probe
```

You should see the following response:

```
NAME             READY     STATUS     RESTARTS     AGE
readiness-probe  0/1       Running    0            8s
```

We can see that the pod is not ready yet.

4. Now, let's try to find more information about this pod using the **describe** command. If we wait for more than 10 seconds after the container starts, we will see that the readiness probe starts failing:

```
kubectl describe pod readiness-probe
```

You should see the following output:

```
Name:                readiness-probe
Namespace:           default
Priority:            0
PriorityClassName:   <none>
Node:                minikube/10.0.2.15
Start Time:          Fri, 05 Jul 2019 00:40:14 +0200
Labels:              <none>
Annotations:         <none>
Status:              Running
IP:                  172.17.0.8
Containers:
  ubuntu-container:
    Container ID:  docker://58d6c9d12f16e81269ce4679ca9e54f750a4b997d6407976162085c82293cfef
    Image:         ubuntu
    Image ID:      docker-pullable://ubuntu@sha256:9b1702dcfe32c873a770a32cfd306dd7fc1c4fd134adfb783db68defc8894b3c
    Port:          <none>
    Host Port:     <none>
    Command:
      /bin/bash
      -ec
      sleep 30; touch /tmp/ready; sleep 600
    State:          Running
      Started:      Fri, 05 Jul 2019 00:40:17 +0200
    Ready:          False
    Restart Count:  0
    Readiness:      exec [cat /tmp/ready] delay=10s timeout=1s period=5s #success=1 #failure=3
    Environment:    <none>
    Mounts:
      /var/run/secrets/kubernetes.io/serviceaccount from default-token-7rmnp (ro)
Conditions:
  Type              Status
  Initialized       True
  Ready             False
  ContainersReady   False
  PodScheduled      True
Volumes:
  default-token-7rmnp:
    Type:        Secret (a volume populated by a Secret)
    SecretName:  default-token-7rmnp
    Optional:    false
QoS Class:       BestEffort
Node-Selectors:  <none>
Tolerations:     node.kubernetes.io/not-ready:NoExecute for 300s
                 node.kubernetes.io/unreachable:NoExecute for 300s
Events:
  Type     Reason     Age   From                Message
  ----     ------     ----  ----                -------
  Normal   Scheduled  19s   default-scheduler   Successfully assigned default/readiness-probe to minikube
  Normal   Pulling    18s   kubelet, minikube   Pulling image "ubuntu"
  Normal   Pulled     16s   kubelet, minikube   Successfully pulled image "ubuntu"
  Normal   Created    16s   kubelet, minikube   Created container ubuntu-container
  Normal   Started    16s   kubelet, minikube   Started container ubuntu-container
  Warning  Unhealthy  2s    kubelet, minikube   Readiness probe failed: cat: /tmp/ready: No such file or directory
```

Figure 5.15: Describing readiness-probe

That output tells us that the readiness probe has failed once already. If we wait for a while and run that command again, we will see that the readiness probe keeps failing until 30 seconds have elapsed since the starting time of the container. After that, the readiness probe will start succeeding since a file will be created at **`/tmp/ready`**.

5. Let's check the state of the pod again:

```
kubectl get pod readiness-probe
```

You should see the following response:

```
NAME              READY    STATUS     RESTARTS     AGE
readiness-probe   1/1      Running    0            66s
```

We can see that the probe has succeeded, and the pod is now in the **Ready** state.

BEST PRACTICES WHILE USING PROBES

An incorrect use of probes will not help you achieve the intended purpose or may even break a pod. Follow these practices to make proper use of probes:

- For liveness probes, **initialDelaySeconds** should be significantly larger than the time it takes for the application to start up. Otherwise, the container is likely to get stuck in a restart loop where it keeps failing the liveness probe and hence keeps on getting restarted by the controller.
- For readiness probes, **initialDelaySeconds** could be small because we want to enable the traffic to the pod as soon as the container is ready, and polling the container more frequently while it's starting up doesn't cause any harm in most cases.
- For readiness probes, we should be careful with setting **failureThreshold** to make sure our readiness probe doesn't give up prematurely in case of temporary outages or issues with the system.

ACTIVITY 5.01: DEPLOYING AN APPLICATION IN A POD

Imagine you are working with a team of developers who have built an awesome application that they want you to deploy in a pod. The application has a process that starts up and takes approximately 20 seconds to load all the required assets. Once the application starts up, it's ready to start receiving requests. If, for some reason, the application crashes, you would want the pod to restart itself as well. They have given you the task of creating the pod using a configuration that will satisfy these needs for the application developers in the best way possible.

We have provided a pre-made application image to emulate the behavior of the application mentioned above. You can get it by using this line in your pod spec:

```
image: packtworkshops/the-kubernetes-workshop:custom-application-for-
    pods-chapter
```

> **NOTE**
>
> Ideally, you would want to create this pod in a different namespace to keep it separate from the rest of the stuff that you created during the exercises. So, feel free to create a namespace and create the pod in that namespace.

Here are the high-level steps to complete this activity:

1. Create a new namespace for your pod.
2. Create a pod configuration that's suitable for the application requirements. Ensure that you use an appropriate namespace, restart policy, readiness and liveness probes, and container image given by application developers.
3. Create a pod using the configuration you've just created.
4. Make sure the pod is running as per the requirements.

> **NOTE**
>
> The solution to this activity can be found at the following address: https://packt.live/304PEoD.

SUMMARY

In this chapter, we have explored various components of pod configuration and learned when to use what. We should now be able to create a pod and choose the right values of various fields in the pod configuration according to the needs of your application. This ability puts us in a position where we can use our strong understanding of this essential, basic building block and extend it to develop a full-fledged application that's deployed reliably.

In the next chapter, we will discuss how we can add labels and arbitrary metadata to pods and use them to identify or search for pods. That will help us to organize our pods as well as choose a subset of them when required.

6

LABELS AND ANNOTATIONS

OVERVIEW

Metadata is extremely useful for any organization and has its use in managing potentially thousands of resources in a cluster. This chapter teaches you how to add metadata to your pods or any other Kubernetes objects. You will be introduced to the concept of labels and annotations. We will also explain their use cases so that you can decide whether to use labels or annotations for a particular use case. You'll utilize labels to organize your objects by using label selectors to select or filter organized sets of objects. You'll also use annotations to add unstructured metadata information to objects.

INTRODUCTION

In the previous chapter, we created various kinds of pods and managed their life cycles. Once we start working with different pods, ideally, we would want to organize, group, and filter them based on certain properties. To do that, we need to add some information to our pods so that we can later use that information to organize them. We have already seen the use of the **name** and **namespace** fields as metadata for the pods. In addition to those fields, we can also add key-value pairs to the pods in order to add extra information as labels and annotations.

In this chapter, we will assign metadata to these pods in order to identify the pods through queries based on some metadata and then add additional unstructured metadata. We will cover labels and annotations in detail and examine the differences between them. We will use both labels and annotations and see when to use one or the other.

LABELS

Labels are the metadata that contain identifiable information pertaining to the Kubernetes objects. These are basically key-value pairs that can be attached to objects such as pods. Each key must be unique for an object. Labels contain information that is meaningful to users. Labels can be attached to pods at the time of creation and can also be added or modified during their runtime too. Here is an example of how labels in a YAML file would appear:

```
metadata:
  labels:
    key1: value1
    key2: value2
```

CONSTRAINTS FOR LABELS

As noted earlier, labels are key-value pairs. There are certain rules that label keys and values should follow. These constraints exist because this way, the queries using labels can be evaluated faster by using optimized data structures and algorithms internally. Kubernetes internally maintains the mappings of labels to corresponding objects using optimized data structures to make these queries faster.

LABEL KEYS

Here's an example of what a label key looks like:

```
label_prefix.com/worker-node-1
```

As we can see, the label key consists of two parts: the label prefix and the label name. Let's take a closer look at these two parts:

- **Label prefix**: The label prefix is optional and must be a DNS subdomain. It cannot be longer than 253 characters and cannot contain spaces. The label prefix is always followed by a forward slash (/). If no prefix is used, the label key is assumed to be private to the user. Some of the prefixes, such as **kubernetes.io/** and **k8s.io/**, are reserved for use solely by the Kubernetes core systems.

  In our example, **label_prefix.com/** is the prefix for that label key.

- **Label name**: The label name is required and can be up to 63 characters long. The label name can only start and end with alphanumeric characters (a – z, A – Z, 0 – 9); however, it can contain dashes (-), underscores (_), dots (.), and alphanumeric characters in between. A label name cannot have spaces or line breaks.

  In the example of **label_prefix.com/worker-node-1**, the name for the label key is **worker-node-1**.

LABEL VALUES

Label values can be up to 63 characters long. Similar to label names, label values should also start and end with alphanumeric characters. However, they can contain dashes (-), underscores (_), dots (.), and alphanumeric characters in between. A label value cannot have spaces or line breaks.

WHY DO WE NEED LABELS?

Labels are generally used for organizing a subset of objects. These objects can then be filtered on the basis of these labels. With labels, you can also run your specific pods on selected nodes. Both of these scenarios are explained in detail in the following section.

ORGANIZING PODS BY ORGANIZATION/TEAM/PROJECT

One of the use cases for labels could be using labels based on teams or organizations in your company. Let's say that your organization has several teams working on different projects. You can enable different teams to list only their pods and even those specific to certain projects. Expanding on this, if you are an infrastructure service provider, you can use an organization label to apply changes only to the pods associated with a particular client organization. For such use cases, you can use label keys such as **team**, **org**, and **project**. The following is an example **labels** section for such a use case:

```
metadata:
  labels:
    environment: production
    team: devops-infra
    project: test-k8s-infra
```

RUNNING SELECTIVE PODS ON SPECIFIC NODES

Another useful scenario can be when you want your pod to be assigned to a certain node with specific hardware or other properties. This can be achieved by adding labels to the nodes that have special hardware or other properties. We can use **nodeSelector** to assign the pod to any node that has a particular label. Consider the following example:

```
apiVersion: v1
kind: Pod
metadata:
  name: pod-with-node-selector
spec:
  containers:
  - name: first-container
    image: nginx
  nodeSelector:
    region: east-us
    disktype: ssd
```

The preceding pod template can be used to make sure the pod will be assigned to a node that is in the **east-us** region and has **ssd** storage. This check is based on the labels added to the nodes. So, we need to ensure that the appropriate **region** and **disktype** labels are assigned to all nodes where applicable.

> **NOTE**
>
> Please note that the exact node labels to be used in the **nodeSelector** section will be provided by the cloud infrastructure provider and that the label keys and values may change. The values used in this example are just to demonstrate the use case.

In the upcoming exercises, we will show you how you can create pods with labels, add labels to a running pod, and modify and/or delete existing labels for a running pod.

EXERCISE 6.01: CREATING A POD WITH LABELS

In this exercise, we aim to create a pod with some labels. In order to complete this exercise successfully, perform the following steps:

1. Create a file called **pod-with-labels.yaml** with the following content:

```
apiVersion: v1
kind: Pod
metadata:
  name: pod-with-labels
  labels:
    app: nginx
    foo: bar
spec:
  containers:
  - name: first-container
    image: nginx
```

As can be seen in the preceding snippet, we have added the **app** and **foo** labels and assigned them the values of **nginx** and **bar**, respectively. Now, we need to create a pod with these labels and verify whether the labels have actually been included in the pod, which will be the focus of the next few steps.

2. Run the following command in the Terminal to create the pod with the preceding configuration:

```
kubectl create -f pod-with-labels.yaml
```

You should see the following response:

```
pod/pod-with-labels created
```

3. Verify that the pod was created by using the **kubectl get** command:

```
kubectl get pod pod-with-labels
```

The following output indicates that the pod has been created:

```
NAME              READY     STATUS      RESTARTS     AGE
pod-with-labels   1/1       Running     0            4m4s
```

4. Verify that the **labels** metadata was actually added to the pod using the **kubectl describe** command:

```
kubectl describe pod pod-with-labels
```

This should lead to the following output:

```
Name:         pod-with-labels
Namespace:    default
Priority:     0
Node:         minikube/10.0.2.15
Start Time:   Mon, 14 Oct 2019 22:16:58 +0200
Labels:       app=nginx
              foo=bar
Annotations:  <none>
Status:       Running
IP:           172.17.0.4
IPs:
  IP:  172.17.0.4
Containers:
  first-container:
    Container ID:   docker://c10a60006740d0c570ad5112d44fd45be5cf4fe7de7e6970a6fc509ba776bada
    Image:          nginx
    Image ID:       docker-pullable://nginx@sha256:aeded0f2a861747f43a01cf1018cf9efe2bdd02afd57d2b11fc
c7fcadc16ccd1
    Port:           <none>
    Host Port:      <none>
    State:          Running
      Started:      Mon, 14 Oct 2019 22:17:17 +0200
    Ready:          True
    Restart Count:  0
    Environment:    <none>
    Mounts:
      /var/run/secrets/kubernetes.io/serviceaccount from default-token-w6xvp (ro)
Conditions:
  Type              Status
  Initialized       True
  Ready             True
  ContainersReady   True
  PodScheduled      True
Volumes:
  default-token-w6xvp:
    Type:        Secret (a volume populated by a Secret)
    SecretName:  default-token-w6xvp
    Optional:    false
QoS Class:       BestEffort
Node-Selectors:  <none>
Tolerations:     node.kubernetes.io/not-ready:NoExecute for 300s
                 node.kubernetes.io/unreachable:NoExecute for 300s
Events:
  Type    Reason     Age        From               Message
  ----    ------     ----       ----               -------
  Normal  Scheduled  <unknown>  default-scheduler  Successfully assigned default/pod-with-labels to mi
nikube
  Normal  Pulling    5m14s      kubelet, minikube  Pulling image "nginx"
  Normal  Pulled     4m56s      kubelet, minikube  Successfully pulled image "nginx"
  Normal  Created    4m56s      kubelet, minikube  Created container first-container
  Normal  Started    4m56s      kubelet, minikube  Started container first-container
```

Figure 6.1: Describing pod-with-labels

The output shows various details relating to the pod (as we have seen in the previous chapter as well). In this case, we will focus on the highlighted section of the output, which shows that the desired labels, **app=nginx**, and **foo=bar**, were actually added to the pod. Note that, in this exercise, we added labels while creating the pod. However, how can you add labels to a pod when a pod is already running? The next exercise will answer this question.

EXERCISE 6.02: ADDING LABELS TO A RUNNING POD

In this exercise, we aim to create a pod without labels and then add labels once the pod is running. In order to complete this exercise successfully, perform the following steps:

1. Create a file called **pod-without-initial-labels.yaml** with the following content:

```
apiVersion: v1
kind: Pod
metadata:
  name: pod-without-initial-labels
spec:
  containers:
  - name: first-container
    image: nginx
```

   Note that we have not yet added any labels to our pod.

2. Run the following command in the Terminal to create the pod with the configuration mentioned in the previous step:

```
kubectl create -f pod-without-initial-labels.yaml
```

   You should see the following response:

```
pod/pod-without-initial-labels created
```

3. Verify that the pod was created by using the **kubectl get** command:

```
kubectl get pod pod-without-initial-labels
```

   The following output indicates that the pod has been created:

NAME	READY	STATUS	RESTARTS	AGE
pod-without-initial-labels	1/1	Running	0	8s

Figure 6.2: Checking the status of pod-without-initial-labels

4. Check if the **`labels`** metadata was actually added to the pod using the **`kubectl describe`** command:

```
kubectl describe pod pod-without-initial-labels
```

You should see the following output:

```
Name:         pod-without-initial-labels
Namespace:    default
Priority:     0
Node:         minikube/10.0.2.15
Start Time:   Mon, 14 Oct 2019 22:32:42 +0200
Labels:       <none>
Annotations:  <none>
Status:       Running
IP:           172.17.0.5
IPs:
  IP:  172.17.0.5
Containers:
  first-container:
    Container ID:   docker://5f85bacb30f858c80654039e498886d684e635627ae58a199c90669f8a54a29c
    Image:          nginx
    Image ID:       docker-pullable://nginx@sha256:aeded0f2a861747f43a01cf1018cf9efe2bdd02afd57d2b11fcc7fcad
c16ccd1
    Port:           <none>
    Host Port:      <none>
    State:          Running
      Started:      Mon, 14 Oct 2019 22:32:46 +0200
    Ready:          True
    Restart Count:  0
    Environment:    <none>
    Mounts:
      /var/run/secrets/kubernetes.io/serviceaccount from default-token-w6xvp (ro)
Conditions:
  Type              Status
  Initialized       True
  Ready             True
  ContainersReady   True
  PodScheduled      True
Volumes:
  default-token-w6xvp:
    Type:        Secret (a volume populated by a Secret)
    SecretName:  default-token-w6xvp
    Optional:    false
QoS Class:       BestEffort
Node-Selectors:  <none>
Tolerations:     node.kubernetes.io/not-ready:NoExecute for 300s
                 node.kubernetes.io/unreachable:NoExecute for 300s
Events:
  Type    Reason     Age        From               Message
  ----    ------     ----       ----               -------
  Normal  Scheduled  <unknown>  default-scheduler  Successfully assigned default/pod-without-initial-labels
to minikube
  Normal  Pulling    48s        kubelet, minikube  Pulling image "nginx"
  Normal  Pulled     46s        kubelet, minikube  Successfully pulled image "nginx"
  Normal  Created    45s        kubelet, minikube  Created container first-container
  Normal  Started    45s        kubelet, minikube  Started container first-container
```

Figure 6.3: Describing pod-without-initial-labels

In the highlighted section of the output, we can note that the **Labels** field is empty. Hence, we can verify that, by default, no label was added to the pod. In the next few steps, we will add a label and then run the pod again to verify whether the label was actually included in the pod.

5. Add a label using the **kubectl label** command as follows:

```
kubectl label pod pod-without-initial-labels app=nginx
```

You should see the following response:

```
pod/pod-without-initial-labels labeled
```

The output shows that the **pod-without-initial-labels** pod was labeled.

6. Verify that the label was actually added in the last step by using the **kubectl describe** command:

```
kubectl describe pod pod-without-initial-labels
```

You should see the following output:

```
Name:           pod-without-initial-labels
Namespace:      default
Priority:       0
Node:           minikube/10.0.2.15
Start Time:     Mon, 14 Oct 2019 22:32:42 +0200
Labels:         app=nginx
Annotations:    <none>
Status:         Running
IP:             172.17.0.5
IPs:
  IP:  172.17.0.5
Containers:
  first-container:
    Container ID:   docker://5f85bacb30f858c80654039e498886d684e635627ae58a199c90669f8a54a29c
    Image:          nginx
    Image ID:       docker-pullable://nginx@sha256:aeded0f2a861747f43a01cf1018cf9efe2bdd02afd57d2b11fcc7fcadc16
ccd1
    Port:           <none>
    Host Port:      <none>
    State:          Running
      Started:      Mon, 14 Oct 2019 22:32:46 +0200
    Ready:          True
    Restart Count:  0
    Environment:    <none>
    Mounts:
      /var/run/secrets/kubernetes.io/serviceaccount from default-token-w6xvp (ro)
Conditions:
  Type              Status
  Initialized       True
  Ready             True
  ContainersReady   True
  PodScheduled      True
Volumes:
  default-token-w6xvp:
    Type:        Secret (a volume populated by a Secret)
    SecretName:  default-token-w6xvp
    Optional:    false
QoS Class:       BestEffort
Node-Selectors:  <none>
Tolerations:     node.kubernetes.io/not-ready:NoExecute for 300s
                 node.kubernetes.io/unreachable:NoExecute for 300s
Events:
  Type    Reason     Age        From               Message
  ----    ------     ----       ----               -------
  Normal  Scheduled  <unknown>  default-scheduler  Successfully assigned default/pod-without-initial-labels to
minikube
  Normal  Pulling    13m        kubelet, minikube  Pulling image "nginx"
  Normal  Pulled     13m        kubelet, minikube  Successfully pulled image "nginx"
  Normal  Created    13m        kubelet, minikube  Created container first-container
  Normal  Started    13m        kubelet, minikube  Started container first-container
```

Figure 6.4: Verifying that the app=nginx label was added

We can observe in the highlighted section of the output that the **app=nginx** label was actually added to the pod. In the preceding case, we only added a single label. However, you can add multiple labels to a pod, as will be done in the next steps.

7. Next, let's add multiple labels in the same command. We can do this by passing multiple labels in the **key=value** format, separated by spaces:

```
kubectl label pod pod-without-initial-labels foo=bar foo2=baz
```

You should see the following response:

```
pod/pod-without-initial-labels labeled
```

8. Verify that the two labels were added to the pod using the **kubectl describe** command:

```
kubectl describe pod pod-without-initial-labels
```

You should see the following output:

```
Name:         pod-without-initial-labels
Namespace:    default
Priority:     0
Node:         minikube/10.0.2.15
Start Time:   Mon, 14 Oct 2019 22:32:42 +0200
Labels:       app=nginx
              foo=bar
              foo2=baz
Annotations:  <none>
Status:       Running
IP:           172.17.0.5
IPs:
  IP:  172.17.0.5
Containers:
  first-container:
    Container ID:   docker://5f85bacb30f858c80654039e498886d684e635627ae58a199c90669f8a54a29c
    Image:          nginx
    Image ID:       docker-pullable://nginx@sha256:aeded0f2a861747f43a01cf1018cf9efe2bdd02afd57d2b11fcc7fcadc16
ccd1
    Port:           <none>
    Host Port:      <none>
    State:          Running
      Started:      Mon, 14 Oct 2019 22:32:46 +0200
    Ready:          True
    Restart Count:  0
    Environment:    <none>
    Mounts:
      /var/run/secrets/kubernetes.io/serviceaccount from default-token-w6xvp (ro)
Conditions:
  Type              Status
  Initialized       True
  Ready             True
  ContainersReady   True
  PodScheduled      True
Volumes:
  default-token-w6xvp:
    Type:        Secret (a volume populated by a Secret)
    SecretName:  default-token-w6xvp
    Optional:    false
QoS Class:       BestEffort
Node-Selectors:  <none>
Tolerations:     node.kubernetes.io/not-ready:NoExecute for 300s
                 node.kubernetes.io/unreachable:NoExecute for 300s
Events:
  Type    Reason     Age        From               Message
  ----    ------     ----       ----               -------
  Normal  Scheduled  <unknown>  default-scheduler  Successfully assigned default/pod-without-initial-labels to
minikube
  Normal  Pulling    13m        kubelet, minikube  Pulling image "nginx"
  Normal  Pulled     13m        kubelet, minikube  Successfully pulled image "nginx"
  Normal  Created    13m        kubelet, minikube  Created container first-container
  Normal  Started    13m        kubelet, minikube  Started container first-container
```

Figure 6.5: Verifying that the new two labels were also added

In the highlighted section of the output, we can see that the two new labels, **foo=bar,** and **foo2=baz**, were also added to the pod.

In the next exercise, we will see how we can delete and modify the existing labels for a pod that is already running.

EXERCISE 6.03: MODIFYING AND/OR DELETING EXISTING LABELS FOR A RUNNING POD

In this exercise, we aim to create a pod with some labels and modify and delete the labels while the pod is running. In order to complete this exercise successfully, perform the following steps:

1. Create a file called **pod-with-some-labels.yaml** with the following content:

```
apiVersion: v1
kind: Pod
metadata:
  name: pod-with-some-labels
  labels:
    app: nginx
spec:
  containers:
  - name: first-container
    image: nginx
```

   As you can see in the pod definition, we have added just one label, **app**, with the value of **nginx**.

2. Run the following command in the Terminal to create the pod with the preceding configuration:

```
kubectl create -f pod-with-some-labels.yaml
```

   You should see the following response:

```
pod/pod-with-some-labels created
```

3. Verify that the pod was created by using the **kubectl get** command:

```
kubectl get pod pod-with-some-labels
```

The following output indicates that the pod has been created:

```
NAME                   READY   STATUS    RESTARTS   AGE
pod-with-some-labels   1/1     Running   0          9s
```

Figure 6.6: Checking the status of the pod-with-some-labels pod

4. Verify that the labels were added as specified in the pod configuration using the **kubectl describe** command:

```
kubectl describe pod pod-with-some-labels
```

You should see the following output:

```
Name:         pod-with-some-labels
Namespace:    default
Priority:     0
Node:         minikube/10.0.2.15
Start Time:   Mon, 14 Oct 2019 23:25:57 +0200
Labels:       app=nginx
Annotations:  <none>
Status:       Running
IP:           172.17.0.6
IPs:
  IP:  172.17.0.6
Containers:
  first-container:
    Container ID:   docker://3f7a0b43019698205fbd7e549093358e978ef890ad04edefb07c9bf7c85681bf
    Image:          nginx
    Image ID:       docker-pullable://nginx@sha256:aeded0f2a861747f43a01cf1018cf9efe2bdd02afd57d2b11fcc7fcad
c16ccd1
    Port:           <none>
    Host Port:      <none>
    State:          Running
      Started:      Mon, 14 Oct 2019 23:26:00 +0200
    Ready:          True
    Restart Count:  0
    Environment:    <none>
    Mounts:
      /var/run/secrets/kubernetes.io/serviceaccount from default-token-w6xvp (ro)
Conditions:
  Type              Status
  Initialized       True
  Ready             True
  ContainersReady   True
  PodScheduled      True
Volumes:
  default-token-w6xvp:
    Type:        Secret (a volume populated by a Secret)
    SecretName:  default-token-w6xvp
    Optional:    false
QoS Class:       BestEffort
Node-Selectors:  <none>
Tolerations:     node.kubernetes.io/not-ready:NoExecute for 300s
                 node.kubernetes.io/unreachable:NoExecute for 300s
Events:
  Type    Reason     Age        From               Message
  ----    ------     ----       ----               -------
  Normal  Scheduled  <unknown>  default-scheduler  Successfully assigned default/pod-with-some-labels to min
ikube
  Normal  Pulling    5m55s      kubelet, minikube  Pulling image "nginx"
  Normal  Pulled     5m52s      kubelet, minikube  Successfully pulled image "nginx"
  Normal  Created    5m52s      kubelet, minikube  Created container first-container
  Normal  Started    5m52s      kubelet, minikube  Started container first-container
```

Figure 6.7: Verifying that the labels were added to pod-with-some-labels

Once we are sure that the **app=nginx** label is present, we will modify this label in the next step.

5. Modify the **app=nginx** label to **app=nginx-application** using the **kubectl label** command:

```
kubectl label --overwrite pod pod-with-some-labels app=nginx-
application
```

You should see the following response:

```
pod/pod-with-some-labels labeled
```

6. Verify that the value of label was modified from **nginx** to **nginx-application** using the **kubectl describe** command:

```
kubectl describe pod pod-with-some-labels
```

The following screenshot shows the output of this command:

```
Name:         pod-with-some-labels
Namespace:    default
Priority:     0
Node:         minikube/10.0.2.15
Start Time:   Mon, 14 Oct 2019 23:25:57 +0200
Labels:       app=nginx-application
Annotations:  <none>
Status:       Running
IP:           172.17.0.6
IPs:
  IP:  172.17.0.6
Containers:
  first-container:
    Container ID:   docker://3f7a0b43019698205fbd7e549093358e978ef890ad04edefb07c9bf7c85681bf
    Image:          nginx
    Image ID:       docker-pullable://nginx@sha256:aeded0f2a861747f43a01cf1018cf9efe2bdd02afd57d2b11fcc7f
cadc16ccd1
    Port:           <none>
    Host Port:      <none>
    State:          Running
      Started:      Mon, 14 Oct 2019 23:26:00 +0200
    Ready:          True
    Restart Count:  0
    Environment:    <none>
    Mounts:
      /var/run/secrets/kubernetes.io/serviceaccount from default-token-w6xvp (ro)
Conditions:
  Type              Status
  Initialized       True
  Ready             True
  ContainersReady   True
  PodScheduled      True
Volumes:
  default-token-w6xvp:
    Type:        Secret (a volume populated by a Secret)
    SecretName:  default-token-w6xvp
    Optional:    false
QoS Class:       BestEffort
Node-Selectors:  <none>
Tolerations:     node.kubernetes.io/not-ready:NoExecute for 300s
                 node.kubernetes.io/unreachable:NoExecute for 300s
Events:
  Type    Reason     Age        From               Message
  ----    ------     ----       ----               -------
  Normal  Scheduled  <unknown>  default-scheduler  Successfully assigned default/pod-with-some-labels to
minikube
  Normal  Pulling    9m16s      kubelet, minikube  Pulling image "nginx"
  Normal  Pulled     9m13s      kubelet, minikube  Successfully pulled image "nginx"
  Normal  Created    9m13s      kubelet, minikube  Created container first-container
  Normal  Started    9m13s      kubelet, minikube  Started container first-container
```

Figure 6.8: Verifying that the label value has been modified

As highlighted in the output, we can see that the label with the **app** key has a new value, **nginx-application**.

7. Delete the label with the **app** key using the **kubectl label** command:

```
kubectl label pod pod-with-some-labels app-
```

Note the hyphen at the end of the preceding command. You should see the following response:

```
pod/pod-with-some-labels labeled
```

8. Verify that the label with the **`app`** key was actually deleted using the **`kubectl describe`** command:

```
kubectl describe pod pod-with-some-labels
```

You should see the following output:

```
Name:         pod-with-some-labels
Namespace:    default
Priority:     0
Node:         minikube/10.0.2.15
Start Time:   Mon, 14 Oct 2019 23:25:57 +0200
Labels:       <none>
Annotations:  <none>
Status:       Running
IP:           172.17.0.6
IPs:
  IP:  172.17.0.6
Containers:
  first-container:
    Container ID:   docker://3f7a0b43019698205fbd7e549093358e978ef890ad04edefb07c9bf7c85681bf
    Image:          nginx
    Image ID:       docker-pullable://nginx@sha256:aeded0f2a861747f43a01cf1018cf9efe2bdd02afd57d2b11fcc7f
cadc16ccd1
    Port:           <none>
    Host Port:      <none>
    State:          Running
      Started:      Mon, 14 Oct 2019 23:26:00 +0200
    Ready:          True
    Restart Count:  0
    Environment:    <none>
    Mounts:
      /var/run/secrets/kubernetes.io/serviceaccount from default-token-w6xvp (ro)
Conditions:
  Type              Status
  Initialized       True
  Ready             True
  ContainersReady   True
  PodScheduled      True
Volumes:
  default-token-w6xvp:
    Type:        Secret (a volume populated by a Secret)
    SecretName:  default-token-w6xvp
    Optional:    false
QoS Class:       BestEffort
Node-Selectors:  <none>
Tolerations:     node.kubernetes.io/not-ready:NoExecute for 300s
                 node.kubernetes.io/unreachable:NoExecute for 300s
Events:
  Type    Reason     Age        From               Message
  ----    ------     ----       ----               -------
  Normal  Scheduled  <unknown>  default-scheduler  Successfully assigned default/pod-with-some-labels to
minikube
  Normal  Pulling    9m55s      kubelet, minikube  Pulling image "nginx"
  Normal  Pulled     9m52s      kubelet, minikube  Successfully pulled image "nginx"
  Normal  Created    9m52s      kubelet, minikube  Created container first-container
  Normal  Started    9m52s      kubelet, minikube  Started container first-container
```

Figure 6.9: Verifying that the desired label was actually deleted from the pod

As highlighted in the preceding output, we can again note that the label with the **app** key was deleted and, hence, the pod now has no label. Thus, we have learned how to modify and delete an existing label for a running pod.

SELECTING KUBERNETES OBJECTS USING LABEL SELECTORS

In order to group various objects based on their labels, we use a label selector. It allows users to identify a set of objects matching certain criteria.

We can use the following syntax for the **kubectl get** command and pass the label selector using the **-l** or **--label** argument:

```
kubectl get pods -l {label_selector}
```

In the following exercises, we will see how to use this command in an actual scenario. Before that, let's understand what kinds of **{label_selector}** arguments we can use in these commands.

Currently, there are two types of label selectors: equality-based and set-based.

EQUALITY-BASED SELECTORS

Equality-based selectors allow Kubernetes objects to be selected according to label keys and values. These kinds of selectors allow us to match all objects that have specific label values for given label keys. In fact, we have inequality-based selectors as well.

Overall, there are three kinds of operators: **=**, **==**, and **!=**.

The first two are actually identical in operation, and denote equality-based operations, while the third one denotes inequality-based operations. While using these kinds of selectors, we can specify more than one condition using any of the preceding operators.

For example, if we are using label keys such as **environment** and **team**, we may want to use the following selectors:

```
environment=production
```

The preceding selector matches all the objects that have a label key environment and the corresponding **production** value:

```
team!=devops-infra
```

The preceding selector matches all the objects that either doesn't have a **team** label key or those for which a **team** label key exists, and the corresponding value is **not** equal to **devops-infra**.

Similarly, we can also use both the selectors together, separated by commas (**,**):

```
environment=production,team!=devops-infra
```

In the preceding example, the selector will match all the objects that match both the criteria specified by the two selectors. The comma acts as a logical AND (**&&**) operator between the two selectors specified. Let's now try our hands at the implementation of these selectors in the following exercises.

EXERCISE 6.04: SELECTING PODS USING EQUALITY-BASED LABEL SELECTORS

In this exercise, we aim to create some pods with different labels and then select them using equality-based selectors. In order to complete this exercise successfully, perform the following steps:

1. Create a file called **pod-frontend-production.yaml** with the following content:

```
apiVersion: v1
kind: Pod
metadata:
  name: frontend-production
  labels:
    environment: production
    role: frontend
spec:
  containers:
  - name: application-container
    image: nginx
```

   As we can see, this is the template for the pod with the following two labels: **environment=production** and **role=frontend**.

2. Create another file called **pod-backend-production.yaml** with the following content:

```
apiVersion: v1
kind: Pod
metadata:
  name: backend-production
```

```
    labels:
      environment: production
      role: backend
spec:
  containers:
  - name: application-container
    image: nginx
```

This is the template for the pod with the following two labels: **environment=production** and **role=backend**.

3. Create another file called **pod-frontend-staging.yaml** with the following content:

```
apiVersion: v1
kind: Pod
metadata:
  name: frontend-staging
  labels:
    environment: staging
    role: frontend
spec:
  containers:
  - name: application-container
    image: nginx
```

This is the template for the pod with the following two labels: **environment=staging** and **role=frontend**.

4. Create all three pods using the following three commands:

```
kubectl create -f pod-frontend-production.yaml
```

You should see the following response:

```
pod/frontend-production created
```

Now, run the following command:

```
kubectl create -f pod-backend-production.yaml
```

The following response indicates that the pod has been created:

```
pod/backend-production created
```

Now, run the following command:

```
kubectl create -f pod-frontend-staging.yaml
```

This should give the following response:

```
pod/frontend-staging created
```

5. Verify that all three pods are created with correct labels using the **--show-labels** argument to the **kubectl get** command.
First, let's check the **frontend-production** pod:

```
kubectl get pod frontend-production --show-labels
```

The following response indicates that the **frontend-production** pod has been created:

```
NAME                  READY   STATUS    RESTARTS   AGE     LABELS
frontend-production   1/1     Running   0          7m39s   environment=production,role=frontend
```

Figure 6.10: Verifying labels for the frontend-production pod

6. Now, check the **backend-production** pod:

```
kubectl get pod backend-production --show-labels
```

The following response indicates that the **backend-production** pod has been created:

```
NAME                 READY   STATUS    RESTARTS   AGE     LABELS
backend-production   1/1     Running   0          7m39s   environment=production,role=backend
```

Figure 6.11: Verifying labels for the backend-production pod

7. Finally, check the **frontend-staging** pod:

```
kubectl get pod frontend-staging --show-labels
```

The following response indicates that the **frontend-staging** pod has been created:

```
NAME               READY   STATUS    RESTARTS   AGE     LABELS
frontend-staging   1/1     Running   0          7m42s   environment=staging,role=frontend
```

Figure 6.12: Verifying labels for the frontend-staging pod

8. Now, we will use label selectors to see all the pods that are assigned to the production environment. We can do this by using **environment=production** as the label selector with the **kubectl get** command:

```
kubectl get pods -l environment=production
```

In the following output, we can see that it only shows those pods that have a label with the **environment** key and the **production** value:

```
NAME                  READY    STATUS     RESTARTS    AGE
backend-production    1/1      Running    0           67m
frontend-production   1/1      Running    0           68m
```

You can confirm from *Figure 6.10* and *Figure 6.11* that these are the pods with the **environment=production** label.

9. Next, we will use label selectors to see all the pods that have the **frontend** role and the **staging** environment. We can do this by using the label selector with the **kubectl get** command, as shown here:

```
kubectl get pods -l role=frontend,environment=staging
```

In the following output, we can see that it only shows those pods that have **staging** as the environment and **frontend** as the role:

```
NAME                  READY    STATUS     RESTARTS    AGE
frontend-staging      1/1      Running    0           72m
```

In this exercise, we have used label selectors to select particular pods. Such label selectors for the **get** command provide a convenient way to choose the required set of pods based on the labels. This also represents a common scenario, where you would want to apply some changes only to the pods involved in the production or staging environment, or the frontend or backend infrastructure.

SET-BASED SELECTORS

Set-based selectors allow Kubernetes objects to be selected on the basis of a set of values for given keys. These kinds of selectors allow us to match all objects that have a given label key with a value in a given set of values.

There are three kinds of operators: **in**, **notin**, and **exists**. Let's see what these operators mean with the help of some examples:

```
environment in (production, staging)
```

In the preceding example, the selector matches all the objects that have an **environment** label key and the value is either **production** or **staging**:

```
team notin (devops-infra)
```

The selector in the preceding example matches all the objects that have a **team** label key and the value is anything other than **devops-infra**. It also matches those objects that don't have the **team** label key:

```
!critical
```

In the preceding example, the selector is equivalent to the **exists** operation. It matches all the objects that don't have the **critical** label key. It doesn't check for a value at all.

> **NOTE**
>
> The two types of selectors can also be used together, as we will observe in *Exercises 6.06, Selecting Pods Using a Mix of Label Selectors*.

Let's implement the set-based selectors in the following exercise.

EXERCISE 6.05: SELECTING PODS USING SET-BASED LABEL SELECTORS

In this exercise, we aim to create some pods with different labels and then select them using set-based selectors.

> **NOTE**
>
> In this exercise, we assume that you have successfully completed *Exercise 6.04, Selecting Pods Using Equality-Based Label Selectors*. We will be reusing the pods created in that exercise.

In order to complete this exercise successfully, perform the following steps:

1. Open the terminal and verify that the **frontend-production** pod we created in *Exercise 6.04, Selecting Pods Using Equality-Based Label Selectors*, is still running and has the required labels. We will be using the **--show-labels** argument with the **kubectl get** command:

```
kubectl get pod frontend-production --show-labels
```

The following response indicates that the **frontend-production** pod exists:

```
NAME                  READY   STATUS    RESTARTS   AGE     LABELS
frontend-production   1/1     Running   0          7m39s   environment=production,role=frontend
```

Figure 6.13: Verifying labels for the frontend-production pod

2. Verify that the **backend-production** pod we created in *Exercise 6.04, Selecting Pods Using Equality-Based Label Selectors* is still running and has the required labels using the **kubectl get** command with the **--show-labels** argument:

```
kubectl get pod backend-production --show-labels
```

The following response indicates that the **backend-production** pod exists:

```
NAME                 READY   STATUS    RESTARTS   AGE     LABELS
backend-production   1/1     Running   0          7m39s   environment=production,role=backend
```

Figure 6.14: Verifying labels for the backend-production pod

3. Verify that the **frontend-staging** pod we created in *Exercise 6.04, Selecting Pods Using Equality-Based Label Selectors* is still running and has the required labels using the **kubectl get** command with the **--show-labels** argument:

```
kubectl get pod frontend-staging --show-labels
```

The following response indicates that the **frontend-staging** pod exists:

```
NAME               READY   STATUS    RESTARTS   AGE     LABELS
frontend-staging   1/1     Running   0          7m42s   environment=staging,role=frontend
```

Figure 6.15: Verifying labels for the frontend-staging pod

4. Now, we will use the label selectors to match all the pods for which the environment is **production**, and the role is either **frontend** or **backend**. We can do this by using the label selector with the **kubectl get** command as shown here:

```
kubectl get pods -l 'role in (frontend, backend),environment in
(production)'
```

You should see the following response:

```
NAME                   READY     STATUS     RESTARTS    AGE
backend-production     1/1       Running    0           82m
frontend-production    1/1       Running    0           82m
```

5. Next, we will use the label selectors to match all those pods that have the **environment** label and whose role is anything other than **backend**. We also want to exclude those pods that don't have the **role** label set:

```
kubectl get pods -l 'environment,role,role notin (backend)'
```

This should produce the following output:

```
NAME                   READY     STATUS     RESTARTS    AGE
frontend-production    1/1       Running    0           86m
frontend-staging       1/1/      Running    0           86m
```

In this example, we have the set-based selectors that can be used to get the desired pods. We can also combine these with selector-based pods, as we shall see in the following exercise.

EXERCISE 6.06: SELECTING PODS USING A MIX OF LABEL SELECTORS

In this exercise, we aim to create some pods with different labels and then select them using a combination of equality-based and set-based selectors.

> **NOTE**
>
> In this exercise, we assume that you have successfully completed *Exercise 6.04, Selecting Pods Using Equality-Based Label Selectors*. We will be reusing the pods created in that exercise.

In order to complete this exercise successfully, perform the following steps:

1. Open the terminal and verify that the **frontend-production** pod we created in *Exercise 6.04, Selecting Pods Using Equality-Based Label Selectors*, is still running and has the required labels. We will be using the **--show-labels** argument with the **kubectl get** command:

```
kubectl get pod frontend-production --show-labels
```

The following response indicates that the **frontend-production** pod exists:

```
NAME                  READY   STATUS    RESTARTS   AGE     LABELS
frontend-production   1/1     Running   0          7m39s   environment=production,role=frontend
```

Figure 6.16: Verifying labels for the frontend-production pod

2. Verify that the **backend-production** pod we created in *Exercise 6.04, Selecting Pods Using Equality-Based Label Selectors* is still running and has the required labels using the **kubectl get** command with the **--show-labels** argument:

```
kubectl get pod backend-production --show-labels
```

The following response indicates that the **backend-production** pod exists:

```
NAME                 READY   STATUS    RESTARTS   AGE     LABELS
backend-production   1/1     Running   0          7m39s   environment=production,role=backend
```

Figure 6.17: Verifying labels for the backend-production pod

3. Verify that the **frontend-staging** pod we created in *Exercise 6.04, Selecting Pods Using Equality-Based Label Selectors* is still running and has the required labels using the **kubectl get** command with the **--show-labels** argument:

```
kubectl get pod frontend-staging --show-labels
```

The following response indicates that the **frontend-staging** pod exists:

```
NAME               READY   STATUS    RESTARTS   AGE     LABELS
frontend-staging   1/1     Running   0          7m42s   environment=staging,role=frontend
```

Figure 6.18: Verifying labels for the frontend-staging pod

4. Now, we will use the label selectors to match all the pods that have a **frontend** role and whose environment is one of **production**, **staging**, or **dev**:

```
kubectl get pods -l 'role=frontend,environment in 
(production,staging,dev)'
```

This command should give the following list of pods:

```
NAME                  READY   STATUS    RESTARTS   AGE
frontend-production   1/1     Running   0          95m
frontend-staging      1/1     Running   0          95m
```

In the output, we can only see those pods that have a **frontend** role, whereas the **environment** can be any one of the given values. Thus, we have seen that a mix of different types of selectors can be used as required.

ANNOTATIONS

As we have seen previously, labels are used to add the identifying metadata that we can later use to filter or select objects by. However, labels have certain constraints in terms of what we can store in the values, such as the limitation of 63 characters and alphanumeric characters at the beginning and end. Annotations, on the other hand, have fewer constraints in terms of what kind of data can be stored in them. However, we cannot filter or select objects by using annotations.

Annotations are also key-value pairs that can be used to store the unstructured information pertaining to the Kubernetes objects. Here is an example of how annotations in a YAML file would appear:

```
metadata:
  annotations:
    key1: value1
    key2: value2
```

CONSTRAINTS FOR ANNOTATIONS

As noted in the previous section, annotations are key-value pairs, just like labels. However, the rules for annotations are more relaxed than the rules for label keys and values. The reason for more relaxed constraints is the lack of support for filtering or selecting objects using annotations. This is because the key-value pairs of annotations are not stored in a lookup-efficient data structure. Hence, there are fewer restrictions here.

ANNOTATION KEYS

Similar to label keys, annotation keys also have two parts: a prefix and a name. The constraints for both annotation prefixes and names are the same as those for the label prefixes and names, respectively.

Here's an example of how an annotation key may appear:

```
annotation_prefix.com/worker-node-identifier
```

ANNOTATION VALUES

There are no restrictions in terms of what kinds of data annotation values may contain.

USE CASE FOR ANNOTATIONS

Annotations are generally used to add metadata that won't be used to filter or select objects. It's used to add metadata that will be used by users or tools to get more subjective information regarding the Kubernetes objects. Let's look at some of the scenarios where using annotations can be useful:

- Annotations can be used to add timestamps, commit SHA, issue tracker links, or names/information about users who are responsible for specific objects in an organization. In this case, we can use the following type of metadata, depending on our use case:

```
metadata:
  annotations:
    timestamp: 123456789
    commit-SHA: d6s9shb82365yg4ygd782889us28377gf6
    JIRA-issue: "https://your-jira-link.com/issue/ABC-1234"
    owner: "https://internal-link.to.website/username"
```

- Annotations can also be used to add information about client libraries or tools. We can add information such as the name of the library, the version used, and public documentation links. This information can later be used for debugging issues in our application:

```
metadata:
  annotations:
    node-version: 13.1.0
    node-documentation: "https://nodejs.org/en/docs/"
```

- We can also use annotations to store the previous pod configuration deployed. This can be really helpful in figuring out what configuration was deployed before the current revision and what has changed:

```
metadata:
  annotations:
    previous-configuration: "{ some json containing the
      previously deployed configuration of the object }"
```

- Annotations can also be used to store the configuration or checkpoints that can be helpful in the deployment process for our applications.

We will learn how to add annotations to a pod in the following exercise.

Exercise 6.07: Adding Annotations to Help with Application Debugging

In this exercise, we will add some arbitrary metadata to our pod. In order to complete this exercise successfully, perform the following steps:

1. Create a file called **pod-with-annotations.yaml** with the following content:

```
apiVersion: v1
kind: Pod
metadata:
  name: pod-with-annotations
  annotations:
    commit-SHA: d6s9shb82365yg4ygd782889us28377gf6
    JIRA-issue: "https://your-jira-link.com/issue/ABC-1234"
    timestamp: "123456789"
    owner: "https://internal-link.to.website/username"
spec:
  containers:
  - name: application-container
    image: nginx
```

   The highlighted part in the pod definition shows the annotations that we have added.

2. Run the following command in the Terminal to create the pod using the **kubectl create** command:

```
kubectl create -f pod-with-annotations.yaml
```

   You should get the following response:

```
pod/pod-with-annotations created
```

3. Run the following command in the Terminal to verify that the pod was created as desired:

```
kubectl get pod pod-with-annotations
```

You should see the following list of pods:

```
NAME                    READY     STATUS     RESTARTS   AGE
pod-with-annotations    1/1       Running    0          29s
```

4. Run the following command in the Terminal to verify that the created pod has the desired annotations:

```
kubectl describe pod pod-with-annotations
```

You should see the following output of this command:

```
Name:         pod-with-annotations
Namespace:    default
Priority:     0
Node:         minikube/10.0.2.15
Start Time:   Fri, 18 Oct 2019 00:41:17 +0200
Labels:       <none>
Annotations:  JIRA-issue: https://your-jira-link.com/issue/ABC-1234
              commit-SHA: d6s9shb82365yg4ygd782889us28377gf6
              owner: https://internal-link.to.website/username
              timestamp: 123456789
Status:       Running
IP:           172.17.0.11
IPs:
  IP:  172.17.0.11
Containers:
  application-container:
    Container ID:   docker://05663bac94c31f21d5e43bd385dbc028576a0009f4284c7dd83ed92ffcaa9652
    Image:          nginx
    Image ID:       docker-pullable://nginx@sha256:77ebc94e0cec30b20f9056bac1066b09fbdc049401b71850922c63f
c0cc1762e
    Port:           <none>
    Host Port:      <none>
    State:          Running
      Started:      Fri, 18 Oct 2019 00:41:28 +0200
    Ready:          True
    Restart Count:  0
    Environment:    <none>
    Mounts:
      /var/run/secrets/kubernetes.io/serviceaccount from default-token-w6xvp (ro)
Conditions:
  Type              Status
  Initialized       True
  Ready             True
  ContainersReady   True
  PodScheduled      True
Volumes:
  default-token-w6xvp:
    Type:        Secret (a volume populated by a Secret)
    SecretName:  default-token-w6xvp
    Optional:    false
QoS Class:       BestEffort
Node-Selectors:  <none>
Tolerations:     node.kubernetes.io/not-ready:NoExecute for 300s
                 node.kubernetes.io/unreachable:NoExecute for 300s
Events:
  Type    Reason     Age        From                Message
  ----    ------     ----       ----                -------
  Normal  Scheduled  <unknown>  default-scheduler   Successfully assigned default/pod-with-annotations to m
inikube
  Normal  Pulling    56s        kubelet, minikube   Pulling image "nginx"
  Normal  Pulled     45s        kubelet, minikube   Successfully pulled image "nginx"
  Normal  Created    45s        kubelet, minikube   Created container application-container
  Normal  Started    45s        kubelet, minikube   Started container application-container
```

Figure 6.19: Verifying annotations for the pod-with-annotations pod

As we can see in the highlighted section of the preceding output, the desired metadata has been added as annotations to the pod. Now, this data can be used by any deployment tools or clients who may know about the key names used.

WORKING WITH ANNOTATIONS

In the previous exercise, we created a pod with annotations. Similar to labels, we can add annotations to a running pod and modify/delete the annotations of a running pod. This can be achieved by running similar commands as those for labels. The following list presents you with the various operations that can be performed on annotations along with the relevant commands:

- Thus, we can add annotations to a running pod by using the following command:

  ```
  kubectl annotate pod <pod_name> <annotation_key>=<annotation_label>
  ```

  In the preceding command, we can add multiple annotations similar to multiple labels, as in *step 7* of *Exercise 6.02, Adding Labels to a Running Pod*.

- We can also modify (overwrite) an annotation as follows:

  ```
  kubectl annotate --overwrite pod <pod_name> <annotation_
  key>=<annotation_label>
  ```

- Finally, we can delete an annotation using the following command:

  ```
  kubectl annotate pod <pod_name> <annotation_key>-
  ```

Note the hyphen at the end of the preceding command. Now that we have learned about labels and annotations as well as the various ways in which we can use them, let's bring all of this together in the following activity.

ACTIVITY 6.01: CREATING PODS WITH LABELS/ANNOTATIONS AND GROUPING THEM AS PER GIVEN CRITERIA

Consider that you're working on supporting two teams called **`product-development`** and **`infra-libraries`**. Both teams have some application pods for different environments (production or staging). The teams also want to mark their pods as critical if that is indeed the case.

In short, you need to create three pods as per the following metadata requirements:

- An **`arbitrary-product-application`** pod that runs in a production environment and is owned by the **`product-development`** team. This needs to be marked as a non-critical pod.

- An **infra-libraries-application** pod that runs in a production environment and is owned by the **infra-libraries** team. This needs to be marked as a critical pod.
- An **infra-libraries-application-staging** pod that runs in a staging environment and is owned by the **infra-libraries** team. Since it runs in staging, the criticality of the pod does not need to be indicated.

In addition to this, both teams also want to add another piece of metadata - "team-link" in which they want to store the internal link of the team's contact information.

You should be able to perform the following tasks once all three pods have been created:

1. Group all the pods that run in the production environment and are critical.
2. Group all the pods that are not critical among all environments.

> **NOTE**
>
> Ideally, you would want to create this pod to be in a different namespace so as to keep it separate from the rest of the stuff that you created during the exercises. Therefore, feel free to create a namespace and create the pod in that namespace.

The high-level steps to perform this activity are as follows:

1. Create a namespace for this activity.
2. Write the pod configurations for all three pods. Ensure that all the metadata requested is added correctly among the labels and annotations.
3. Create all three pods using the configurations written in the previous step.
4. Make sure that all three pods are running and have all the requested metadata.
5. Group all the pods that run in the production environment and are critical.
6. Group all the pods that are not critical among all environments.

For the first task, your goal should get the **infra-libraries-application** pod once you complete the activity, as shown here:

```
NAME                          READY   STATUS      RESTARTS    AGE
infra-libraries-application   1/1     Running     0           12m
```

For the second task, your goal is to obtain **arbitrary-product-application** and **infra-libraries-application-staging** once you complete the activity, as shown here:

```
NAME                                  READY   STATUS     RESTARTS    AGE
arbitrary-product-application         1/1     Running    0           14m
infra-libraries-application-staging   1/1     Running    0           14m
```

> **NOTE**
>
> The solution to this activity can be found at the following address: https://packt.live/304PEoD.

SUMMARY

In this chapter, we have described labels and annotations and used them to add metadata information, which can either be identifiable information that can be used to filter or select objects, or non-identifiable information that can be used by users or tools to get more context regarding the state of the application. More specifically, we have also organized objects such as pods using labels and annotations. These are important skills that will help you manage your Kubernetes objects more efficiently.

In the following chapters, as we become familiar with more Kubernetes objects such as Deployments and Services, we will see the further application of labels and label selectors while organizing pods for deployment or discovery.

7

KUBERNETES CONTROLLERS

OVERVIEW

This chapter introduces the concept of Kubernetes controllers and explains how to use them to create replicated Deployments. We will describe the use of different types of controllers, such as ReplicaSets, Deployments, DaemonSets, StatefulSets, and Jobs. You will learn how to choose a suitable controller for specific use cases. Using hands-on exercises, we will guide you through how to use these controllers with the desired configuration to deploy several replicas of Pods for your application. You will also learn how to manage them using various commands.

INTRODUCTION

In previous chapters, we created different Pods, managed their life cycle manually, and added metadata (labels or annotations) to them to help organize and identify various Pods. In this chapter, we will take a look at a few Kubernetes objects that help you manage several replica Pods declaratively.

When deploying your application in production, there are several reasons why you would want to have more than one replica of your Pods. Having more than one replica ensures that your application continues to work in cases where one or more Pods fail. In addition to handling failures, replication also allows you to balance the load across the different replicas so that one Pod is not overloaded with a lot of requests, thereby allowing you to easily serve higher traffic than what a single Pod can serve.

Kubernetes supports different controllers that you can use for replication, such as ReplicaSets, Deployments, DaemonSets, StatefulSets, and Jobs. A controller is an object that ensures that your application runs in the desired state for its entire runtime. Each of these controllers is useful for specific use cases. In this chapter, we will explore some of the most commonly used controllers one by one and understand how and when to use them in real-life scenarios.

REPLICASETS

As discussed earlier, having multiple replicas of our application ensures that it is still available even if a few replicas fail. This also makes it easy for us to scale our application to balance the load to serve more traffic. For example, if we are building a web application that's exposed to users, we'd want to have at least two replicas of the application in case one of them fails or dies unexpectedly. We would also want the failed replica to recover on its own. In addition to that, if our traffic starts growing, we would want to increase the number of Pods (replicas) running our application. A ReplicaSet is a Kubernetes controller that keeps a certain number of Pods running at any given time.

ReplicaSet acts as a supervisor for multiple Pods across the different nodes in a Kubernetes cluster. A ReplicaSet will terminate or start new Pods to match the configuration specified in the ReplicaSet template. For this reason, it is a good idea to use them even if your application only needs one Pod. Even if someone deletes the only running Pod, the ReplicaSet will ensure that a new Pod is created to replace it, thereby ensuring that one Pod is always running.

A ReplicaSet can be used to reliably run a single Pod indefinitely or to run multiple instances of the same Pod.

REPLICASET CONFIGURATION

Let's first look at an example of the configuration of a ReplicaSet, and then we will cover what the different fields mean:

```
apiVersion: apps/v1
kind: ReplicaSet
metadata:
  name: nginx-replicaset
  labels:
    app: nginx
spec:
  replicas: 2
  selector:
    matchLabels:
      environment: production
  template:
    metadata:
      labels:
        environment: production
    spec:
      containers:
      - name: nginx-container
        image: nginx
```

As with Pod configuration, a ReplicaSet also needs fields such as **apiVersion**, **kind**, and **metadata**. For a ReplicaSet, the API version, **apps/v1**, is the current version and the **kind** field will always be **ReplicaSet**. One field that is different from what we have seen in Pod configuration so far is the **spec**.

Now, we will see what information we need to specify in the **spec** field.

REPLICAS

The **replicas** field under **spec** specifies how many Pods the ReplicaSet should keep running concurrently. You can see the following value in the preceding example:

```
replicas: 2
```

The ReplicaSet will create or delete Pods in order to match this number. The default value for this field, if not specified, is **1**.

POD TEMPLATE

In the **template** field, we will specify the template of the Pod that we want to run using this ReplicaSet. This Pod template will be exactly the same as the Pod templates we used in the previous two chapters. As usual, we can add metadata in the form of labels and annotations to the Pods. The ReplicaSet will use this Pod template to create new Pods whenever there is a need for them. The following section from the previous example comprises the template:

```
template:
  metadata:
    labels:
      environment: production
  spec:
    containers:
    - name: nginx-container
      image: nginx
```

POD SELECTOR

This is a really important section. In the **selector** field under **spec**, we can specify the label selectors that will be used by the ReplicaSet to identify which Pods to manage:

```
selector:
  matchLabels:
    environment: production
```

The preceding example ensures that our controller will only manage Pods with an **environment: production** label.

Let's now proceed to create our first ReplicaSet.

EXERCISE 7.01: CREATING A SIMPLE REPLICASET WITH NGINX CONTAINERS

In this exercise, we will create a simple ReplicaSet and examine the Pods created by it. To successfully complete this exercise, perform the following steps:

1. Create a file called **replicaset-nginx.yaml** with the following content:

```
apiVersion: apps/v1
kind: ReplicaSet
metadata:
  name: nginx-replicaset
  labels:
    app: nginx
spec:
  replicas: 2
  selector:
    matchLabels:
      environment: production
  template:
    metadata:
      labels:
        environment: production
    spec:
      containers:
      - name: nginx-container
        image: nginx
```

   As you can see in the highlighted part of the configuration, we have three fields: **replicas**, **selector**, and **template**. We have set the number of replicas to **2**. The Pod selector has been set in such a way that this ReplicaSet will manage the Pods with the **environment: production** label. The Pod template has the simple Pod configuration that we used in previous chapters. We have ensured that the Pod label selector matches the Pod's labels in the template exactly.

2. Run the following command to create the ReplicaSet using the preceding configuration:

```
kubectl create -f replicaset-nginx.yaml
```

You should see the following response:

```
replicaset.apps/nginx-replicaset created
```

3. Verify that the ReplicaSet was created by using the **kubectl get** command:

```
kubectl get rs nginx-replicaset
```

Note that **rs** is a short form of **replicaset** in all kubectl commands.

You should see the following response:

```
NAME               DESIRED    CURRENT    READY    AGE
nginx-replicaset   2          2          2        30s
```

As you can see, we have a ReplicaSet with two desired replicas, as we defined in **replicaset-nginx.yaml** in *step 1*.

4. Verify that the Pods were actually created by using the following command:

```
kubectl get pods
```

You should get the following response:

```
NAME                     READY    STATUS    RESTARTS    AGE
nginx-replicaset-b8fwt   1/1      Running   0           51s
nginx-replicaset-k4h9r   1/1      Running   0           51s
```

We can see that the names of the Pods created by the ReplicaSet take the name of the ReplicaSet as a prefix.

5. Now that we have created our first ReplicaSet, let's look at it in more detail to understand what actually happened during its creation. To do that, we can describe the ReplicaSet we just created by using the following command in the terminal:

```
kubectl describe rs nginx-replicaset
```

You should see output similar to the following:

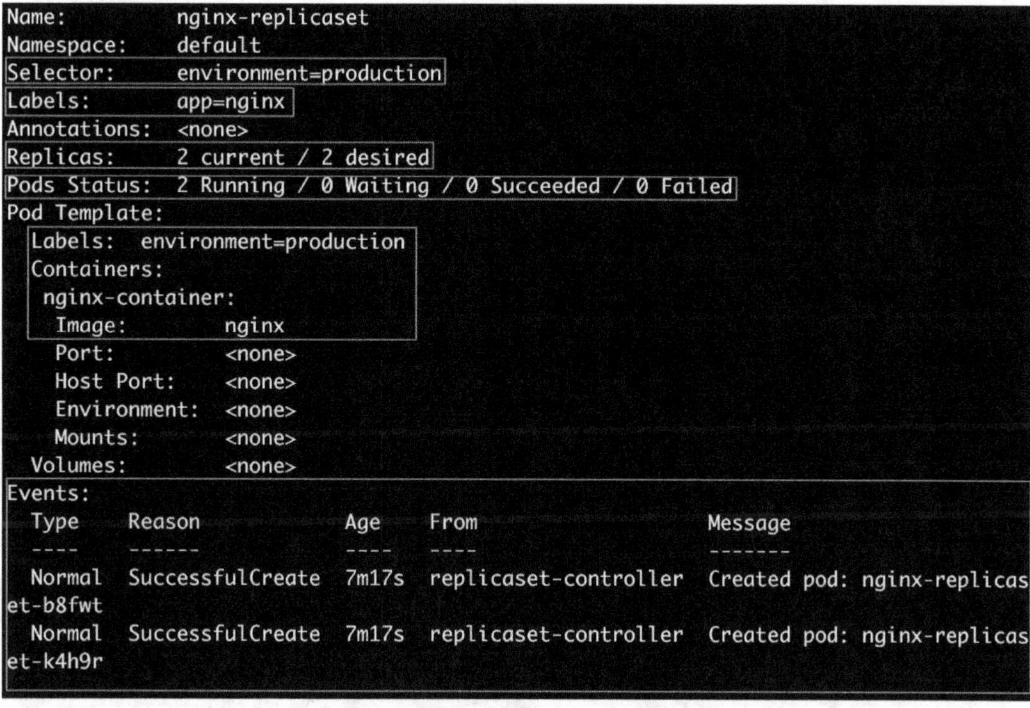

Figure 7.1: Describing nginx-replicaset

6. Next, we will inspect the Pods created by this ReplicaSet and verify that they have been created with the correct configuration. Run the following command to get a list of the Pods that are running:

```
kubectl get pods
```

You should see a response as follows:

```
NAME                       READY    STATUS    RESTARTS   AGE
nginx-replicaset-b8fwt     1/1      Running   0          38m
nginx-replicaset-k4h9r     1/1      Running   0          38m
```

7. Run the following command to describe one of the Pods by copying its name:

```
kubectl describe pod <pod_name>
```

You should see output similar to the following:

```
Name:           nginx-replicaset-b8fwt
Namespace:      default
Priority:       0
Node:           minikube/10.0.2.15
Start Time:     Sat, 09 Nov 2019 15:18:24 +0100
Labels:         environment=production
Annotations:    <none>
Status:         Running
IP:             172.17.0.4
IPs:
  IP:             172.17.0.4
Controlled By:  ReplicaSet/nginx-replicaset
Containers:
  nginx-container:
    Container ID:   docker://6c7ea0fd9afe4c48023b6afe0fcc7ffeb394ab3bee6836aefea5849874d978d4
    Image:          nginx
    Image ID:       docker-pullable://nginx@sha256:922c815aa4df050d4df476e92daed4231f466acc8ee90e0e77495
1b0fd7195a4
    Port:           <none>
    Host Port:      <none>
    State:          Running
      Started:      Sat, 09 Nov 2019 15:18:28 +0100
    Ready:          True
```

Figure 7.2: Listing Pods

In the highlighted sections of the preceding output, we can clearly see that the pod has the **environment=production** label and is controlled by **ReplicaSet/nginx-replicaset**.

So, we have created a simple ReplicaSet in this exercise. In the following subtopics, we will go through the highlighted sections of the preceding output to understand the ReplicaSet that's running.

LABELS ON THE REPLICASET

Consider the following line from the output shown in *Figure 7.1*:

```
Labels:         app=nginx
```

It shows that, as desired, the ReplicaSet was created with a label key called **app** with a value of **nginx**.

SELECTORS FOR THE REPLICASET

Now, consider the following line from the output shown in *Figure 7.1*:

```
Selector:       environment=production
```

This shows that the ReplicaSet is configured with an **environment=production** Pod selector. This means that this ReplicaSet will try to acquire Pods that have this label.

REPLICAS

Consider the following line from the output shown in *Figure 7.1*:

```
Replicas:       2 current / 2 desired
```

We can see that the ReplicaSet has the desired count of **2** for the Pods, and it also shows that there are currently two replicas present.

PODS STATUS

While the **Replicas** field only shows the number of Pods currently present, **Pods Status** shows the actual status of those Pods:

```
Pods Status:    2 Running / 0 Waiting / 0 Succeeded / 0 Failed
```

We can see that there are currently two Pods running under this ReplicaSet.

PODS TEMPLATE

Now, let's consider the **Pod Template** section of the output shown in *Figure 7.1*. We can see that the Pod template is the same as was described in the configuration.

EVENTS

In the last section of the output shown in *Figure 7.1*, we can see that there are two events, which denotes that two pods were created to get to the desired count of two Pods for the ReplicaSet.

In the last exercise, we created a ReplicaSet to maintain a number of running replicas. Now, let's consider a scenario where some nodes or Pods fail for some reason. We will see how the ReplicaSet will behave in this situation.

EXERCISE 7.02: DELETING PODS MANAGED BY A REPLICASET

In this exercise, we will delete one of the Pods managed by a ReplicaSet to see how it responds. This way, we will be simulating a single or multiple Pods failing during the runtime of a ReplicaSet:

> **NOTE**
>
> In this exercise, we will assume that you have successfully completed the previous exercise as we will be reusing the ReplicaSet created in that exercise.

1. Verify that the Pods created by the ReplicaSet are still running:

   ```
   kubectl get pods
   ```

   You should see something similar to the following response:

   ```
   NAME                      READY    STATUS    RESTARTS   AGE
   nginx-replicaset-9tgb9    1/1      Running   0          103s
   nginx-replicaset-zdjb5    1/1      Running   0          103s
   ```

2. Delete the first Pod to replicate Pod failure during runtime by using the following command:

   ```
   kubectl delete pod <pod_name>
   ```

   You should see a response similar to the following:

   ```
   pod "nginx-replicaset-9tgb9" deleted
   ```

3. Describe the ReplicaSet and check the events:

   ```
   kubectl describe rs nginx-replicaset
   ```

You should see output similar to the following:

```
Name:         nginx-replicaset
Namespace:    default
Selector:     environment=production
Labels:       app=nginx
Annotations:  <none>
Replicas:     2 current / 2 desired
Pods Status:  2 Running / 0 Waiting / 0 Succeeded / 0 Failed
Pod Template:
  Labels:  environment=production
  Containers:
   nginx-container:
    Image:        nginx
    Port:         <none>
    Host Port:    <none>
    Environment:  <none>
    Mounts:       <none>
  Volumes:        <none>
Events:
  Type    Reason            Age    From                   Message
  ----    ------            ----   ----                   -------
  Normal  SuccessfulCreate  2m51s  replicaset-controller  Created pod: nginx-replicase
t-9tgb9
  Normal  SuccessfulCreate  2m51s  replicaset-controller  Created pod: nginx-replicase
t-zdjb5
  Normal  SuccessfulCreate  22s    replicaset-controller  Created pod: nginx-replicase
t-46spq
```

Figure 7.3: Describing the ReplicaSet

As highlighted in the preceding output, we can see that after a Pod is deleted, the ReplicaSet creates a new Pod using the Pod configuration in the **Template** section of the ReplicaSet configuration. Even if we delete all the Pods managed by the ReplicaSet, they will be recreated. So, to delete all the Pods permanently and to avoid the recreation of the Pods, we need to delete the ReplicaSet itself.

4. Run the following command to delete the ReplicaSet:

```
kubectl delete rs nginx-replicaset
```

You should see the following response:

```
replicaset.apps "nginx-replicaset" deleted
```

As shown in the preceding output, the **nginx-replicaset** ReplicaSet was deleted.

5. Run the following command to verify that the Pods managed by the ReplicaSet were also deleted:

```
kubectl get pods
```

You should get the following response:

```
No resources found in default namespace
```

As you can see from this output, we can verify that the Pods were deleted.

Consider a scenario where you have already deployed a single Pod for testing. Now, it is ready to go live. You apply the required label changes from development to production, and now you want to control this using a ReplicaSet. We will see how to do this in the following exercise.

EXERCISE 7.03: CREATING A REPLICASET GIVEN THAT A MATCHING POD ALREADY EXISTS

In this exercise, we will create a Pod that matches the Pod template in the ReplicaSet and then create the ReplicaSet. Our aim is to prove that the newly created ReplicaSet will acquire the existing Pod and start managing it as if it created that Pod itself.

In order to successfully complete this exercise, perform the following steps:

1. Create a file called **pod-matching-replicaset.yaml** with the following content:

```
apiVersion: v1
kind: Pod
metadata:
  name: pod-matching-replicaset
  labels:
    environment: production
spec:
  containers:
  - name: first-container
    image: nginx
```

2. Run the following command to create the Pod using the preceding configuration:

```
kubectl create -f pod-matching-replicaset.yaml
```

You should see the following response:

```
pod/pod-matching-replicaset created
```

3. Create a file called **replicaset-nginx.yaml** with the following content:

```
apiVersion: apps/v1
kind: ReplicaSet
metadata:
  name: nginx-replicaset
  labels:
    app: nginx
spec:
  replicas: 2
  selector:
    matchLabels:
      environment: production
  template:
    metadata:
      labels:
        environment: production
    spec:
      containers:
      - name: nginx-container
        image: nginx
```

4. Run the following command to create the ReplicaSet using the preceding configuration:

```
kubectl create -f replicaset-nginx.yaml
```

You should see a response similar to the following:

```
replicaset.apps/nginx-replicaset created
```

This output indicates that the Pod has been created.

5. Run the following command to check the status of the ReplicaSet:

```
kubectl get rs nginx-replicaset
```

You should get the following response:

```
NAME               DESIRED    CURRENT    READY    AGE
nginx-replicaset   2          2          2        2
```

We can see that there are currently two Pods managed by the ReplicaSet, as desired.

6. Next, let's check what Pods are running by using the following command:

```
kubectl get pods
```

You should see output similar to the following:

```
NAME                       READY    STATUS    RESTARTS    AGE
nginx-replicaset-4dr7s     1/1      Running   0           28s
pod-matching-replicaset    1/1      Running   0           81s
```

In this output, we can see that the manually created Pod named **pod-matching-replicaset** is still running and that there was only one new Pod created by the **nginx-replicaset** ReplicaSet.

7. Next, we will use the **kubectl describe** command to check whether the Pod named **pod-matching-replicaset** is being managed by the ReplicaSet:

```
kubectl describe pod pod-matching-replicaset
```

You should see output similar to the following:

```
Name:         pod-matching-replicaset
Namespace:    default
Priority:     0
Node:         minikube/10.0.2.15
Start Time:   Sat, 09 Nov 2019 23:23:29 +0100
Labels:       environment=production
Annotations:  <none>
Status:       Running
IP:           172.17.0.4
IPs:
  IP:           172.17.0.4
Controlled By:  ReplicaSet/nginx-replicaset
Containers:
  first-container:
    Container ID:   docker://7b8d0f4660b8b9bf8b54a4886b6db31388e6f142075aae8bcb074d78d7c47810
    Image:          nginx
```

Figure 7.4: Describing the Pod

In the highlighted section of the truncated output, we can see that even though this Pod was created manually before the ReplicaSet event existed, this Pod is now managed by the ReplicaSet itself.

8. Next, we will describe the ReplicaSet to see how many Pod creations were triggered by it:

```
kubectl describe rs nginx-replicaset
```

You should see output similar to the following:

```
Name:           nginx-replicaset
Namespace:      default
Selector:       environment=production
Labels:         app=nginx
Annotations:    <none>
Replicas:       2 current / 2 desired
Pods Status:    2 Running / 0 Waiting / 0 Succeeded / 0 Failed
Pod Template:
  Labels:  environment=production
  Containers:
   nginx-container:
    Image:        nginx
    Port:         <none>
    Host Port:    <none>
    Environment:  <none>
    Mounts:       <none>
  Volumes:        <none>
Events:
  Type    Reason            Age   From                   Message
  ----    ------            ----  ----                   -------
  Normal  SuccessfulCreate  13m   replicaset-controller  Created pod: ngi
nx-replicaset-4dr7s
```

Figure 7.5: Describing the ReplicaSet

9. Run the following command to delete the ReplicaSet for cleanup:

```
kubectl delete rs nginx-replicaset
```

You should see the following response:

```
replicaset.apps "nginx-replicaset" deleted
```

So, we can see that a ReplicaSet is capable of acquiring existing Pods as long as they match the label selector criteria. In cases where there are more matching Pods than the desired count, the ReplicaSet will terminate some of the Pods in order to maintain the total count of running Pods.

Another common operation is horizontally scaling a ReplicaSet that you previously created. Let's say that you create a ReplicaSet with a certain number of replicas and later you need to have more or fewer replicas to manage increased or decreased demand. Let's see how you can scale the number of replicas in the next exercise.

EXERCISE 7.04: SCALING A REPLICASET AFTER IT IS CREATED

In this exercise, we will create a ReplicaSet with two replicas and then modify it to increase the number of replicas. Then, we will reduce the number of replicas.

In order to successfully complete this exercise, perform the following steps:

1. Create a file called **replicaset-nginx.yaml** with the following content:

```
apiVersion: apps/v1
kind: ReplicaSet
metadata:
  name: nginx-replicaset
  labels:
    app: nginx
spec:
  replicas: 2
  selector:
    matchLabels:
      environment: production
  template:
    metadata:
      labels:
        environment: production
    spec:
      containers:
      - name: nginx-container
        image: nginx
```

2. Run the following command to create the ReplicaSet using the **kubectl apply** command, as described in the preceding code:

```
kubectl apply -f replicaset-nginx.yaml
```

You should get the following response:

```
replicaset.apps/nginx-replicaset created
```

3. Run the following command to check all the existing Pods:

```
kubectl get pods
```

You should get a response similar to the following:

```
NAME                      READY    STATUS    RESTARTS    AGE
nginx-replicaset-99tj7    1/1      Running   0           23s
nginx-replicaset-s4stt    1/1      Running   0           23s
```

We can see that there are two Pods created by the replica set.

4. Run the following command to scale up the number of replicas for the ReplicaSet to **4**:

```
kubectl scale --replicas=4 rs nginx-replicaset
```

You should see the following response:

```
replicaset.apps/nginx-replicaset scaled
```

5. Run the following command to check all the Pods that are running:

```
kubectl get pods
```

You should see output similar to the following:

```
NAME                      READY    STATUS    RESTARTS    AGE
nginx-replicaset-99tj7    1/1      Running   0           75s
nginx-replicaset-klh6k    1/1      Running   0           21s
nginx-replicaset-lrqsk    1/1      Running   0           21s
nginx-replicaset-s4stt    1/1      Running   0           75s
```

We can see that now there are a total of four Pods. The ReplicaSet created two new Pods after we applied the new configuration.

6. Next, let's run the following command to scale down the number of replicas to **1**:

```
kubectl scale --replicas=1 rs nginx-replicaset
```

   You should see the following response:

```
replicaset.apps/nginx-replicaset scaled
```

7. Run the following command to check all the Pods that are running:

```
kubectl get pods
```

   You should see a response similar to the following:

```
nginx-replicaset-s4stt   1/1       Running   0           11m
```

   We can see that this time, the ReplicaSet deleted all the Pods exceeding the count from the desired count of **1** and kept only one replica running.

8. Run the following command to delete the ReplicaSet for cleanup:

```
kubectl delete rs nginx-replicaset
```

   You should see the following response:

```
replicaset.apps "nginx-replicaset" deleted
```

In this exercise, we have managed to scale the number of replicas up and down. This could be particularly useful if the traffic to your application grows or decreases for any reason.

DEPLOYMENT

A Deployment is a Kubernetes object that acts as a wrapper around a ReplicaSet and makes it easier to use. In general, in order to manage replicated services, it's recommended that you use Deployments that, in turn, manage the ReplicaSet and the Pods created by the ReplicaSet.

The major motivation for using a Deployment is that it maintains a history of revisions. Every time a change is made to the ReplicaSet or the underlying Pods, a new revision of the ReplicaSet is recorded by the Deployment. This way, using a Deployment makes it easy to roll back to a previous state or version. Keep in mind that every rollback will also create a new revision for the Deployment. The following diagram provides an overview of the hierarchy of the different objects managing your containerized application:

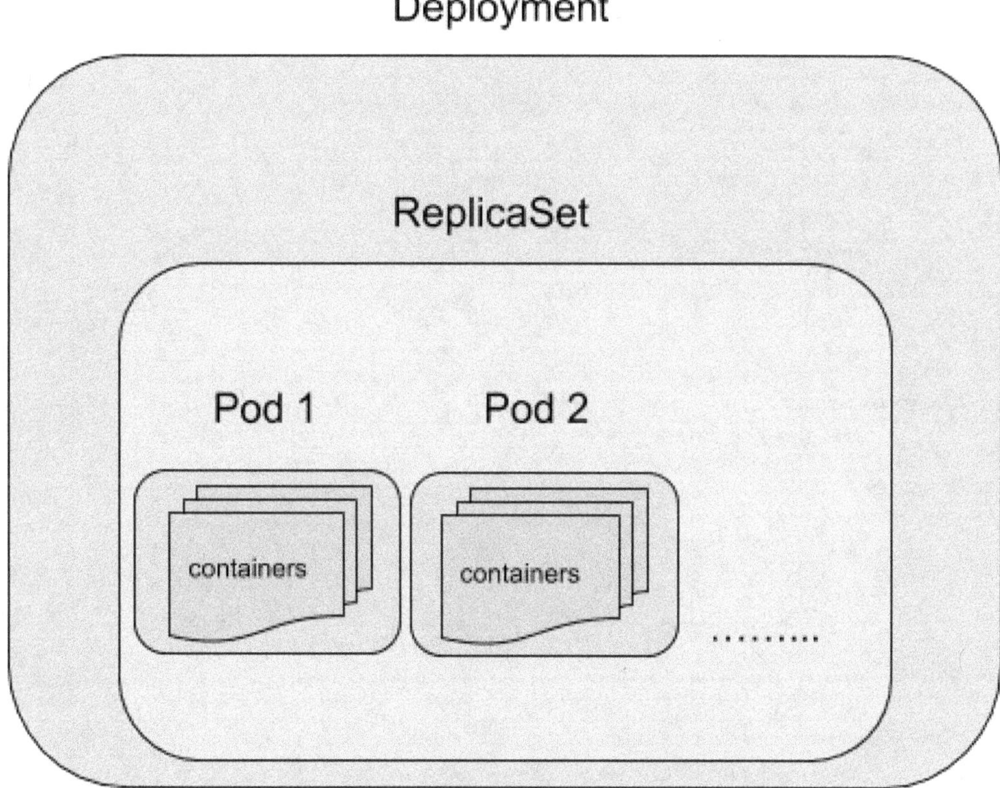

Figure 7.6: Hierarchy of Deployment, ReplicaSet, Pods, and containers

DEPLOYMENT CONFIGURATION

The configuration of a Deployment is actually very similar to that of a ReplicaSet. Here's an example of a Deployment configuration:

```
apiVersion: apps/v1
kind: Deployment
metadata:
  name: nginx-deployment
  labels:
    app: nginx
spec:
  replicas: 3
  strategy:
    type: RollingUpdate
    rollingUpdate:
      maxUnavailable: 1
      maxSurge: 1
  selector:
    matchLabels:
      app: nginx
      environment: production
  template:
    metadata:
      labels:
        app: nginx
        environment: production
    spec:
      containers:
      - name: nginx-container
        image: nginx
```

The value for the **`kind`** field is **`Deployment`**. The rest of the configuration remains the same as that for ReplicaSets. Deployments also have the **`replicas`**, **`selector`**, and Pod **`template`** fields used in the same way as ReplicaSets.

STRATEGY

In the **strategy** field under **spec**, we can specify which strategy the Deployment should use when it replaces old pods with new ones. This can either be **RollingUpdate** or **Recreate**. The default value is **RollingUpdate**.

RollingUpdate

This is a strategy used to update a Deployment without having any downtime. With the **RollingUpdate** strategy, the controller updates the Pods one by one. Hence, at any given time, there will always be some Pods running. This strategy is particularly helpful when you want to update the Pod template without incurring any downtime for your application. However, be aware that having a rolling update means that there may be two different versions of Pods (old and new) running at the same time.

If applications serve static information, this is usually fine because there's usually no harm in serving traffic using two different versions of an application, so long as the information that is served is the same. So, **RollingUpdate** is usually a good strategy for these applications. In general, we can use **RollingUpdate** for applications for which the data stored by a new version can be read and handled by the old version of the application.

Here's an example configuration for setting the strategy to **RollingUpdate**:

```
strategy:
  type: RollingUpdate
  rollingUpdate:
    maxUnavailable: 1
    maxSurge: 1
```

maxUnavailable is the maximum number of Pods that can be unavailable during the update. This field can be specified as either an integer representing the maximum number of unavailable Pods or a string representing the percentage of total replicas that can be unavailable. For the preceding example configuration, Kubernetes will ensure that no more than one replica becomes unavailable while applying an update. The default value for **maxUnavailable** is **25%**.

maxSurge is the maximum number of Pods that can be scheduled/created above the desired number of Pods (as specified in the **replicas** field). This field can also be specified as either an integer or a percentage string, as with **maxUnavailable**. The default value for **maxSurge** is also **25%**.

Hence, in the preceding example, we are telling the Kubernetes controller to update the Pods one at a time, in such a way that no more than one Pod is ever unavailable and that no more than four Pods are ever scheduled.

The two parameters—**maxUnavailable** and **maxSurge**—can be tuned for availability and the speed of scaling up or down the Deployment. For example, **maxUnavailable: 0** and **maxSurge: "30%"** ensure a rapid scale-up while maintaining the desired capacity at all times. **maxUnavailable: "15%"** and **maxSurge: 0** ensure that the deployment can be performed without using any extra capacity at the cost of having, at worst, 15% fewer Pods running.

Recreate

In this strategy, all the existing pods are killed before creating the new Pods with an updated configuration. This means there will be some downtime during the update. This, however, ensures that all the Pods running in the Deployment will be on the same version (old or new). This strategy is particularly useful when working with application Pods that need to have a shared state and so we can't have two different versions of Pods running at the same time. This strategy can be specified as follows:

```
strategy:
  type: Recreate
```

A good use case for using the **Recreate** update strategy is if we need to run some data migration or data processing before the new code can be used. In this case, we will need to use the **Recreate** strategy because we can't afford to have any new code running along with the old one without running the migration or processing first for all the Pods.

Now that we have studied the different fields in the configuration of a Deployment, let's implement them in the following exercise.

EXERCISE 7.05: CREATING A SIMPLE DEPLOYMENT WITH NGINX CONTAINERS

In this exercise, we will create our first Deployment Pod using the configuration described in the previous section.

To successfully complete this exercise, perform the following steps:

1. Create a file called **nginx-deployment.yaml** with the following content:

```
apiVersion: apps/v1
kind: Deployment
metadata:
  name: nginx-deployment
  labels:
    app: nginx
spec:
  replicas: 3
  selector:
    matchLabels:
      app: nginx
      environment: production
  template:
    metadata:
      labels:
        app: nginx
        environment: production
    spec:
      containers:
      - name: nginx-container
        image: nginx
```

   In this configuration, we can see that the Deployment will have three replicas of Pods running with the **app: nginx** and **environment: production** labels.

2. Run the following command to create the Deployment defined in the previous step:

```
kubectl apply -f nginx-deployment.yaml
```

You should see the following response:

```
deployment.apps/nginx-deployment created
```

3. Run the following command to check the status of the Deployment:

```
kubectl get deployment nginx-deployment
```

You should see a response similar to the following:

```
NAME               READY    UP-TO-DATE    AVAILABLE    AGE
nginx-deployment   3/3      3             3            26m
```

4. Run the following command to check all the Pods that are running:

```
kubectl get pods
```

You should see a response similar to the following:

```
NAME                                 READY   STATUS    RESTARTS   AGE
nginx-deployment-588765684f-6wkkc    1/1     Running   0          19s
nginx-deployment-588765684f-7hq4q    1/1     Running   0          19s
nginx-deployment-588765684f-82wpf    1/1     Running   0          19s
```

Figure 7.7: A list of Pods created by the Deployment

We can see that the Deployment has created three Pods, as desired.

Let's try to understand the names given to the Pods automatically. **nginx-deployment** creates a ReplicaSet named **nginx-deployment-588765684f**. The ReplicaSet then creates three replicas of Pods, each of which has a name that is prefixed with the name of the ReplicaSet followed by a unique identifier.

5. Now that we have created our first Deployment, let's look at it in more detail to understand what actually happened during its creation. To do that, we can describe the Deployment we just created using the following command in the terminal:

```
kubectl describe rs nginx-deployment
```

You should see output similar to this:

```
Name:                   nginx-deployment
Namespace:              default
CreationTimestamp:      Sun, 10 Nov 2019 01:06:20 +0100
Labels:                 app=nginx
Annotations:            deployment.kubernetes.io/revision: 1
                        kubectl.kubernetes.io/last-applied-configuration:
                          {"apiVersion":"apps/v1","kind":"Deployment","metadata":{"a
nnotations":{},"labels":{"app":"nginx"},"name":"nginx-deployment","namespace":"d...
Selector:               app=nginx,environment=production
Replicas:               3 desired | 3 updated | 3 total | 3 available | 0 unavailabl
e
StrategyType:           RollingUpdate
MinReadySeconds:        0
RollingUpdateStrategy:  25% max unavailable, 25% max surge
Pod Template:
  Labels:  app=nginx
           environment=production
  Containers:
   nginx-container:
    Image:        nginx
    Port:         <none>
    Host Port:    <none>
    Environment:  <none>
    Mounts:       <none>
  Volumes:        <none>
Conditions:
  Type           Status  Reason
  ----           ------  ------
  Available      True    MinimumReplicasAvailable
  Progressing    True    NewReplicaSetAvailable
OldReplicaSets:  <none>
NewReplicaSet:   nginx-deployment-588765684f (3/3 replicas created)
Events:
  Type    Reason             Age   From                   Message
  ----    ------             ----  ----                   -------
  Normal  ScalingReplicaSet  38s   deployment-controller  Scaled up replica set ngin
x-deployment-588765684f to 3
```

Figure 7.8: Describing nginx-deployment

This output shows various details about the Deployment we just created. In the following subtopics, we will go through the highlighted sections of the preceding output to understand the Deployment that's running.

LABELS AND ANNOTATIONS ON THE DEPLOYMENT

Similar to ReplicaSets, we can see the following line highlighted in the output shown in *Figure 7.8*:

```
Labels:     app=nginx
```

This indicates that the Deployment was created with an **app=nginx** label. Now, let's consider the next field in the output:

```
Annotations:     deployment.kubernetes.io/revision: 1
                 kubectl.kubernetes.io/last-applied-configuration:
{"apiVersion":"apps/v1","kind":"Deployment","metadata":{"annotations":{},
"labels":{"app":"nginx"},"name":"nginx-deployment","namespace":"d...
```

There are two annotations added to the Deployment automatically.

The Revision annotation

The Kubernetes controller adds an annotation with the **deployment.kubernetes.io/revision** key, which contains information about how many revisions have been there for a particular Deployment.

The last-applied-configuration annotation

Another annotation added by the controller has the **kubectl.kubernetes.io/last-applied-configuration** key, which contains the last configuration (in JSON format) that was applied to the Deployment. This annotation is particularly helpful in rolling back a Deployment to a previous revision if a new revision doesn't work well.

SELECTORS FOR THE DEPLOYMENT

Now, consider the following line from the output shown in *Figure 7.8*:

```
Selector:     app=nginx,environment=production
```

This shows which Pod selectors the Deployment is configured with. So, this Deployment will try to acquire the Pods that have both of these labels.

REPLICAS

Consider the following line from the output shown in *Figure 7.8*:

```
Replicas:     3 desired | 3 updated | 3 total | 3 available | 0
unavailable
```

We can see that the Deployment has the desired count of **3** for the Pods, and it also shows that there are currently **3** replicas present.

ROLLING BACK A DEPLOYMENT

In a real-life scenario, you may make a mistake when making a change in the Deployment configuration. You can easily undo a change and roll back to a previous stable revision of the Deployment.

We can use the **kubectl rollout** command to check the revision history and rollback. But to make this work, we also need to use the **--record** flag when we use any **apply** or **set** commands to modify the Deployment. This flag records the rollout history. Then, you can view the rollout history using the following command:

```
kubectl rollout history deployment <deployment_name>
```

Then, we can undo any updates by using the following command:

```
kubectl rollout undo deployment <deployment_name>
```

Let's take a closer look at how this works in the following exercise:

EXERCISE 7.06: ROLLING BACK A DEPLOYMENT

In this exercise, we will update the Deployment twice. We will make an intentional mistake in the second update and try to roll back to a previous revision:

1. Create a file called **app-deployment.yaml** with the following content:

```
apiVersion: apps/v1
kind: Deployment
metadata:
  name: app-deployment
  labels:
    environment: production
spec:
  replicas: 3
  selector:
    matchLabels:
      app: nginx
      environment: production
  template:
    metadata:
      labels:
```

```
        app: nginx
        environment: production
    spec:
      containers:
      - name: nginx-container
        image: nginx
```

2. Run the following command to create the Deployment:

```
kubectl apply -f app-deployment.yaml
```

You should see the following response:

```
deployment.apps/app-deployment created
```

3. Run the following command to check the rollout history of the newly created Deployment:

```
kubectl rollout history deployment app-deployment
```

You should see the following response:

```
deployment.apps/app-deployment
REVISION     CHANGE-CAUSE
1            <none>
```

This output shows that the Deployment has no rollout history as of now.

4. For the first update, let's change the name of the container to **nginx** instead of **nginx-container**. Update the content of the **app-deployment.yaml** file with the following:

```
apiVersion: apps/v1
kind: Deployment
metadata:
  name: app-deployment
  labels:
    environment: production
spec:
  replicas: 3
  selector:
    matchLabels:
      app: nginx
      environment: production
  template:
    metadata:
```

```
      labels:
        app: nginx
        environment: production
    spec:
      containers:
      - name: nginx
        image: nginx
```

As you can see, the only thing that has changed in this template is the container name.

5. Apply the changed configuration using the **kubectl apply** command with the **--record** flag. The **--record** flag ensures that the update to the Deployment is recorded in the rollout history of the Deployment:

```
kubectl apply -f app-deployment.yaml --record
```

You should see the following response:

```
deployment.apps/app-deployment configured
```

Note that the rollout history maintained by the **--record** flag is different from the past configs stored in the annotations, which we saw in the *Labels and Annotations on the Deployment* subsection.

6. Wait for a few seconds to allow the Deployment to recreate the Pods with the updated Pod configuration, and then run the following command to check the rollout history of the Deployment:

```
kubectl rollout history deployment app-deployment
```

You should see the following response:

```
deployment.apps/app-deployment
REVISION  CHANGE-CAUSE
1         <none>
2         kubectl apply --filename=app-deployment.yaml --record=true
```

Figure 7.9: Checking the deployment history

In the output, we can see that the second revision of the Deployment was created. It also keeps track of what command was used to update the Deployment.

7. Next, let's update the Deployment and assume that we made a mistake while doing so. In this example, we will update the container image to **ngnx** (note the intentional spelling error) instead of **nginx** using the **set image** command:

```
kubectl set image deployment app-deployment nginx=ngnx --record
```

You should see the following response:

```
deployment.apps/app-deployment image updated
```

8. Wait for a few seconds for Kubernetes to recreate the new containers, and then check the status of the Deployment rollout using the **kubectl rollout status** command:

```
kubectl rollout status deployment app-deployment
```

You should see the following response:

```
Waiting for deployment "app-deployment" rollout to finish: 1 out of 3
new replicas have been updated...
```

In this output, we can see that none of the new replicas are ready yet. Press *Ctrl* + *C* to exit and proceed.

9. Run the following command to check the state of the Pods:

```
kubectl get pods
```

You should see the following output:

```
NAME                              READY   STATUS             RESTARTS   AGE
app-deployment-6d85cc6748-8n5h9   0/1     ImagePullBackOff   0          2m42s
app-deployment-d4f979c99-6qltn    1/1     Running            0          4m
app-deployment-d4f979c99-ts6n8    1/1     Running            0          3m57s
app-deployment-d4f979c99-zpbrf    1/1     Running            0          3m54s
```

Figure 7.10: Checking the status of Pods

We can see in the output that the newly created Pod has failed with an **ImagePullBackOff** error, which means that the Pods aren't able to pull the image. This is expected because we have a typo in the name of the image.

10. Next, check the revision history of the Deployment again by using the following command:

```
kubectl rollout history deployment app-deployment
```

You should see the following response:

```
deployment.apps/app-deployment
REVISION  CHANGE-CAUSE
1         <none>
2         kubectl apply --filename=app-deployment.yaml --record=true
3         kubectl set image deployment app-deployment nginx=ngnx --record=true
```

Figure 7.11: Checking the rollout history of the Deployment

We can see that a third revision of the Deployment was created using the **set image** command containing the typo. Now that we have pretended to have made a mistake in updating the Deployment, we will see how to undo this and roll back to the last stable revision of the Deployment.

11. Run the following command to roll back to the previous revision:

```
kubectl rollout undo deployment app-deployment
```

You should see the following response:

```
deployment.apps/app-deployment rolled back
```

As we can see in this output, the Deployment has not been rolled back to the previous revision. To practice, we may want to roll back to a revision different from the previous revision. We can use the **--to-revision** flag to specify the revision number to which we want to roll back. For example, in the preceding case, we could have used the following command and the result would have been exactly the same:

```
kubectl rollout undo deployment app-deployment --to-revision=2
```

12. Run the following command to check the rollout history of the Deployment again:

```
kubectl rollout history deployment app-deployment
```

You should see the following output:

```
deployment.apps/app-deployment
REVISION  CHANGE-CAUSE
1         <none>
3         kubectl set image deployment app-deployment nginx=ngnx --record=true
4         kubectl apply --filename=app-deployment.yaml --record=true
```

Figure 7.12: The rollout history for the Deployment after rollback

We can see in this output that a new revision was created, which applied the revision that was previously revision 2. We can see that revision 2 is no longer present in the list of revisions. This is because rollouts are always done in a rolling-forward manner. This means that any time we update a revision, a new revision of a higher number is created. Similarly, in the case of a rollback to revision 2, revision 2 became revision 4.

In this exercise, we explored a lot of different possible operations relating to updating a Deployment, rolling it forward with some changes, tracking the history of a Deployment, undoing some changes, and rolling back to a previous revision.

STATEFULSETS

StatefulSets are used to manage stateful replicas. Similar to a Deployment, a StatefulSet creates and manages the specified number of Pod replicas from an identical Pod template. However, where StatefulSets differ from Deployments is that they maintain a unique identity for each of their Pods. So, even if all the Pods are of identical specs, they are not interchangeable. Each of the Pods has a sticky identity that can be used by the application code to manage the state of the application on a particular Pod. For a StatefulSet with *n* replicas, each Pod is assigned a unique integer ordinal between *0* and *n – 1*. The names of the Pods reflect the integer identity assigned to them. When a StatefulSet is created, all the Pods are created in the order of their integer ordinal.

Each of the Pods managed by a StatefulSet will persist their sticky identity (integer ordinal) even if the Pod restarts. For example, if a particular Pod crashes or is deleted, a new Pod will be created and assigned the same sticky identity as that of the old Pod.

STATEFULSET CONFIGURATION

The configuration of a StatefulSet is also very similar to that of a ReplicaSet. Here's an example of StatefulSet configuration:

```
apiVersion: apps/v1
kind: StatefulSet
metadata:
  name: example-statefulset
spec:
  replicas: 3
  selector:
    matchLabels:
      environment: production
```

```
template:
  metadata:
    labels:
      environment: production
  spec:
    containers:
    - name: name-container
      image: image_name
```

As we can see in the preceding configuration, **apiVersion** for a StatefulSet is **apps/v1** and **kind** is **StatefulSet**. The rest of the fields are used in the same way as for ReplicaSets.

> **NOTE**
>
> You will learn how to implement StatefulSets on a multi-node cluster in *Chapter 14, Running Stateful Components in Kubernetes*.

USE CASES FOR STATEFULSETS

- StatefulSets are useful if you need persistent storage. Using a StatefulSet, you can partition the data and store it in different Pods. In this case, it would also be possible for a Pod to go down and a new Pod come up with the same identity and have the same partition of data previously stored by the old Pod.
- A StatefulSet can also be used if you require ordered updates or scaling. For example, if you want to create or update your Pods in the order of the identities assigned to them, using a StatefulSet is a good idea.

DAEMONSETS

DaemonSets are used to manage the creation of a particular Pod on all or a selected set of nodes in a cluster. If we configure a DaemonSet to create Pods on all nodes, then if new nodes are added to the cluster, new pods will be created to run on these new nodes. Similarly, if some nodes are removed from the cluster, the Pods running on these nodes will be destroyed.

USE CASES FOR DAEMONSETS

- Logging: One of the most common use cases for a DaemonSet is to manage running a log collection Pod on all nodes. These Pods can be used to collect logs from all the nodes and then process them in a log processing pipeline.
- Local data caching: A DaemonSet can also be used to manage caching Pods on all the nodes. These Pods can be used by other application Pods to store the cached data temporarily.
- Monitoring: Another use case for a DaemonSet is to manage running monitoring Pods on all the nodes. This can be used to collect system- or application-level metrics for Pods running on a particular node.

DAEMONSET CONFIGURATION

The configuration of a DaemonSet is also very similar to that of a ReplicaSet or a Deployment. Here's an example of DaemonSet configuration:

```
apiVersion: apps/v1
kind: DaemonSet
metadata:
  name: daemonset-example
  labels:
    app: daemonset-example
spec:
  selector:
    matchLabels:
      app: daemonset-example
  template:
    metadata:
      labels:
        app: daemonset-example
    spec:
      containers:
      - name: busybox-container
        image: busybox
        args:
        - /bin/sh
        - -c
        - sleep 10000
```

As we can see in the preceding configuration, **`apiVersion`** for a DaemonSet is set to **`apps/v1`** and **`kind`** is set to **`DaemonSet`**. The rest of the fields are used in the same way as for ReplicaSets.

To limit the scope of this book, we will not cover the details for implementing DaemonSets.

Up until now in this chapter, you have learned about ReplicaSets, which help us manage several replicas of Pods running an application, and how a Deployment acts as a wrapper on a ReplicaSet to add some features to control rolling out updates and maintaining the update history, with the option of rolling back if needed. Then, we learned about StatefulSets, which are handy if we need to treat each replica as a unique entity. We also learned how DaemonSets allow us to schedule a Pod on each of our nodes.

All of these controllers have one common characteristic—they are useful for applications or workloads that are to be run continually. However, some workloads have a graceful conclusion, and there is no need to keep the Pods running after the task is done. For this, Kubernetes has a controller called a Job. Let's take a look at this in the following section.

JOBS

A Job is a supervisor in Kubernetes that can be used to manage Pods that are supposed to run a determined task and then terminate gracefully. A Job creates the specified number of Pods and ensures that they successfully complete their workloads or tasks. When a Job is created, it creates and tracks the Pods that were specified in its configuration. When a specified number of Pods complete successfully, the Job is considered complete. If a Pod fails because of underlying node failures, the Job will create a new Pod to replace it. This also means that the application or code running on the Pod should be capable of gracefully handling a case where a new Pod comes up during the runtime of the process.

The Pods created by a Job aren't deleted following completion of the job. The Pods run to completion and stay in the cluster with a **`Completed`** status.

A Job can be used in several different ways:

- The simplest use case is to create a Job that runs only one Pod to completion. The Job will only create additional new Pods if the running pod fails. For example, a Job can be used for one-off or recurring data analysis work or for the training of a machine learning model.
- Jobs can also be used for parallel processing. We can specify more than one successful Pod completion to ensure that the Job will complete only when a certain number of Pods have terminated successfully.

JOB CONFIGURATION

The configuration of a Job follows a similar pattern to that of a ReplicaSet or a Deployment. Here's an example of Job configuration:

```
apiVersion: batch/v1
kind: Job
metadata:
  name: one-time-job
spec:
  template:
    spec:
      containers:
      - name: busybox-container
        image: busybox
        args:
        - /bin/sh
        - -c
        - date
      restartPolicy: OnFailure
```

The **`apiVersion`** field for a Job object is set to **`batch/v1`**. The **`batch`** API group contains objects relating to batch processing jobs. The **`kind`** field is set to **`Job`**.

A USE CASE FOR JOBS IN MACHINE LEARNING

Jobs are perfect for batch processes—processes that run for a certain amount of time before exiting. This makes Jobs ideal for many types of production machine learning tasks, such as feature engineering, cross-validation, model training, and batch inference. For instance, you can create a Kubernetes Job that trains a machine learning model and persists the model and training metadata to external storage. Then, you can create another Job to perform batch inference. This Job would create a Pod that fetches the pre-trained model from storage, loads both the model and data into memory, performs inference, and stores the predictions.

EXERCISE 7.07: CREATING A SIMPLE JOB THAT FINISHES IN FINITE TIME

In this exercise, we will create our first Job, which will run a container that simply waits for 10 seconds and then finishes.

To successfully complete this exercise, perform the following steps:

1. Create a file called **`one-time-job.yaml`** with the following content:

```
apiVersion: batch/v1
kind: Job
metadata:
  name: one-time-job
spec:
  template:
    spec:
      containers:
      - name: busybox-container
        image: busybox
        args:
        - /bin/sh
        - -c
        - date; sleep 20; echo "Bye"
      restartPolicy: OnFailure
```

2. Run the following command to create the Deployment using the **`kubectl apply`** command:

```
kubectl apply -f one-time-job.yaml
```

You should see the following response:

```
job.batch/one-time-job created
```

3. Run the following command to check the status of the Job:

```
kubectl get jobs
```

You should see a response similar to this:

```
NAME           COMPLETIONS    DURATION    AGE
one-time-job   0/1            3s          3s
```

We can see that the Job requires one completion and is not yet completed.

4. Run the following command to check the Pod running the Job:

```
kubectl get pods
```

Note that you should run this before the Job is complete to see the response shown here:

```
NAME                 READY     STATUS     RESTARTS     AGE
one-time-job-bzz8l   1/1       Running    0            7s
```

We can see that the Job has created a Pod named **one-time-job-bzz8l** to run the task specified in the Job template.

5. Next, run the following command to check the logs for the Pod created by the Job:

```
kubectl logs -f <pod_name>
```

You should see logs similar to the following:

```
Sun   Nov 10 15:20:19 UTC 2019
Bye
```

We can see that the Pod printed the date, waited for 20 seconds, and then printed **Bye** in the terminal.

6. Let's check the status of the Job again by using the following command:

```
kubectl get job one-time-job
```

You should see a response similar to this:

```
NAME           COMPLETIONS    DURATION    AGE
one-time-job   1/1            24s         14m
```

We can see that the Job has now been completed.

7. Run the following command to verify that the Pod has run to completion:

```
kubectl get pods
```

You should see a response similar to this:

```
NAME                 READY     STATUS      RESTARTS    AGE
one-time-job-whw79   0/1       Completed   0           32m
```

We can see that the Pod has a **Completed** status.

8. Run the following command to delete the job (as well as the Pod it created) for cleanup:

```
kubectl delete job one-time-job
```

You should see the following response:

```
job.batch "one-time-job" deleted
```

In this exercise, we created a one-time Job and verified that the Pod created by the Job runs to completion. Implementing Jobs for parallel tasks is a bit more complicated, and we will leave that out of this workshop for brevity.

Next, let's wrap this chapter up with an activity where we will create a Deployment and bring together several ideas learned in this chapter.

ACTIVITY 7.01: CREATING A DEPLOYMENT RUNNING AN APPLICATION

Consider a scenario where the product/application team you're working with is now ready to put their application in production and they need your help to deploy it in a replicated and reliable manner. For the scope of this exercise, consider the following requirements for the application:

- The default number of replicas should be 6.
- For simplicity, you can use the **nginx** image for the container running in the Pod.
- Make sure all the Pods have the following two labels with corresponding values:

```
chapter=controllers
activity=1
```

- The update strategy for the Deployment should be **RollingUpdate**. At worst, no more than half of the Pods can be down, and similarly, at no point should there be more than 150% of the desired count of Pods.

You should be able to perform the following tasks once the Deployment has been created:

- Scale up the number of replicas to 10.
- Scale down the number of replicas to 5.

> **NOTE**
>
> Ideally, you would want to create this Deployment to be in a different namespace to keep it separate from the rest of the stuff that you created during the previous exercises. So, feel free to create a namespace and create the Deployment in that namespace.

The following are the high-level steps to perform this activity:

1. Create a namespace for this activity.
2. Write the Deployment configuration. Ensure that it meets all the requirements that are specified.
3. Create the Deployment using the configuration from the previous step.
4. Verify that six Pods were created by the Deployment.
5. Perform both of the tasks mentioned previously and verify the number of Pods after performing each step.

You should be able to get the list of Pods to check whether you can scale up the number of Pods, as shown in the following image:

```
NAME                                  READY   STATUS    RESTARTS   AGE
activity-deployment-54b9c6ff99-45shk  1/1     Running   0          4m39s
activity-deployment-54b9c6ff99-57kls  1/1     Running   0          18s
activity-deployment-54b9c6ff99-cl2hc  1/1     Running   0          4m39s
activity-deployment-54b9c6ff99-dswsb  1/1     Running   0          18s
activity-deployment-54b9c6ff99-g6t7v  1/1     Running   0          4m39s
activity-deployment-54b9c6ff99-h2vb2  1/1     Running   0          4m39s
activity-deployment-54b9c6ff99-njnzc  1/1     Running   0          4m39s
activity-deployment-54b9c6ff99-vl2md  1/1     Running   0          18s
activity-deployment-54b9c6ff99-z2fxg  1/1     Running   0          4m39s
activity-deployment-54b9c6ff99-zp5zj  1/1     Running   0          18s
```

Figure 7.13: Checking whether the number of Pods is scaled up

Similarly, you should also be able to scale down and check the number of Pods, as shown here:

```
NAME                                  READY   STATUS    RESTARTS   AGE
activity-deployment-54b9c6ff99-45shk  1/1     Running   0          9m14s
activity-deployment-54b9c6ff99-cl2hc  1/1     Running   0          9m14s
activity-deployment-54b9c6ff99-g6t7v  1/1     Running   0          9m14s
activity-deployment-54b9c6ff99-h2vb2  1/1     Running   0          9m14s
activity-deployment-54b9c6ff99-njnzc  1/1     Running   0          9m14s
```

Figure 7.14: Checking whether the number of Pods is scaled down

> **NOTE**
>
> The solution to this activity can be found at the following address: https://packt.live/304PEoD.

SUMMARY

Kubernetes treats Pods as ephemeral entities, and ideally you would not deploy any application or a microservice in an individual Pod. Kubernetes offers various controllers to leverage various benefits, including automatic replication, health monitoring, and automatic scaling.

In this chapter, we covered different kinds of controllers and understood when to use each of them. We created ReplicaSets and observed how they manage Pods. We learned when to use DaemonSets and StatefulSets. We also created a Deployment and learned how we can scale up and down the number of replicas and roll back to an earlier version of the Deployment. Finally, we learned how to create Jobs for one-time tasks. All of these controllers come into play when you want to deploy a production-ready application or workload, as you will see in the upcoming chapters.

In the next chapter, we will see how we can discover and access the Pods or replicas managed by a Deployment or a ReplicaSet.

8

SERVICE DISCOVERY

OVERVIEW

In this chapter, we will take a look at how to route traffic between the various kinds of objects that we have created in previous chapters and make them discoverable from both within and outside our cluster. This chapter also introduces the concept of Kubernetes Services and explains how to use them to expose the application deployed using controllers such as Deployments. By the end of this chapter, you will be able to make your application accessible to the external world. You will also know about the different types of Services and be able to use them to make different sets of pods interact with each other.

INTRODUCTION

In the past few chapters, we learned about Pods and Deployments, which help us run containerized applications. Now that we are equipped to deploy our applications, in this chapter, we will take a look at some API objects that help us with the networking setup to ensure that our users can reach our application and that the different components of our application, as well as different applications, can work together.

As we have seen in the previous chapters, each Kubernetes Pod gets its IP address. However, setting up networking and connecting everything is not as simple as coding in Pod IP addresses. We can't rely on a single Pod to run our applications reliably. Due to this, we use a Deployment to ensure that, at any given moment, we will have a fixed number of specific kinds of Pods running in the cluster. However, this means that during the runtime of our application, we can tolerate the failure of a certain number of Pods as new pods are automatically created to replace them. Hence, the IP addresses of these Pods don't stay the same. For example, if we have a set of Pods running the frontend application that need to talk to another set of Pods running the backend application inside our cluster, we need to find a way to make the Pods discoverable.

To solve this problem, we use Kubernetes Services. Services allow us to make a logical set of Pods (for example, all pods managed by a Deployment) discoverable and accessible for other Pods running inside the same cluster or to the external world.

SERVICE

A Service defines policies by which a logical set of Pods can be accessed. Kubernetes Services enable communication between various components of our application, as well as between different applications. Services help us connect the application with other applications or users. For example, let's say we have a set of Pods running the frontend of an application, a set of Pods running the backend, and another set of Pods connecting the data source. The frontend is the one that users need to interact with directly. The frontend then needs to connect to the backend, which, in turn, needs to talk to the external data source.

Consider you are making a survey app that also allows users to make visualizations based on their survey results. Using a bit of simplification, we can imagine three Deployments – one that runs the forms' frontend to collect the data, another that validates and stores the data, and a third one that runs the data visualization application. The following diagram should help you visualize how Services would come into the picture for routing traffic and exposing different components:

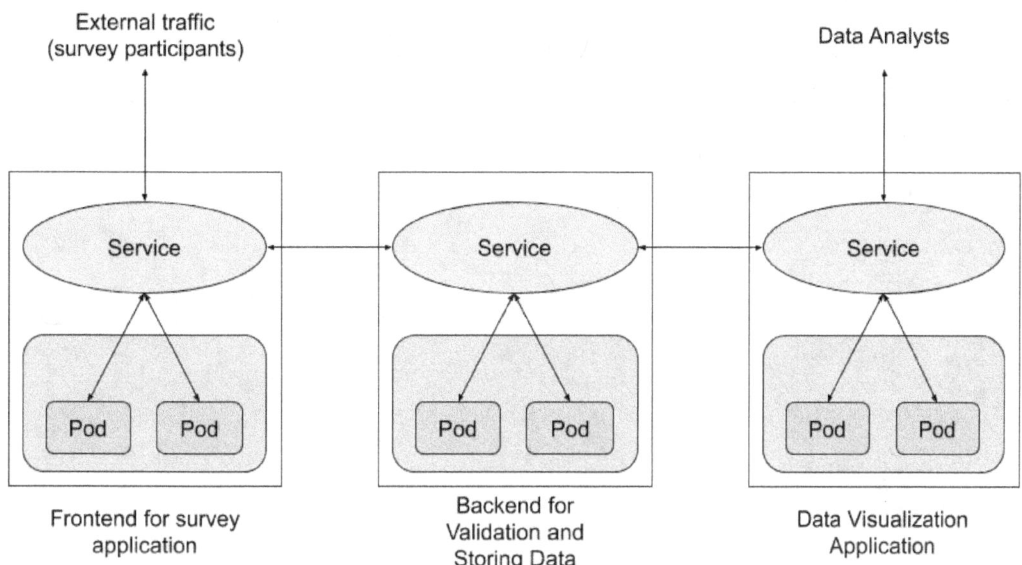

Figure 8.1: Using Services to route traffic into and within the cluster

Hence, the abstraction of Services helps in keeping the different parts of the application decoupled and enables communication between them. In legacy (non-Kubernetes) environments, you may expect different components to be linked together by the IP addresses of different VMs or bare-metal machines running different resources. When working with Kubernetes, the predominant way of linking different resources together is using labels and label selectors, which allows a Deployment to easily replace failed Pods or scale the number of Deployments as needed. Thus, you can think of a Service as a translation layer between the IP addresses and label selector-based mechanism of linking different resources. Hence, you just need to point toward a Service, and it will take care of routing the traffic to the appropriate application, regardless of how many replica Pods are associated with the application or which nodes these Pods are running on.

SERVICE CONFIGURATION

Similar to the configuration of Pods, ReplicaSets, and Deployments, the configuration for a Service also contains four high-level fields; that is, **`apiVersion`**, **`kind`**, **`metadata`**, and **`spec`**.

Here is an example manifest for a Service:

```
apiVersion: v1
kind: Service
metadata:
  name: sample-service
spec:
  ports:
    - port: 80
      targetPort: 80
  selector:
      key: value
```

For a Service, **`apiVersion`** is **`v1`** and **`kind`** will always be **`Service`**. In the **`metadata`** field, we will specify the name of the Service. In addition to the name, we can also add **`labels`** and **`annotations`** in the **`metadata`** field.

The content of the **`spec`** field depends on the type of Service we want to create. In the next section, we will go through the different types of Services and understand various parts of the **`spec`** field regarding the configuration.

TYPES OF SERVICES

There are four different types of Services:

- **NodePort**: This type of Service makes internal Pod(s) accessible on a port on the node on which the Pod(s) are running.
- **ClusterIP**: This type of Service exposes the Service on a certain IP inside the cluster. This is the default type of Service.
- **LoadBalancer**: This type of Service exposes the application externally using the load balancer provided by the cloud provider.
- **ExternalName**: This type of Service points to a DNS rather than a set of Pods. The other types of Services use label selectors to select the Pods to be exposed. This is a special type of Service that doesn't use any selectors by default.

We will take a closer look at all these Services in the following sections.

NODEPORT SERVICE

A NodePort Service exposes the application on the same port on all the nodes in the cluster. The Pods may be running across all or some of the nodes in the cluster.

In a simplified case where there's only one node in the cluster, the Service exposes all the selected Pods on the port configured in the Service. However, in a more practical case, where the Pods may be running on multiple nodes, the Service spans across all the nodes and exposes the Pods on the specific port on all the nodes. This way, the application can be accessed from outside the Kubernetes cluster using the following IP/port combination: **`<NodeIP>:<NodePort>`**.

A **`config`** file for a sample Service would look like this:

```
apiVersion: v1
kind: Service
metadata:
  name: nginx-service
spec:
  type: NodePort
  ports:
    - targetPort: 80
      port: 80
      nodePort: 32023
  selector:
      app: nginx
      environment: production
```

As we can see, there are three ports involved in the definition of a **`NodePort`** Service. Let's take a look at these:

- **`targetPort`**: This field represents the port where the application running on the Pods is exposed. This is the port that the Service forwards the request to. By default, **`targetPort`** is set to the same value as the **`port`** field.
- **`port`**: This field represents the port of the Service itself.
- **`nodePort`**: This field represents the port on the node that we can use to access the Service itself.

Besides the ports, there's also another field called **selector** in the Service **spec** section. This section is used to specify the labels that a Pod needs to have in order to be selected by a Service. Once this Service is created, it will identify all the Pods that have the **app: nginx** and **environment: production** labels and add endpoints for all such Pods. We will look at endpoints in more detail in the following exercise.

EXERCISE 8.01: CREATING A SIMPLE NODEPORT SERVICE WITH NGINX CONTAINERS

In this exercise, we will create a simple NodePort Service with Nginx containers. Nginx containers, by default, expose port **80** on the Pod with an HTML page saying **Welcome to nginx!**. We will make sure that we can access that page from a browser on our local machine.

To successfully complete this exercise, perform the following steps:

1. Create a file called **nginx-deployment.yaml** with the following content:

```
apiVersion: apps/v1
kind: Deployment
metadata:
  name: nginx-deployment
  labels:
    app: nginx
spec:
  replicas: 3
  strategy:
    type: Recreate
  selector:
    matchLabels:
      app: nginx
      environment: production
  template:
    metadata:
      labels:
        app: nginx
        environment: production
    spec:
      containers:
      - name: nginx-container
        image: nginx
```

2. Run the following command to create the Deployment using the **kubectl apply** command:

```
kubectl apply -f nginx-deployment.yaml
```

You should get the following output:

```
deployment.apps/nginx-deployment created
```

As we can see, **nginx-deployment** has been created.

3. Run the following command to verify that the Deployment has created three replicas:

```
kubectl get pods
```

You should see a response similar to the following:

```
NAME                               READY   STATUS    RESTARTS   AGE
nginx-deployment-588765684f-4dzvv  1/1     Running   0          113s
nginx-deployment-588765684f-n8ltl  1/1     Running   0          113s
nginx-deployment-588765684f-qxcqh  1/1     Running   0          113s
```

Figure 8.2: Getting all Pods

4. Create a file called **nginx-service-nodeport.yaml** with the following content:

```
apiVersion: v1
kind: Service
metadata:
  name: nginx-service-nodeport
spec:
  type: NodePort
  ports:
    - port: 80
      targetPort: 80
      nodePort: 32023
  selector:
      app: nginx
      environment: production
```

5. Run the following command to create the Service:

```
kubectl create -f nginx-service-nodeport.yaml
```

You should see the following output:

```
service/nginx-service-nodeport created
```

Alternatively, we can use the **kubectl expose** command to expose a Deployment or a Pod using a Kubernetes Service. The following command will also create a NodePort Service named **nginx-service-nodeport**, with **port** and **targetPort** set to **80**. The only difference is that this command doesn't allow us to customize the **nodePort** field. **nodePort** is automatically allocated when we create the Service using the **kubectl expose** command:

```
kubectl expose deployment nginx-deployment --name=nginx-service-
nodeport --port=80 --target-port=80 --type=NodePort
```

If we use this command to create the Service, we will be able to figure out what **nodePort** was automatically assigned to the Service in the following step.

6. Run the following command to verify that the Service was created:

```
kubectl get service
```

This should give a response similar to the following:

NAME	TYPE	CLUSTER-IP	EXTERNAL-IP	PORT(S)	AGE
kubernetes	ClusterIP	10.96.0.1	<none>	443/TCP	54d
nginx-service-nodeport	NodePort	10.97.8.85	<none>	80:32023/TCP	3m21s

Figure 8.3: Getting the NodePort Service

You can ignore the additional Service named **kubernetes**, which already existed before we created our Service. This Service is used to expose the Kubernetes API of the cluster internally.

7. Run the following command to verify that the Service was created with the correct configuration:

```
kubectl describe service nginx-service-nodeport
```

This should give us the following output:

```
Name:                     nginx-service-nodeport
Namespace:                default
Labels:                   <none>
Annotations:              <none>
Selector:                 app=nginx,environment=production
Type:                     NodePort
IP:                       10.97.8.85
Port:                     <unset>  80/TCP
TargetPort:               80/TCP
NodePort:                 <unset>  32023/TCP
Endpoints:                172.17.0.3:80,172.17.0.4:80,172.17.0.5:80
Session Affinity:         None
External Traffic Policy:  Cluster
Events:                   <none>
```

Figure 8.4: Describing the NodePort Service

In the highlighted sections of the output, we can confirm that the Service was created with the correct **`Port`**, **`TargetPort`**, and **`NodePort`** fields.

There's also another field called **`Endpoints`**. We can see that the value of this field is a list of IP addresses; that is, **`172.17.0.3:80`**, **`172.17.0.4:80`**, and **`172.17.0.5:80`**. Each of these IP addresses points to the IP addresses allocated to the three Pods created by **`nginx-deployment`**, along with the target ports exposed by all of those Pods. We can use the **`custom-columns`** output format alongside the **`kubectl get pods`** command to get the IP addresses for all three pods. We can create a custom column output using the **`status.podIP`** field, which contains the IP address of a running Pod.

8. Run the following command to see the IP addresses of all three Pods:

```
kubectl get pods -o custom-columns=IP:status.podIP
```

You should see the following output:

```
IP
172.17.0.4
172.17.0.3
172.17.0.5
```

Hence, we can see that the **`Endpoints`** field of the Service actually points to the IP addresses of our three Pods.

As we know in the case of a NodePort Service, we can access the Pod's application using the IP address of the node and the port exposed by the Service on the node. To do this, we need to find out the IP address of the node in the Kubernetes cluster.

9. Run the following command to get the IP address of the Kubernetes cluster running locally:

```
minikube ip
```

You should see the following response:

```
192.168.99.100
```

10. Run the following command to send a request to the IP address we obtained from the previous step at port **32023** using **curl**:

```
curl 192.168.99.100:32023
```

You should get a response from Nginx like so:

```
<!DOCTYPE html>
<html>
<head>
<title>Welcome to nginx!</title>
<style>
    body {
        width: 35em;
        margin: 0 auto;
        font-family: Tahoma, Verdana, Arial, sans-serif;
    }
</style>
</head>
<body>
<h1>Welcome to nginx!</h1>
<p>If you see this page, the nginx web server is successfully installed and
working. Further configuration is required.</p>

<p>For online documentation and support please refer to
<a href="http://nginx.org/">nginx.org</a>.<br/>
Commercial support is available at
<a href="http://nginx.com/">nginx.com</a>.</p>

<p><em>Thank you for using nginx.</em></p>
</body>
</html>
```

Figure 8.5: Sending a curl request to check the NodePort Service

11. Finally, open your browser and enter **192.168.99.100:32023** to make sure we can get to the following page:

Welcome to nginx!

If you see this page, the nginx web server is successfully installed and working. Further configuration is required.

For online documentation and support please refer to nginx.org.
Commercial support is available at nginx.com.

Thank you for using nginx.

Figure 8.6: Accessing the application in a browser

> **NOTE**
>
> Ideally, you would want to create the objects for each exercise and activity in different namespaces to keep them separate from the rest of your objects. So, feel free to create a namespace and create the Deployment in that namespace. Alternatively, you can ensure that you clean up any objects shown in the following commands so that there is no interference.

12. Delete both the Deployment and the Service to ensure you're working on the clean ground for the rest of the exercises in this chapter:

```
kubectl delete deployment nginx-deployment
```

You should see the following response:

```
deployment.apps "nginx-deployment" deleted
```

Now, delete the Service using the following command:

```
kubectl delete service nginx-service-nodeport
```

You should see this response:

```
service "nginx-service-nodeport" deleted
```

In this exercise, we have created a Deployment with three replicas of the Nginx container (this can be replaced with any real application running in the container) and exposed the application using the NodePort Service.

CLUSTERIP SERVICE

As we mentioned earlier, a ClusterIP Service exposes the application running on the Pods on an IP address that's accessible from inside the cluster only. This makes the ClusterIP Service a good type of Service to use for communication between different types of Pods inside the same cluster.

For example, let's consider our earlier example of a simple survey application. Let's say we have a survey application that serves the frontend to show the forms to the users where they can fill in the surveys. It's running on a set of Pods managed by the **survey-frontend** Deployment. We also have another application that is responsible for validating and storing the data filled by the users. It's running on a set of Pods managed by the **survey-backend** Deployment. This backend application needs to be accessed internally by the survey frontend application. We can use a ClusterIP Service to expose the backend application so that the frontend Pods can easily access the backend application using a single IP address for that ClusterIP Service.

SERVICE CONFIGURATION

Here's an example of what the configuration for a ClusterIP Service looks like:

```
apiVersion: v1
kind: Service
metadata:
  name: nginx-service
spec:
  type: ClusterIP
  ports:
    - targetPort: 80
      port: 80
  selector:
      app: nginx
      environment: production
```

The **type** of Service is set to **ClusterIP**. Only two ports are needed for this type of the Service: **targetPort** and **port**. These represent the port where the application is exposed on the Pod and the port where the Service is created on a given cluster IP, respectively.

Similar to the NodePort Service, the ClusterIP Service's configuration also needs a **selector** section, which is used to decide which Pods to select by the Service. In this example, this Service will select all the Pods that have both **app: nginx** and **environment: production** labels. We will create a simple ClusterIP Service in the following exercise based on a similar example.

EXERCISE 8.02: CREATING A SIMPLE CLUSTERIP SERVICE WITH NGINX CONTAINERS

In this exercise, we will create a simple ClusterIP Service with Nginx containers. Nginx containers, by default, expose port **80** on the Pod with an HTML page saying **Welcome to nginx!**. We will make sure that we can access that page from inside the Kubernetes cluster using the **curl** command. Let's get started:

1. Create a file called **nginx-deployment.yaml** with the following content:

```
apiVersion: apps/v1
kind: Deployment
metadata:
  name: nginx-deployment
  labels:
    app: nginx
spec:
  replicas: 3
  strategy:
    type: Recreate
  selector:
    matchLabels:
      app: nginx
      environment: production
  template:
    metadata:
      labels:
        app: nginx
        environment: production
    spec:
      containers:
      - name: nginx-container
        image: nginx
```

2. Run the following command to create the Deployment using the **kubectl apply** command:

```
kubectl create -f nginx-deployment.yaml
```

You should see the following response:

```
deployment.apps/nginx-deployment created
```

3. Run the following command to verify that the Deployment has created three replicas:

```
kubectl get pods
```

You should see output similar to the following:

```
NAME                                READY   STATUS    RESTARTS   AGE
nginx-deployment-588765684f-cg6n4   1/1     Running   0          43s
nginx-deployment-588765684f-fcsj4   1/1     Running   0          43s
nginx-deployment-588765684f-m5bdk   1/1     Running   0          43s
```

Figure 8.7: Getting all the Pods

4. Create a file called **nginx-service-clusterip.yaml** with the following content:

```
apiVersion: v1
kind: Service
metadata:
  name: nginx-service-clusterip
spec:
  type: ClusterIP
  ports:
    - port: 80
      targetPort: 80
  selector:
      app: nginx
      environment: production
```

5. Run the following command to create the Service:

```
kubectl create -f nginx-service-clusterip.yaml
```

You should see the following response:

```
service/nginx-service-clusterip created
```

6. Run the following command to verify that the Service was created:

```
kubectl get service
```

You should see the following response:

```
NAME                       TYPE        CLUSTER-IP    EXTERNAL-IP   PORT(S)   AGE
kubernetes                 ClusterIP   10.96.0.1     <none>        443/TCP   54d
nginx-service-clusterip    ClusterIP   10.99.11.74   <none>        80/TCP    82m
```

Figure 8.8: Getting the ClusterIP Service

7. Run the following command to verify that the Service has been created with the correct configuration:

```
kubectl describe service nginx-service-clusterip
```

You should see the following response:

```
Name:               nginx-service-clusterip
Namespace:          default
Labels:             <none>
Annotations:        <none>
Selector:           app=nginx,environment=production
Type:               ClusterIP
IP:                 10.99.11.74
Port:               <unset>  80/TCP
TargetPort:         80/TCP
Endpoints:          172.17.0.3:80,172.17.0.4:80,172.17.0.5:80
Session Affinity:   None
Events:             <none>
```

Figure 8.9: Describing the ClusterIP Service

We can see that the Service has been created with the correct **`Port`** and **`TargetPort`** fields. In the **`Endpoints`** field, we can see the IP addresses of the Pods, along with the target ports on those Pods.

8. Run the following command to see the IP addresses of all three Pods:

```
kubectl get pods -o custom-columns=IP:status.podIP
```

You should see the following response:

```
IP
172.17.0.5
172.17.0.3
172.17.0.4
```

Hence, we can see that the **Endpoints** field of the Service actually points to the IP addresses of our three Pods.

9. Run the following command to get the cluster IP of the Service:

```
kubectl get service nginx-service-clusterip
```

This results in the following output:

NAME	TYPE	CLUSTER-IP	EXTERNAL-IP	PORT(S)	AGE
nginx-service-clusterip	ClusterIP	10.99.11.74	<none>	80/TCP	6d6h

Figure 8.10: Getting the cluster IP from the Service

As we can see, the Service has a cluster IP of **10.99.11.74**.

We know that, in the case of a ClusterIP Service, we can access the application running on its endpoints from inside the cluster. So, we need to go inside the cluster to be able to check whether this really works.

10. Run the following command to access the **minikube** node via SSH:

```
minikube ssh
```

You will see the following response:

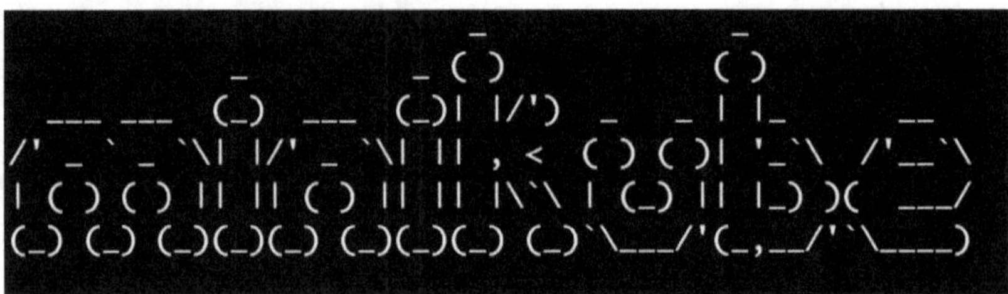

Figure 8.11: SSHing into the minikube node

11. Now that we are inside the cluster, we can try to access the cluster IP address of the Service and see whether we can access the Pods running Nginx:

```
curl 10.99.11.74
```

You should see the following response from Nginx:

```
<!DOCTYPE html>
<html>
<head>
<title>Welcome to nginx!</title>
<style>
    body {
        width: 35em;
        margin: 0 auto;
        font-family: Tahoma, Verdana, Arial, sans-serif;
    }
</style>
</head>
<body>
<h1>Welcome to nginx!</h1>
<p>If you see this page, the nginx web server is successfully installed and
working. Further configuration is required.</p>

<p>For online documentation and support please refer to
<a href="http://nginx.org/">nginx.org</a>.<br/>
Commercial support is available at
<a href="http://nginx.com/">nginx.com</a>.</p>

<p><em>Thank you for using nginx.</em></p>
</body>
</html>
```

Figure 8.12: Sending a curl request to the Service from inside the cluster

Here, we can see that **`curl`** returns the HTML code for the default Nginx landing page. Thus, we can successfully access our Nginx Pods. Next, we will delete the Pods and Services.

12. Run the following command to exit the SSH session inside minikube:

```
exit
```

13. Delete the Deployment and the Service to ensure you're working on the clean ground for the following exercises in this chapter:

```
kubectl delete deployment nginx-deployment
```

You should see the following response:

```
deployment.apps "nginx-deployment" deleted
```

Delete the Service using the following command:

```
kubectl delete service nginx-service-clusterip
```

You should see the following response:

```
service "nginx-service-clusterip" deleted
```

In this exercise, we were able to expose the application running on multiple Pods on a single IP address. This can be accessed by all the other Pods running inside the same cluster.

CHOOSING A CUSTOM IP ADDRESS FOR THE SERVICE

In the previous exercise, we saw that the Service was created with a random available IP address inside the Kubernetes cluster. We can also specify an IP address if we want. This may be particularly useful if we already have a DNS entry for a particular address and we want to reuse that for our Service.

We can do this by setting the **spec.clusterIP** field with a value of the IP address we want the Service to use. The IP address specified in this field should be a valid IPv4 or IPv6 address. If an invalid IP address is used to create the Service, the API server will return an error.

EXERCISE 8.03: CREATING A CLUSTERIP SERVICE WITH A CUSTOM IP

In this exercise, we will create a ClusterIP Service with a custom IP address. We will try a random IP address. As in the previous exercise, we will make sure that we can access the default Nginx page from inside the Kubernetes cluster by using the **curl** command to the set IP address. Let's get started:

1. Create a file called **nginx-deployment.yaml** with the same content that we used in the previous exercises in this chapter.

2. Run the following command to create the Deployment:

```
kubectl create -f nginx-deployment.yaml
```

You should see the following response:

```
deployment.apps/nginx-deployment created
```

3. Create a file named **nginx-service-custom-clusterip.yaml** with the following content:

```
apiVersion: v1
kind: Service
metadata:
  name: nginx-service-custom-clusterip
spec:
  type: ClusterIP
  ports:
    - port: 80
      targetPort: 80
  clusterIP: 10.90.10.70
  selector:
      app: nginx
      environment: production
```

   This uses a random ClusterIP value at the moment.

4. Run the following command to create a Service with the preceding configuration:

```
kubectl create -f nginx-service-custom-clusterip.yaml
```

   You should see the following response:

```
The Service "nginx-service-custom-clusterip" is invalid: spec.clusterIP: Inva
lid value: "10.90.10.70": provided IP is not in the valid range. The range of
 valid IPs is 10.96.0.0/12
```

Figure 8.13: Service creation failure due to incorrect IP address

As we can see, the command gives us an error because the IP address we used (**10.90.10.70**) isn't in the valid IP range. As highlighted in the preceding output, the valid IP range is **10.96.0.0/12**.

We can actually find this valid range of IP addresses before creating the Service using the **kubectl cluster-info dump** command. It provides a lot of information that can be used for cluster debugging and diagnosis. We can filter for the **service-cluster-ip-range** string in the output of the command to find out the valid ranges of IP addresses we can use in a cluster. The following command will output the valid IP range:

```
kubectl cluster-info dump | grep -m 1 service-cluster-ip-range
```

You should see the following output:

```
"--service-cluster-ip-range=10.96.0.0/12",
```

We can then use the appropriate IP address for **clusterIP** for our Service.

5. Modify the **nginx-service-custom-clusterip.yaml** file by changing the value of **clusterIP** to **10.96.0.5** since that's one of the valid values:

```
apiVersion: v1
kind: Service
metadata:
  name: nginx-service-custom-clusterip
spec:
  type: ClusterIP
  ports:
    - port: 80
      targetPort: 80
  clusterIP: 10.96.0.5
  selector:
      app: nginx
      environment: production
```

6. Run the following command to create the Service again:

```
kubectl create -f nginx-service-custom-clusterip.yaml
```

You should see the following output:

```
service/nginx-service-custom-clusterip created
```

We can see that the Service has been created successfully.

7. Run the following command to ensure that the Service was created with the custom ClusterIP we specified in the configuration:

```
kubectl get service nginx-service-custom-clusterip
```

You should see the following output:

NAME	TYPE	CLUSTER-IP	EXTERNAL-IP	PORT(S)	AGE
nginx-service-custom-clusterip	ClusterIP	10.96.0.5	<none>	80/TCP	14m

Figure 8.14: Getting the ClusterIP from the Service

Here, we can confirm that the Service was indeed created with the IP address mentioned in the configuration; that is, **`10.96.0.5`**.

8. Next, let's confirm that we can access the Service using the custom IP address from inside the cluster:

```
minikube ssh
```

You should see the following response:

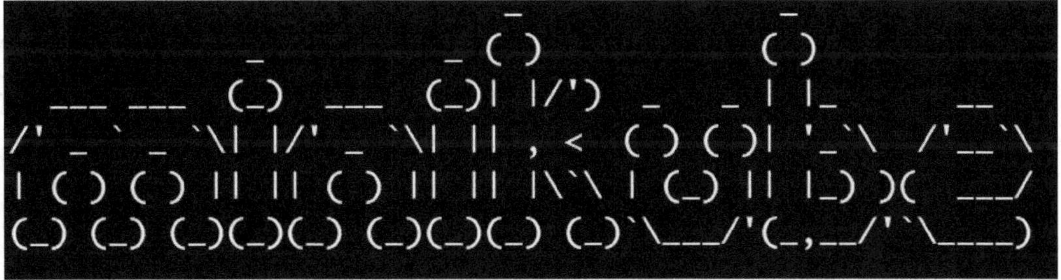

Figure 8.15: SSHing into the minikube node

9. Now, run the following command to send a request to **`10.96.0.5:80`** using **`curl`**:

```
curl 10.96.0.5
```

We intentionally skipped the port number (**80**) in the **curl** request because, by default, curl assumes the port number to be **80**. If the Service were using a different port number, we would have to specify that in the curl request explicitly. You should see the following output:

```
<!DOCTYPE html>
<html>
<head>
<title>Welcome to nginx!</title>
<style>
    body {
        width: 35em;
        margin: 0 auto;
        font-family: Tahoma, Verdana, Arial, sans-serif;
    }
</style>
</head>
<body>
<h1>Welcome to nginx!</h1>
<p>If you see this page, the nginx web server is successfully installed and
working. Further configuration is required.</p>

<p>For online documentation and support please refer to
<a href="http://nginx.org/">nginx.org</a>.<br/>
Commercial support is available at
<a href="http://nginx.com/">nginx.com</a>.</p>

<p><em>Thank you for using nginx.</em></p>
</body>
</html>
```

Figure 8.16: Sending a curl request to a Service from the minikube node

Thus, we can see that we are able to access our Service from inside the cluster and that that service can be accessed at the IP address that we defined for **clusterIP**.

LOADBALANCER SERVICE

A LoadBalancer Service exposes the application externally using the load balancer provided by the cloud provider. This type of Service has no default local implementation and can only be deployed using a cloud provider. The cloud providers provision a load balancer when a Service of the **LoadBalancer** type is created.

Thus, a LoadBalancer Service is basically a superset of the NodePort Service. The LoadBalancer Service uses the implementation offered by the cloud provider and assigns an external IP address to the Service.

The configuration of a **LoadBalancer** Service depends on the cloud provider. Each cloud provider requires you to add a particular set of metadata in the form of annotations. Here's a simplified example of the configuration for a **LoadBalancer** Service:

```
apiVersion: v1
kind: Service
metadata:
  name: loadbalancer-service
spec:
  type: LoadBalancer
  clusterIP: 10.90.10.0
  ports:
    - targetPort: 8080
      port: 80
  selector:
    app: nginx
    environment: production
```

EXTERNALNAME SERVICE

The ExternalName Service maps a Service to a DNS name. In the case of the ExternalName Service, there's no proxying or forwarding. Redirecting the request happens at the DNS level instead. When a request comes for the Service, a CNAME record is returned with the value of the DNS name that was set in the Service configuration.

The configuration of the ExternalName Service doesn't contain any selectors. It looks as follows:

```
apiVersion: v1
kind: Service
metadata:
  name: externalname-service
spec:
  type: ExternalName
  externalName: my.example.domain.com
```

The preceding Service template maps **`externalname-service`** to a DNS name; for example, **`my.example.domain.com`**.

Let's say you're migrating your production applications to a new Kubernetes cluster. A good approach is to start with stateless parts and move them to a Kubernetes cluster first. During the migration process, you will need to make sure those stateless parts in the Kubernetes cluster can still access the other production Services, such as database storage or other backend Services/APIs. In such a case, we can simply create an ExternalName Service so that our Pods from the new cluster can still access resources from the old cluster, which are outside the bounds of the new cluster. Hence, ExternalName provides communication between Kubernetes applications and external Services running outside the Kubernetes cluster.

INGRESS

Ingress is an object that defines rules that are used to manage external access to the Services in a Kubernetes cluster. Typically, Ingress acts like a middleman between the internet and the Services running inside a cluster:

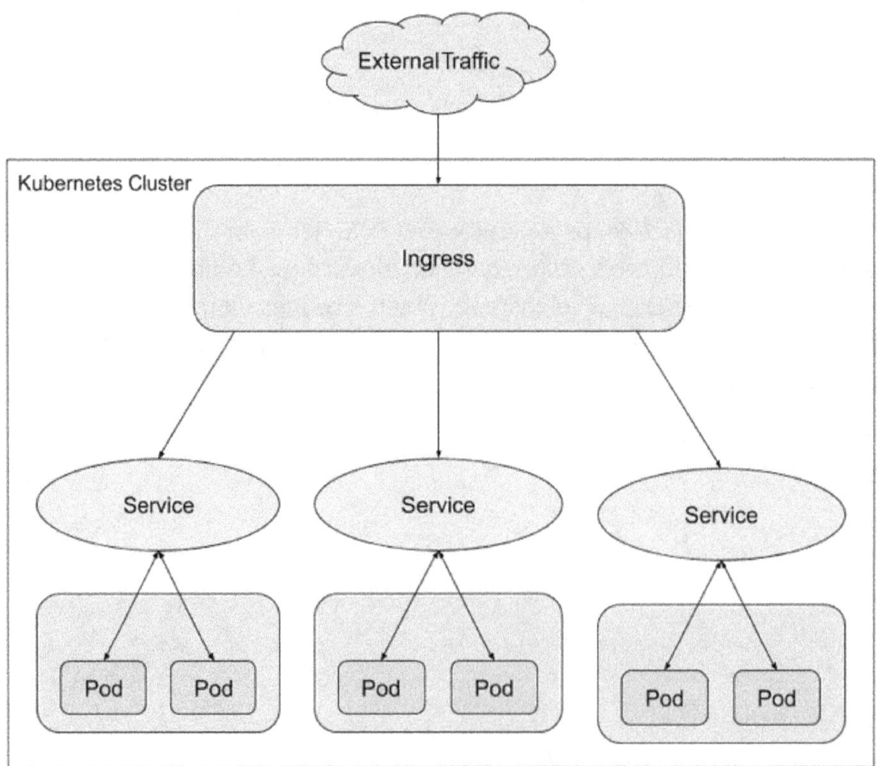

Figure 8.17: Ingress

You will learn much more about Ingress and the major motivations for using it in *Chapter 12, Your Application and HA*. Due to this, we will not cover the implementation of Ingress here.

Now that we have learned about the different types of Services in Kubernetes, we will implement all of them to get an idea of how they would work together in a real-life scenario.

ACTIVITY 8.01: CREATING A SERVICE TO EXPOSE THE APPLICATION RUNNING ON A POD

Consider a scenario where the product team you're working with has created a survey application that has two independent and decoupled components – a frontend and a backend. The frontend component of the survey application renders the survey forms and needs to be exposed to external users. It also needs to communicate with the backend component, which is responsible for validating and storing the survey's responses.

For the scope of this activity, consider the following tasks:

1. To avoid overcomplicating this activity, you can deploy the Apache server (https://hub.docker.com/_/httpd) as the frontend, and we can treat its default placeholder home page as the component that should be visible to the survey applicants. Expose the frontend application so that it's accessible on the host node at port **31000**.

2. For the backend application, deploy an Nginx server. We will treat the default home page of Nginx as the page that you should be able to see from the backend. Expose the backend application so that it's accessible for the frontend application Pods in the same cluster.

   Both Apache and Nginx are exposed at port **80** on the Pods by default.

   > **NOTE**
   >
   > We are using Apache and Nginx here to keep the activity simple. In a real-world scenario, these two would be replaced with the frontend survey site and the backend data analysis component of your survey application, along with a database component for storing all the survey data.

3. To make sure frontend applications are aware of the backend application Service, add an environment variable to the frontend application Pods that contain the IP and the port address of the backend Service. This will ensure that the frontend applications know where to send a request to backend applications.

   To add environment variables to a Pod, we can add a field named **env** to the **spec** section of a Pod configuration that contains a list of name and value pairs for all the environment variables we want to add. Here's an example of how to add an environment variable called **APPLICATION_TYPE** with a value of **Frontend**:

```
apiVersion: v1
kind: Pod
metadata:
  name: environment-variables-example
  labels:
    application: frontend
spec:
  containers:
  - name: apache-httpd
    image: httpd
    env:
    - name: APPLICATION_TYPE
      value: "Frontend"
```

> **NOTE**
>
> We used something called a **ConfigMap** to add an environment variable here. We will learn more about them in *Chapter 10, ConfigMaps and Secrets*.

4. Let's assume that, based on load testing the application, you have estimated that you'll initially need five replicas of the frontend application and four replicas of the backend application.

The following are the high-level steps you will need to perform in order to complete this activity:

1. Create a namespace for this activity.
2. Write an appropriate Deployment configuration for the backend application and create the Deployment.

3. Write an appropriate Service configuration for the backend application with the appropriate Service type and create the Service.
4. Ensure that the backend application is accessible, as expected.
5. Write an appropriate Deployment configuration for the frontend application. Make sure it has the environment variables set for the IP address and the port address for the backend application Service.
6. Create a deployment for the frontend application.
7. Write an appropriate Service configuration for the frontend application with the appropriate service type and create the Service.
8. Ensure that the frontend application is accessible as expected on port **31000** on the host node.

Expected Output:

At the end of the exercise, you should be able to access the frontend application in the browser using the host IP address at port **31000**. You should see the following output in your browser:

It works!

Figure 8.18: Expected output of Activity 8.01

> **NOTE**
>
> The solution to this activity can be found at the following address: https://packt.live/304PEoD.

SUMMARY

In this chapter, we covered the different ways in which we can expose our application running on Pods. We have seen how we can use a ClusterIP Service to expose an application inside the cluster. We have also seen how we can use a NodePort Service to expose an application outside the cluster. We have also covered the LoadBalancer and ExternalName Services in brief.

Now that we have created a Deployment and learned how to make it accessible from the external world, in the next chapter, we will focus on storage aspects. There, we will cover reading and storing data on disk, in and across Pods.

9

STORING AND READING DATA ON DISK

OVERVIEW

This chapter introduces the concept of using Volumes to store or read data from the containers running inside pods. By the end of this chapter, you will be able to create Volumes to temporarily store data in a pod independent of a container's life cycle, as well as share the data among different containers inside the same pod. You will also learn how to use **PersistentVolumes** (**PVs**) to store data on your cluster independent of the pod life cycle. We will also cover how to create **PersistentVolumeClaims** (**PVCs**) to dynamically provision volumes and use them inside a pod.

INTRODUCTION

In previous chapters, we created Deployments to create multiple replicas of our application and exposed our application using Services. However, we have not yet properly explored how Kubernetes facilitates applications to store and read data, which is the subject of this chapter.

In practice, most applications interact with data in some way. It's possible that we may have an application that needs to read data from a file. Similarly, our application may need to write some data locally in order for other parts of the application, or different applications, to read it. For example, if we have a container running our main application that produces some logs locally, we would want to have a sidecar container (which is a second container running inside the pod along with the main application container) that can run inside the same pod to read and process the local logs produced by the main application. However, to enable this, we need to find a way to share the storage among different containers in the same pod.

Let's say we are training a machine learning model in a pod. During the intermediate stages of the model training, we would need to store some data locally on a disk. Similarly, the end result – the trained model – will need to be stored on a disk, such that it can be retrieved later even once the pod terminates. For this use case, we need some way of allocating some storage to the pod such that the data written in that storage exists even beyond the life cycle of the pod.

Similarly, we may have some data that needs to be written or read by multiple replicas of the same application. This data should also persist when some of such pod replicas crash and/or restart. For example, if we have an e-commerce website, we may want to store the user data, as well as inventory records, in a database. This data will need to be persisted across pod restarts as well as Deployment updates or rollbacks.

To serve these purposes, Kubernetes provides an abstraction called Volume. A **PersistentVolume** (**PV**) is the most common type of Volume that you will encounter. In this chapter, we will cover this, as well as many other types of Volumes. We will learn how to use them and provision them on-demand.

VOLUMES

Let's say we have a pod that stores some data locally on a disk. Now, if the container that's storing the data crashes and is restarted, the data will be lost. The new container will start with an empty disk space allocated. Thus, we cannot rely on containers themselves even for the temporary storage of data.

We may also have a case where one container in a pod stores some data that needs to be accessed by other containers in the same pod as well.

The Kubernetes Volume abstraction solves both of these problems. Here's a diagram showing Volumes and their interaction with physical storage and the application:

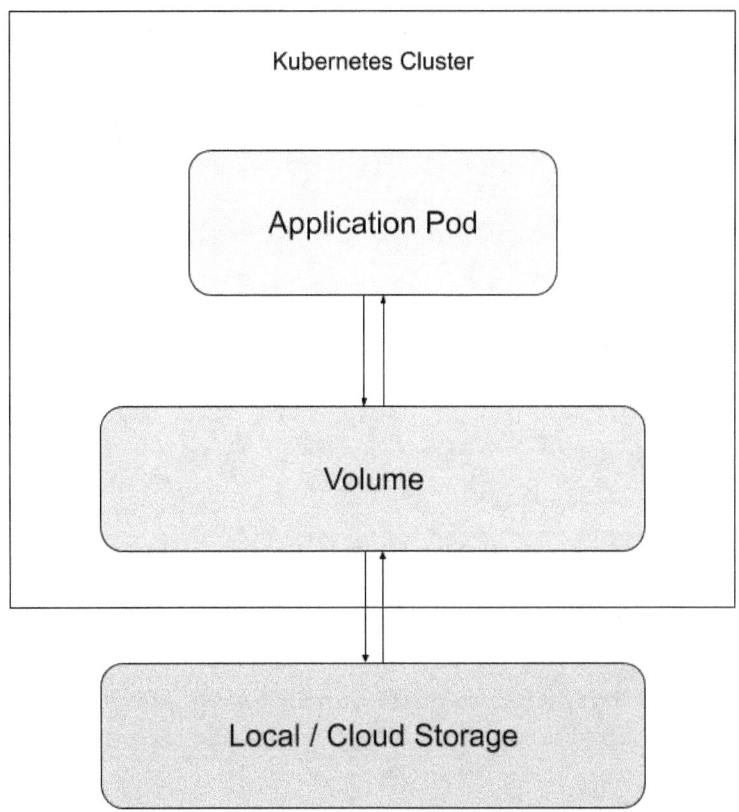

Figure 9.1: Volume as a storage abstraction for applications

As you can see from this diagram, a Volume is exposed to the applications as an abstraction, which eventually stores the data on any type of physical storage that you may be using.

The lifetime of a Kubernetes Volume is the same as that of the pod that uses it. In other words, even if the containers within a pod restart, the same Volume will be used by the new container as well. Hence, the data isn't lost across container restarts. However, once a pod terminates or is restarted, the Volume ceases to exist, and the data is lost. To solve this problem, we can use PVs, which we will cover later in this chapter.

HOW TO USE VOLUMES

A Volume is defined in the pod spec. Here's an example of a pod configuration with Volumes:

```
apiVersion: v1
kind: Pod
metadata:
  name: pod-with-emptydir-volume
spec:
  restartPolicy: Never
  containers:
  - image: ubuntu
    name: ubuntu-container
    volumeMounts:
    - mountPath: /data
      name: data-volume
  volumes:
  - name: data-volume
    emptyDir: {}
```

As we can see in the preceding configuration, to define a Volume, a pod configuration needs to set two fields:

- The **`.spec.volumes`** field defines what Volumes this pod is planning to use.
- The **`.spec.containers.volumeMounts`** defines where to mount those Volumes in individual containers. This will be defined separately for all the containers.

DEFINING VOLUMES

In the preceding example, the **`.spec.volumes`** field has two fields that define the configuration of a Volume:

- **`name`**: This is the name of the Volume by which it will be referred to in the containers' **`volumeMounts`** fields when it will be mounted. It has to be a valid DNS name. The name of the Volume must be unique within a single pod.
- **`emptyDir`**: This varies based on the type of the Volume being used (which, in the case of the preceding example, is **`emptyDir`**). This defines the actual configuration of the Volume. We will go through the types of Volumes in the next section with some examples.

MOUNTING VOLUMES

Each container needs to specify **`volumeMounts`** separately to mount the volume. In the preceding example, you can see that the **`.spec.containers[*].volumeMounts`** configuration has the following fields:

- **`name`**: This is the name of the Volume that needs to be mounted for this container.
- **`mountPath`**: This is the path inside the container where the Volume should be mounted. Each container can mount the same Volume on different paths.

Other than these, there are two other notable fields that we can set:

- **`subPath`**: This is an optional field that contains the path from the Volume that needs to be mounted on the container. By default, the volume is mounted from its root directory. This field can be used to mount only a sub-directory in the volume and not the entire volume. For example, if you're using the same Volume for multiple users, it's useful to mount a sub-path on the containers, rather than the root directory of the Volume.
- **`readonly`**: This is an optional flag that determines whether the mounted volume will be read-only or not. By default, the volumes are mounted with read-write access.

TYPES OF VOLUMES

As mentioned earlier, Kubernetes supports several types of Volumes and the availability of most of them depends on the cloud provider that you use. AWS, Azure, and Google Cloud all have different types of Volumes supported.

Let's take a look at some common types of Volumes in detail.

EMPTYDIR

An **`emptyDir`** Volume refers to an empty directory that's created when a pod is assigned to a node. It only exists as long as the pod does. All the containers running inside the pod have the ability to write and read files from this directory. The same **`emptyDir`** Volume can be mounted on different paths for different containers.

Here's an example of pod configuration using the **emptyDir** Volume:

```
apiVersion: v1
kind: Pod
metadata:
  name: pod-with-emptydir-volume
spec:
  restartPolicy: Never
  containers:
  - image: ubuntu
    name: ubuntu-container
    volumeMounts:
    - mountPath: /data
      name: data-volume
  volumes:
  - name: data-volume
    emptyDir: {}
```

In this example, **{}** indicates that the **emptyDir** Volume will be defined in the default manner. By default, the **emptyDir** Volumes are stored on the disk or SSD, depending on the environment. We can change it to use RAM instead by setting the **.emptyDir.medium** field to **Memory**.

Thus, we can modify the **volumes** section of the preceding pod configuration to use the **emptyDir** Volume backed by memory, as follows:

```
  volumes:
  - name: data-volume
    emptyDir:
      medium: Memory
```

This informs Kubernetes to use a RAM-based filesystem (tmpfs) to store the Volume. Even though tmpfs is very fast compared to data on a disk, there are a couple of downsides to using in-memory Volume. First, the tmpfs storage is cleared on the system reboot of the node on which the pod is running. Second, the data stored in a memory-based Volume counts against the memory limits of the container. Hence, we need to be careful while using memory-based Volumes.

We can also specify the size limit of the storage to be used in the **emptyDir** Volume by setting the **.volumes.emptyDir.sizeLimit** field. This size limit applies to both disk-based and memory-based **emptyDir** Volumes. In the case of memory-based Volumes, the maximum usage allowed will be either the **sizeLimit** field value or the sum of memory limits on all containers in the pod – whichever is lower.

Use Cases

Some of the use cases for **emptyDir** Volumes are as follows:

- Temporary scratch space for computations requiring a lot of space, such as on-disk merge sort
- Storage required for storing checkpoints for a long computation, such as training machine learning models where the progress needs to be saved to recover from crashes

HOSTPATH

A **hostPath** Volume is used to mount a file or a directory from the host node's filesystem to a pod.

Here's an example of pod configuration using the **hostPath** Volume:

```
apiVersion: v1
kind: Pod
metadata:
  name: pod-with-hostpath-volume
spec:
  restartPolicy: Never
  containers:
  - image: ubuntu
    name: ubuntu-container
    volumeMounts:
    - mountPath: /data
      name: data-volume
  volumes:
  - name: data-volume
    hostPath:
      path: /tmp
      type: Directory
```

In this example, the **/home/user/data** directory from the host node will be mounted on the **/data** path on the container. Let's look at the two fields under **hostPath**:

- **path**: This is the path of the directory or the file that will be mounted on the containers mounting this Volume. It can also be a symlink (symbolic link) to a directory or a file, the address of a UNIX socket, or a character or block device, depending on the **type** field.
- **type**: This is an optional field that allows us to specify the type of the Volume. If this field is specified, certain checks will be performed before mounting the **hostPath** Volume.

The **type** field supports the following values:

- **""** (an empty string): This is the default value implying that no checks will be performed before mounting the **hostPath** Volume. If the path specified doesn't exist on the node, the pod will still be created without verifying the existence of the path. Hence, the pod will keep crashing indefinitely because of this error.
- **DirectoryOrCreate**: This implies that the directory path specified may or may not already exist on the host node. If it doesn't exist, an empty directory is created.
- **Directory**: This implies that a directory must exist on the host node at the path specified. If the directory doesn't exist at the path specified, there will be a **FailedMount** error while creating the pod, indicating that the **hostPath** type check has failed.
- **FileOrCreate**: This implies that the file path specified may or may not already exist on the host node. If it doesn't exist, an empty file is created.
- **File**: This implies that a file must exist on the host node at the path specified.
- **Socket**: This implies that a UNIX socket must exist at the path specified.
- **CharDevice**: This implies that a character device must exist at the path specified.
- **BlockDevice**: This implies that a block device must exist at the path specified.

Use Cases

In most cases, your application won't need a **hostPath** Volume. However, there are some niche use cases where the **hostPath** Volume may be particularly useful. Some of these use cases for the **hostPath** Volume are as follows:

- Allowing pods to be created only if a particular host path exists on the host node before running the pod. For example, a pod may require some Secrets or credentials to be present in a file on the host before it can run.
- Running a container that needs access to Docker internals. We can do that by setting **hostPath** to **/var/lib/docker**.

> **NOTE**
>
> In addition to the two types of Volumes covered here, Kubernetes supports many more, some of which are specific to certain cloud platforms. You can find more information about them at https://kubernetes.io/docs/concepts/storage/volumes/#types-of-volumes.

In the previous sections, we learned about Volumes and how to use their different types. In the following exercises, we will put these concepts into action and use Volumes with pods.

EXERCISE 9.01: CREATING A POD WITH AN EMPTYDIR VOLUME

In this exercise, we will create a basic pod with an **emptyDir** Volume. We will also simulate data being written manually, and then make sure that the data stored in the Volume is kept across container restarts:

1. Create a file called **pod-with-emptydir-volume.yaml** with the following content:

```
apiVersion: v1
kind: Pod
metadata:
  name: pod-with-emptydir-volume
spec:
  containers:
  - image: nginx
    name: nginx-container
    volumeMounts:
```

```
    - mountPath: /mounted-data
      name: data-volume
  volumes:
  - name: data-volume
    emptyDir: {}
```

In this pod configuration, we have used an **emptyDir** Volume mounted at the **/mounted-data** directory.

2. Run the following command to create the pod using the preceding configuration:

```
kubectl create -f pod-with-emptydir-volume.yaml
```

You should see the following response:

```
pod/pod-with-emptydir-volume created
```

3. Run the following command to confirm that the pod was created and is ready:

```
kubectl get pod pod-with-emptydir-volume
```

You should see the following response:

```
NAME                       READY   STATUS    RESTARTS   AGE
pod-with-emptydir-volume   1/1     Running   0          20s
```

4. Run the following command to describe the pod so that we can verify that the correct Volume was mounted on this pod:

```
kubectl describe pod pod-with-emptydir-volume
```

This will give a long output. Look for the following section in the terminal output:

```
Containers:
  nginx-container:
    Container ID:   docker://9def64e1e059e6fcfd865650cd0029fdb59570f25048d9ad2387da5cff67e277
    Image:          nginx
    Image ID:       docker-pullable://nginx@sha256:8aa7f6a9585d908a63e5e418dc5d14ae7467d2e36e1a
b4f0d8f9d059a3d071ce
    Port:           <none>
    Host Port:      <none>
    State:          Running
      Started:      Mon, 20 Jan 2020 16:29:58 +0100
    Ready:          True
    Restart Count:  0
    Environment:    <none>
    Mounts:
      /mounted-data from data-volume (rw)
      /var/run/secrets/kubernetes.io/serviceaccount from default-token-w6xvp (ro)
Conditions:
  Type              Status
  Initialized       True
  Ready             True
  ContainersReady   True
  PodScheduled      True
Volumes:
  data-volume:
    Type:       EmptyDir (a temporary directory that shares a pod's lifetime)
    Medium:
    SizeLimit:  <unset>
```

Figure 9.2: Describing the pod with a mounted emptyDir volume

As highlighted in the preceding image, the **emptyDir** Volume named **data-volume** was created and it was mounted on **nginx-container** at the **/mounted-data** path. We can see that the Volume has been mounted in **rw** mode, which stands for read-write.

Now that we have verified that the pod was created with the correct Volume configured, we will manually write some data to this path. In practice, this writing will be done by your application code.

5. Now, we will use the **kubectl exec** command to run the Bash shell inside the pod:

```
kubectl exec pod-with-emptydir-volume -it /bin/bash
```

You should see the following on your terminal screen:

```
root@pod-with-emptydir-volume:/#
```

This will now allow you to run commands via an SSH connection on the Bash shell running in the **nginx-container**. Note that we are running as a root user.

> **NOTE**
>
> If you had a sidecar container running in the pod (or any number of multiple containers in a pod), then you can control where the **kubectl exec** command will execute by adding the **-c** parameter to specify the container, as you will see in the next exercise.

6. Run the following command to check the content of the root directory of the pod:

```
ls
```

You should see an output similar to this one:

```
bin   dev  home  lib64  mnt          opt   root  sbin   sys   usr
boot  etc  lib   media  mounted-data proc  run   srv    tmp   var
```

Notice that there's a directory called **mounted-data**.

7. Run the following commands to go to the **mounted-data** directory and check its content:

```
cd mounted-data
ls
```

You should see a blank output, as follows:

```
root@pod-with-emptydir-volume:/mounted-data#
```

This output indicates that the **mounted-data** directory is empty as expected because we don't have any code running inside the pod that would write to this path.

8. Run the following command to create a simple text file inside the **mounted-data** directory:

```
echo "Manually stored data" > manual-data.txt
```

9. Now, run the **ls** command again to check the content of the directory:

```
ls
```

You should see the following output:

```
manual-data.txt
```

Thus, we have created a new file with some content in the mounted volume directory. Now, our aim will be to verify that this data will still exist if the container is restarted.

10. In order to restart the container, we will kill the **nginx** process, which will trigger a restart. Run the following commands to install the procps package so that we can use the **ps** command to find out the process ID (PID) of the process that we want to kill. First, update the package lists:

```
sudo apt-get update
```

You should see an output similar to the following:

```
Get:2 http://deb.debian.org/debian buster InRelease [122 kB]
Get:3 http://deb.debian.org/debian buster-updates InRelease [49.3 kB]
Get:1 http://security-cdn.debian.org/debian-security buster/updates InRelease [65.4 kB]
Get:4 http://deb.debian.org/debian buster/main amd64 Packages [7908 kB]
Get:5 http://security-cdn.debian.org/debian-security buster/updates/main amd64 Packages [171 kB]
Get:6 http://deb.debian.org/debian buster-updates/main amd64 Packages [5792 B]
Fetched 8321 kB in 4s (2319 kB/s)
Reading package lists... Done
```

Figure 9.3: An apt-get update

Our package lists are up to date and we are now ready to install procps.

11. Use the following command to install procps:

```
sudo apt-get install procps
```

Enter *Y* when prompted to confirm the installation, and then the installation will proceed with an output similar to the following:

```
Reading package lists... Done
Building dependency tree
Reading state information... Done
The following additional packages will be installed:
  libgpm2 libncurses6 libprocps7 psmisc
Suggested packages:
  gpm
The following NEW packages will be installed:
  libgpm2 libncurses6 libprocps7 procps psmisc
0 upgraded, 5 newly installed, 0 to remove and 0 not upgraded.
Need to get 584 kB of archives.
After this operation, 1931 kB of additional disk space will be used.
Do you want to continue? [Y/n]
Get:1 http://deb.debian.org/debian buster/main amd64 libncurses6 amd64 6.1+20181013-2+deb10u2 [10
2 kB]
```

Figure 9.4: Using apt-get to install procps

12. Now, run the following command to check the list of processes running on the container:

```
ps aux
```

You should see the following output:

```
USER       PID %CPU %MEM    VSZ   RSS TTY      STAT START   TIME COMMAND
root         1  0.0  0.2  10632  5020 ?        Ss   15:45   0:00 nginx: master process nginx -g d
nginx        6  0.0  0.1  11088  2560 ?        S    15:45   0:00 nginx: worker process
root         7  0.0  0.1   3988  3216 pts/0    Ss   15:46   0:00 /bin/bash
root       338  0.0  0.1   7640  2684 pts/0    R+   15:55   0:00 ps aux
```

Figure 9.5: A list of the running processes

In the output, we can see that among several other processes, the **nginx** master process is running with a **PID** of **1**.

13. Run the following command to kill the **nginx** master process:

```
kill 1
```

You should see the following response:

```
root@pod-with-emptydir-volume:/mounted-data# command terminated with exit code 137
```

Figure 9.6: Killing the container

The output shows that the terminal exited the Bash session on the pod. This is because the container was killed. The **137** exit code indicates that the session was killed by manual intervention.

14. Run the following command to get the status of the pod:

```
kubectl describe pod pod-with-emptydir-volume
```

Observe the following section in the output that you get:

```
Ready:            True
Restart Count:    1
Environment:      <none>
Mounts:
  /mounted-data from data-volume (rw)
  /var/run/secrets/kubernetes.io/serviceaccount from default-token-w6xvp (ro)
```

Figure 9.7: Describing the pod

You will see that there's now a **Restart Count** field for **nginx-container** that has a value of **1**. That means that the container was restarted after we killed it. Please note that restarting a container doesn't trigger a restart of a pod. Hence, we should expect the data stored in the Volume to still exist. Let's verify that in the next step.

15. Let's run Bash inside the pod again and go to the **/mounted-data** directory:

```
kubectl exec pod-with-emptydir-volume -it /bin/bash
cd mounted-data
```

You will see the following output:

```
root@pod-with-emptydir-volume:/# cd mounted data/
```

16. Run the following command to check the contents of **/mounted-data** directory:

```
ls
```

You will see the following output:

```
manual-data.txt
```

This output indicates that the file we created before killing the container still exists in the Volume.

17. Run the following command to verify the contents of the file we created in the Volume:

```
cat manual-data.txt
```

You will see the following output:

```
Manually stored data
```

This output indicates that the data we stored in the Volume stays intact even when the container gets restarted.

18. Run the following command to delete the pod:

```
kubectl delete pod pod-with-emptydir-volume
```

You will see the following output confirming that the pod has been deleted:

```
pod "pod-with-emptydir-volume" deleted
```

In this exercise, we created a pod with the **emptyDir** Volume, checked that the pod was created with an empty directory mounted at the correct path inside the container, and verified that we can write the data inside that directory and that the data stays intact across the container restarts as long as the pod is still running.

Now, let's move to a scenario that lets us observe some more uses for Volumes. Let's consider a scenario where we have an application pod that runs a total of three containers. We can assume that two of the three containers are serving traffic and they dump the logs into a shared file. The third container acts as a sidecar monitoring container that reads the logs from the file and dumps them into an external log storage system where the logs can be preserved for further analysis and alerting. Let's consider this scenario in the next exercise and understand how we can utilize an **emptyDir** Volume shared between the three containers of a pod.

EXERCISE 9.02: CREATING A POD WITH AN EMPTYDIR VOLUME SHARED BY THREE CONTAINERS

In this exercise, we will show some more uses of the **emptyDir** Volume and share it among three containers in the same pod. Each container will mount the same volume at a different local path:

1. Create a file called **shared-emptydir-volume.yaml** with the following content:

```
apiVersion: v1
kind: Pod
metadata:
  name: shared-emptydir-volume
spec:
  containers:
  - image: ubuntu
    name: container-1
    command: ['/bin/bash', '-ec', 'sleep 3600']
    volumeMounts:
    - mountPath: /mounted-data-1
      name: data-volume
  - image: ubuntu
    name: container-2
    command: ['/bin/bash', '-ec', 'sleep 3600']
    volumeMounts:
    - mountPath: /mounted-data-2
      name: data-volume
  - image: ubuntu
    name: container-3
    command: ['/bin/bash', '-ec', 'sleep 3600']
    volumeMounts:
    - mountPath: /mounted-data-3
      name: data-volume
  volumes:
  - name: data-volume
    emptyDir: {}
```

In this configuration, we have defined an **emptyDir** Volume named **data-volume**, which is being mounted on three containers at different paths.

Note that each of the containers has been configured to run a command on startup that makes them sleep for 1 hour. This is intended to keep the **ubuntu** container running so that we can perform the following operations on the containers. By default, an **ubuntu** container is configured to run whatever command is specified and exit upon completion.

2. Run the following command to create the pod with the preceding configuration:

```
kubectl create -f shared-emptydir-volume.yaml
```

You will see the following output:

```
pod/shared-emptydir-volume created
```

3. Run the following command to check the status of the pod:

```
kubectl get pod shared-emptydir-volume
```

You will see the following output:

```
NAME                     READY   STATUS    RESTARTS   AGE
shared-emptydir-volume   3/3     Running   0          13s
```

This output indicates that all three containers inside this pod are running.

4. Next, we will run the following command to run Bash in the first container:

```
kubectl exec shared-emptydir-volume -c container-1 -it -- /bin/bash
```

Here, the **-c** flag is used to specify the container that we want to run Bash in. You will see the following in the terminal:

```
root@shared-emptydir-volume:/#
```

5. Run the following command to check the content of the root directory on the container:

```
ls
```

You will see the following output:

```
bin   dev  home  lib32  libx32  mnt              opt   root  sbin  sys  usr
boot  etc  lib   lib64  media   mounted-data-1   proc  run   srv   tmp  var
```

Figure 9.8: Listing the content of the root directory inside the container

We can see that the **mounted-data-1** directory has been created on the container. Also, you can see the list of directories you would see in a typical Ubuntu root directory, in addition to the **mounted-data-1** directory that we created.

6. Now, we will go to the **mounted-data-1** directory and create a simple text file with some text in it:

```
cd mounted-data-1
echo 'Data written on container-1' > data-1.txt
```

7. Run the following command to verify that the file has been stored:

```
ls
```

You will see the following output:

```
data-1.txt
```

8. Run the following command to exit **container-1** and go back to your host terminal:

```
exit
```

9. Now, let's run Bash inside the second container, which is named **container-2**:

```
kubectl exec shared-emptydir-volume -c container-2 -it -- /bin/bash
```

You will see the following in your terminal:

```
root@shared-emptydir-volume:/#
```

10. Run the following command to locate the mounted directory in the root directory on the container:

```
ls
```

You will see the following output:

```
bin   dev  home  lib32  libx32  mnt              opt   root  sbin  sys  usr
boot  etc  lib   lib64  media   mounted-data-2   proc  run   srv   tmp  var
```

Figure 9.9: Listing the content of the root directory inside the container

Note the directory called **mounted-data-2**, which is the mount point for our Volume inside **container-2**.

11. Run the following command to check the content of the **mounted-data-2** directory:

```
cd mounted-data-2
ls
```

You will see the following output:

```
data-1.txt
```

This output indicates that there's already a file called **data-1.txt**, which we created in **container-1** earlier.

12. Let's verify that it's the same file that we created in earlier steps. Run the following command to check the content of this file:

```
cat data-1.txt
```

You will see the following output:

```
Data written on container-1
```

This output verifies that this is the same file that we created in earlier steps of this exercise.

13. Run the following command to write a new file called **data-2.txt** into this directory:

```
echo 'Data written on container-2' > data-2.txt
```

14. Now, let's confirm that the file has been created:

```
ls
```

You should see the following output:

```
data-1.txt   data-2.txt
```

As you can see in this screenshot, the new file has been created and there are now two files - **data-1.txt** and **data-2.txt** - in the mounted directory.

15. Run the following command to exit the Bash session on this container:

```
exit
```

16. Now, let's run Bash inside **container-3**:

```
kubectl exec shared-emptydir-volume -c container-3 -it -- /bin/bash
```

You will see the following in your terminal:

```
root@shared-empty-dir-volume:/#
```

17. Go to the **/mounted-data-3** directory and check its content:

```
cd mounted-data-3
ls
```

You will see the following output:

```
data-1.txt   data-2.txt
```

This output shows that this container can see the two files - **data-1.txt** and **data-2.txt** - that we created in earlier steps from **container-1** and **container-2**, respectively.

18. Run the following command to verify the content of the first file, **data-1.txt**:

```
cat data-1.txt
```

You should see the following output:

```
Data written on container-1
```

19. Run the following commands to verify the content of the second file, **data-2.txt**:

```
cat data-2.txt
```

You should see the following output:

```
Data written on container-2
```

The output of the last two commands proves that the data written by any container on the mounted volume is accessible by other containers for reading. Next, we will verify that other containers have write access to the data written by a particular container.

20. Run the following command to overwrite the content of the **data-2.txt** file:

```
echo 'Data updated on container 3' > data-2.txt
```

21. Next, let's exit **container-3**:

```
exit
```

22. Run the following command to run Bash inside **container-1** again:

```
kubectl exec shared-emptydir-volume -c container-1 -it -- /bin/bash
```

You should see the following in your terminal:

```
root@shared-emptydir-volume:/#
```

23. Run the following command to check the content of the **data-2.txt** file:

```
cat mounted-data-1/data-2.txt
```

You should see the following output:

```
Data updated on container 3
```

This output indicates that the data overwritten by **container-3** becomes available for other containers to read as well.

24. Run the following command to come out of the SSH session inside **container-3**:

```
exit
```

25. Run the following command to delete the pod:

```
kubectl delete pod shared-emptydir-volume
```

You should see the following output, indicating that the pod has been deleted:

```
pod "shared-emptydir-volume" deleted
```

In this exercise, we learned how to use Volumes and verified that the same Volume can be mounted at different paths in different containers. We also saw that the containers using the same Volume can read or write (or overwrite) content of the Volume.

PERSISTENT VOLUMES

The Volumes we have seen so far have the limitation that their life cycle depends on the life cycle of pods. Volumes such as emptyDir or hostPath get deleted when the pod using them is deleted or gets restarted. For example, if we use Volumes to store user data and inventory records for our e-commerce website, the data will be deleted when the application pod restarts. Hence, Volumes are not suited to store data that you want to persist.

To solve this problem, Kubernetes supports persistent storage in the form of a **Persistent Volume** (**PV**). A PV is a Kubernetes object that represents a block of storage in the cluster. It can either be provisioned beforehand by the cluster administrators or be dynamically provisioned. A PV can be considered a cluster resource just like a node and, hence, it is not scoped to a single namespace. These Volumes work similarly to the Volumes we have seen in previous sections. The life cycle of a PV doesn't depend on the life cycle of any pod that uses the PV. From the pod's perspective, however, there's no difference between using a normal Volume and a PV.

In order to use a PV, a **PersistentVolumeClaim** (**PVC**) needs to be created. A PVC is a request for storage by a user or a pod. A PVC can request a specific size of storage and specific access modes. A PVC is effectively an abstract way of accessing the various storage resources by users. PVCs are scoped by namespaces, so pods can only access the PVCs created within the same namespace.

> **NOTE**
>
> At any time, a PV can be bound to one PVC only.

Here's a diagram showing how an application interacts with a PV and PVC:

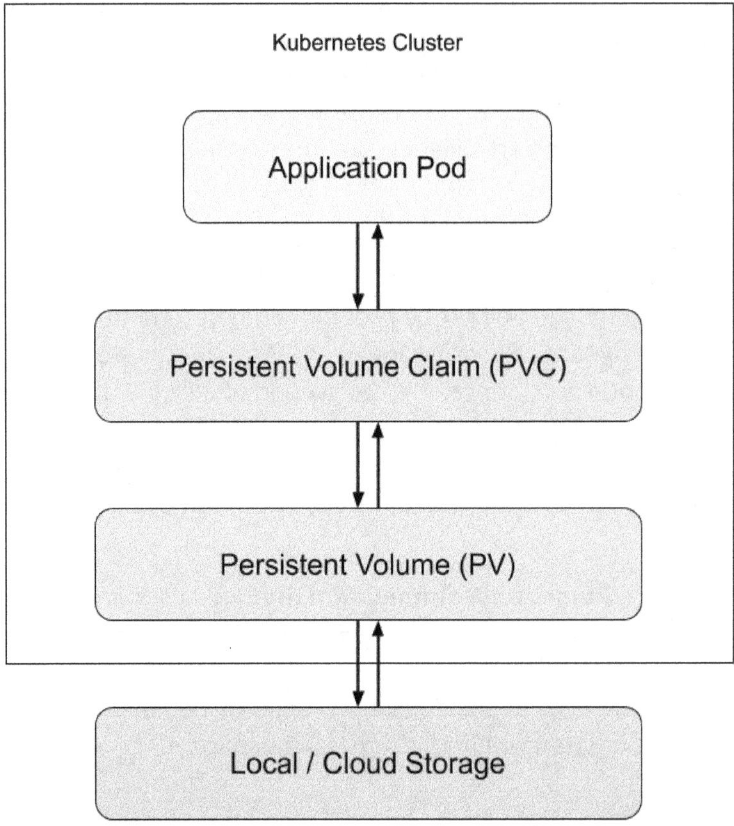

Figure 9.10: How PV and PVC work together to provide storage to your application pod

As you can see in this diagram, Kubernetes uses a combination of PV and PVC to make storage available to your applications. A PVC is basically a request to provide a PV that meets certain criteria.

This is a notable variation from what we saw in the previous exercises, where we created Volumes directly in the pod definitions. This separation of the request (PVC) and the actual storage abstraction (PV) allows an application developer to not worry about the specifics and the statuses of all the different PVs present on the cluster; they can simply create a PVC with the application requirements and then use it in the pod. This kind of loose binding also allows the entire system to be resilient and remain stable in the case of pod restarts.

Similar to Volumes, Kubernetes supports several types of PVs. Some of them may be specific to your cloud platform. You can find a list of the different supported types at this link: https://kubernetes.io/docs/concepts/storage/persistent-volumes/#types-of-persistent-volumes

PersistentVolume Configuration

Here's an example of PV configuration:

```
apiVersion: v1
kind: PersistentVolume
metadata:
  name: example-persistent-volume
spec:
  storageClassName: standard
  capacity:
    storage: 10Gi
  volumeMode: Filesystem
  accessModes:
    - ReadWriteMany
  persistentVolumeReclaimPolicy: Retain
  nfs:
    server: 172.10.1.1
    path: /tmp/pv
```

As usual, the PV object also has the three fields that we have already seen: **apiVersion**, **kind**, and **metadata**. Since this is an **nfs** type of PV, we have the **nfs** section in the configuration. Let's go through some important fields in the PV **spec** section one by one.

storageClassName

Each PV belongs to a certain storage class. We define the name of the storage class that the PV is associated with using the **storageClassName** field. A StorageClass is a Kubernetes object that provides a way for administrators to describe the different types or profiles of storages they support. In the preceding example, **standard** is just an example of a storage class.

Different storage classes allow you to allocate different types of storage based on performance and capacity to different applications based on the specific needs of the application. Each cluster administrator can configure their own storage classes. Each storage class can have its own provisioners, backup policies, or reclamation policies determined by administrators. A provisioner is a system that determines how to provision a PV of a particular type. Kubernetes supports a set of internal provisioners as well as external ones that can be implemented by users. The details about how to use or create a provisioner are, however, beyond the scope of this book.

A PV belonging to a certain storage class can only be bound to a PVC requesting that particular class. Note that this is an optional field. Any PV without the storage class field will only be available to PVCs that do not request a specific storage class.

CAPACITY

This field denotes the storage capacity of the PV. We can set this field in a similar way as we would define constraints used by memory and CPU limit fields in a pod spec. In the preceding example spec, we have set the capacity to 10 GiB.

VOLUMEMODE

The **`volumeMode`** field denotes how we want the storage to be used. It can have two possible values: **`Filesystem`** (default) and **`Block`**. We can set the **`volumeMode`** field to **`Block`** in order to use the raw block device as storage, or **`Filesystem`** to use a traditional filesystem on the persistent volume.

ACCESSMODES

The access mode for a PV represents the capabilities allowed for a mounted Volume. A Volume can be mounted using only one of the supported access modes at a time. There are three possible access modes:

- **`ReadWriteOnce`** (**RWO**): Mounted as read-write by a single node only
- **`ReadOnlyMany`** (**ROX**): Mounted as read-only by many nodes
- **`ReadWriteMany`** (**RWX**): Mounted as read-write by many nodes

Note that not all the types of volumes support all the access modes. Please check the reference for the allowed access modes for the specific type of volume you are using.

PERSISTENTVOLUMERECLAIMPOLICY

Once a user is done with a volume, they can delete their PVC, and that allows the PV resource to be reclaimed. The reclaim policy field denotes the policy that will be used to allow a PV to be claimed after its release. A PV being *released* implies that the PV is no longer associated with the PVC since that PVC is deleted. Then, the PV is available for any other PVCs to use, or in other words, *reclaim*. Whether a PV can be reused or not depends on the reclaim policy. There can be three possible values for this field:

- **`Retain`**: This reclaim policy indicates that the data stored in the PV is kept in storage even after the PV has been released. The administrator will need to delete the data in storage manually. In this policy, the PV is marked as **`Released`** instead of **`Available`**. Thus, a **`Released`** PV may not necessarily be empty.
- **`Recycle`**: Using this reclaim policy means that once the PV is released, the data on the volume is deleted using a basic **`rm -rf`** command. This marks the PV as **`Available`** and hence ready to be claimed again. Using dynamic provisioning is a better alternative to using this reclaim policy. We will discuss the dynamic provisioning in the next section.
- **`Delete`**: Using this reclaim policy means that once the PV is released, both the PV as well as the data stored in the underlying storage will be deleted.

> **NOTE**
>
> Various cloud environments have different default values for reclaim policies. So, make sure you check the default value of the reclaim policy for the cloud environment you're using to avoid the accidental deletion of data in PVs.

PV STATUS

At any moment of its life cycle, a PV can have one of the following statuses:

- **`Available`**: This indicates that the PV is available to be claimed.
- **`Bound`**: This indicates that the PV has been bound to a PVC.
- **`Released`**: This indicates that the PVC bound to this resource has been deleted; however, it's yet to be reclaimed by some other PVC.
- **`Failed`**: This indicates that there was a failure during reclamation.

Now that we have taken a look at the various aspects of the PV, let's take a look at the PVC.

PERSISTENTVOLUMECLAIM CONFIGURATION

Here's an example of PVC configuration:

```
apiVersion: v1
kind: PersistentVolumeClaim
metadata:
  name: example-persistent-volume-claim
spec:
  storageClassName: standard
  resources:
    requests:
      storage: 500Mi
  volumeMode: Filesystem
  accessModes:
    - ReadWriteMany
  selector:
    matchLabels:
      environment: "prod"
```

Again, as usual, the PVC object also has three fields that we have already seen: **apiVersion**, **kind**, and **metadata**. Let's go through some important fields in the PVC **spec** section one by one.

STORAGECLASSNAME

A PVC can request a particular class of storage by specifying the **storageClassName** field. Only the PVs of the specified storage class can be bound to such a PVC.

If the **storageClassName** field is set to an empty string (**""**), these PVCs will only be bound to PVs that have no storage class set.

On the other hand, if the **storageClassName** field in the PVC is not set, then it depends on whether **DefaultStorageClass** has been enabled by the administrator. If a default storage class is set for the cluster, the PVCs with no **storageClassName** field set will be bound to PVs with that default storage class. Otherwise, PVCs with no **storageClassName** field set will only be bound to PVs that have no storage class set.

RESOURCES

Just as we learned that pods can make specific resource requests, PVCs can also request resources in a similar manner by specifying the **requests** and **limits** fields, which are optional. Only the PVs satisfying the resource requests can be bound to a PVC.

VOLUMEMODE

PVCs follow the same convention as PVs to indicate the use of storage as a filesystem or a raw block device. A PVC can only be bound to a PV that has the same Volume mode as the one specified in the PVC configuration.

ACCESSMODE

A PVC should specify the access mode that it needs, and a PV is assigned as per the availability based on that access mode.

SELECTORS

Similar to pod selectors in Services, PVCs can use the **matchLabels** and/or **matchExpressions** fields to specify the criteria of volumes that can satisfy a particular claim. Only the PVs whose labels satisfy the conditions specified in the **selectors** field are considered for a claim. When both of these fields are used together as selectors, the conditions specified by the two fields are combined using an AND operation.

HOW TO USE PERSISTENT VOLUMES

In order to use a PV, we have the following three steps: provisioning the volume, binding it to a claim (PVC), and using the claim as a volume on a pod. Let's go through these steps in detail.

STEP 1 – PROVISIONING THE VOLUME

A Volume can be provisioned in two ways – statically and dynamically:

- **Static**: In static provisioning, the cluster administrator has to provision several PVs beforehand, and only then are they available to PVCs as available resources.

- **Dynamic**: If you are using dynamic provisioning, the administrator doesn't need to provision all the PVs beforehand. In this kind of provisioning, the cluster will dynamically provision the PV for the PVC based on the storage class requested. Thus, as the applications or microservices demand more storage, Kubernetes can automatically take care of it and expand the cloud infrastructure as needed.

  We will go through dynamic provisioning in more detail in a later section.

STEP 2 – BINDING THE VOLUME TO A CLAIM

In this step, a PVC is to be created with the requested storage limits, a certain access mode, and a specific storage class. Whenever a new PVC is created, the Kubernetes controller will search for a PV matching its criteria. If a PV matching all of the PVC criteria is found, it will bind the claim to the PV. Each PV can be bound to only one PVC at a time.

STEP 3 – USING THE CLAIM

Once the PV has been provisioned and bound to a PVC, the PV can be used by the pod as a Volume. Next, when a pod uses a PVC as a Volume, Kubernetes will take the PV bound to that PVC and mount that PV for the pod.

Here's an example of pod configuration using a PVC as a Volume:

```
apiVersion: v1
kind: Pod
metadata:
  name: pod-pvc-as-volume
spec:
  containers:
  - image: nginx
    name: nginx-application
    volumeMounts:
    - mountPath: /data/application
      name: example-storage
  volumes:
  - name: example-storage
    persistentVolumeClaim:
      claimName: example-claim
```

In this example, we assume that we have a PVC named **`example-claim`** that has already been bound to **`PersistentVolume`**. The pod configuration specifies **`persistentVolumeClaim`** as the type of the Volume and specifies the name of the claim to be used. Kubernetes will then find the actual PV bound to this claim and mount it on **`/data/application`** inside the container.

> **NOTE**
>
> The pod and the PVC have to be in the same namespace for this to work. This is because Kubernetes will look for the claim inside the pod's namespace only, and if the PVC isn't found, the pod will not be scheduled. In this case, the pod will be stuck in a **`Pending`** state until deleted.

Now, let's put these concepts into action by creating a pod that uses PV in the following exercise.

EXERCISE 9.03: CREATING A POD THAT USES PERSISTENTVOLUME FOR STORAGE

In this exercise, we will first provision the PV pretending that the cluster administrator does it in advance. Next, assuming the role of a developer, we will create a PVC that is bound to the PV. After that, we will create a pod that will use this claim as a Volume mounted on one of the containers:

1. First of all, we will access the host node via SSH. In the case of Minikube, we can do so by using the following command:

```
minikube ssh
```

You should see an output similar to this one:

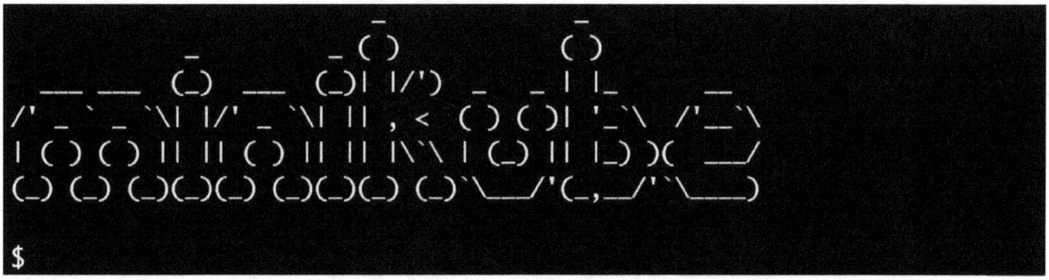

```
                         _             _
            _         _ ( )           ( )
  ___ ___  (_)  ___  (_)| |/')  _   _ | |_      __
/' _ ` _ `\| |/' _ `\| || , <  ( ) ( )| '_`\  /'__`\
| ( ) ( ) || || ( ) || || |\`\ | (_) || |_) )(  ___/
(_) (_) (_)(_)(_) (_)(_)(_) (_)`\___/'(_,__/'`\____)

$
```

Figure 9.11: SSH to the minikube node

2. Run the following command to create a directory named **data** inside the **/mnt** directory:

```
sudo mkdir /mnt/data
```

3. Run the following command to create a file called **data.txt** inside the **/mnt/data** directory:

```
sudo bash -ec 'echo "Data written on host node" > /mnt/data/data.txt'
```

   This command should create a file, **data.txt**, with the **Data written on host node** content. We will use the content of this file to verify at a later stage that we can successfully mount this directory on a container using a PV and a PVC.

4. Run the following command to exit the host node:

```
exit
```

   That will bring us back to the local machine terminal where we can run **kubectl** commands.

5. Create a file called **pv-hostpath.yaml** with the following content:

```
apiVersion: v1
kind: PersistentVolume
metadata:
  name: pv-hostpath
spec:
  storageClassName: local-pv
  capacity:
    storage: 500Mi
  accessModes:
    - ReadWriteOnce
  hostPath:
    path: /mnt/data
```

   In this PV configuration, we have used the **local-pv** storage class. The Volume will be hosted at the **/mnt/data** path on the host node. The size of the volume will be **500Mi** and the access mode will be **ReadWriteOnce**.

6. Run the following command to create the PV using the preceding configuration:

```
kubectl create -f pv-hostpath.yaml
```

You should see the following output:

```
persistentvolume/pv-hostpath created
```

7. Run the following command to check the status of the PV we just created:

```
kubectl get pv pv-hostpath
```

As you can see in this command, **pv** is an accepted shortened name for **PersistentVolume**. You should see the following output:

```
NAME          CAPACITY   ACCESS MODES   RECLAIM POLICY   STATUS      CLAIM   STORAGECLASS   REASON   AGE
pv-hostpath   500Mi      RWO            Retain           Available           local-pv                113s
```

Figure 9.12: Checking the status of the PV

In the preceding output, we can see that the Volume was created with the required configuration and that its status is **Available**.

8. Create a file called **pvc-local.yaml** with the following content:

```
apiVersion: v1
kind: PersistentVolumeClaim
metadata:
  name: pvc-local
spec:
  storageClassName: local-pv
  accessModes:
    - ReadWriteOnce
  resources:
    requests:
      storage: 100Mi
```

In this configuration, we have a claim that requests a Volume with the **local-pv** storage class, the **ReadWriteOnce** access mode and a storage size of **100Mi**.

9. Run the following command to create this PVC:

```
kubectl create -f pvc-local.yaml
```

You should see the following output:

```
persistentvolumeclaim/pvc-local created
```

Once we create this PVC, Kubernetes will search for a matching PV to satisfy this claim.

10. Run the following command to check the status of this PVC:

```
kubectl get pvc pvc-local
```

You should see the following output:

```
NAME        STATUS   VOLUME        CAPACITY   ACCESS MODES   STORAGECLASS   AGE
pvc-local   Bound    pv-hostpath   500Mi      RWO            local-pv       103s
```

Figure 9.13: Checking the status of the claim

As we can see in this output, the PVC has been created with the required configuration and has been immediately bound to the existing PV named **pv-hostpath** that we created in earlier steps of this exercise.

11. Next, we can create a pod that will use this PVC as a Volume. Create a file called **pod-local-pvc.yaml** with the following content:

```
apiVersion: v1
kind: Pod
metadata:
  name: pod-local-pvc
spec:
  restartPolicy: Never
  containers:
  - image: ubuntu
    name: ubuntu-container
    command: ['/bin/bash', '-ec', 'cat /data/application/data.txt']
    volumeMounts:
    - mountPath: /data/application
      name: local-volume
  volumes:
  - name: local-volume
    persistentVolumeClaim:
      claimName: pvc-local
```

The pod will use a PVC named **pvc-local** as a Volume and mount it at the **/data/application** path in the container. Also, we have a container that will run the **cat /data/application/data.txt** command on startup. This is just a simplified example where we will showcase that the data we wrote in the PV directory on the host node initially is now available to this pod.

12. Run the following command to create this pod:

```
kubectl create -f pod-local-pvc.yaml
```

You should see the following output:

```
pod/pod-local-pvc created
```

This output indicates that the pod was created successfully.

13. Run the following command to check the status of the pod we just created:

```
kubectl get pod pod-local-pvc
```

You should see the following output:

```
NAME              READY     STATUS      RESTARTS    AGE
pod-local-pvc     0/1       Completed   1           7s
```

In this output, we can see that the pod has run to completion since we didn't add any sleep commands this time.

14. Run the following command to check the logs. We expect to see the output of the **cat /data/application/data.txt** command in the logs:

```
kubectl logs pod-local-pvc
```

You should see the following output:

```
Data written on host node
```

This output clearly indicates that this pod has access to the file that we created at **/mnt/data/data.txt**. This file is a part of the directory mounted at **/data/application** in the container.

15. Now, let's clean up the resources created in this exercise. Use the following command to delete the pod:

```
kubectl delete pod pod-local-pvc
```

You should see the following output, indicating that the pod has been deleted:

```
pod "pod-local-pvc" deleted
```

16. Use this command to delete the PVC:

```
kubectl delete pvc pvc-local
```

You should see the following output, indicating that the PVC has been deleted:

```
persistentvolumeclaim "pvc-local" deleted
```

Note that if we try to delete the PV before the PVC is deleted, the PV will be stuck in the **Terminating** phase and will wait for it to be released by the PVC. Hence, we need to first delete the PVC bound to the PV before the PV can be deleted.

17. Now that our PVC has been deleted, we can safely delete the PV by running the following command:

```
kubectl delete pv pv-hostpath
```

You should see the following output, indicating that the PV has been deleted:

```
persistentvolume "pv-hostpath" deleted
```

In this exercise, we learned how to provision PVs, create claims to use these volumes, and then use those PVCs as volumes inside pods.

DYNAMIC PROVISIONING

In previous sections of this chapter, we saw that the cluster administrator needs to provision PVs for us before we can use them as storage for our application. To solve this problem, Kubernetes supports dynamic volume provisioning as well. Dynamic volume provisioning enables the creation of storage volumes on-demand. This eliminates the need for administrators to create volumes before creating any PVCs. The volume is provisioned only when there's a claim requesting it.

In order to enable dynamic provisioning, the administrator needs to create one or more storage classes that users can use in their claims to make use of dynamic provisioning. These **StorageClass** objects need to specify what provisioner will be used along with its parameters. The provisioner depends on the environment. Every cloud provider supports different provisioners, so make sure you check with your cloud provider if you happen to create this kind of storage class in your cluster.

Here's an example of the configuration for creating a new **StorageClass** on the AWS platform:

```
apiVersion: storage.k8s.io/v1
kind: StorageClass
metadata:
  name: example-storage-class
provisioner: kubernetes.io/aws-ebs
parameters:
  type: io1
  iopsPerGB: "10"
  fsType: ext4
```

In this configuration, the **kubernetes.io/aws-ebs** provisioner is used – EBS stands for Elastic Block Store and is only available on AWS. This provisioner takes various parameters, including **type**, which we can use to specify what kind of disk we want to use for this storage class. Please check the AWS docs to find out more about the various parameters we can use and their possible values. The provisioner and the parameters required will change based on what cloud provider you use.

Once a storage class is created by the cluster administrator, users can create a PVC, requesting storage with that storage class name set in the **storageClassName** field. Kubernetes will then automatically provision the storage volume, create a PV object with that storage class satisfying the claim, and bind it to the claim:

Here's an example of the configuration for a PVC using the storage class we defined previously:

```
apiVersion: v1
kind: PersistentVolumeClaim
metadata:
  name: example-pvc
spec:
  storageClassName: example-storage-class
  accessModes:
    - ReadWriteOnce
  resources:
    requests:
      storage: 1Gi
```

As we can see, the configuration of the PVC stays the same, except that now, we have to use a storage class that has already been created by the cluster administrator for us.

Once the claim has been bound to an automatically created Volume, we can create pods using that PVC as a Volume, as we saw in the previous section. Once the claim is deleted, the Volume is automatically deleted.

ACTIVITY 9.01: CREATING A POD THAT USES A DYNAMICALLY PROVISIONED PERSISTENTVOLUME

Consider that you are a cluster administrator, at first, and are required to create a custom storage class that will enable the developers using your cluster to provision PVs dynamically. To create a storage class on a minikube cluster, you can use the **`k8s.io/minikube-hostpath`** provisioner without any extra parameters, similar to what we showed in the **`StorageClass`** example in the *Dynamic Provisioning* section.

Next, acting as a developer or a cluster user, claim a PV with a storage request of 100Mi and mount it on the containers inside the pod created using the following specifications:

1. The pod should have two containers.
2. Both the containers should mount the same PV locally.
3. The first container should write some data into the PV and the second container should read and print out the data written by the first container.

For simplicity, consider writing a simple string to a file in the PV from the first container. For the second container, add a bit of wait time so that the second container does not start reading data until it is fully written. Then, the latter container should read and print out the content of the file written by the first container.

> **NOTE**
>
> Ideally, you would want to create this deployment to be in a different namespace to keep it separate from the rest of the stuff that you created during these exercises. So, feel free to create a namespace and create all the objects in this activity in that namespace.

The high-level steps to perform this activity are as follows:

1. Create a namespace for this activity.
2. Write the appropriate configuration for the storage class using the given information, and create the **StorageClass** object.
3. Write the appropriate configuration for the PVC using the storage class created in the previous step. Create the PVC using this configuration.
4. Verify that the claim was bound to an automatically created PV of the same storage class that we created in *step 2*.
5. Write the appropriate configuration for the pod using the given information and the PVC from the previous step as a Volume. Create the pod using this configuration.
6. Verify that one of the containers can read the content of the file written to PV by another container.

You should be able to check the logs of the second container and verify that the data written by the first container in the PV can be read by the second container, as shown in the following output:

```
Data written by container-1
```

> **NOTE**
>
> The solution to this activity can be found at the following address: https://packt.live/304PEoD.

SUMMARY

As we mentioned in the introduction, most applications need to store or retrieve data for a lot of different reasons. In this chapter, we saw that Kubernetes provides various ways of provisioning storage for not just storing the state of an application, but also for the long-term storage of data.

We have covered ways to use storage for our application running inside pods. We saw how we can use the different types of Volumes to share temporary data among containers running in the same pod. We also learned how to persist data across pod restarts. We learned how to manually provision PVs to create PVCs to bind to those Volumes, as well as how to create pods that can use these claims as Volumes mounted on their containers. Next, we learned how to request storage dynamically using only the PVCs with pre-created storage classes. We also learned about the life cycle of these volumes with respect to that of the pods.

In the next chapter, we will extend these concepts further and learn how to store application configurations and secrets.

10

CONFIGMAPS AND SECRETS

OVERVIEW

In this chapter, we will learn how to decouple application configuration data from the application itself and the advantages of taking this approach. By the end of this chapter, you will be able to define Kubernetes ConfigMap and Secret objects, run a simple Pod that uses data from ConfigMaps and Secrets, describe the advantages of decoupling configuration data from applications, and use ConfigMaps and Secrets to decouple application configuration data from the application container.

INTRODUCTION

In *Chapter 5, Pods*, we learned that Pods are the minimal unit of deployment in Kubernetes. Pods can have multiple containers, and each container can have a container image associated with it. This container image generally packages the target application that you plan to run. Once the developers are satisfied that the code is running as expected, the next step is to promote the code to testing, integration, and production environments.

Easy, right? One problem, however, is that as we move our packaged container from one environment to another, although the application remains the same, it needs environment-specific data, for example, the database URL to connect to. To overcome this problem, we can write our applications in such a way that the environment-specific data is provided to the application by the environment it is being deployed into.

In this chapter, we will discover what Kubernetes provides to associate **environment-specific data** with our application containers without changing our container image. There are multiple ways to provide **environment-specific configuration** data to our application:

1. Provide command-line arguments to the Pods.
2. Provide environment variables to the Pods.
3. Mount configuration files in the containers.

First, we need to define our configuration data using an object called **ConfigMap**. Once the data is defined and loaded into Kubernetes, the second step is to provide the defined data to your application.

However, what if you have sensitive data, such as database passwords, that you want to provide to your application container? Well, Kubernetes **Secret** provides a way to define sensitive data to an application.

ConfigMap and Secret objects both serve a similar purpose. Both provide a way to define data that can be injected into your applications so that the same container can be used across different environments. There is little difference between them, which we will learn in detail later on in this chapter. As a quick rule, Secrets are designed to hold confidential data (such as passwords, private keys, and more), while ConfigMaps are more suited for general configuration data such as a database location. ConfigMaps and Secrets reside in the specific namespace in which they are created. They can only be referenced by Pods residing in the same namespace.

Kubernetes uses an internal key-value store called **etcd** as its database to store all the objects defined in Kubernetes. As ConfigMaps and Secrets are Kubernetes objects, they get stored in the internal key-value store.

Let's dig a bit deeper into ConfigMaps first.

WHAT IS A CONFIGMAP?

A ConfigMap allows us to define application-related data. A ConfigMap decouples the application data from the application so that the same application can be ported across different environments. It also provides a way to inject customized data into running services from the same container image.

ConfigMaps can be created through a literal value or from a file or all the files in a directory. Note that the primary data we stored in ConfigMaps is for non-sensitive configuration, for example, config files or environment variables.

Once a ConfigMap is defined, it will be loaded to the application via an environment variable or a set of files. The application can then see the files as local files and can read from them. It is important to note that (from 1.9.6 version onward of Kubernetes), files loaded from ConfigMaps are read-only. ConfigMaps can also hold configuration data for system applications such as operators and controllers.

In the following exercises, you will see different ways of defining ConfigMaps and different ways to make the ConfigMap data available to the running Pods.

Let's see what Kubernetes offers us in terms of ConfigMap creation. Kubernetes help commands provide a good starting point:

```
kubectl create configmap --help
```

You should see the following response:

```
Create a configmap based on a file, directory, or specified literal value.

A single configmap may package one or more key/value pairs.

When creating a configmap based on a file, the key will default to the basename of the file, and the value will default
to the file content.  If the basename is an invalid key, you may specify an alternate key.

When creating a configmap based on a directory, each file whose basename is a valid key in the directory will be
packaged into the configmap.  Any directory entries except regular files are ignored (e.g. subdirectories, symlinks,
devices, pipes, etc).

Aliases:
configmap, cm

Examples:
  # Create a new configmap named my-config based on folder bar
  kubectl create configmap my-config --from-file=path/to/bar

  # Create a new configmap named my-config with specified keys instead of file basenames on disk
  kubectl create configmap my-config --from-file=key1=/path/to/bar/file1.txt --from-file=key2=/path/to/bar/file2.txt

  # Create a new configmap named my-config with key1=config1 and key2=config2
  kubectl create configmap my-config --from-literal=key1=config1 --from-literal=key2=config2

  # Create a new configmap named my-config from the key=value pairs in the file
  kubectl create configmap my-config --from-file=path/to/bar

  # Create a new configmap named my-config from an env file
  kubectl create configmap my-config --from-env-file=path/to/bar.env
```

Figure 10.1: Kubernetes built-in help for creating ConfigMap

As you can see from the preceding output, ConfigMaps can be created for a single value, a list of values, or from an entire file or directory. We will learn exactly how to do each of these in the exercises in this chapter. Note that the command to create a ConfigMap has the following format:

```
kubectl create configmap <map-name> <data-source>
```

Here, **<map-name>** is the name you want to assign to the ConfigMap and **<data-source>** is the directory, file, or literal value to draw the data from.

The data source corresponds to a key-value pair in the ConfigMap, where:

- **Key** is the filename or the key you provided on the command line
- **Value** is the file content or the literal value you provided on the command line

Before we start with the exercises, let's make sure that you have Kubernetes running and that you can issue commands to it. We will use minikube to easily run a single-node cluster on your local computer.

Start up minikube using the following command:

```
minikube start
```

You should see the following response as minikube starts up:

```
There is a newer version of minikube available (v1.2.0).  Download it here:
https://github.com/kubernetes/minikube/releases/tag/v1.2.0

To disable this notification, run the following:
minikube config set WantUpdateNotification false
    minikube v1.1.1 on darwin (amd64)

⚠ Ignoring --vm-driver=virtualbox, as the existing "minikube" VM was created using the vmwarefusion driver.
⚠ To switch drivers, you may create a new VM using `minikube start -p <name> --vm-driver=virtualbox`
⚠ Alternatively, you may delete the existing VM using `minikube delete -p minikube`

    Restarting existing vmwarefusion VM for "minikube" ...
    Waiting for SSH access ...
    Configuring environment for Kubernetes v1.14.3 on Docker 18.09.6
    Relaunching Kubernetes v1.14.3 using kubeadm ...

    Verifying: apiserver proxy etcd scheduler controller dns
    Done! kubectl is now configured to use "minikube"
```

Figure 10.2: Starting up minikube

For all of the exercises in this chapter, we recommend creating a new namespace. Recall from *Chapter 5, Pods*, that namespaces are Kubernetes' way to group components of the solution together. Namespaces can be used to apply policies, quotas, and could also be used to separate resources if the same Kubernetes resources are being used by different teams.

In the following exercise, we will create a ConfigMap from literal values using the kubectl CLI commands. The idea is that we have some configuration data (for example, the master database name) that we can inject into, for example, a MySQL Pod, and it will create the database as per the given environment variable. This set of commands can also be used in the automated code pipelines that are responsible for application deployments across multiple environments.

EXERCISE 10.01: CREATING A CONFIGMAP FROM LITERAL VALUES AND MOUNTING IT ON A POD USING ENVIRONMENT VARIABLES

In this exercise, we will create a ConfigMap in the Kubernetes cluster. This exercise shows how to create ConfigMaps using a key-value pattern. Please follow these steps to complete the exercise:

1. First, let's begin by creating a namespace for all of the exercises in this chapter.

   ```
   kubectl create namespace configmap-test
   ```

   You should see a response like this:

   ```
   namespace/configmap-test created
   ```

   > **NOTE**
   >
   > We will use the **`configmap-test`** namespace for all the exercises in this chapter unless mentioned otherwise.

2. First, let's create a ConfigMap that contains a single name-value pair. Use the command shown here:

   ```
   kubectl create configmap singlevalue-map --from-literal=partner-
   url=https://www.auppost.com.au --namespace configmap-test
   ```

   You should see the following output in the terminal:

   ```
   configmap/singlevalue-map created
   ```

3. Once we create the ConfigMap, let's confirm that it is created by issuing a command to get all the ConfigMaps in the namespace:

   ```
   kubectl get configmaps --namespace configmap-test
   ```

   As **`singlevalue-map`** is the only ConfigMap in the **`configmap-test`** namespace, you should see an output that looks something like this:

   ```
   NAME                DATA    AGE
   singlevalue-map     1       111s
   ```

4. Let's see what the Kubernetes ConfigMap object looks like. Enter the Kubernetes **get** command as follows:

```
kubectl get configmap singlevalue-map -o yaml --namespace configmap-test
```

The full object should be described something like this:

```
apiVersion: v1
data:
  partner-url: https://www.auppost.com.au
kind: ConfigMap
metadata:
  creationTimestamp: "2019-07-24T01:48:32Z"
  name: singlevalue-map
  namespace: configmap-test
  resourceVersion: "547609"
  selfLink: /api/v1/namespaces/configmap-test/configmaps/singlevalue-map
  uid: 24d1f3ab-adb5-11e9-89ac-000c2917147b
$
```

Figure 10.3: Describing singlevalue-map

As you can see in the third line of the preceding output, the ConfigMap is created and the literal value we entered is available as a key-value pair in the **data** section of the ConfigMap.

5. Now, we will create a YAML file named **configmap-as-env.yaml** to create a Pod into which we will inject fields from our ConfigMap as an environment variable. Using your favorite text editor, create a YAML file with the following content:

```
apiVersion: v1
kind: Pod
metadata:
  name: configmap-env-pod
spec:
  containers:
    - name: configmap-container
      image: k8s.gcr.io/busybox
      command: [ "/bin/sh", "-c", "env" ]
      envFrom:
      - configMapRef:
          name: singlevalue-map
```

You can see that the **envFrom** section in the preceding file is loading the data from the ConfigMap.

6. Let's create a Pod from the preceding specification. This Pod is using the **busybox** container image, which runs the command specified in the **command** section of the YAML file mentioned in the previous step:

```
kubectl create -f configmap-as-env.yaml --namespace configmap-test
```

You should see an output like this:

```
pod/configmap-env-pod created
```

7. Let's check the logs for this Pod using the following command:

```
kubectl logs -f configmap-env-pod --namespace configmap-test
```

You should see the logs as shown here:

```
KUBERNETES_PORT=tcp://10.96.0.1:443
KUBERNETES_SERVICE_PORT=443
HOSTNAME=configmap-env-pod
SHLVL=1
HOME=/root
partner-url=https://www.auppost.com.au
KUBERNETES_PORT_443_TCP_ADDR=10.96.0.1
PATH=/usr/local/sbin:/usr/local/bin:/usr/sbin:/usr/bin:/sbin:/bin
KUBERNETES_PORT_443_TCP_PORT=443
KUBERNETES_PORT_443_TCP_PROTO=tcp
KUBERNETES_PORT_443_TCP=tcp://10.96.0.1:443
KUBERNETES_SERVICE_PORT_HTTPS=443
PWD=/
KUBERNETES_SERVICE_HOST=10.96.0.1
```

Figure 10.4: Getting logs for configmap-env-pod

The **["/bin/sh", "-c", "env"]** command will display all the environment variables loaded into the Pod. In the ConfigMap, we have defined the property name as **partner-url**, which is part of the output.

In this exercise, the name of the environment variable, **partner-url**, is the same as the key in our key-value pair. We can also make the name of the environment variable different from the key. For example, if we want to have **partner-server-location** as the name of our environment variable, we can replace the content of the YAML file in the exercise with the following:

```
apiVersion: v1
kind: Pod
metadata:
  name: configmap-multi-env-pod
spec:
  containers:
    - name: configmap-container
      image: k8s.gcr.io/busybox
      command: [ "/bin/sh", "-c", "echo $(partner-server-location)"
        ]
      env:
        - name: partner-server-location
          valueFrom:
            configMapKeyRef:
              name: singlevalue-map
              key: partner-url
```

Pay special attention to the **env** section in the preceding YAML file. The first **name** field after **env** defines the name of the environment variable, and the **key** field under **configMapKeyRef** defines the name of the key in the ConfigMap.

DEFINING A CONFIGMAP FROM A FILE AND LOADING IT ONTO A POD

In this section, we will create a ConfigMap from a file and then load the file onto the application Pod. As mentioned previously, this newly mounted file will be accessible as a local file to the application running inside the Pod.

This is common when applications store their configuration data externally, allowing easier upgrades, as well as patches of the container image across different environments. We can have such a file in our source control repository, and we load the correct file in the correct container using a ConfigMap.

Let's understand this through an example. Imagine that you have written a web application that connects to a database to store information. When you deploy the application in a development environment, you will want to connect to the development database. Once you are satisfied that the application is working correctly, you will want to deploy the application to a testing environment. Since the application is packaged in a container, you would not want to change the container to deploy the application to the testing environment. But to run the application in the testing environment, you need to connect to a different database. An easy solution to this is that you configure your application to read the database server URL from a file, and that file can be mounted through a ConfigMap. This way, the file is not packaged as part of the container, but injected from outside via Kubernetes; thus, you do not need to modify your containerized application. Another use case would be that external software vendors can provide a container image, and any specific configuration settings can be mounted on the image as per a specific client's requirements.

EXERCISE 10.02: CREATING A CONFIGMAP FROM A FILE

In this exercise, we will create a ConfigMap from a file, which can be mounted onto any Pods later on:

1. First, create a file named **application.properties** containing the following configuration details. You may use your preferred text editor:

```
partner-url=https://www.fedex.com
partner-key=1234
```

2. Now, create a ConfigMap from the file using the following command:

```
kubectl create configmap full-file-map --from-file=./application.
properties --namespace configmap-test
```

   You should see the following output indicating that the ConfigMap has been created:

```
configmap/full-file-map created
```

3. Get the list of all ConfigMaps to confirm that our ConfigMap has been created:

```
kubectl get configmaps --namespace configmap-test
```

You should see a list of all ConfigMaps, as shown here:

```
NAME                DATA      AGE
full-file-map       1         109m
singlevalue-map     1         127m
```

You can see that the names of the ConfigMaps are displayed alongside the number of keys they have.

You might be wondering, why does this output show only one key, even though we have added two keys? Let's understand this in the next step.

4. Let's see how the ConfigMap is being stored by using the following command:

```
kubectl get configmap full-file-map -o yaml --namespace configmap-test
```

You should see the following output:

```
apiVersion: v1
data:
  application.properties: |
    partner-url=https://www.fedex.com
    partner-key=1234
kind: ConfigMap
metadata:
  creationTimestamp: "2019-07-29T11:56:14Z"
  name: full-file-map
  namespace: configmap-test
  resourceVersion: "1220"
  selfLink: /api/v1/namespaces/configmap-test/configmaps/full-file-map
  uid: e47d88da-4082-4101-9dbf-37b40063aae1
```

Figure 10.5: Getting details of full-file-map

Note that the name of the file, **`application.properties`**, becomes the **key** under the **`data`** section, and the entire file payload is the **value** of the key.

5. Now that we have defined our ConfigMap, the next step is to mount it onto a container. Create a YAML file named **`mount-configmap-as-volume.yaml`** to be used as our Pod configuration using the following content:

```
apiVersion: v1
kind: Pod
metadata:
  name: configmap-test-pod
spec:
  containers:
    - name: configmap-container
```

```
      image: k8s.gcr.io/busybox
      command: [ "/bin/sh", "-c", "ls /etc/appconfig/" ]
      volumeMounts:
      - name: config-volume
        mountPath: /etc/appconfig
  volumes:
    - name: config-volume
      configMap:
        # Provide the name of the ConfigMap containing the
          files you want
        # to add to the container
        name: full-file-map
  restartPolicy: Never
```

First, let's focus on the **volumes** section in the preceding file. In this section, we are instructing Kubernetes to define a volume from our ConfigMap named **full-file-map**.

Secondly, in the **volumeMounts** section, we are defining that Kubernetes should mount the volume in the **/etc/appconfig** directory.

Note that the **command** field in the container allows us to configure what command we want the container to execute when it starts. In this example, we are running the **ls** command, which is a Linux command to list the contents of a directory. This is similar to the Windows **dir** command. This will print the contents of directory **/etc/appconfig**, where we have mounted the ConfigMap.

> **NOTE**
>
> The **name** field under the **volume** and **volumeMounts** sections has to be the same so that Kubernetes can identify which **volume** is associated with which **volumeMounts**.

6. Now, use the following command to start a Pod using the YAML file we just created:

```
kubectl create -f mount-configmap-as-volume.yaml --namespace configmap-
test
```

You should get a response saying that the Pod has been created:

```
pod/configmap-test-pod created
```

7. The YAML file we used specifies the name of the Pod as **configmap-test-pod** and configures it to just display the content of the folder. To verify this, just issue the following command to get the output logs of the Pod:

```
kubectl logs -f configmap-test-pod --namespace configmap-test
```

This should print **application.properties**, which is the file we placed in the folder:

```
application.properties
```

As you can see, we get the contents of **/etc/appconfig**, which is the output of the **ls** command in the Pod.

You have just successfully defined a ConfigMap and mounted it as a file in a Pod that printed the name of the file.

EXERCISE 10.03: CREATING A CONFIGMAP FROM A FOLDER

In this exercise, we will load all the files in a folder as a ConfigMap. Each filename becomes a key for the ConfigMap, and when you mount it, all the files will be mounted at the **volumeMounts** location (as defined in the YAML file for the container):

1. Create two files in a new folder. Name one of them **fileone.txt**, with its contents as **file one**, and name the other **filetwo.txt**, with its contents as **file two**. The folder name can be anything for this exercise. You can confirm that the files have been created using the **ls** command:

```
ls
```

You will see the following list of files:

```
fileone.txt     filetwo.txt
```

2. Use the following command to create ConfigMap from a folder. Note that instead of specifying the filename, we just mentioned the name of the folder:

```
kubectl create configmap map-from-folder --from-file=./ -n configmap-
test
```

You should see the following response:

```
configmap/map-from-folder created
```

3. Now, let's describe the ConfigMap to see what it contains:

```
kubectl describe configmap map-from-folder -n configmap-test
```

You should see the following output:

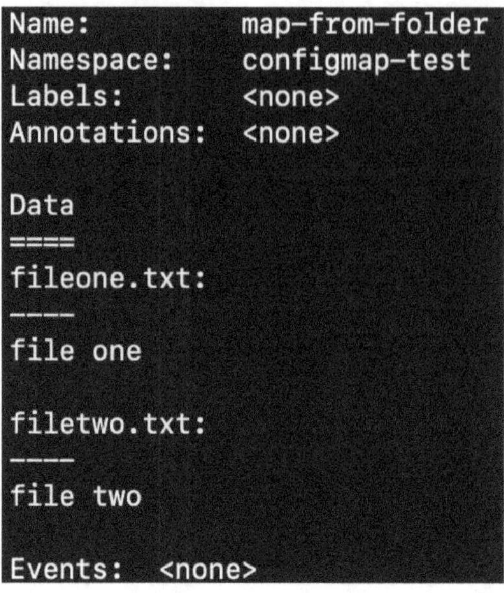
```
Name:         map-from-folder
Namespace:    configmap-test
Labels:       <none>
Annotations:  <none>

Data
====
fileone.txt:
----
file one

filetwo.txt:
----
file two

Events:  <none>
```

Figure 10.6: Describing the map-from-folder ConfigMap

Notice that there are two keys in the ConfigMap – one for each file, that is, **fileone.txt** and **filetwo.txt**. The values of the keys are the contents of the files. Thus, we can see that a ConfigMap can be created from all the files in a folder.

WHAT IS A SECRET?

A ConfigMap provides a way to decouple application configuration data from the application itself. However, the problem with a ConfigMap is that it stores the data in plain text as a Kubernetes object. What if we want to store some **sensitive data** such as a database password? Kubernetes Secret provides a way to store sensitive data that can then be made available to the applications that require it.

SECRET VERSUS CONFIGMAP

You can think of a Secret as the same as a ConfigMap with the following differences:

1. Unlike a ConfigMap, a Secret is intended to store a small amount (1 MB for a Secret) of sensitive data. A Secret is **base64**-encoded, so we cannot treat it as secure. It can also store binary data such as a public or private key.
2. Kubernetes ensures that Secrets are passed only to the nodes that are running the Pods that need the respective Secrets.

> **NOTE**
>
> Another way to store sensitive data is a vault solution, such as HashiCorp Vault. We have left such implementation out of the scope of the workshop.

But wait; if the Kubernetes Secrets are not secure enough due to their base64 encoding, then what is the solution for storing extremely sensitive data? One way is to encrypt it and then store it in Secrets. The data can be decrypted while it is being loaded to the Pod, though we are leaving this implementation out of the scope of this workshop.

Once we define our Secrets, we need to expose them to the applications Pods. The way we expose Secrets to the running application is the same as for ConfigMaps, that is, by mounting them as an environment variable or as a file.

As for ConfigMaps, let's use the built-in **`help`** command for **`secret`** to see what types of Secrets are offered by Kubernetes:

```
kubectl create secret --help
```

The **help** command should show the following:

```
Create a secret using specified subcommand.

Available Commands:
  docker-registry Create a secret for use with a Docker registry
  generic         Create a secret from a local file, directory or literal value
  tls             Create a TLS secret

Usage:
  kubectl create secret [flags] [options]

Use "kubectl <command> --help" for more information about a given command.
Use "kubectl options" for a list of global command-line options (applies to all commands).
```

Figure 10.7: Output of the built-in help command for Secret

As you can see in the preceding output, the **Available Commands** section lists three types of Secrets:

- **generic**: A generic Secret holds any custom-defined key-value pair.
- **tls**: A TLS Secret is a special kind of Secret for holding a public-private key pair for communication using the TLS protocol.
- **docker-registry**: This is a special kind of Secret that stores the username, password, and email address to access a Docker registry.

We will take a deeper dive into the implementation and uses of these Secrets in the following exercises.

EXERCISE 10.04: DEFINING A SECRET FROM LITERAL VALUES AND LOADING THE VALUES ONTO THE POD AS AN ENVIRONMENT VARIABLE

In this exercise, we will define a Secret from a literal value and load it as an environment variable in the running Pod on Kubernetes. This literal value maybe something like a password to your internal database. Since we are creating this Secret from a literal value, it would be categorized as a **generic** Secret. Follow these steps to perform the exercise:

1. First, create a Secret that will hold a simple password by using the following command:

   ```
   kubectl create secret generic test-secret --from-
   literal=password=secretvalue --namespace configmap-test
   ```

   You should get a response as follows:

   ```
   secret/test-secret created
   ```

2. Once we define our Secret, we can use the Kubernetes **describe** command to obtain more details about it:

```
kubectl describe secret test-secret --namespace configmap-test
```

```
Name:         test-secret
Namespace:    configmap-test
Labels:       <none>
Annotations:  <none>

Type:  Opaque

Data
====
password:  11 bytes
```

Figure 10.8: Describing test-secret

You can see that it stored our value against the **password** key:

3. Now that our Secret is created, we will mount it as an environment variable in a Pod. To create a Pod, make a YAML file named **mount-secret-as-env.yaml** with the following content:

```
apiVersion: v1
kind: Pod
metadata:
  name: secret-env-pod
spec:
  containers:
    - name: secret-container
      image: k8s.gcr.io/busybox
      command: [ "/bin/sh", "-c", "env" ]
      envFrom:
      - secretRef:
          name: test-secret
```

Pay attention to the **envFrom** section, which mentions the Secret to load. In the **command** section for the container, we specify the **env** command, which will make the container display all the environment variables loaded into the Pod.

4. Now, let's use the YAML configuration to create a Pod and see it in action:

```
kubectl create -f mount-secret-as-env.yaml --namespace=configmap-test
```

You should see a response as follows:

```
pod/secret-env-pod created
```

5. Now, let's get the logs for the Pod to see all the environment variables displayed by our container:

```
kubectl logs -f secret-env-pod --namespace=configmap-test
```

You should see the logs similar to the following screenshot:

```
KUBERNETES_PORT=tcp://10.96.0.1:443
KUBERNETES_SERVICE_PORT=443
HOSTNAME=secret-env-pod
SHLVL=1
HOME=/root
KUBERNETES_PORT_443_TCP_ADDR=10.96.0.1
PATH=/usr/local/sbin:/usr/local/bin:/usr/sbin:/usr/bin:/sbin:/bin
KUBERNETES_PORT_443_TCP_PORT=443
KUBERNETES_PORT_443_TCP_PROTO=tcp
password=secretvalue
KUBERNETES_PORT_443_TCP=tcp://10.96.0.1:443
KUBERNETES_SERVICE_PORT_HTTPS=443
PWD=/
KUBERNETES_SERVICE_HOST=10.96.0.1
```

Figure 10.9: Getting logs from secret-env-pod

As you can see in the highlighted line of the preceding output, the **password** key is displayed with its value as **secretvalue**, which was what we had specified.

The following exercise demonstrates how to use a public-private key combination and mount the private key file into a Pod. The public key can then be made available to any other service connecting to this Pod, but that is not demonstrated in this exercise. Using a separate file as a Secret enables us to use any kind of file instead of simple key-value strings. This opens up the possibility of using binary files like private key stores.

EXERCISE 10.05: DEFINING A SECRET FROM A FILE AND LOADING THE VALUES ONTO THE POD AS A FILE

In this exercise, we will create a private key, store it in a new Secret, and then load it onto a Pod as a file:

1. First, let's create a private key. We will use a tool used to create SSH keys. Enter the following command in the terminal:

   ```
   ssh-keygen -f ~/test_rsa -t rsa -b 4096 -C "test@example.com"
   ```

   If prompted, do not provide any password for the key.

   > **NOTE**
   >
   > If you require more information about the SSH protocol and its uses, please refer to https://www.ssh.com/ssh/protocol/.

   After this is executed successfully, you will see two files named **test_rsa** and **test_rsa.pub**. You should see an output similar to the one shown here:

```
Generating public/private rsa key pair.
Enter passphrase (empty for no passphrase):
Enter same passphrase again:
Your identification has been saved in /Users/faisalmasood/test_rsa.
Your public key has been saved in /Users/faisalmasood/test_rsa.pub.
The key fingerprint is:
SHA256:AXDE/3UZ4oVjT168TJZgURTU7QVsZ3bR54k+8K7OgYw test@example.com
The key's randomart image is:
+---[RSA 4096]----+
|     .++     *BOB|
|     ...    * *+&|
|      ..   o O=X*|
|       .. .o.=+o|
|        S. .+.   |
|        o o  +   |
|       E o .. .  |
|          . ..   |
|          .+.    |
+----[SHA256]-----+
```

Figure 10.10: Creating SSH keys

Your output may not be exactly the same as shown here because the keys are randomized.

> **NOTE**
>
> Most Linux distros include the **ssh-keygen** tool. However, if you don't have or cannot use **ssh-keygen**, you can use any other file instead of the private key to proceed with this exercise.

2. Now, let's load the newly created private key as a Secret. This time, we will use the **from-file** argument of the **create secret** command:

```
kubectl create secret generic test-key-secret --from-file=private-
key=/Users/faisalmassod/test_rsa --namespace=configmap-test
```

You should get a response like this:

```
secret/test-key-secret created
```

3. Once the Secret is created, we can get its details using the **describe** command:

```
kubectl describe secret test-key-secret --namespace=configmap-test
```

The Secret should be described as follows:

```
Name:         test-key-secret
Namespace:    configmap-test
Labels:       <none>
Annotations:  <none>

Type:  Opaque

Data
====
private-key:  3381 bytes
```

Figure 10.11: Describing test-key-secret

4. Now that our Secret is created, let's mount it onto a Pod. The process is similar to mounting a ConfigMap. First, create a YAML file named **mount-secret-as-volume.yaml** with the following content:

```
apiVersion: v1
kind: Pod
metadata:
  name: secret-test-pod
spec:
  containers:
    - name: secret-container
      image: k8s.gcr.io/busybox
      command: [ "/bin/sh", "-c", "ls /etc/appconfig/; cat 
        /etc/appconfig/private-key" ]
      volumeMounts:
      - name: secret-volume
        mountPath: /etc/appconfig
  volumes:
    - name: secret-volume
      secret:
        # Provide the name of the Secret containing the files 
          you want
        # to add to the container
        secretName: test-key-secret
```

In the preceding Pod specification, note that **volumes** are mounted the same way as we mounted the earlier ConfigMap. In the volumes section, we are instructing Kubernetes to define a volume from our Secret. In the **volumeMounts** section, we are defining the specific path on which Kubernetes should mount the volume. The **"/bin/sh", "-c", "ls /etc/appconfig/; cat /etc/appconfig/private-key"** command will print out the contents of the file loaded onto it as a Secret.

> **NOTE**
>
> The **name** field in the **volume** and **volumeMounts** sections has to be the same so that Kubernetes can identify which **volume** is associated with which **volumeMounts**. For this example, we have used **secret-volume** as the name in both places.

5. Now, let's create a Pod using the YAML file as the Pod definition using the following command:

```
kubectl create -f mount-secret-as-volume.yaml --namespace=configmap-
test
```

If the Pod is successfully created, you should see the following output:

```
pod/secret-test-pod created
```

6. To check whether our Pod has the Secret loaded, we can get its logs and examine them. Use the following command:

```
kubectl logs -f secret-test-pod --namespace=configmap-test
```

The logs should show the contents of the private key, as follows:

```
private-key
-----BEGIN OPENSSH PRIVATE KEY-----
b3BlbnNzaC1rZXktdjEAAAAABG5vbmUAAAAEbm9uZQAAAAAAAAABAAACFwAAAAdzc2gtcn
NhAAAAAwEAAQAAAgEAuyK4s7tLoRtEzdIr1o6FWA8qW7N9rMCFfPsVh7M8s7J2iYA/HhS8
WQS+RzhliTlaYfTdbjwaVJZhhgEVN6PCqAWZGCRCiw+UBKWe0uGm4whDIDhdnXF3y20/BS
bhb+iIBLlKj7Z4+1wdQRT28AsytY9iNZPA22ApWxeAsHi/qffIUp+hhITJ9ije0IUQeQLC
8qwvEHx89CP1+rVSP02DrCd1RmbbGRsd2uPeWfE9aKKkxFwoR7XXK24vmkTyL+2elUODdH
i3pJXMpo1hFcYhFr/4vml4m6qRyRWwhnMieYzHX70xmGTu/ta6TjQLJxtSzDvIj+/dEKIt
iPGkLhSoon3rnGa20xltTBci/m86JhGpob3/6H03UuhOZv8+XNO7eMj7ev8Mat/7sOSS62
K4+z2hZovk9i9zuMfDmJAqJqoRlMl55V3EPyM/ouHNB0fjxkODZ1bApLxz1KicpeKJBMUF
DAmxBKHYjFgam02Mxci9EIvCNymfjFQFnPkUSFj+mFCwTt1RLD/+hP4WeSiHJRHIyibUfa
sD2cN8mN3CE1TV/ONez431QKaWPJFa6tMlngcrcgDA3jYYI8HzrNuIJCYEc7rBkNAe4NZm
GCKfT0nRQAUhApxMoQmc9qtkFhLNO/AbrKMfZfR3gCm1AkN/zo9uCpxxL/VC9MUam43S9c
cAAAdITMfpVUzH6VUAAAAHc3NoLXJzYQAAAgEAuyK4s7tLoRtEzdIr1o6FWA8qW7N9rMCF
fPsVh7M8s7J2iYA/HhS8WQS+RzhliTlaYfTdbjwaVJZhhgEVN6PCqAWZGCRCiw+UBKWe0u
Gm4whDIDhdnXF3y20/BSbhb+iIBLlKj7Z4+1wdQRT28AsytY9iNZPA22ApWxeAsHi/qffI
Up+hhITJ9ije0IUQeQLC8qwvEHx89CP1+rVSP02DrCd1RmbbGRsd2uPeWfE9aKKkxFwoR7
```

Figure 10.12: Getting logs of secret-test-pod

As you can see from the log, the container is displaying the contents of the Secret mounted onto the Pod.

> **NOTE**
>
> Since the SSH key is randomized, your output may not look exactly the same as the one shown here.

7. The SSH key is randomized, so each time you will get a different output. You can try this exercise multiple times and see for yourself. Make sure to either delete the Pod or change the name every time. You can delete the Pod using the following command:

```
kubectl delete pod secret-test-pod --namespace=configmap-test
```

You will see the following output if the Pod is successfully deleted:

```
pod "secret-test-pod" deleted
```

In this exercise, we created a key pair using another tool and loaded the private key onto our Pod by mounting it as a binary file. However, public-private key pairs are used for encryption in the TLS protocol, which is a cryptographic standard for securing web traffic.

> **NOTE**
>
> To learn more about TLS, please refer to https://www.cloudflare.com/learning/ssl/transport-layer-security-tls/.

Kubernetes provides its own way of creating a key pair and storing keys for TLS. Let's see how to create a TLS Secret in the following exercise.

EXERCISE 10.06: CREATING A TLS SECRET

In this exercise, we will see how to create a Secret that can store a cryptographic key for TLS:

1. Use the following command to create a pair of private-public keys:

```
openssl req -x509 -nodes -days 365 -newkey rsa:2048 -keyout tls.key
-out tls.crt -subj "/CN=kube.example.com"
```

This command creates the private key in the file named **`tls.key`**, and the public certificate in the file named **`tls.crt`**.

> **NOTE**
>
> For more details on how the **openssl** tool is used here, you can refer to https://www.openssl.org/docs/manmaster/man1/req.html.

If the key is successfully generated, you should see an output like this:

```
Generating a 2048 bit RSA private key
..................................+++
.....................................................+++
writing new private key to 'tls.key'
-----
```

Figure 10.13: Creating SSL keys

2. Once it is successful, we can create a Secret to hold the files using the following command:

```
kubectl create secret tls test-tls --key="tls.key" --cert="tls.crt"
--namespace=configmap-test
```

Once the Secret is successfully created, you will see the following output:

```
secret/test-tls created
```

3. Verify that our Secret is created by listing down all Secrets in the **configmap-test** namespace using the following command:

```
kubectl get secrets --namespace configmap-test
```

Our Secret must be listed in the following output:

```
NAME                  TYPE                                  DATA   AGE
default-token-hvn5s   kubernetes.io/service-account-token   3      27m
test-key-secret       Opaque                                1      5m2s
test-secret           Opaque                                1      7m34s
test-tls              kubernetes.io/tls                     2      17s
```

Figure 10.14: Listing down all secrets in configmap-test

4. If we issue the **describe** command for the newly created Secret, you can see that it stores the two parts, the public and the private key, as two different keys of the Secret:

```
kubectl describe secrets test-tls --namespace configmap-test
```

You should see the following response:

```
Name:           test-tls
Namespace:      configmap-test
Labels:         <none>
Annotations:    <none>

Type:  kubernetes.io/tls

Data
====
tls.key:  1704 bytes
tls.crt:  997 bytes
```

Figure 10.15: Describing test-tls

Thus, we have created a set of public-private keys for TLS using a special set of commands provided by Kubernetes. This Secret can be mounted in a similar way as demonstrated in *Exercise 10.05, Defining a Secret from a File and Loading the Values onto the Pod as a File*.

Another common task is to fetch Docker images from an external Docker registry. Many organizations use **enterprise container registries** (for example, Nexus) for their applications, which can then be fetched and deployed as needed. Kubernetes also provides a special type of Secret to store authentication information for accessing these Docker registries. Let's see how to implement it in the following exercise.

EXERCISE 10.07: CREATING A DOCKER-REGISTRY SECRET

In this exercise, we will create a **docker-registry** Secret that can be used for authentication while fetching a Docker image from a registry:

1. We can create the Secret directly using the following command:

```
kubectl create secret docker-registry test-docker-registry-secret
--docker-username=test --docker-password=testpassword --docker-
email=example@a.com --namespace configmap-test
```

   As you can see in the command arguments, we need to specify the username, password, and email address for the Docker account. Once the Secret is created, you should see the following response:

```
secret/test-docker-registry-secret created
```

2. Verify that it is created by using this command:

```
kubectl get secrets test-docker-registry-secret --namespace configmap-
test
```

   You should see **test-docker-registry-secret** as displayed in the following output:

```
NAME                          TYPE                             DATA   AGE
test-docker-registry-secret   kubernetes.io/dockerconfigjson   1      30s
```

Figure 10.16: Checking test-docker-registry-secret

3. Let's use the **describe** command and get more details about our Secret:

```
kubectl describe secrets test-docker-registry-secret --namespace
configmap-test
```

   The command should return the following details:

```
Name:         test-docker-registry-secret
Namespace:    configmap-test
Labels:       <none>
Annotations:  <none>

Type:  kubernetes.io/dockerconfigjson

Data
====
.dockerconfigjson:  145 bytes
```

Figure 10.17: Describing test-docker-registry-secret

As you can see under the **Data** section of the preceding output, a single key with the name **.dockerconfigjson** has been created.

> **NOTE**
>
> This exercise is just an easy way to load a **.dockerconfigjson** file. You can create and load the file manually using other methods and achieve the same objective as we have in this exercise.

ACTIVITY 10.01: USING A CONFIGMAP AND SECRET TO PROMOTE AN APPLICATION THROUGH DIFFERENT STAGES

Let's assume that we have an application and we want to promote it to different environments. Your task is to promote the application from testing to production environments, and each environment has different configuration data.

In this activity, we will use the ConfigMap and Secret to easily reconfigure the application for different stages in its life cycle. It should also give you an idea of how the separation of ConfigMap data and Secret data from the application can help in the easier transition of an application through various stages of development and deployment.

These guidelines should help you to complete the activity:

1. Define a namespace called **my-app-test**.
2. Define a ConfigMap named **my-app-data** in the **my-app-test** namespace with the following key values:

```
external-system-location=https://testvendor.example.com
external-system-basic-auth-username=user123
```

3. Define a Secret named **my-app-secret** in the **my-app-test** namespace with the following key values:

```
external-system-basic-auth-password=password123
```

4. Define a Pod specification and deploy the ConfigMap in the **/etc/app-data** folder with the filename **application-data.properties**.
5. Define a Pod specification and deploy the Secret in the **/etc/secure-data** folder with the filename **application-secure.properties**.

6. Run the Pod so that it displays all the contents from the ConfigMap and the Secret. You should see something like this:

```
external-system-location=https://testvendor.example.com
external-system-basic-auth-username=user123
external-system-basic-auth-password=password123
```

Figure 10.18: Key values for the test environment

7. Define another namespace called **my-app-production**.
8. Define a ConfigMap named **my-app-data** in **my-app-production** with the following key values:

```
external-system-location=https://vendor.example.com
external-system-basic-auth-username=activityapplicationuser
```

9. Define a Secret named **my-app-secret** in **my-app-production** with the following key values:

```
external-system-basic-auth-password=A#4b*(1=B88%tFr3
```

10. Use the same Pod specification as defined in *step 5* and run the Pod in the **my-app-production** namespace.
11. Check whether the application running in **my-app-production** displays the correct data. You should see output like this:

```
external-system-location=https://vendor.example.com
external-system-basic-auth-username=activityapplicationuser
external-system-basic-auth-password=A#4b*(1=B88%tFr3
```

Figure 10.19: Key values for the production environment

> **NOTE**
>
> The solution to this activity can be found at the following address: https://packt.live/304PEoD. The GitHub repository also includes a Bash script for this activity, which will execute all these solution steps automatically. However, please take a look at the detailed steps provided in the solution to get a complete understanding of how to perform the activity.

SUMMARY

In this chapter, we have seen the different ways that Kubernetes provides to associate environment-specific data with our applications running as containers.

Kubernetes provides ways to store sensitive data as Secrets and normal application data as ConfigMaps. We have also seen how to create ConfigMaps and Secrets and associate them with our containers via CLI. Running everything via the command line will facilitate the automation of these steps and improve the overall agility of your application.

Associating data with containers enables us to use the same container across different environments in our IT systems (for example, in test and production). Using the same container across different environments provides a way for secure and trusted code promotion techniques for IT processes. Each team can use a container as a unit of deployment and sign the container so that other parties can trust the container. This also provides a trusted way of distributing code not only across the same IT organizations but also across multiple organizations. For example, a software vendor can just provide you with a container as packaged software. ConfigMaps and Secrets can then be used to provide specific configurations for using the packaged software in your organization.

The next set of chapters is all about deploying Kubernetes and running it in high availability mode. These chapters will provide you with fundamental and practical knowledge regarding how to run stable clusters for Kubernetes.

11

BUILD YOUR OWN HA CLUSTER

OVERVIEW

In this chapter, we will learn how Kubernetes enables us to deploy infrastructure with remarkable resilience and how to set up a high-availability Kubernetes cluster in the AWS cloud. This chapter will help you understand what enables Kubernetes to be used for highly available deployments and, in turn, enable you to make the right choices while architecting a production environment for your use case. By the end of the chapter, you will be able to set up a suitable cluster infrastructure on AWS to support your **highly available** (**HA**) Kubernetes cluster. You will also be able to deploy an application in a production environment.

INTRODUCTION

In the previous chapters, you learned about application containerization, how Kubernetes works, and some of the "proper nouns" or "objects" in Kubernetes that allow you to create a declarative-style application architecture that Kubernetes will execute on your behalf.

Software and hardware instability are a reality in all environments. As applications need higher and higher availability, shortcomings in the infrastructure become more obvious. Kubernetes was purpose-built to help solve this challenge for containerized applications. But what about Kubernetes itself? As cluster operators, do we shift from watching our individual servers like hawks to watching our single Kubernetes control infrastructure?

As it turns out, this aspect was one of the design considerations for Kubernetes. One of the design goals of Kubernetes is to be able to withstand instability in its own infrastructure. This means that when set up properly, the Kubernetes control plane could withstand quite a few disasters, including:

- Network splits/partitions
- Control plane (master) server failure
- Data corruption in etcd
- Many other less severe events that impact availability events

Not only can Kubernetes help your application tolerate failure, but you can rest easy at night knowing that Kubernetes can also tolerate failures in its own control infrastructure. In this chapter, we are going to build a cluster of our very own and make sure that it is highly available. High availability implies that the system is very reliable and almost always available. This does not mean that everything in it always works perfectly; it just means that whenever the user or client wants something, the architecture stipulates that the API server should be **available** to do the job. This means that we have to design a system for our applications to automatically respond to and take corrective measures in response to any faults.

In this chapter, we will look at how Kubernetes integrates such measures to tolerate faults in its own control architecture. Then, you will have the chance to extend this concept a bit further by designing your application to take advantage of this horizontally scalable, fault-tolerant architecture. But first, let's look at how the different cogs in the machine turn together to enable it to be highly available.

HOW THE COMPONENTS OF KUBERNETES WORK TOGETHER TO ACHIEVE HIGH AVAILABILITY

You have learned in *Chapter 2, An Overview of Kubernetes*, how the pieces of Kubernetes work together to provide a runtime for your application containers. But we need to investigate deeper how these components work together to achieve high availability. To do that, we'll start with the memory bank of Kubernetes, otherwise known as etcd.

ETCD

As you have learned in earlier chapters, etcd is the place where all Kubernetes configuration is stored. This makes it arguably the single most important component of the cluster since changes in etcd affect the state of everything. More specifically, any change to a key-value pair in etcd will cause the other components of Kubernetes to react to this change, which could mean disruptions to your application. In order to achieve high availability for Kubernetes, it is wise to have more than one etcd node.

But many more challenges arise when you add multiple nodes to an eventually consistent datastore like etcd. Do you have to write to every node to persist a change of state? How does replication work? Do we read from just one node or as many as are available? How does it handle networking failures and partitions? Who is the master of the cluster and how does leader election work? The short answer is that, by design, etcd makes these challenges either non-existent or easy to deal with. etcd uses a consensus algorithm called **Raft** to achieve replication and fault tolerance in relation to many of the aforementioned issues. Thus, if we're building a Kubernetes HA cluster, we need to make sure that we set up multiple nodes (preferably an odd number to make leader election tie-breaking easier) of an etcd cluster properly, and we can rely on that from there.

> **NOTE**
>
> Leader election in etcd is a process where multiple instances of the database software collectively vote on which host will be an authority for dealing with any issues that arise in achieving database consensus. For more details, refer to this link: https://raft.github.io/

NETWORKING AND DNS

Many of the applications that run on Kubernetes require some form of network to be useful. Therefore, networking is an important consideration when designing a topology for your clusters. For example, your network should be able to support all of the protocols that your application uses, including the ones for Kubernetes. Kubernetes itself uses TCP for all of its communication between masters, nodes, and etcd, and it uses UDP for internal domain name resolution, which is otherwise known as service discovery. Your network should also be provisioned to have at least as many IP addresses as the number of nodes that you plan to have in the cluster. For example, if you planned to have more than 256 machines (nodes) in your cluster, you probably shouldn't use an IP CIDR address space of /24 or higher since that only has 255 or fewer available IP addresses.

Later in this workshop, we will talk about the security decisions you will need to make as a cluster operator. However, in this section, we will not discuss them because they do not directly relate to Kubernetes' ability to achieve high availability. We will deal with the security of Kubernetes in *Chapter 13, Runtime and Network Security in Kubernetes*.

One final thing to take into consideration about the network where your master and worker nodes will run is that every master node should be able to communicate with every worker node. The reason this is important is that each master node communicates with the Kubelet process running on the worker node in order to determine the state of the full cluster.

NODES' AND MASTER SERVERS' LOCATIONS AND RESOURCES

Because of the design of etcd's Raft algorithm, which allows distributed consensus to happen in the key-value store of Kubernetes, we are able to run multiple master nodes, each of which is capable of controlling the entire cluster without the fear of them behaving independently from each other (in other words, going rogue). As a reminder of why master nodes being out of sync is a problem in Kubernetes, consider that the runtime of your application is being controlled by commands that Kubernetes issues on your behalf. If those commands conflict with each other because of state sync problems between master nodes, then your application runtime will suffer as a result. By introducing multiple master nodes, we again provide resistance to faults and network partitions that could potentially sacrifice the availability of the cluster.

Kubernetes is actually able to run in a "headless" mode. This means whatever instructions the Kubelets (worker nodes) have last received from the master nodes will continue to be carried out until communication with the master nodes can be re-established. In theory, this means an application that was deployed on Kubernetes could run indefinitely, even if the entire control plane (all master nodes) went down and nothing else changed on the worker nodes where the Pods running the application were scheduled. Obviously, this is a worst-case scenario for the availability of a cluster, but it is reassuring to know that, even in the worst case, applications don't necessarily have to suffer downtime.

When you are planning the design and capacity for a high-availability deployment of Kubernetes, it is important to know a few things about the design of your network, which we discussed previously. For example, if you are running a cluster in a popular cloud provider, they likely have a concept of "availability zones". A similar concept for data center environments would be physically isolated data centers. If possible, there should be at least one master node and multiple worker nodes per availability zone. This is important because, in the event of an availability zone (data center) outage, your cluster is still able to operate within the remaining availability zones. This is illustrated in the following diagrams:

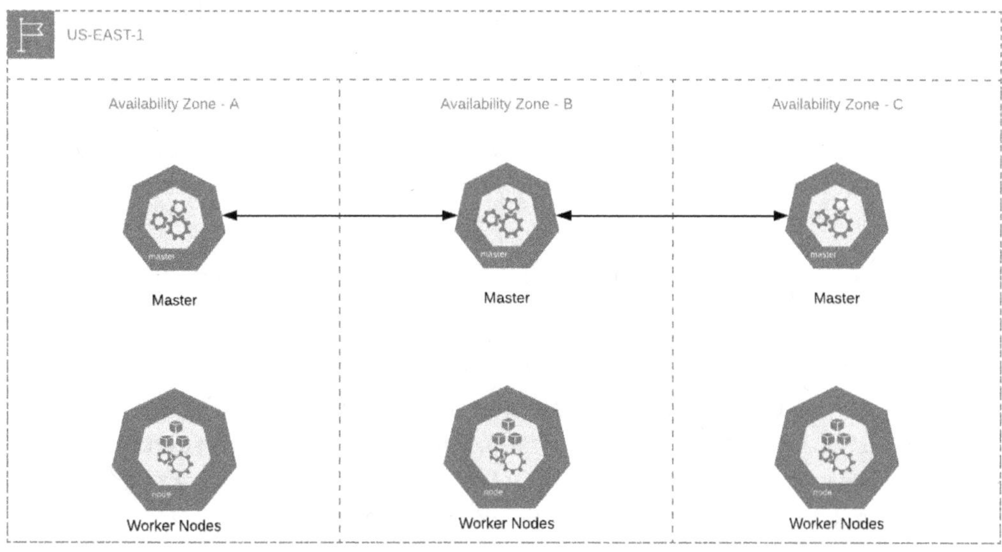

Figure 11.1: The cluster before the outage of an availability zone

Let's assume that there is a total outage of Availability Zone – C, or at least we are no longer able to communicate with any servers that are running inside it. Here is how the cluster now behaves:

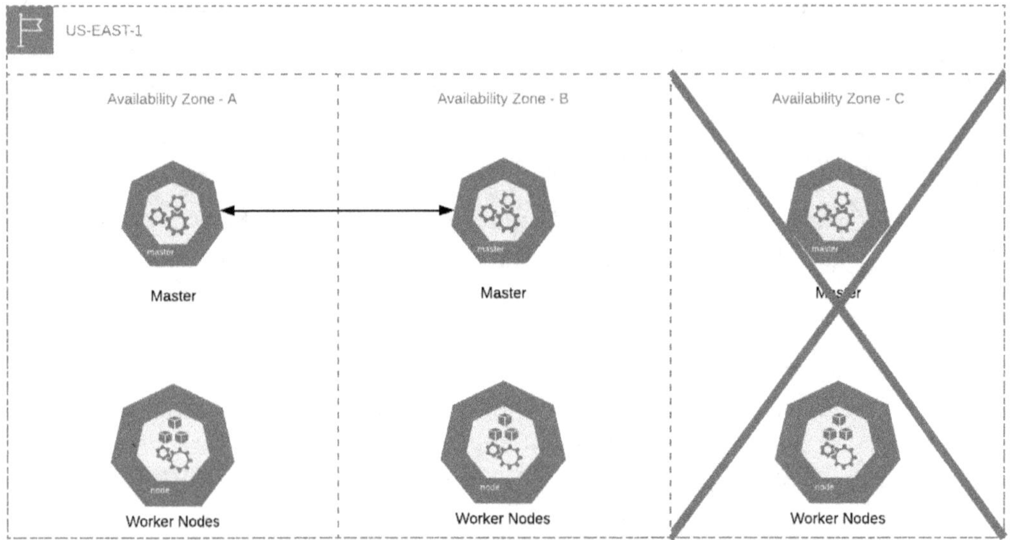

Figure 11.2: The cluster following the outage of an availability zone

As you can see in the diagram, Kubernetes can still execute. Additionally, if the loss of the nodes running in Availability Zone - C causes an application to no longer be in its desired state, which is dictated by the application's Kubernetes manifest, the remaining master nodes will work to schedule the interrupted workload on the remaining worker nodes.

> **NOTE**
>
> Depending on the number of worker nodes in your Kubernetes cluster, you may have to plan for additional resource constraints because of the amount of CPU power needed to run a master connected to several worker nodes. You can use the chart at this link to determine the resource requirements of the master nodes you should deploy for controlling your cluster: https://kubernetes.io/docs/setup/best-practices/cluster-large/

CONTAINER NETWORK INTERFACE AND CLUSTER DNS

The next decision you need to make with respect to your cluster is how the containers themselves communicate across each of the nodes. Kubernetes itself has a container network interface called **kubenet**, which is what we will use in this chapter.

For smaller deployments and simple operations, kubenet more than exceeds the needs of those clusters from a **Container Network Interface** (**CNI**) perspective. However, it does not work for every workload and network topology. So, Kubernetes provides support for several different CNIs. When considering container network interfaces from a high-availability perspective, you will want the most performant and stable option possible. It is beyond the scope of this introduction to Kubernetes to discuss each of the CNI offerings at length.

> **NOTE**
>
> If you plan to use a managed Kubernetes service provider or plan to have a more complex network topology such as multiple subnets inside a single VPC, kubenet will not work for you. In this case, you will have to pick one of the more advanced options. More information on selecting the right CNI for your environment can be found here: https://chrislovecnm.com/kubernetes/cni/choosing-a-cni-provider/

CONTAINER RUNTIME INTERFACES

One of the final decisions you will have to make is how your containers will run on your worker nodes. The Kubernetes default for this is the Docker container runtime interface, and Kubernetes was initially built to work with Docker. Since then, however, open standards have been developed and other container runtime interfaces are now compatible with the Kubernetes API. Generally, cluster operators tend to stick with Docker because it is extremely well established. Even if you want to explore alternatives, keep in mind when designing a topology capable of maintaining high availability for your workloads and Kubernetes that you'll probably want to go with more established and stable options like Docker.

> **NOTE**
>
> You can find some of the other container runtime interfaces that are compatible with Kubernetes on this page: https://kubernetes.io/docs/setup/production-environment/container-runtimes/

CONTAINER STORAGE INTERFACES

Recent versions of Kubernetes have introduced improved ways of interacting with the persistence tools that are available in data centers and cloud providers such as storage arrays and blob storage. The most important improvement has been the introduction and standardization of the container storage interface for managing **`StorageClass`**, **`PersistentVolume`**, and **`PersistentVolumeClaim`** in Kubernetes. The consideration for highly available clusters you will need to make with regard to storage is more specific per application. For example, if your application makes use of Amazon EBS volumes, which must reside within an availability zone, then you will have to ensure appropriate redundancy is available in your worker nodes so that the Pod that depends on that volume can be rescheduled in the event of an outage. More information on CSI drivers and implementations can be found here: https://kubernetes-csi.github.io/docs/

BUILDING A HIGH-AVAILABILITY FOCUSED KUBERNETES CLUSTER

Hopefully, by reading the previous section, you're starting to realize that Kubernetes is less magical than it may seem when you first approached the topic. It is an extremely powerful tool on its own, but Kubernetes really shines when we take full advantage of its capability of running in a highly available configuration. So now we're going to see how to implement it and actually build a cluster using a cluster life cycle management tool. But before we do that, we need to know the different ways that we can deploy and manage a Kubernetes cluster.

SELF-MANAGED VERSUS VENDOR-MANAGED KUBERNETES SOLUTIONS

Amazon Web Services, Google Cloud Platform, Microsoft Azure, and practically every other major cloud services provider has a managed Kubernetes offering. So, when you are deciding how you are going to build and run your cluster, you should consider some of the different managed providers and their strategic offerings to see whether or not they align with your business needs and goals. For example, if you use Amazon Web Services, then Amazon EKS might be a viable solution for you.

There are trade-offs with choosing a managed service provider over an open-source and self-managed solution. For example, a lot of the hard work of cluster assembly is done for you, but you forfeit a great deal of control in the process. So, you need to decide how much value you place on being able to control the Kubernetes master plane and whether or not you would like to be able to pick your container networking interface or container runtime interface. For the purposes of this tutorial, we are going to use an open-source solution because it can be deployed anywhere, and it also helps us understand how Kubernetes works and how it is supposed to be configured.

> **NOTE**
>
> Please ensure that you have an AWS account and are able to access it using the AWS CLI: https://aws.amazon.com/cli.
>
> If you are unable to access it, then please follow the instructions at the preceding link.

Assuming for now that we want more control over our cluster and are comfortable with managing it by ourselves, let's look at some open-source tools that can be used for setting up a cluster.

KOPS

We will use one of the more popular open-source installation tools to do this called **kops**, which stands for **Kubernetes Operations**. It is a complete cluster life cycle management tool and has a very easy API to understand. As a part of the cluster creation/updating process, kops can generate Terraform configuration files so you can run the infrastructure upgrade process as part of your own pipeline. It also has good tooling to support the upgrade path between versions of Kubernetes.

> **NOTE**
>
> Terraform is an infrastructure life cycle management tool that we will briefly learn about in the next chapter.

Some of the drawbacks of kops are that it tends to be about two versions of Kubernetes behind, it has not always been able to respond to vulnerability announcements as fast as other tools, and it is currently limited to creating clusters in AWS, GCP, and OpenStack.

The reason we have decided to use kops for our cluster life cycle management in this chapter is four-fold:

- We wanted to select a tool that would abstract away some of the more confusing bits of the Kubernetes setup as we ease you into cluster administration.
- It supports more cloud platforms than just AWS, so you don't have to be locked into Amazon if you choose not to be.
- It supports a broad array of customizations to the Kubernetes infrastructure, such as choosing CNI providers, deciding on a VPC network topology, and node instance group customizations.
- It has first-class support for zero-downtime cluster version upgrades and handles the process automatically.

OTHER COMMONLY USED TOOLS

Besides kops, there are several other tools that can be used to set up a Kubernetes cluster. You can find the full list at this link: https://kubernetes.io/docs/setup/#production-environment.

We will mention a couple of them here so you get an idea of what's available:

- **kubeadm**: This is generated from the Kubernetes source code and is the tool that will allow the greatest level of control over each component of Kubernetes. It can be deployed in any environment.

  Using kubeadm requires an expert level knowledge of Kubernetes to be useful. It gives cluster administrators little room for error, and it is complicated to upgrade a cluster using kubeadm.

- **Kubespray**: This uses Ansible/Vagrant-style configuration management, which is familiar to many IT professionals. It is better for environments where the infrastructure is more static rather than dynamic (such as the cloud). Kubespray is very composable and configurable from a tooling perspective. It also allows the deployment of a cluster on bare-metal servers. The key to watch out for here is coordinating software upgrades of cluster components and hardware and operating systems. Since you are providing much of the functionality a cloud provider does, you have to make sure your upgrade processes won't break the applications running on top of the cluster.

  Because Kubespray uses Ansible for provisioning, you are restricted by the underlying limitations of Ansible for provisioning large clusters and keeping them in spec. Currently, Kubespray is limited to the following environments: AWS, GCP, Azure, OpenStack, vSphere, Packet, Oracle Cloud Infrastructure, or your own bare-metal installations.

AUTHENTICATION AND IDENTITY IN KUBERNETES

Kubernetes uses two concepts for authentication: ServiceAccounts are meant to identify processes running inside Pods, and User Accounts are meant to identify human users. We will take a look at ServiceAccounts in a later topic in this chapter, but first, let's understand User Accounts.

From the very beginning, Kubernetes has tried to remain incredibly agnostic to any form of authentication and identity for user accounts, because most companies have a very specific way of authenticating users. Some use Microsoft Active Directory and Kerberos, some may use Unix passwords and UGW permission sets, and some may use a cloud provider or software as a service-based IAM solution. In addition, there are a number of different authentication strategies that may be used by an organization.

Because of this, Kubernetes does not have built-in identity management or a required single way of authenticating those identities. Instead, it has a concept of authentication "strategies." A strategy is essentially a way for Kubernetes to delegate the verification of identity to another system or method.

In this chapter, we will be using x509 certificate-based authentication. X509 certificate authentication essentially makes use of the Kubernetes Certificate Authority and common names/organization names. Since Kubernetes RBAC rules use **`usernames`** and **`group names`** to map authenticated identities to permission sets, x509 **`common names`** become the **`usernames`** of Kubernetes, and **`organization names`** become the **`group names`** in Kubernetes. kops automatically provisions x509-based authentication certificates for you so there is little to worry about; but when it comes to adding your own users, you will want to be aware of this.

> **NOTE**
>
> Kubernetes RBAC stands for Role-Based Access Control, which allows us to allow or deny certain access to our users based on their roles. This will be covered in more depth in *Chapter 13*, *Runtime and Network Security in Kubernetes*.

An interesting feature of kops is that you can use it in a similar way to manage cluster resources as you would use kubectl to manage cluster resources. kops handles a node similar to how Kubernetes would handle a Pod. Just as Kubernetes has a resource called "Deployment" to manage a bunch of Pods, kops has a resource called **InstanceGroup** (which can also be referred to by its short form, **`ig`**) to manage a bunch of nodes. In the case of AWS, a kops InstanceGroup effectively creates an AWS EC2 Autoscaling group.

Extending this comparison, **`kops get instancegroups`** or **`kops get ig`** is analogous to **`kubectl get deployments`**, and **`kops edit`** works similarly to **`kubectl edit`**. We will make use of this feature in the activity later in the chapter, but first, let's get our basic HA cluster infrastructure up and running in the following exercise.

> **NOTE**
>
> In this chapter, the commands have been run using the Zsh shell. However, they are completely compatible with Bash.

EXERCISE 11.01: SETTING UP OUR KUBERNETES CLUSTER

> **NOTE**
>
> This exercise will exceed the free tier of AWS that is normally given to new account holders for the first 12 months. Pricing information on EC2 can be found here: https://aws.amazon.com/ec2/pricing/
>
> Also, you should remember to delete your instances at the end of the chapter to stop being billed for your consumed AWS resources.

In this exercise, we will prepare our infrastructure for running a Kubernetes cluster on AWS. There's nothing particularly special about the choice of AWS; Kubernetes is platform-agnostic, though it already has code that allows it to integrate with native AWS services (EBS, EC2, and IAM) on behalf of cluster operators. This is also true for Azure, GCP, IBM Cloud, and many other cloud platforms.

We will set up a cluster with the following specifications:

- Three master nodes
- Three etcd nodes (to keep things simple, we will run these on the master nodes)
- Two worker nodes
- At least two availability zones

Once we have our cluster set up, we will deploy an application on it in the next exercise. Now follow these steps to complete this exercise:

1. Ensure that you have installed kops as per the instructions in the *Preface*. Verify that kops is properly installed and configured using the following command:

```
kops version
```

You should see the following response:

```
Version 1.15.0 (git-9992b4055)
```

Now before we move on to the following steps, we need to do some setup in AWS. Most of the following settings are configurable, but we will be making a few decisions for you for the sake of convenience.

2. First, we will set up an AWS IAM user that kops will use to provision your infrastructure. Run the following commands one after the other in your terminal:

```
aws iam create-group --group-name kops

aws iam attach-group-policy --policy-arn arn:aws:iam::aws:policy/
AmazonEC2FullAccess --group-name kops

aws iam attach-group-policy --policy-arn arn:aws:iam::aws:policy/
AmazonRoute53FullAccess --group-name kops

aws iam attach-group-policy --policy-arn arn:aws:iam::aws:policy/
AmazonS3FullAccess --group-name kops

aws iam attach-group-policy --policy-arn arn:aws:iam::aws:policy/
IAMFullAccess --group-name kops

aws iam attach-group-policy --policy-arn arn:aws:iam::aws:policy/
AmazonVPCFullAccess --group-name kops

aws iam create-user --user-name kops

aws iam add-user-to-group --user-name kops --group-name kops

aws iam create-access-key --user-name kops
```

You should see output similar to this:

```
aws iam attach-group-policy --policy-arn arn:aws:iam::aws:policy/AmazonEC2FullAccess
 --group-name kops
aws iam attach-group-policy --policy-arn arn:aws:iam::aws:policy/AmazonRoute53FullAc
cess --group-name kops
aws iam attach-group-policy --policy-arn arn:aws:iam::aws:policy/AmazonS3FullAccess
--group-name kops
aws iam attach-group-policy --policy-arn arn:aws:iam::aws:policy/IAMFullAccess --gro
up-name kops
aws iam attach-group-policy --policy-arn arn:aws:iam::aws:policy/AmazonVPCFullAccess
 --group-name kops

aws iam create-user --user-name kops

aws iam add-user-to-group --user-name kops --group-name kops

aws iam create-access-key --user-name kops
{
    "Group": {
        "Path": "/",
        "GroupName": "kops",
        "GroupId": "AGPA5YQUHQAPQUSWCU2CR",
        "Arn": "arn:aws:iam::946008981535:group/kops",
        "CreateDate": "2020-01-25T12:52:43Z"
    }
}
{
    "User": {
        "Path": "/",
        "UserName": "kops",
        "UserId": "AIDA5YQUHQAPSUUYXUSU3",
        "Arn": "arn:aws:iam::946008981535:user/kops",
        "CreateDate": "2020-01-25T12:52:51Z"
    }
}
{
    "AccessKey": {
        "UserName": "kops",
        "AccessKeyId": "AKIA5YQUHQAP5GNU7NWF",
        "Status": "Active",
        "SecretAccessKey": "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",
        "CreateDate": "2020-01-25T12:52:54Z"
    }
}
```

Figure 11.3: Setting up an IAM user for kops

Note the highlighted **AccessKeyID** and **SecretAccessKey** fields you will receive for your output. This is sensitive information, and the keys in the preceding screenshot will, of course, be invalidated by the author. We will need the highlighted information for our next step.

3. Next, we need to export the created credentials for kops as environment variables for our terminal session. Use the highlighted information from the screenshot in the previous step:

```
export AWS_ACCESS_KEY_ID=<AccessKeyId>
export AWS_SECRET_ACCESS_KEY=<SecretAccessKey>
```

4. Next, we need to create an S3 bucket for kops to store its state. To create a random bucket name, run the following command:

```
export BUCKET_NAME="kops-$(LC_ALL=C tr -dc 'a-z0-9' </dev/urandom |
head -c 13 ; echo)" && echo $BUCKET_NAME
```

The second command outputs the name of the S3 bucket created, and you should see a response similar to the following:

```
kops-aptjv0e9o2wet
```

5. Run the following command to create the required bucket using the AWS CLI:

```
aws s3 mb s3://$BUCKET_NAME --region us-west-2
```

Here, we are using the **us-west-2** region. You can use a region closer to you if you want. You should see the following response for a successful bucket creation:

```
make_bucket: kops-aptjv0e9o2wet
```

Now that we have our S3 bucket, we can begin to set our cluster up. There are numerous options we can choose, but right now we're going to work with the defaults.

6. Export the name of your cluster and the S3 bucket that kops will use to store its state:

```
export NAME=myfirstcluster.k8s.local
export KOPS_STATE_STORE=s3://$BUCKET_NAME
```

7. Generate all the config and store it in the S3 bucket from earlier to create a Kubernetes cluster using the following command:

```
kops create cluster --zones us-west-2a,us-west-2b,us-west-2c
--master-count=3 --kubernetes-version=1.15.0 --name $NAME
```

By passing the **--zones** argument, we are specifying the availability zones we want our cluster to span, and by specifying the **master-count=3** parameter, we are effectively saying we want to use a highly available Kubernetes cluster. By default, kops will create two worker nodes.

Note that this did not actually create the cluster, but it created a pre-flight set of checks so we can create a cluster in just a moment. It is informing us that in order to access our AWS instances, we need to provide a public key – the default search location is **~/.ssh/id_rsa.pub**.

8. Now, we need to create an SSH key to be added to all of the master and worker nodes so we can log in to them with SSH. Use the following command:

```
kops create secret --name myfirstcluster.k8s.local sshpublickey admin
-i ~/.ssh/id_rsa.pub
```

The type of secret (**sshpublickey**) is a special keyword reserved to kops for this operation. More information can be found at this link: https://github.com/kubernetes/kops/blob/master/docs/cli/kops_create_secret_sshpublickey.md.

> **NOTE**
>
> The key being specified here at **~/.ssh/id_rsa.pub** will be the key that kops is going to distribute to all master and worker nodes and can be used for SSH from your local computer to the running server for diagnostic or maintenance purposes.

You can use the following command to use the key to log in with an admin account:

```
ssh -i ~/.ssh/id_rsa admin@<public_ip_of_instance>
```

While this is not required for this exercise, you will find this useful for a later chapter.

9. To view our configuration, let's run the following command:

```
kops edit cluster $NAME
```

This will open your text editor with the definition of our cluster, as shown here:

```
apiVersion: kops.k8s.io/v1alpha2
kind: Cluster
metadata:
  creationTimestamp: "2020-01-25T13:37:24Z"
  name: myfirstcluster.k8s.local
spec:
  api:
    loadBalancer:
      type: Public
  authorization:
    rbac: {}
  channel: stable
  cloudProvider: aws
  configBase: s3://kops-abze1cw4wsf0t/myfirstcluster.k8s.local
  etcdClusters:
  - cpuRequest: 200m
    etcdMembers:
    - instanceGroup: master-us-west-2a
      name: a
    memoryRequest: 100Mi
    name: main
  - cpuRequest: 100m
    etcdMembers:
    - instanceGroup: master-us-west-2a
      name: a
    memoryRequest: 100Mi
    name: events
  iam:
    allowContainerRegistry: true
    legacy: false
```

Figure 11.4: Examining the definition of our cluster

We have truncated this screenshot for brevity. At this point, you can make any edits, though, for this exercise, we will proceed without making any changes. We will keep the description of this spec out of the scope of this workshop for brevity. If you want more details about the various elements in the **clusterSpec** of kops, you can find more details here: https://github.com/kubernetes/kops/blob/master/docs/cluster_spec.md.

10. Now, take the configuration we generated and stored in S3 and actually run commands to reconcile the AWS infrastructure with what we said we wanted it to be in our config files:

```
kops update cluster $NAME --yes
```

> **NOTE**
>
> All commands in kops are dry-run (nothing will actually happen except some validation steps) by default unless you specify the **`--yes`** flag. This is a protectionary measure, so you don't accidentally do something harmful to your cluster in production.

This will take a long time, but after it's done, we'll have a working Kubernetes HA cluster. You should see the following response:

```
I0125 15:14:35.716296   10817 apply_cluster.go:556] Gossip DNS: skipping DNS validation
I0125 15:14:39.522404   10817 executor.go:103] Tasks: 0 done / 95 total; 43 can run
I0125 15:14:43.191821   10817 vfs_castore.go:729] Issuing new certificate: "etcd-manager-ca-events"
I0125 15:14:43.271673   10817 vfs_castore.go:729] Issuing new certificate: "etcd-peers-ca-main"
I0125 15:14:43.305705   10817 vfs_castore.go:729] Issuing new certificate: "etcd-peers-ca-events"
I0125 15:14:43.410568   10817 vfs_castore.go:729] Issuing new certificate: "etcd-manager-ca-main"
I0125 15:14:43.760330   10817 vfs_castore.go:729] Issuing new certificate: "ca"
I0125 15:14:44.406332   10817 vfs_castore.go:729] Issuing new certificate: "apiserver-aggregator-ca"
I0125 15:14:45.177145   10817 vfs_castore.go:729] Issuing new certificate: "etcd-clients-ca"
I0125 15:14:48.989778   10817 executor.go:103] Tasks: 43 done / 95 total; 26 can run
I0125 15:14:54.592041   10817 vfs_castore.go:729] Issuing new certificate: "kube-scheduler"
I0125 15:14:54.644617   10817 vfs_castore.go:729] Issuing new certificate: "kube-controller-manager"
I0125 15:14:54.654585   10817 vfs_castore.go:729] Issuing new certificate: "apiserver-aggregator"
I0125 15:14:54.782827   10817 vfs_castore.go:729] Issuing new certificate: "kube-proxy"
I0125 15:14:54.783214   10817 vfs_castore.go:729] Issuing new certificate: "kops"
I0125 15:14:54.896238   10817 vfs_castore.go:729] Issuing new certificate: "apiserver-proxy-client"
I0125 15:14:54.999278   10817 vfs_castore.go:729] Issuing new certificate: "kubelet"
I0125 15:14:55.263693   10817 vfs_castore.go:729] Issuing new certificate: "kubelet-api"
I0125 15:14:56.427218   10817 vfs_castore.go:729] Issuing new certificate: "kubecfg"
I0125 15:15:01.674217   10817 executor.go:103] Tasks: 69 done / 95 total; 22 can run
I0125 15:15:09.663504   10817 executor.go:103] Tasks: 91 done / 95 total; 3 can run
I0125 15:15:14.581826   10817 vfs_castore.go:729] Issuing new certificate: "master"
I0125 15:15:17.656541   10817 executor.go:103] Tasks: 94 done / 95 total; 1 can run
I0125 15:15:24.768284   10817 executor.go:103] Tasks: 95 done / 95 total; 0 can run
I0125 15:15:31.422504   10817 update_cluster.go:294] Exporting kubecfg for cluster
kops has set your kubectl context to myfirstcluster.k8s.local

Cluster is starting.  It should be ready in a few minutes.

Suggestions:
 * validate cluster: kops validate cluster
 * list nodes: kubectl get nodes --show-labels
 * ssh to the master: ssh -i ~/.ssh/id_rsa admin@api.myfirstcluster.k8s.local
 * the admin user is specific to Debian. If not using Debian please use the appropriate user based on your OS.
 * read about installing addons at: https://github.com/kubernetes/kops/blob/master/docs/addons.md.
```

Figure 11.5: Updating the cluster to match the generated definition

11. To validate that our cluster is running, let's run the following command. This may take up to 5-10 minutes to fully work:

```
kops validate cluster
```

You should see the following response:

```
Using cluster from kubectl context: myfirstcluster.k8s.local

Validating cluster myfirstcluster.k8s.local

INSTANCE GROUPS
NAME                    ROLE    MACHINETYPE     MIN     MAX     SUBNETS
master-us-west-2a       Master  m3.medium       1       1       us-west-2a
master-us-west-2b       Master  m3.medium       1       1       us-west-2b
master-us-west-2c       Master  m3.medium       1       1       us-west-2c
nodes                   Node    t2.medium       2       2       us-west-2a,us-west-2b,us-west-2c

NODE STATUS
NAME                                            ROLE    READY
ip-172-20-105-193.us-west-2.compute.internal    node    True
ip-172-20-113-65.us-west-2.compute.internal     master  True
ip-172-20-62-164.us-west-2.compute.internal     master  True
ip-172-20-68-181.us-west-2.compute.internal     node    True
ip-172-20-78-59.us-west-2.compute.internal      master  True

Your cluster myfirstcluster.k8s.local is ready
```

Figure 11.6: Validating our cluster

From this screenshot, we can see we have three Kubernetes master nodes running in separate availability zones, and two worker nodes spread across two of the three availability zones (making this a highly available cluster). Also, all of the nodes as well as the cluster appear to be healthy.

> **NOTE**
>
> Remember your cluster resources are still running. If you plan to proceed to the next exercise after a significant amount of time, you may want to delete this cluster to stop the billing for the AWS resources. To delete this cluster, you can use the following command:
>
> **`kops delete cluster --name ${NAME} --yes`**

KUBERNETES SERVICE ACCOUNTS

As we learned earlier, a Kubernetes ServiceAccount object serves as an identification marker for a process inside a Pod. While Kubernetes does not manage and authenticate the identity of human users, it does manage and authenticate ServiceAccount objects. And then, similar to users, you can allow role-based access to Kubernetes resources for ServiceAccount.

ServiceAccount acts as a way of authenticating to the cluster using **JSON Web Token (JWT)** style, header-based authentication. Every ServiceAccount is paired with a token stored in a secret that is created by the Kubernetes API and then mounted into the Pod associated with that ServiceAccount. Whenever any process in the Pod needs to make an API request, it passes the token along with it to the API server, and Kubernetes maps that request to the ServiceAccount. Based on that identity, Kubernetes can then determine the level of access to the resources/objects (authorization) that a process should be granted. Typically, service accounts are given to Pods inside the cluster as they are intended only to be used internally. A ServiceAccount is a Kubernetes namespace-scoped object.

An example spec for a ServiceAccount would look as follows:

```
apiVersion: v1
kind: ServiceAccount
metadata:
  name: admin-user
  namespace: kube-system
```

We will use this example in the next exercise. You would attach this ServiceAccount to an object by including this field in the definition of an object such as a Kubernetes deployment:

```
serviceAccountName: admin-user
```

If you create a Kubernetes object without specifying a service account, it will be created with the **`default`** service account. A **`default`** service account is created by Kubernetes for each namespace.

In the following exercise, we will deploy the Kubernetes Dashboard on our cluster. Kubernetes Dashboard is arguably one of the most helpful tools to have running in any Kubernetes cluster. It is useful for debugging issues with configuring workloads in Kubernetes.

> **NOTE**
>
> You can find more information about it here: https://kubernetes.io/docs/tasks/access-application-cluster/web-ui-dashboard/.

EXERCISE 11.02: DEPLOYING AN APPLICATION ON OUR HA CLUSTER

In this exercise, we will use the same cluster that we deployed in the previous exercise and deploy Kubernetes Dashboard. If you have deleted your cluster resources, then please rerun the previous exercise. kops will automatically add the required information to connect to the cluster in your local Kube config file (found at **~/.kube/config**) and set that cluster as the default context.

Since the Kubernetes Dashboard is an application that helps us in administration tasks, the **default** ServiceAccount does not have sufficient privileges. We will be creating a new ServiceAccount with generous privileges in this exercise:

1. To begin with, we will apply the Kubernetes Dashboard manifest sourced directly from the official Kubernetes repository. This manifest defines all the objects that we will need for our application. Run the following command:

```
kubectl apply -f https://raw.githubusercontent.com/kubernetes/
dashboard/v2.0.0-beta1/aio/deploy/recommended.yaml
```

   You should see the following response:

```
namespace/kubernetes-dashboard created
serviceaccount/kubernetes-dashboard created
service/kubernetes-dashboard created
secret/kubernetes-dashboard-certs created
secret/kubernetes-dashboard-csrf created
secret/kubernetes-dashboard-key-holder created
configmap/kubernetes-dashboard-settings created
role.rbac.authorization.k8s.io/kubernetes-dashboard created
clusterrole.rbac.authorization.k8s.io/kubernetes-dashboard created
rolebinding.rbac.authorization.k8s.io/kubernetes-dashboard created
clusterrolebinding.rbac.authorization.k8s.io/kubernetes-dashboard created
deployment.apps/kubernetes-dashboard created
service/dashboard-metrics-scraper created
deployment.apps/kubernetes-metrics-scraper created
```

Figure 11.7: Applying the manifest for Kubernetes Dashboard

2. Next, we need to configure a ServiceAccount to access the dashboard. To do this, create a file called **sa.yaml** with the following content:

```
apiVersion: v1
kind: ServiceAccount
metadata:
  name: admin-user
  namespace: kube-system
---
apiVersion: rbac.authorization.k8s.io/v1
kind: ClusterRoleBinding
metadata:
  name: admin-user
roleRef:
  apiGroup: rbac.authorization.k8s.io
  kind: ClusterRole
  name: cluster-admin
subjects:
- kind: ServiceAccount
  name: admin-user
  namespace: kube-system
```

> **NOTE**
>
> We are giving this user very liberal permissions, so please treat the access token with care. ClusterRole and ClusterRoleBinding objects are a part of RBAC policies, which are covered in *Chapter 13*, *Runtime and Network Security in Kubernetes*.

3. Next, run the following command:

```
kubectl apply -f sa.yaml
```

You should see this response:

```
serviceaccount/admin-user created
clusterrolebinding.rbac.authorization.k8s.io/admin-user created
```

4. Now, let's confirm the ServiceAccount details by running the following command:

```
kubectl describe serviceaccount -n kube-system admin-user
```

You should see the following response:

```
Name:                admin-user
Namespace:           kube-system
Labels:              <none>
Annotations:         kubectl.kubernetes.io/last-applied-configuration:
                       {"apiVersion":"v1","kind":"ServiceAccount","metadata":{"a
nnotations":{},"name":"admin-user","namespace":"kube-system"}}
Image pull secrets:  <none>
Mountable secrets:   admin-user-token-vx84g
Tokens:              admin-user-token-vx84g
Events:              <none>
```

Figure 11.8: Examining our ServiceAccount

When you create a ServiceAccount in Kubernetes, it will also create a Secret in the same namespace with the contents of the JWT needed to make API calls against the API server. As we can see from the previous screenshot, the Secret in this case is named **admin-user-token-vx84g**.

5. Let's examine the **secret** object:

```
kubectl get secret -n kube-system -o yaml admin-user-token-vx84g
```

You should see the following output:


```
  namespace: a3ViZS1zeXN0ZW0=
  token: ZXlKaGJHY2lPaUpTVXpJMU5pSXNJbXRwWkNJNklpSjkuZXlKcGMzTWlPaUpyZFdKbGNtNWx
kR1Z6TDNObGNuWnBZMlZoWTJOdmRXNTBJaXdpYTNWaVpYSnVaWFJsY3k1cGJ5OXpaWEoyYVdObFlXTmp
iM1Z1ZEM5dVlXMWxjM0JoWTJVaU9pSnJkV0psTFhONWMzUmxiU0lzSW10MVlmVnlibVYwWlhNdWFXOHZ
jM1Z5ZG1salpXRmpZMjkxYm5RdmMyVmpjbVYwTG01aGJXVWlPaUpoWkcxcGJpMTFjM1Z5TFhSdmEyVnV
MWFo0T0RSbklpd2lhM1ZpWlhKdVpYUmxjeTVwYnk5elpYSjhV05sWVdOamIzVnVkQzl6WlhKMmFXTmx
MV0ZqWTI5MWJuUXVibUZ0WlNJNkltRmtiV2x1TFhWelpYSWlMQ0pyZFdKbGNtNWxkR1Z6TG1sdkwzTmx
jblpwWTJWaFkyTnZkVzUwTDNObGNuWnBZMlV0WVdOamIzVnVkQzUxYVdRaU9pSmlPVFExTkRNMk5TMHl
OR0prTFRSak5ETXRZakpsT1Mxa05tUTVNV1JpT1RNMk1UVWlMQ0p6ZFdJaU9pSnplWE4wWlcwNmMyVnl
kbWxqWldGalkyOTFiblE2YTNWaVpTMXplWE4wWlcwNllXUnRhVzR0ZFhObGNpSjkuQ0hvNmRHY0V6Mm8
5dlBONXdreFVKSThiZTlMQUJRX2JOMC02RnU4dkNpaXRDX19VZ2RDZjdQdExDWnd5M1JHTlhkNFFKWW1
tUGpfSXZjQ3pKb1hwVWVtclg2cEY0WlNSU2VPc2xaUkYyMWQycXdPVTdmSGtmX0JMbmxzbVhVcFFuN1B
pdFMwZFpGRXFwVEllUUhENGN6eE5GaUYwZ2ZTZTRPWEYzVkNvMTcxd3lpNWl6QWVLc01GNzBkSHkwdFJ
kNS1wTjlNejNCcnlDMFJSalFLNnVaeTFZbGczZkpQNjUzZ1F2elllOGdpbE9VeFZreGdLTDFMSEpxNzk
1Y3kxc1BPcHpNNFdua2NyNm5Od2lvSnR5eVlzcVVhVzdmNzZLVU5yVDg5dC1FVU9vNjBuSGlzcGxYWll
JOXVPVUNaWjVNR19UdEcxLTJEb2ZaVWNkZGhEdkxn
kind: Secret
metadata:
  annotations:
    kubernetes.io/service-account.name: admin-user
    kubernetes.io/service-account.uid: b9454365-24bd-4c43-b2e9-d6d91db93615
  creationTimestamp: "2020-05-03T00:11:22Z"
  name: admin-user-token-vx84g
  namespace: kube-system
  resourceVersion: "174327"
  selfLink: /api/v1/namespaces/kube-system/secrets/admin-user-token-vx84g
  uid: d8b89a20-e3a9-4147-a9f1-c14d5f397dd3
type: kubernetes.io/service-account-token
```


Figure 11.9: Examining the token in our ServiceAccount

This is a truncated screenshot of the output. As we can see, we have a token here in this secret. Note that this is Base64 encoded, which we will decode in the next step.

6. Now we need the content of the token for the account Kubernetes just created for us, so let's use this command:

```
kubectl -n kube-system get secret $(kubectl -n kube-system get secret
| grep admin-user | awk '{print $1}') -o jsonpath='{.data.token}' |
base64 --decode
```

   Let's break this command down. The command gets the secret called **admin-user** because we created a ServiceAccount with that name. When a ServiceAccount is created in Kubernetes, it places a secret named the same with the token we use to authenticate to the cluster. The rest of the command is syntactic sugar to decode the result in a useful form for copying and pasting into the dashboard. You should get an output as shown in the following screenshot:


```
eyJhbGciOiJSUzI1NiIsImtpZCI6IiJ9.eyJpc3MiOiJrdWJlcm5ldGVzL3NlcnZpY2VhY2NvdW50Iiw
ia3ViZXJuZXRlcy5pby9zZXJ2aWNlYWNjb3VudC9uYW1lc3BhY2UiOiJrdWJlLXN5c3RlbSIsImt1YmV
ybmV0ZXMuaW8vc2VydmljZWFjY291bnQvc2VjcmV0Lm5hbWUiOiJhZG1pbi11c2VyLXRva2VuLWc5OWZ
iIiwia3ViZXJuZXRlcy5pby9zZXJ2aWNlYWNjb3VudC9zZXJ2aWNlLWFjY291bnQubmFtZSI6ImFkbWl
uLXVzZXIiLCJrdWJlcm5ldGVzLmlvL3NlcnZpY2VhY2NvdW50L3NlcnZpY2UtYWNjb3VudC51aWQiOiJ
kMTlkNGQzYi1iOTQ4LTQ0ZWYtODA2Ni1iMGMzZGNiM2U1YmQiLCJzdWIiOiJzeXN0ZW06c2VydmljZWF
jY291bnQ6a3ViZS1zeXN0ZW06YWRtaW4tdXNlciJ9.C5IRqbTNVFeMI4L80SslseAbiDHE8s8U01Dih-
91VIyrVTcS1VSVifXeTg5zcn8FlEbp-VDPvVhZjSmIQJYRnNJk5zQxlhftjVOcLmyYapOzwORS2JMRCH
e5OMauczAdBvX3MzAHhDGjyZsNEDQRPa8E_CGjZQlZvWSSuAHvff8FDr8nnXnufbuzNLOWJyRskZiPSx
FbEQa2FEQguFtC_LX5oeX3wkugkzlPm3JzPjgAN-xLQUPf7uXyCU7R03gdcGaiOvir67h_ul211m5T0j
ZUW6zufGX_fvvVqkyap3ewInP-06pj1EfqeOaR9ulEA4rSO4Z2t2TwSdL618USbA%
```


Figure 11.10: Getting the content of the token associated with the admin-user ServiceAccount

   Copy the output you receive, while being careful not to copy the **$** or **%** signs (seen in Bash or Zsh, respectively) seen at the very end of the output.

7. By default, Kubernetes Dashboard is not exposed to the public internet outside our cluster. So, in order to access it with our browser, we need a way to allow our browser to communicate with Pods inside the Kubernetes container network. One useful way is to use the proxy built into **kubectl**:

```
kubectl proxy
```

   You should see this response:

```
Starting to serve on 127.0.0.1:8001
```

8. Open your browser and navigate to the following URL:

```
http://localhost:8001/api/v1/namespaces/kubernetes-dashboard/
services/https:kubernetes-dashboard:/proxy/
```

You should see the following prompt:

Kubernetes Dashboard

Authentication method:

Kubeconfig

Token

Token *

SIGN IN   SKIP

Figure 11.11: Entering the token to sign in to Kubernetes Dashboard

Paste your token copied from *step 4*, and then click on the **`SIGN IN`** button.

After logging in successfully, you should see the dashboard as shown in the following screenshot:

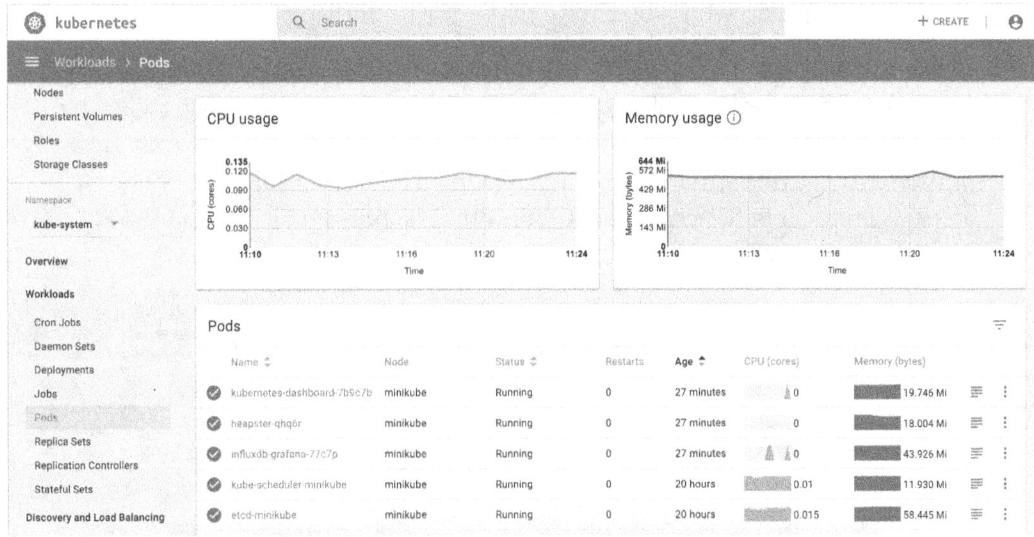

Figure 11.12: Kubernetes Dashboard landing page

In this exercise, we have deployed Kubernetes Dashboard to the cluster to allow you to administer your application from a convenient GUI. During the course of deploying this application, we have seen how we can create ServiceAccounts for our cluster.

Throughout this chapter, you've learned how to create the cloud infrastructure using kops to make a highly available Kubernetes cluster. Then, we deployed the Kubernetes Dashboard and learned about ServiceAccounts in the process. Now that you have seen the steps required to make a cluster and get an application running on it, we will make another cluster and see its resilience in action in the following activity.

ACTIVITY 11.01: TESTING THE RESILIENCE OF A HIGHLY AVAILABLE CLUSTER

In this activity, we will test out the resiliency of a Kubernetes cluster we create ourselves. Here are some guidelines for proceeding with this activity:

1. Deploy Kubernetes Dashboard. But this time, set the replica count of the deployment running the application to something higher than **1**.

   The Kubernetes Dashboard application is run on Pods managed by a deployment named **kubernetes-dashboard**, which runs in a namespace called **kubernetes-dashboard**. This is the deployment that you need to manipulate.

2. Now, start shutting down various nodes from the AWS console to remove nodes, delete Pods, and do what you can to make the underlying system unstable.

3. After each attempt you make to take down the cluster, refresh the Kubernetes console if the console is still accessible. So long as you get any response from the application, this means that the cluster and our application (in this case, Kubernetes Dashboard) is still online. As long as the application is online, you should be able to access the Kubernetes Dashboard as shown in the following screenshot:

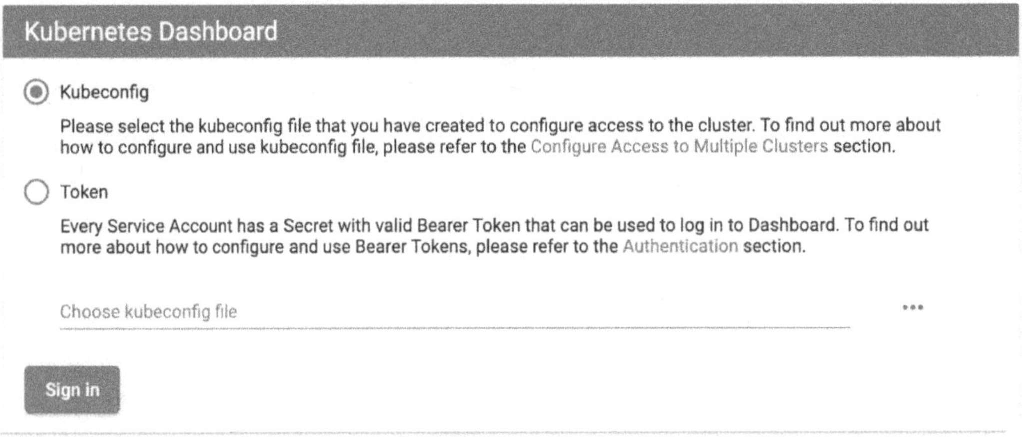

Kubernetes Dashboard

Kubeconfig

Please select the kubeconfig file that you have created to configure access to the cluster. To find out more about how to configure and use kubeconfig file, please refer to the Configure Access to Multiple Clusters section.

Token

Every Service Account has a Secret with valid Bearer Token that can be used to log in to Dashboard. To find out more about how to configure and use Bearer Tokens, please refer to the Authentication section.

Choose kubeconfig file

Sign in

Figure 11.13: Kubernetes Dashboard prompt for entering a token

This screenshot shows just the prompt where you need to enter your token, but it is a good enough indicator that our application is online. If your request times out, this means that our cluster is no longer functional.

4. Join another node to this cluster.

   To achieve this, you need to find and edit the InstanceGroup resource that is managing the nodes. The spec contains **maxSize** and **minSize** fields, which you can manipulate to control the number of nodes. When you update your cluster to match the modified specification, you should be able to see three nodes, as shown in the following screenshot:

```
Using cluster from kubectl context: myfirstcluster.k8s.local

NAME                    STATUS  NEEDUPDATE      READY   MIN     MAX     NODES
master-us-west-2a       Ready   0               1       1       1       1
master-us-west-2b       Ready   0               1       1       1       1
master-us-west-2c       Ready   0               1       1       1       1
nodes                   Ready   0               3       3       3       3

No rolling-update required.
```

Figure 11.14: Number of master and worker nodes in the cluster

> **NOTE**
>
> The solution to this activity can be found at the following address: https://packt.live/304PEoD. Make sure you have deleted your clusters once you have completed the activity. More details on how to delete your clusters are presented in the following section (*Deleting Our Cluster*).

DELETING OUR CLUSTER

Once we're done with all the exercises and activities in this chapter, you should delete the cluster by running the following command:

```
kops delete cluster --name ${NAME} --yes
```

You should see this response:

```
zarnold@Zachs-MacBook-Pro ~ % kops delete cluster --name ${NAME} --yes
TYPE                    NAME                                                                            ID
autoscaling-config      master-us-west-2a.masters.myfirstcluster.k8s.local-20200125141503               master-us-wes
t-2a.masters.myfirstcluster.k8s.local-20200125141503
autoscaling-config      nodes.myfirstcluster.k8s.local-20200125141502                                   nodes.myfirst
cluster.k8s.local-20200125141502
autoscaling-group       master-us-west-2a.masters.myfirstcluster.k8s.local                              master-us-wes
t-2a.masters.myfirstcluster.k8s.local
autoscaling-group       nodes.myfirstcluster.k8s.local                                                  nodes.myfirst
cluster.k8s.local
dhcp-options            myfirstcluster.k8s.local                                                        dopt-04c4f21f
c0df41b7c
iam-instance-profile    masters.myfirstcluster.k8s.local                                                masters.myfir
stcluster.k8s.local
iam-instance-profile    nodes.myfirstcluster.k8s.local                                                  nodes.myfirst
cluster.k8s.local
iam-role                masters.myfirstcluster.k8s.local                                                masters.myfir
stcluster.k8s.local
iam-role                nodes.myfirstcluster.k8s.local                                                  nodes.myfirst
cluster.k8s.local
instance                master-us-west-2a.masters.myfirstcluster.k8s.local                              i-0ab79446268
47d457
instance                nodes.myfirstcluster.k8s.local                                                  i-03c7899843c
3f07dc
instance                nodes.myfirstcluster.k8s.local                                                  i-076dae19068
fb6b44
internet-gateway        myfirstcluster.k8s.local                                                        igw-05db8a701
ac04de81
keypair                 kubernetes.myfirstcluster.k8s.local-b9:cc:eb:0b:89:46:94:ea:d9:6a:0c:4f:89:35:b8:34     kubernetes.my
firstcluster.k8s.local-b9:cc:eb:0b:89:46:94:ea:d9:6a:0c:4f:89:35:b8:34
load-balancer           api.myfirstcluster.k8s.local                                                    api-myfirstcl
uster-k8s-lo-hqulii
route-table             myfirstcluster.k8s.local                                                        rtb-0e8f84277
6aedec81
security-group          api-elb.myfirstcluster.k8s.local                                                sg-0d3dec708d
22ece7a
security-group          masters.myfirstcluster.k8s.local                                                sg-0989ebcbf9
11364e7
security-group          nodes.myfirstcluster.k8s.local                                                  sg-0ffbed1bd6
28d8913
subnet                  us-west-2a.myfirstcluster.k8s.local                                             subnet-0f2d1d
ebb852d607b
subnet                  us-west-2b.myfirstcluster.k8s.local                                             subnet-0251d1
3ad6c2a2736
subnet                  us-west-2c.myfirstcluster.k8s.local                                             subnet-0d4914
652626e27ce
volume                  a.etcd-events.myfirstcluster.k8s.local                                          vol-0446119f9
a30d4a57
volume                  a.etcd-main.myfirstcluster.k8s.local                                            vol-0a1ecbebd
fa7be875
vpc                     myfirstcluster.k8s.local                                                        vpc-053038985
730552fa
```

Figure 11.15: Deleting our cluster

At this point, you should no longer be receiving charges from AWS for the Kubernetes infrastructure you have spun up in this chapter.

SUMMARY

Highly available infrastructure is one of the key components to achieving high availability for applications. Kubernetes is an extremely well-designed tool and has many built-in resiliency features that make it able to withstand major networking and compute events. It works to keep those events from impacting your application. During our exploration of high-availability systems, we investigated some components of Kubernetes and how they work together to achieve high availability. Then, we constructed a cluster of our own on AWS that was designed to be highly available using the kops cluster life cycle management tool.

In the next chapter, we're going to take a look at how we make our applications more resilient by leveraging Kubernetes primitives to ensure high availability.

12

YOUR APPLICATION AND HA

OVERVIEW

In this chapter, we will explore Kubernetes cluster life cycle management through the use of Terraform and Amazon **Elastic Kubernetes Service** (**EKS**). We will also deploy an application and learn some principles to make applications better suited to the Kubernetes environment.

This chapter will walk you through using Terraform to create a fully functioning, highly available Kubernetes environment. You will deploy an application to the cluster and modify its functionality to make it suitable for a highly available environment. We will also learn how to get traffic from the internet to an application running in a cluster by using a Kubernetes ingress resource.

INTRODUCTION

In the previous chapter, we set up our first multi-node Kubernetes cluster in a cloud environment. In this section, we're going to talk about how we operationalize a Kubernetes cluster for our application—that is, we will use the cluster to run a containerized application other than the dashboard.

Since Kubernetes has as many uses as can be imagined by a cluster operator, no two use cases for Kubernetes are alike. So, we're going to make some assumptions about the type of application that we're operationalizing our cluster for. We're going to optimize a workflow for deploying a stateless web application with a stateful backend that has high-availability requirements in a cloud-based environment. In doing so, we're hopefully going to cover a large percentage of what people generally use Kubernetes clusters for.

Kubernetes can be used for just about anything. Even if what we cover does not exactly match your use case for Kubernetes, it's worth studying since this point is important. What we're going to be doing in this chapter is merely running through an example workflow for running a web application on Kubernetes in the cloud. Once you have studied the principles that we will use for running the example workflow in this chapter, you can look up many other resources on the internet that can help you discover other ways of optimizing your workflow with Kubernetes if this doesn't fit your use case.

But before we move on to ensure the high availability of the application that we will be running on the cluster, let's take a step back and consider the high-availability requirements for your cloud infrastructure. In order to maintain high availability at an application level, it is also imperative that we manage our infrastructure with the same goal in mind. This brings us to a discussion about infrastructure life cycle management.

AN OVERVIEW OF INFRASTRUCTURE LIFE CYCLE MANAGEMENT

In simple words, infrastructure life cycle management refers to how we manage our servers through each phase of its useful life. This involves provisioning, maintaining, and decommissioning physical hardware or cloud resources. Since we are leveraging cloud infrastructure, we should leverage infrastructure life cycle management tools to provision and de-provision resources programmatically. To understand why this is important, let's consider the following example.

Imagine for a moment that you work as a system administrator, DevOps engineer, site reliability engineer, or any other role that requires you to deal with server infrastructure for a company that is in the digital news industry. What that means is that the primary output of the people who are working for this company is the information that they publish on their website. Now, imagine that the entirety of the website runs on one server in your company's server room. The application running on the server is a PHP blog site with a MySQL backend. One day, an article goes viral and suddenly you are handling an exponentially higher amount of traffic than you were handling the day before. What do you do? The website keeps crashing (if it loads at all) and your company is losing money while you try to figure out a solution.

Your solution is to start separating concerns and isolating single points of failure. The first thing you do is buy a lot more hardware and start configuring it to hopefully scale the website horizontally. After doing this, you're running five servers, with one running HAProxy, which is load-balancing connections to your PHP application running on three servers and a database server. OK, now you think that you have it under control. However, not all of the server hardware is the same—they run different distributions of Linux, the resource requirements are different for each machine, and patching, upgrading, and maintaining each server individually becomes difficult. Well, as luck would have it, another article goes viral and suddenly you're experiencing five times more requests than the current hardware can handle. What do you do now? Keep scaling it out horizontally? You're only one person, though, so you're bound to make a mistake in configuring the next set of servers. Due to that mistake, you've crashed the website in new and exciting ways that no one in management is happy about. Are you feeling as stressed reading this as I was writing it?

It's because of misconfigurations that engineers began to leverage tools and configuration written in source code to define their topologies. That way, if a mutation in the infrastructure state is required, it can be tracked, controlled, and rolled out in a way that makes the code responsible for resolving differences between your declared infrastructure state and what it observes in reality.

Infrastructure is only as good as the life cycle management tools that surround it and the application that runs atop it. What this means is that if your cluster is well-built but there is no tool that exists to successfully update your application on that cluster, then it won't serve you well. In this chapter, we're going to take a look at an application-level view of how we can leverage a continuous integration build pipeline to be able to roll out new updates to our application in a zero-downtime, cloud-native manner.

In this chapter, we will provide a test application for you to manage. We will also be using an infrastructure life cycle management tool called **Terraform** in order to manage the Deployment of Kubernetes cloud infrastructure more efficiently. This chapter should help you develop an effective skill set that will allow you to begin creating your own application delivery pipeline in your own environment in Kubernetes very quickly.

TERRAFORM

In the last chapter, we used **kops** to create a Kubernetes cluster from scratch. However, this process can be viewed as tedious and difficult to replicate, which creates a high probability of misconfiguration, resulting in unexpected events at application runtime. Luckily, there is a very powerful community-supported tool that solves this issue very well for Kubernetes clusters running on **Amazon Web Services** (**AWS**), as well as several other cloud platforms, such as Azure, **Google Cloud Platform** (**GCP**), and many more.

Terraform is a general-purpose infrastructure life cycle management tool; that is, Terraform can manage the state of your infrastructure as defined through code. The goal of Terraform, when it was initially created, was to create both a language (**HashiCorp Configuration Language** (**HCL**)) and runtime that can create infrastructure in a repeatable manner and control changes to that infrastructure in the same way that we control changes to application source code—through pull requests, reviews, and version control. Terraform has since grown considerably, and it is now a general-purpose configuration management tool. In this chapter, we will be using its original functionality of infrastructure life cycle management in its most classical sense.

Terraform files are written in a language called HCL. HCL looks a lot like YAML and JSON, but with a few differences. For example, HCL supports the interpolation of references to other resources in its files and is capable of determining the order in which resources need to be created so as to ensure that resources that depend on the creation of other resources won't be created in the wrong order. Terraform files have the `.tf` file extension.

You can think of a Terraform file as specifying the desired state of your entire infrastructure in a similar way as, for example, a Kubernetes YAML file would specify the desired state of a Deployment. This allows the declarative management of your entire infrastructure. So, we arrive at the idea of managing **Infrastructure as Code** (**IaC**).

Terraform works in two stages—**plan** and **apply**. This is to ensure that you have the chance to review infrastructure changes before making them. Terraform assumes that it alone is responsible for all state changes to your infrastructure. So, if you are using Terraform to manage your infrastructure, it would be inadvisable to make infrastructure changes by any other means (for example, by adding a resource via the AWS console). This is because if you make a change and don't make sure that it is updated in the Terraform file, then the next time the Terraform file is applied, it will remove your one-time change. It isn't a bug, it's a feature, for real this time. The reason for this is that when you track infrastructure as code, every change can be tracked, reviewed, and managed with automated tooling, such as a CI/CD pipeline. So, if the state of your system drifts away from what is written down, then Terraform will be responsible for reconciling your observed infrastructure to what you have written down.

In this chapter, we will introduce you to Terraform as it is very commonly used in the industry as a convenient way to manage infrastructure as code. However, we will not dive deep into creating every single AWS resource with Terraform to keep our discussion focused on Kubernetes. We will just carry out a quick demo to ensure that you understand some basic principles.

> **NOTE**
>
> You can learn more about using Terraform for AWS in this book: https://www.packtpub.com/networking-and-servers/getting-started-terraform-second-edition

EXERCISE 12.01: CREATING AN S3 BUCKET WITH TERRAFORM

In this exercise, we will implement some common commands that you will use when working with Terraform and introduce you to a Terraform file that will be the definition of our infrastructure as code

> **NOTE**
>
> Terraform will create resources on our behalf in AWS, which will cost you money.

1. First, let's make a directory where we're going to make our Terraform changes, and then we will navigate to that directory:

```
mkdir -p ~/Desktop/eks_terraform_demo

cd Desktop/eks_terraform_demo/
```

2. Now, we're going to make our first Terraform file. Terraform files have a **.tf** file extension. Create a file named **main.tf** (there is no significance to the word **main**, unlike some other languages) with the following content:

```
resource "aws_s3_bucket" "my_bucket" {
  bucket = "<<NAME>>-test-bucket"
  acl    = "private"
}
```

This block has a definition called **aws_s3_bucket**, which means that it will create an Amazon S3 bucket with the name specified in the **bucket** field. The **acl="private"** line indicates that we are not allowing public access to this bucket. Be sure to replace **<<NAME>>** with a unique name of your own.

3. To get started with Terraform, we need to initialize it. So, let's do that with the following command:

```
terraform init
```

You should see the following response:

```
Initializing the backend...

Initializing provider plugins...

The following providers do not have any version constraints in configuration,
so the latest version was installed.

To prevent automatic upgrades to new major versions that may contain breaking
changes, it is recommended to add version = "..." constraints to the
corresponding provider blocks in configuration, with the constraint strings
suggested below.

* provider.aws: version = "~> 2.46"

Terraform has been successfully initialized!

You may now begin working with Terraform. Try running "terraform plan" to see
any changes that are required for your infrastructure. All Terraform commands
should now work.

If you ever set or change modules or backend configuration for Terraform,
rerun this command to reinitialize your working directory. If you forget, other
commands will detect it and remind you to do so if necessary.
```

Figure 12.1: Initializing Terraform

4. Run the following command to have Terraform determine a plan to create resources defined by the **main.tf** file that we created earlier:

```
terraform plan
```

You will be prompted to enter an AWS region. Use the one that's closest to you. In the following screenshot, we are using **us-west-2**:

```
provider.aws.region
  The region where AWS operations will take place. Examples
  are us-east-1, us-west-2, etc.

  Enter a value: us-west-2

Refreshing Terraform state in-memory prior to plan...
The refreshed state will be used to calculate this plan, but will not be
persisted to local or remote state storage.


------------------------------------------------------------------------

An execution plan has been generated and is shown below.
Resource actions are indicated with the following symbols:
  + create

Terraform will perform the following actions:

  # aws_s3_bucket.my_bucket will be created
  + resource "aws_s3_bucket" "my_bucket" {
      + acceleration_status         = (known after apply)
      + acl                         = "private"
      + arn                         = (known after apply)
      + bucket                      = "zparnold-test-bucket"
      + bucket_domain_name          = (known after apply)
      + bucket_regional_domain_name = (known after apply)
      + force_destroy               = false
      + hosted_zone_id              = (known after apply)
      + id                          = (known after apply)
      + region                      = (known after apply)
      + request_payer               = (known after apply)
      + website_domain              = (known after apply)
      + website_endpoint            = (known after apply)

      + versioning {
          + enabled    = (known after apply)
          + mfa_delete = (known after apply)
        }
    }

Plan: 1 to add, 0 to change, 0 to destroy.

------------------------------------------------------------------------

Note: You didn't specify an "-out" parameter to save this plan, so Terraform
can't guarantee that exactly these actions will be performed if
"terraform apply" is subsequently run.
```

Figure 12.2: Calculating the required changes to the cluster resources for creating an S3 bucket

So, we can see that Terraform has accessed our AWS account using the access keys that we set up in *Exercise 11.01, Setting Up Our Kubernetes Cluster* of the previous chapter and calculated what it will need to do in order to make our AWS environment look like what we have defined in our Terraform file. As we can see in the screenshot, it's planning to add an S3 bucket for us, which is what we want.

> **NOTE**
>
> Terraform will try to apply all the files with a **.tf** extension in your current working directory.

In the previous screenshot, we can see that the **terraform** command is indicating that we haven't specified an **-out** parameter, so it won't guarantee that the exact calculated plan will be applied. This is because something in your AWS infrastructure could have changed from the time of planning to the time of applying. Let's say that you calculate a plan today. Then, later, you add or remove a few resources. So, the required modifications to achieve the given state would be different. So, unless you specify the **-out** parameter, Terraform will recalculate its plan before applying it.

5. Run the following command to apply the configuration and create the resources specified in our Terraform file:

```
terraform apply
```

Terraform will give us one more chance to review the plan and decide what we want to do before making the changes to the AWS resources for us:

```
provider.aws.region
  The region where AWS operations will take place. Examples
  are us-east-1, us-west-2, etc.

  Enter a value: us-west-2


An execution plan has been generated and is shown below.
Resource actions are indicated with the following symbols:
  + create

Terraform will perform the following actions:

  # aws_s3_bucket.my_bucket will be created
  + resource "aws_s3_bucket" "my_bucket" {
      + acceleration_status         = (known after apply)
      + acl                         = "private"
      + arn                         = (known after apply)
      + bucket                      = "zparnold-test-bucket"
      + bucket_domain_name          = (known after apply)
      + bucket_regional_domain_name = (known after apply)
      + force_destroy               = false
      + hosted_zone_id              = (known after apply)
      + id                          = (known after apply)
      + region                      = (known after apply)
      + request_payer               = (known after apply)
      + website_domain              = (known after apply)
      + website_endpoint            = (known after apply)

      + versioning {
          + enabled    = (known after apply)
          + mfa_delete = (known after apply)
        }
    }

Plan: 1 to add, 0 to change, 0 to destroy.

Do you want to perform these actions?
  Terraform will perform the actions described above.
  Only 'yes' will be accepted to approve.

  Enter a value: yes
```

Figure 12.3: Calculation of the changes and confirmation prompt for creating an S3 bucket

As mentioned earlier, Terraform calculated the required changes even when we used the **apply** command. Confirm the actions displayed by Terraform, and then enter **yes** to proceed with the plan displayed. Now, Terraform has made an S3 bucket for us:

```
Do you want to perform these actions?
  Terraform will perform the actions described above.
  Only 'yes' will be accepted to approve.

  Enter a value: yes

aws_s3_bucket.my_bucket: Creating...
aws_s3_bucket.my_bucket: Still creating... [10s elapsed]
aws_s3_bucket.my_bucket: Creation complete after 14s [id=zparnold-test-bucket]

Apply complete! Resources: 1 added, 0 changed, 0 destroyed.
```

Figure 12.4: Creating an S3 bucket after confirmation

6. Now, we're going to destroy all the resources that we created to clean up before we move on to the next exercise. To destroy them, run the following command:

```
terraform destroy
```

Again, to confirm this action, you must explicitly allow Terraform to destroy your resources by entering **yes** when prompted, as in the following screenshot:

```
provider.aws.region
  The region where AWS operations will take place. Examples
  are us-east-1, us-west-2, etc.

  Enter a value: us-west-2

aws_s3_bucket.my_bucket: Refreshing state... [id=zparnold-test-bucket]

An execution plan has been generated and is shown below.
Resource actions are indicated with the following symbols:
  - destroy

Terraform will perform the following actions:

  # aws_s3_bucket.my_bucket will be destroyed
  - resource "aws_s3_bucket" "my_bucket" {
      - acl                         = "private" -> null
      - arn                         = "arn:aws:s3:::zparnold-test-bucket" -> nul
l
      - bucket                      = "zparnold-test-bucket" -> null
      - bucket_domain_name          = "zparnold-test-bucket.s3.amazonaws.com" ->
 null
      - bucket_regional_domain_name = "zparnold-test-bucket.s3.us-west-2.amazona
ws.com" -> null
      - force_destroy               = false -> null
      - hosted_zone_id              = "Z3BJ6K6RIION7M" -> null
      - id                          = "zparnold-test-bucket" -> null
      - region                      = "us-west-2" -> null
      - request_payer               = "BucketOwner" -> null
      - tags                        = {} -> null

      - versioning {
          - enabled    = false -> null
          - mfa_delete = false -> null
        }
    }

Plan: 0 to add, 0 to change, 1 to destroy.

Do you really want to destroy all resources?
  Terraform will destroy all your managed infrastructure, as shown above.
  There is no undo. Only 'yes' will be accepted to confirm.

  Enter a value: yes
```

Figure 12.5: Destroying resources created using Terraform

In this exercise, we demonstrated how to create a single resource (an S3 bucket) using Terraform, and also how to destroy a bucket. This should have familiarized you with the simple tooling of Terraform, and we will now expand on these concepts further.

Now, let's make a Kubernetes cluster with Terraform. Last time, we built and managed our own cluster control plane. Since almost every cloud provider provides this service to their customers, we will be leveraging Amazon **Elastic Kubernetes Service** (**EKS**), a **managed service** for Kubernetes provided by AWS.

When we use a managed Kubernetes service, the following is taken care of by the cloud service vendor:

- Managing and securing etcd
- Managing and securing user authentication
- Managing the control plane components, such as the controller manager(s), the scheduler, and the API server
- Provisioning the CNI running between Pods in your network

The control plane is exposed to your nodes through elastic network interfaces bound to your VPC. You still need to manage the worker nodes and they run as EC2 instances in your account. So, using a managed service allows you to focus on the work that you want to get done using Kubernetes, but the drawback is not having very granular control of the control plane.

> **NOTE**
>
> Since AWS handles user authentication for the cluster, we will have to use AWS IAM credentials to access our Kubernetes clusters. We can leverage the AWS IAM Authenticator binary on our machines to do that. More on this in the upcoming sections.

EXERCISE 12.02: CREATING A CLUSTER WITH EKS USING TERRAFORM

For this exercise, we will use the **main.tf** file that we have already provided to create a production-ready, highly available Kubernetes cluster.

> **NOTE**
>
> This Terraform file is adapted from the examples available at https://github.com/terraform-aws-modules/terraform-aws-eks/tree/master/examples.

This will enable Terraform to create the following:

- A VPC with IP address space **10.0.0.0/16**. It will have three public subnets with **/24**s (**255**) worth of IP addresses each.
- Route tables and an internet gateway for the VPC to work properly.
- Security groups for the control plane to communicate with the nodes, as well as to receive traffic from the outside world on the allowed and required ports.
- IAM roles for both the EKS control plane (to perform tasks such as creating **ELB** (**Elastic Load Balancer**) for services on your behalf) and the nodes (to handle EC2 API-related concerns).
- The EKS control plane and a setup of all the necessary connections to your VPC and nodes.
- An **ASG** (**Autoscaling Group**) for nodes to join the cluster (it will provision two **m4.large** instances).
- Generate both a kubeconfig file and a ConfigMap, which are necessary for the nodes to join the cluster and for you to communicate with the cluster.

This is a relatively secure and stable way for you to create a Kubernetes cluster that is capable of reliably handling production workloads. Let's begin with the exercise:

1. Use the following command to fetch the **main.tf** file that we have provided:

```
curl -O https://raw.githubusercontent.com/PacktWorkshops/Kubernetes-Workshop/master/Chapter12/Exercise12.02/main.tf
```

   This will replace the existing **main.tf** file, if you still have it from the previous exercise. Note that you should not have any other Terraform files in the directory.

2. Now, we need Terraform to apply the state defined in the **main.tf** file to your cloud infrastructure. To do that, use the following command:

```
terraform apply
```

> **NOTE**
>
> You should not use the AWS IAM user we generated for kops in the previous chapter to execute these commands, but rather a user with Administrative access to your AWS account so there is no chance of accidental permissions issues.

   This may take around 10 minutes to complete. You should see a very long output similar to the following:

```
aws_eks_cluster.demo: Still creating... [3m20s elapsed]
aws_eks_cluster.demo: Still creating... [3m30s elapsed]
aws_eks_cluster.demo: Still creating... [3m40s elapsed]
aws_eks_cluster.demo: Still creating... [3m50s elapsed]
aws_eks_cluster.demo: Still creating... [4m0s elapsed]
aws_eks_cluster.demo: Still creating... [4m10s elapsed]
aws_eks_cluster.demo: Still creating... [4m20s elapsed]
aws_eks_cluster.demo: Still creating... [4m30s elapsed]
aws_eks_cluster.demo: Still creating... [4m40s elapsed]
```

Figure 12.6: Creating resources for our EKS cluster

Once this is done, there will be two terminal outputs—a ConfigMap for nodes and a kubeconfig file for accessing the cluster, as demonstrated in the following screenshot:

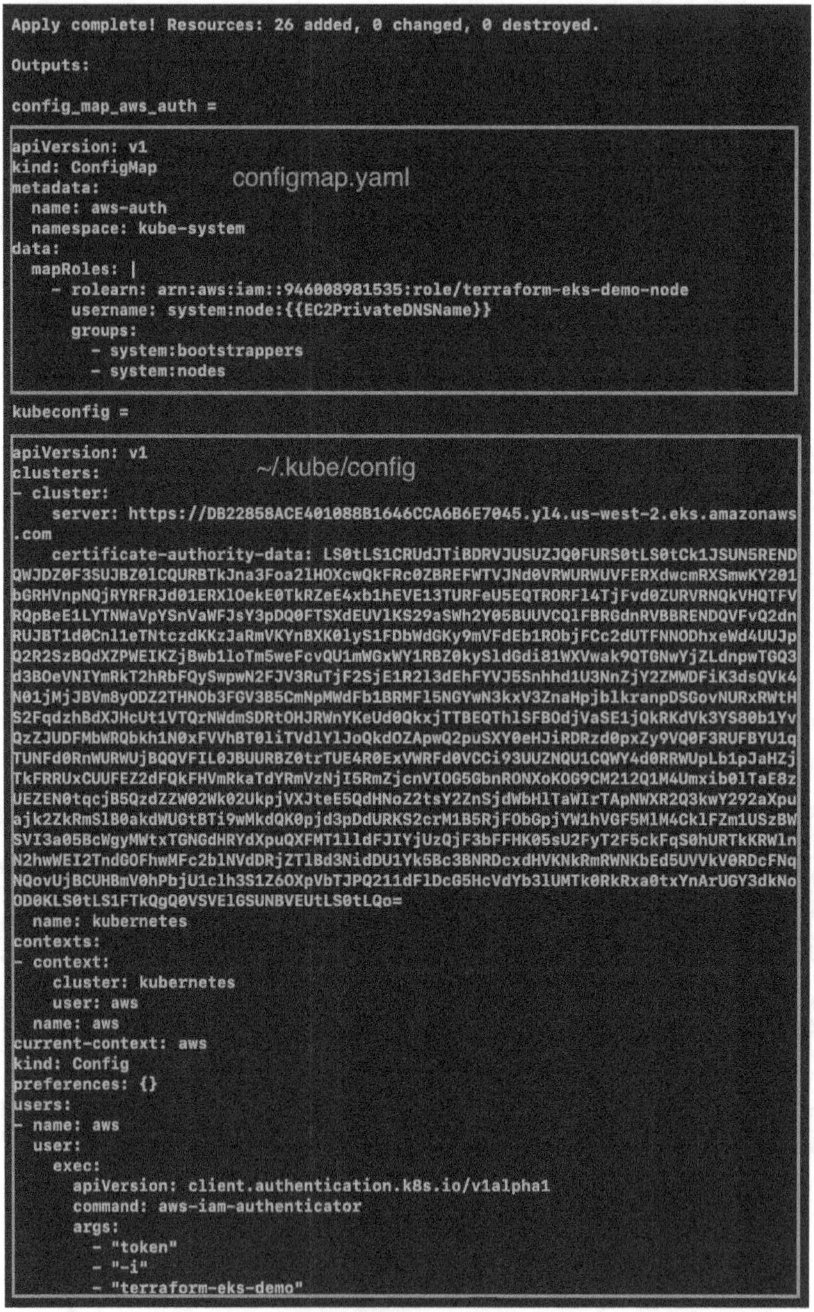

```
Apply complete! Resources: 26 added, 0 changed, 0 destroyed.

Outputs:

config_map_aws_auth =

apiVersion: v1
kind: ConfigMap                    configmap.yaml
metadata:
  name: aws-auth
  namespace: kube-system
data:
  mapRoles: |
    - rolearn: arn:aws:iam::946008981535:role/terraform-eks-demo-node
      username: system:node:{{EC2PrivateDNSName}}
      groups:
        - system:bootstrappers
        - system:nodes

kubeconfig =

apiVersion: v1
clusters:                          ~/.kube/config
- cluster:
    server: https://DB22858ACE401088B1646CCA6B6E7045.yl4.us-west-2.eks.amazonaws
.com
    certificate-authority-data: LS0tLS1CRUdJTiBDRVJUSUZJQ0FURS0tLS0tCk1JSUN5REND
QWJDZ0F3SUJBZ01CQURBTkJna3Foa2lHOXcwQkFRc0ZBREFWTVJNd0VRWURWUVFERXdwcmRXSmwKY201
bGRHVnpNQjRYRFRJd01ERXlOekE0TkRZeE4xb1hEVE13TURFeU5EQTRORFl4TjFvd0ZURVRNQkVHQTFV
RQpBeE1LYTNWaVpYSnVaWFJsY3pDQ0FTSXdEUVlKS29aSWh2Y05BUUVCQlFBRGdnRVBBRENDQVFvQ2dn
RUJBT1d0Cnl1eTNtczdKKzJaRmVKYnBXK0lyS1FDbWdGKy9mVFdEb1RObjFCc2dUTFNNODhxeWd4UUJp
Q2R2SzBQdXZPWEIKZjBwb1loTm5weFcvQU1mWGxWY1RBZ0kySldGdi81WXVwak9QTGNwYjZLdnpwTGQ3
d3BOeVNIYmRkT2hRbFQySwpwN2FJV3RuTjF2SjE1R2l3dEhFYVJ5Snhhd1U3NnZjY2ZMWDFiK3dsQVk4
N01jMjJBVm8yODZ2THNOb3FGV3B5CmNpMWdFb1BRMFl5NGYwN3kxV3ZnaHpjblkranpDSGovNURxRWtH
S2FqdzhBdXJHcUt1VTQrNWdmSDRtOHJRWnYKeUd0QkxjTTBEQThlSFBOdjVaSE1jQkRKdVk3YS80b1Yv
QzZJUDFMbWRQbkh1N0xFVVhBT0liTVdlYlJoQkdOZApwQ2puSXY0eHJiRDRzd0pxZy9VQ0F3RUFBYU1q
TUNFd0RnWURWUjBQQVFIL0JBUURBZ0trTUE4R0ExVWRFd0VCCi93UUZNQU1CQWY4d0RRWUpLb1pJaHZj
TkFRRUxCUUFEZ2dFQkFHVmRkaTdYRmVzNjI5RmZjcnVIOG5GbnRONXoKOG9CM212Q1M4UmxibDlTaE8z
UEZEN0tqcjB5QzdZZW02Wk02UkpjVXJteE5QdHNoZ2tsY2ZnSjdWbHlTaWIrTApNWXR2Q3kwY292aXpu
ajk2ZkRmS1B0akdWUGtBTi9wMkdQK0pjd3pDdURKS2crM1B5RjFObGpjYW1hVGF5M1M4CklFZm1USzBW
SVI3a05BcWgyMWtxTGNGdHRYdXpuQXFMT1lldFJIYjUzQjF3bFFHK05sU2FyT2F5ckFqS0hURTkKRWln
N2hwWEI2TndGOFhwMFc2blNVdDRjZTlBd3NidDU1Yk5Bc3BNRDcxdHVKNkRmRWNKbEd5UVVkV0RDcFNq
NQovUjBCUHBmV0hPbjU1clh3S1Z6OXpVbTJPQ211dFlDcG5HcVdYb3lUMTk0RkRxa0txYnArUGY3dkNo
OD0KLS0tLS1FTkQgQ0VSVElGSUNBVEUtLS0tLQo=
  name: kubernetes
contexts:
- context:
    cluster: kubernetes
    user: aws
  name: aws
current-context: aws
kind: Config
preferences: {}
users:
- name: aws
  user:
    exec:
      apiVersion: client.authentication.k8s.io/v1alpha1
      command: aws-iam-authenticator
      args:
        - "token"
        - "-i"
        - "terraform-eks-demo"
```


Figure 12.7: Getting the information required to access our cluster

Copy the ConfigMap to a file and name it **configmap.yaml**, and then copy the kubeconfig file and write it to the **~/.kube/config** file on your computer.

3. Now, we need to apply the changes to allow our worker nodes to communicate with the control plane. This is a YAML-formatted file for joining the worker nodes to your EKS cluster; we already saved this as **configmap.yaml**. Run the following command:

```
kubectl apply -f configmap.yaml
```

> **NOTE**
>
> To run this command, you need the **aws-iam-authenticator** binary installed on your computer. To do that, follow the instructions here: https://docs.aws.amazon.com/eks/latest/userguide/install-aws-iam-authenticator.html.

This applies the ConfigMap that allows the Kubernetes cluster to communicate with the nodes. You should see the following response:

```
configmap/aws-auth created
```

4. Now, let's verify that everything is running OK. Run the following command in the terminal:

```
kubectl get node
```

You should see the following output:

```
NAME                                          STATUS   ROLES    AGE   VERSION
ip-10-0-0-205.us-west-2.compute.internal     Ready    <none>   34s   v1.14.8-eks-b
8860f
ip-10-0-2-229.us-west-2.compute.internal     Ready    <none>   33s   v1.14.8-eks-b
8860f
```

Figure 12.8: Checking whether our nodes are accessible

At this stage, we have a running Kubernetes cluster using EKS as the control plane and two worker nodes.

> **NOTE**
>
> Remember that your cluster resources will stay online until you delete them. If you plan to come back to the following exercises later, you may want to delete your cluster to minimize your bill. To do that, run **`terraform destroy`**. To get your cluster back online, run this exercise again.

Now that we have our cluster set up, in the next section, let's take a look at an efficient and flexible way to bring traffic to any application to be run on our cluster.

KUBERNETES INGRESS

In the early days of the Kubernetes project, the Service object was used to get traffic from outside the cluster to the running Pods. You had only two options to get that traffic from outside in—using either a NodePort service or a LoadBalancer service. The latter option was preferred in public cloud provider environments because the cluster would automatically manage setting up security groups/firewall rules and to point the LoadBalancer to the correct ports on your worker nodes. However, there is one slight problem with that approach, especially for those who are just getting started with Kubernetes or those who have tight cloud budgets. The problem is that one LoadBalancer can only point toward a single Kubernetes service object.

Now, imagine that you have 100 microservices running in Kubernetes, all of which need to be exposed publicly. In AWS, the average cost of an ELB (a load balancer provided by AWS) is roughly $20 per month. So, in this scenario, you're paying $2,000 per month just to have the option of getting traffic into your cluster, and we still have not factored in the additional costs for networking.

Let's also understand another limitation of the one-to-one relationship between Kubernetes Service objects and AWS load balancers. Let's say that for your project, you need to have a path-based mapping to internal Kubernetes services from the same load-balancing endpoint. Let's suppose that you have a web service running at **`api.example.io`** and you want **`api.example.io/users`** to go to one microservice and **`api.examples.io/weather`** to go to another completely separate microservice. Before the arrival of Ingress, you would need to set up your own Kubernetes Service and do the internal path resolution to your app.

This is now no longer a problem due to the advent of the Kubernetes Ingress resource. The Kubernetes Ingress resource is meant to operate in conjunction with an Ingress controller (which is an application running in your cluster watching the Kubernetes API server for changes to the Ingress resource). Together, these two components allow you to define multiple Kubernetes services, which do not have to be exposed externally themselves to be routed through a single load-balancing endpoint. Let's examine the following diagram to understand this a bit better:

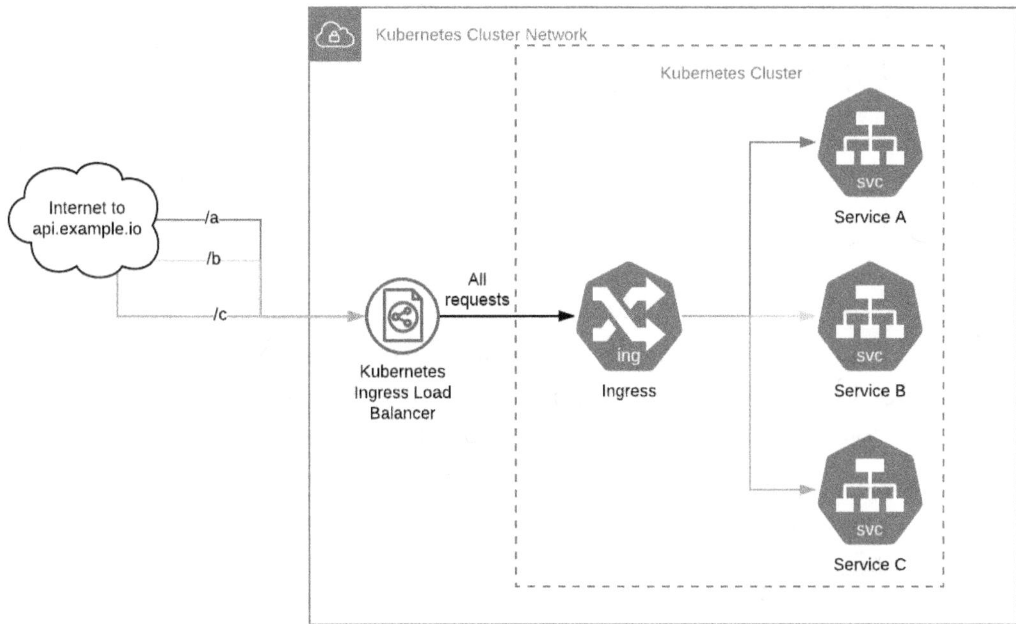

Figure 12.9: Using Ingress to route traffic to our services

In this example, all requests are being routed to **`api.example.io`** from the internet. One request is going to **`api.example.io/a`**, another is going to **`api.example.io/b`**, and the last to **`api.example.io/c`**. The requests are going to a single load balancer and a Kubernetes Service, which is controlled through a Kubernetes Ingress resource. This Ingress resource forwards the traffic from the single Ingress endpoint to the services it was configured to forward traffic to. In the following sections, we will set up the **`ingress-nginx`** Ingress controller, which is a commonly used open-source tool used in the Kubernetes community for ingress. Then, we will configure the Ingress to allow traffic into our cluster to access our highly available application.

HIGHLY AVAILABLE APPLICATIONS RUNNING ON TOP OF KUBERNETES

Now that you've had a chance to spin up an EKS cluster and learn about Ingress, let's introduce you to our application. We have provided an example application that has a flaw that prevents it from being cloud-native and really being able to be horizontally scaled in Kubernetes. We will deploy this application in the following exercise and observe its behavior. Then, in the next section, we will deploy a modified version of this application and observe how it is more suited to achieve our stated objective of being highly available.

EXERCISE 12.03: DEPLOYING A MULTI-REPLICA NON-HA APPLICATION IN KUBERNETES

In this exercise, we will deploy a version of the application that's not horizontally scalable. We will try to scale it and observe the problem that prevents it from being scaled horizontally:

> **NOTE**
>
> We have provided the source code for this application in the GitHub repository for reference. However, since our focus is on Kubernetes, we will use commands to fetch it directly from the repository in this exercise.

1. Use the following command to get the manifest for all of the objects required to run the application:

```
curl https://raw.githubusercontent.com/PacktWorkshops/Kubernetes-
Workshop/master/Chapter12/Exercise12.03/without_redis.yaml > without_
redis.yaml
```

This should download the manifest to your current directory:

```
  % Total    % Received % Xferd  Average Speed   Time    Time     Time  Current
                                 Dload  Upload   Total   Spent    Left  Speed
100   895  100   895    0     0   2193      0 --:--:-- --:--:-- --:--:--  2188
```

Figure 12.10: Downloading the application manifest

If you take a look at the manifest, it has a Deployment running a single replica of a Pod and a Service of the ClusterIP type to route traffic to it.

2. Then, create a Kubernetes Deployment and Service object so that we can run our application:

```
kubectl apply -f without_redis.yaml
```

You should see the following response:

```
deployment.apps/kubernetes-test-ha-application-without-redis-deployment created
service/kubernetes-test-ha-application-without-redis created
```

Figure 12.11: Creating the resources for our application

3. Now, we need to add a Kubernetes Ingress resource to be able to access this website. To get started with Kubernetes Ingress, we need to run the following commands:

```
kubectl apply -f https://raw.githubusercontent.com/kubernetes/
ingress-nginx/nginx-0.30.0/deploy/static/mandatory.yaml

kubectl apply -f https://raw.githubusercontent.com/kubernetes/
ingress-nginx/nginx-0.30.0/deploy/static/provider/aws/service-l4.yaml

kubectl apply -f https://raw.githubusercontent.com/kubernetes/
ingress-nginx/nginx-0.30.0/deploy/static/provider/aws/patch-
configmap-l4.yaml
```

These three commands will deploy the Nginx Ingress controller implementation for EKS. You should see the following response:

```
zarnold@zachs-mbp ~ % kubectl apply -f https://raw.githubusercontent.com/kuberne
tes/ingress-nginx/nginx-0.30.0/deploy/static/mandatory.yaml
namespace/ingress-nginx created
configmap/nginx-configuration created
configmap/tcp-services created
configmap/udp-services created
serviceaccount/nginx-ingress-serviceaccount created
clusterrole.rbac.authorization.k8s.io/nginx-ingress-clusterrole created
role.rbac.authorization.k8s.io/nginx-ingress-role created
rolebinding.rbac.authorization.k8s.io/nginx-ingress-role-nisa-binding created
clusterrolebinding.rbac.authorization.k8s.io/nginx-ingress-clusterrole-nisa-bind
ing created
deployment.apps/nginx-ingress-controller created
limitrange/ingress-nginx created
zarnold@zachs-mbp ~ % kubectl apply -f https://raw.githubusercontent.com/kuberne
tes/ingress-nginx/nginx-0.30.0/deploy/static/provider/aws/service-l4.yaml
service/ingress-nginx created
zarnold@zachs-mbp ~ % kubectl apply -f  https://raw.githubusercontent.com/kubern
etes/ingress-nginx/nginx-0.30.0/deploy/static/provider/aws/patch-configmap-l4.ya
ml
configmap/nginx-configuration configured
```

Figure 12.12: Implementing the Ingress controllers

> **NOTE**
>
> This command is to be run for the AWS cloud provider only. If you are running your cluster on another platform, you will need to find the appropriate link from https://kubernetes.github.io/ingress-nginx/deploy/#aws.

4. Then, we need to create an Ingress for ourselves. In the same folder we are in, let's create a file named **ingress.yaml** with the following content:

```
apiVersion: networking.k8s.io/v1beta1
kind: Ingress
metadata:
  name: ingress
  annotations:
    nginx.ingress.kubernetes.io/rewrite-target: /
spec:
  rules:
    - host: counter.com
      http:
        paths:
          - path: /
            backend:
              serviceName: kubernetes-test-ha-application-
                without-redis
              servicePort: 80
```

5. Now, run the Ingress using the following command:

```
kubectl apply -f ingress.yaml
```

   You should see the following response:

```
ingress.networking.k8s.io/ingress created
```

6. Now, we will configure the Ingress controller such that when a request arrives at the load balancer that has a **Host:** header of **counter.com**, it should be forwarded to the **kubernetes-test-ha-application-without-redis** service on port **80**.

First, let's find the URL that we need to access:

```
kubectl describe svc -n ingress-nginx ingress-nginx
```

You should see an output similar to the following:

```
Selector:                  app.kubernetes.io/component=controller,app.kubernetes.
io/instance=ingress-nginx,app.kubernetes.io/name=ingress-nginx
Type:                      LoadBalancer
IP:                        172.20.159.113
LoadBalancer Ingress:      a0c805e36932449eab6c966b16b6cf1-13eb0d593e468ded.elb.
us-east-1.amazonaws.com
Port:                      http  80/TCP
TargetPort:                http/TCP
NodePort:                  http  30653/TCP
Endpoints:                 10.0.0.135:80
Port:                      https  443/TCP
TargetPort:                https/TCP
NodePort:                  https  32416/TCP
Endpoints:                 10.0.0.135:443
Session Affinity:          None
External Traffic Policy:   Local
HealthCheck NodePort:      31186
```

Figure 12.13: Checking the URL to access the Ingress load balancer endpoint

From the preceding screenshot, note that the Ingress load balancer endpoint that Kubernetes created for us in AWS is as follows:

```
a0c805e36932449eab6c966b16b6cf1-13eb0d593e468ded.elb.us-east-1.
amazonaws.com
```

Your value will likely be different from the preceding one and you should use the one that you get for your setup.

7. Now, let's access the endpoint using **`curl`**:

```
curl -H 'Host: counter.com' a0c805e36932449eab6c966b16b6cf1-
13eb0d593e468ded.elb.us-east-1.amazonaws.com/get-number
```

You should get a response similar to the following:

```
{number: 1}%
```

If you run it multiple times, you'll see that the number increases by 1 each time:

```
[zarnold@zachs-mbp kubernetes-test-ha-application % curl -H 'Host: counter.com' a
0c805e36932449eab6c966b16b6c6f1-13eb0d593e468ded.elb.us-east-1.amazonaws.com/get
-number
[{number: 1}%
zarnold@zachs-mbp kubernetes-test-ha-application % curl -H 'Host: counter.com' a
0c805e36932449eab6c966b16b6c6f1-13eb0d593e468ded.elb.us-east-1.amazonaws.com/get
-number
[{number: 2}%
zarnold@zachs-mbp kubernetes-test-ha-application % curl -H 'Host: counter.com' a
0c805e36932449eab6c966b16b6c6f1-13eb0d593e468ded.elb.us-east-1.amazonaws.com/get
-number
[{number: 3}%
zarnold@zachs-mbp kubernetes-test-ha-application % curl -H 'Host: counter.com' a
0c805e36932449eab6c966b16b6c6f1-13eb0d593e468ded.elb.us-east-1.amazonaws.com/get
-number
[{number: 4}%
zarnold@zachs-mbp kubernetes-test-ha-application % curl -H 'Host: counter.com' a
0c805e36932449eab6c966b16b6c6f1-13eb0d593e468ded.elb.us-east-1.amazonaws.com/get
-number
{number: 5}%
```

Figure 12.14: Repeatedly accessing our application

8. Now, let's discover the problem with the application. In order to make the application highly available, we need to have multiple replicas of it running simultaneously so that we can allow at least one replica to be unavailable. This, in turn, enables the app to tolerate failure. To scale the app, we're going to run the following command:

```
kubectl scale deployment --replicas=3 kubernetes-test-ha-application-
without-redis-deployment
```

You should see the following response:

```
deployment.extensions/kubernetes-test-ha-application-without-redis-deployment scaled
```

Figure 12.15: Scaling the application Deployment

9. Now, try accessing the application again multiple times, as we did in *step 7*:

```
curl -H 'Host: counter.com'
a3960d10c980e40f99887ea068f41b7b-1447612395.us-east-1.elb.amazonaws.
com/get-number
```

You should see a response similar to the following:

```
zarnold@zachs-mbp kubernetes-test-ha-application % curl -H 'Host: counter.com' a
3960d10c980e40f99887ea068f41b7b-1447612395.us-east-1.elb.amazonaws.com/get-numbe
r
{number: 1}%
zarnold@zachs-mbp kubernetes-test-ha-application % curl -H 'Host: counter.com' a
3960d10c980e40f99887ea068f41b7b-1447612395.us-east-1.elb.amazonaws.com/get-numbe
r
{number: 1}%
zarnold@zachs-mbp kubernetes-test-ha-application % curl -H 'Host: counter.com' a
3960d10c980e40f99887ea068f41b7b-1447612395.us-east-1.elb.amazonaws.com/get-numbe
r
{number: 2}%
zarnold@zachs-mbp kubernetes-test-ha-application % curl -H 'Host: counter.com' a
3960d10c980e40f99887ea068f41b7b-1447612395.us-east-1.elb.amazonaws.com/get-numbe
r
{number: 2}%
zarnold@zachs-mbp kubernetes-test-ha-application % curl -H 'Host: counter.com' a
3960d10c980e40f99887ea068f41b7b-1447612395.us-east-1.elb.amazonaws.com/get-numbe
r
{number: 1}%
zarnold@zachs-mbp kubernetes-test-ha-application % curl -H 'Host: counter.com' a
3960d10c980e40f99887ea068f41b7b-1447612395.us-east-1.elb.amazonaws.com/get-numbe
r
{number: 2}%
```

Figure 12.16: Repeatedly accessing the scaled application to observe the behavior

> **NOTE**
>
> This output may not be exactly the same for you, but if you see the number increasing with the first few attempts, keep accessing the application again. You will be able to observe the problem behavior after a few attempts.

This output highlights the problem with our application—the number isn't always increasing. Why is that? That is because the load balancer may pass the request to any one of the replicas, and the replica that receives the request returns a response based on its local state.

WORKING WITH STATEFUL APPLICATIONS

The previous exercise demonstrates the challenge of working with stateful applications in a distributed context. As a brief overview, a stateless app is an application program that does not save client data generated in one session for use in the next session with that client. This means that in general, a stateless application depends entirely on the input to derive its output. Imagine a server displaying a static web page that does not need to change for any reason. In the real world, stateless applications typically need to be combined with stateful applications in order to create a useful experience for clients or consumers of the application. There are, of course, exceptions to this.

A stateful application is one whose output depends on multiple factors, such as user input, input from other applications, and past saved events. These factors are called the "state" of the application, which determines its behavior. One of the most important parts of creating distributed applications with multiple replicas is that any state that is used to generate output needs to be shared among all the replicas. If the different replicas of your application are working with different states, then your application is going to exhibit random behavior based on which replica your request is routed to. This effectively defeats the purpose of horizontally scaling an application using replicas.

In the use case from the previous exercise, for each replica to respond with the correct number, we need to move the storage of that number outside each replica. To do this, we need to modify the application. Let's think for a second about how this can be done. Could we communicate the numbers between the replicas using another request? Could we assign each replica to only respond with multiples of the number it is assigned? (If we had three replicas, one would only respond with **1**, **4**, **7**..., while another would respond with **2**, **5**, **8**..., and the last one would respond with **3**, **6**, **9**....) Or, might we share the number in an external state store, such as a database? Regardless of what we choose, the path forward will involve updating our running application in Kubernetes. So, we will need to talk briefly about a strategy to do this.

THE CI/CD PIPELINE

With the help of containerization technology and a container image tag revision policy, we can push an incremental update to our application in a fairly easy manner. Just as with source code and infrastructure as code, we can keep the scripts and Kubernetes manifests that execute steps of our build and deploy a pipeline versioned in a tool such as **git**. This allows us to have tremendous visibility into, and flexibility to control, how software updates happen in our cluster using approaches such as CI and CD.

For the uninitiated, **CI/CD** stands for **Continuous Integration and Continuous Deployment/Delivery**. The CI aspect uses tooling, such as Jenkins or Concourse CI, to integrate new changes to our source code in a repeatable process for testing and assembling our code into a final artifact for deployment. The goal of CI is manifold, but here are a few benefits:

- Defects in the software are found earlier in the process (if testing is adequate).
- Repeatable steps create reproducible results when we are deploying to an environment.
- Visibility exists to communicate the status of a feature with stakeholders.
- It encourages frequent software updates to give developers confidence that their new code is not breaking existing functionality.

The other part, CD, is the incorporation of automated mechanisms to constantly deliver small updates to end-users, such as updating Deployment objects in Kubernetes and tracking rollout statuses. The CI/CD pipeline is the prevalent DevOps model today.

Ideally, a CI/CD pipeline should be able to reliably and predictably take code from a developer's machine and bring it all the way to a production environment with as few manual interventions as possible. A CI pipeline should ideally have components for compilation (where necessary), testing, and final application assembly (in the case of a Kubernetes cluster, this is a container).

A CD pipeline should have some way of automating its interactions with an infrastructure to take the application revision and deploy it, along with any dependent configurations and one-off deployment tasks, in such a way that the desired version of the software becomes the running version of the software via some kind of strategy (such as using a Deployment object in Kubernetes). It should also include telemetry tooling to observe the immediate impact of the Deployment on the surrounding environment.

The problem that we observed in the previous section with our application is that each replica is working off of its local state to return a number via HTTP. To solve this problem, we propose that we should use an external state store (database) to manage the information (the number) shared between each replica of our application. We have several options of state stores to choose from. We chose Redis simply because it's easy to get started with and it's simple to understand. Redis is a high-performance key-value database, much like etcd. In our example refactor, we will be sharing the state between the replicas by setting a key with the **`num`** name and the value is the increasing integer value that we want to return. During each request, this value will be incremented and stored back into the database so that each replica can work off the most up-to-date information.

Every company and individual has a different process that they use to manage new versions of code being deployed. Therefore, we are going to use simple commands to perform our steps, which can be automated via Bash with the tool of your choice.

EXERCISE 12.04: DEPLOYING AN APPLICATION WITH STATE MANAGEMENT

In this exercise, we will deploy a modified version of the application that we deployed in the previous exercise. As a reminder, this application counts how many times it has been accessed and returns that value in JSON format to the requestor. However, at the end of the previous exercise, we observed in *Figure 12.16* that when we scale this application horizontally with multiple replicas, we get numbers that are not always increasing.

> **NOTE**
>
> We have provided the source code for this application in the GitHub repository for your reference. However, since our focus is on Kubernetes, we will use commands to directly fetch it from the repository in this exercise.

In this modified version of the application, we have refactored our code to add the capability of storing this increasing count in a Redis database. This allows us to have multiple replicas of our application, but always have the count increase each time we make a request to the endpoint:

> **NOTE**
>
> In our implementation of Redis, we are not using a transaction to set the count after getting it. So, there is a very small chance that we are getting and acting on old information when we update the value set in the database, which may lead to unexpected results.

1. Use the following command to get the manifest of all the objects required for this application:

```
curl https://raw.githubusercontent.com/PacktWorkshops/Kubernetes-Workshop/master/Chapter12/Exercise12.04/with_redis.yaml > with_redis.yaml
```

You should see a response similar to the following:

```
  % Total    % Received % Xferd  Average Speed   Time    Time     Time  Current
                                 Dload  Upload   Total   Spent    Left  Speed
100  1549  100  1549    0     0   3723      0 --:--:-- --:--:-- --:--:--  3723
```

Figure 12.17: Downloading the manifest for the modified application

If you open this manifest, you will see that we have a Deployment for our app running three replicas: a ClusterIP Service to expose it, a Deployment for Redis running one replica, and another ClusterIP Service to expose Redis. We are also modifying the Ingress object created earlier to point to the new Service.

2. Now, it is time to deploy it on Kubernetes. We can run the following command:

```
kubectl apply -f with_redis.yaml
```

You should see a response similar to the following:

```
deployment.apps/kubernetes-test-ha-application-with-redis-deployment created
service/kubernetes-test-ha-application-with-redis created
deployment.apps/redis created
service/redis created
ingress.networking.k8s.io/ingress configured
```

Figure 12.18: Creating the resources required for our cluster

3. Now, let's see what this application gives us by using the following command:

```
curl -H 'Host: counter.com'
a3960d10c980e40f99887ea068f41b7b-1447612395.us-east-1.elb.amazonaws.
com/get-number
```

Run this command repeatedly. You should be able to see an increasing number, as shown:

```
zarnold@zachs-mbp kubernetes % curl -H 'Host: counter.com' a3960d10c980e40f99887]
ea068f41b7b-1447612395.us-east-1.elb.amazonaws.com/get-number
zarnold@zachs-mbp kubernetes % curl -H 'Host: counter.com' a3960d10c980e40f99887]
ea068f41b7b-1447612395.us-east-1.elb.amazonaws.com/get-number
{number: 1}%                                                                      ]
zarnold@zachs-mbp kubernetes % curl -H 'Host: counter.com' a3960d10c980e40f99887
ea068f41b7b-1447612395.us-east-1.elb.amazonaws.com/get-number
{number: 2}%                                                                      ]
zarnold@zachs-mbp kubernetes % curl -H 'Host: counter.com' a3960d10c980e40f99887
ea068f41b7b-1447612395.us-east-1.elb.amazonaws.com/get-number
{number: 3}%                                                                      ]
zarnold@zachs-mbp kubernetes % curl -H 'Host: counter.com' a3960d10c980e40f99887
ea068f41b7b-1447612395.us-east-1.elb.amazonaws.com/get-number
{number: 4}%                                                                      ]
zarnold@zachs-mbp kubernetes % curl -H 'Host: counter.com' a3960d10c980e40f99887
ea068f41b7b-1447612395.us-east-1.elb.amazonaws.com/get-number
{number: 5}%
```

Figure 12.19: Predictable output with consistently increasing numbers

As you can see in the preceding output, the program now outputs numbers in sequence because all of the replicas of our Deployment now share a single datastore responsible for managing the application state (Redis).

There are a lot of other paradigms that need to be shifted if you want to create a truly highly available, fault-tolerant software system, and it is beyond the scope of this book to explore them in detail. However, for more information, you can check out Packt's book on distributed systems at this link: https://www.packtpub.com/virtualization-and-cloud/hands-microservices-kubernetes.

> **NOTE**
>
> Again, remember that your cluster resources are still running at this point. Don't forget to tear down your cluster using **`terraform destroy`** if you expect to continue with the activity later.

Now that we have built our application with the ability to persist and share its state among different replicas, we will expand it further in the following activity.

ACTIVITY 12.01: EXPANDING THE STATE MANAGEMENT OF OUR APPLICATION

Right now, our application can leverage a shared Redis database running inside our Kubernetes cluster to manage the variable counter that we return to the user when it is fetched.

But let's suppose for a moment that we don't trust Kubernetes to reliably manage the Redis container (since it's a volatile in-memory datastore) and instead we want to use AWS ElastiCache to do so. Your goal in this activity is to use the tools we have learned in this chapter to modify our application to work with AWS ElastiCache.

You can use the following guidelines to complete this activity:

1. Use Terraform to provision ElastiCache.

   You can find the required parameter values for provisioning ElastiCache at this link: https://www.terraform.io/docs/providers/aws/r/elasticache_cluster.html#redis-instance.

2. Change the application to connect to Redis. You will need to use an environment variable in your Kubernetes Deployment for that. You can find the required information in the **`redis_address`** field when you run the **`terraform apply`** command.

3. Add the ElastiCache endpoint to the appropriate Kubernetes manifest environment variable.

4. Roll out the new version of code onto the Kubernetes cluster using any tool you want.

By the end, you should be able to observe the application responding similarly to what we saw in the previous exercise, but this time, it will use ElastiCache for its state management:

```
[zarnold@zachs-mbp kubernetes % curl -H 'Host: counter.com' a3960d10c980e40f99887]
ea068f41b7b-1447612395.us-east-1.elb.amazonaws.com/get-number
[zarnold@zachs-mbp kubernetes % curl -H 'Host: counter.com' a3960d10c980e40f99887]
ea068f41b7b-1447612395.us-east-1.elb.amazonaws.com/get-number
[{number: 1}%                                                                    ]
zarnold@zachs-mbp kubernetes % curl -H 'Host: counter.com' a3960d10c980e40f99887
ea068f41b7b-1447612395.us-east-1.elb.amazonaws.com/get-number
[{number: 2}%                                                                    ]
zarnold@zachs-mbp kubernetes % curl -H 'Host: counter.com' a3960d10c980e40f99887
ea068f41b7b-1447612395.us-east-1.elb.amazonaws.com/get-number
[{number: 3}%                                                                    ]
zarnold@zachs-mbp kubernetes % curl -H 'Host: counter.com' a3960d10c980e40f99887
ea068f41b7b-1447612395.us-east-1.elb.amazonaws.com/get-number
[{number: 4}%                                                                    ]
zarnold@zachs-mbp kubernetes % curl -H 'Host: counter.com' a3960d10c980e40f99887
ea068f41b7b-1447612395.us-east-1.elb.amazonaws.com/get-number
{number: 5}%
```

Figure 12.20: Expected output of the Activity 12.01

> **NOTE**
>
> The solution to this activity can be found at the following address: https://packt.live/304PEoD. Remember that your cluster resources will stay online until you delete them. To delete the cluster, you need to run **`terraform destroy`**.

SUMMARY

In an earlier chapter of this book, we explored how Kubernetes works favorably with a declarative approach to application management; that is, you define your desired state and let Kubernetes take care of the rest. Throughout this chapter, we took a look at some tools that help us manage our cloud infrastructure in a similar way. We introduced Terraform as a tool that can help us manage the state of our infrastructure and introduced the idea of treating your infrastructure as code.

We then created a mostly secure, production-ready Kubernetes cluster using Terraform in Amazon EKS. We took a look at the Ingress object and learned about the major motivations for using it, as well as the various advantages that it provides. Then, we deployed two versions of an application on a highly available Kubernetes cluster and explored some concepts that allow us to improve at horizontally scaling stateful applications. This gave us a glimpse of the challenges that come with running stateful applications, and we will explore some more ways of dealing with them in *Chapter 14, Running Stateful Components in Kubernetes*.

In the next chapter, we're going to take a look at continuing our production readiness by further securing our cluster.

13

RUNTIME AND NETWORK SECURITY IN KUBERNETES

OVERVIEW

In this chapter, we will look at various resources that we can use to secure workloads running in our cluster. We will also understand a rough threat model and apply it to architect a secure cluster so that we can defend our cluster and application against various types of threats. By the end of this chapter, you will be able to create Role and ClusterRole, as well as RoleBinding and ClusterRoleBinding to control the access of any process or user to the Kubernetes API server and objects. Then, you will learn how to create a NetworkPolicy to restrict communication between your application and the database. You will also learn how to create a PodSecurityPolicy to ensure that the running components of your application are conforming to the defined limits.

INTRODUCTION

In the last couple of chapters, we had our DevOps hat on and learned how to set up a cluster, as well as how to roll out new application versions safely and without downtime in Kubernetes.

Now, it's time to switch gears a bit, take our DevOps hat off, and put on our security analyst hat. First, we will look at where someone might attack our Kubernetes cluster and how an unauthorized user could potentially wreak havoc in our cluster. After that, we're going to introduce a few of the security primitives of Kubernetes and how we can combat the most common forms of attack. Finally, we'll further modify our application and demonstrate how some of these security primitives work.

But before we get to any of it, let's begin by taking a brief look at the various areas of concern for security in a modern web application, as well as a basic paradigm for implementing effective security for our cluster. We'll start by examining what we call the "4Cs of Cloud Native Security."

THREAT MODELING

It is far beyond the scope of this chapter to adequately teach many of the necessary disciplines of security so that you have a rigorous understanding of how modern workload security should be implemented and orchestrated. However, we will briefly gain an idea of how we should be thinking about it. Threat modeling is a discipline where we examine the various areas where our applications could be subject to an attack or unauthorized usage.

For example, consider an HTTP web server. It will typically have ports 80 and 443 exposed for serving web traffic, but it also acts as an entry point for any potential attackers. It may have a web management console exposed at a certain port. It may have certain other management ports open and API access to allow other software to manage it for automation purposes. The application runtime may need to regularly handle sensitive data. The entire end-to-end pipeline meant to create and deliver the application could expose various points that are vulnerable to compromise. The encryption algorithms that an application relies on may be compromised or made obsolete due to the increased sophistication of brute-force attacks. All these represent the various areas where our application could be subject to an attack.

An easy way to organize some of the attack vectors of our application is to remember the acronym **STRIDE**. It stands for the following types of attacks:

- **S**poofing: A user or an application disguising themselves as someone else.
- **T**ampering: Changing any data without seeking consent from or providing information to the concerned stakeholders.
- **R**epudiation: Being able to deny your involvement in your actions and/or the lack of ability to trace any actions to a particular user.
- **I**nformation disclosure: Exfiltrating privileged or sensitive information you were not intended to have.
- **D**enial of service: Flooding a server with bogus requests to saturate its resources and deny it the ability to serve its intended purpose.
- **E**levation of privilege: Getting access to a restricted resource or privilege by exploiting bugs.

Many of the attacks that hackers carry out are designed to do one or more of the preceding, usually to jeopardize the confidentiality, integrity, and availability of our data. With this in mind, we can use a mental model of how we can think about where threats to our system might exist in various parts of a modern cloud native application stack. This mental model is called "The 4Cs of Cloud Native Security," and we'll be using it to organize our exploration of the security primitives of Kubernetes. Ideally, by leveraging all these primitives, this should give you a good level of confidence in your application's resistance to STRIDE-like attacks, specifically within the context of Kubernetes.

THE 4CS OF CLOUD NATIVE SECURITY

Security can and should be organized into layers. This is considered a "defense in depth" approach to security and it is widely regarded by the technology community as the best way to prevent the compromise of any single component from exposing the whole system. When it comes to cloud native applications, we think of security in four layers: securing your code, containers, cluster, and cloud. The following diagram shows how they are organized. This helps us visualize that if a compromise happens at a lower level, it will most assuredly compromise a higher level that depends on it:

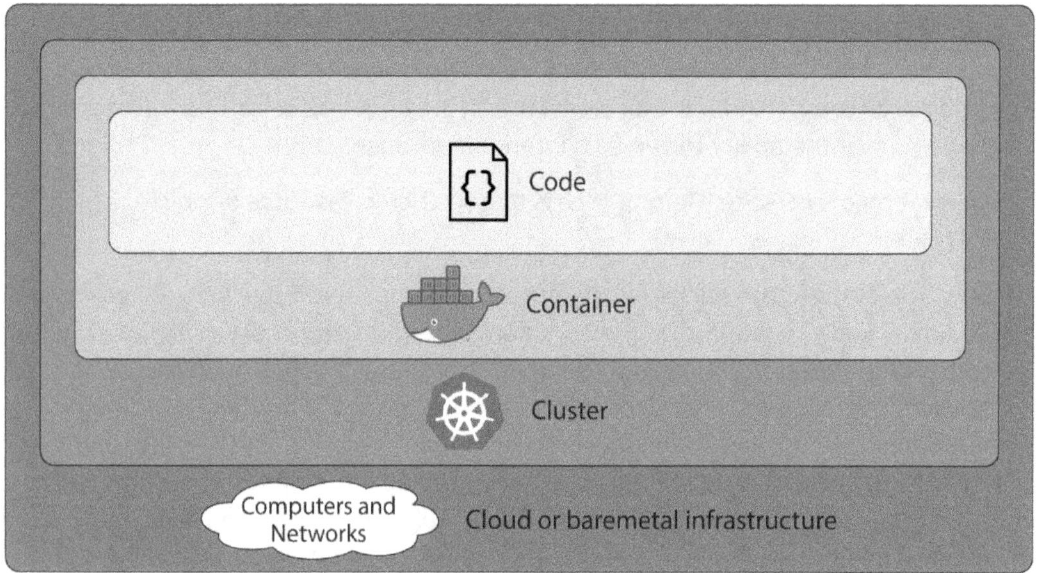

Figure 13.1: The 4Cs of Cloud Native Security

Since this book is focused on Kubernetes, we'll zoom into cluster security and then begin to implement some of the suggestions in our example application.

> **NOTE**
>
> For suggestions on the other C's, take a look at this link: https://kubernetes.io/docs/concepts/security/overview/.

CLUSTER SECURITY

One way to think about Kubernetes is as a gigantic self-orchestrating pool of compute, networking, and storage. As such, in many respects, Kubernetes is *exactly like a cloud platform*. It is important to understand this equivalence because this mental abstraction allows us to reason differently as a cluster operator versus a cluster developer. A cluster operator would want to ensure that all the components *of* the cluster were secure and hardened against any workload. A cluster developer would concern themselves with ensuring that the workload they are defining for Kubernetes is running securely inside the cluster.

Here is where your work becomes a bit easy – most cloud provider offerings from Kubernetes will ensure the security of the Kubernetes control plane for you. If, for whatever reason, you're not able to leverage a cloud provider offering, you'll want to read more in the documentation about securing your cluster at this link: https://kubernetes.io/docs/tasks/administer-cluster/securing-a-cluster/.

Even when you are using a cloud provider's offering, just because they are securing your control plane does not mean that your Kubernetes cluster is secure. The reason you cannot rely on your cloud provider's security is that your application, its container, or a poor policy implementation could leave your infrastructure very exposed to attacks. So, now, we need to talk about securing workloads within our cluster.

> **NOTE**
>
> There is active work being done in the Kubernetes community to improve security concepts and implementations. The relevant Kubernetes documentation should be revisited often to determine whether improvements have been made.

To fortify our internal cluster security, we need to take a look at the following three concepts:

- **Kubernetes RBAC**: This is the main policy engine of Kubernetes. It defines a system of roles and permissions, as well as how permissions are granted to those roles.
- **NetworkPolicies**: These are (depending on your Container Network Interface plugin) policies that act as a "firewall" between Pods. Think of them as a Kubernetes-aware network access control list.
- **PodSecurityPolicies**: These are defined at a particular scope (namespace, whole cluster) and serve as a definition of how a Pod is allowed to run in Kubernetes.

We will not be covering encrypting Kubernetes Secrets at rest in etcd as most cloud providers either handle that for you or the implementation is specific to that cloud provider (such as AWS KMS).

KUBERNETES RBAC

Before we dive into RBAC, recall from *Chapter 4, How to Communicate with Kubernetes (API Server)*, how Kubernetes authorizes requests to the API. We learned that there are three stages – Authentication, Authorization, and AdmissionControl. We will learn more about Admission Controllers in *Chapter 16, Kubernetes Admission Controllers*.

Kubernetes supports multiple different methods of authenticating with the cluster, and you'll want to reference your cloud provider's documentation to get more details on their specific implementation.

Authorization logic is handled through something called **RBAC**. It stands for **role-based access control** and it's the foundation of how we constrain certain users and groups to the minimum necessary permissions to perform their job. This is based on a concept in software security called "the principle of least privilege." For example, if you are a software engineer for a credit card processing company, **Payment Card Industry Data Security Standard** (**PCI DSS**) compliance requires that you shouldn't have access to production clusters and customer data. Therefore, if you did have access to a cluster in production, you should have a role that has no privileges.

RBAC is implemented by cluster administrators through four different API objects: **Roles**, **RoleBindings**, **ClusterRoles**, and **ClusterRoleBindings**. Let's look at how they work together by examining a diagram:

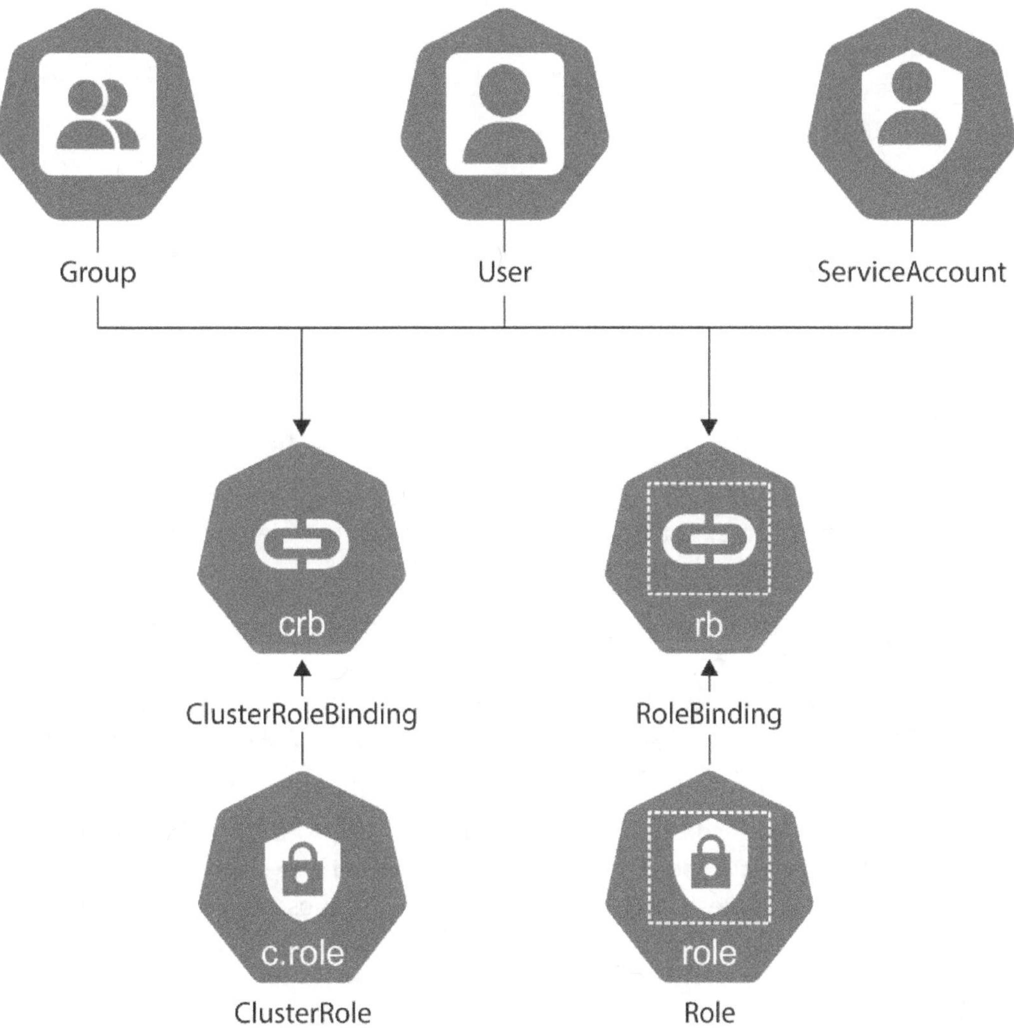

Figure 13.2: Different objects interacting to implement RBAC

In this diagram, we can see that Kubernetes **User/Group** and **ServiceAccount** objects obtain their permissions by being bound to a **Role** or **ClusterRole**. Let's understand these objects individually.

ROLE

Here is a sample spec for a Role:

```
apiVersion: rbac.authorization.k8s.io/v1
kind: Role
metadata:
  namespace: default
  name: test-role
rules:
  - verbs:
      - "list"
    apiGroups:
      - ""
    resources:
      - "pods"
```

The various fields define the permissions that a Role should have:

- **`namespace`**: Roles are scoped to a Kubernetes namespace, which is defined in this field. This makes a Role different from a ClusterRole, whose permissions apply for any namespace in the cluster.
- **`verbs`**: These describe which Kubernetes actions we are allowing. Some examples of commonly used verbs include **`get`**, **`list`**, **`watch`**, **`create`**, **`update`**, and **`delete`**. There are more, but these are usually good enough for most use cases. For a refresher on this, please refer to *The Kubernetes API* section of *Chapter 4, How to Communicate with Kubernetes (API Server)*.
- **`apiGroups`**: These describe which Kubernetes API groups the Role will have access to. These are specified as **`<group>/<version>`** (such as **`apps/v1`**). If you use CustomResourceDefinitions, these API groups can be referenced here as well.

> **NOTE**
>
> A full list of API groups that ship with Kubernetes can be found here (as of version 1.18): https://kubernetes.io/docs/reference/generated/kubernetes-api/v1.18/.

- **`resources`**: These describe which API objects we are talking about and are defined by the value in the **`Kind`** field of the object definition; for example, **`deployment`**, **`secret`**, **`configmap`**, **`pod`**, **`node`**, and others.

ROLEBINDING

As shown in the preceding diagram, a RoleBinding binds or associates a Role to ServiceAccounts, users, or groups of users. Here's a sample spec for a RoleBinding:

```
apiVersion: rbac.authorization.k8s.io/v1
kind: RoleBinding
metadata:
  name: test-role-binding
  namespace: default
roleRef:
  name: test-role
  kind: ClusterRole
  apiGroup: rbac.authorization.k8s.io
subjects:
  - kind: ServiceAccount
    name: test-sa
    namespace: default
```

This spec defines the subjects that should be able to use a Role to perform an action that requires authorization in Kubernetes:

- **`subjects`**: This refers to an authenticated ServiceAccount, user, or group that should be able to use this Role.
- **`roleRef`**: This refers to the Role they can assume.

CLUSTERROLE

A ClusterRole is identical to a Role in every way except one. Instead of granting permissions only inside one Kubernetes namespace, it grants this set of permissions cluster-wide.

CLUSTERROLEBINDING

This is identical to a RoleBinding except that it must be bound to a ClusterRole and not a Role. You cannot bind a ClusterRoleBinding to a Role, nor a RoleBinding to a ClusterRole.

SOME IMPORTANT NOTES ABOUT RBAC POLICIES

- RBAC policy documents are allow-only. This means that, by default, a subject has no access, and only via RoleBinding or ClusterRoleBinding will it have the specific access set forth in the corresponding Role or ClusterRole.
- Bindings are immutable. This means that once you have bound a subject to a Role or ClusterRole, it cannot be changed. This is to prevent privilege escalation. As such, an entity can be granted permission to modify objects (which is good enough for many use cases) while preventing it from elevating its own privileges. If you need to modify a binding, simply delete and recreate it.
- A ClusterRole or Role that can create other ClusterRoles and Roles will only be able to grant, at most, the same permissions it has. Otherwise, it would be a clear privilege escalation path.

SERVICEACCOUNT

In the previous chapters, when we learned about authentication in terms of Minikube and Kops, we saw that Kubernetes generated certificates that we used. In the case of EKS, AWS IAM roles and the AWS IAM Authenticator were used.

As it turns out, Kubernetes has a special object type for allowing resources within the cluster to authenticate with the API server.

We can use the ServiceAccount resource to allow Pods to receive a Kubernetes-generated token that it will pass to the API server for authentication. All official Kubernetes client libraries support this type of authentication, so it is the preferred method for programmatic Kubernetes cluster access from within the cluster.

When you are running as a cluster admin, you can use **kubectl** to authenticate using a particular ServiceAccount using the **--as** parameter. For the example ServiceAccount shown previously, this would look something like this:

```
kubectl --as=system:serviceaccount:default:test-sa get pods
```

We'll learn how these objects work together so that we can control access in the following exercise.

EXERCISE 13.01: CREATING A KUBERNETES RBAC CLUSTERROLE

In this exercise, we will create a ClusterRole and ClusterRoleBinding. Then, we will become the user and inherit their permissions, as defined by the ClusterRole, and demonstrate how Kubernetes prevents access to certain APIs based on rules. Let's get started:

1. To begin with, we will recreate the EKS cluster from the Terraform file we used in *Exercise 12.02, Creating a Cluster with EKS Using Terraform*. If you already have the **main.tf** file, you can work with it. Otherwise, you can run the following command to get it:

```
curl -O https://raw.githubusercontent.com/PacktWorkshops/Kubernetes-
Workshop/master/Chapter12/Exercise12.02/main.tf
```

   Now, use the following two commands, one after the other, to get your cluster resources up and running:

```
terraform init

terraform apply
```

> **NOTE**
>
> After performing any of these exercises, if you plan to continue working through the following exercises after a significant amount of time, it might be a good idea to deallocate your cluster resources to stop AWS billing. You can do that using the **terraform destroy** command. Then, you can run this step to get everything back online again when you are ready to perform an exercise or activity.
>
> If any exercise or activity relies on objects that were created in the previous exercises, you will need to recreate those objects as well.

2. Now, we're going to create three YAML files for our RBAC resources. The first is a ServiceAccount that lets us have identity and authentication tokens granted to us by the cluster. Create a file called **sa.yaml** with the following content:

```
apiVersion: v1
kind: ServiceAccount
metadata:
  name: test-sa
  namespace: default
```

3. Next, we are going to create a ClusterRole object and assign it some permissions. Create a file called **cr.yaml** with the following content:

```
apiVersion: rbac.authorization.k8s.io/v1
kind: ClusterRole
metadata:
  namespace: default
  name: test-sa-cluster-role
rules:
  - verbs:
      - "list"
    apiGroups:
      - ""
    resources:
      - "pods"
```

   We are defining a **ClusterRole** with the ability to list all the Pods in any namespace, but nothing else.

4. Next, we are going to create a **ClusterRoleBinding** object that will bind the created ServiceAccount and ClusterRole. Create a file called **crb.yaml** with the following content:

```
apiVersion: rbac.authorization.k8s.io/v1
kind: ClusterRoleBinding
metadata:
  name: test-sa-cluster-role-binding
  namespace: default
roleRef:
  name: test-sa-cluster-role
  kind: ClusterRole
  apiGroup: rbac.authorization.k8s.io
subjects:
  - kind: ServiceAccount
    name: test-sa
    namespace: default
```

In these files, we are defining three objects: a **ServiceAccount**, a **ClusterRole**, and a **ClusterRoleBinding**.

5. Run the following command to create this RBAC policy, as well as our ServiceAccount:

```
kubectl apply -f sa.yaml -f cr.yaml -f crb.yaml
```

You should see the following response:

```
serviceaccount/test-sa created
clusterrole.rbac.authorization.k8s.io/test-sa-cluster-role created
clusterrolebinding.rbac.authorization.k8s.io/test-sa-cluster-role-binding create
d
```

Figure 13.3: Creating a ServiceAccount, a ClusterRole, and a ClusterRoleBinding

6. In the following steps, we will demonstrate that using our service account's ClusterRole will prevent us from describing Pods. But before that, let's get a list of the Pods and prove that everything still works. Do this by running the following command:

```
kubectl get pods --all-namespaces
```

You should see the following response:

```
NAMESPACE     NAME                       READY   STATUS    RESTARTS   AGE
kube-system   aws-node-fzr6m             1/1     Running   0          37m
kube-system   aws-node-z4r2r             1/1     Running   0          37m
kube-system   coredns-5b9879fcff-4989r   1/1     Running   0          45m
kube-system   coredns-5b9879fcff-nb425   1/1     Running   0          45m
kube-system   kube-proxy-rnwsw           1/1     Running   0          37m
kube-system   kube-proxy-xlfbj           1/1     Running   0          37m
```

Figure 13.4: Getting the list of Pods

7. Now, let's describe the first Pod. The name of the first Pod here is **aws-node-fzr6m**. The **describe** command, in this case, would be as follows:

```
kubectl describe pod -n kube-system aws-node-fzr6m
```

Please use the Pod name that you have for your cluster. You should see a response similar to the following:

```
                 node.kubernetes.io/memory-pressure:NoSchedule
                 node.kubernetes.io/network-unavailable:NoSchedule
                 node.kubernetes.io/not-ready:NoExecute
                 node.kubernetes.io/pid-pressure:NoSchedule
                 node.kubernetes.io/unreachable:NoExecute
                 node.kubernetes.io/unschedulable:NoSchedule
Events:
  Type    Reason     Age   From                                                    Mes
sage
  ----    ------     ----  ----                                                    ---
----
  Normal  Scheduled  39m   default-scheduler                                       Suc
cessfully assigned kube-system/aws-node-fzr6m to ip-10-0-0-61.us-west-2.compute.
internal
  Normal  Pulling    39m   kubelet, ip-10-0-0-61.us-west-2.compute.internal  Pul
ling image "602401143452.dkr.ecr.us-west-2.amazonaws.com/amazon-k8s-cni:v1.5.3"
  Normal  Pulled     39m   kubelet, ip-10-0-0-61.us-west-2.compute.internal  Suc
cessfully pulled image "602401143452.dkr.ecr.us-west-2.amazonaws.com/amazon-k8s-
cni:v1.5.3"
  Normal  Created    39m   kubelet, ip-10-0-0-61.us-west-2.compute.internal  Cre
ated container aws-node
  Normal  Started    39m   kubelet, ip-10-0-0-61.us-west-2.compute.internal  Sta
rted container aws-node
zarnold@Zachs-MBP ~ %
```

Figure 13.5: Describing the aws-node-fzr6m Pod

The preceding screenshot shows the truncated version of the output of the **describe** command.

8. Now, we will run the same commands we used previously, but this time pretending to be the user using the ServiceAccount that is currently bound to the ClusterRole and ClusterRoleBinding that we created. We'll do this by using the **--as** parameter with **kubectl**. Thus, the command will look like this:

```
kubectl --as=system:serviceaccount:default:test-sa get pods
--all-namespaces
```

Note that we can assume the ClusterRole because we are an admin in the cluster that we created. You should see the following response:

```
NAMESPACE     NAME                       READY   STATUS    RESTARTS   AGE
kube-system   aws-node-fzr6m             1/1     Running   0          42m
kube-system   aws-node-z4r2r             1/1     Running   0          42m
kube-system   coredns-5b9879fcff-4989r   1/1     Running   0          50m
kube-system   coredns-5b9879fcff-nb425   1/1     Running   0          50m
kube-system   kube-proxy-rnwsw           1/1     Running   0          42m
kube-system   kube-proxy-xlfbj           1/1     Running   0          42m
```

Figure 13.6: Getting the list of Pods while assuming the test-sa ServiceAccount

Sure enough, that still works. As you may recall from *step 3*, we mentioned the **list** as an allowed verb, which is what's used for fetching the list of all resources of a certain kind.

9. Now, let's see what happens if a user with the ClusterRole we created attempts to describe a Pod:

```
kubectl --as=system:serviceaccount:default:test-sa describe pod -n
kube-system aws-node-fzr6m
```

You should see the following response:

```
Error from server (Forbidden): pods "aws-node-fzr6m" is forbidden: User "system:
serviceaccount:default:test-sa" cannot get resource "pods" in API group "" in th
e namespace "kube-system"
```

Figure 13.7: Forbidden error

The kubectl **describe** command uses the **get** verb. Recall from *step 3* that it was not on the allowed list of verbs for our ClusterRole.

If this were a user (or a hacker) trying to use any command not allowed for them, we would have successfully stopped it. There are many practical RBAC examples available on the Kubernetes documentation website. It is beyond the scope of this chapter to talk about all the design patterns for RBAC in Kubernetes. All we can say is this: wherever possible, you should be practicing the "principle of least privilege" to limit unnecessary access to the Kubernetes API server. That is, everyone should get the minimum level of access required to do their job; not everyone needs to be a cluster admin.

While we cannot make specific recommendations about security at your company, we can say that there are a few good "rules of thumb," which can be stated as follows:

- Whenever possible, try to make cluster contributors/users inside of a Role instead of a ClusterRole. Since a Role is constrained to a namespace, this will prevent that user from gaining unauthorized access to another namespace.
- Only cluster admins should have access to ClusterRoles, which should be limited and temporary in scope. For example, if you do on-call rotations where engineers are responsible for the availability of your services, then they should only have an admin ClusterRole for the time they are on call.

NETWORKPOLICIES

NetworkPolicy objects in Kubernetes are essentially Network Access Control Lists but at the Pod and namespace level. They work by using label selection (such as Services) or by indicating a CIDR IP address range to allow on a particular port/protocol.

This is immensely helpful for ensuring security, especially when you have multiple microservices running on a cluster. Now, imagine you have a cluster that hosts many applications for your company. It hosts a marketing website that runs an open-source library, a database server with sensitive data, and an application server that controls access to that data. If the marketing website doesn't need to access the database, then there should be no reason for it to be allowed access to the database. By using a NetworkPolicy, we can prevent an exploit or a bug in the marketing website from allowing an attacker to expand that attack so that they can access your business data by preventing the marketing website Pod from even being able to talk to the database. Let's take a look at a sample NetworkPolicy document and decipher it:

```
apiVersion: networking.k8s.io/v1
kind: NetworkPolicy
metadata:
  name: sample-network-policy
  namespace: my-namespace
spec:
  podSelector:
    matchLabels:
      role: db
  policyTypes:
  - Ingress
  - Egress
  ingress:
```

```
  - from:
    - ipBlock:
        cidr: 192.18.0.0/16
        except:
        - 192.18.1.0/24
    - namespaceSelector:
        matchLabels:
          project: sample-project
    - podSelector:
        matchLabels:
          role: frontend
    ports:
    - protocol: TCP
      port: 3257
  egress:
  - to:
    - ipBlock:
        cidr: 10.0.0.0/24
    ports:
    - protocol: TCP
      port: 5832
```

Let's examine some of the fields of this NetworkPolicy:

- It contains the standard **`apiVersion`**, **`kind`**, and **`metadata`** fields that we described earlier in this chapter.
- **`podSelector`**: The labels it should look for in the namespace to apply the policy.
- **`policyTypes`**: Can be either ingress, egress, or both. This means that the network policy applies to either traffic coming into the Pods being selected, leaving the Pods being selected, or both.
- **`Ingress`**: This takes a **`from`** block that defines where traffic can originate from in the policy. This can be a namespace, a Pod selector, or an IP address block and port combination.
- **`Egress`**: This takes a **`to`** block and defines where traffic is allowed to go to in the network policy. This can be a namespace, a Pod selector, or an IP address block and port combination.

Your CNI may not have a mature implementation of NetworkPolicies, so be sure to consult your cloud provider's documentation for more information. In the case of the cluster we set up using EKS, it is using the Amazon CNI. We can use **Calico**, an open-source project, to augment the existing EKS CNI and make up for deficiencies with respect to enforcing NetworkPolicy declarations. It is worth mentioning that Calico can be used as a CNI as well, but we will only be using the supplementary functionality for NetworkPolicy enforcement in the following exercise.

EXERCISE 13.02: CREATING A NETWORKPOLICY

In this exercise, we will implement Calico to augment the out-of-the-box enforcement of NetworkPolicy declarations available with Amazon CNI in EKS. Let's get started:

1. Run the following command to install the Amazon CNI with Calico:

```
kubectl apply -f https://raw.githubusercontent.com/aws/amazon-vpc-cni-k8s/release-1.5/config/v1.5/calico.yaml
```

You should see a response similar to the following:

```
daemonset.apps/calico-node created
customresourcedefinition.apiextensions.k8s.io/felixconfigurations.crd.projectcalico.org created
customresourcedefinition.apiextensions.k8s.io/ipamblocks.crd.projectcalico.org created
customresourcedefinition.apiextensions.k8s.io/blockaffinities.crd.projectcalico.org created
customresourcedefinition.apiextensions.k8s.io/bgpconfigurations.crd.projectcalico.org created
customresourcedefinition.apiextensions.k8s.io/bgppeers.crd.projectcalico.org created
customresourcedefinition.apiextensions.k8s.io/ippools.crd.projectcalico.org created
customresourcedefinition.apiextensions.k8s.io/hostendpoints.crd.projectcalico.org created
customresourcedefinition.apiextensions.k8s.io/clusterinformations.crd.projectcalico.org created
customresourcedefinition.apiextensions.k8s.io/globalnetworkpolicies.crd.projectcalico.org created
customresourcedefinition.apiextensions.k8s.io/globalnetworksets.crd.projectcalico.org created
customresourcedefinition.apiextensions.k8s.io/networkpolicies.crd.projectcalico.org created
customresourcedefinition.apiextensions.k8s.io/networksets.crd.projectcalico.org created
serviceaccount/calico-node created
clusterrole.rbac.authorization.k8s.io/calico-node created
clusterrolebinding.rbac.authorization.k8s.io/calico-node created
deployment.apps/calico-typha created
poddisruptionbudget.policy/calico-typha created
clusterrolebinding.rbac.authorization.k8s.io/typha-cpha created
clusterrole.rbac.authorization.k8s.io/typha-cpha created
configmap/calico-typha-horizontal-autoscaler created
deployment.apps/calico-typha-horizontal-autoscaler created
role.rbac.authorization.k8s.io/typha-cpha created
serviceaccount/typha-cpha created
rolebinding.rbac.authorization.k8s.io/typha-cpha created
service/calico-typha created
```

Figure 13.8: Installing Amazon CNI with Calico

2. To verify that you have deployed the DaemonSet corresponding to Calico successfully, use the following command:

```
kubectl get daemonset calico-node --namespace kube-system
```

You should see the **calico-node** DaemonSet, as shown here:

```
NAME          DESIRED   CURRENT   READY   UP-TO-DATE   AVAILABLE   NODE SELECTOR
                AGE
calico-node   2         2         0       2            0           beta.kubernet
es.io/os=linux    24s
```

Figure 13.9: Checking the calico-node DaemonSet

3. Now, let's create our NetworkPolicy object. First, create a file named **net_pol_all_deny.yaml** with the following content:

```
apiVersion: networking.k8s.io/v1
kind: NetworkPolicy
metadata:
  name: default-deny
spec:
  podSelector: {}
  policyTypes:
    - Ingress
    - Egress
```

This policy is a very simple NetworkPolicy. It says that no traffic to and from Pods is allowed in or out of the cluster. This is the secure base on which we're going to continue expanding our application.

4. Let's apply our policy using the following command:

```
kubectl apply -f net_pol_all_deny.yaml
```

You should see the following response:

```
networkpolicy.networking.k8s.io/default-deny created
```

Now, there is no traffic flowing through our cluster. We can prove this by deploying our application since it needs the network to communicate with itself.

5. As a test application, we will use the same application we used in *Exercise 12.04, Deploying an Application Version Update*. If you already have the YAML file for that, you can use it. Otherwise, run the following command to get the file in your working directory:

```
curl -O https://raw.githubusercontent.com/PacktWorkshops/Kubernetes-
Workshop/master/Chapter12/Exercise12.04/with_redis.yaml
```

Then, use the following command to deploy the application:

```
kubectl apply -f with_redis.yaml
```

```
deployment.apps/kubernetes-test-ha-application-with-redis-deployment created
service/kubernetes-test-ha-application-with-redis created
deployment.apps/redis created
service/redis created
```

Figure 13.10: Deploying our application

6. Now, let's check the status of our deployment using the following command:

```
kubectl describe deployment kubernetes-test-ha-application-with-
redis-deployment
```

You should see the following response:

```
Name:                   kubernetes-test-ha-application-with-redis-deployment
Namespace:              default
CreationTimestamp:      Thu, 05 Dec 2019 20:10:18 -0800
Labels:                 app=kubernetes-test-ha-application-with-redis
Annotations:            deployment.kubernetes.io/revision: 1
                        kubectl.kubernetes.io/last-applied-configuration:
                          {"apiVersion":"apps/v1","kind":"Deployment","metadata":{"an
notations":{},"labels":{"app":"kubernetes-test-ha-application-with-redis"},"nam...
Selector:               app=kubernetes-test-ha-application-with-redis
Replicas:               3 desired | 3 updated | 3 total | 0 available | 3 unavailable
StrategyType:           RollingUpdate
MinReadySeconds:        0
RollingUpdateStrategy:  25% max unavailable, 25% max surge
```

Figure 13.11: Checking the status of our application

This is a truncated screenshot. As you can see, we have an issue that we are unable to communicate with Redis. Fixing this will be a part of *Activity 13.01, Going Beyond Primitives*.

7. We are going to test network access now, so in a separate Terminal window, let's start our proxy:

```
kubectl proxy
```

You should see this response:

```
Starting to serve on 127.0.0.1:8001
```

Another way to verify that the NetworkPolicy is preventing traffic is to use our **`curl`** command:

```
curl localhost:8001/api/v1/namespaces/default/services/kubernetes-
test-ha-application-with-redis:/proxy/get-number
```

You should see a response similar to this:

```
Error: 'dial tcp 10.0.0.193:8080: i/o timeout'
Trying to reach: 'http:10.0.0.193:8080/get-number'%
```

As we can see, we are able to prevent unauthorized communication between Pods in our Kubernetes cluster. By leveraging NetworkPolicies, we can prevent attackers from doing further damage if they are able to compromise some of the components of our cluster, containers, or source code.

PodSecurityPolicy

So far, we have learned about and tested Kubernetes RBAC to prevent unauthorized API server access, and also applied a NetworkPolicy to prevent unnecessary network communication. The next most important area of security outside the network is the application runtime. Attackers need access to the network to get in and out, but they also need a vulnerable runtime to do anything more serious. This is where Kubernetes PodSecurityPolicy objects help prevent that from happening.

PodSecurityPolicy objects overlap with a specific type of AdmissionController and allow a cluster operator to dynamically define the minimum runtime requirements of a Pod that's been admitted for scheduling on the cluster.

To understand exactly how PodSecurityPolicies can be useful, let's consider the following scenario. You are a Kubernetes cluster admin at a large financial institution. Your company uses ticket-based change management software in an ITIL-compliant fashion (ITIL is a standardized change management framework for IT services) to ensure that changes that are made to the environment are stable. This prevents developers from doing anything disastrous in production. To keep up with the change of pace in the market that your customers are demanding, you need a programmatic way to enable developers to do more change management autonomously. But you also need to do so in a way that is secure and compliant with certain standards. PodSecurityPolicies help us do this because they allow administrators to create policy definitions in software that are enforced when a Pod is being admitted to a cluster. This means that developers can move more rapidly, and cluster admins can still certify that their environment is fully compliant with the set standards.

Further extending this scenario, you might want to prevent users from running their container as the root user so that attackers can't exploit any vulnerabilities in Docker. By applying a PodSecurityPolicy, you can prevent your users from accidentally deploying unsecured containers.

Now that we have seen how they can be useful, let's consider a sample PodSecurityPolicy and examine it:

```
apiVersion: policy/v1beta1
kind: PodSecurityPolicy
metadata:
  name: psp-example
  namespace: default
spec:
  privileged: true
  seLinux:
    rule: RunAsAny
  supplementalGroups:
    rule: MustRunAs
    ranges:
      - min: 1
        max: 2500
  runAsUser:
    rule: MustRunAsNonRoot
  fsGroup:
    rule: MustRunAs
    ranges:
      - min: 655
        max: 655
  volumes:
    - '*'
```

Let's examine a few noteworthy fields here:

- **metadata.namespace**: This is going to create the PodSecurityPolicy in the **default** namespace and will apply to Pods in the same namespace.
- **privileged**: This controls whether containers are allowed to run in a privileged execution context on the node, which effectively grants the container root-level access to the host. You can find more information about privileged containers here: https://docs.docker.com/engine/reference/run/#runtime-privilege-and-linux-capabilities.
- **seLinux**: This defines any SELinux settings. Some Kubernetes clusters run in SELinux environments, which implement something called "mandatory access control" outside of the cluster. This allows those controls to be projected into the cluster. By stating **RunAsAny**, we are allowing any SELinux user.

- **supplementalGroups**: This is a mandatory field of the policy. It essentially tells us that we are allowing any Linux user group ID (GID). In this sample spec, we are saying that users from any Linux user group with IDs 1 to 2500 are allowed.
- **runAsUser**: This allows us to specify specific Linux users who are permitted to run any process in the Pod. By stating **MustRunAsNonRoot**, we are saying that any process in the Pod must not run with root privileges.
- **fsGroup**: This is the Linux group ID the container process must be running as to interact with certain volumes on the cluster. Thus, even if a volume exists on a Pod, we can restrict certain processes in that Pod from accessing it. In this sample spec, we are saying that only Linux users in the **devops** group with a GID of 655 can access the volume. This is applied regardless of the location of the Pod in the cluster or where the volume is.
- **volumes**: This allows us to permit the different types of volume that can be mounted to that Pod, such as a **configmap** or a **persistentVolumeClaim**. In this sample spec, we have specified ***** (an asterisk), which implies that all kinds of volumes are allowed to be used by the processes in this Pod.

Now that we have understood what the different fields in the spec mean, we'll create a PodSecurityPolicy in the following exercise.

EXERCISE 13.03: CREATING AND TESTING A PODSECURITYPOLICY

In this exercise, we're going to be creating a PodSecurityPolicy and applying it to our cluster to demonstrate the types of functionalities Pods must now comply with in our cluster after we apply it. Let's get started:

1. Create a file named **pod_security_policy_example.yaml** with the following content:

```
apiVersion: policy/v1beta1
kind: PodSecurityPolicy
metadata:
  name: psp-example
  namespace: default
spec:
  privileged: false
  seLinux:
    rule: RunAsAny
  supplementalGroups:
```

```
    rule: MustRunAs
    ranges:
      - min: 1
        max: 2500
  runAsUser:
    rule: MustRunAsNonRoot
  fsGroup:
    rule: MustRunAs
    ranges:
      - min: 655
        max: 655
  volumes:
    - '*'
```

2. To apply this to the cluster, run the following command:

```
kubectl apply -f pod_security_policy_example.yaml
```

You should see the following response:

```
podsecuritypolicy.policy/psp-example created
```

To check that our policy is enforced, let's try to create a Pod that doesn't comply with this policy. Now we have a policy called **MustRunAsNonRoot**, so we should try to run a container as root and see what happens.

3. To create a Docker container that would violate this PodSecurityPolicy, first, create a file named **Dockerfile** with the following content:

```
FROM debian:latest
USER 0
CMD echo $(whoami)
```

The second line of this **Dockerfile** switches to the root user (indicated by the UID of **0**), and then the **echo** command should tell us what user is running in this container when it starts.

4. Build the Docker image by running the following command:

```
docker build -t root .
```

You should see the following response:

```
Sending build context to Docker daemon  3.072kB
Step 1/3 : FROM debian:latest
 ---> 3de0e2c97e5c
Step 2/3 : USER 0
 ---> Using cache
 ---> 16326e22a5e9
Step 3/3 : CMD echo $(whoami)
 ---> Using cache
 ---> ecf183764859
Successfully built ecf183764859
Successfully tagged root:latest
```

Figure 13.12: Building our Docker image

5. Let's run our Docker container:

```
docker run root:latest
```

You should see the following response:

```
root
```

As we can see, this container is going to run as root.

6. Now, we need to create a Pod from this container. Create a file named **pod.yaml** with the following content:

```
apiVersion: v1
kind: Pod
metadata:
  name: rooter
spec:
  containers:
    - name: rooter
      image: packtworkshops/the-kubernetes-workshop:root-tester
```

You can push your own image to your Docker Hub repository and replace this link, or you can use the container that we have already provided for convenience. As a general rule of thumb, you should always be careful when downloading something that is supposed to run with root access.

7. By default, a PodSecurityPolicy does nothing until the **use** permission is installed on a user, group, or ServiceAccount that will be creating the Pod. To mimic this, we will quickly create a ServiceAccount:

```
kubectl create serviceaccount fake-user
```

You should see the following response:

```
serviceaccount/fake-user created
```

8. Now, let's create a Role that will be subject to this PodSecurityPolicy:

```
kubectl create role psp:unprivileged --verb=use
--resource=podsecuritypolicy --resource-name=psp-example
```

Note that this is another quick way to create a Role. Here, **psp:unprivileged** corresponds to the name of the role, while the flags correspond to the fields that we studied earlier. We are using the **--resource-name** flag to apply the Role to our specific PodSecurityPolicy. You should get the following response:

```
role.rbac.authorization.k8s.io/psp:unprivileged created
```

9. Let's bind this role to our ServiceAccount using a RoleBinding:

```
kubectl create rolebinding fake-user:psp:unprivileged
--role=psp:unprivileged --serviceaccount=psp-example:fake-user
```

Here, we are using a command similar to the one we used in the previous step. You should see the following response:

```
rolebinding.rbac.authorization.k8s.io/fake-user: psp:unprivileged
created
```

10. Now, let's masquerade as this user and try to create this Pod:

```
kubectl --as=system:serviceaccount:psp-example:fake-user apply -f
pod.yaml
```

You should see the following response:

```
Error from server (Forbidden): error when creating "STDIN": pods "privileged" is
 forbidden: unable to validate against any pod security policy: [spec.containers
[0].securityContext.privileged: Invalid value: true: Privileged containers are n
ot allowed]
```

Figure 13.13: Trying to create a Pod while assuming the fake-user ServiceAccount

At the beginning of this chapter, we explored the 4Cs of cluster security, and then throughout this chapter, we have seen different ways in which Kubernetes allows us to harden our cluster against various areas of attack. We learned that RBAC policies allow us to control access to our API and objects, NetworkPolicy allows us to harden the networking topology, and PodSecurityPolicy helps us protect against compromised runtimes.

Now, let's bring these concepts together in the following activity.

ACTIVITY 13.01: SECURING OUR APP

As it stands, our application from the previous chapter is already quite secure for the use case. What we need to do, though, is prevent users from deploying Pods that are privileged (so that they can't escalate their permissions) and make sure that our app can communicate with both the outside world and its datastore. A correct solution to this application would be to have the following functionality:

- The application should work seamlessly, as we demonstrated in the previous chapter, but now, it should prevent any unnecessary network traffic. Unnecessary here refers to the fact that the only Pod communicating with the Redis server should be the app, and that the app should only be communicating with other IP ranges.
- In *Exercise 13.02, Creating a NetworkPolicy*, we saw that our application did not work due to the highly restrictive NetworkPolicy. However, in this case, you should see the application running with an output similar to the following:

```
zarnold@zachs-mbp kubernetes % curl -H 'Host: counter.com' a3960d10c980e40f99887
ea068f41b7b-1447612395.us-east-1.elb.amazonaws.com/get-number
zarnold@zachs-mbp kubernetes % curl -H 'Host: counter.com' a3960d10c980e40f99887
ea068f41b7b-1447612395.us-east-1.elb.amazonaws.com/get-number
{number: 1}%
zarnold@zachs-mbp kubernetes % curl -H 'Host: counter.com' a3960d10c980e40f99887
ea068f41b7b-1447612395.us-east-1.elb.amazonaws.com/get-number
{number: 2}%
zarnold@zachs-mbp kubernetes % curl -H 'Host: counter.com' a3960d10c980e40f99887
ea068f41b7b-1447612395.us-east-1.elb.amazonaws.com/get-number
{number: 3}%
zarnold@zachs-mbp kubernetes % curl -H 'Host: counter.com' a3960d10c980e40f99887
ea068f41b7b-1447612395.us-east-1.elb.amazonaws.com/get-number
{number: 4}%
zarnold@zachs-mbp kubernetes % curl -H 'Host: counter.com' a3960d10c980e40f99887
ea068f41b7b-1447612395.us-east-1.elb.amazonaws.com/get-number
{number: 5}%
```

Figure 13.14: Expected output for Activity 13.01

Here are some steps that can help you complete this activity:

1. Ensure that you have a cluster infrastructure and all the objects from *Exercise 13.01, Creating a Kubernetes RBAC ClusterRole*.
2. Create a file named **pod_security_policy.yaml** (and then apply it). Keep in mind the functionality as described in the first bullet point above when creating this file. You might want to re-visit the section *PodSecurityPolicy* where we describe each of the fields used in such a file in detail.
3. Create a file named **network_policy.yaml**. Keep in mind the requirement as listed in the second bullet point above when creating this file. You might want to re-visit the section *NetworkPolicies* where we describe each of the fields used in such a file in detail. Make sure to apply this policy once you have created it.
4. If you have the application from *Exercise 14.02, Creating a NetworkPolicy* still deployed in your cluster, you can move on to the next step. Otherwise, rerun *steps 5* and *6* from that exercise.
5. Now, test the application.

> **NOTE**
>
> The solution to this activity can be found at the following address: https://packt.live/304PEoD.
>
> Also, consider deleting the NetworkPolicy and PodSecurityPolicy after you are done with this chapter to avoid any interference with later chapters.

SUMMARY

In our journey of building a production-ready Kubernetes environment, security is a critical aspect. With that in mind, in this chapter, we examined how threat modeling allows us to think in an adversarial way about our application infrastructure and how it informs us of how we can defend it from attack. Then, we looked at the 4Cs of Cloud Native Security to understand where our attack surfaces are, followed by how Kubernetes can help us run workloads securely in the cluster.

Kubernetes has several security features that we can leverage to secure our cluster. We learned about three security measures that are important to leverage: RBAC, NetworkPolicies, and PodSecurityPolicies. We also learned about their various applications when it comes to securing access to your cluster, securing your container network, and securing your container runtimes.

In the next chapter, we're going to examine how to manage storage objects in Kubernetes and deal with apps that are stateful.

14

RUNNING STATEFUL COMPONENTS IN KUBERNETES

OVERVIEW

In this chapter, we will expand our skills to go beyond stateless applications and learn how to deal with stateful applications. We will learn about the various forms of state preservation mechanisms available to Kubernetes cluster operators and derive a mental model for where certain options can be invoked to run applications well. We will also introduce Helm, a useful tool for deploying complex applications with various Kubernetes objects.

By the end of this chapter, you will be able to use StatefulSets and PersistentVolumes in conjunction to run apps that require disk-based state to be retained in between pod interruptions. You will also be able to deploy applications using Helm charts.

INTRODUCTION

From everything that you have learned up until this point, you know that pods and the containers that run in them are considered ephemeral. This means that they are not to be depended upon for stability as Kubernetes will intervene and move them around the cluster in order to comply with the desired state specified by the various manifests in the cluster. But there's a problem in this - what do we do with the parts of our applications that depend on the state being persisted from one interaction to the next? Without certain guarantees such as predictable naming for the pods and dependable storage operations, which we will learn about later in the chapter, such stateful components may fail if Kubernetes restarts the relevant pods or moves them around. However, before diving into the details of the aforementioned topics, let's talk briefly about stateful apps and why it's challenging to run them in a containerized environment.

STATEFUL APPS

We briefly introduced the concept of statefulness in *Chapter 12, Your Application and HA.* Stateful components of applications are a necessity to just about all information technology systems in the world. They're necessary to keep account details, records of transactions, information on HTTP requests, and a whole host of other purposes. The challenging part of running these applications in a production environment almost always has to do with either the network or the persistence mechanism. Whether it's spinning metal disks, flash storage, block storage, or some other yet-to-be-invented tool, persistence is notoriously difficult to deal with in all forms. Part of why this is difficult is because all of these forms have a non-zero probability of failure, which can become very significant once you need to have hundreds or even thousands of storage devices in a production environment. These days, many cloud providers will give assistance to customers and offer managed services to account for this difficulty. In the case of AWS, we have tools such as S3, EBS, RDS, DynamoDB, Elasticache, and many others that help developers and operators run stateful applications smoothly without much heavy lifting (provided you are OK with vendor lock-in.)

Another trade-off that some companies face with running stateful applications and the persistence mechanisms they depend on is between either training and maintaining a large body of staff capable of keeping these systems of record online, healthy, and up to date, or attempting to develop a set of tools and programmatically enforced processes for common operational scenarios. These two approaches differ in the amount of human maintenance effort needed as the organization scales.

For example, a human-centric approach to operations will allow things to move swiftly at first, but all operational costs scale linearly with the application scale, and eventually, the bureaucracy causes diminishing productivity returns with each new hire. Software-centric approaches are a higher upfront investment, but costs scale logarithmically with application scale and have a higher probability of cascading failures in the event of an unexpected bug.

Some examples of these operational scenarios are provisioning and configuration, normal operations, scaling input/output, backups, and abnormal operations. Examples of abnormal operations include network failures, hard drive failures, corruption of data on disk, security breaches, and application-specific irregularities. Examples of application-specific irregularities could be handling MySQL-specific collation concerns, handling S3 eventually consistent read failures, etcd Raft protocol resolution errors, and so on.

Many companies find it easier to pay for vendor support, use cloud-managed product offerings, or re-train their staff rather than developing programmatic state management processes and software.

One of the benefits of a Kubernetes-enabled development life cycle is on the workload definition side. The more effort a company puts into rigorously defining the smallest logical unit of compute (a pod template or PersistentVolume definition), the better they will be prepared for Kubernetes to intervene in irregular operations and appropriately orchestrate the entire application. This is largely because Kubernetes orchestration is a classical dynamic **constraint satisfaction problem** (**CSP**). The more information in the form of constraints the CSP solver has to work with at its disposal, the more predictable workload orchestration will become because the number of feasible steady-state solutions is reduced. So, using the end goal of predictable workload orchestration, is it then possible to run state-bearing components of our application in Kubernetes? The answer is an unequivocal yes. It is common to be hesitant to run stateful workloads in Kubernetes. We've said from the beginning of this book that pods are ephemeral and should not be depended on for stability because, in the event of a node failure, they will be moved and restarted. So, before you decide that it's too risky to run a database in Kubernetes, consider this – the world's largest search engine company runs databases in a very similar tool to Kubernetes. This tells us that it's not only possible but in reality, it's preferable to work on defining workloads well enough that they can be run by an orchestrator because it can likely handle application failures much faster than a human.

So, how do we accomplish this? The answer to that question is the use of a combination of two Kubernetes objects that you have learned about earlier – **PersistentVolumes** and **StatefulSets**. These are introduced in *Chapters 7* and *9*, so we won't belabor their usage here except to say that we're going to be bringing together all of the introductory topics into an example relevant to *our application*.

The key to effective stateful workload orchestration is modularization and abstraction. These are fundamental software concepts that are taught to engineers so they can design well-architected software systems, and the same holds for well-architected infrastructure systems. Let's consider the following diagram as an example of modularization when it comes to running a database in Kubernetes:

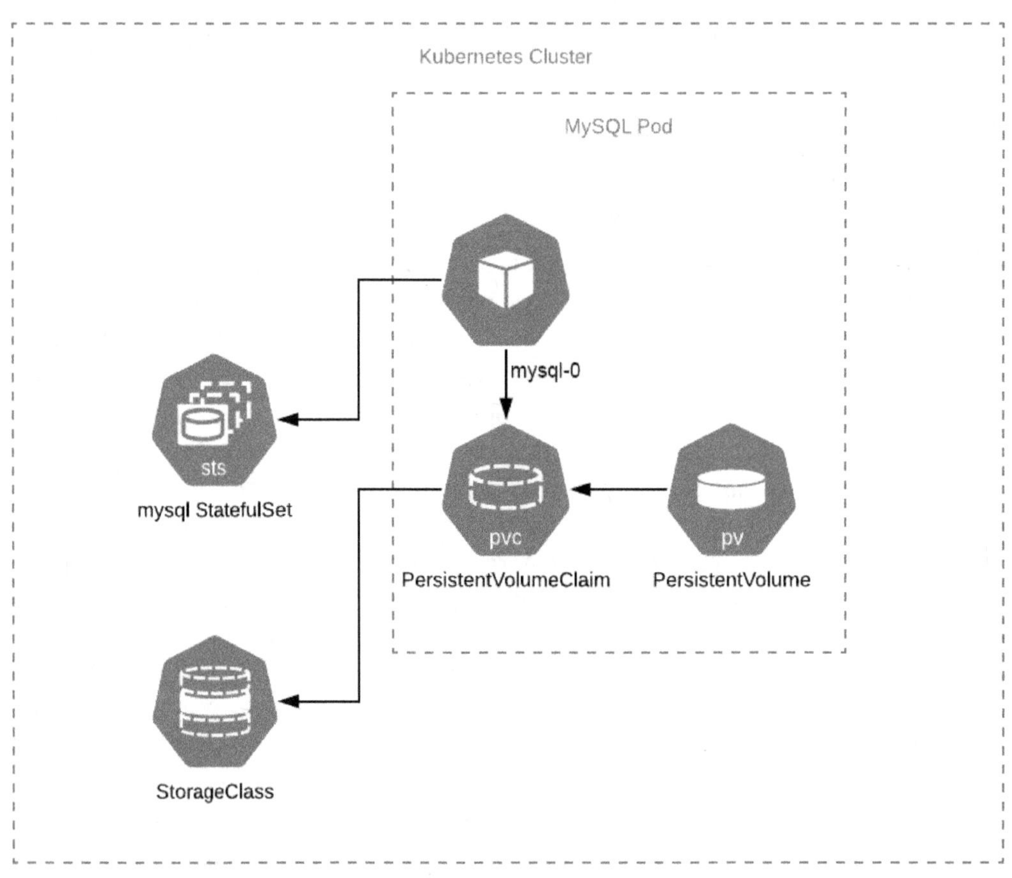

Figure 14.1: Modular stateful components in Kubernetes

As you can see in the preceding diagram, and as you have learned up until now in this book, Kubernetes is made up of modular components. Thus, by leveraging the StatefulSet resource, we can compose the usage of PersistentVolumes, PersistentVolumeClaims, StorageClasses, pods, and some special rules around their life cycles that make much stronger guarantees about the condition that the persistence layers of our app are in.

UNDERSTANDING STATEFULSETS

In *Figure 14.1*, we can see that a StatefulSet is invoked to be able to manage pod life cycles. A StatefulSet (in older versions of Kubernetes, this was called a PetSet) operates very similarly to a Deployment in that we provide a pod template of what we want to run and how many instances of it we want to run. What differs between a StatefulSet and a Deployment is the following:

- **A clear naming scheme that can be depended upon by pods in DNS queries**:

  This means that in the preceding diagram when we name a StatefulSet **`mysql`**, the first pod in that StatefulSet will always be **`mysql-0`**. This is unlike a traditional deployment where pod IDs are assigned randomly. It also means that if you had a pod named **`mysql-2`** and it crashed, it would be resurrected on the cluster using exactly the same name.

- **A clearly ordered way in which updates must proceed**:

  Depending on the update strategy in this StatefulSet, each pod will be taken down in a very specific order. So, if you have a well-known upgrade path (such as in the case of minor software revisions in MySQL), you should be able to leverage one of the Kubernetes-provided software update strategies.

- **Dependable storage operations**:

  Since storage is the most critical part of a stateful solution, having deterministic actions taken by a StatefulSet is imperative. By default, any PersistentVolume provisioned for a StatefulSet will be retained, even if that StatefulSet has been deleted. While this behavior is meant to prevent accidental deletion of data, it can lead to significant charges from your cloud provider during testing, so you should monitor this closely.

- **A serviceName field that must be defined in the StatefulSet**:

  This **serviceName** field must refer to something called a "headless" service that points to this group of pods. This exists to allow the pods to be individually addressable using the common Kubernetes DNS syntax. So for example, if my StatefulSet is running in the default namespace and has the name **zachstatefulset**, then the first pod will have the DNS entry **zachstatefulset-0.default.svc.cluster.local**. The same DNS entry will be used by any replacement pod if this one fails.

  More on headless services can be found at this link: https://kubernetes.io/docs/concepts/services-networking/service/#headless-services.

DEPLOYMENTS VERSUS STATEFULSETS

Now that you've been introduced to StatefulSets at a slightly more granular level, on what basis should you choose between a StatefulSet and a Deployment that uses a PersistentVolumeClaim? The answer to that depends on what you're looking to orchestrate.

In theory, you could achieve similar behavior using both types of Kubernetes object. Both create pods, both have update strategies, and both can use PVCs to create and manage PersistentVolume objects. The reason StatefulSets were designed was to give the guarantees laid out in the preceding bullet points. Typically, you would want these guarantees when orchestrating databases, file servers, and other forms of sensitive persistence-dependent applications.

As we understand how StatefulSets are useful to predictably run the stateful components of our applications, let's look at a specific example that's relevant to us. As you'll recall from previous chapters, we have a little counter app that we are refactoring to leverage as many cloud-native principles as possible as we go along. In this chapter, we will be replacing the state persistence mechanism and testing out a new engine.

FURTHER REFACTORING OUR APPLICATION

We'd like to now take our application a little further into cloud-native principles. Let's consider that the product manager for our counter app said that we're getting insane amounts of load (and you can confirm this through your observability toolset), and some people are not always getting a strictly increasing number; sometimes, they are getting duplicates of the same number. So, you confer with your colleagues and come to the conclusion that in order to guarantee the increasing number, you will need guarantees around how data is accessed and persisted in your app.

Specifically, you need a guarantee that operations against this datastore are atomically unique, consistent between operations, isolated from other operations, and durable against failure. That is, you are looking for an ACID-compliant database.

> **NOTE**
>
> More on what ACID compliance is can be found at this link: https://database.guide/what-is-acid-in-databases/.

The team wants to be able to use a database, but they'd rather not pay for that database to be run by AWS. They would also rather not be locked into AWS if they find better deals on GCP or Azure later.

So, after a brief look at Google for some options, your team settles on using MySQL. MySQL is one of the more popular open-source RDBMS solutions, and as such has a lot of documentation, support, and community suggestions for implementation as a database solution in Kubernetes.

Now the work begins on changing your code to support incrementing the counter using a transaction supported by MySQL. So, to do this, we need to change a few things:

- Change our application code to use SQL instead of Redis to access the data and increment the counter.
- Modify our Kubernetes cluster to run MySQL instead of Redis.
- Ensure the durability of the storage underneath the database in case of catastrophic failure.

You may be asking yourself why a cluster operator or administrator would need to be able to understand and refactor code. The advent of Kubernetes accelerated a trend in the software industry of leveraging DevOps tooling, practices, and culture to begin to deliver value to customers more rapidly and more predictably. This means beginning to scale our operations using software and not people. We need robust automation to take the place of human-centric processes to be able to make guarantees around functionalities and delivery speed. Thus, an infrastructure designer or administrator having systems-level software engineering experience to allow them to assist in refactoring a codebase to leverage more cloud-native practices is a huge benefit for them in their careers, and it may soon become a job requirement for all DevOps engineers. So, let's take a look at how to refactor our application for StatefulSets using MySQL for the transactions.

> **NOTE**
>
> If you are not yet comfortable programming or you are not familiar with the syntax of the language the authors chose (Golang in this example), you don't have to worry – all of the solutions have been worked out and are ready to be used.

First, let's examine our code for *Exercise 12.04, Deploying an Application with State Management*:

main.go

```
if r.Method == "GET" {
    val, err := client.Get("num").Result()
    if err == redis.Nil {
        fmt.Println("num does not exist")
        err := client.Set("num", "0", 0).Err()
        if err != nil {
            panic(err)
        }
    } else if err != nil {
        w.WriteHeader(500)
        panic(err)
    } else {
        fmt.Println("num", val)
        num, err := strconv.Atoi(val)
        if err != nil {
            w.WriteHeader(500)
            fmt.Println(err)
        } else {
            num++
            err := client.Set("num", strconv.Itoa(num), 0).Err()
            if err != nil {
                panic(err)
            }
            fmt.Fprintf(w, "{number: %d}", num)
        }
}
```

The complete code for this step can be found at https://packt.live/3jSWTHB.

Highlighted in the preceding code are the two instances where we are accessing our persistence layer. As you can see, not only are we not using a transaction, but we are manipulating the value in the code and therefore cannot guarantee the constraint that this is a strictly incrementing counter. To do this, we must change our strategy.

> **NOTE**
>
> You can find the required information for using a MySQL container at this link: https://hub.docker.com/_/mysql?tab=description.

We have provided the refactored application that uses SQL. Let's take a look at the code of the refactored application:

main.go

```
fmt.Println("Starting HTTP server")
http.HandleFunc("/get-number", func(w http.ResponseWriter, r
  *http.Request) {
    if r.Method == "GET" {
        tx, err := db.Begin()
            if err != nil {
        panic(err)
        }
        _, err = tx.Exec(t1)
        if err != nil {
            tx.Rollback()
            fmt.Println(err)
        }
        err = tx.Commit()
        if err != nil {
            fmt.Println(err)
        }
        row := db.QueryRow(t2, 1)
        switch err := row.Scan(&num); err {
        case sql.ErrNoRows:
            fmt.Println("No rows were returned!")
        case nil:
            fmt.Fprintf(w, "{number: %d}\n", num)
        default:
            panic(err)
        }
    } else {
        w.WriteHeader(400)
        fmt.Fprint(w, "{\"error\": \"Only GET HTTP method is
            supported.\"}")
    }
}
```

The complete code for this step can be found at https://packt.live/35ck7nX.

As you can see, it's roughly the same as the Redis code, except now our value is being set in a transaction. Unlike Redis, MySQL is not a volatile in-memory datastore, so operations against the database must be persisted to disk to succeed, and ideally, they are persisted to a disk that won't disappear when the pod is interrupted. Let's set up the other required components of our application in the following exercise.

EXERCISE 14.01: DEPLOYING A COUNTER APP WITH A MYSQL BACKEND

In this exercise, we will reconfigure our counter app to work with a MySQL backend instead of Redis:

1. To begin with, we will recreate your EKS cluster from the Terraform file in *Exercise 12.02, Creating a Cluster with EKS Using Terraform*. If you already have the **main.tf** file, you can work with it. Otherwise, you can run the following command to get it:

```
curl -O https://raw.githubusercontent.com/PacktWorkshops/Kubernetes-Workshop/master/Chapter12/Exercise12.02/main.tf
```

Now, use the following two commands one after the other to get your cluster resources up and running:

```
terraform init

terraform apply
```

> **NOTE**
>
> After performing any of the exercises, if you plan to continue to the following exercises after a significant amount of time, it might be a good idea to deallocate your cluster resources to stop AWS from billing you. You can do that using the **terraform destroy** command. Then, you can run this step to get everything back online again when you are ready to perform an exercise or an activity.
>
> If any exercise or activity relies on objects created in the previous exercises, you will need to recreate those objects as well.

2. Run the following command to get the manifest file, **with_mysql.yaml**, which defines all the required objects:

```
curl -O https://raw.githubusercontent.com/PacktWorkshops/Kubernetes-Workshop/master/Chapter14/Exercise14.01/with_mysql.yaml
```

Open the file for inspection so we can examine this StatefulSet:

with_mysql.yaml

```
apiVersion: apps/v1
kind: StatefulSet
metadata:
  name: mysql
spec:
  selector:
   matchLabels:
      app: mysql
  serviceName: mysql
  replicas: 1
  template:
    metadata:
      labels:
        app: mysql
    spec:
```

The complete code for this step can be found at https://packt.live/2R2WN3x.

> **NOTE**
>
> Here, a PersistentVolumeClaim is automatically binding a 10 GiB volume from Amazon EBS on startup to each pod. Kubernetes will automatically provision the EBS volume using the IAM role that we defined in our Terraform file.

When the pod gets interrupted for any reason, Kubernetes will automatically re-bind the appropriate PersistentVolume to the pod when it restarts, even if it is on a different worker node, so long as it is in the same availability zone.

3. Let's apply this to our cluster by running the following command:

```
kubectl apply -f with_mysql.yaml
```

You should see this response:

```
deployment.apps/kubernetes-test-ha-application-with-mysql-deployment created
service/kubernetes-test-ha-application-with-mysql created
statefulset.apps/mysql created
service/mysql created
secret/mysql-secret-config created
```

Figure 14.2: Deploying the refactored application that uses a MySQL backend

4. Now run **kubectl proxy** in this window and let's open up another terminal window:

```
kubectl proxy
```

You should see this response:

```
Starting to serve on 127.0.0.1:8001
```

5. In the other window, run the following command to access our application:

```
curl localhost:8001/api/v1/namespaces/default/services/kubernetes-test-ha-application-with-mysql:/proxy/get-number
```

You should see this response:

```
{number: 1}
```

You should see the app running as expected, as we have seen in the previous chapters. And just like that, we have a working StatefulSet with our application using MySQL that is persisting data.

As we've said, one of the things that will cause cluster operators to not pursue StatefulSets as a way of being able to manage their data infrastructure is a mistaken belief that the information in PersistentVolumes is as ephemeral as the pods they are bound to. This is not true. The PersistentVolumeClaims created by a StatefulSet will not be deleted if a pod or even the StatefulSet is deleted. This is to protect the data contained in these volumes at all costs. Thus, for cleanup, we need to delete the PersistentVolume separately. Cluster operators also have other tools at their disposal to prevent this from happening, such as changing the reclamation policy of the PersistentVolumes (or the StorageClass it was created from) that you are creating.

EXERCISE 14.02: TESTING THE RESILIENCE OF STATEFULSET DATA IN PERSISTENTVOLUMES

In this exercise, we will continue from where we left off in the last exercise and test the resilience of the data that is in our application by deleting a resource and seeing how Kubernetes responds:

1. Now for the fun part, let's try to test the resilience of our persistence mechanism by deleting the MySQL pod:

```
kubectl delete pod mysql-0
```

You should see this response:

```
pod "mysql-0" deleted
```

2. The app may crash at this point, but if you keep trying the preceding **curl** command again after a few seconds, it should automatically continue counting from the number it had before we deleted the pod. We can verify this by trying to access the application again:

```
curl localhost:8001/api/v1/namespaces/default/services/kubernetes-
test-ha-application-with-mysql:/proxy/get-number
```

You should see a response similar to the following:

```
{number: 2}
```

As you can see, we not only get a valid response from the application, but we also get the next number in the sequence (**2**), meaning that no data was lost when we lost our MySQL pod and Kubernetes recovered it.

After you've created this StatefulSet, cleaning it up is not as simple as running **kubectl delete -f with_mysql.yaml**. This is because Kubernetes will not automatically destroy a PersistentVolume created by a StatefulSet.

> **NOTE**
>
> This also means that even if we try to delete all of our AWS resources using **terraform destroy**, we will still be paying for orphaned EBS volumes in AWS indefinitely (and we don't want that in this example).

3. So, to clean up, we need to find out what PersistentVolumes are bound to this StatefulSet. Let's list the PersistentVolumes in the default namespace of our cluster:

```
kubectl get pv
```

You should see a response similar to the following:

```
NAME                                       CAPACITY   ACCESS MODES   RECLAIM POL
ICY   STATUS   CLAIM                      STORAGECLASS   REASON   AGE
pvc-5e4418e0-a4f3-40ad-9f2a-57376ba1d1d1   10Gi       RWO            Delete
      Bound    default/data-mysql-0       gp2                     2m46s
```

Figure 14.3: Getting the list of PersistentVolumes

4. It looks like we have a PersistentVolume named **data-mysql-0**, which is the one we want to delete. First, we need to remove the objects that created this. Thus, let's first delete our application and all of its components:

```
kubectl delete -f with_mysql.yaml
```

You should see this response:

```
deployment.apps "kubernetes-test-ha-application-with-mysql-deployment" deleted
service "kubernetes-test-ha-application-with-mysql" deleted
statefulset.apps "mysql" deleted
service "mysql" deleted
secret "mysql-secret-config" deleted
```

Figure 14.4: Deleting the PersistentVolume associated with MySQL

5. Let's check on the PersistentVolume that we were trying to remove:

```
kubectl get pv
```

You should see a response similar to this:

```
NAME                                       CAPACITY   ACCESS MODES   RECLAIM POL
ICY   STATUS   CLAIM                    STORAGECLASS   REASON   AGE
pvc-5e4418e0-a4f3-40ad-9f2a-57376ba1d1d1   10Gi       RWO            Delete
      Bound    default/data-mysql-0     gp2                     5m24s
```

Figure 14.5: Getting the list of PersistentVolumes

From this image, it appears that our volume is still there.

6. We need to remove both the PersistentVolume and the PersistentVolumeClaim that created it. To do this, let's run the following command:

```
kubectl delete pvc data-mysql-0
```

You should see this response:

```
persistentvolumeclaim "data-mysql-0" deleted
```

Once we delete the PersistentVolumeClaim, the PersistentVolume becomes **unbound** and is subject to its reclaim policy, which we can see in the screenshot of the previous step. In this case, the policy is to delete the underlying storage volume.

7. To verify that the PV is deleted, let's run the following:

```
kubectl get pv
```

You should see the following response:

```
No resources found in default namespace.
```

As is apparent in this screenshot, our PersistentVolume has now been deleted.

> **NOTE**
>
> If the reclaim policy for your case is anything other than **`Delete`**, you will need to manually delete the PersistentVolume as well.

8. Now that we have cleaned up our PersistentVolumes and PersistentVolumeClaims, we can continue to clean up as we would normally by running the following command:

```
terraform destroy
```

You should see a response that ends as in this screenshot:

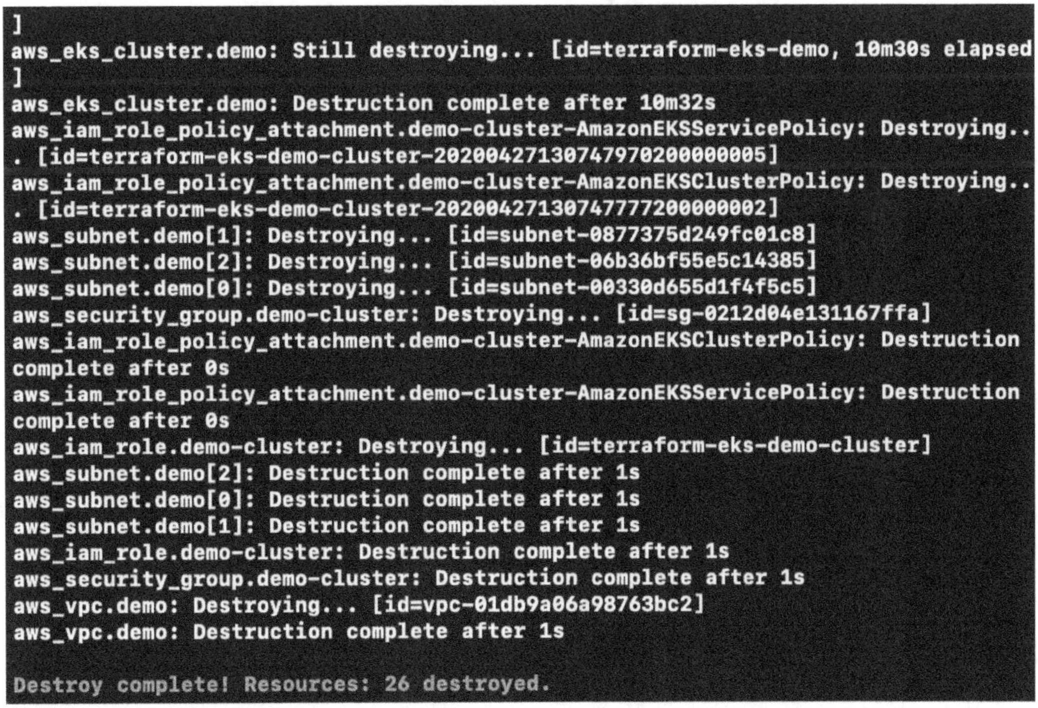

```
]
aws_eks_cluster.demo: Still destroying... [id=terraform-eks-demo, 10m30s elapsed
]
aws_eks_cluster.demo: Destruction complete after 10m32s
aws_iam_role_policy_attachment.demo-cluster-AmazonEKSServicePolicy: Destroying..
. [id=terraform-eks-demo-cluster-20200427130747970200000005]
aws_iam_role_policy_attachment.demo-cluster-AmazonEKSClusterPolicy: Destroying..
. [id=terraform-eks-demo-cluster-20200427130747777200000002]
aws_subnet.demo[1]: Destroying... [id=subnet-0877375d249fc01c8]
aws_subnet.demo[2]: Destroying... [id=subnet-06b36bf55e5c14385]
aws_subnet.demo[0]: Destroying... [id=subnet-00330d655d1f4f5c5]
aws_security_group.demo-cluster: Destroying... [id=sg-0212d04e131167ffa]
aws_iam_role_policy_attachment.demo-cluster-AmazonEKSClusterPolicy: Destruction
complete after 0s
aws_iam_role_policy_attachment.demo-cluster-AmazonEKSServicePolicy: Destruction
complete after 0s
aws_iam_role.demo-cluster: Destroying... [id=terraform-eks-demo-cluster]
aws_subnet.demo[2]: Destruction complete after 1s
aws_subnet.demo[0]: Destruction complete after 1s
aws_subnet.demo[1]: Destruction complete after 1s
aws_iam_role.demo-cluster: Destruction complete after 1s
aws_security_group.demo-cluster: Destruction complete after 1s
aws_vpc.demo: Destroying... [id=vpc-01db9a06a98763bc2]
aws_vpc.demo: Destruction complete after 1s

Destroy complete! Resources: 26 destroyed.
```

Figure 14.6: Cleaning up resources created by Terraform

In this exercise, we have seen how Kubernetes tries to preserve PersistentVolumes even when we delete the StatefulSet. We have also seen how to proceed when we actually want to remove a PersistentVolume.

Now that we have seen how to set up a StatefulSet and run a MySQL database attached to it, we will extend the principle of high availability further in the following activity. Before we do this, though, we need to address the problem of Kubernetes manifest sprawl, because it seems to take more and more YAML manifests to achieve our objective of building highly available stateful applications. In the following section, we will learn about a tool that will help us better organize and manage the manifests for our applications.

HELM

In this section, we are going to be taking a look at a tool that is very helpful in the Kubernetes ecosystem called Helm. Helm was created by Microsoft after it quickly became apparent that for any sizeable deployment of Kubernetes (for example, those involving 20 or more separate components, observability tools, services, and other objects), there are a lot of YAML manifests to keep track of. Couple that with the fact that many companies run multiple environments other than production, which you need to be able to keep in sync with each other, and you start to have an unwieldy problem on your hands.

Helm allows you to write Kubernetes manifest templates, to which you supply arguments that override any defaults, and then Helm creates the appropriate Kubernetes manifests for you. Thus, you can use Helm as a sort of package manager, where your entire application can be deployed using a Helm chart, and you can tweak a few small parameters before installing. Another way to use Helm is as a templating engine. It allows an experienced Kubernetes operator to write a good template only one time and then it can be used by people not familiar with the Kubernetes manifest syntax to successfully create Kubernetes resources. A Helm chart can be created with any number of fields set by arguments, and a base template can be adapted to deploy vastly different implementations of a piece of software or a microservice to suit different needs.

Helm packages are called "charts" and they have a specific folder structure. You can either use a shared Helm chart repository from Git, an Artifactory server, or a local filesystem. In the upcoming exercise, we're going to look at a Helm chart and install it on our clusters.

This is a good point to be introduced to Helm in your journey of learning Kubernetes because if you've been following along, you've written quite a bit of YAML and applied it to your cluster. Also, a lot of what we've written is a repeat of things that we've seen before. So, leveraging Helm's templating functionality will be helpful for packaging up similar components and delivering them using Kubernetes. You don't have to leverage the templating components of Helm to use it, but it helps so that you can reuse the chart for multiple different permutations of the resulting Kubernetes object.

> **NOTE**
>
> We will be using Helm 3, which has significant differences from its predecessor, Helm 2, and was only recently released. If you are familiar with Helm 2 and want to know about the differences, you can refer to the documentation at this link: https://v3.helm.sh/docs/faq/#changes-since-helm-2.

Detailed coverage of Helm is beyond the scope of this book, but the fundamentals covered here serve as a great starting point, and also put into perspective how different tools and technologies can work together to remove several hurdles of complex application orchestration in Kubernetes.

Let's see how we can create a chart (which is the Helm term for a package) and apply it to a cluster. Then, we will understand how Helm generates Kubernetes manifest files from a Helm chart.

Let's make a new Helm chart by running the following command:

```
helm create chart-dev
```

You should see the following response:

```
Creating chart-dev
```

When you create a new chart, Helm will generate a chart for NGINX as a placeholder application by default. This will create a new folder and skeleton chart for us to examine.

> **NOTE**
>
> For the following section, make sure that you have `tree` installed as per the instructions in the *Preface*.

Let's use the Linux **tree** command and take a look at what Helm has made for us:

```
tree .
```

You should see a response similar to the following:

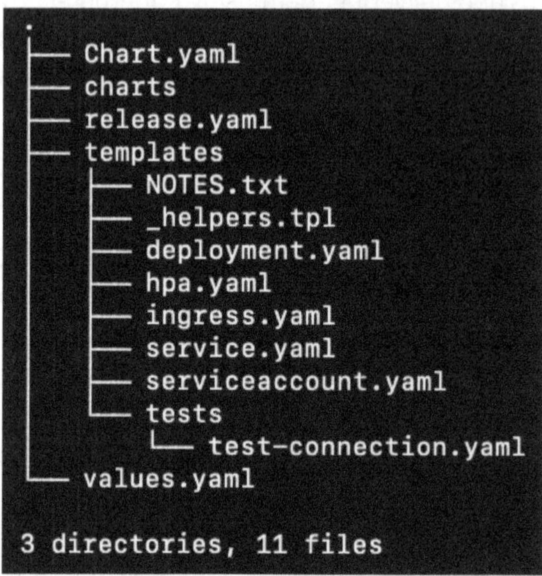

Figure 14.7: Directory structure of a Helm chart

Pay attention to the **templates** folder and the **values.yaml** file. Helm works by using the values found in the **values.yaml** file and fills those values into the corresponding placeholders in the files inside the **templates** folder. Let's examine a part of the **values.yaml** file:

values.yaml

```
# Default values for chart-dev.
# This is a YAML-formatted file.
# Declare variables to be passed into your templates.

replicaCount: 1

image:
  repository: nginx
  pullPolicy: IfNotPresent
  # Overrides the image tag whose default is the chart appVersion.
  tag: ""

imagePullSecrets: []
nameOverride: ""
fullnameOverride: ""
```

The complete code for this step can be found at https://packt.live/33ej2cO.

As we can see here, this is not a Kubernetes manifest, but it looks like it has many of the same fields. In the preceding snippet, we have highlighted the entire **image** block. This has three fields (**repository**, **pullPolicy**, and **tag**), each with their corresponding values.

Another notable file is **Chart.yaml**. The following line from this file is relevant to our discussion:

```
appVersion: 1.16.0
```

> **NOTE**
>
> You can find the complete file at this link: https://packt.live/2FboR2a.

The comment in the file is pretty descriptive of what this means: *"This is the version number of the application being deployed. This version number should be incremented each time you make changes to the application. Versions are not expected to follow Semantic Versioning. They should reflect the version the application is using."*

So, how does Helm assemble these into the traditional Kubernetes manifest format that we expect? To understand that, let's inspect the corresponding section of the **deployment.yaml** file in the **templates** folder:

deployment.yaml

```
containers:
  - name: {{ .Chart.Name }}
    securityContext:
      {{- toYaml .Values.securityContext | nindent 12 }}
    image: "{{ .Values.image.repository }}:{{ .Values.image.tag |
       default .Chart.AppVersion }}"
    imagePullPolicy: {{ .Values.image.pullPolicy }}
```

The complete code for this step can be found at https://packt.live/3k0OGRL.

This file looks a lot more like a Kubernetes manifest with a bunch of variables added into it. Comparing the template placeholders from **deployment.yaml** to the observations from **values.yaml** and **Chart.yaml**, we can infer the following:

- **{{ .Values.image.repository }}** will be interpreted as **nginx**.
- **{{ .Values.image.tag | default .Chart.AppVersion }}** will be interpreted as **1.16.0**.

Thus, we get the resultant field for our deployment spec as **image: nginx:1.16.0**.

This is our first glimpse into the Helm templating language. For those familiar with templating engines such as Jinja, Go templating, or Twig, this syntax should look familiar. As mentioned earlier, we will not dive into too many details about Helm, but you can find more on the Helm documentation at this link: https://helm.sh/docs/chart_template_guide/.

Now, let's install the sample chart **chart-dev** that we have generated. This chart will deploy an example NGINX app to our Kubernetes cluster. To install a Helm chart, the command would look as follows:

```
helm install [NAME] [CHART] [flags]
```

We can use **--generate-name** to get a random name. Also, since we are already in the **chart-dev** directory, we can directly use **values.yaml** from the root of the current working directory:

```
helm install --generate-name -f values.yaml .
```

You should see the following response:

```
NAME: chart-1589678730
LAST DEPLOYED: Sat May 16 21:25:31 2020
NAMESPACE: default
STATUS: deployed
REVISION: 1
NOTES:
1. Get the application URL by running these commands:
  export POD_NAME=$(kubectl get pods --namespace default -l "app.kubernetes.io/n
ame=chart-dev,app.kubernetes.io/instance=chart-1589678730" -o jsonpath="{.items[
0].metadata.name}")
  echo "Visit http://127.0.0.1:8080 to use your application"
  kubectl --namespace default port-forward $POD_NAME 8080:80
```

Figure 14.8: Installing a Helm chart

Notice that in the output, you are given instructions on what to do next. These are customizable instructions from the **templates/NOTES.txt** file. When you make your own Helm chart, you can use these to guide whoever is using the chart. Now, let's run these commands.

> **NOTE**
>
> The exact values in this output are customized to your particular environment, so you should copy the commands from your terminal output. This applies to the following command.

The first command sets the pod name into an environment variable named **POD_NAME**:

```
export POD_NAME=$(kubectl get pods --namespace default -l "app.
kubernetes.io/name=chart-dev,app.kubernetes.io/instance=chart-1589678730"
-o jsonpath="{.items[0].metadata.name}")
```

We'll skip the **echo** command; it just tells you how to access your application. The reason this **echo** command exists is to show what the next commands are going to be in the terminal output.

Now before we access our application, we need to do some port forwarding. The next command maps port **8080** on your host to port **80** on the pod:

```
kubectl --namespace default port-forward $POD_NAME 8080:80
```

You should see this response:

```
Forwarding from 127.0.0.1:8080 ->80
Forwarding from [::1]:8080 -> 80
```

Now let's try to access NGINX. In a browser, go to **localhost:8080**. You should be able to see the default NGINX landing page:

Welcome to nginx!

If you see this page, the nginx web server is successfully installed and working. Further configuration is required.

For online documentation and support please refer to nginx.org.
Commercial support is available at nginx.com.

Thank you for using nginx.

Figure 14.9: Accessing our default NGINX test application

You can clean this up by deleting our resources. First, let's get the generated name of this release by getting a list of all the releases installed by Helm in your cluster:

```
helm ls
```

You should see a response similar to this:

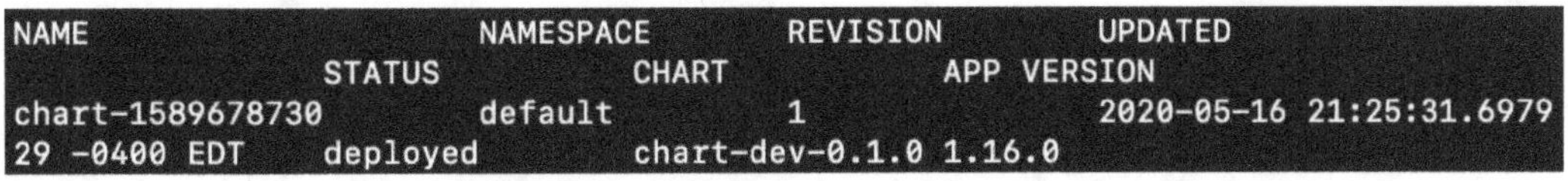

```
NAME                        NAMESPACE        REVISION        UPDATED
                    STATUS           CHART               APP VERSION
chart-1589678730            default          1               2020-05-16 21:25:31.6979
29 -0400 EDT        deployed         chart-dev-0.1.0 1.16.0
```

Figure 14.10: Getting a list of all applications installed by Helm

Now, we can remove the release as follows:

```
helm uninstall chart-1589678730
```

Use the name from the previous output. You should see this response:

```
release "chart-1589678730" uninstalled
```

And just like that, we've written our first chart. So, let's proceed to the following exercise, where we will learn exactly how Helm can make our job easier.

EXERCISE 14.03: CHART-IFYING OUR REDIS-BASED COUNTER APPLICATION

We created a generic Helm chart in the previous section, but what if we want to make our own chart for our software? In this exercise, we will create a Helm chart that will deploy our HA Redis-based solution from *Chapter 12, Your Application and HA*, using Helm.

1. If you are inside the **chart-dev** directory, navigate to the parent directory:

   ```
   cd ..
   ```

2. Let's start by making a fresh Helm chart:

   ```
   helm create redis-based-counter && cd redis-based-counter
   ```

   You should see this response:

   ```
   Creating redis-based-counter
   ```

3. Now let's remove the unnecessary files from our chart:

   ```
   rm templates/NOTES.txt; \
   rm templates/*.yaml; \
   rm -r templates/tests/; \
   cd templates
   ```

4. Now, we need to navigate into the **templates** folder of our chart and copy in the files from our repo for the Redis-based counter application:

```
curl -O https://raw.githubusercontent.com/PacktWorkshops/Kubernetes-
Workshop/master/Chapter14/Exercise14.03/templates/redis-deployment.
yaml; \
curl -O https://raw.githubusercontent.com/PacktWorkshops/Kubernetes-
Workshop/master/Chapter14/Exercise14.03/templates/deployment.yaml;\
curl -O https://raw.githubusercontent.com/PacktWorkshops/Kubernetes-
Workshop/master/Chapter14/Exercise14.03/templates/redis-service.yaml;
\
curl -O https://raw.githubusercontent.com/PacktWorkshops/Kubernetes-
Workshop/master/Chapter14/Exercise14.03/templates/service.yaml
```

   You may recall from previous chapters that we had multiple Kubernetes manifests sharing one file, separated by the **---** YAML file separator string. Now that we have a tool for managing Kubernetes manifests, it's better to keep them in separate files so that we can manage them independently. The job of bundling will now be handled by Helm.

5. There should be four files in the **templates** folder. Let's confirm that as follows:

```
tree .
```

   You should see the following response:

```
.
├── Chart.yaml
├── charts
├── templates
│   ├── _helpers.tpl
│   ├── deployment.yaml
│   ├── redis-deployment.yaml
│   ├── redis-service.yaml
│   └── service.yaml
└── values.yaml

2 directories, 7 files
```

Figure 14.11: Expected file structure for our application

6. ow we need to modify the **values.yaml** file. Delete all contents from that file and copy only the following into it:

```
deployment:
  replicas: 3
redis:
  version: 3
```

7. Now, to wire them together, we need to edit both **deployment.yaml** and **redis-deployment.yaml**. The one we will edit first is **deployment.yaml**. We should replace **replicas: 3** with the template, as shown in the highlighted line in the following manifest:

```
apiVersion: apps/v1
kind: Deployment
metadata:
  name: kubernetes-test-ha-application-with-redis-deployment
  labels:
    app: kubernetes-test-ha-application-with-redis
spec:
  replicas: {{ .Values.deployment.replicas }}
  selector:
    matchLabels:
      app: kubernetes-test-ha-application-with-redis
  template:
    metadata:
      labels:
        app: kubernetes-test-ha-application-with-redis
    spec:
      containers:
        - name: kubernetes-test-ha-application-with-redis
          image: packtworkshops/the-kubernetes-workshop:demo-app-
            with-redis
          imagePullPolicy: Always
          ports:
            - containerPort: 8080
          env:
            - name: REDIS_SVC_ADDR
              value: "redis.default:6379"
```

8. Next, edit the **redis-deployment.yaml** file and add a similar block of templating language, as shown in the highlighted line in the following manifest:

```
apiVersion: apps/v1 # for versions before 1.9.0 use apps/v1beta2
kind: Deployment
metadata:
  name: redis
  labels:
    app: redis
spec:
  selector:
    matchLabels:
      app: redis
  replicas: 1
  template:
    metadata:
      labels:
        app: redis
    spec:
      containers:
      - name: master
        image: redis:{{ .Values.redis.version }}
        resources:
          requests:
            cpu: 100m
            memory: 100Mi
        ports:
        - containerPort: 6379
```

9. Now let's install our application using Helm:

```
helm install --generate-name -f values.yaml .
```

You should see a response similar to this:

```
NAME: chart-1589680252
LAST DEPLOYED: Sat May 16 21:50:53 2020
NAMESPACE: default
STATUS: deployed
REVISION: 1
TEST SUITE: None
```

Figure 14.12: Installing our Helm chart with an auto-generated name

10. To check whether our application is online, we can get the list of deployments:

```
kubectl get deployment
```

You should see the following output:

```
NAME                                                    READY   UP-TO-DATE   AVAI
LABLE   AGE
kubernetes-test-ha-application-with-redis-deployment   3/3     3            3
        49s
redis                                                   1/1     1            1
        49s
```

Figure 14.13: Getting the list of deployments

As you can see, Helm has deployed our application deployment, as well as the Redis backend for it. With these skills in the bag, you are soon to be a captain of Helm.

In the following activity, we will bring together the two things we learned in this chapter – refactoring our application for stateful components and then deploying it as a Helm chart.

ACTIVITY 14.01: CHART-IFYING OUR STATEFULSET DEPLOYMENT

Now that you have experience with MySQL, StatefulSets, and Helm for resource management, your activity is to take what you learned in *Exercises 14.01*, *14.02*, and *14.03* and combine them together.

For this activity, we will refactor our Redis-based application to use MySQL as the backend datastore using StatefulSets, and then deploy it using Helm.

Follow these high-level guidelines to complete the activity:

1. Set up the required cluster infrastructure as shown in *step 1* of *Exercise 14.01, Deploying a Counter App with a MySQL Backend*.
2. Introduce a new Helm chart called **counter-mysql**.
3. Create a template for our counter application that uses MySQL as its backend.
4. Create a template for our MySQL StatefulSet.
5. Wire everything together with Kubernetes Service objects wherever appropriate.
6. Configure the template such that the **values.yaml** file is able to change the version of MySQL.

7. Test the application. You should see a similar output to that which we've seen in previous exercises with our counter application:

```
{number: 1}
zarnold@zachs-mbp counter-mysql % curl localhost:8080/get-number
{number: 2}
zarnold@zachs-mbp counter-mysql % curl localhost:8080/get-number
{number: 3}
zarnold@zachs-mbp counter-mysql % curl localhost:8080/get-number
{number: 4}
zarnold@zachs-mbp counter-mysql % curl localhost:8080/get-number
{number: 5}
zarnold@zachs-mbp counter-mysql % curl localhost:8080/get-number
{number: 6}
zarnold@zachs-mbp counter-mysql % curl localhost:8080/get-number
{number: 7}
zarnold@zachs-mbp counter-mysql % curl localhost:8080/get-number
{number: 8}
zarnold@zachs-mbp counter-mysql % curl localhost:8080/get-number
{number: 9}
zarnold@zachs-mbp counter-mysql % curl localhost:8080/get-number
{number: 10}
zarnold@zachs-mbp counter-mysql % curl localhost:8080/get-number
{number: 11}
zarnold@zachs-mbp counter-mysql % curl localhost:8080/get-number
{number: 12}
```

Figure 14.14: Expected output of Activity 14.01

> **NOTE**
>
> The solution to this activity can be found at the following address: https://packt.live/304PEoD.
>
> Also, don't forget to clean up your cloud resources using the **terraform destroy** command to stop AWS from billing you after you are done with the activity.

SUMMARY

Over the course of this chapter, we have applied our skills to be able to leverage StatefulSets in our example application. We have looked at how to think about running stateful portions of our software programmatically and how to refactor applications to leverage that change in state persistence. Finally, we learned how to create and run Kubernetes StatefulSets that will allow us to run stateful components in our cluster and make guarantees about how that workload will be run.

Being equipped with the skills needed to manage stateful components on our Kubernetes cluster is a major step in being able to operate effectively in many real-world applications that you are likely to come across.

In the next chapter, we're going to talk more about data-driven application orchestration with the use of Metrics Server, HorizontalPodAutoscalers, and ClusterAutoscaler. We will learn how these objects help us respond to varying levels of demand on our application running on a Kubernetes cluster.

15

MONITORING AND AUTOSCALING IN KUBERNETES

OVERVIEW

This chapter will introduce you to how Kubernetes enables you to monitor your cluster and workloads, and then use the data collected to automatically drive certain decisions. You will learn about the Kubernetes Metric Server, which aggregates all cluster runtime information, allowing you to use this information to drive application runtime scaling decisions. We will walk you through setting up monitoring using the Kubernetes Metrics server and Prometheus and then use Grafana to visualize those metrics. By the end of this chapter, you will also have learned how to automatically scale up your application to completely utilize the resources on the provisioned infrastructure, as well as automatically scale your cluster infrastructure as needed.

INTRODUCTION

Let's take a moment to reflect on our progress through this series of chapters beginning from *Chapter 11, Build Your Own HA Cluster*. We started by setting up a Kubernetes cluster using kops to configure AWS infrastructure in a highly available manner. Then, we used Terraform and some scripting to improve the stability of our cluster and deploy our simple counter app. After this, we began hardening the security and increasing the availability of our app using Kubernetes/cloud-native principles. Finally, we learned how to run a stateful database responsible for using transactions to ensure that we always get a series of increasing numbers from our application.

In this chapter, we are going to explore how to leverage the data that already exists in Kubernetes about our applications to drive and automate decision-making processes around scaling them so that they are always the right size for our load. Because it takes time to observe application metrics, schedule and start containers, and bootstrap nodes from scratch, this scaling is not instantaneous but will eventually (usually within minutes) balance the number of pods and nodes needed to perform the work of the load on the cluster. To achieve this, we need a way of getting this data, understanding/interpreting this data, and feeding back instructions to Kubernetes with this data. Luckily, there are already tools in Kubernetes that will help us do this. These are the **Kubernetes Metric Server**, **HorizontalPodAutoscalers** (**HPAs**), and the **ClusterAutoscaler**.

KUBERNETES MONITORING

Kubernetes has built-in support for providing useful monitoring information about infrastructure components as well as various Kubernetes objects. The Kubernetes Metrics server is a component (which does not come built-in) that gathers and exposes the metrics data at an API endpoint on the API server. Kubernetes uses this data to manage the scaling of Pods, but this data can also be scraped by a third-party tool such as Prometheus for use by cluster operators. Prometheus has a few very basic data visualization functions and primarily serves as a metric-gathering and storage tool, so you can use a more powerful and useful data visualization tool such as Grafana. Grafana allows cluster admins to create useful dashboards to monitor their clusters. You can learn more about how monitoring in Kubernetes is architected at this link: https://github.com/kubernetes/community/blob/master/contributors/design-proposals/instrumentation/monitoring_architecture.md.

Here's how this will look for us in a diagram:

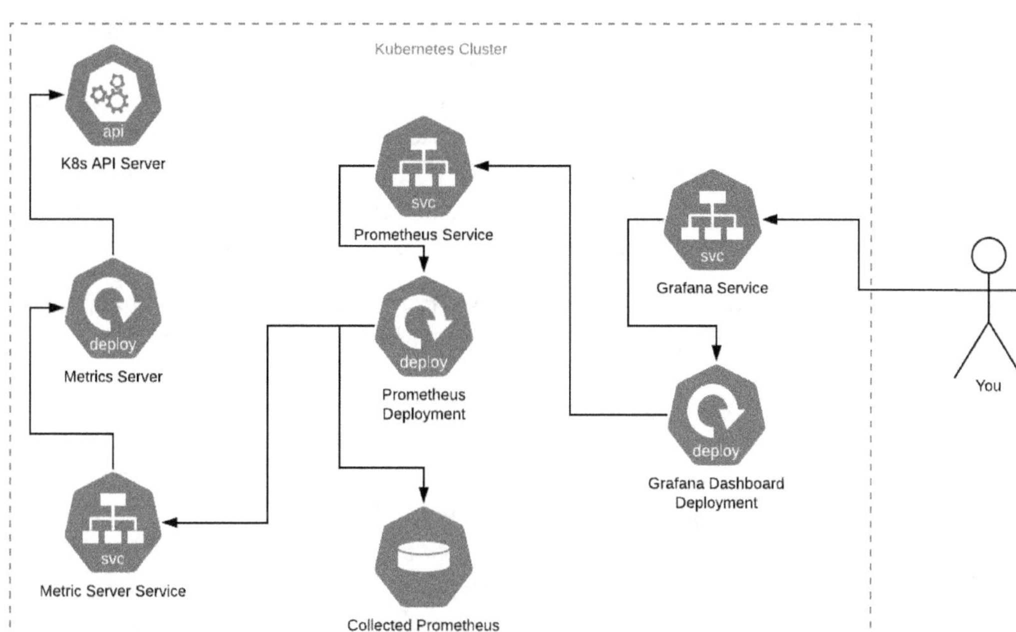

Figure 15.1: An overview of the monitoring pipeline that we will implement in this chapter

This diagram represents how the monitoring pipeline is going to be implemented through various Kubernetes objects. In summary, the monitoring pipeline will work as follows:

1. The various components of Kubernetes are already instrumented to provide various metrics. The Kubernetes Metrics server will fetch these metrics from the components.
2. The Kubernetes Metrics server will then expose these metrics on an API endpoint.
3. Prometheus will access this API endpoint, scrape these metrics, and add it to its special database.
4. Grafana will query the Prometheus database to gather these metrics and present it in a neat dashboard with graphs and other visual representations.

Now, let's look at each of the previously mentioned components to understand them better.

KUBERNETES METRICS API/METRICS SERVER

The Kubernetes Metrics server (formerly known as Heapster) gathers and exposes metric data on the running state of all Kubernetes components and objects in Kubernetes. Nodes, control plane components, running pods, and really any Kubernetes objects are all observable via the Metrics server. Some examples of the metrics that it collects are the number of pods that are desired in a Deployment/ReplicaSet, the number of pods posting a **Ready** status in that Deployment, and the CPU and memory utilization of each container.

We will mostly be using the default exposed metrics while gathering the information relevant to the Kubernetes objects that we are orchestrating our application.

PROMETHEUS

Prometheus is a metric collector, a time-series database, and an alert manager for just about anything. It makes use of a scraping function to pull metrics from running processes that expose those metrics in Prometheus format at a defined interval. Those metrics are then stored in their own time-series database and you can run queries on this data to get a snapshot of the state of your running applications.

It also comes with an alert manager function, which allows you to set up triggers to alert your on-call admins. As an example, you can configure the alert manager to automatically trigger an alert if the CPU utilization on one of your nodes is above 90% for 15 minutes. The alert manager can interface with several third-party services to send the alert via various means, such as email, chat messages, or SMS phone alerts.

> **NOTE**
>
> If you want to learn more about Prometheus, you can refer to this book: https://www.packtpub.com/virtualization-and-cloud/hands-infrastructure-monitoring-prometheus.

GRAFANA

Grafana is an open-source tool that can be used to visualize data and create useful dashboards. Grafana will query the Prometheus database for metrics and graph them on dashboard charts that are easier for humans to understand and spot trends or discrepancies. These tools are indispensable when running a production cluster as they help us spot issues in the infrastructure quickly and resolve issues.

MONITORING YOUR APPLICATIONS

While application monitoring is beyond the scope of this book, we will provide some rough guidelines so that you can explore more on this topic. We would recommend that you expose your application's metrics in Prometheus format and use Prometheus to scrape them; there are many libraries for most languages that can help with this.

Another way is to use Prometheus exporters that are available for various applications. Exporters gather the metrics from an application and expose them to an API endpoint so that Prometheus can scrape it. You can find several open-source exporters for common applications at this link: https://prometheus.io/docs/instrumenting/exporters/.

For your custom applications and frameworks, you can create your own exporters using the libraries provided by Prometheus. You can find the relevant guidelines at this link: https://prometheus.io/docs/instrumenting/writing_exporters/.

Once you have exposed and scraped the metrics from your applications, you can present them in a Grafana dashboard, similar to the one we will create for monitoring Kubernetes components.

EXERCISE 15.01: SETTING UP THE METRICS SERVER AND OBSERVING KUBERNETES OBJECTS

In this exercise, we are going to be setting up monitoring for Kubernetes objects in our cluster and running a few queries and creating visualizations to see what's going on. We're going to be installing Prometheus, Grafana, and the Kubernetes Metrics server:

1. To begin with, we will recreate your EKS cluster from the Terraform file in *Exercise 12.02, Creating a Cluster with EKS Using Terraform*. If you already have the **main.tf** file, you can work with it. Otherwise, you can run the following command to get it:

```
curl -O https://github.com/PacktWorkshops/Kubernetes-Workshop/blob/
master/Chapter12/Exercise12.02/main.tf
```

Now, use the following two commands one after the other to get your cluster resources up and running:

```
terraform init

terraform apply
```

> **NOTE**
>
> You will need **jq** for the following command. **jq** is a simple tool to manipulate JSON data. If you don't already have it installed, you can do so by using this command: **sudo apt install jq**.

2. To set up the Kubernetes Metrics server in our cluster, we need to run the following in sequence:

```
curl -O https://raw.githubusercontent.com/PacktWorkshops/Kubernetes-
Workshop/master/Chapter15/Exercise15.01/metrics_server.yaml

kubectl apply -f metrics_server.yaml
```

You should see a response similar to the following:

```
zarnold@zachs-mbp kubernetes-test-ha-application % DOWNLOAD_URL=$(curl -Ls "https://api.github.com/repos/kubernetes-sigs/metrics-server/releases/latest" | jq -r .tarball_url)
DOWNLOAD_VERSION=$(grep -o '[^/v]*$' <<< $DOWNLOAD_URL)
curl -Ls $DOWNLOAD_URL -o metrics-server-$DOWNLOAD_VERSION.tar.gz
mkdir metrics-server-$DOWNLOAD_VERSION
tar -xzf metrics-server-$DOWNLOAD_VERSION.tar.gz --directory metrics-server-$DOWNLOAD_VERSION --strip-components 1
kubectl apply -f metrics-server-$DOWNLOAD_VERSION/deploy/1.8+/
clusterrole.rbac.authorization.k8s.io/system:aggregated-metrics-reader created
clusterrolebinding.rbac.authorization.k8s.io/metrics-server:system:auth-delegator created
rolebinding.rbac.authorization.k8s.io/metrics-server-auth-reader created
apiservice.apiregistration.k8s.io/v1beta1.metrics.k8s.io created
serviceaccount/metrics-server created
deployment.apps/metrics-server created
service/metrics-server created
clusterrole.rbac.authorization.k8s.io/system:metrics-server created
clusterrolebinding.rbac.authorization.k8s.io/system:metrics-server created
zarnold@zachs-mbp kubernetes-test-ha-application %
```

Figure 15.2: Deploying all the objects required for the Metrics server

3. To test this, let's run the following command:

```
kubectl get --raw "/apis/metrics.k8s.io/v1beta1/nodes"
```

> **NOTE**
>
> If you are getting a **ServiceUnavailable** error, please check whether your firewall rules are allowing the API server to communicate with the node running the Metrics server.

We have been frequently using the **kubectl get** commands by naming the object. We have seen in *Chapter 4, How to Communicate with Kubernetes (API Server)*, that Kubectl interprets the request, points the request to the appropriate endpoint, and formats the results in a readable format. But here, since we have created a custom endpoint at our API server, we have to point toward it using the **--raw** flag. You should see a response similar to the following:

```
zarnold@zachs-mbp terraform % kubectl get --raw "/apis/metrics.k8s.io/v1beta1/nodes"
```

```
{"kind":"NodeMetricsList","apiVersion":"metrics.k8s.io/v1beta1","metadata":{"selfLink":"/apis/metrics.k8s.io/v1beta1/nodes"},"items":[{"metadata":{"name":"ip-10-0-0-192.us-west-2.compute.internal","selfLink":"/apis/metrics.k8s.io/v1beta1/nodes/ip-10-0-0-192.us-west-2.compute.internal","creationTimestamp":"2019-12-15T08:03:51Z"},"timestamp":"2019-12-15T08:03:39Z","window":"30s","usage":{"cpu":"33912299n","memory":"424080Ki"}},{"metadata":{"name":"ip-10-0-2-152.us-west-2.compute.internal","selfLink":"/apis/metrics.k8s.io/v1beta1/nodes/ip-10-0-2-152.us-west-2.compute.internal","creationTimestamp":"2019-12-15T08:03:51Z"},"timestamp":"2019-12-15T08:03:38Z","window":"30s","usage":{"cpu":"38985507n","memory":"556972Ki"}}]}
```

```
zarnold@zachs-mbp terraform %
```

Figure 15.3: Response from the Kubernetes Metrics server

As we can see here, the response contains JSON blobs that define a metric namespace, metric values, and metric metadata, such as a node name and availability zones. However, these metrics are not very readable. We will make use of Prometheus to aggregate them and then use Grafana to present the aggregated metrics in a concise dashboard.

4. Now, we have metric data being aggregated. Let's start scraping and visualizing with Prometheus and Grafana. For this, we will install Prometheus and Grafana using Helm. Run the following command:

```
helm install --generate-name stable/prometheus
```

> **NOTE**
>
> If you are installing and running helm for the first time, you will need to run the following command to get stable repos:
>
> **help repo add stable https://kubernetes-charts.storage.googleapis.com/**

You should see an output similar to the following:

```
terraform — -zsh — 121×62
[zarnold@zachs-mbp terraform % helm install --generate-name stable/prometheus
NAME: prometheus-1576397083
LAST DEPLOYED: Sun Dec 15 00:04:46 2019
NAMESPACE: default
STATUS: deployed
REVISION: 1
TEST SUITE: None
NOTES:
The Prometheus server can be accessed via port 80 on the following DNS name from within your cluster:
prometheus-1576397083-server.default.svc.cluster.local


Get the Prometheus server URL by running these commands in the same shell:
  export POD_NAME=$(kubectl get pods --namespace default -l "app=prometheus,component=server" -o jsonpath="{.items[0].met
adata.name}")
  kubectl --namespace default port-forward $POD_NAME 9090


The Prometheus alertmanager can be accessed via port 80 on the following DNS name from within your cluster:
prometheus-1576397083-alertmanager.default.svc.cluster.local


Get the Alertmanager URL by running these commands in the same shell:
  export POD_NAME=$(kubectl get pods --namespace default -l "app=prometheus,component=alertmanager" -o jsonpath="{.items[
0].metadata.name}")
  kubectl --namespace default port-forward $POD_NAME 9093
#################################################################################
######   WARNING: Pod Security Policy has been moved to a global property.  #####
######            use .Values.podSecurityPolicy.enabled with pod-based      #####
######            annotations                                               #####
######            (e.g. .Values.nodeExporter.podSecurityPolicy.annotations) #####
#################################################################################


The Prometheus PushGateway can be accessed via port 9091 on the following DNS name from within your cluster:
prometheus-1576397083-pushgateway.default.svc.cluster.local


Get the PushGateway URL by running these commands in the same shell:
  export POD_NAME=$(kubectl get pods --namespace default -l "app=prometheus,component=pushgateway" -o jsonpath="{.items[0
].metadata.name}")
  kubectl --namespace default port-forward $POD_NAME 9091

For more information on running Prometheus, visit:
https://prometheus.io/
zarnold@zachs-mbp terraform %
```

Figure 15.4: Installing the Helm chart for Prometheus

5. Now, let's install Grafana in a similar fashion:

```
helm install --generate-name stable/grafana
```

You should see the following response:

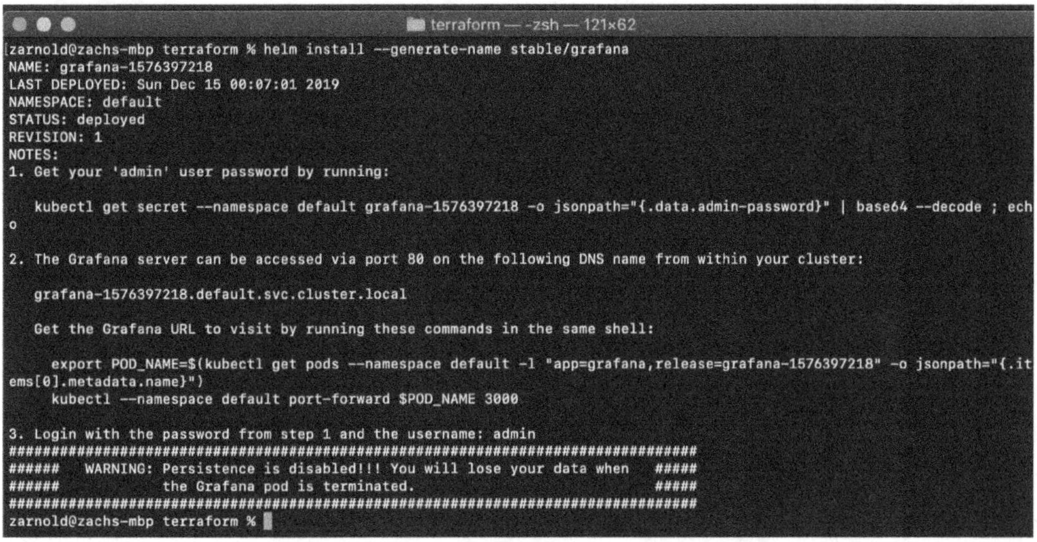

Figure 15.5: Installing the Helm chart for Grafana

In this screenshot, notice the **NOTES:** section, which lists two steps. Follow these steps to get your Grafana admin password and your endpoint to access Grafana.

6. Here, we are running the first command that Grafana showed in the output of the previous step:

```
kubectl get secret --namespace default grafana-1576397218 -o
jsonpath="{.data.admin-password}" | base64 --decode ; echo
```

Please use the version of the commands that you got; the command will be customized for your instance. This command gets your password, which is stored in a Secret, decodes it, and echoes it in your terminal output so that you can copy it for use in further steps. You should see a response similar to the following:

```
brM8aEVPCJtRtu0XgHVLWcBwJ76wBixUqkCmwUK)
```

7. Now, let's run the next two commands that Grafana asked us to run, as seen in *Figure 15.5*:

```
export POD_NAME=$(kubectl get pods --namespace default
-l "app.kubernetes.io/name=grafana,app.kubernetes.io/
instance=grafana-1576397218" -o jsonpath="{.items[0].metadata.name}")
kubectl --namespace default port-forward $POD_NAME 3000
```

Again, use the command that you obtain for your instance as this will be customized. These commands find the Pod that Grafana is running on and then map a port from our local machine to it so that we can easily access it. You should see the following response:

```
Forwarding from 127.0.0.1:3000 -> 3000
Forwarding from [::1]:3000 -> 3000
```

> **NOTE**
>
> At this step, if you are facing any issues with getting the proper Pod name, you can simply run **`kubectl get pods`** to find the name of the Pod running Grafana and use that name instead of the shell (**`$POD_NAME`**) variable. So, your command will look similar to this:
>
> **`kubectl --namespace default port-forward grafana-1591658222-7cd4d8b7df-b2hlm 3000`**.

8. Now, open your browser and visit **`http://localhost:3000`** to access Grafana. You should see the following landing page:

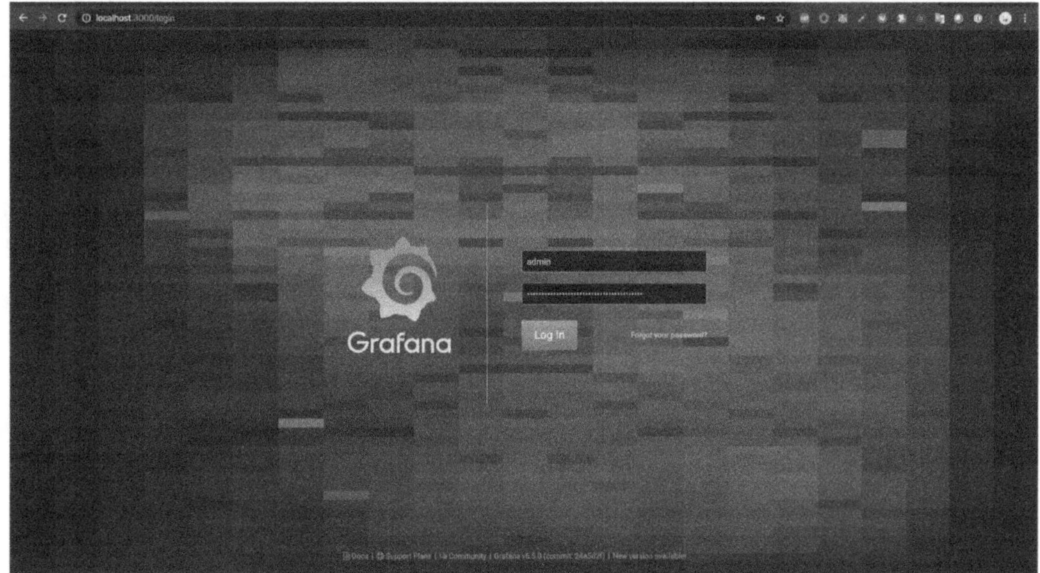

Figure 15.6: The log-in page for the Grafana dashboard

The default username is **`admin`** and the password is the value echoed in the output of *step 6*. Use that to log in.

9. After a successful login, you should see this page:

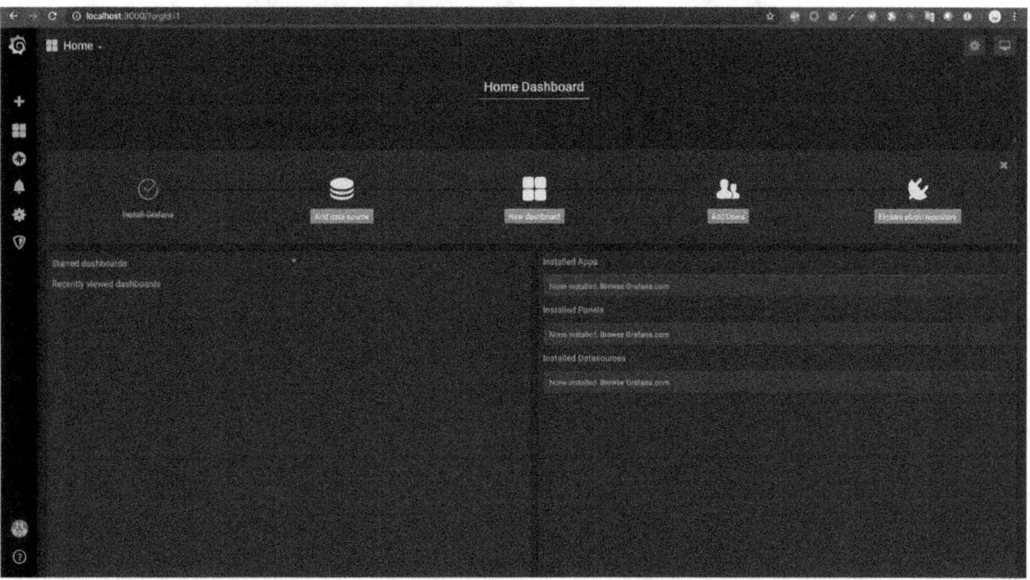

Figure 15.7: The Grafana Home dashboard

10. Now, let's create a dashboard for Kubernetes metrics. To do so, we need to set up Prometheus as a data source for Grafana. On the left sidebar, click on **Configuration** and then on **Data Sources**:

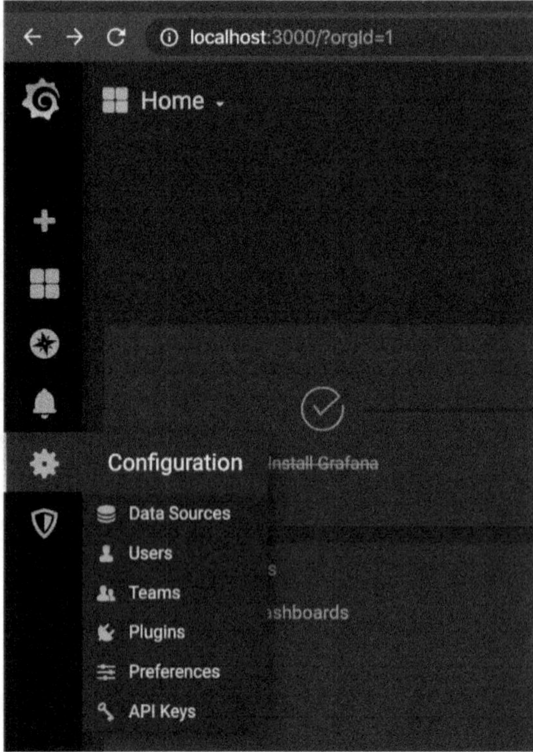

Figure 15.8: Selecting Data Sources from the Configuration menu

11. You will see this page:

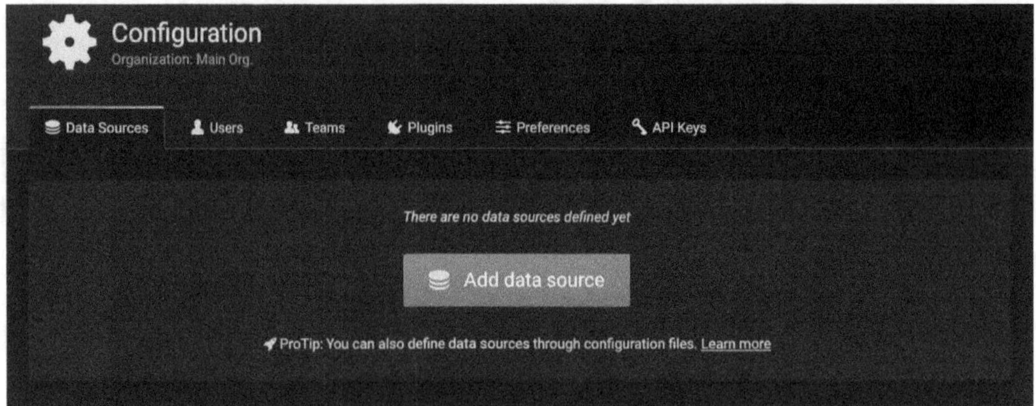

Figure 15.9: The Add data source option

Now, click on the **Add data source** button.

12. You should see this page with several database options. Prometheus should be on top. Click on that:

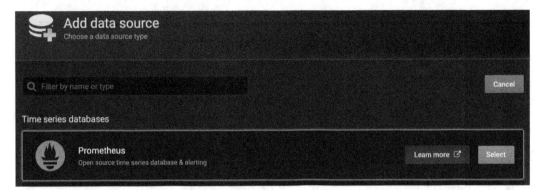

Figure 15.10: Choosing Prometheus as our data source for the Grafana dashboard

Now, before we move on to the next screen, here, we need to get the URL that Grafana will use to access the Prometheus database from inside the cluster. We will do that in the next step.

13. Open a new terminal window and run the following command:

```
kubectl get svc --all-namespaces
```

You should see a response similar to the following:

```
NAMESPACE       NAME                                          TYPE           CLUSTER-IP      EXTERNAL-IP
default         grafana-1576397218                            ClusterIP      172.20.110.18   <none>
default         kubernetes                                    ClusterIP      172.20.0.1      <none>
default         kubernetes-test-ha-application-with-redis     ClusterIP      172.20.173.13   <none>
default         prometheus-1576397083-alertmanager            ClusterIP      172.20.11.35    <none>
default         prometheus-1576397083-kube-state-metrics      ClusterIP      None            <none>
default         prometheus-1576397083-node-exporter           ClusterIP      None            <none>
default         prometheus-1576397083-pushgateway             ClusterIP      172.20.84.75    <none>
default         prometheus-1576397083-server                  ClusterIP      172.20.179.12   <none>
default         redis                                         ClusterIP      172.20.85.223   <none>
ingress-nginx   ingress-nginx                                 LoadBalancer   172.20.197.38   a6726be641f0511
kube-system     kube-dns                                      ClusterIP      172.20.0.10     <none>
kube-system     metrics-server                                ClusterIP      172.20.16.234   <none>
zarnold@zachs-mbp terraform %
```

Figure 15.11: Getting the list of all services

Copy the name of the service that starts with **prometheus** and ends in **server**.

14. After *step 12*, you will have arrived at the screen shown in the following screenshot:

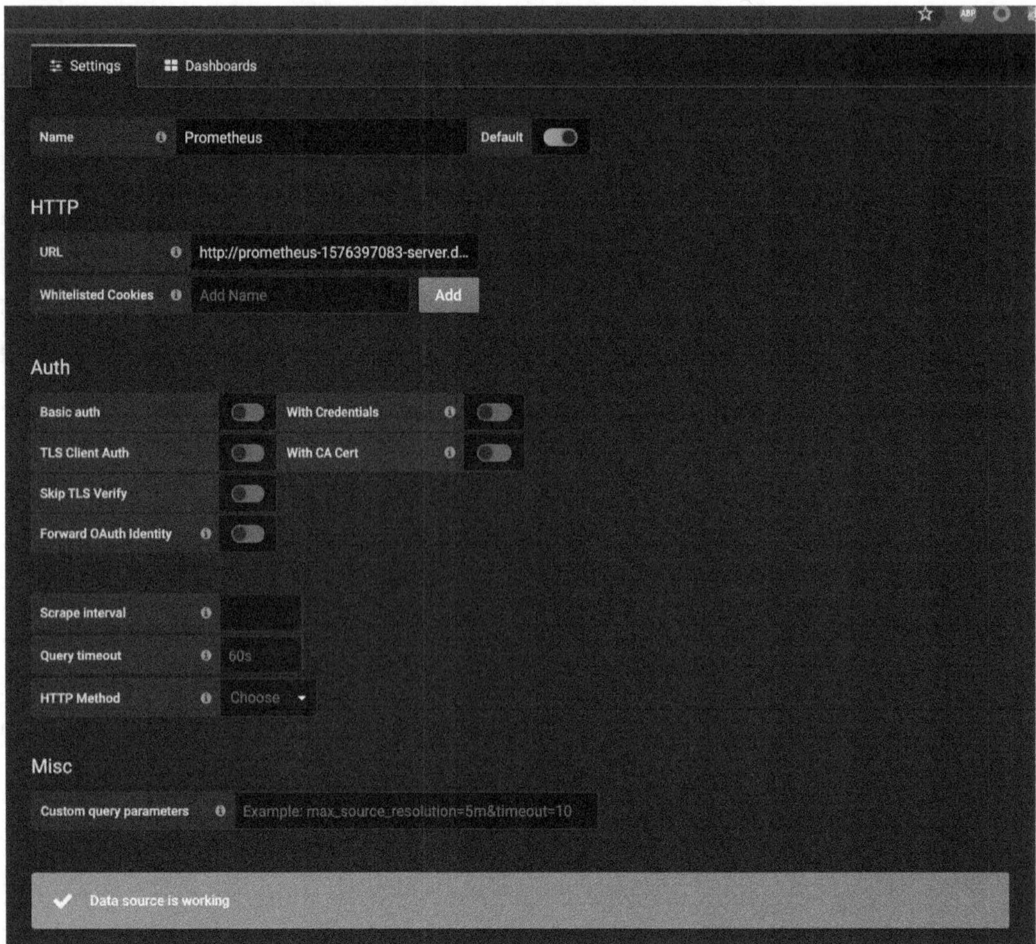

Figure 15.12: Entering the address of our Prometheus service in Grafana

In the **URL** field of the **HTTP** section, enter the following value:

```
http://<YOUR_PROMETHEUS_SERVICE_NAME>.default
```

Note that you should see **Data source is working**, as shown in the preceding screenshot. Then, click on the **Save and Test** button at the bottom. The reason we have added **.default** to our URL is that we deployed this Helm chart to the **default** Kubernetes namespace. If you deployed it to another namespace, you should replace **default** with the name of your namespace.

15. Now, let's set up the dashboard. Back on the Grafana home page (**http://localhost:3000**), click on the **+** symbol on the left sidebar, and then click on **Import**, as shown here:

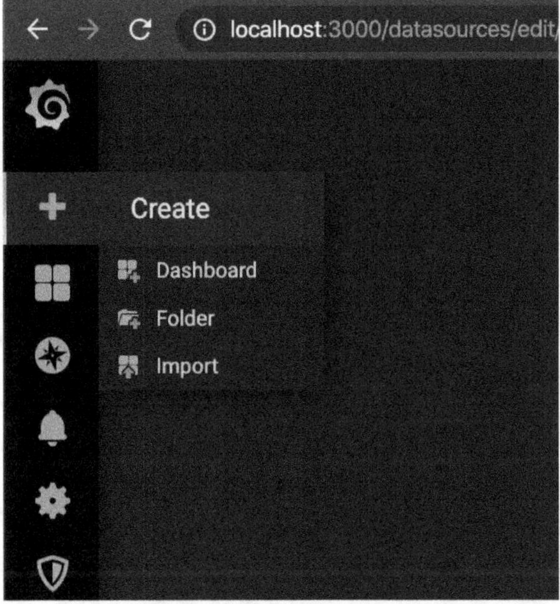

Figure 15.13: Navigating to import Dashboard option

16. On the next page, you should see the **Grafana.com Dashboard** field, as shown here:

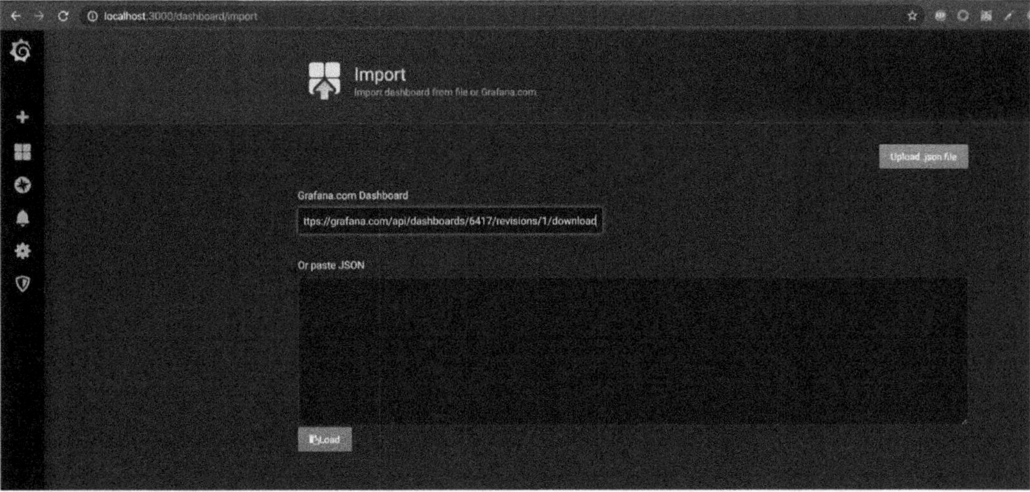

Figure 15.14: Entering the source to import the dashboard from

Paste the following link into the **Grafana.com Dashboard** field:

```
https://grafana.com/api/dashboards/6417/revisions/1/download
```

This is an officially supported Kubernetes dashboard. Once you click anywhere outside the file, you should automatically advance to the next screen.

17. The previous step should lead you to this screen:

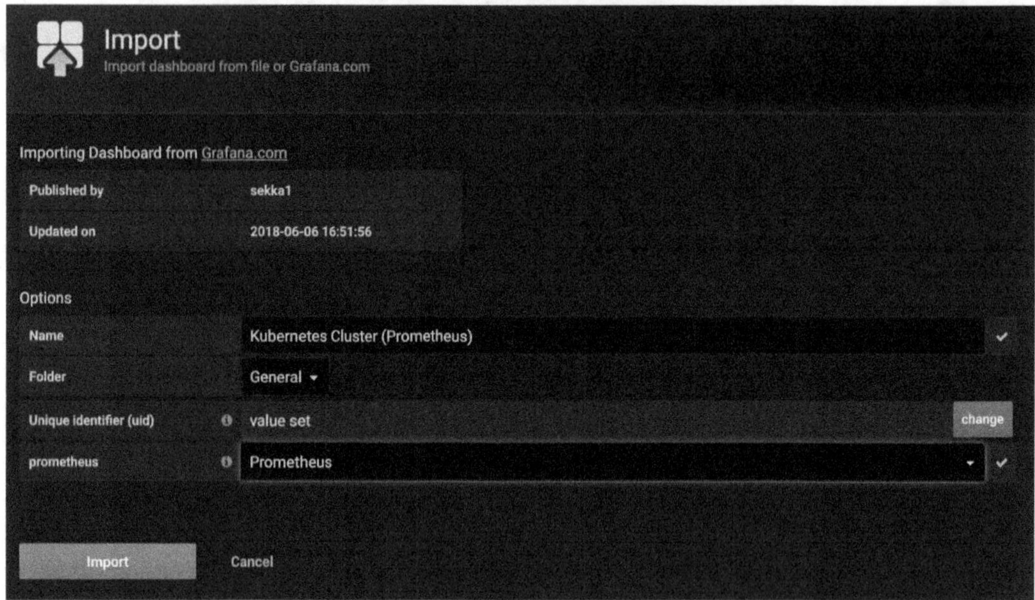

Figure 15.15: Setting Prometheus as the data source for the imported dashboard

Where you see the **prometheus**, click on the drop-down list next to it, select **Prometheus**, and hit **Import**.

18. The result should look like this:

Figure 15.16: The Grafana dashboard to monitor our cluster

As you can see, we have a concise dashboard for monitoring workloads in Kubernetes. In this exercise, we deployed our Metric Server to collect and expose Kubernetes object metrics, then we deployed Prometheus to store those metrics and Grafana to help us visualize the collected metrics in Prometheus, which will inform us as to what's going on in our cluster at any point in time. Now, it's time to use that information to scale things.

AUTOSCALING IN KUBERNETES

Kubernetes allows you to automatically scale your workloads to adapt to changing demands on your applications. The information gathered from the Kubernetes Metrics server is the data that is used for driving the scaling decisions. In this book, we will be covering two types of scaling action—one that impacts the number of running pods in a Deployment and another that impacts the number of running nodes in a cluster. Both are examples of horizontal scaling. Let's briefly gain an intuition for what both the horizontal scaling of pods and the horizontal scaling of nodes would entail:

- **Pods**: Assuming that you filled out the **`resources:`** section of **`podTemplate`** when creating a Deployment in Kubernetes, each container within that pod will have the **`requests`** and **`limits`** fields, as designated by the corresponding **`cpu`** and **`memory`** fields. When the resources needed to process a workload exceed that which you have allocated, then by adding additional replicas of a pod to the Deployment, you are horizontally scaling to add capacity to your Deployment. By letting a software process decide the number of replicas of a Pod in a Deployment for you based on load, you are *autoscaling* your deployment to keep the number of replicas consistent with the metric you have defined to express your application's load. One such metric for application load could be the percentage of the allocated CPU that is currently being consumed.
- **Nodes**: Every node has a certain amount of CPU (typically expressed by the number of cores) and memory (typically expressed in gigabytes) that it has available for consumption by Pods. When the total capacity of all worker nodes is exhausted by all running pods (meaning that the CPU and memory requests/limits for all the Pods are equal to or greater than that of the whole cluster), then we have saturated the resources of our cluster. In order to allow more Pods to be run on the cluster, or to allow more autoscaling to take place in the cluster, we need to add capacity in the form of additional worker nodes. When we allow a software process to make this decision for us, we are considered to be *autoscaling* the total capacity of our cluster. In Kubernetes, this is handled by the ClusterAutoscaler.

> **NOTE**
>
> When you increase the number of pod replicas of an application, it is known as horizontal scaling and is handled by the **HorizontalPodAutoscaler**. If, instead, you were to increase the resource limits for your replicas, that would be called vertical scaling. Kubernetes also offers **VerticalPodAutoscaler**, but we are leaving it out for brevity, and due to the fact that it is not yet generally available and safe for use in production.

Using both HPAs and ClusterAutoscalers in conjunction with each other can be an effective way for companies to ensure that they always have the right amount of application resources deployed for their load and that they aren't paying too much for it at the same time. Let's examine both of them in the following subsections.

HorizontalPodAutoscaler

HPAs are responsible for making sure that the number of replicas of your application in a Deployment match whatever the current demand as measured by a metric. This is useful because we can use real-time metric data, which is already gathered by Kubernetes, to always ensure that our application is meeting the demands we have set forth in our thresholds. This may be a new concept to some application owners who are not used to running applications using data, but once you begin to leverage tools that can right-size your deployments, you will never want to go back.

Kubernetes has an API resource in the **`autoscaling/v1`** and **`autoscaling/v2beta2`** groups to provide a definition of autoscaling triggers that can run against another Kubernetes resource, which is most often a Kubernetes Deployment object. In the case of **`autoscaling/v1`**, the only supported metric is the current CPU consumption, and in the case of **`autoscaling/v2beta2`**, there is support for any custom metrics.

HPA queries the Kubernetes Metric Server to look at the metrics for the particular deployment. Then, the autoscaling resource will determine whether or not the currently observed metric is beyond the threshold for a scaling target. If it is, then it will change the number of Pods desired by the deployment to be higher or lower depending on the load.

As an example, consider a shopping cart microservice hosted by an e-commerce company. The shopping cart service experiences a heavy load during the coupon code-entry process because it must traverse all items in the cart and search for active coupons on them before validating a coupon code. On a random Tuesday morning, there are many shoppers online using the service and they all want to use coupons. Normally, the service would become overwhelmed and requests would start to fail. However, if you were able to use an HPA, Kubernetes would use the spare computing power of your cluster to ensure that there are enough Pods of this shopping cart service to be able to handle the load.

Note that simply autoscaling a Deployment is not a "one-size-fits-all" solution to performance problems in an application. There are many places in modern applications where slowdowns can occur, so careful consideration should be made about your application architecture to see where you can identify other bottlenecks not solved by simple autoscaling. One such example would be slow query performance on a database. However, for this chapter, we will be focusing on application problems that can be solved by autoscaling in Kubernetes.

Let's look at the structure of an HPA to understand a bit better:

with_autoscaler.yaml

```
apiVersion: autoscaling/v1
kind: HorizontalPodAutoscaler
metadata:
  name: shopping-cart-hpa
spec:
  scaleTargetRef:
    apiVersion: apps/v1
    kind: Deployment
    name: shopping-cart-deployment
  minReplicas: 20
  maxReplicas: 50
  targetCPUUtilizationPercentage: 50
```

You can find the full code at this link: https://packt.live/3bE9v28.

In this spec, observe the following fields:

- **`scaleTargetRef`**: This is the reference to the object that is being scaled. In this case, it is a pointer to the Deployment of a shopping-cart microservice.
- **`minReplicas`**: The minimum replicas in the Deployment, regardless of scaling triggers.
- **`maxReplicas`**: The maximum number of replicas in the Deployment, regardless of scaling triggers.

- **`targetCPUUtilizationPercentage`**: The goal percentage of average CPU utilization across all Pods in this deployment. Kubernetes will re-evaluate this metric constantly and increase and decrease the number of pods so that the actual average CPU utilization matches this target.

To simulate stress on our application, we will use **wrk**, because it is simple to configure and has a Docker container already made for us. wrk is an HTTP load-testing tool. It is simple to use and only has a few options; however, it will be able to generate large amounts of load by making requests over and over using multiple simultaneous HTTP connections against a specified endpoint.

> **NOTE**
>
> You can find out more about wrk at this link: https://github.com/wg/wrk.

For the following exercise, we will use a modified version of the application we've been running to help drive scaling behavior. In this revision of our application, we have modified it such that the application will perform a Fibonacci sequence calculation in a naïve way out to the 10,000,000th entry so that it will be slightly more computationally expensive and exceed our CPU autoscaling trigger. If you examine the source code, you can see that we have added this function:

`main.go`

```
func FibonacciLoop(n int) int {
  f := make([]int, n+1, n+2)
  if n < 2 {
        f = f[0:2]
  }
  f[0] = 0
  f[1] = 1
  for i := 2; i <= n; i++ {
        f[i] = f[i-1] + f[i-2]
  }
  return f[n]
}
```

`You can find the full code at this link:` https://packt.live/3h5wCEd.

Other than this, we will be using an Ingress, which we learned about in *Chapter 12, Your Application and HA*, and the same SQL database that we built in the previous chapter.

Now, with all of that said, let's dig into the implementation of these autoscalers in the following exercise.

EXERCISE 15.02: SCALING WORKLOADS IN KUBERNETES

In this exercise, we're going to be putting together a few different pieces from before. Since our application has several moving parts at this point, we need to lay out some steps that we're going to take so that you understand where we're headed:

1. We need to have our EKS cluster set up as we have in *Exercise 12.02, Creating a Cluster with EKS Using Terraform*.
2. We need to have the required components for the Kubernetes Metrics server set up.

> **NOTE**
>
> Considering these two points, you need to complete the previous exercise successfully to be able to perform this exercise.

3. We need to install our counter application using a modification so that it will be a computationally intensive exercise to get the next number in a sequence.
4. We need to install the HPA and set a metric target for the CPU percentage.
5. We need to install the ClusterAutoscaler and give it the permissions to change the **Autoscaling Group** (**ASG**) size in AWS.
6. We need to stress test our application by generating enough load to be able to scale the application out and cause the HPA to trigger a cluster-scaling action.

We will use a Kubernetes Ingress resource to load test using traffic external to our cluster so that we can create an even more realistic simulation.

After doing this, you'll be a Kubernetes captain, so let's dive in:

1. Now, let's deploy the **`ingress-nginx`** setup by running the following commands one after the other:

```
kubectl apply -f https://raw.githubusercontent.com/kubernetes/
ingress-nginx/nginx-0.30.0/deploy/static/mandatory.yaml

kubectl apply -f https://raw.githubusercontent.com/kubernetes/
ingress-nginx/nginx-0.30.0/deploy/static/provider/aws/service-l4.yaml

kubectl apply -f https://raw.githubusercontent.com/kubernetes/
ingress-nginx/nginx-0.30.0/deploy/static/provider/aws/patch-
configmap-l4.yaml
```

You should see the following responses:

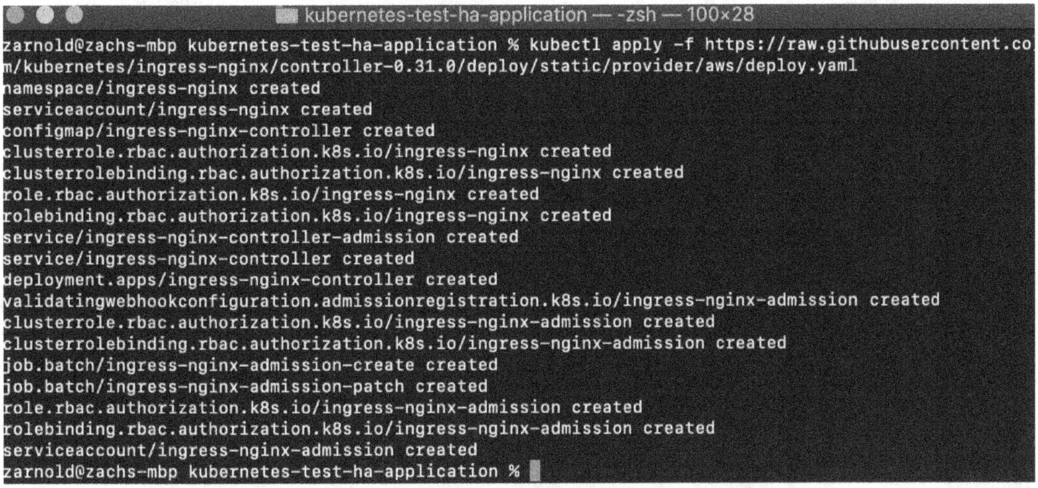

```
kubernetes-test-ha-application — -zsh — 100×28
zarnold@zachs-mbp kubernetes-test-ha-application % kubectl apply -f https://raw.githubusercontent.co
m/kubernetes/ingress-nginx/controller-0.31.0/deploy/static/provider/aws/deploy.yaml
namespace/ingress-nginx created
serviceaccount/ingress-nginx created
configmap/ingress-nginx-controller created
clusterrole.rbac.authorization.k8s.io/ingress-nginx created
clusterrolebinding.rbac.authorization.k8s.io/ingress-nginx created
role.rbac.authorization.k8s.io/ingress-nginx created
rolebinding.rbac.authorization.k8s.io/ingress-nginx created
service/ingress-nginx-controller-admission created
service/ingress-nginx-controller created
deployment.apps/ingress-nginx-controller created
validatingwebhookconfiguration.admissionregistration.k8s.io/ingress-nginx-admission created
clusterrole.rbac.authorization.k8s.io/ingress-nginx-admission created
clusterrolebinding.rbac.authorization.k8s.io/ingress-nginx-admission created
job.batch/ingress-nginx-admission-create created
job.batch/ingress-nginx-admission-patch created
role.rbac.authorization.k8s.io/ingress-nginx-admission created
rolebinding.rbac.authorization.k8s.io/ingress-nginx-admission created
serviceaccount/ingress-nginx-admission created
zarnold@zachs-mbp kubernetes-test-ha-application %
```

Figure 15.17: Deploying the nginx Ingress controller

2. Now, let's fetch the manifest for our application with HA MySQL, Ingress, and an HPA:

```
curl -O https://raw.githubusercontent.com/PacktWorkshops/Kubernetes-Workshop/master/Chapter15/Exercise15.02/with_autoscaler.yaml
```

Before we apply it, let's look at our autoscaling trigger:

with_autoscaler.yaml

```
apiVersion: autoscaling/v1
kind: HorizontalPodAutoscaler
metadata:
  name: counter-hpa
spec:
  scaleTargetRef:
    apiVersion: apps/v1
    kind: Deployment
    name: kubernetes-test-ha-application-with-autoscaler-
      deployment
  minReplicas: 2
  maxReplicas: 1000
  targetCPUUtilizationPercentage: 10
```

The full code can be found at this link: https://packt.live/3bE9v28.

Here, we are starting with two replicas of this deployment and allowing ourselves to grow up to 1000 replicas while trying to keep the CPU at a constant 10% utilization. Recall from our Terraform template that we are using m4.large EC2 instances to run these Pods.

3. Let's deploy this application by running the following command:

```
kubectl apply -f with_autoscaler.yaml
```

You should see the following response:

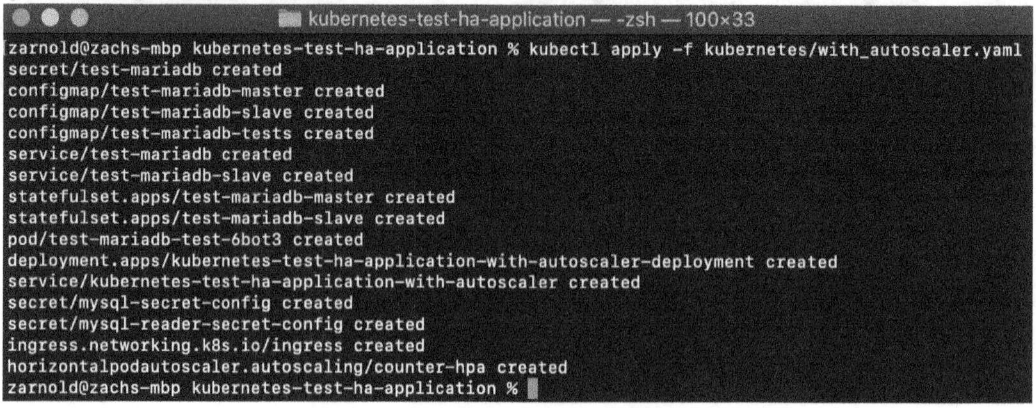

```
kubernetes-test-ha-application — -zsh — 100×33
zarnold@zachs-mbp kubernetes-test-ha-application % kubectl apply -f kubernetes/with_autoscaler.yaml
secret/test-mariadb created
configmap/test-mariadb-master created
configmap/test-mariadb-slave created
configmap/test-mariadb-tests created
service/test-mariadb created
service/test-mariadb-slave created
statefulset.apps/test-mariadb-master created
statefulset.apps/test-mariadb-slave created
pod/test-mariadb-test-6bot3 created
deployment.apps/kubernetes-test-ha-application-with-autoscaler-deployment created
service/kubernetes-test-ha-application-with-autoscaler created
secret/mysql-secret-config created
secret/mysql-reader-secret-config created
ingress.networking.k8s.io/ingress created
horizontalpodautoscaler.autoscaling/counter-hpa created
zarnold@zachs-mbp kubernetes-test-ha-application %
```

Figure 15.18: Deploying our application

4. With that, we are ready to load test. Before we begin, let's check on the number of Pods in our deployment:

```
kubectl describe hpa counter-hpa
```

This may take up to 5 minutes to show a percentage, after which you should see something like this:

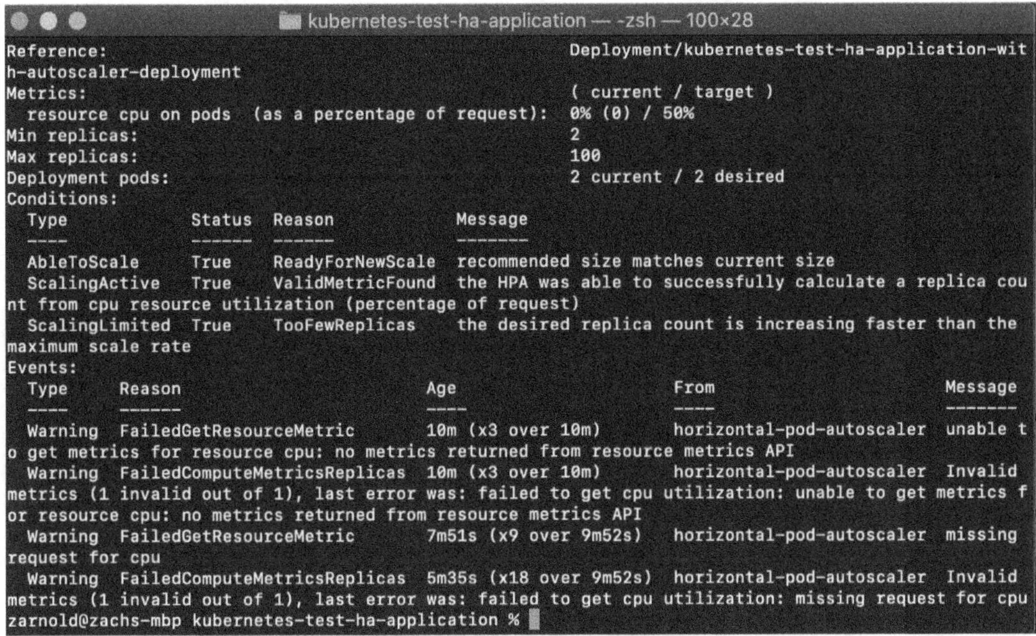

```
Reference:                                              Deployment/kubernetes-test-ha-application-wit
h-autoscaler-deployment
Metrics:                                                ( current / target )
  resource cpu on pods  (as a percentage of request):  0% (0) / 50%
Min replicas:                                           2
Max replicas:                                           100
Deployment pods:                                        2 current / 2 desired
Conditions:
  Type            Status  Reason            Message
  ----            ------  ------            -------
  AbleToScale     True    ReadyForNewScale  recommended size matches current size
  ScalingActive   True    ValidMetricFound  the HPA was able to successfully calculate a replica cou
nt from cpu resource utilization (percentage of request)
  ScalingLimited  True    TooFewReplicas    the desired replica count is increasing faster than the
maximum scale rate
Events:
  Type     Reason                         Age                     From                       Message
  ----     ------                         ----                    ----                       -------
  Warning  FailedGetResourceMetric        10m (x3 over 10m)       horizontal-pod-autoscaler  unable t
o get metrics for resource cpu: no metrics returned from resource metrics API
  Warning  FailedComputeMetricsReplicas  10m (x3 over 10m)       horizontal-pod-autoscaler  Invalid
metrics (1 invalid out of 1), last error was: failed to get cpu utilization: unable to get metrics f
or resource cpu: no metrics returned from resource metrics API
  Warning  FailedGetResourceMetric        7m51s (x9 over 9m52s)   horizontal-pod-autoscaler  missing
request for cpu
  Warning  FailedComputeMetricsReplicas  5m35s (x18 over 9m52s)  horizontal-pod-autoscaler  Invalid
metrics (1 invalid out of 1), last error was: failed to get cpu utilization: missing request for cpu
zarnold@zachs-mbp kubernetes-test-ha-application %
```

Figure 15.19: Getting details about our HPA

The **`Deployment pods:`** field shows **`2 current / 2 desired`**, meaning our HPA has changed the desired replica count from 3 to 2 because we have a CPU utilization of 0%, which is below the target of 10%.

Now, we need to get some load going. We're going to run a load test from our computer to the cluster using wrk as a Docker container. But first, we need to get the Ingress endpoint to access our cluster.

5. Run the following command to first get your Ingress endpoint:

```
kubectl get svc ingress-nginx -n ingress-nginx -o jsonpath='{.status.
loadBalancer.ingress[0].hostname}'
```

You should see the following response:

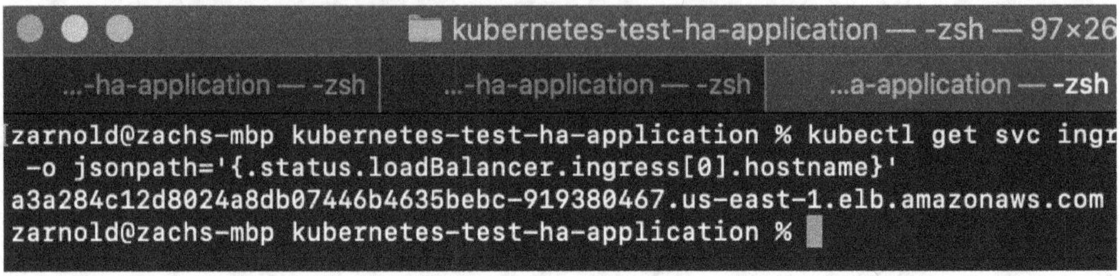

```
kubernetes-test-ha-application — -zsh — 97×26
...-ha-application — -zsh | ...-ha-application — -zsh | ...a-application — -zsh
zarnold@zachs-mbp kubernetes-test-ha-application % kubectl get svc ingr
 -o jsonpath='{.status.loadBalancer.ingress[0].hostname}'
a3a284c12d8024a8db07446b4635bebc-919380467.us-east-1.elb.amazonaws.com
zarnold@zachs-mbp kubernetes-test-ha-application %
```

Figure 15.20: Checking our Ingress endpoint

6. In another terminal session, run a **wrk** load test using the following command:

```
docker run --rm skandyla/wrk -t10 -c1000 -d600 -H ,Host: counter.
com'  http://YOUR_HOSTNAME/get-number
```

Let's quickly understand these parameters:

-t10: The number of threads to use for this test, which is 10 in this case.

-c1000: The total number of connections to hold open. In this case, each thread is handling 1,000 connections each.

-d600: The number of seconds to run this test (which in this case is 600 seconds or 10 minutes).

You should get output like the following:

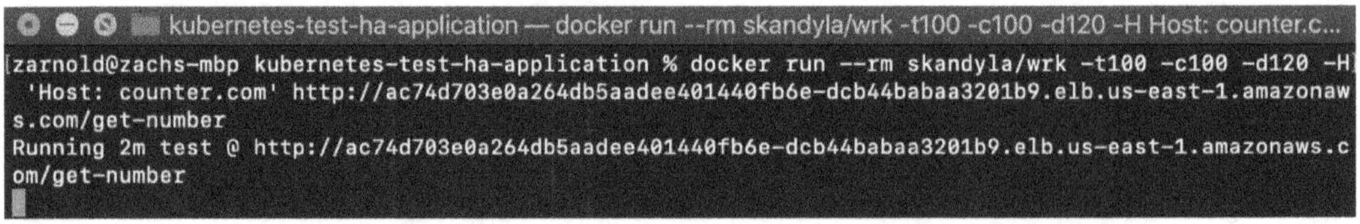

```
kubernetes-test-ha-application — docker run --rm skandyla/wrk -t100 -c100 -d120 -H Host: counter.c...
zarnold@zachs-mbp kubernetes-test-ha-application % docker run --rm skandyla/wrk -t100 -c100 -d120 -H
 'Host: counter.com' http://ac74d703e0a264db5aadee401440fb6e-dcb44babaa3201b9.elb.us-east-1.amazonaw
s.com/get-number
Running 2m test @ http://ac74d703e0a264db5aadee401440fb6e-dcb44babaa3201b9.elb.us-east-1.amazonaws.c
om/get-number
```

Figure 15.21: Running a load test to our Ingress endpoint

7. In another session, let's keep an eye on the pods for our application:

```
kubectl get pods --watch
```

You should be able to see a response similar to this:

```
zarnold — kubectl get pods --watch — 80×24
g             0             14m
kubernetes-test-ha-application-with-autoscaler-deployment-7vbk4    0/1     Pendin
g             0             14m
kubernetes-test-ha-application-with-autoscaler-deployment-t7mdt    0/1     Pendin
g             0             14m
kubernetes-test-ha-application-with-autoscaler-deployment-mx7mb    0/1     Pendin
g             0             14m
kubernetes-test-ha-application-with-autoscaler-deployment-bp972    0/1     Pendin
g             0             14m
kubernetes-test-ha-application-with-autoscaler-deployment-rq86x    0/1     Pendin
g             0             14m
prometheus-1593096646-node-exporter-48ngg                          0/1     Pendin
g             0             6s
prometheus-1593096646-node-exporter-48ngg                          0/1     Contai
nerCreating   0             6s
kubernetes-test-ha-application-with-autoscaler-deployment-w4cxf    0/1     Pendin
g             0             14m
kubernetes-test-ha-application-with-autoscaler-deployment-2jhkk    0/1     Pendin
g             0             6m43s
kubernetes-test-ha-application-with-autoscaler-deployment-p5pbt    0/1     Pendin
g             0             6m42s
kubernetes-test-ha-application-with-autoscaler-deployment-b7kfr    0/1     Pendin
g             0             6m43s
```

Figure 15.22: Watching pods backing our application

In this terminal window, you should see the number of Pods increasing. Note that we can also check the same in our Grafana dashboard.

Here, it is increased by 1; but soon, these pods will exceed all the available space.

8. In yet another terminal session, you can again set up port forwarding to Grafana to observe the dashboard:

```
kubectl --namespace default port-forward $POD_NAME 3000
```

You should see the following response:

```
Forwarding from 127.0.0.1:3000 -> 3000
Forwarding from [::1]:3000 -> 3000
```

9. Now, access the dashboard on your browser at **`localhost:3000`**:

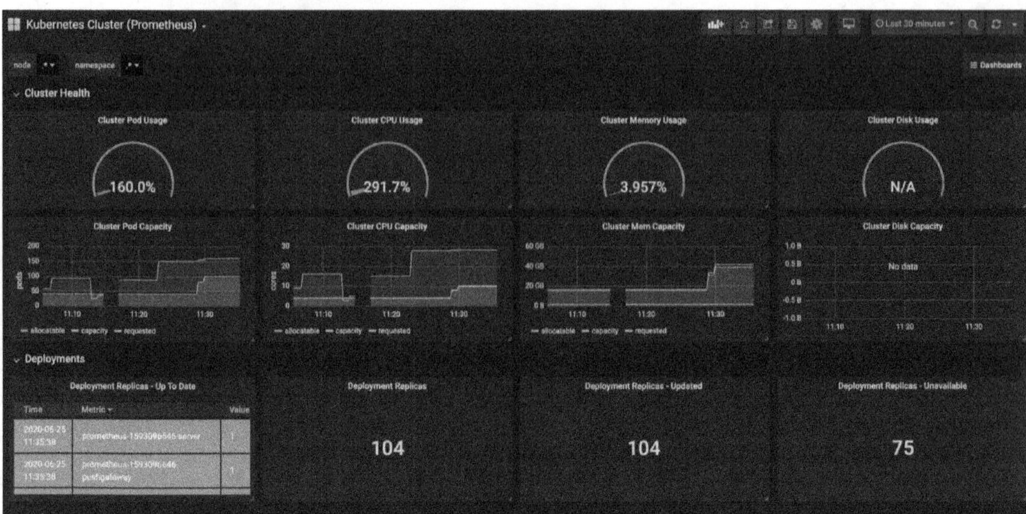

Figure 15.23: Observing our cluster in the Grafana dashboard

You should be able to see the number of Pods increasing here as well. Thus, we have successfully deployed an HPA that is automatically scaling up the number of Pods as the load on our application increases.

ClusterAutoscaler

If the HPA ensures that there are always the right number of Pods running in a Deployment, then what happens when we run out of capacity on the cluster for all of those Pods? We need more of them, but we also don't want to be paying for that additional cluster capacity when we don't need it. This is where the ClusterAutoscaler comes in.

The ClusterAutoscaler will work inside your cluster to ensure that the number of nodes running in the ASG (in the case of AWS) always has enough capacity to run the currently deployed application components of your cluster. So, if 10 pods in a Deployment can fit on 2 nodes, then when you need an 11th Pod, the ClusterAutoscaler will ask AWS to add a 3rd node to your Kubernetes cluster to get that Pod scheduled. When that Pod is no longer needed, that Node goes away, too. Let's look at a brief architecture diagram to understand how the ClusterAutoscaler works:

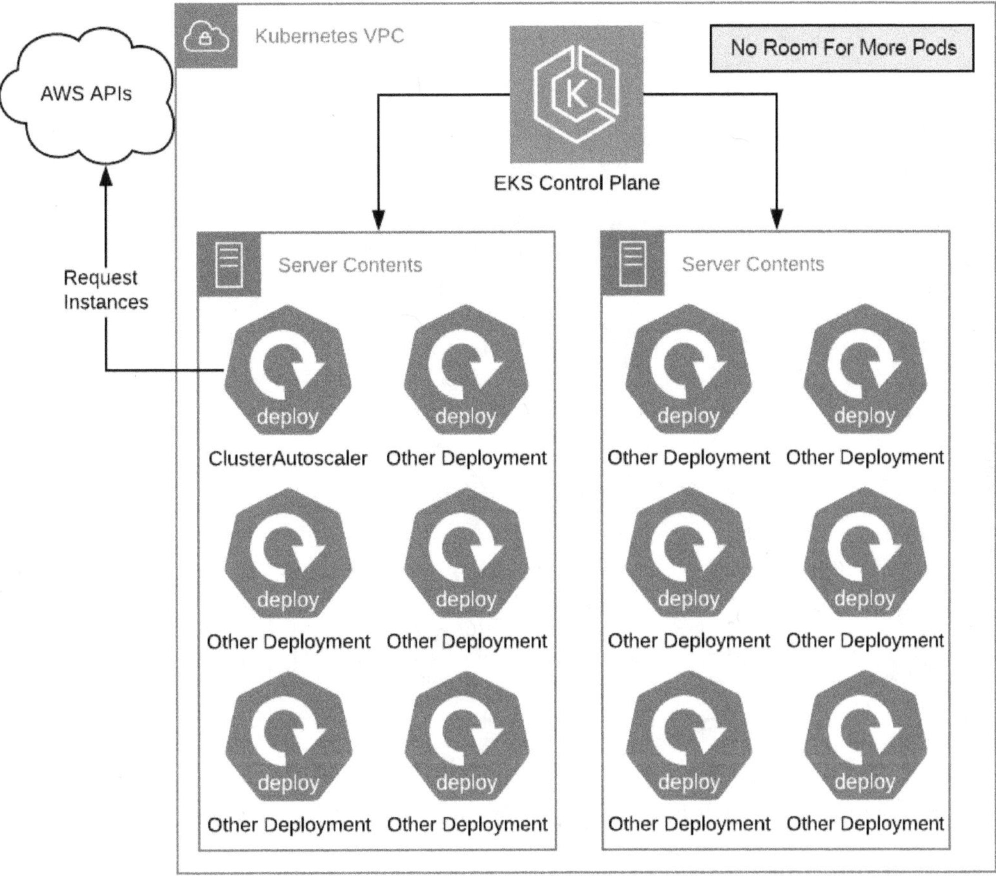

Figure 15.24: Cluster with nodes at full capacity

Note that in this example, we have an EKS cluster running two worker nodes and all available cluster resources are taken up. So, here's what the ClusterAutoscaler does.

When a request for a Pod that won't fit arrives at the control plane, it remains in a `Pending` state. When the ClusterAutoscaler observes this, it will communicate with the AWS EC2 API and request for the ASG, which has our worker nodes deployed in them, to scale up by another node. This requires the ClusterAutoscaler to be able to communicate with the API for the cloud provider it is running in in order to change worker node count. In the case of AWS, this also means that we will either have to generate IAM credentials for the ClusterAutoscaler or allow it to use the IAM role of the machine to access the AWS APIs.

A successful scaling action should look like the following:

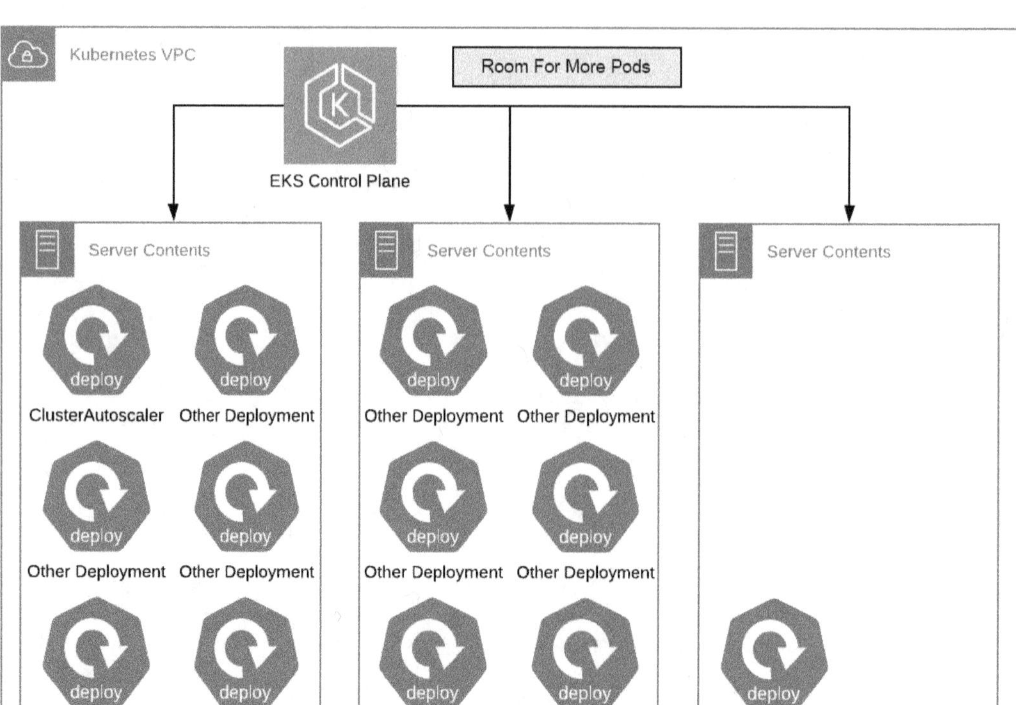

Figure 15.25: Additional node provisioned to run the additional pods

We will implement the ClusterAutoscaler in the following exercise, and then load test it in the activity after that.

EXERCISE 15.03: CONFIGURING THE CLUSTERAUTOSCALER

So, now that we've seen our Kubernetes Deployment scale, it's time to see it scale to the point where it needs to add more node capacity to the cluster. We will be continuing where the last lesson left off and run the exact same application and load test but let it run a little longer:

1. To create a ClusterAutoscaler, first, we need to create an AWS IAM account and give it the permissions to manage our ASGs. Create a file called **`permissions.json`** with the following contents:

```
{
  "Version": "2012-10-17",
  "Statement": [
```

```
        {
          "Effect": "Allow",
          "Action": [
            "autoscaling:DescribeAutoScalingGroups",
            "autoscaling:DescribeAutoScalingInstances",
            "autoscaling:DescribeLaunchConfigurations",
            "autoscaling:SetDesiredCapacity",
            "autoscaling:TerminateInstanceInAutoScalingGroup",
            "autoscaling:DescribeLaunchConfigurations",
            "ec2:DescribeLaunchTemplateVersions",
            "autoscaling:DescribeTags"
          ],
          "Resource": "*"
        }
      ]
    }
```

2. Now, let's run the following command to create an AWS IAM policy:

```
aws iam create-policy --policy-name k8s-autoscaling-policy --policy-
document file://permissions.json
```

You should see the following response:

```
kubernetes-test-ha-application — -zsh — 97×26
...-ha-application — -zsh | ...-ha-application — -zsh | ...a-application — -zsh | ...erraform destroy
zarnold@zachs-mbp kubernetes-test-ha-application % aws iam create-policy --policy-name k8s-autosc
aling-policy --policy-document file://permissions.json
{
    "Policy": {
        "PolicyName": "k8s-autoscaling-policy",
        "PolicyId": "ANPA5YQUHQAP6KQLQJL2B",
        "Arn": "arn:aws:iam::946008981535:policy/k8s-autoscaling-policy",
        "Path": "/",
        "DefaultVersionId": "v1",
        "AttachmentCount": 0,
        "PermissionsBoundaryUsageCount": 0,
        "IsAttachable": true,
        "CreateDate": "2020-04-27T00:45:46+00:00",
        "UpdateDate": "2020-04-27T00:45:46+00:00"
    }
}
zarnold@zachs-mbp kubernetes-test-ha-application %
```

Figure 15.26: Creating an AWS IAM policy

Note down the value of the `Arn:` field from the output that you get.

3. Now, we need to create an IAM user and then attach a policy to it. First, let's create the user:

```
aws iam create-user --user-name k8s-autoscaler
```

You should see this response:

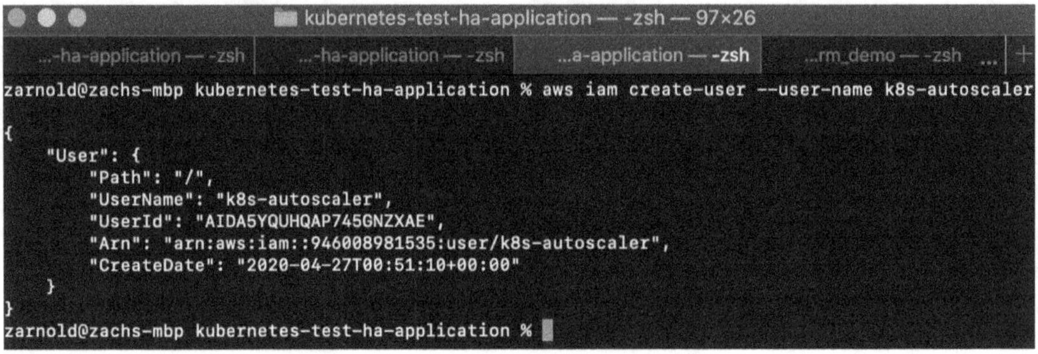

```
zarnold@zachs-mbp kubernetes-test-ha-application % aws iam create-user --user-name k8s-autoscaler
{
    "User": {
        "Path": "/",
        "UserName": "k8s-autoscaler",
        "UserId": "AIDA5YQUHQAP745GNZXAE",
        "Arn": "arn:aws:iam::946008981535:user/k8s-autoscaler",
        "CreateDate": "2020-04-27T00:51:10+00:00"
    }
}
zarnold@zachs-mbp kubernetes-test-ha-application %
```

Figure 15.27: Creating an IAM user to use our policy

4. Now, let's attach the IAM policy to the user:

```
aws iam attach-user-policy --policy-arn <ARN_VALUE> --user-name
k8s-autoscaler
```

Use the ARN value that you obtained in *step 2*.

5. Now, we need the secret access key for this IAM user. Run the following command:

```
aws iam create-access-key --user-name k8s-autoscaler
```

You should get this response:

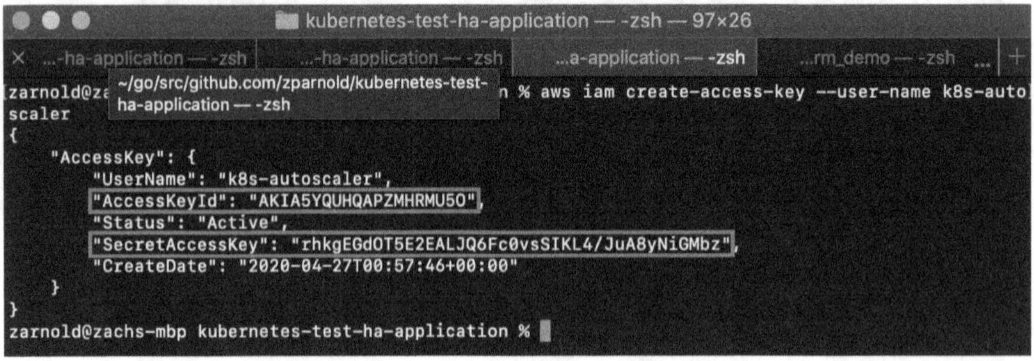

```
zarnold@zachs-mbp kubernetes-test-ha-application % aws iam create-access-key --user-name k8s-auto
scaler
{
    "AccessKey": {
        "UserName": "k8s-autoscaler",
        "AccessKeyId": "AKIA5YQUHQAPZMHRMU5O",
        "Status": "Active",
        "SecretAccessKey": "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",
        "CreateDate": "2020-04-27T00:57:46+00:00"
    }
}
zarnold@zachs-mbp kubernetes-test-ha-application %
```

Figure 15.28: Fetching the secret access key for the created IAM user

In the output of this command, note **AccessKeyId** and **SecretAccessKey**.

6. Now, get the manifest file for ClusterAutoscaler that we have provided:

```
curl -O https://raw.githubusercontent.com/PacktWorkshops/Kubernetes-Workshop/master/Chapter15/Exercise15.03/cluster_autoscaler.yaml
```

7. We need to create a Kubernetes Secret to expose these credentials to the ClusterAutoscaler. Open the **cluster_autoscaler.yaml** file. In the first entry, you should see the following:

cluster_autoscaler.yaml

```
apiVersion: v1
kind: Secret
metadata:
  name: aws-secret
  namespace: kube-system
type: Opaque
data:
  aws_access_key_id: YOUR_AWS_ACCESS_KEY_ID
  aws_secret_access_key: YOUR_AWS_SECRET_ACCESS_KEY
```

You can find the full code at this link: https://packt.live/2DCDfzZ.

You need to replace **YOUR_AWS_ACCESS_KEY_ID** and **YOUR_AWS_SECRET_ACCESS_KEY** with the Base64-encoded versions of the values returned by AWS in *step 5*.

8. To encode in Base64 format, run the following command:

```
echo -n <YOUR_VALUE> | base64
```

Run this twice, using **AccessKeyID** and **SecretAccessKey** in place of **<YOUR_VALUE>** to get the corresponding Base64-encoded version that you need to enter into the secret fields. Here's what it should look like when complete:

```
aws_access_key_id: QUtJQU1PU0ZPRE5ON0VYQU1QTEUK
aws_secret_access_key:
d0phbHJYVXRuRkVNSS9LN01ERU5HL2JQeFJmaUNZRVhBTVBMRUtFWQo=
```

9. Now, in the same **cluster_autoscaler.yaml** file, go to line 188. You will need to replace the value of **YOUR_AWS_REGION** with the value of the region you deployed your EKS cluster into, such as **us-east-1**:

cluster_autoscaler.yaml

```
176    env:
177    - name: AWS_ACCESS_KEY_ID
178      valueFrom:
179        secretKeyRef:
180          name: aws-secret
181          key: aws_access_key_id
182    - name: AWS_SECRET_ACCESS_KEY
183      valueFrom:
184        secretKeyRef:
185          name: aws-secret
186          key: aws_secret_access_key
187    - name: AWS_REGION
188      value: <YOUR_AWS_REGION>
```

You can find the entire code at this link: https://packt.live/2F8erkb.

10. Now, apply this file by running the following:

```
kubectl apply -f cluster_autoscaler.yaml
```

You should see a response similar to the following:

```
zarnold — -zsh — 80×24
zarnold@zachs-mbp ~ % kubectl apply -f cluster_autoscaler.yaml
secret/aws-secret created
serviceaccount/cluster-autoscaler created
clusterrole.rbac.authorization.k8s.io/cluster-autoscaler created
role.rbac.authorization.k8s.io/cluster-autoscaler created
clusterrolebinding.rbac.authorization.k8s.io/cluster-autoscaler created
rolebinding.rbac.authorization.k8s.io/cluster-autoscaler created
deployment.apps/cluster-autoscaler created
zarnold@zachs-mbp ~ %
```

Figure 15.29: Deploying our ClusterAutoscaler

11. Note that we need to now modify our ASG in AWS to allow for a scale-up; otherwise, the ClusterAutoscaler will not attempt to add any nodes. To do this, we have provided a modified **main.tf** file that has only one line changed: **max_size = 5** (*line 299*). This will allow the cluster to add up a maximum of five EC2 nodes to itself.

Navigate to the same location where you downloaded the previous Terraform file, and then run the following command:

```
curl -O https://raw.githubusercontent.com/PacktWorkshops/Kubernetes-Workshop/master/Chapter15/Exercise15.03/main.tf
```

You should see this response:

```
zarnold@zachs-mbp eks_terraform_demo % curl -O https://raw.githubusercontent.com
/PacktWorkshops/Kubernetes-Workshop/master/Chapter15/Exercise15.03/main.tf
  % Total    % Received % Xferd  Average Speed   Time    Time     Time  Current
                                 Dload  Upload   Total   Spent    Left  Speed
100  8203  100  8203    0     0  18771      0 --:--:-- --:--:-- --:--:-- 18728
zarnold@zachs-mbp eks_terraform_demo %
```

Figure 15.30: Downloading the modified Terraform file

12. Now, apply the modifications to the Terraform file:

```
terraform apply
```

Verify that the changes are only applied to the ASG max capacity, and then type **yes** when prompted:

```
            "subnet-054e3ef257162b98d",
            "subnet-07c7f338e17cd3e06",
        ]
        wait_for_capacity_timeout = "10m"

        tag {
            key                 = "Name"
            propagate_at_launch = true
            value               = "terraform-eks-demo"
        }
        tag {
            key                 = "kubernetes.io/cluster/terraform-eks-demo"
            propagate_at_launch = true
            value               = "owned"
        }
    }

Plan: 0 to add, 1 to change, 0 to destroy.

Do you want to perform these actions?
  Terraform will perform the actions described above.
  Only 'yes' will be accepted to approve.

  Enter a value:
```

Figure 15.31: Applying our Terraform modifications

> **NOTE**
>
> We will test this ClusterAutoscaler in the following activity. Hence, do not delete your cluster and API resources for now.

At this point, we have deployed our ClusterAutoscaler and configured it to access the AWS API. Thus, we should be able to scale the number of nodes as required.

Let's proceed to the following activity, where we will load test our cluster. You should plan to do this activity as soon as possible in order to keep costs down.

ACTIVITY 15.01: AUTOSCALING OUR CLUSTER USING CLUSTERAUTOSCALER

In this activity, we are going to run another load test and this time, we are going to run it for longer and observe the changes to the infrastructure as the cluster expands to meet demands. This activity should repeat the previous steps (as shown in *Exercise 15.02, Scaling Workloads in Kubernetes*) to run the load test but this time, it should be done with the ClusterAutoscaler installed so that when your cluster runs out of capacity for the Pods, it will scale the number of nodes to fit the new Pods. The goal of this is to see a load test increase the node count.

Follow these guidelines to complete your activity:

1. We will use the Grafana dashboard to observe the cluster metrics, paying close attention to the number of running Pods and the number of nodes.
2. Our HPA should be set up so that when our application receives more load, we can scale the number of Pods to meet the demand.
3. Ensure that your ClusterAutoscaler has been successfully set up.

> **NOTE**
>
> To fulfill the three aforementioned requirements, you will need to have successfully completed all the exercises in this chapter. We will be using the resources created in those exercises.

4. Run a load test, as shown in *step 2* of *Exercise 15.02*. You may choose a longer or more intense test if you wish.

By the end of this activity, you should be able to observe an increase in the number of nodes by describing the AWS ASG like so:

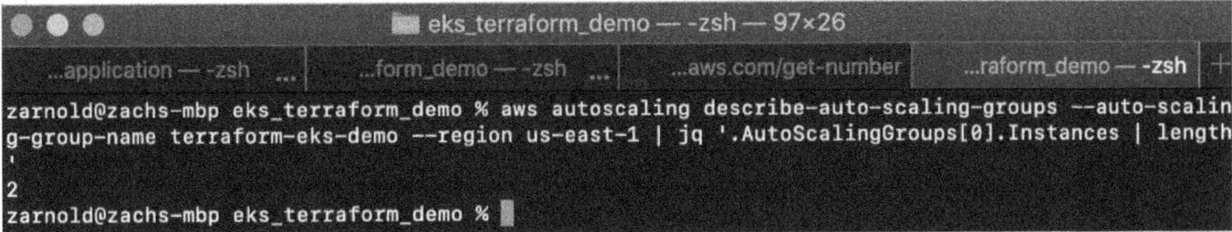

Figure 15.32: Increase in the number of nodes observed by describing the AWS scaling group

You should also be able to observe the same in your Grafana dashboard:

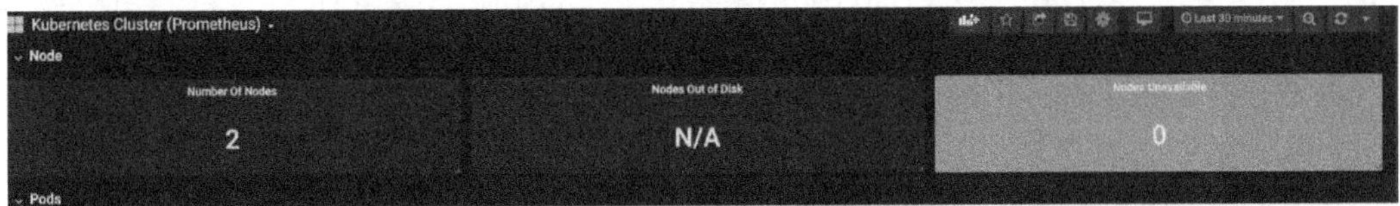

Figure 15.33: Increase in the number of nodes observed in the Grafana dashboard

> **NOTE**
>
> The solution to this activity can be found at the following address: https://packt.live/304PEoD. Make sure you delete the EKS cluster by running the command **`terraform destroy`**.

DELETING YOUR CLUSTER RESOURCES

This is the last chapter where we will use our EKS cluster. Hence, we recommend that you delete your cluster resources using the following command:

```
terraform destroy
```

This should stop the billing for the EKS cluster that we created using Terraform.

SUMMARY

Let's reflect a bit on how far we've come from *Chapter 11, Build Your Own HA Cluster*, when we started to talk about running Kubernetes in a highly available manner. We covered how to set up a production cluster that was secure in the cloud and created using infrastructure as code tools such as Terraform, as well as secured the workloads that it runs. We also looked at necessary modifications to our applications in order to scale them well—both for the stateful and stateless versions of the application.

Then, in this chapter, we looked at how we can extend the management of our application runtimes using data specifically when introducing Prometheus, Grafana, and the Kubernetes Metrics server. We then used that information to leverage the HPA and the ClusterAutoscaler so that we can rest assured that our cluster is always appropriately sized and ready to respond to spikes in demand automatically without having to pay for hardware that is overprovisioned.

In the following series of chapters, we will explore some advanced concepts in Kubernetes, starting with admission controllers in the next chapter.

16

KUBERNETES ADMISSION CONTROLLERS

OVERVIEW

In this chapter, we will learn about Kubernetes admission controllers and use them to modify or validate incoming API requests. This chapter describes the utility of Kubernetes admission controllers and how they offer to extend the capabilities of your Kubernetes cluster. You will learn about several built-in admission controllers and the difference between mutating and validating controllers. By the end of this chapter, you will be able to create your own custom admission controllers and apply this knowledge to build a controller for your required scenario.

INTRODUCTION

In *Chapter 4, How to Communicate with Kubernetes (API Server)*, we learned how Kubernetes exposes its **Application Programming Interface** (**API**) to interact with the Kubernetes platform. You also studied how to use kubectl to create and manage various Kubernetes objects. The kubectl tool is simply a client to the Kubernetes API server. Kubernetes master nodes host the API server through which anyone can communicate with the cluster. The API server provides a way to communicate with Kubernetes for not only external actors but also all internal components, such as the kubelet running on a worker node.

The API server is the central access point to our cluster. If we want to make sure that our organization's default set of best practices and policies are enforced, there is no better place to check for and apply them than at the API server. Kubernetes provides this exact capability via **admission controllers**.

Let's take a moment to understand why admission controllers are useful. Consider, for example, that we have a policy of a standard set of labels in all the objects to assist in the reporting of groups of objects per business unit. This might be important for getting specific data, such as how many Pods are being executed by the integration team. If we are managing and monitoring objects based on their labels, then any objects without the required labels can hamper our management and monitoring practices. Therefore, we would want to implement a policy that will prevent an object from being created if these labels are not defined in the object specification. This requirement can be easily implemented using admission controllers.

> **NOTE**
>
> Open Policy Agent is a good example of how webhooks can be used to build an extensible platform to apply standards on the Kubernetes objects. You can find more details about it at this link: https://www.openpolicyagent.org/docs/latest/kubernetes-admission-control.

Admission controllers are a set of components that intercept all calls to the Kubernetes API server and provide a way to make sure that any requests are meeting the desired criteria. It is important to note that the controllers are invoked after the API call is authenticated and authorized and before the objects are actioned and stored in etcd. This provides a perfect opportunity to implement control and governance, apply standards, and accept or reject the API requests to keep the cluster in the desired shape. Let's take a look at how admission controllers work in the Kubernetes cluster.

HOW ADMISSION CONTROLLERS WORK

Kubernetes provides a set of more than 25 admission controllers. A set of admission controllers is enabled by default and the cluster administrator can pass flags to the API server to control enabling/disabling the additional controllers (configuring the API server in a production-grade cluster is outside the scope of this book). These can be broadly divided into two types:

- **Mutating admission controllers** allow you to modify the request before it gets applied to the Kubernetes platform. **`LimitRanger`** is one such example, which applies the **`defaultRequests`** to the Pod if it is undefined by the Pod itself.
- **Validating admission controllers** validate the request and cannot change the request object. If this controller rejects the request, it will not be actioned by the Kubernetes platform. An example of this would be the **`NamespaceExists`** controller, which rejects the request if the namespace referenced in the request is not available.

Essentially, admission controllers are executed in two phases. In the first phase, mutating admission controllers are executed, and, in the second phase, validating admission controllers are executed.

> **NOTE**
>
> Depending on the situation, it might be a good idea to avoid using mutating controllers because they change the state of the request, and the caller may not be aware of the changes. Instead, you can use a validating controller to reject an invalid request and let the caller fix the request.

A high-level overview of admission controllers is illustrated in the following figure:

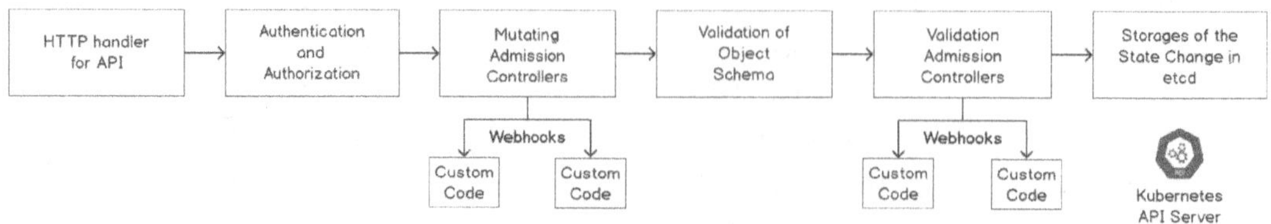

Figure 16.1: Stages of an API request for creating an object

When the Kubernetes API server receives an API call (which can be made via kubectl or the kubelet running on other nodes), it passes the call through the following phases:

1. Perform authentication and authorization of the call to make sure that the caller is authenticated and RBAC policies are applied.
2. Run the payload through all of the existing mutating controllers. Mutating controllers are those that can change the object sent by the client.
3. Check whether the object abides by the defined schema and whether all of the fields are valid.
4. Run the payload through all of the existing validating controllers. These controllers validate the final objects.
5. Store the objects in the etcd datastore.

You can see from *Figure 16.1* that some admission controllers have something called **webhooks** attached to them. This might not be true for all admission controllers. We will learn more about webhooks in the later sections of this chapter.

Note that some of the controllers provide functionality both as mutating and validating controllers. In fact, a few Kubernetes functions are implemented as admission controllers. For example, when a Kubernetes namespace enters the terminating state, the **`NamespaceLifecycle`** admission controller prevents new objects from being created in the terminating namespace.

> **NOTE**
>
> We will only cover a few admission controllers in this chapter for brevity. Please refer to this link for a complete list of the controllers that are available: https://kubernetes.io/docs/reference/access-authn-authz/admission-controllers/#what-does-each-admission-controller-do.

Let's confirm that our Minikube setup is configured to run admission controllers. Run the following command to start Minikube with all of the required plugins enabled:

```
minikube stop
minikube start --extra-config=apiserver.enable-admission-plugins="LimitRan
ger,NamespaceExists,NamespaceLifecycle,ResourceQuota,ServiceAccount,Defau
ltStorageClass,MutatingAdmissionWebhook,ValidatingAdmissionWebhook"
```

You should see a response like the following screenshot:

```
😄  minikube v1.9.2 on Darwin 10.15.5
✨  Using the hyperkit driver based on existing profile
👍  Starting control plane node m01 in cluster minikube
🔄  Restarting existing hyperkit VM for "minikube" ...
🐳  Preparing Kubernetes v1.18.0 on Docker 19.03.8 ...
    ▪ apiserver.enable-admission-plugins=LimitRanger,NamespaceExists,NamespaceL
ifecycle,ResourceQuota,ServiceAccount,DefaultStorageClass,MutatingAdmissionWebh
ook,ValidatingAdmissionWebhook
🌟  Enabling addons: default-storageclass, storage-provisioner
🏄  Done! kubectl is now configured to use "minikube"
```

Figure 16.2: Starting up Minikube with all of the required plugins to run admission controllers

Now that we have had an overview of the built-in admission controllers, let's take a look at how we can make an admission controller using our own custom logic.

CREATING CONTROLLERS WITH CUSTOM LOGIC

As mentioned earlier, Kubernetes provides a list of controllers with predefined functionality. These controllers are baked into the Kubernetes server binary. However, what happens if you need to have your own policy or standard to check against, and none of the admission controllers fit your requirements?

To address such a requirement, Kubernetes provides something called **admission webhooks**. There are two types of admission webhooks, which we will study in the following sections.

THE MUTATING ADMISSION WEBHOOK

The **mutating admission webhook** is a type of mutating admission controller that doesn't have any logic of its own. Instead, it allows you to define a URL that will be called by the Kubernetes API server. This URL is the address to our webhook. Functionally, a webhook is an HTTPS server that accepts requests, processes them, and then responds back.

If multiple URLs are defined, they are processed in a chain, that is, the output of the first webhook becomes the input for the second webhook.

The Kubernetes API server sends a payload (the AdmissionReview object) to the webhook URL with the request being processed. You can modify the request as per your requirement (for example, by adding a custom annotation) and send back a modified request. The Kubernetes API server will use the modified object in the next stages of creating the resource.

The execution flow will be as follows:

1. The Kubernetes API receives a request for creating an object. For example, let's say you want to create a Pod that is defined as follows:

```
apiVersion: v1
kind: Pod
metadata:
  name: configmap-env-pod
spec:
  containers:
    - name: configmap-container
      image: k8s.gcr.io/busybox
      command: [ "/bin/sh", "-c", "sleep 5" ]
```

2. Kubernetes calls a webhook, defined as **MutatingAdmissionWebHook**, and passes the object definition to it. In this case, it's the Pod specification.

3. The webhook (which is the custom code written by you) receives the object and modifies it as per the custom rules. Let's say, for example, it adds the custom annotation, **podModified="true"**. After modification, the object will look like this:

```
apiVersion: v1
kind: Pod
metadata:
  name: configmap-env-pod
  annotations:
    podModified: "true"
spec:
  containers:
    - name: configmap-container
      image: k8s.gcr.io/busybox
      command: [ "/bin/sh", "-c", "sleep 5" ]
```

4. The webhook returns the modified object.
5. Kubernetes will treat the modified object as if it was the original request and move on.

The flow mentioned earlier can be visualized as follows. Note that the flow is simplified so that you can understand the major stages:

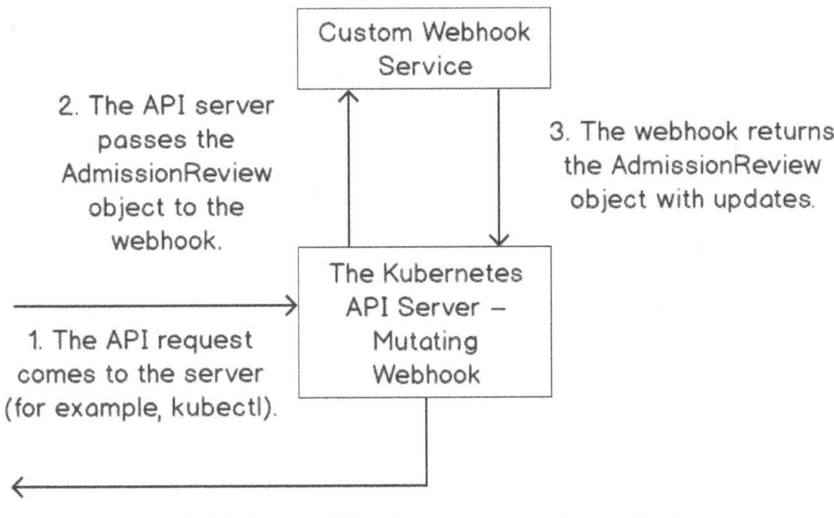

Figure 16.3: Process flow for the mutating admission webhook

THE VALIDATING ADMISSION WEBHOOK

The second type of webhook is the validating admission webhook. This hook, similar to a mutating admission webhook, doesn't have any logic of its own. Following the same pattern, it allows us to define a URL, which ultimately provides the logic that decides to accept or reject this call.

The main difference is that a validating webhook cannot modify the request and can only allow or reject a request. If this webhook rejects the request, Kubernetes will send an error back to the caller; otherwise, it will proceed to execute the request further.

HOW A WEBHOOK WORKS

Webhooks are deployed as Pods in the Kubernetes cluster, and the Kubernetes API server calls them over SSL using the **AdmissionReview** object. This object defines the **AdmissionRequest** and **AdmissionResponse** objects. The webhook reads the request payload from the AdmissionRequest object and provides the success flag and optional changes in the AdmissionResponse object.

The following is a top-level definition of the AdmissionReview object. Note that AdmissionRequest and AdmissionResponse are both part of the AdmissionReview object. The following is an excerpt from the definition of the AdmissionReview object in the Kubernetes source code:

```
// AdmissionReview describes an admission review request/response.
type AdmissionReview struct {
     metav1.TypeMeta `json:",inline"`
     // Request describes the attributes for the admission request.
     // +optional
     Request *AdmissionRequest `json:"request,omitempty"
       protobuf:"bytes,1,opt,name=request"`
     // Response describes the attributes for the admission response.
     // +optional
     Response *AdmissionResponse `json:"response,omitempty"
protobuf:"bytes,2,opt,name=response"`
}
```

> **NOTE**
>
> This snippet is an extract from the Kubernetes source code. You can view more details of the AdmissionReview objects at this link: https://github.com/kubernetes/api/blob/release-1.16/admission/v1beta1/types.go.

The same AdmissionReview object is used for both mutating and validating admission webhooks. A mutating webhook calculates the changes required to meet the custom requirements that you have coded in the webhook. These changes (defined as a patch) are passed in the `patch` field, along with a `patchType` field in the AdmissionResponse object. The API server then applies that patch to the original object and the resultant object is persisted in the API server. To validate the webhook, these two fields are kept empty.

A validating admission webhook would simply set a flag to accept or reject a request, while a mutating admission webhook would set a flag whether or not the request was successfully modified as per the request.

First, let's take a closer look at how we can manually patch an object, which will help you to build a webhook that can patch an object.

You can manually patch an object using the **kubectl patch** command. As an example, let's say that you want to add a field to the **.metadata.annotation** section in an object. To do that, the command would look like this:

```
kubectl patch configmap simple-configmap -n webhooks -p '{"metadata":
{"annotations":  {"new":"annotation"}  } }'
```

Note the double space before and after the field that we want to add (shown in the preceding command as **{"new":"annotation"}**). Let's implement this in an exercise where we will also learn how this command can be used with a JSON payload.

EXERCISE 16.01: MODIFYING A CONFIGMAP OBJECT THROUGH A PATCH

In this exercise, we will patch a ConfigMap using kubectl. We will add an annotation to the ConfigMap object. This annotation can later be used to group objects, similar to the use case that we mentioned in the *Introduction* section. Therefore, if multiple teams are using a cluster, we would want to track which teams are using which resources. Let's begin the exercise:

1. Create a namespace with the name **webhooks**:

   ```
   kubectl create ns webhooks
   ```

   You should see the following response:

   ```
   namespace/webhooks created
   ```

2. Next, create a ConfigMap using the following command:

   ```
   kubectl create configmap simple-configmap --from-literal=url=google.com
   -n webhooks
   ```

   You will see the following response:

   ```
   configmap/simple-configmap created
   ```

3. Check the contents of the ConfigMap using the following command:

```
kubectl get configmap simple-configmap -o yaml -n webhooks
```

You should see the following response:

```
apiVersion: v1
data:
  url: google.com
kind: ConfigMap
metadata:
  creationTimestamp: "2019-08-14T00:29:44Z"
  name: simple-configmap
  namespace: webhooks
  resourceVersion: "708072"
  selfLink: /api/v1/namespaces/webhooks/configmaps/simple-configmap
  uid: 9ce14ece-be2a-11e9-adfa-000c2917147b
```

Figure 16.4: Getting the contents of the ConfigMap in YAML format

4. Now, let's patch the ConfigMap with an annotation. The annotation we want to add is **teamname** with the value of **kubeteam**:

```
kubectl patch configmap simple-configmap -n webhooks -p '{"metadata":
{"annotations":  {"teamname":"kubeteam"}  } }'
```

You will get the following response:

```
configmap/simple-configmap patched
```

In *Chapter 6, Labels and Annotations*, we learned that annotations are stored as key-value pairs. Therefore, a key can have only a value, and if a value already exists for the key (in this case, **teamname**), then the value will be overwritten by the new value. Therefore, ensure your webhook logic excludes the objects that already have the desired configuration.

5. Now, let's apply another patch using detailed patch instructions using JSON format to provide the required field:

```
kubectl patch configmap simple-configmap -n webhooks --type='json'
-p='[{"op": "add", "path": "/metadata/annotations/custompatched",
"value": "true"}]'
```

Note that there are three components of the patch: **op** (for operations such as **add**), **path** (for the location of the fields to patch), and **value** (which is the new value). You should see the following response:

```
configmap/simple-configmap patched
```

This is another way to apply the patch. You can see the preceding command, which is instructing Kubernetes to add a new annotation with the key as **custompatched** and the value as **true**.

6. Now, let's see whether the patch has been applied. Use the following command:

```
kubectl get configmap simple-configmap -n webhooks -o yaml
```

You should see the following output:

```
apiVersion: v1
data:
  url: google.com
kind: ConfigMap
metadata:
  annotations:
    custompatched: "true"
    teamname: kubeteam
  creationTimestamp: "2019-10-18T05:50:50Z"
  name: simple-configmap
  namespace: webhooks
  resourceVersion: "22786"
  selfLink: /api/v1/namespaces/webhooks/configmaps/simple-configmap
  uid: 3d793d1e-f16b-11e9-b05a-000c2917147b
```

Figure 16.5: Checking the modified annotations on our ConfigMap

As you can see from the **annotations** field under **metadata**, both annotations have been applied to our ConfigMap. The platform team now knows who owns this ConfigMap object.

GUIDELINES FOR BUILDING A MUTATING ADMISSION WEBHOOK

We now know all the parts of a working mutating admission webhook. Remember that the webhook is just a simple HTTPS server, and you can write it in your language of choice. Webhooks are deployed in the cluster as Pods. The Kubernetes API server will call these Pods over SSL on port 443 to mutate or validate the objects.

The pseudocode for building a webhook Pod will look like this:

1. A simple HTTPS server (the webhook) is set up in a Pod to accept POST calls. Note that the call must be over SSL.
2. Kubernetes will send the AdmissionReview object to the webhook through an HTTPS POST call.
3. The webhook code will process the AdmissionRequest object to get the details of the object in the request.
4. The webhook code will optionally patch the object and set the response flag to indicate success or failure.
5. The webhook code will populate the AdmissionResponse section in the AdmissionReview object with the updated request.
6. The webhook will respond to the POST call (received in *step 2*) with the AdmissionReview object.
7. The Kubernetes API server will assess the response and, based on the flag, accept or reject the client request.

In the code for the webhook, we will specify the path and required modifications using JSON. Keep in mind from the previous exercise that, while patching, our patch object definition will contain the following:

- **`op`** specifies operations such as **`add`** and **`replace`**.
- **`path`** specifies the location of the field we are trying to modify. Refer to the output of the command in *Figure 16.5* and note that different fields are located in different places. For example, the name is inside the metadata field, so the path for this will be **`/metadata/name`**.
- **`value`** specifies the value of the field.

A simple mutating webhook written in Go should look like the following:

mutatingcontroller.go

```
func MutateCustomAnnotation(admissionRequest *v1beta1.AdmissionRequest ) (*v1beta1.AdmissionResponse, error){

    // Parse the Pod object.
    raw := admissionRequest.Object.Raw
    pod := corev1.Pod{}
    if _, _, err := deserializer.Decode(raw, nil, &pod); err != nil{
            return nil, errors.New("unable to parse pod")
    }

    //create annotation to add
    annotations := map[string]string{"podModified" : "true"}

    //prepare the patch to be applied to the object
    var patch []patchOperation
    patch = append(patch, patchOperation{
            Op:    "add",
            Path: "/metadata/annotations",
            Value: annotations,
    })

    //convert patch into bytes
    patchBytes, err := json.Marshal(patch)
    if err != nil {
            return nil, errors.New("unable to parse the patch")
    }

    //create the response with patch bytes
    var admissionResponse *v1beta1.AdmissionResponse
    admissionResponse = &v1beta1.AdmissionResponse {
            Allowed: true,
            Patch:   patchBytes,
            PatchType: func() *v1beta1.PatchType {
                pt := v1beta1.PatchTypeJSONPatch
                return &pt
            }(),
    }

    //return the response
    return admissionResponse, nil

}
```

The complete code for this example can be found at https://packt.live/2GFRCot.

As you can see in the preceding code, the three main parts are the **AdmissionRequest** object, the **patch**, and the **AdmissionResponse** object with the patched information.

So far, in this chapter, we have learned what the admission webhook is and how it interacts with the Kubernetes API server. We have also demonstrated that one way to change the requested objects is by using a patch. Now, let's apply what we have learned until now and deploy a webhook in our Kubernetes cluster.

Remember that all communications between the API server and the webhook are over SSL. SSL is a protocol that is used for secure communication over a network. To do this, we need to create public and private keys, as you will see in the following exercise.

Note that we have not yet built the code that goes into the webhook. First, let's demonstrate how to deploy the Pods (using Deployment) for a webhook using a pre-built container, and then we will go on to build the code that goes into the Pod to get the webhook up and running.

EXERCISE 16.02: DEPLOYING A WEBHOOK

In this exercise, we'll deploy a simple pre-built webhook server to Kubernetes. Remember that a webhook is just an HTTPS server, and that is exactly what we are going to create. When Kubernetes has to call the webhook endpoint over SSL, we will need to create a certificate for our call. Once we create our certificates for SSL communication, we will use the Kubernetes Deployment object to deploy our webhook:

1. Create a **Certificate Authority** (**CA**) for a self-signed certificate. This CA will be later used to create trust between the Kubernetes and our webhook server for the HTTPS call:

```
openssl req -nodes -new -x509 -keyout controller_ca.key -out
controller_ca.crt -subj "/CN=Mutating Admission Controller Webhook
CA"
```

This should give you the following response:

```
Generating a 2048 bit RSA private key
.............................+++
.........................................+++
writing new private key to 'controller_ca.key'
-----
```

Figure 16.6: Generating a self-signed certificate

> **NOTE**
>
> You can learn more about self-signed certificates at this link: https://aboutssl.org/what-is-self-sign-certificate/.

2. Create the private key for the SSL call:

```
openssl genrsa -out tls.key 2048
```

You should see the following response:

```
$openssl genrsa -out tls.key 2048
Generating RSA private key, 2048 bit long modulus
........+++
...........+++
e is 65537 (0x10001)
$
```

Figure 16.7: Creating the private key for the SSL call

3. Now sign the server certificate with the CA:

```
openssl req -new -key tls.key -subj "/CN=webhook-server.webhooks.svc"
\
    | openssl x509 -req -CA controller_ca.crt -CAkey controller_
ca.key -CAcreateserial -out tls.crt
```

Note that the name of the service in this command is the service that is going to expose our webhook within the cluster so that the API server can access it. We will revisit this name in *step 7*. You should see the following response:

```
Signature ok
subject=/CN=webhook-server.webhooks.svc
Getting CA Private Key
```

4. Now we have created a certificate that our server can use. Next, we will just create a Kubernetes Secret to load the private key and certificate to our webhook server:

```
kubectl -n webhooks create secret tls webhook-server-tls \
    --cert "tls.crt" \
    --key "tls.key"
```

You should see the following response:

```
secret/webhook-server-tls created
```

5. Our webhook will run as a Pod, which we will create using a Deployment. To do that, first, create a file named **mutating-server.yaml** with the following content:

```
apiVersion: apps/v1
kind: Deployment
metadata:
  name: webhook-server
  labels:
    app: webhook-server
spec:
  replicas: 1
  selector:
    matchLabels:
      app: webhook-server
  template:
    metadata:
      labels:
        app: webhook-server
    spec:
      containers:
      - name: server
        image: packtworkshops/the-kubernetes-
          workshop:mutating-webhook
        imagePullPolicy: Always
        ports:
        - containerPort: 8443
          name: webhook-api
        volumeMounts:
        - name: webhook-tls-certs
          mountPath: /etc/secrets/tls
          readOnly: true
      volumes:
      - name: webhook-tls-certs
        secret:
          secretName: webhook-server-tls
```

Note that we are linking to the premade image for the server that we have provided.

6. Create a Deployment using the YAML file that we created in the previous step:

```
kubectl create -f mutating-server.yaml -n webhooks
```

You should see the following response:

```
deployment.apps/webhook-server created
```

7. Once the server is created, we need to create a Kubernetes Service. Note that the Service is accessible through **webhook-server.webhooks.svc**. This string, which we used in *step 3* while creating the certificate, is based on the fields defined in the following specification, in the format of **<SERVICENAME>.<NAMESPACENAME>.svc**.

   Create a file, named **mutating-serversvc.yaml**, to define a Service with the following specification:

```
apiVersion: v1
kind: Service
metadata:
  labels:
    app: webhook-server
  name: webhook-server
  namespace: webhooks
spec:
  ports:
  - port: 443
    protocol: TCP
    targetPort: 8443
  selector:
    app: webhook-server
  sessionAffinity: None
  type: ClusterIP
```

8. Using the definition from the previous step, create the Service using the following command:

```
kubectl create -f mutating-serversvc.yaml -n webhooks
```

You should see the following response:

```
service/webhook-server created
```

In this exercise, we have deployed a pre-built webhook and configured certificates such that our webhook is ready to accept calls from the Kubernetes API server.

CONFIGURING THE WEBHOOK TO WORK WITH KUBERNETES

At this stage, we have created and deployed the webhook using a Deployment. Now, we need to register the webhook with Kubernetes so that Kubernetes knows about it. The way to do this is by creating a **MutatingWebHookConfiguration** object.

> **NOTE**
>
> You can find more details about MutatingConfigurationWebhook at https://kubernetes.io/docs/reference/access-authn-authz/extensible-admission-controllers/.

The following snippet shows an example of what the configuration object for **MutatingWebhookConfiguration** would look like:

```
apiVersion: admissionregistration.k8s.io/v1beta1
kind: MutatingWebhookConfiguration
metadata:
  name: pod-annotation-webhook
webhooks:
- name: webhook-server.webhooks.svc
   clientConfig:
     service:
       name: webhook-server
       namespace: webhooks
       path: "/mutate"
     caBundle: "LS0..."    #The caBundle is truncated for brevity
   rules:
     - operations: [ "CREATE" ]
       apiGroups: [""]
       apiVersions: ["v1"]
       resources: ["pods"]
```

Here are a few notable definitions from the preceding object:

1. The **clientConfig.service** section defines the location of the mutating webhook (which we deployed in *Exercise 16.02, Deploying a Webhook*).
2. The **caBundle** section contains the certificate through which SSL trust will be established. This is the certificate, encoded in Base64 format. We will explain how to encode it in the next section.
3. The **rules** section defines what operations need to be intercepted. Here, we are instructing Kubernetes to intercept any calls to create a new Pod.

HOW TO ENCODE A CERTIFICATE IN BASE64 FORMAT

As pointed out earlier, when the Kubernetes API server calls the webhook, the call is encrypted over SSL, and we need to provide the SSL trust certificate in the webhook definition. This can be seen in the **caBundle** field in the definition of **MutatingWebhookConfiguration** shown in the previous section. The data in this field is Base64-encoded, as you learned in *Chapter 10, ConfigMaps and Secrets*. The following commands can be used to encode a certificate in Base64 format.

First, convert the generated file into Base64 format using the following command:

```
openssl base64 -in controller_ca.crt -out controller_ca-base64.crt
```

Since we need to convert the generated CA bundle into the Base64 format and put it in the YAML file (as mentioned earlier), we need to remove the newline (**\n**) characters. The following commands could be used to do this:

```
cat controller_ca-base64.crt | tr -d '\n' > onelinecert.pem
```

Both of these commands do not show any response in the terminal upon successful execution. At this stage, you will have the CA bundle inside the **onelinecert.pem** file, which you can copy to create your YAML definitions.

ACTIVITY 16.01: CREATING A MUTATING WEBHOOK THAT ADDS AN ANNOTATION TO A POD

In this activity, we are using the knowledge we have acquired in this and earlier chapters to create a mutating webhook that adds a custom annotation to a Pod. There can be many use cases for such a webhook. For example, you might want to record whether the container image is coming from the previously approved repository or not, for future reporting. Extending this further, you can also schedule Pods from different repositories on different nodes.

The high-level steps for completing this activity are as follows:

1. Create a new namespace named **webhooks**. If it exists already, delete the existing namespace and then create it again.
2. Generate the self-signed CA certificate.
3. Generate a private/public key pair for SSL and sign it with the CA certificate.
4. Create a secret that holds the private/public key pair generated in the previous step.
5. Write the webhook code to add a custom annotation in the Pod.
6. Package the webhook server code as a Docker container.
7. Push the Docker container to a public repository of your choice.

> **NOTE**
>
> If you have any difficulty building your own webhook, you can use the code available at this link as a reference: https://packt.live/2R1vJlk.
>
> If you want to avoid building and packaging a webhook, we have provided a pre-built container so that you can use it directly in your Deployment. You can use this image from Docker Hub: **packtworkshops/the-kubernetes-workshop:webhook**.
>
> Using this image allows you to skip *steps 5* to *7*.

8. Create a Deployment that deploys the webhook server.
9. Expose the webhooks Deployment as a Kubernetes Service.

10. Create a Base64-encoded version of the CA certificate.

11. Create a **MutatingWebHookConfiguration** object so that Kubernetes can intercept the API call and call our webhook.

At this stage, our webhook has been created. Now, to test whether our webhook is working, create a simple Pod with no annotations.

Once the Pod is created, make sure that the annotation is added to the Pod by describing it. Here is a truncated version of the expected output. Note that the annotation here is supposed to be added by our webhook:

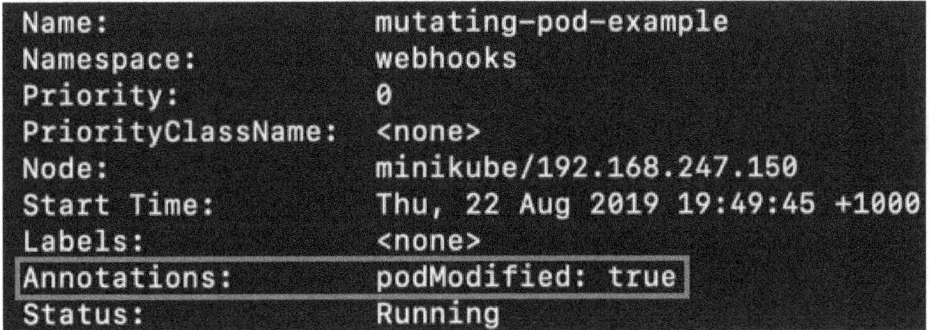

Name: mutating-pod-example
Namespace: webhooks
Priority: 0
PriorityClassName: <none>
Node: minikube/192.168.247.150
Start Time: Thu, 22 Aug 2019 19:49:45 +1000
Labels: <none>
Annotations: podModified: true
Status: Running

Figure 16.8: Expected output of Activity 16.01

> **NOTE**
>
> The solution to this activity can be found on page 799.

VALIDATING A WEBHOOK

We have learned that the mutating webhook essentially allows the modification of Kubernetes objects. The other kind of webhook is called a validating webhook. As the name suggests, this webhook does not allow any change in the Kubernetes objects; instead, it works as a gatekeeper to our cluster. It allows us to write code that can validate any Kubernetes object being requested and allow or reject the request based on the conditions that we specify.

Let's understand how this can be helpful using an example. Let's assume that our Kubernetes cluster is used by many teams, and we want to know which Pods are associated with which teams. One solution is to ask all the teams to add a label on their Pod (for example, a label with the key as **teamName** and the name of the team as the value). As you can guess, it is not a standard Kubernetes feature to enforce a set of labels. In this case, we would need to create our own logic to disallow Pods that do not have these labels.

One way to achieve this is to write a validating webhook that looks for this label in any requests for Pods and reject the creation of the requested Pods if this label does not exist. You are going to do exactly this in *Activity 16.02, Creating a Validating Webhook that Checks for a Label in a Pod* later in the chapter. For now, let's take a look at what the code for a validating webhook will look like.

CODING A SIMPLE VALIDATING WEBHOOK

Let's take a look at an excerpt from the code for a simple validating webhook:

```
func ValidateTeamAnnotation(admissionRequest
  *v1beta1.AdmissionRequest ) (*v1beta1.AdmissionResponse, error){

      // Get the AdmissionReview Object
      raw := admissionRequest.Object.Raw
      pod := corev1.Pod{}

     // Parse the Pod object.
      if _, _, err := deserializer.Decode(raw, nil, &pod);
        err != nil {
            return nil, errors.New("unable to parse pod")
      }

      //Get all the Labels of the Pod
      podLabels := pod.ObjectMeta.GetLabels()

      //Logic to check if label exists
      //check if the teamName label is available, if not
        generate an error.
      if podLabels == nil || podLabels[teamNameLabel] == "" {
           return nil, errors.New("teamName label not found")
      }

      //Populate the Allowed flag
      //if the teamName label exists, return the response with
```

```
        //Allowed flag set to true.
        var admissionResponse *v1beta1.AdmissionResponse
        admissionResponse = &v1beta1.AdmissionResponse {
            Allowed: true,
        }

        //Return the response with Allowed set to true
        return admissionResponse, nil

}
const (
        //This is the name of the label that is expected to be
          part of the pods to allow them to be created.
        teamNameLabel = `teamName`

)
```

The three main parts that you can observe in this snippet are the AdmissionRequest object, the logic to check whether the label exists, and creating the AdmissionResponse object with the Allowed flag.

Now that we understand all the different components required for a validating webhook, let's build one in the following activity.

ACTIVITY 16.02: CREATING A VALIDATING WEBHOOK THAT CHECKS FOR A LABEL IN A POD

In this activity, we will use the knowledge that we have acquired in this and earlier chapters to write a validating webhook that verifies whether a label is present in the requested Pod.

The required steps are as follows:

1. Create a new namespace named **webhooks**. If it exists already, delete the existing namespace and then create it again.
2. Generate the self-signed CA certificate.
3. Generate a private/public key pair for SSL and sign it with the CA certificate.
4. Create a secret that holds the private/public key pair generated in the previous step.

> **NOTE**
>
> Even if you have the certificates and secrets from the previous activity, we recommend that you discard them and start afresh to avoid any conflicts.

5. Write the webhook code to check whether a label with the key **`teamName`** is present. If it is not present, reject the request.
6. Package the webhook code as a Docker container.
7. Push the Docker container to a public repository of your choice (quay.io allows you to create a free public repository).

> **NOTE**
>
> If you have any difficulty in building your own webhook, you can use the code available at this link as a reference: https://packt.live/2FbL7Jv.
>
> If you want to avoid building and packaging a webhook, we have provided a pre-built container so that you can use it directly in your Deployment. You can use this image from Docker Hub: **`packtworkshops/the-kubernetes-workshop:webhook`**.
>
> Using this image allows you to skip *steps 5* to *7*.

8. Create a Deployment that deploys the webhook server.
9. Expose the webhooks Deployment as a Kubernetes service.
10. Create a Base64-encoded version of the CA certificate.
11. Create **`ValidtingWebhookConfiguration`** so that Kubernetes can intercept the API call and call our webhook.
12. Create a simple Pod with no labels and verify that it is being rejected.
13. Create a simple Pod with the desired labels and verify that it is being created.
14. Once the Pod is created, make sure that the label is part of the Pod specifications.

You can test your validating webhook by trying to create a Pod without the **teamName** label. It should get rejected with the following message:

```
Error from server: error when creating "target-validating-pod.yaml":
 admission webhook "webhook-server.webhooks.svc" denied the request:
 labels not found
```

Figure 16.9: Expected output of the Activity 16.02

> **NOTE**
>
> The solution to this activity can be found at the following address: https://packt.live/304PEoD.

CONTROLLING THE EFFECT OF A WEBHOOK ON SELECTED NAMESPACES

When you define any webhook (mutating or validating), you can control which namespaces will be affected by the webhook by defining the **namespaceSelector** parameter. Note that this is only applicable to objects that are namespace-scoped. For cluster-scoped objects, such as persistent volumes, this parameter will make no difference, and the webhook will be applied.

> **NOTE**
>
> Not all admission controllers (mutating or validating) can be restricted to a namespace.

Just like many Kubernetes objects, namespaces can also have labels. We will use this property of namespaces to apply a webhook on specific namespaces, as you will see in the following exercise.

EXERCISE 16.03: CREATING A VALIDATING WEBHOOK WITH THE NAMESPACE SELECTOR DEFINED

In this exercise, we will define a validating webhook that enforces a custom rule to be applied to Pods created in a **webhooks** namespace. The rule is that the Pod must define a label called **teamName**. Since the rule is applicable to Pods created in the **webhooks-demo** namespace, all other namespaces can create Pods without the label defined.

> **NOTE**
>
> Before running this exercise, make sure that you have completed *Activity 16.02, Creating a Validating Webhook that Checks for a Label in a Pod* as we are reusing the objects created there. You can refer to the solution in the *Appendix* if you are facing any issues with the activity.

1. Verify that the validating webhook we created in *Activity 16.02, Creating a Validating Webhook that Checks for a Label in a Pod*, still exists:

```
kubectl get ValidatingWebHookConfiguration -n webhooks
```

You will see the following response:

```
NAME                         CREATED AT
pod-label-verify-webhook     201908-23T13:59:30Z
```

2. Now, delete the preexisting validating webhook defined in *Activity 16.02, Creating a Validating Webhook that Checks for a Label in a Pod*:

```
kubectl delete ValidatingWebHookConfiguration pod-label-verify-webhook
-n webhooks
```

> **NOTE**
>
> The **ValidatingWebHookConfiguration** is a cluster scoped object, and specifying the **-n** flag is optional for this command.

You will get the following response:

```
validatingwebhookconfiguration.admissionregistration.k8s.io "pod-label-verify-webhook" deleted
```

Figure 16.10: Deleting the existing validating webhook

3. Delete the **webhooks** namespace:

```
kubectl delete ns webhooks
```

You will get the following response:

```
namespace "webhooks" deleted
```

4. Create the **webhooks** namespace:

```
kubectl create ns webhooks
```

You will get the following response:

```
namespace/webhooks created
```

Now we should have a clean slate to continue with this exercise.

5. Create a new CA bundle and a private/public key pair to be used in this webhook. Generate a self-signed certificate using this command:

```
openssl req -nodes -new -x509 -keyout controller_ca.key -out
controller_ca.crt -subj "/CN=Mutating Admission Controller Webhook
CA"
```

You will get an output similar to the following:

```
Generating a 2048 bit RSA private key
.........................+++
...............................................................................................+++
writing new private key to 'controller_ca.key'
-----
```

Figure 16.11: Generating a self-signed certificate

> **NOTE**
>
> Even if you have created the CA and keys in the previous activity, you will need to recreate them for this exercise to work properly.

6. Generate a private/public key pair and sign it with the CA certificate using the following two commands, one after the other:

```
openssl genrsa -out tls.key 2048


openssl req -new -key tls.key -subj "/CN=webhook-server.webhooks.svc"
\
    | openssl x509 -req -CA controller_ca.crt -CAkey controller_
ca.key -CAcreateserial -out tls.crt
```

You will get an output that is similar to the following response:

```
Generating RSA private key, 2048 bit long modulus
.........................................................................................+++
......+++
e is 65537 (0x10001)
$openssl req -new -key tls.key -subj "/CN=webhook-server.webhooks.svc" \
>     | openssl x509 -req -CA controller_ca.crt -CAkey controller_ca.key -CAcreateserial -out tls.crt
Signature ok
subject=/CN=webhook-server.webhooks.svc
Getting CA Private Key
```

Figure 16.12: Signing a private/public key pair with our certificate

7. Create a secret that holds the private/public key pair:

```
kubectl -n webhooks create secret tls webhook-server-tls \
--cert "tls.crt" \
--key "tls.key"
```

You should get the following response:

```
secret/webhook-server-tls created
```

8. Next, we need to deploy the webhook in the **webhooks** namespace. Create a file named **validating-server.yaml** with the following content:

```
apiVersion: apps/v1
kind: Deployment
metadata:
  name: webhook-server
  labels:
    app: webhook-server
spec:
  replicas: 1
  selector:
    matchLabels:
      app: webhook-server
  template:
    metadata:
      labels:
        app: webhook-server
    spec:
      containers:
      - name: server
        image: packtworkshops/the-kubernetes-workshop:webhook
        imagePullPolicy: Always
```

```
        ports:
        - containerPort: 8443
          name: webhook-api
        volumeMounts:
        - name: webhook-tls-certs
          mountPath: /etc/secrets/tls
          readOnly: true
      volumes:
      - name: webhook-tls-certs
        secret:
          secretName: webhook-server-tls
```

> **NOTE**
>
> You can use the same webhook image created in *Activity 16.02, Creating a Validating Webhook That Checks for a Label in a Pod*. In this reference YAML, we are using the image that we have provided in our repository.

9. Deploy the webhook server by using the definition from the previous step:

```
kubectl create -f validating-server.yaml -n webhooks
```

You should see the following response:

```
deployment.apps/webhook-server created
```

10. You might need to wait a bit and check whether the webhook Pods have been created. Keep checking the status of the Pods:

```
kubectl get pods -n webhooks -w
```

You should see the following response:

```
NAME                              READY   STATUS              RESTARTS   AGE
webhook-server-68b8d6b987-fbv95   0/1     ContainerCreating   0          12s
webhook-server-68b8d6b987-fbv95   1/1     Running             0          15s
^C$
```

Figure 16.13: Checking whether our webhook is online

Note that the **-w** flag continuously watches the Pods. You can end the watch when all of the Pods are ready.

11. Now, we have to expose the deployed webhook server via the Kubernetes service. Create a file named **validating-serversvc.yaml** with the following content:

```
apiVersion: v1
kind: Service
metadata:
  labels:
    app: webhook-server
  name: webhook-server
  namespace: webhooks
spec:
  ports:
  - port: 443
    protocol: TCP
    targetPort: 8443
  selector:
    app: webhook-server
  sessionAffinity: None
  type: ClusterIP
```

Note that the webhook service has to be running on port **443**, as this is the standard for TLS communication.

12. Use the definition from the previous step to create the service using the following command:

```
kubectl create -f validating-serversvc.yaml -n webhooks
```

You will see the following output:

```
service/webhook-server created
```

13. Create a Base64-encoded version of the CA certificate. Use the following commands, one after the other:

```
openssl x509 -inform PEM -in controller_ca.crt > controller_ca.crt.
pem

openssl base64 -in controller_ca.crt.pem -out controller_ca-base64.
crt.pem
```

The first command is to convert the certificate into a PEM format. And the second one is to convert the PEM certificate into Base64. These commands show no response. You can inspect the file using the following command:

```
cat controller_ca-base64.crt.pem
```

The file contents should be something like this:


```
LS0tLS1CRUdJTiBDRVJUSUZJQ0FURS0tLS0tCk1JSUM0akNDQWNvQ0NRRHNPMFph
Q0swMDVUQU5CZ2txaGtpRzl3MEJBUXNGQURBek1URXdMd1lEVlFRRERDaE4KZFhS
aGRHbHVaeUJCWkcxcGMzTnBiMjRnUTI5dWRISnZiR3hsY21lCWFpXSm9iMjlySUVO
Qk1CNFhEVEU1TURneQpNakEwTWpBeU0xb1hEVEU1TURreU1UQTBNakF5TTFvd016
RXhNQzhHQTFVRUF3d29UWFYwWVhScGJtY2dRV1J0CmFYTnphVzl1SUVOdmJuUnli
MnhzWlhJZ1YyVmlhRzl2YXlCRFFUQ0NBU0l3RFFZSktvWklodmNOQVFFQkJRQUQK
Z2dFUEFEQ0NBUW9DZ2dFQkFLbnVhT1pIcml2TDNIZ3oxbHhrVVdnczY0ei9DVFRV
OTRjOGhLTkdNdHdvMGt6SwpxWXR4NnQ5MTIxNWc0Q0dsbE0zM0pEamljd21XRUJW
dkNDNWFYbEtDc1d6STlHS1ZtVEFESW80RFpDSXhvaHBNClR5TkhPZUxTbDJlSllY
c2V2cEowRnRBSlRJZ0ZkRm52UUlYYUNYUkJyYVdNV3JpUWZnZGsvaThyQzJveWsw
blEKRElQb3ljVEFBcmlSZ0FvZnBTek9nZnVqc3ZJeEViaDYvMnNRaHY5M25icFFR
TWNHKzNkWHVpWjZweTFTRDArYQplSThXRUFoMDQ0MXpaWGRDOEI5OHlndldCWWdo
QUN3dUIzdHFKeEdjbzdDZ011NkVWQXZVTFNvSlA3a0VQS3VTCnRtbHYvUm16Vm5P
NWx5NkI1Y1BjOGRKYk1WKzROZVNObngxNmc0MENBd0VBQVRBTkJna3Foa2lHOXcw
QkFRc0YKQUFPQ0FRRUFpVC96Q0F1dVR6OFhsSlduczIwWGIwSmJGcE4vZDZKN3hU
VGp5S0k3SU9rRW9zaUZaSDg3ZDB3NgpYd3JBTnZiR2NIdlhOZHRRTkY3S3ArZ1k1
RzFSeFV3V3BEUnpjdVlrOEVWWnJCMDNhM2JDVXl4ejZmRkUxanlUCmcvMmdKSFhV
d005Yy92LzhOZ2NNa2ZtdFlLeGErREV6anQ3V2oxbDFUYlVFM3NCK1ZFalVYYWFt
Z3pyZEJFRHQKQmhVejhVZE1sUUVONVNEVWtHNlJzTkV1MWJ1dml0cHlYVGdOb0tB
ZWVQWkU5Rk5NME51SmJVbVVacWsyejhTNgpDUVRjOUtSU0piR203bGUrV1ptYnBy
NzJGcG9GbmZhbXdHUDJVODIxOTQ2TWVROXFiRGVwSXNFSURlTXlUeEdOClcxZWdr
eFVodVdSdTVGbmZkd2ZYT1ZlaEhiMDlwdz09Ci0tLS0tRU5EIENFUlRJRklDQVRF
LS0tLS0K
```


Figure 16.14: Contents of the Base64-encoded CA certificate

Please note that the TLS certificates you generate will not look exactly like what is shown here.

14. Use the following two commands to clean up the blank lines from our CA certificate and add the contents to a new file:

```
cat controller_ca-base64.crt.pem | tr -d '\n' > onelinecert.pem

cat onelinecert.pem
```

The first command shows no response, and the second one prints out the contents of **onlinecert.pem**. You should see the following response:


```
$cat controller_ca-base64.crt.pem | tr -d '\n' > onelinecert.txt
$cat onelinecert.txt
LS0tLS1CRUdJTiBDRVJUSUZJQ0FURS0tLS0tCk1JSUM0akNDQWNvQ0NRRHNPMFphQ0swMDVUQU5CZ2txaGtpRzl3MEJBUXNGQURBek1URXd
Md1lEVlFRRERDaE4KZFhSaGRHbHVaeUJCWkcxcGMzTnBiMjRnUTI5dWRISnZiR3hsY2lCWFpXSm9iMjlySUVOQk1CNFhEVEU1TURneQpNak
EwTWpBeU0xb1hEVEU1TURreU1UQTBNakF5TTFvd016RXhNQzhHQTFVRUF3d29UWFYwWVhScGJtY2dRV1J0CmFYTnphVzl1SUVOdmJuUnliiM
hhzWlhJZ1YyVmlhRzl2YXlCRFFUQ0NBU013RFFZSktvWklodmNOQVFFQkJRQUQKZ2dFUEFEQ0NBUW9DZ2dFQkFLbnVhT1pIcml2TDNIZ3ox
bHhrVVdnczY0ei9DVFRVOTRjOGhLTkdNdHdvMGt6SwpxWXR4NnQ5MTIxNWc0Q0dsbE0zM0pEamljd21XRUJWdkNDNWFYbEtDc1d6STlHS1Z
tVEFESW80RFpDSXhvaHBNClR5TkhPZUxTbDJlSllYc2V2cEowRnRBS1RJZ0ZkRm52UUlYYUNYUkJyYVdNV3JpUWZnZGsvaThyQzJveWswbl
EKRElQb3ljVEFBcmlSZ0FvZnBTek9nZnVqc3ZJeEViaDYvMnNRaHY5M25icFFRTWNHKzNkWHVpWjZweTFTRDArYQplSThXRUFoMDQ0MXpaW
GRDOEI5OHlndldCWWdoQUN3dUIzdHFKeEdjbzdDZ011NkVWQXZVTFNvSlA3a0VQS3VTCnRtbHYvUm16Vm5PNWx5NkI1Y1BjOGRKYk1WKzRO
ZVNObngxNmc0MENBd0VBQVRBTkJna3Foa2lHOXcwQkFRc0YKQUFPQ0FRRUFpVC96Q0F1dVR6OFhsSlducz IwWGIwSmJGcE4vZDZKN3hUVGp
5S0k3SU9rRW9zaUZaSDg3ZDB3NgpYd3JBTnZiR2NIdlhOZHRRTkY3S3ArZ1k1RzFSeFV3V3BEUnpjdVlrOEVWWnJCMDNhM2JDVXl4ejZmRk
UxanlUCmcvMmdKSFhVd005Yy92LzhOZ2NNa2ZtdFlLeGErREV6anQ3V2oxbDFUYlVFM3NCK1ZFalVYYWFtZ3pyZEJFRHQKQmhVejhVZE1sU
UVONVNEVWtHNlJzTkVlMWJ1dml0cHlYVGdOb0tBZWVQWkU5Rk5NME51SmJVbVVacWsyejhTNgpDUVRjOUtSU0piR203bGUrV1ptYnByNzJG
cG9GbmZhbXdHUDJVODIxOTQ2TWVROXFiRGVwSXNFSURlTXlUeEdOClcxZWdreFVodVdSdTVGbmZkd2ZYT1ZlaEhiMDlwdz09Ci0tLS0tRU5
EIENFUlRJRklDQVRFLS0tLS0K$
```


Figure 16.15: Base64-encoded CA certificate with the line breaks removed

Now we have the Base64-encoded certificate with no blank lines. For the next step, we will copy the value that you get in this output, being careful not to copy the **$** (which would be **%**, in the case of Zsh) at the end of the value. Paste this value in place of **CA_BASE64_PEM** (a placeholder for **caBundle**) in **validation-config-namespace-scoped.yaml**, which will be created in the next step.

15. Create a file, named **validation-config-namespace-scoped.yaml**, using the following **ValidatingWebHookConfiguration** specification to configure the Kubernetes API server to call our webhook:

```
apiVersion: admissionregistration.k8s.io/v1beta1
kind: ValidatingWebhookConfiguration
metadata:
  name: pod-label-verify-webhook
webhooks:
  - name: webhook-server.webhooks.svc
    namespaceSelector:
      matchExpressions:
      - key: applyValidation
        operator: In
        values: ["true","yes", "1"]

    clientConfig:
      service:
        name: webhook-server
        namespace: webhooks
```

```
      path: "/validate"
    caBundle: "CA_BASE64_PEM"     #Retain the quotes when you
      copy the caBundle here. Please read the note below on
      how to add specific values here.
  rules:
    - operations: [ "CREATE" ]
      apiGroups: [""]
      apiVersions: ["v1"]
      resources: ["pods"]
      scope: "Namespaced"
```

> **NOTE**
>
> The **CA_BASE64_PEM** placeholder will be replaced with the contents of **onelinecert.pem** from the previous step. Be careful not to copy any line breaks.

16. Create the webhook, as defined in the previous step. Make sure that you replace the **caBundle** field with the certificates created in the earlier steps:

```
kubectl create -f validation-config-namespace-scoped.yaml
```

You should see the following response:

```
validatingwebhookconfiguration.admissionregistration.k8s.io/pod-label-verify-webhook created
```

Figure 16.16: Creating the ValidatingWebhookConfiguration

17. Create a new namespace, called **webhooks-demo**, as follows:

```
kubectl create namespace webhooks-demo
```

You should see the following response:

```
namespace/webhooks-demo created
```

18. Apply the **applyValidation=true** label to the **webhooks** namespace, as shown here:

```
kubectl label namespace webhooks applyValidation=true
```

You should see the following response:

```
namespace/webhooks labeled
```

This label will match the selector defined in *step 14* and make sure our validation criteria (enforced by the webhook) applies to this namespace. Note that we don't label the **webhooks-demo** namespace, so the validation will *not* apply to this namespace.

19. Now define a Pod without the **teamName** label. Create a file named **target-validating-pod.yaml** with the following content:

```
apiVersion: v1
kind: Pod
metadata:
  name: validating-pod-example
spec:
  containers:
    - name: validating-pod-example-container
      image: k8s.gcr.io/busybox
      command: [ "/bin/sh", "-c", "while :; do echo '.'; sleep
        5 ; done" ]
```

20. Based on the definition from the previous step, create the Pod in the **webhooks** namespace:

```
kubectl create -f target-validating-pod.yaml -n webhooks
```

The creation of the Pod should get rejected as follows:

```
Error from server: error when creating "target-validating-pod.yaml": admission webhook "web
hook-server.webhooks.svc" denied the request: teamName label not found
```

Figure 16.17: Pod rejected due to the absence of the required label

Keep in mind that our webhook just checks the **teamName** label in the Pod. The Pod creation is rejected as per our namespace selector in the definition from *step 14*.

21. Now, try creating the same Pod in the **webhooks-demo** namespace to see whether things go differently:

```
kubectl create -f target-validating-pod.yaml -n webhooks-demo
```

You should get this response:

```
pod/validating-pod-example created
```

We were able to successfully create the Pod in the **webhooks-demo** namespace, but we were not able to do so in the **webhooks** namespace.

22. Let's describe the Pod to get more details:

```
kubectl describe pod validating-pod-example -n webhooks-demo
```

You should see a response similar to this:

```
Name:                validating-pod-example
Namespace:           webhooks-demo
Priority:            0
PriorityClassName:   <none>
Node:                minikube/192.168.247.150
Start Time:          Sun, 25 Aug 2019 00:14:21 +1000
Labels:              <none>
Annotations:         podModified: true
Status:              Running
IP:                  172.17.0.8
```

Figure 16.18: Checking the specification of our Pod

As you can see, this Pod does not have any labels, and yet we were able to create it. This is because our validating webhook is not watching the **webhooks-demo** namespace.

In this exercise, you have learned how a webhook can be configured to make changes at the namespace level. This could be useful to test functionality and provide different functionality to different teams that might own different namespaces.

SUMMARY

In this chapter, we learned that admission controllers provide a way to enforce the mutation and validation of objects during create, update, and delete operations. It is an easy way to extend the Kubernetes platform to adhere to the standards of your organization. They can be used to apply the best practices and policies onto the Kubernetes cluster.

Next, we learned what mutating and validating webhooks are, how to configure them, and how to deploy them on the Kubernetes platform. Webhooks provide a simple way to extend Kubernetes and help you to adapt to the requirements of a particular enterprise.

In the previous series of chapters, starting from *Chapter 11, Build Your Own HA Cluster*, to *Chapter 15, Monitoring and Autoscaling in Kubernetes*, you learned how to set up your highly-available cluster on AWS and run stateless, as well as stateful, applications. In the next few chapters, you will learn many advanced skills that will help you go beyond just running applications, and enable you to leverage many of the powerful administration features offered by Kubernetes and maintain the health of your cluster.

Specifically, in the next chapter, you will learn about the Kubernetes scheduler. This is a component that decides the nodes on which a Pod will be scheduled. You will also learn how to configure the scheduler to adhere to your needs and how you can control Pod placement on a node.

17

ADVANCED SCHEDULING IN KUBERNETES

OVERVIEW

This chapter focuses on scheduling, which is the process by which Kubernetes selects a node for running a Pod. In this chapter, we will take a closer look at this process and the Kubernetes Scheduler, which is the default Kubernetes component responsible for this process.

By the end of this chapter, you will be able to use different ways to control the behavior of the Kubernetes Scheduler to suit the requirements of an application. The chapter will equip you to be able to choose appropriate Pod scheduling methods to control which nodes you want to run your Pods on based on your business needs. You will learn about the different ways to control the scheduling of Pods on the Kubernetes cluster.

INTRODUCTION

We have seen that we package our applications as containers and deploy them as a Pod in Kubernetes, which is the minimal unit of Deployment. With the help of the advanced scheduling capabilities provided by Kubernetes, we can optimize the deployment of these Pods with respect to our hardware infrastructure to meet our needs and get the most out of the available resources.

Kubernetes clusters generally have more than a few nodes (or machines or hosts) where the Pod can be executed. Consider that you are managing a few of the machines and you have been assigned to execute an application on these machines. What would you do to decide which machine is the best fit for the given application? Until now in this workshop, whenever you wanted to run a Pod on a Kubernetes cluster, have you mentioned which node(s) the Pod should run on?

That's right – we don't need to; Kubernetes comes with a smart component that finds the best node to run your Pod. This component is the **Kubernetes Scheduler**. In this chapter, we will look a bit more deeply into how the Kubernetes Scheduler works, and how to adapt it to better control our cluster to suit different needs.

THE KUBERNETES SCHEDULER

As mentioned in the introduction, a typical cluster has several nodes. When you create a Pod, Kubernetes has to choose a node and assign the Pod to it. This process is known as **Pod scheduling**.

The Kubernetes component that is responsible for deciding which node a Pod should be assigned to for execution is called a scheduler. Kubernetes comes with a default scheduler that suffices for most use cases. For example, the default Kubernetes Scheduler spreads the load evenly in the cluster.

Now, consider a scenario in which two different Pods are expected to communicate with each other very often. As a system architect, you may want them to be on the same node to reduce latency and free up some internal networking bandwidth. The Scheduler does not know the relationship between different types of Pods, but Kubernetes provides ways to inform the Scheduler about this relationship and influence the scheduling behavior so that these two different Pods can be hosted on the same node. But first, let's take a closer look at the Pod **scheduling process**.

THE POD SCHEDULING PROCESS

The scheduler works in a three-step process: **filtering**, **scoring**, and **assigning**. Let's take a look at what happens during the execution of each of these steps. An overview of the process is described in the following diagram:

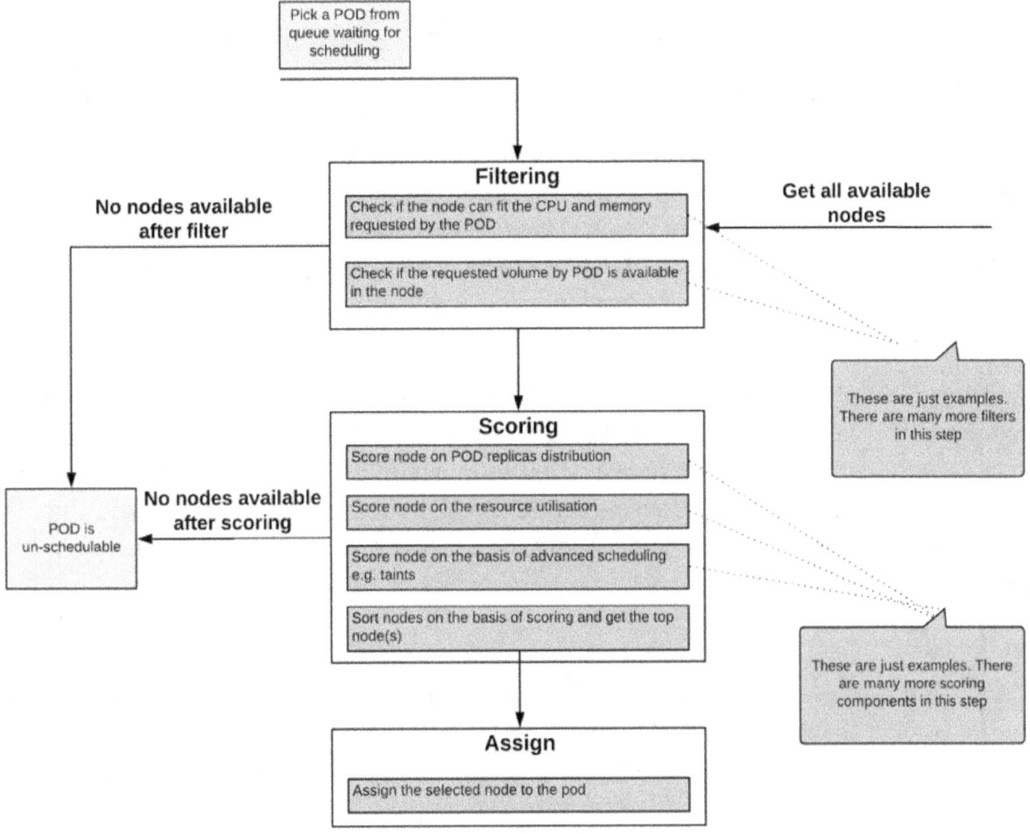

Figure 17.1: An overview of how the Kubernetes Scheduler selects a suitable node

FILTERING

Filtering is a process in which the **Kubernetes Scheduler** runs a series of checks or filters to see which nodes are not suitable to run the target Pod. An example of a filter is to see if the node has enough CPU and memory to host the Pod, or if the storage volume requested by the Pod can be mounted on the host. If the cluster has no node that's suitable to meet the requirements of the Pod, then the Pod is deemed un-schedulable and is not executed on the cluster.

SCORING

Once the **Kubernetes Scheduler** has a list of feasible nodes, the second step is to score the nodes and find the best node(s) to host the target Pod. The node is passed through several priority functions and assigned a priority score. Each function assigns a score between 0 and 10, where 0 is the lowest and 10 is the highest.

To understand priority functions, let's take **`SelectorSpreadPriority`** as an example. This priority function uses label selectors to find the Pods that are associated together. Let's say, for example, that a bunch of Pods is created by the same Deployment. As the name SpreadPriority suggests, this function tries to spread the Pods across different nodes so that in case of a node failure, we will still have replicas running on other nodes. Under this priority function, the Kubernetes Scheduler selects the nodes that have the fewest Pods running using the same label selectors as the requested Pod. These nodes will be assigned the highest score and vice versa.

Another example of a priority function is **`LeastRequestedPriority`**. This tries to spread the workload on the nodes that have the most resources available. The scheduler gets the nodes that have the lowest amount of memory and CPU allocated to existing Pods. These nodes are assigned the highest scores. In other words, this priority function will assign a higher score for a larger amount of free resources.

> **NOTE**
>
> There are far too many priority functions to cover within the limited scope of this chapter. The full list of priority functions can be found at the following link: https://kubernetes.io/docs/concepts/scheduling/kube-scheduler/#scoring.

ASSIGNING

Lastly, the Scheduler informs the API server about the node that has been selected based on the highest score. If there are multiple nodes with the same score, the Scheduler picks a random node and effectively applies a tiebreaker.

The default Kubernetes Scheduler runs as a Pod in the **`kube-system`** namespace. You can see it running by listing all the Pods in the **`kube-system`** namespace:

```
kubectl get pods -n kube-system
```

You should see the following list of Pods:

```
NAME                                 READY   STATUS    RESTARTS   AGE
coredns-fb8b8dccf-6kf4g              1/1     Running   1          3m5s
coredns-fb8b8dccf-gfvmf              1/1     Running   1          3m5s
etcd-minikube                        1/1     Running   0          113s
kube-addon-manager-minikube          1/1     Running   0          112s
kube-apiserver-minikube              1/1     Running   0          2m11s
kube-controller-manager-minikube     1/1     Running   0          2m3s
kube-proxy-gqzxj                     1/1     Running   0          3m5s
kube-scheduler-minikube              1/1     Running   0          110s
storage-provisioner                  1/1     Running   0          3m4s
```

Figure 17.2: Listing Pods in the kube-system namespace

In our Minikube environment, the Kubernetes Scheduler Pod is named **kube-scheduler-minikube**, as you can see in this screenshot.

TIMELINE OF POD SCHEDULING

Let's dig into the timeline of the **Pod scheduling** process. When you request a Pod to be created, different Kubernetes components get invoked to assign the Pod to the right node. There are three steps involved, from requesting a Pod to assigning a node. The following diagram gives an overview of this process, and we will elaborate and break down the process into more detailed steps after the diagram:

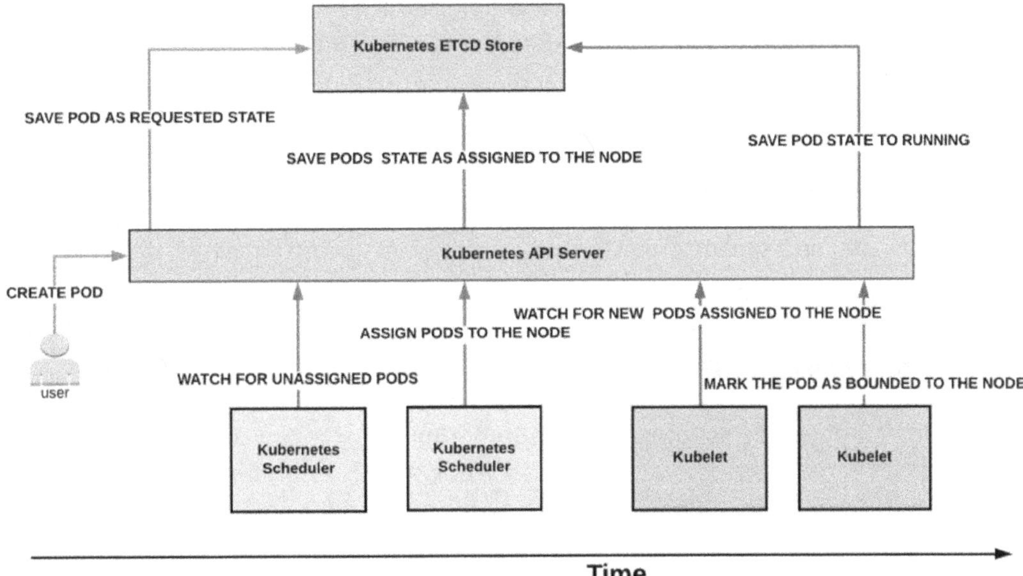

Figure 17.3: Timeline of the Pod scheduling process

Step 1: When a request is raised for creating and running a Pod, for instance, through a kubectl command or by a Kubernetes Deployment, the API server responds to this request. It updates the Kubernetes internal database (etcd) with a Pod pending entry to be executed. Note that at this stage, there is no guarantee that Pod will be scheduled.

Step 2: The **Kubernetes Scheduler** constantly watches the Kubernetes data store through the API server. As soon as a Pod creation request is available (or a Pod is in the pending state), the Scheduler tries to schedule it. It is important to note that the Scheduler is not responsible for running the Pod. It simply calculates the best node for hosting the Pod and informs the Kubernetes API server, which then stores this information in etcd. In this step, the Pod is assigned to the optimal node, and the association is stored in etcd.

Step 3: The Kubernetes agent (kubelet) constantly watches the Kubernetes data store through the API server. As soon as a new Pod is assigned to a node, it tries to execute the Pod on the node. When the Pod is successfully up and running, it is marked as running in etcd through the API server, and now the process is complete.

Now that we have an idea of the scheduling process, let's see how we can tweak it to suit our needs in the following topic.

MANAGING THE KUBERNETES SCHEDULER

Kubernetes provides many parameters and objects through which we can manage the behavior of the **Kubernetes Scheduler**. We will look into the following ways of managing the scheduling process:

- Node affinity and anti-affinity
- Pod affinity and anti-affinity
- Pod priority and preemption
- Taints and tolerations

NODE AFFINITY AND ANTI-AFFINITY

Using node affinity rules, a Kubernetes cluster administrator can control the placement of Pods on specific sets of nodes. Node affinity or anti-affinity allows you to constrain which nodes a Pod can run on based on the labels of the nodes.

Imagine that you are an administrator of the shared Kubernetes cluster in a bank. Multiple teams are running their applications on the same cluster. Your organization's security group has identified nodes that can run data-sensitive applications and would like you to make sure that no other applications run on those nodes. Node affinity or anti-affinity rules provide a solution to this requirement to only associate specific Pods to a set of nodes.

Node affinity rules are defined through two components. First, you assign a label to a set of nodes. The second part is to configure the Pods to associate them only with the nodes with certain labels. Another way to think about this is that the Pod defines where it should be placed, and the Scheduler matches the labels in this definition with the node labels.

There are two types of node affinity/anti-affinity rules:

- **Required rules** are hard rules. If these rules are not met, the Pod cannot be scheduled on a node. It is defined as the **`requiredDuringSchedulingIgnoredDuringExecution`** section in the Pod specification. Please see *Exercise 17.01, Running a Pod with Node Affinity* as an example of this.
- **Preferred rules** are soft rules. The Scheduler tries to enforce preferred rules whenever possible, but it goes ahead to ignore them when the rules cannot be enforced, that is, the Pod would be rendered unschedulable if these rules were followed as rigidly. Preferred rules are defined as the **`preferredDuringSchedulingIgnoredDuringExecution`** section in the Pod specification.

Preferred rules have weights associated with each criterion. The Scheduler will create a score based on these weights to schedule a Pod at the right node. The value of the weight field ranges from 1 to 100. The Scheduler calculates the priority score for all the suitable nodes to find the optimal one. Note that the score can be impacted by other priority functions, such as **`LeastRequestedPriority`**.

If you define a weight that is too low (compared to the other weights), then the overall score will be most affected by other priority functions, and our preferred rule may have little effect on the scheduling process. If you have multiple rules defined, then you can alter the weights of the rules that are the most important to you.

Affinity rules are defined in the Pod specification. Based on the labels of our desired/undesired nodes, we would provide the first part of the selection criteria in the Pod spec. It consists of the set of labels and, optionally, their values.

The other part of the criteria is to provide the way we want to match the labels. We define these matching criteria as the **operator** in the affinity definition. This operator can have the following values:

- The **In** operator instructs the Scheduler to schedule the Pods on the nodes that match the label and one of the specified values.
- The **NotIn** operator instructs the Scheduler to not schedule the Pods on the nodes that do not match the label and any of the specified values. This is a negative operator and denotes the anti-affinity configuration.
- The **Exists** operator instructs the Scheduler to schedule the Pods on the nodes that match the label. The value of the label does not matter in this case. Thus, this operator is satisfied even if the specified label exists and the value of the label does not match.
- The **DoesNotExist** operator instructs the Scheduler to not schedule the Pods on the nodes that do not match the label. The value of the label does not matter in this case. This is a negative operator and denotes the anti-affinity configuration.

Note that affinity and anti-affinity rules are defined based on the labels on the nodes. If the labels on a node are changed, it is possible that a node affinity rule may no longer be applied. In this case, the Pods that are running will continue to run on the node. If a Pod is restarted, or if it dies and a new Pod is created, Kubernetes considers this a new Pod. In this case, if the node labels have been modified, the Scheduler may not put the Pod on the same node. This is something that you would want to be mindful of when you modify node labels. Let's implement these rules for a Pod in the following exercise.

EXERCISE 17.01: RUNNING A POD WITH NODE AFFINITY

In this exercise, we will configure a Pod to be scheduled on the node available in our Minikube environment. We will also see, if the labels do not match, the Pod will be in the **Pending** state. Think of this state in which the scheduler is unable to find the right node to assign to the Pod:

1. Create a new namespace called **schedulerdemo** using the following command:

   ```
   kubectl create ns schedulerdemo
   ```

   You should see the following response:

   ```
   namespace/schedulerdemo created
   ```

2. Now we need to create a Pod with node affinity defined. Create a file named **pod-with-node-affinity.yaml** with the following specification:

```
apiVersion: v1
kind: Pod
metadata:
  name: pod-with-node-affinity
spec:
  affinity:
   nodeAffinity:
     requiredDuringSchedulingIgnoredDuringExecution:
       nodeSelectorTerms:
       - matchExpressions:
         - key: data-center
           operator: In
           values:
           - sydney
  containers:
    - name: pod-with-node-affinity-container
      image: k8s.gcr.io/busybox
      command: [ "/bin/sh", "-c", "while :; do echo '.'; sleep
        5 ; done" ]
```

Note that in the Pod specification, we have added the new **affinity** section. This rule is configured as **requiredDuringSchedulingIgnoredDuringExecution**. This means if the node with a matching label does not exist, this Pod will not get scheduled. Also note that as per the **In** operator, the expressions mentioned here are to be matched with the node labels. In this example, a matching node would have the label **data-center=sydney**.

3. Try to create this Pod and see if it gets scheduled and executed:

```
kubectl create -f pod-with-node-affinity.yaml -n schedulerdemo
```

You should see the following response:

```
pod/pod-with-node-affinity created
```

Note that the response you see here does not necessarily imply that the Pod has successfully been executed on a node. Let's check that in the following step.

4. Check the status of the Pod using this command:

```
kubectl get pods -n schedulerdemo
```

You will see the following response:

```
NAME                      READY     STATUS     RESTARTS    AGE
pod-with-node-affinity    0/1       Pending    0           10s
```

From this output, you can see that the Pod is in the **Pending** state and it is not being executed.

5. Check the **events** to see why the Pod is not being executed:

```
kubectl get events -n schedulerdemo
```

You will see the following response:

```
LAST SEEN   TYPE      REASON             OBJECT                       MESSAGE
<unknown>   Warning   FailedScheduling   pod/pod-with-node-affinity   0/1 nodes are availabl
e: 1 node(s) didn't match node selector.
```

Figure 17.4: Getting the list of events

You can see that Kubernetes is saying that there is no node to match the selector for this Pod.

6. Let's delete the Pod before proceeding further:

```
kubectl delete pod pod-with-node-affinity -n schedulerdemo
```

You should see the following response:

```
pod "pod-with-node-affinity" deleted
```

7. Now, let's see what nodes are available in our cluster:

```
kubectl get nodes
```

You will see the following response:

```
NAME        STATUS    ROLES     AGE     VERSION
minikube    Ready     master    105d    v1.14.3
```

Since we are using Minikube, there is only one node available called **minikube**.

8. Check the label for the **minikube** node. Use the **describe** command as shown here:

```
kubectl describe node minikube
```

You should see the following response:

```
Name:               minikube
Roles:              master
Labels:             beta.kubernetes.io/arch=amd64
                    beta.kubernetes.io/os=linux
                    kubernetes.io/arch=amd64
                    kubernetes.io/hostname=minikube
                    kubernetes.io/os=linux
                    node-role.kubernetes.io/master=
Annotations:        kubeadm.alpha.kubernetes.io/cri-socket: /var/run/dockershim.sock
                    node.alpha.kubernetes.io/ttl: 0
                    volumes.kubernetes.io/controller-managed-attach-detach: true
```

Figure 17.5: Describing the minikube node

As you can see, the label that we want, **`data-center=sydney`**, does not exist.

9. Now, let's apply the desired label to our node using this command:

```
kubectl label node minikube data-center=sydney
```

You will see the following response indicating that the node was labeled:

```
node/minikube labeled
```

10. Verify whether the label is applied to the node using the **`describe`** command:

```
kubectl describe node minikube
```

You should see the following response:

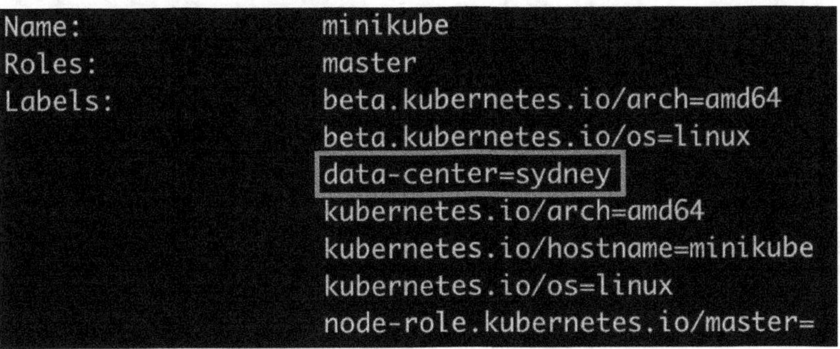

Figure 17.6: Checking the label on the minikube node

As you can see in this image, our label has now been applied.

11. Now try to run the Pod again and see if it can be executed:

```
kubectl create -f pod-with-node-affinity.yaml -n schedulerdemo
```

You should see the following response:

```
pod/pod-with-node-affinity created
```

12. Now, let's check whether the Pod is successfully running:

```
kubectl get pods -n schedulerdemo
```

You should see the following response:

```
NAME                        READY      STATUS       RESTARTS    AGE
pod-with-node-affinity    1/1       Running     0            5m22s
```

Thus, our Pod is successfully running.

13. Let's check out how Pod scheduling is displayed in **`events`**:

```
kubectl get events -n schedulerdemo
```

You will get the following response:

```
LAST SEEN    TYPE       REASON             OBJECT                         MESSAGE
<unknown>    Warning    FailedScheduling   pod/pod-with-node-affinity     0/1 nodes are availabl
e: 1 node(s) didn't match node selector.
<unknown>    Warning    FailedScheduling   pod/pod-with-node-affinity     0/1 nodes are availabl
e: 1 node(s) didn't match node selector.
<unknown>    Warning    FailedScheduling   pod/pod-with-node-affinity     skip schedule deleting
 pod: schedulerdemo/pod-with-node-affinity
<unknown>    Normal     Scheduled          pod/pod-with-node-affinity     Successfully assigned
schedulerdemo/pod-with-node-affinity to minikube
16s          Normal     Pulling            pod/pod-with-node-affinity     Pulling image "k8s.gcr
.io/busybox"
16s          Normal     Pulled             pod/pod-with-node-affinity     Successfully pulled im
age "k8s.gcr.io/busybox"
16s          Normal     Created            pod/pod-with-node-affinity     Created container pod-
with-node-affinity-container
15s          Normal     Started            pod/pod-with-node-affinity     Started container pod-
with-node-affinity-container
```

Figure 17.7: Checking out scheduling events

As you can see in the preceding output, the Pod has been successfully scheduled.

14. Now, let's do some housekeeping to avoid conflicts with further exercises and activities. Delete the Pod using this command:

```
kubectl delete pod pod-with-node-affinity -n schedulerdemo
```

You should see the following response:

```
pod "pod-with-node-affinity" deleted
```

15. Remove the label from the node using the following command:

```
kubectl label node minikube data-center-
```

Note that the syntax for deleting the label from the Pod has an additional hyphen (**-**) after the label name. You should see the following response:

```
node/minikube labeled
```

In this exercise, we have seen how node affinity works by labeling a node and then scheduling a Pod on the labeled node. We have also seen how Kubernetes events can be used to see the status of Pod scheduling.

The **data-center=sydney** label that we used in this exercise also hints at an interesting use case. We can use node affinity and anti-affinity rules to target not just a specific Pod, but also specific server racks or data centers. We would simply assign specific labels to all nodes in a specific server rack, data center, availability zone, and so on. Then, we can simply pick and choose the desired targets for our Pods.

POD AFFINITY AND ANTI-AFFINITY

Pod affinity and Pod anti-affinity allow your Pods to check what other Pods are running on a given node before they are scheduled on that node. Note that other Pods in this context do not mean a new copy of the same Pod, but Pods related to different workloads.

Pod affinity allows you to control on which node your Pod is eligible to be scheduled based on the labels of the other Pods that are already running on that node. The idea is to cater to the need to place two different types of containers relative to each other at the same place or to keep them apart.

Consider that your application has two components: a frontend part (for example, a GUI) and a backend (for example, an API). Let's assume that you want to run them on the same host because the communications between frontend and backend Pods would be faster if they are hosted on the same node. By default, on a multi-node cluster (not Minikube), the Scheduler will schedule such Pods on different nodes. Pod affinity provides a way to control the scheduling of Pods relative to each other so that we can ensure the optimal performance of our application.

There are two components that are required to define Pod affinity. The first component defines how the scheduler will relate the target Pod (in our previous example, the frontend Pod) to the already running Pods (the backend Pod). This is done through labels on the Pod. In the Pod affinity rules, we mention which labels of the other Pods should be used to relate to the new Pod. Label selectors have similar operators, as described in the Node Affinity and Anti-Affinity section, for matching the labels of the Pods.

The second component describes where you want to run the target Pods. Just as we have seen in the previous exercise, we can use Pod affinity rules to schedule a Pod on the same node as the other Pod (in our example, we are assuming that the backend Pod is the other Pod that is already running), any node on the same rack as the other Pod, any node on the same data center as the other Pod, and so on. This component defines the set of nodes where the Pods can be allocated. To achieve this, we label our group of nodes and define this label as **topologyKey** in the Pod specification. For example, if we use the hostname as the value for **topologyKey**, the Pods will be placed on the same node.

If we label our nodes with the rack name on which they are hosted and define the rack name as **topologyKey**, then the candidate Pods will be scheduled for one of the nodes with the same rack name label.

Similar to the node affinity rules defined in the previous section, there are hard and soft Pod affinity rules as well. Hard rules are defined with **requiredDuringSchedulingIgnoredDuringExecution** while soft rules are defined with **preferredDuringSchedulingIgnoredDuringExecution**. It is possible to have multiple combinations of hard and soft rules in the Pod affinity configuration.

EXERCISE 17.02: RUNNING PODS WITH POD AFFINITY

In this exercise, we will see how Pod affinity can help the Scheduler to see the relationships between different Pods and assign them to suitable nodes. We will place Pods using the **preferred** option. In a later part of this exercise, we will configure the Pod anti-affinity using the **required** option and see that that Pod will not be scheduled until all the criteria are met. We will use the same example of frontend and backend Pods that we mentioned earlier:

1. We need to create and run the backend Pod first. Create a file named **pod-with-pod-affinity-first.yaml** with the following contents:

```
apiVersion: v1
kind: Pod
metadata:
  name: pod-with-pod-affinity
  labels:
      application-name: banking-app
spec:
  containers:
    - name: pod-with-node-pod-container
      image: k8s.gcr.io/busybox
      command: [ "/bin/sh", "-c", "while :; do echo 'this is
        backend pod'; sleep 5 ; done" ]
```

   This Pod is a simple Pod with just a loop printing a message. Notice that we have assigned a label to the Pod so that it can be related to the frontend pod.

2. Let's create the Pod defined in the previous step:

```
kubectl create -f pod-with-pod-affinity-first.yaml -n schedulerdemo
```

   You should see the following response:

```
pod/pod-with-pod-affinity created
```

3. Now, let's see if the Pod has been successfully created:

```
kubectl get pods -n schedulerdemo
```

   You should see a response like this:

```
NAME                         READY     STATUS     RESTARTS    AGE
pod-with-pod-affinity     1/1       Running    0           22s
```

4. Now, let's check the labels on the **minikube** node:

```
kubectl describe node minikube
```

You should see the following response:

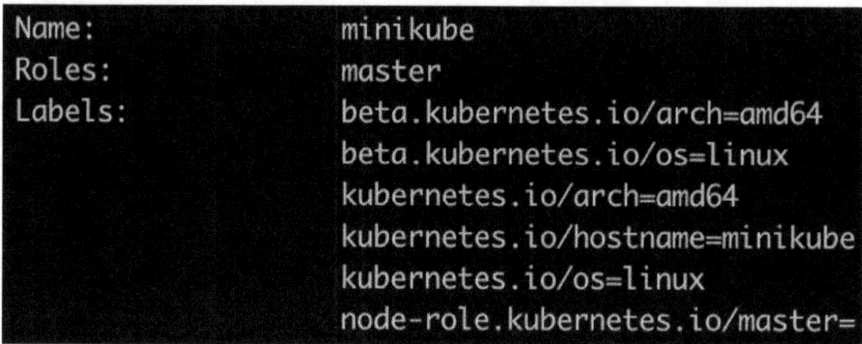

```
Name:        minikube
Roles:       master
Labels:      beta.kubernetes.io/arch=amd64
             beta.kubernetes.io/os=linux
             kubernetes.io/arch=amd64
             kubernetes.io/hostname=minikube
             kubernetes.io/os=linux
             node-role.kubernetes.io/master=
```

Figure 17.8: Describing the minikube node

Since we want to run both the Pods on the same host, we can use the **kubernetes.io/hostname** label of the node.

5. Now, let's define the second Pod. Create a file named **pod-with-pod-affinity-second.yaml** with the following contents:

```
apiVersion: v1
kind: Pod
metadata:
  name: pod-with-pod-affinity-fe
  labels:
     application-name: banking-app
spec:
  affinity:
   podAffinity:
     preferredDuringSchedulingIgnoredDuringExecution:
     - weight: 100
       podAffinityTerm:
         labelSelector:
           matchExpressions:
           - key: application-name
             operator: In
             values:
             - banking-app
         topologyKey: kubernetes.io/hostname
```

```
  containers:
    - name: pod-with-node-pod-container-fe
      image: k8s.gcr.io/busybox
      command: [ "/bin/sh", "-c", "while :; do echo 'this is
        frontend pod'; sleep 5 ; done" ]
```

Consider this Pod as the frontend application. Notice that we have defined a **preferredDuringSchedulingIgnoredDuringExecution** rule in the **podAffinity** section. We have also defined the **labels** and the **topologyKey** for the Pods and the nodes.

6. Let's create the Pod defined in the previous step:

```
kubectl create -f pod-with-pod-affinity-second.yaml -n schedulerdemo
```

You should see the following response:

```
pod/pod-with-pod-affinity-fe created
```

7. Verify the status of the Pods using the **get** command:

```
kubectl get pods -n schedulerdemo
```

You should see the following response:

```
NAME                        READY   STATUS    RESTARTS   AGE
pod-with-pod-affinity       1/1     Running   0          7m33s
pod-with-pod-affinity-fe    1/1     Running   0          21s
```

As you can see, the **pod-with-pod-affinity-fe** Pod is running. This is not much different than the normal Pod placement. This is because we have only one node in the Minikube environment and we have defined the Pod affinity using **preferredDuringSchedulingIgnoredDuringExecution**, which is the soft variation of the matching criteria.

The next steps of this exercise will talk about anti-affinity using **requiredDuringSchedulingIgnoredDuringExecution** or the hard variation of the matching criteria, and you will see that the Pod does not reach the **Running** state.

8. First, let's delete the **pod-with-pod-affinity-fe** Pod:

```
kubectl delete pod pod-with-pod-affinity-fe -n schedulerdemo
```

You should see the following response:

```
pod "pod-with-pod-affinity-fe" deleted
```

9. Confirm that the Pod has been deleted by listing all the Pods:

```
kubectl get pods -n schedulerdemo
```

You should see the following response:

```
NAME                        READY   STATUS    RESTARTS   AGE
pod-with-pod-affinity    1/1     Running   0          10m
```

10. Now create another Pod definition with the following contents and save it as **pod-with-pod-anti-affinity-second.yaml**:

```
apiVersion: v1
kind: Pod
metadata:
  name: pod-with-pod-anti-affinity-fe
  labels:
     application-name: backing-app
spec:
  affinity:
   podAntiAffinity:
     requiredDuringSchedulingIgnoredDuringExecution:
     - labelSelector:
         matchExpressions:
         - key: application-name
           operator: In
           values:
           - banking-app
       topologyKey: kubernetes.io/hostname
  containers:
    - name: pod-with-node-pod-anti-container-fe
      image: k8s.gcr.io/busybox
      command: [ "/bin/sh", "-c", "while :; do echo 'this is
        frontend pod'; sleep 5 ; done" ]
```

As you can see, the configuration is for **podAntiAffinity** and it uses the **requiredDuringSchedulingIgnoredDuringExecution** option, which is the hard variation of Pod affinity rules. Here, the Scheduler will not schedule any Pod if the condition is not met. We are using the **In** operator so that our Pod will not run on the same host as any Pod with the parameters defined in the **labelSelector** component of the configuration.

11. Try creating the Pod with the preceding specification:

```
kubectl create -f pod-with-pod-anti-affinity-second.yaml -n
schedulerdemo
```

You should see the following response:

```
pod/pod-with-pod-anti-affinity-fe created
```

12. Now, check the status of this Pod:

```
kubectl get pods -n schedulerdemo
```

You should see the following response:

```
NAME                             READY   STATUS     RESTARTS   AGE
pod-with-pod-affinity            1/1     Running    0          14m
pod-with-pod-anti-affinity-fe    1/1     Pending    0          3s
```

From this output, you can see the Pod is in the **`Pending`** state.

13. You can verify that the Pod is not being scheduled because of Pod anti-affinity by checking events:

```
kubectl get events -n schedulerdemo
```

You should see the following response:

```
<unknown>   Warning   FailedScheduling   pod/pod-with-pod-anti-affinity-fe   0/1 nodes are a
vailable: 1 node(s) didn't match pod affinity/anti-affinity, 1 node(s) didn't match pod anti
-affinity rules.
```

Figure 17.9: Checking out the event for failed scheduling

In this exercise, we have seen how Pod affinity can help place two different Pods on the same node. We have also seen how Pod anti-affinity options can help us schedule the Pods on different sets of hosts.

POD PRIORITY

Kubernetes allows you to associate a priority with a Pod. If there are resource constraints, if a new Pod with high priority is requested to be scheduled, the Kubernetes scheduler may evict the Pods with lower priority in order to make room for the new high-priority Pod.

Consider an example where you are a cluster administrator and you run both critical and non-critical workloads in the cluster. An example is a Kubernetes cluster for a bank. In this case, you would have a payment service as well as the bank's website. You may decide that processing payments are of higher importance than running the website. By configuring Pod priority, you can prevent lower-priority workloads from impacting critical workloads in your cluster, especially in cases where the cluster starts to reach its resource capacity. This technique of evicting lower-priority Pods to schedule more critical Pods could be faster than adding additional nodes and would help you better manage traffic spikes on the cluster.

The way we associate a priority with a Pod is to define an object known as **PriorityClass**. This object holds the priority, which is defined as a number between 1 and 1 billion. The higher the number, the higher the priority. Once we have defined our priority classes, we assign a priority to a Pod by associating a **PriorityClass** with the Pod. By default, if there is no priority class associated with the Pod, the Pod either gets assigned the default priority class if it is available, or it gets assigned the priority value of 0.

You can get the list of priority classes similarly to any other objects:

```
kubectl get priorityclasses
```

You should see a response like this:

```
NAME                      VALUE        GLOBAL-DEFAULT   AGE
system-cluster-critical   2000000000   false            9d
system-node-critical      2000001000   false            9d
```

Note that in Minikube, there are two priority classes predefined in the environment. Let's learn more about the **system-cluster-critical** class. Issue the following command to get the details about it:

```
kubectl get pc system-cluster-critical -o yaml
```

You should see the following response:

```
apiVersion: scheduling.k8s.io/v1
description: Used for system critical pods that must run in the cluster, but can be
  moved to another node if necessary.
kind: PriorityClass
metadata:
  creationTimestamp: "2019-10-01T07:46:47Z"
  generation: 1
  name: system-cluster-critical
  resourceVersion: "42"
  selfLink: /apis/scheduling.k8s.io/v1/priorityclasses/system-cluster-critical
  uid: 9f0701d3-e41f-11e9-b737-000c2917147b
value: 2000000000
```

Figure 17.10: Describing the system-cluster-critical PriorityClass

The output here mentions that this class is reserved for the Pods that are absolutely critical for the cluster. etcd is one such Pod. Let's see if this priority class is associated with it.

Issue the following command to get details about the etcd Pod running in Minikube:

```
kubectl get pod etcd-minikube -n kube-system -o yaml
```

You should see the following response:

```
dnsPolicy: ClusterFirst
enableServiceLinks: true
hostNetwork: true
nodeName: minikube
priority: 2000000000
priorityClassName: system-cluster-critical
restartPolicy: Always
schedulerName: default-scheduler
securityContext: {}
terminationGracePeriodSeconds: 30
```

Figure 17.11: Getting information about the etcd-minikube Pod

You can see from this output that the Pod has been associated with the **`system-cluster-critical`** priority.

In the following exercise, we will add a default priority class and a higher-priority class to better understand the behavior of the Kubernetes scheduler.

It is important to understand that Pod priority works in coordination with other rules, such as Pod affinity. If the Scheduler determines that a high-priority Pod cannot be scheduled even if lower-priority Pods are evicted, it will not evict lower-priority Pods.

Similarly, if high-priority and low-priority Pods are waiting to be scheduled and the scheduler determines that high-priority Pods cannot be scheduled due to affinity or anti-affinity rules, the scheduler will schedule the suitable low-priority Pods.

EXERCISE 17.03: POD PRIORITY AND PREEMPTION

In this exercise, we shall define two priority classes: default (low priority) and high priority. We will then create 10 Pods with default priority and allocate some CPU and memory to each Pod. After this, we will check how much capacity is being used from our local cluster. We will then create 10 more Pods with high priority and allocate resources to them. We will see that the Pods with the default priority will be terminated and the higher-priority Pods will be scheduled on the cluster. We will then reduce the number of high-priority Pods from 10 to 5 and then see that some of the low-priority Pods are being scheduled again. This is because reducing the number of high-priority Pods should free up some resources:

1. First, let's create the definition for the default priority class. Create a file named **priority-class-default.yaml** with the following contents:

   ```
   apiVersion: scheduling.k8s.io/v1
   kind: PriorityClass
   metadata:
     name: default-priority
   value: 1
   globalDefault: true
   description: "Default Priority class."
   ```

   Note that we have marked this priority class as default by setting the value of **globalDefault** as **true**. Also, the priority number, **1**, is very low.

2. Create this priority class using the following command:

   ```
   kubectl create -f priority-class-default.yaml
   ```

   You should see the following response:

   ```
   priorityclass.scheduling.k8s.io/default-priority
   ```

   Note that we have not mentioned the namespace as this object is not a namespace-level object. A priority class is a cluster scope object in Kubernetes.

3. Let's check whether our priority class has been created:

```
kubectl get priorityclasses
```

You should see the following list:

```
NAME                     VALUE        GLOBAL-DEFAULT   AGE
default-priority         1            true             5m46s
system-cluster-critical  2000000000   false            105d
system-node-critical     2000001000   false            105d
```

In this output, you can see the priority class that we just created under the name **default-priority**, and it is the global default as you can see in the **GLOBAL-DEFAULT** column. Now create another priority class with higher priority.

4. Create a file named **priority-class-highest.yaml** with the following contents:

```
apiVersion: scheduling.k8s.io/v1
kind: PriorityClass
metadata:
  name: highest-priority
value: 100000
globalDefault: false
description: "This priority class should be used for pods with
  the highest of priority."
```

Note the very high value of the **value** field in this object.

5. Use the definition from the previous step to create a Pod priority class using the following command:

```
kubectl create -f priority-class-highest.yaml
```

You should see the following response:

```
priorityclass.scheduling.k8s.io/highest-priority created
```

6. Now let's create a definition for a Deployment with **10** Pods and a default priority. Create a file named **pod-with-default-priority.yaml** using the following contents to define our Deployment:

```
apiVersion: apps/v1
kind: Deployment
metadata:
  name: pod-default-priority-deployment
spec:
  replicas: 10
  selector:
    matchLabels:
      app: priority-test

  template:
    metadata:
      labels:
        app: priority-test
    spec:
      containers:
      - name: pod-default-priority-deployment-container
        image: k8s.gcr.io/busybox
        command: [ "/bin/sh", "-c", "while :; do echo 'this is
          backend pod'; sleep 5 ; done" ]
      priorityClassName: default-priority
```

7. Let's create the Deployment that we defined in the previous step:

```
kubectl create -f pod-with-default-priority.yaml -n schedulerdemo
```

You should see this response:

```
deployment.apps/pod-default-priority-deployment created
```

8. Now, increase the memory and CPU allocated to each of them to 128 MiB and 1/10 of the CPU by using the following commands:

```
kubectl set resources deployment/pod-default-priority-deployment
--limits=cpu=100m,memory=128Mi -n schedulerdemo
```

You should see the following response:

```
deployment.extensions/pod-default-priority-deployment resource
requirements updated
```

> **NOTE**
>
> You may need to adjust this resource allocation as per the resources available on your computer. You can start with 1/10 CPU and verify the resources as mentioned in *step 10*.

9. Verify that the Pods are running using the following command:

```
kubectl get pods -n schedulerdemo
```

You should see the following list of Pods:

```
NAME                                                READY   STATUS    RESTAR
TS    AGE
pod-default-priority-deployment-57c965b8cd-4z944    1/1     Running   0
      3m9s
pod-default-priority-deployment-57c965b8cd-6k4gf    1/1     Running   0
      3m4s
pod-default-priority-deployment-57c965b8cd-c7tg4    1/1     Running   0
      3m34s
pod-default-priority-deployment-57c965b8cd-gk8kv    1/1     Running   0
      3m34s
pod-default-priority-deployment-57c965b8cd-gwm9k    1/1     Running   0
      3m34s
pod-default-priority-deployment-57c965b8cd-hsn9r    1/1     Running   0
      3m34s
pod-default-priority-deployment-57c965b8cd-j5jxm    1/1     Running   0
      3m34s
pod-default-priority-deployment-57c965b8cd-q2cnw    1/1     Running   0
      3m11s
pod-default-priority-deployment-57c965b8cd-qcjnv    1/1     Running   0
      3m6s
pod-default-priority-deployment-57c965b8cd-zjhjd    1/1     Running   0
      3m3s
```

Figure 17.12: Getting the list of Pods

10. Check the resource usage in our cluster. Note that we have only one node, and thus we can easily see the values by issuing the **describe** command:

```
kubectl describe node minikube
```

The following screenshot is truncated for a better presentation. Find the **Allocated resources** section in your output:

```
Allocated resources:
  (Total limits may be over 100 percent, i.e., overcommitted.)
  Resource           Requests      Limits
  --------           --------      ------
  cpu                1555m (77%)   800m (40%)
  memory             1214Mi (64%)  1364Mi (72%)
  ephemeral-storage  0 (0%)        0 (0%)
```

Figure 17.13: Checking the resource utilization on the minikube node

Note that CPU usage is at 77% and memory at 64% for the **minikube** host. Please note that the resource utilization is dependent on the hardware of your computer and the resources allocated to Minikube. If your CPU is too powerful or if you have a huge amount of memory (or even if you have a slower CPU and less memory), you may see resource utilization values vastly different from what we see here. Please adjust the CPU and memory resources as mentioned in *step 8* so that we get similar resource utilization as we see here. This will enable you to see a similar result to the one we have demonstrated in the following steps of this exercise.

11. Now let's schedule Pods with high priority. Create 10 Pods using the Kubernetes Deployment object. For this, create a file named **pod-with-high-priority.yaml** with the following contents:

```
apiVersion: apps/v1
kind: Deployment
metadata:
  name: pod-highest-priority-deployment
```

```
spec:
  replicas: 10
  selector:
    matchLabels:
      app: priority-test

  template:
    metadata:
      labels:
        app: priority-test
    spec:
      containers:
      - name: pod-highest-priority-deployment-container
        image: k8s.gcr.io/busybox
        command: [ "/bin/sh", "-c", "while :; do echo 'this is
          backend pod'; sleep 5 ; done" ]
      priorityClassName: highest-priority
```

Note that **priorityClassName** has been set to the **highest-priority** class in the preceding specification.

12. Now create the Deployment that we created in the previous step:

```
kubectl create -f pod-with-high-priority.yaml -n schedulerdemo
```

You should get the following output:

```
deployment.apps/pod-with-highest-priority-deployment created
```

13. Allocate a similar amount of CPU and memory to these Pods as you did for the Pods with default priority:

```
kubectl set resources deployment/pod-highest-priority-deployment
--limits=cpu=100m,memory=128Mi -n schedulerdemo
```

You should see the following response:

```
deployment.apps/pod-highest-priority-deployment resource requirements
updated
```

14. After a minute or so, run the following command to see which Pods are running:

```
kubectl get pods -n schedulerdemo
```

You should see a response similar to this:

```
NAME                                               READY   STATUS    RESTARTS   AGE
pod-default-priority-deployment-57c965b8cd-2qlvp   0/1     Pending   0          2m30s
pod-default-priority-deployment-57c965b8cd-6f6f2   0/1     Pending   0          2m25s
pod-default-priority-deployment-57c965b8cd-bssnv   0/1     Pending   0          2m30s
pod-default-priority-deployment-57c965b8cd-bx85k   0/1     Pending   0          104s
pod-default-priority-deployment-57c965b8cd-dbsd8   0/1     Pending   0          2m30s
pod-default-priority-deployment-57c965b8cd-hz7qj   0/1     Pending   0          2m31s
pod-default-priority-deployment-57c965b8cd-ng22k   0/1     Pending   0          2m27s
pod-default-priority-deployment-57c965b8cd-qcjnv   1/1     Running   0          7m51s
pod-default-priority-deployment-57c965b8cd-tzqsq   0/1     Pending   0          102s
pod-default-priority-deployment-57c965b8cd-zjhjd   1/1     Running   0          7m48s
pod-highest-priority-deployment-6df898d4c4-2jk8p   1/1     Running   0          2m31s
pod-highest-priority-deployment-6df898d4c4-cjc8r   1/1     Running   0          102s
pod-highest-priority-deployment-6df898d4c4-gc4tr   1/1     Running   0          2m31s
pod-highest-priority-deployment-6df898d4c4-gmh2j   1/1     Running   0          2m31s
pod-highest-priority-deployment-6df898d4c4-hdpr4   1/1     Running   0          104s
pod-highest-priority-deployment-6df898d4c4-jmnjb   1/1     Running   0          2m31s
pod-highest-priority-deployment-6df898d4c4-l2nsz   1/1     Running   0          2m25s
pod-highest-priority-deployment-6df898d4c4-mhq2x   1/1     Running   0          2m27s
pod-highest-priority-deployment-6df898d4c4-qmj5w   1/1     Running   0          105s
pod-highest-priority-deployment-6df898d4c4-wm6rs   1/1     Running   0          2m31s
```

Figure 17.14: Getting the list of Pods

You can see that most of our high-priority Pods are in the **Running** state and the Pods with low-priority Pods are moved to the **Pending** state. This tells us the Kubernetes Scheduler has actually terminated the lower-priority Pods, and it is now waiting for the resources to be available to schedule them again.

15. Try changing the number of high-priority Pods from 10 to 5 and see if additional low-priority Pods can be scheduled. Change the number of replicas using this command:

```
kubectl scale deployment/pod-highest-priority-deployment --replicas=5
-n schedulerdemo
```

You should see the following response:

```
deployment.extensions/pod-highest-priority-deployment scaled
```

16. Verify that high-priority Pods are reduced from 10 to 5 using the following command:

```
kubectl get pods -n schedulerdemo
```

```
NAME                                             READY   STATUS    RESTARTS   AGE
pod-default-priority-deployment-57c965b8cd-2qlvp 1/1     Running   0          8m23s
pod-default-priority-deployment-57c965b8cd-6f6f2 0/1     Pending   0          8m18s
pod-default-priority-deployment-57c965b8cd-bssnv 1/1     Running   0          8m23s
pod-default-priority-deployment-57c965b8cd-bx85k 0/1     Pending   0          7m37s
pod-default-priority-deployment-57c965b8cd-dbsd8 1/1     Running   0          8m23s
pod-default-priority-deployment-57c965b8cd-hz7qj 0/1     Pending   0          8m24s
pod-default-priority-deployment-57c965b8cd-ng22k 1/1     Running   0          8m20s
pod-default-priority-deployment-57c965b8cd-qcjnv 1/1     Running   0          13m
pod-default-priority-deployment-57c965b8cd-tzqsq 1/1     Running   0          7m35s
pod-default-priority-deployment-57c965b8cd-zjhjd 1/1     Running   0          13m
pod-highest-priority-deployment-6df898d4c4-gc4tr 1/1     Running   0          8m24s
pod-highest-priority-deployment-6df898d4c4-gmh2j 1/1     Running   0          8m24s
pod-highest-priority-deployment-6df898d4c4-jmnjb 1/1     Running   0          8m24s
pod-highest-priority-deployment-6df898d4c4-l2nsz 1/1     Running   0          8m18s
pod-highest-priority-deployment-6df898d4c4-wm6rs 1/1     Running   0          8m24s
```

Figure 17.15: Getting the list of Pods

As you can see in this screenshot, some more low-priority Pods changed from the `Pending` state to the `Running` state. Thus, we can see that the Scheduler is working to make optimal use of the available resources based on the priority of workloads.

In this exercise, we have used the Pod priority rules and seen how the Kubernetes Scheduler may choose to terminate the Pods with a lower priority if there are requests for a Pod with a higher priority to be fulfilled.

TAINTS AND TOLERATIONS

Previously, we have seen how Pods can be configured to control which node they run on. Now we will see how nodes can control which Pods can run on them using taints and tolerations.

A taint prevents the scheduling of a pod unless that Pod has a matching toleration for the Pod. Think of taint as an attribute of a node and a toleration is an attribute of a Pod. The Pod will get scheduled on the node only if the Pod's toleration matches the node's taint. The taints on a node tell the scheduler to check which Pods tolerate the taint and run only those Pods that match their toleration with the node's taint.

A taint definition contains the key, value, and effect. The key and value will match the Pod toleration definition in the Pod specification, while the effect instructs the scheduler what should be done once the node's taint matches the Pod's toleration.

The following diagram provides an overview of how the process of controlling scheduling based on taints and tolerations works. Notice that a Pod with toleration can also be scheduled on a node with no taint.

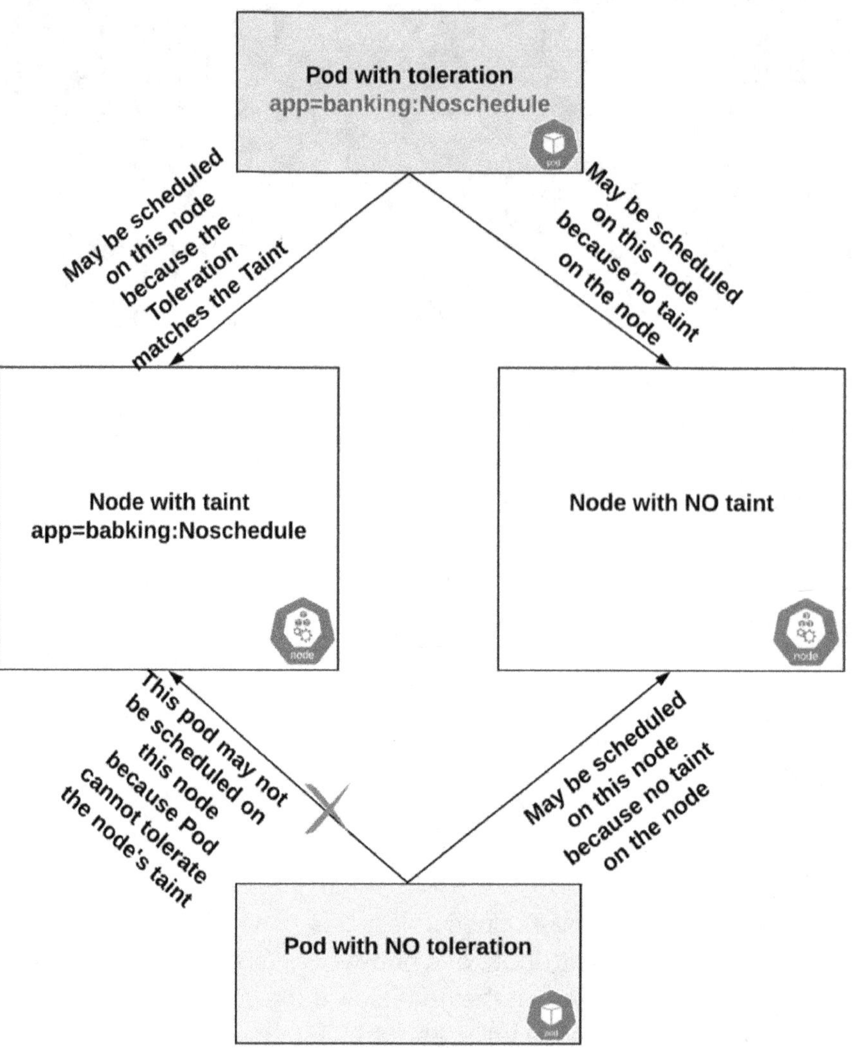

Figure 17.16: Overview of how taints and tolerations are used to influence scheduling

When we define a taint, we also need to specify the behavior of the taint. This can be specified by the following values:

- **NoSchedule** provides the ability to reject the scheduling of new Pods on the node. Existing Pods that were scheduled before the taint was defined will continue to run on the node.
- **NoExecute** taint provides the ability to resist new Pods that do not have a toleration that matches the taint. It further checks whether all the existing Pods running on the node match this taint, and removes the ones that don't.
- **PreferNoSchedule** instructs the scheduler to avoid scheduling Pods that do not tolerate the taint on the node. This is a soft rule, where the scheduler will try to find the right node but it will still schedule the Pods on the node if it cannot find any other node that is appropriate as per the defined taint and toleration rules.

In order to apply a taint to a node, we can use the **kubectl taint** command as follows:

```
kubectl taint nodes <NODE_NAME> <TAINT>:<TAINT_TYPE>
```

There can be many reasons why you would want certain Pods (applications) not to be run on specific nodes. An example use case could be the requirement of specialized hardware, such as a GPU for machine learning applications. Another case could be when a license restriction for software on the Pod dictates that it needs to run on specific nodes. For example, out of 10 worker nodes in your cluster, only 2 nodes are allowed to run particular software. Using the taints and tolerations combination, you can help the scheduler to schedule Pods on the right node.

EXERCISE 17.04: TAINTS AND TOLERATIONS

In this exercise, we will see how taints and tolerations can allow us to schedule Pods on the nodes we desire. We will define a taint and try to schedule a Pod on the node. We then showcase the **NoExecute** functionality in which a Pod can be removed from a node if that taint on the node changes:

1. Get the list of nodes using the following command:

   ```
   kubectl get nodes
   ```

   You should see the following list of nodes:

   ```
   NAME       STATUS   ROLES    AGE   VERSION
   minikube   Ready    master   44h   v1.14.3
   ```

   Recall that in our Minikube environment, we have only one node.

2. Create a taint for the **minikube** node using the following command:

   ```
   kubectl taint nodes minikube app=banking:NoSchedule
   ```

   You should see the following response:

   ```
   node/minikube tainted
   ```

3. Verify that the node has been tainted correctly. You can use the **describe** command to see what taints are applied to the node:

   ```
   kubectl describe node minikube
   ```

   You should see the following response:

```
Name:               minikube
Roles:              master
Labels:             beta.kubernetes.io/arch=amd64
                    beta.kubernetes.io/os=linux
                    kubernetes.io/arch=amd64
                    kubernetes.io/hostname=minikube
                    kubernetes.io/os=linux
                    node-role.kubernetes.io/master=
Annotations:        kubeadm.alpha.kubernetes.io/cri-socket: /var/run/dockershim.sock
                    node.alpha.kubernetes.io/ttl: 0
                    volumes.kubernetes.io/controller-managed-attach-detach: true
CreationTimestamp:  Tue, 01 Oct 2019 17:46:46 +1000
Taints:             app=banking:NoSchedule
```

Figure 17.17: Checking the taints on the minikube node

4. Now we need to create a Pod with toleration defined as per the taint. Create a file named **pod-toleration-noschedule.yaml** with the following contents:

```
apiVersion: v1
kind: Pod
metadata:
  name: pod-with-node-toleration-noschedule
spec:
  tolerations:
  - key: "app"
    operator: "Equal"
    value: "banking"
    effect: "NoSchedule"
  containers:
    - name: pod-with-node-toleration-noschedule-container
      image: k8s.gcr.io/busybox
      command: [ "/bin/sh", "-c", "while :; do echo '.'; sleep
        5 ; done" ]
```

Notice that the toleration value is the same as the taint defined in *step 1*, that is, **app=banking**. The **effect** attribute controls the type of toleration behavior. Here, we have defined **effect** as **NoSchedule**.

5. Let's create the Pod as per the preceding specification:

```
kubectl create -f pod-toleration-noschedule.yaml -n schedulerdemo
```

This should give the following response:

```
pod/pod-with-node-toleration-noschedule created
```

6. Verify that the Pod is running using the following command:

```
kubectl get pods -n schedulerdemo
```

```
NAME                                  READY   STATUS    RESTARTS   AGE
pod-with-node-toleration-noschedule   1/1     Running   0          2m2s
```

Figure 17.18: Getting the list of Pods

7. Now let's define a different Pod with a toleration that does not match the taint on the node. Create a file named **pod-toleration-noschedule2.yaml** with the following contents:

```
apiVersion: v1
kind: Pod
metadata:
  name: pod-with-node-toleration-noschedule2
spec:
  tolerations:
  - key: "app"
    operator: "Equal"
    value: "hr"
    effect: "NoSchedule"
  containers:
    - name: pod-with-node-toleration-noschedule-container2
      image: k8s.gcr.io/busybox
      command: [ "/bin/sh", "-c", "while :; do echo '.'; sleep
        5 ; done" ]
```

Notice that here we have the toleration set to **app=hr**. We need a Pod with the same taint to match this toleration. Since we have tainted our node with **app=banking**, this Pod should not be scheduled by the scheduler. Let's try this in the following steps.

8. Create the Pod using the definition from the previous step:

```
kubectl create -f pod-toleration-noschedule2.yaml -n schedulerdemo
```

This should give the following response:

```
pod/pod-with-node-toleration-noschedule2 created
```

9. Check the status of the Pod using the following command:

```
kubectl get pods -n schedulerdemo
```

You should see this response:

```
NAME                                   READY   STATUS    RESTARTS   AGE
pod-with-node-toleration-noschedule    1/1     Running   0          5m7s
pod-with-node-toleration-noschedule2   0/1     Pending   0          20s
```

Figure 17.19: Getting the list of Pods

You can see that Pod is in the **Pending** state and not in the **Running** state.

10. In the remaining part of this exercise, we shall see how the **NoExecute** effect instructs the scheduler to even remove Pods after they have been scheduled to the node. Before that, we need to do some cleanup. Delete both Pods using the following command:

```
kubectl delete pod pod-with-node-toleration-noschedule pod-with-node-toleration-noschedule2 -n schedulerdemo
```

    You should see the following response:

```
pod "pod-with-node-toleration-noschedule" deleted
pod "pod-with-node-toleration-noschedule2" deleted
```

11. Let's remove the taint from the node using the following command:

```
kubectl taint nodes minikube app:NoSchedule-
```

    Note the hyphen (**-**) at the end of the command, which tells Kubernetes to remove this label. You should see the following response:

```
node/minikube untainted
```

    Our node is in the state where there is no taint defined. Now, we want to run a Pod first with the toleration as **app=banking** and allocate the Pod. Once the Pod is in the **Running** state, we will remove the taint from the node and see whether the Pod has been removed.

12. Now, taint the node again with the **NoExecute** type as follows:

```
kubectl taint nodes minikube app=banking:NoExecute
```

    You should see the following response:

```
node/minikube tainted
```

13. Now, we need to define a Pod with matching toleration. Create a file called **pod-toleration-noexecute.yaml** with the following contents:

```
apiVersion: v1
kind: Pod
metadata:
  name: pod-with-node-toleration-noexecute
spec:
  tolerations:
  - key: "app"
    operator: "Equal"
    value: "banking"
```

```
    effect: "NoExecute"
  containers:
    - name: pod-with-node-toleration-noexecute-container
      image: k8s.gcr.io/busybox
      command: [ "/bin/sh", "-c", "while :; do echo '.'; sleep
        5 ; done" ]
```

Note that the **tolerations** section defines the label as **app=banking** and the **effect** as **NoExecute**.

14. Create the Pod that we defined in the previous step using the following command:

```
kubectl create -f pod-toleration-noexecute.yaml -n schedulerdemo
```

You should see the following response:

```
pod/pod-with-node-toleration-noexecute created
```

15. Verify that the Pod is in the **Running** state using the following command:

```
kubectl get pods -n schedulerdemo
```

You should see the following response:

```
NAME                                 READY   STATUS    RESTARTS   AGE
pod-with-node-toleration-noexecute   1/1     Running   0          32s
```

Figure 17.20: Getting the list of Pods

16. Now remove the taint from the node using this command:

```
kubectl taint nodes minikube app:NoExecute-
```

Note the hyphen (**-**) at the end of this command, which tells Kubernetes to remove the taint. You will see the following response:

```
node/minikube untainted
```

As mentioned earlier, Pods with tolerations can be attached to nodes with no taints. After you remove the taint, the Pod will still be executed. Note that we have not deleted the Pod and it is still running.

17. Now, if we add a new taint with **NoExecute** to the node, the Pod should be removed from it. To see this in action, add a new taint that is different than the Pod toleration:

```
kubectl taint nodes minikube app=hr:NoExecute
```

As you can see, we have added the **app=hr** taint to the Pod. You should see the following response:

```
node/minikube tainted
```

18. Now, let's check the status of the Pod:

```
kubectl get pods -n schedulerdemo
```

You will see the following response:

```
NAME                                READY   STATUS        RESTARTS   AGE
pod-with-node-toleration-noexecute  0/1     Terminating   0          2m41s
```

Figure 17.21: Checking the status of our Pod

The Pod will either be removed or go into the **Terminating** (marked for removal) state. After a few seconds, Kubernetes will remove the Pod.

In this exercise, you have seen how we can configure taints on nodes so that they accept only specific Pods. You have also configured the taint to affect the running Pods.

USING A CUSTOM KUBERNETES SCHEDULER

Building your own fully featured scheduler is out of the scope of this workshop. However, it is important to understand that the Kubernetes platform allows you to write your own scheduler if your use case requires it, although it is not recommended to use a custom scheduler unless you have a very specialized use case.

A custom scheduler runs as a normal Pod. You can specify in the definition of the Pod running your application to use the custom scheduler. You can add a **schedulerName** field in the Pod specification with the name of the custom scheduler as shown in this sample definition:

```
apiVersion: v1
kind: Pod
metadata:
  name: pod-with-custom-scheduler
spec:
  containers:
    - name: mutating-pod-example-container
      image: k8s.gcr.io/busybox
      command: [ "/bin/sh", "-c", "while :; do echo '.'; sleep 5 ;
        done" ]
  schedulerName: "custom-scheduler"
```

For this configuration to work, it is assumed that a custom scheduler called **custom-scheduler** is available in the cluster.

ACTIVITY 17.01: CONFIGURING A KUBERNETES SCHEDULER TO SCHEDULE PODS

Consider you are the administrator of a Kubernetes cluster and you have the following scenario:

1. There is an API Pod that provides the current currency conversion rate.
2. There is a GUI Pod that displays the conversion rate on a website.
3. There is a Pod that provides services for stock exchanges to get the real-time currency conversion rate.

You have been tasked to make sure that the API and GUI Pods run on the same node. You have also been asked to give higher priority to the real-time currency converter Pod if the traffic spikes. In this activity, you will control the behavior of the Kubernetes Scheduler to complete the activity.

Each of the Pods in this activity should have 0.1 CPU and 100 MiB of memory allocated to it. Note that we have named the Pods API, GUI, and real-time to make things easier. The Pods in this activity are expected to be just printing expressions on the console. You can use the **k8s.gcr.io/busybox** image for all of them.

> **NOTE**
>
> Before starting this activity, make sure that the nodes are not tainted from the previous exercises. To see how to remove a taint, please see *step 15* of *Exercise 17.01*, *Running a Pod with Node Affinity* in this chapter.

Here are some guidelines for the activity:

1. Create a namespace called **scheduleractivity**.
2. Create the Pod priority for the API Pods.
3. Deploy and make sure that the API and GUI Pods are using Pod affinity to be on the same node. The GUI Pod should define the affinity to be on the same node as the API pod.
4. Scale the replicas of the API and GUI Pod to two each.

5. Create a Pod priority for the real-time currency converter Pod. Make sure that the API Pod priority, defined earlier, is less than the real-time Pod but greater than 0.
6. Deploy and run the real-time currency converter Pod with one replica.
7. Make sure that all Pods are in the **Running** state.
8. Now, increase the number of replicas for the real-time currency converter Pod from 1 to 10.
9. See whether the real-time currency converter Pods are being started and whether the GUI Pods are being evicted. If not, keep on increasing the real-time Pods by a factor of 5.
10. Depending on your resources and the number of Pods, the scheduler may start evicting API Pods.
11. Reduce the number of replicas of the real-time Pod from 10 to 1 and see that the API and GUI Pods are scheduled back on the cluster.

Once you have completed the activity, two Pods each of the API and GUI Pods are expected to be in the **Running** state, along with one real-time Pod as shown in the following screenshot:

```
NAME                              READY   STATUS    RESTARTS   AGE
api-pod-c644d44b8-f5xq2           1/1     Running   0          2m16s
api-pod-c644d44b8-wztg6           1/1     Running   0          2m16s
gui-pod-6c494b5888-54vxp          1/1     Running   0          5m22s
gui-pod-6c494b5888-lzcbh          1/1     Running   0          5m22s
realtime-pod-59d4c8b768-dgnvr     1/1     Running   0          12m
```

Figure 17.22: Expected output of Activity 17.01

Note that your output will vary as per your system resources, and hence, you may not see exactly what you see in this screenshot.

> **NOTE**
>
> The solution to this activity can be found at the following address: https://packt.live/304PEoD.

SUMMARY

The Kubernetes Scheduler is a powerful software that abstracts the work of selecting the appropriate node for a Pod on a cluster. The Scheduler watches for unscheduled Pods and attempts to find suitable nodes for them. Once it finds a suitable node for a Pod, it updates etcd (via the API server) that the Pod has been bound to the node.

The scheduler has matured with every release of Kubernetes. The default behavior of the scheduler is sufficient for a variety of workloads, although you have also seen many ways to customize the way that the Scheduler associates resources with Pods. You have seen how node affinity can help you schedule Pods on your desired nodes. Pod affinity can help you schedule a Pod relative to another Pod, and it is a good tool for applications where multiple modules are targeted to be placed next to each other. Taints and tolerations can also help you assign specific workloads to specific nodes. You have also seen that Pod priority can help you schedule the workloads as per the total resources available in the cluster.

In the next chapter, we will upgrade a Kubernetes cluster with no downtime. If you have configured custom scheduling in your cluster using any of the techniques shown in this chapter, you may need to plan your upgrade accordingly. Since the upgrade will take down one worker node at a time, it may be possible that some of your Pods may become non-schedulable because of your configuration, and that may not be an acceptable solution.

18

UPGRADING YOUR CLUSTER WITHOUT DOWNTIME

OVERVIEW

In this chapter, we will discuss how to upgrade your cluster without downtime. We will first understand the need to keep your Kubernetes cluster up to date. Then, we will understand basic application deployment strategies that can help zero-downtime upgrades of the Kubernetes cluster. We will then put these strategies into action by performing an upgrade on a Kubernetes cluster with no downtime for your application.

INTRODUCTION

We learned how to set up a multi-node Kubernetes platform on AWS using kops in *Chapter 11, Build Your Own HA Cluster*. In this chapter, you will learn about upgrading the Kubernetes platform to a new version. We will walk you through hands-on examples of the steps that are required to upgrade the Kubernetes platform. These exercises will also equip you with the skills required to maintain a Kubernetes cluster.

Different organizations set up and maintain their Kubernetes clusters in different ways. You saw in *Chapter 12, Your Application and HA*, that there are numerous ways to set up a cluster. We will present a simple technique to upgrade your cluster and, depending on the cluster you are dealing with, the exact techniques and steps that you will need to take for upgrading may be different, although the basic principles and precautions that we will mention here will be applicable regardless of how you go about upgrading your cluster.

THE NEED TO UPGRADE YOUR KUBERNETES CLUSTER

Building up your business application and putting it out in the world is only half the game. Making your application usable by customers in a secure, scalable, and consistent way is the other half and the one that you have to keep working on. To be able to execute this other half well, you need a rock-solid platform.

In today's highly competitive environment, delivery of the latest features to customers in a timely manner is important to give your business an edge. This platform has to not only be dependable but also provide new and updated features to keep up with the demands of running modern applications. Kubernetes is a fast-moving platform and is well suited for such a dynamic environment. The pace of development and advancement of Kubernetes is evidenced by the number of commits in the official Kubernetes GitHub repository. Let's take a look at the following screenshot:

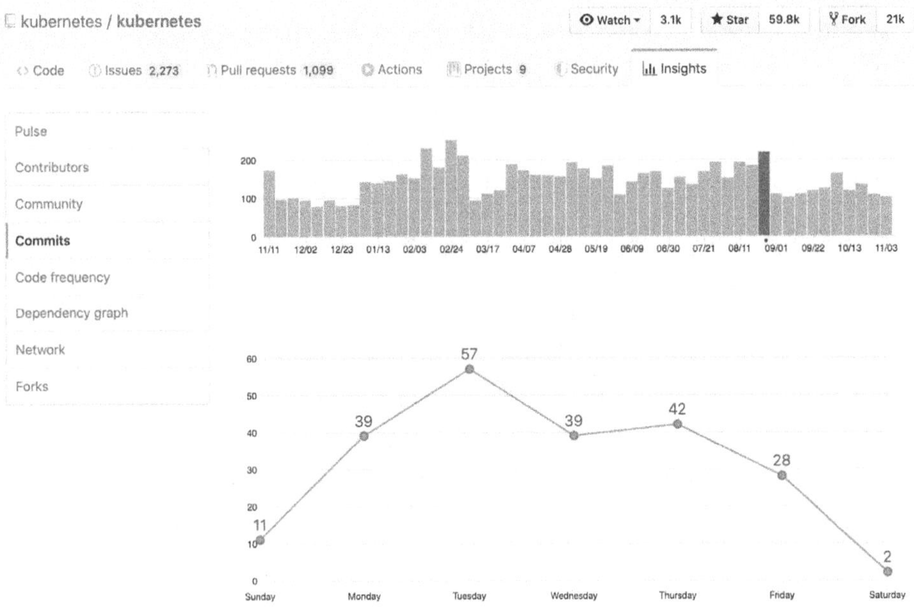

Figure 18.1: Daily commits to the Kubernetes project during the period August 25-31, 2019

The orange bar graph represents the commits per week and, as you can see, they are averaging over 100 per week. The green line graph underneath shows the commits for the week of August 25 through August 31. That's more than 50 commits just on a Tuesday.

By now, it's clear that Kubernetes is advancing at a fast pace, but you may still be unsure about whether you need to update the version of Kubernetes on your cluster. The following are some of the reasons why it is important to keep the platform up to date:

- **New features**: The Kubernetes community is continuously adding new features to satisfy the needs of modern applications. Your software team may come up with a new software component that may be dependent on a newer Kubernetes feature. Thus, sticking to an older version of Kubernetes will hold back the development of *your* software.

- **Security patches**: There are many moving parts in the Kubernetes platform. It has not only the Kubernetes binaries that need to be patched but also lots of Linux features, such as iptables and cgroups. If there are vulnerabilities in any of the components used by Kubernetes, you may need to patch the underlying component, such as the OS itself. Having a consistent way to upgrade is extremely important in keeping the Kubernetes ecosystem as secure as possible.

  For example, there was a vulnerability in versions 1.0–1.12 of the Kubernetes API server that resulted in the API server possibly consuming lots of resources due to an invalid YAML or JSON payload. You can find more details about this vulnerability at this link: https://cve.mitre.org/cgi-bin/cvename.cgi?name=CVE-2019-11253

- **Better handling of existing features**: The Kubernetes team not only adds new features but also keeps on improving existing features for stability and performance. These improvements may be useful for your existing applications or your automation scripts. So, keeping your platform updated is a good idea from this perspective, too.

KUBERNETES COMPONENTS – REFRESHER

By now, you are already aware of the basic components of the Kubernetes platform. Just as a refresher, let's revisit the major components:

- The API server is responsible for exposing RESTful Kubernetes APIs and is stateless. All users on your cluster, Kubernetes master components, kubectl clients, worker nodes, and maybe even your application all need to interact with the API server.
- A key-value store (the etcd server) stores the objects and provides a persistent backend to the API server.
- The scheduler and controller manager act to attain the state of the cluster and objects stored in etcd.
- kubelet is a program that runs on every worker node and behaves like an agent to perform the work as directed by Kubernetes master components.

When we update the platform, as you will see in the later sections, we are going to utilize these components and upgrade them as separate modules.

A WORD OF CAUTION

Kubernetes versions are marked as **A.B.C** and follow the semantic versioning concepts. **A** is the major version, **B** is the minor version, and **C** is the patch release. As per the Kubernetes documentation, "*in highly available (HA) clusters, the newest and oldest kube-apiserver instances must be within one minor version.*'

The following is the safest approach when planning your upgrade:

- Always upgrade to the latest patched release of your current minor version first. For example, if you are on **1.14.X**, first upgrade to the latest available version for the **1.14.X** release train. This will make sure that the platform has all the available fixes applied for the version of your cluster. The latest patch may have bug fixes, which might provide you with a smoother path toward the next minor version, which, in our example, would be **1.15.X**.
- Upgrade to the next minor version. Avoid jumping over multiple minor versions, even if this is possible, as generally, API compatibility is within one minor release. During the upgrade, the Kubernetes platform will be running two different versions of an API because we upgrade one node at a time. For example, it is better to go from **1.14** to **1.15**, and not to **1.16**.

Another important thing to consider is to see whether the newer version needs some updated libraries from the underlying Linux OS. Although, in general, patch releases don't require any underlying component upgrades, keeping the underlying OS up to date should also be on top of your list to provide a safe and consistent environment for the Kubernetes platform.

THE UPGRADE PROCESS

In this section, you will see the steps required to upgrade the Kubernetes platform. Note that upgrading the underlying OS is not covered here. To meet the requirement of zero-downtime upgrades, you must have an HA Kubernetes cluster with a minimum of three masters and etcd servers, which enables frictionless upgrades. The process will take one node out of the three and upgrade it. The upgraded component then will rejoin the cluster, and then we take the second node and apply the upgrade process to it. Since, at any given time, at least two of the servers are kept available, the cluster will remain available during the upgrade.

SOME CONSIDERATIONS FOR KOPS

We have guided you through the creation of an HA Kubernetes cluster in *Chapter 11, Build Your Own HA Cluster*. Hence, in this chapter, we will walk you through upgrading the same cluster.

As mentioned in that chapter, there are various ways of deploying and managing a Kubernetes cluster. We have opted for kops, which has built-in tools for upgrading Kubernetes components. We will be leveraging them in this chapter.

The versioning of kops is set to be analogous to the minor version of Kubernetes it implements. For example, kops version **1.14.x** implements Kubernetes version **1.14.x**. For more details on this, please refer to this link: https://kops.sigs.k8s.io/welcome/releases/.

> **NOTE**
>
> In the HA cluster we created in *Chapter 11*, *Build Your Own HA Cluster*, we deployed three master nodes, which host all the Kubernetes master plane components, including the etcd.

AN OVERVIEW OF THE UPGRADE PROCESS

The entire upgrade process can be diagrammatically summarized as follows:

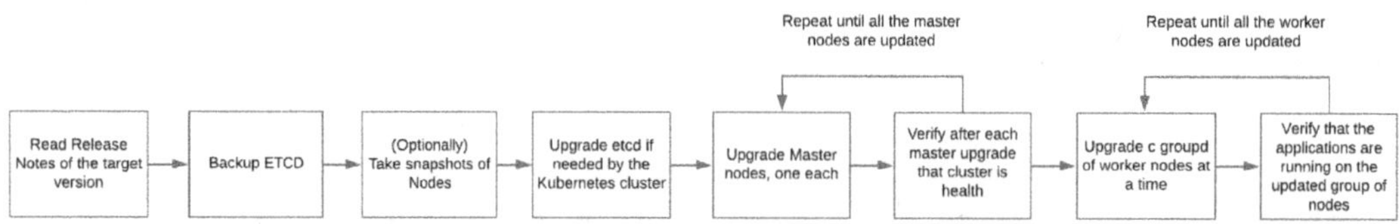

Figure 18.2: The recommended upgrade process

Let's take a quick look at each step before we move on to the implementation:

1. **Read the release notes**

   These will indicate any special considerations that might be necessary during an upgrade. The release notes for each version are available on GitHub at this link: https://github.com/kubernetes/kubernetes/tree/master/CHANGELOG.

2. **Back up the etcd datastore**

   As you have learned earlier, etcd stores the entire state of the cluster. A backup of etcd would allow you to restore the state of your datastore, if needed.

3. **Back up the nodes as an optional failsafe**

   This may come in handy if the upgrade process does not go as planned and you want to revert to a previous state. Cloud vendors (such as AWS, GCP, Azure, and others) enable you to take a snapshot of the hosts. If you are running in a private data center and using hypervisors for your machines, your hypervisor provider (for example, VMware) may provide tools to take snapshots of the nodes. Taking snapshots is beyond the scope of this book, but nonetheless, it is a useful step before you start upgrading your Kubernetes platform.

4. **Upgrade the etcd if required**

   The more recent versions of the tools used to deploy and manage a Kubernetes cluster (such as kops in our case) usually take care of this automatically. Even so, this is an important consideration, especially if you are not using any tools such as kops.

   Check and verify whether the new version of Kubernetes needs a different version of the etcd store. This is not always necessary, but may be required depending on your version. For example, Kubernetes version `1.13` needs etcd v3, while prior versions work with etcd v2.

   You will know whether you need to upgrade etcd from reading the release notes (*step 1*). For example, when the earlier version of etcd was phased out in version 1.13, it was explicitly mentioned in the release notes: https://github.com/kubernetes/kubernetes/blob/master/CHANGELOG/CHANGELOG-1.13.md#urgent-upgrade-notes.

5. **Upgrade the master components**

   Log in to the bastion host and upgrade the version of kops based on the desired version of Kubernetes. This compatibility matrix should be a useful guide: https://kops.sigs.k8s.io/welcome/releases/#compatibility-matrix.

   Run the upgrade on the first master node, verify that it is updated correctly, and then repeat the same steps for all other master nodes.

6. **Upgrade the worker node groups**

   As you have seen in *Chapter 11, Build Your Own HA Cluster*, kops allows you to manage the nodes using instance groups, which is tied to the autoscaling group, in the case of AWS. Run the upgrade on the first instance group of worker nodes. To verify that the nodes were successfully upgraded, you need to check that the nodes are upgraded to the desired version of Kubernetes and whether pods are scheduled on the upgraded nodes. Repeat the same steps for all other instance groups of worker nodes.

7. **Verify that the upgrade process succeeded**

   Check whether all the nodes are upgraded and all your applications are running as intended.

THE IMPORTANCE OF AUTOMATION

As you have seen from this overview, there are several steps required to upgrade the cluster. Given the number of releases and patches, you may need to do this often. Since the process is well documented, it is highly recommended that you consider using an automation tool, such as Ansible or Puppet, to automate this whole process. All the preceding steps can be fully automated, and you have a repeatable way to upgrade your cluster. Automation, however, will not be covered in this chapter as this is beyond the scope of this book.

BACKING UP THE ETCD DATASTORE

etcd stores the state of the entire cluster. So, taking a snapshot of etcd allows us to restore the entire cluster to the state when the snapshot was taken. This may come in handy if you want to revert the cluster to a previous state.

> **NOTE**
>
> Before you begin with any exercises, make sure that the cluster is set up and available as per the instructions in *Chapter 11, Build Your Own HA Cluster*, and that you can access the nodes from your computer via SSH. It is also recommended that you take snapshots of the nodes before starting the upgrade process. This is especially beneficial because in this chapter, you will upgrade the cluster two times – once during the exercises and once during the activity.

Now, before we move on to the first exercise, we need to understand a bit more about etcd. The way that it works is that it runs as a pod on your cluster in the **kube-system** namespace (as you have seen in *Chapter 2, An Overview of Kubernetes*) and exposes an API, which is used to write data to it. Whenever the Kubernetes API server wants to persist any data to etcd, it will use etcd's API to access it.

For backing up etcd, we will also need to access its API and use a built-in function to save a snapshot. For that, we will use a command-line client called **etcdctl**, which is already present in the etcd pod. Detailed coverage of this tool and the etcd API is not necessary for our purposes and so we are not including it in this book. You can learn more about it at this link: https://github.com/etcd-io/etcd/tree/master/etcdctl.

Now, let's see how we can use etcdctl to back up etcd in the following exercise.

Exercise 18.01: Taking a Snapshot of the etcd Datastore

In this exercise, we will see how to take a snapshot of the etcd store. As mentioned in the previous section, a manual upgrade of etcd may not be required, depending on your upgrade path. However, backing up etcd is essential. For this, and all the following exercises and activities, use the same machine (your laptop or desktop) that you used to perform *Exercise 11.01, Setting Up Our Kubernetes Cluster*:

1. We have used kops to install the cluster. Kops uses two different etcd clusters – one for events generated by Kubernetes components, and the second one for everything else. You can see these pods by issuing the following command:

```
kubectl get pods -n kube-system | grep etcd-manager
```

This should get the details of the etcd pods. You should see an output similar to the following:

```
$kubectl get pods -n kube-system | grep etcd-manager
etcd-manager-events-ip-172-20-115-0.us-west-2.compute.internal     1/1     Running   0          97m
etcd-manager-events-ip-172-20-46-185.us-west-2.compute.internal    1/1     Running   0          97m
etcd-manager-events-ip-172-20-80-162.us-west-2.compute.internal    1/1     Running   0          97m
etcd-manager-main-ip-172-20-115-0.us-west-2.compute.internal       1/1     Running   0          97m
etcd-manager-main-ip-172-20-46-185.us-west-2.compute.internal      1/1     Running   0          96m
etcd-manager-main-ip-172-20-80-162.us-west-2.compute.internal      1/1     Running   0          97m
```

Figure 18.3: Getting the list of etcd-manager pods

2. By default, kops' **etcd-manager** function creates backups every 15 minutes. The location of the backups is the same S3 storage used by the kops tool. In *Exercise 11.01*, you configured the S3 bucket to store kops' state. Let's query the bucket to see whether a backup is available there:

```
aws s3api list-objects --bucket $BUCKET_NAME | grep backups/etcd/main
```

You should see a response similar to this:

```
"Key": "myfirstcluster.k8s.local/backups/etcd/main/2020-06-14T02:06:33Z-000001/_etcd_backup.meta",
"Key": "myfirstcluster.k8s.local/backups/etcd/main/2020-06-14T02:06:33Z-000001/etcd.backup.gz",
"Key": "myfirstcluster.k8s.local/backups/etcd/main/2020-06-14T02:21:37Z-000002/_etcd_backup.meta",
"Key": "myfirstcluster.k8s.local/backups/etcd/main/2020-06-14T02:21:37Z-000002/etcd.backup.gz",
"Key": "myfirstcluster.k8s.local/backups/etcd/main/2020-06-14T02:36:40Z-000003/_etcd_backup.meta",
"Key": "myfirstcluster.k8s.local/backups/etcd/main/2020-06-14T02:36:40Z-000003/etcd.backup.gz",
"Key": "myfirstcluster.k8s.local/backups/etcd/main/2020-06-14T02:51:41Z-000001/_etcd_backup.meta",
"Key": "myfirstcluster.k8s.local/backups/etcd/main/2020-06-14T02:51:41Z-000001/etcd.backup.gz",
"Key": "myfirstcluster.k8s.local/backups/etcd/main/2020-06-14T03:06:44Z-000004/_etcd_backup.meta",
"Key": "myfirstcluster.k8s.local/backups/etcd/main/2020-06-14T03:06:44Z-000004/etcd.backup.gz",
"Key": "myfirstcluster.k8s.local/backups/etcd/main/2020-06-14T03:21:45Z-000005/_etcd_backup.meta",
"Key": "myfirstcluster.k8s.local/backups/etcd/main/2020-06-14T03:21:45Z-000005/etcd.backup.gz",
"Key": "myfirstcluster.k8s.local/backups/etcd/main/2020-06-14T03:36:47Z-000001/_etcd_backup.meta",
"Key": "myfirstcluster.k8s.local/backups/etcd/main/2020-06-14T03:36:47Z-000001/etcd.backup.gz",
"Key": "myfirstcluster.k8s.local/backups/etcd/main/2020-06-14T03:51:48Z-000002/_etcd_backup.meta",
"Key": "myfirstcluster.k8s.local/backups/etcd/main/2020-06-14T03:51:48Z-000002/etcd.backup.gz",
```

Figure 18.4: Getting a list of available backups

You can see that the backups are taken automatically every 15 minutes and timestamps of the backups are marked. We will use the **Key** of the latest backup, highlighted in the preceding screenshot, in the next step.

3. The next step is to get the backup from the S3 bucket. We can use AWS CLI commands to get the backup that we need:

```
aws s3api get-object --bucket $BUCKET_NAME --key "myfirstcluster.k8s.
local/backups/etcd/main/2020-06-14T02:06:33Z-000001/etcd.backup.
gz'  etcd-backup-$(date +%Y-%m-%d_%H:%M:%S_%Z).db
```

Note that this command contains the name of the bucket, the **Key** of the file from the previous step, and the filename that we want to use while saving the file. Use the **Key** that you get for your instance in the output of the previous step. You should see a response similar to this:


```
{
    "AcceptRanges": "bytes",
    "LastModified": "Sun, 14 Jun 2020 02:06:34 GMT",
    "ContentLength": 688,
    "ETag": "\"366b9e91913c43799ab2d1e99e044339\"",
    "ContentType": "binary/octet-stream",
    "ServerSideEncryption": "AES256",
    "Metadata": {}
}
```


Figure 18.5: Saving the etcd backup from our S3 bucket

Note that we have used the **date** command to generate the filename. This is a very common technique used by system administrators to make sure that any files are not overwritten.

> **NOTE**
>
> If you want to recover your etcd instance using this backup, you can find the recovery instructions at this link: https://kops.sigs.k8s.io/operations/etcd_backup_restore_encryption/.

4. Verify that the backup file is created:

```
ls -lrt
```

You should see the following response:

```
$ls -rlt
total 8
-rw-r--r--  1 faisalmasood  wheel  688 14 Jun 14:15 etcd-backup-2020-06-14_14:15:45_AEST.db
```

Figure 18.6: Confirming the saved etcd backup

You should be able to see the snapshot that we created in the response.

In this exercise, you have seen how to generate a backup of the etcd datastore. This backup is the state of Kubernetes and could be useful not only if your upgrade is hit by any issues, but also to restore the cluster for any other reason, such as **Disaster Recovery** (**DR**) scenarios.

DRAINING A NODE AND MAKING IT NON-SCHEDULABLE

Before we start to upgrade any nodes (master or worker), we need to make sure that no pods (including the pods for the master components) are running on this node. This is an important step to prepare any node to be upgraded. Furthermore, the node needs to be marked as unschedulable. An unschedulable node is a flag for the scheduler to not schedule any pods in this node.

We can use the **drain** command to mark the node as un-schedulable and to evict all the pods. The **drain** command will not delete any DaemonSet pods unless we tell the flag to do so. One of the reasons for this behavior is that DaemonSet pods cannot be scheduled on any other nodes.

Note that the **drain** command waits for the graceful termination of the pods and it is highly recommended to wait for all the pods to terminate gracefully in production environments. Let's see this in action in the following exercise.

EXERCISE 18.02: DRAINING ALL THE PODS FROM THE NODES

In this exercise, we will remove all the pods running on a node. Once all the pods are removed, we will change the node back to schedulable so that it can accept new workloads. This is when the node has been upgraded and ready to take new pods:

1. Get a list of all the nodes:

```
kubectl get nodes
```

You should see a response similar to this:

```
kube-group-1-54cx   Ready    master   71m   v1.14.8
kube-group-1-gxwc   Ready    master   67m   v1.14.8
kube-group-1-lb51   Ready    master   69m   v1.14.8
kube-group-1-mdlr   Ready    worker   47m   v1.14.8
kube-group-1-v627   Ready    worker   48m   v1.14.8
```

Figure 18.7: Getting a list of nodes

In this example, we have two worker nodes and three master nodes.

2. Create a new namespace called **upgrade-demo**:

```
kubectl create ns upgrade-demo
```

You should see the following response:

```
namespace/upgrade-demo created
```

3. Run a bunch of pods to simulate a workload. Create a file named **multiple-pods.yaml** with the following content:

```
apiVersion: apps/v1
kind: Deployment
metadata:
  name: sleep
spec:
  replicas: 4
  selector:
    matchLabels:
      app.kubernetes.io/name: sleep
```

```
  template:
    metadata:
      labels:
        app.kubernetes.io/name: sleep
    spec:
      containers:
      - name: sleep
        image: k8s.gcr.io/busybox
        command: [ "/bin/sh', "-c', "while :; do echo 'this is
          backend pod'; sleep 5 ; done' ]
        imagePullPolicy: IfNotPresent
```

The deployment will create four replicas of the pods.

4. Now, use the config to create the deployment:

```
kubectl create -f multiple-pod.yaml -n upgrade-demo
```

You should see this response:

```
deployment.apps/sleep created
```

5. Verify that they are running on the worker pods:

```
kubectl get pods -n upgrade-demo -o wide
```

Your output should look like this:

NAME	READY	STATUS	RESTARTS	AGE	IP	NODE
sleep-868969c989-5jwmh	1/1	Running	0	77s	10.40.0.1	kube-group-1-v627
sleep-868969c989-hfsvc	1/1	Running	0	77s	10.40.0.2	kube-group-1-v627
sleep-868969c989-vm2bm	1/1	Running	0	76s	10.42.0.2	kube-group-1-mdlr
sleep-868969c989-vtndb	1/1	Running	0	77s	10.42.0.1	kube-group-1-mdlr

Figure 18.8: Verifying whether the pods are running on the worker nodes

Note that the pods are distributed among both worker nodes by the default scheduler behavior.

6. Use the **drain** command to evict all the pods from any of the nodes. This command will also mark the node as unschedulable:

```
kubectl drain kube-group-1-mdlr --ignore-daemonsets
```

Use the name of your node that you obtain from the output of the previous step. Note that we have passed a flag to ignore the daemon sets. You should see the following response:

```
node/kube-group-1-mdlr already cordoned
WARNING: ignoring DaemonSet-managed Pods: kube-system/kube-proxy-4h9m2, kube-system/weave-net-wrrdq
evicting pod "sleep-868969c989-vtndb"
evicting pod "sleep-868969c989-vm2bm"
```

Figure 18.9: Draining a node

If we don't set the **--ignore-daemonsets** flag and there are some DaemonSet pods on the node, **drain** will not proceed without this flag. We recommend using this flag because your cluster may be running some essential pods as a DaemonSet –for example, a Fluentd pod that collects logs from all other pods on the node and sends them to the central logging server. You may want this log collection pod to be available until the very last minute.

7. Verify that all the pods are drained from this node. To do that, get a list of the pods:

```
kubectl get pods -n upgrade-demo -o wide
```

You should see the following response:

```
NAME                    READY   STATUS    RESTARTS   AGE     IP          NODE
sleep-868969c989-5jwmh  1/1     Running   0          4m52s   10.40.0.1   kube-group-1-v627
sleep-868969c989-c9s8z  1/1     Running   0          113s    10.40.0.3   kube-group-1-v627
sleep-868969c989-hfsvc  1/1     Running   0          4m52s   10.40.0.2   kube-group-1-v627
sleep-868969c989-v8k51  1/1     Running   0          113s    10.40.0.4   kube-group-1-v627
```

Figure 18.10: Checking whether the pods have been moved away from the drained node

In the preceding screenshot, you can see that all the pods are running on the other node. We only had two worker nodes in our cluster, and so all the pods were scheduled on the lone schedulable node. If we had several available worker nodes, the pods would have been distributed among them by the scheduler.

8. Let's describe our drained node and make a few important observations:

```
kubectl describe node kube-group-1-mdlr
```

Use the name of the node that you drained in *step 6*. This will give a pretty long output, but there are two sections worth observing:

```
Labels:             beta.kubernetes.io/arch=amd64
                    beta.kubernetes.io/os=linux
                    kubernetes.io/arch=amd64
                    kubernetes.io/hostname=instance-2
                    kubernetes.io/os=linux
Annotations:        kubeadm.alpha.kubernetes.io/cri-socket: /var/run/dockershim.sock
                    node.alpha.kubernetes.io/ttl: 0
                    volumes.kubernetes.io/controller-managed-attach-detach: true
CreationTimestamp:  Sun, 24 Nov 2019 13:39:42 +0000
Taints:             node.kubernetes.io/unschedulable:NoSchedule
Unschedulable:      true
```

Figure 18.11: Checking taints and the unschedulable status of our drained node

The preceding screenshot shows that our node is marked as unschedulable. Next, find the section like the following in your output:

```
Non-terminated Pods:          (2 in total)
  Namespace                   Name                    CPU Requests  CPU Limits  Memory Requests  Memory Limits  AGE
  ---------                   ----                    ------------  ----------  ---------------  -------------  ---
  kube-system                 kube-proxy-9ljcz        0 (0%)        0 (0%)      0 (0%)           0 (0%)         7m7s
  kube-system                 weave-net-gkbfv         20m (1%)      0 (0%)      0 (0%)           0 (0%)         5m27s
```

Figure 18.12: Examining the non-terminated pods on the drained node

This shows that the only non-terminated pods running on our system have names starting with **`kube-proxy`** and **`weave-net`**. The first pod implements **`kube-proxy`**, which is the component that manages pod and service network rules on nodes. The second pod is **`weave-net`**, which implements virtual networking for our cluster (note that your networking provider depends on the type of network you have selected). Since we added a flag to exclude DaemonSets in *step 6*, these pods, which are managed by a DaemonSet, are still running.

9. Once you drain the pod in *step 6*, you will be able to upgrade the node. Even though upgrading is not part of this exercise, we just want to make the node schedulable again. For that, use the following command:

```
kubectl uncordon kube-group-1-mdlr
```

You should see a response similar to this:

```
node/kube-group-1-mdlr uncordoned
```

10. Verify that the node is schedulable again. Check the **`Taints`** section in the following output:

```
kubectl describe node kube-group-1-mdlr
```

You should see a response similar to the following:

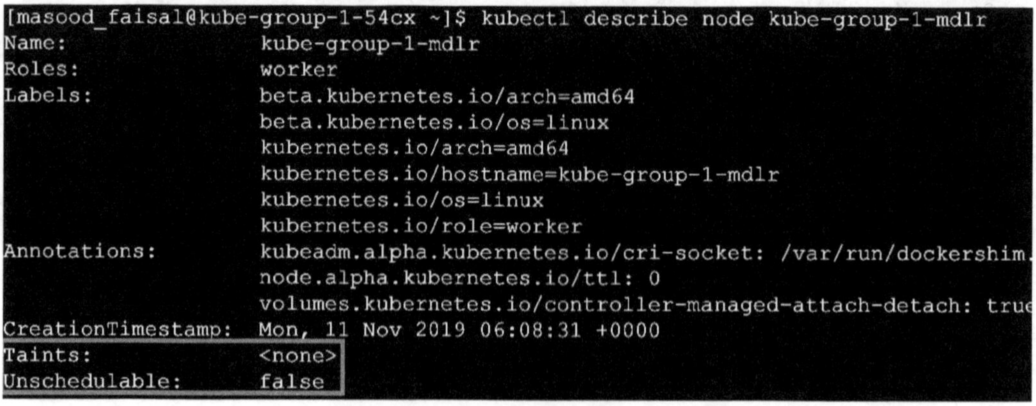

```
[masood_faisal@kube-group-1-54cx ~]$ kubectl describe node kube-group-1-mdlr
Name:               kube-group-1-mdlr
Roles:              worker
Labels:             beta.kubernetes.io/arch=amd64
                    beta.kubernetes.io/os=linux
                    kubernetes.io/arch=amd64
                    kubernetes.io/hostname=kube-group-1-mdlr
                    kubernetes.io/os=linux
                    kubernetes.io/role=worker
Annotations:        kubeadm.alpha.kubernetes.io/cri-socket: /var/run/dockershim.
                    node.alpha.kubernetes.io/ttl: 0
                    volumes.kubernetes.io/controller-managed-attach-detach: tru
CreationTimestamp:  Mon, 11 Nov 2019 06:08:31 +0000
Taints:             <none>
Unschedulable:      false
```

Figure 18.13: Checking the taints and unschedulable statuses of our uncordoned node

The preceding screenshot shows that the node is now schedulable, and the taint that we observed in *step 8* has been removed.

In this exercise, you have seen how to remove all the pods from the node and mark the node as unschedulable. This will make sure that no new pod will be scheduled in this node and we can work on upgrading this node. We also learned how to make the node schedulable again so that we can continue using it after completing the upgrade.

UPGRADING KUBERNETES MASTER COMPONENTS

When you are running Kubernetes in any capacity that is important for your organization, you will be running the platform in an HA configuration. To achieve that, the typical configuration is at least three replicas of master components, running on three different nodes. This allows you to upgrade single nodes from one minor version to the next, one by one, while still maintaining API compatibility when an upgraded node rejoins the cluster because Kubernetes provides compatibility across one minor version. This means the master components can be on different versions when you are upgrading each node at a time. The following table provides a logical flow of the versions. Let's assume you are upgrading from version 1.14 to 1.15:

Timeline	Kubernetes version on node 1	Kubernetes version on node 2	Kubernetes version on node 3
Before starting the upgrade	1.14	1.14	1.14
After upgrading the first node	1.15	1.14	1.14
After upgrading the second node	1.15	1.15	1.14
After upgrading the third node	1.15	1.15	1.15

Figure 18.14: Upgrade plan for three master nodes

In the following exercise, we will proceed with upgrading the Kubernetes master components.

EXERCISE 18.03: UPGRADING KUBERNETES MASTER COMPONENTS

In this exercise, you will upgrade all the master components on the Kubernetes master nodes. This exercise assumes that you are still logged in to the bastion host of your cluster.

In this exercise, we are demonstrating the process on a smaller number of nodes for the sake of simplicity, but the process of upgrading a large number of nodes would be the same. However, for a seamless upgrade, three master nodes are a minimum, and your applications should be HA and running on at least two worker nodes:

1. Run the kops validator to validate the existing cluster:

```
kops validate cluster
```

You should see a response similar to the following:

```
Using cluster from kubectl context: myfirstcluster.k8s.local

Validating cluster myfirstcluster.k8s.local

I0315 00:59:45.180939    3785 gce_cloud.go:273] Scanning zones: [australia-so
utheast1-b australia-southeast1-c australia-southeast1-a]
INSTANCE GROUPS
INSTANCE GROUPS
NAME                            ROLE    MACHINETYPE     MIN     MAX     SUBNETS
master-australia-southeast1-a   Master  n1-standard-1   1       1       australia
-southeast1
master-australia-southeast1-b   Master  n1-standard-1   1       1       australia
-southeast1
master-australia-southeast1-c   Master  n1-standard-1   1       1       australia
-southeast1
nodes                           Node    n1-standard-2   3       3       australia
-southeast1
```

Figure 18.15: Validating our kops cluster

This is a truncated version of the output. It shows the major infrastructure components of your cluster.

2. List all the nodes in your cluster:

```
kubectl get nodes
```

You should see a response similar to this:

```
NAME                                 STATUS   ROLES    AGE    VERSION
master-australia-southeast1-a-q2pw   Ready    master   93s    v1.15.7
master-australia-southeast1-b-4jll   Ready    master   102s   v1.15.7
master-australia-southeast1-c-0ndl   Ready    master   103s   v1.15.7
nodes-6htd                           Ready    node     63s    v1.15.7
nodes-71x0                           Ready    node     60s    v1.15.7
nodes-wjth                           Ready    node     60s    v1.15.7
```

Figure 18.16: Getting a list of the nodes

Notice that we have three master nodes and all of them are on version 1.15.7.

> **NOTE**
>
> In this exercise, we are showcasing the upgrade from Kubernetes version 1.15.7 to 1.15.10. You can apply the same steps to upgrade to the version of Kubernetes supported by kops at the time when you perform this exercise. Just remember our earlier advice of upgrading to the latest patch version first (which is what we are doing here).

3. Use the **`kops upgrade cluster`** command to see what update is available:

```
kops upgrade cluster ${NAME}
```

Note that this command will not directly run the update, but it will give you the latest update version possible. The **`NAME`** environment variable holds the name of your cluster. You should see an output similar to the following:

```
I0315 01:03:16.106957    3832 upgrade_cluster.go:216] Custom image (cos-cloud/cos
-stable-65-10323-99-0) has been provided for Instance Group "master-australia-sou
theast1-a"; not updating image
I0315 01:03:16.107009    3832 upgrade_cluster.go:216] Custom image (cos-cloud/cos
-stable-65-10323-99-0) has been provided for Instance Group "master-australia-sou
theast1-b"; not updating image
I0315 01:03:16.107026    3832 upgrade_cluster.go:216] Custom image (cos-cloud/cos
-stable-65-10323-99-0) has been provided for Instance Group "master-australia-sou
theast1-c"; not updating image
I0315 01:03:16.107047    3832 upgrade_cluster.go:216] Custom image (cos-cloud/cos
-stable-65-10323-99-0) has been provided for Instance Group "nodes"; not updating
 image
ITEM    PROPERTY                 OLD     NEW
Cluster KubernetesVersion        1.15.7  1.15.10

Must specify --yes to perform upgrade
```

Figure 18.17: Checking the available cluster version

You can see from the preceding screenshot that the **`OLD`** version is **`1.15.7`**, which is our current version, and an update is available to the **`NEW`** version of **`1.15.10`**, which is our target version.

4. Once you verify the changes from the command in *step 4*, run the same command with a **--yes** flag. This will mark the desired state of the cluster in the kops state store:

```
kops upgrade cluster --yes
```

You should see an output similar to the following:

```
I0315 01:04:22.847381    3842 upgrade_cluster.go:216] Custom image (cos-cloud/cos
-stable-65-10323-99-0) has been provided for Instance Group "master-australia-sou
theast1-a"; not updating image
I0315 01:04:22.847411    3842 upgrade_cluster.go:216] Custom image (cos-cloud/cos
-stable-65-10323-99-0) has been provided for Instance Group "master-australia-sou
theast1-b"; not updating image
I0315 01:04:22.847422    3842 upgrade_cluster.go:216] Custom image (cos-cloud/cos
-stable-65-10323-99-0) has been provided for Instance Group "master-australia-sou
theast1-c"; not updating image
I0315 01:04:22.847440    3842 upgrade_cluster.go:216] Custom image (cos-cloud/cos
-stable-65-10323-99-0) has been provided for Instance Group "nodes"; not updating
 image
ITEM     PROPERTY                 OLD      NEW
Cluster  KubernetesVersion        1.15.7   1.15.10

Updates applied to configuration.
You can now apply these changes, using `kops update cluster myfirstcluster.k8s.lo
cal`
```

Figure 18.18: Upgrading the kops cluster configuration

This output indicates that the desired version of the Kubernetes cluster is recorded in the updated kops configuration. In the next step, we will ask kops to update the cloud or cluster resources to match the new specifications – that is, Kubernetes version **1.15.10**.

5. Now, let's run the following command so that kops updates the cluster to match the updated kops configuration:

```
kops update cluster ${NAME} --yes
```

This will give a long output that will end in a similar way to the following screenshot:

```
W0315 01:05:17.698551    3859 autoscalinggroup.go:106] enabling storage-rw for etcd backups
W0315 01:05:17.698649    3859 autoscalinggroup.go:106] enabling storage-rw for etcd backups
I0315 01:05:28.135766    3859 executor.go:103] Tasks: 0 done / 76 total; 43 can run
I0315 01:05:29.245349    3859 executor.go:103] Tasks: 43 done / 76 total; 27 canrun
I0315 01:05:29.563841    3859 instancetemplate.go:226] We should be using NVME for GCE
I0315 01:05:29.566522    3859 instancetemplate.go:226] We should be using NVME for GCE
I0315 01:05:29.570846    3859 instancetemplate.go:226] We should be using NVME for GCE
I0315 01:05:29.573952    3859 instancetemplate.go:226] We should be using NVME for GCE
I0315 01:05:29.578939    3859 instancetemplate.go:226] We should be using NVME for GCE
I0315 01:05:29.579948    3859 instancetemplate.go:226] We should be using NVME for GCE
I0315 01:05:29.675463    3859 instancetemplate.go:226] We should be using NVME for GCE
I0315 01:05:29.677909    3859 instancetemplate.go:226] We should be using NVME for GCE
I0315 01:05:34.867830    3859 executor.go:103] Tasks: 70 done / 76 total; 6 can run
I0315 01:05:49.036234    3859 executor.go:103] Tasks: 76 done / 76 total; 0 can run
I0315 01:05:49.396688    3859 update_cluster.go:294] Exporting kubecfg for cluster
kops has set your kubectl context to myfirstcluster.k8s.local

Cluster changes have been applied to the cloud.


Changes may require instances to restart: kops rolling-update cluster
```

Figure 18.19: Updating our cluster infrastructure as per the requirements of our cluster upgrade

This has updated the cluster infrastructure to match the updated kops configuration. Next, we need to perform an upgrade of the Kubernetes master components running on this infrastructure.

6. If you are running several instances of your master/worker nodes on different instance groups, then you can control which instance group is receiving the updates. For that, let's get the name of our instance group first. Use the following command to get the names:

```
kops get instancegroups
```

You should see a response as follows:

```
Using cluster from kubectl context: myfirstcluster.k8s.local

NAME                             ROLE     MACHINETYPE     MIN     MAX     ZONES
master-australia-southeast1-a    Master   n1-standard-1   1       1       australia-southeast1
-a
master-australia-southeast1-b    Master   n1-standard-1   1       1       australia-southeast1
-b
master-australia-southeast1-c    Master   n1-standard-1   1       1       australia-southeast1
-c
nodes                            Node     n1-standard-2   3       3       australia-southeast1
-a,australia-southeast1-b,australia-southeast1-c
```

Figure 18.20: Getting a list of the instance groups

7. In this step, kops will update the Kubernetes cluster to match the kops specifications. Let's upgrade the first master node to the new version using a rolling update:

```
kops rolling-update cluster ${NAME} --instance-group master-
australia-southeast1-a --yes
```

Note that this command will only apply changes if you specify the **--yes** flag. This command may take time based on your node configuration. Be patient and watch the logs to see whether there are any errors. After some time, you should see a successful message similar to the one in the following screenshot:

```
I0315 01:13:38.099246    3885 instancegroups.go:275] Cluster did not pass validation,
will try again in "30s" until duration "15m0s" expires: machine "https://www.googleapi
s.com/compute/beta/projects/kube-test-258704/zones/australia-southeast1-a/instances/ma
ster-australia-southeast1-a-q2pw" has not yet joined cluster.
I0315 01:14:04.521005    3885 gce_cloud.go:273] Scanning zones: [australia-southeast1-
b australia-southeast1-c australia-southeast1-a]
I0315 01:14:08.347291    3885 instancegroups.go:278] Cluster validated.
I0315 01:14:08.347343    3885 rollingupdate.go:184] Rolling update completed for clust
er "myfirstcluster.k8s.local"!
```

Figure 18.21: Applying a rolling update to our first instance group

8. Verify that the node is upgraded to the target version, which is **1.15.10**, in our case:

```
kubectl get nodes
```

This should give a response similar to the following:

```
NAME                                 STATUS   ROLES    AGE     VERSION
master-australia-southeast1-a-q2pw   Ready    master   2m54s   v1.15.10
master-australia-southeast1-b-4jll   Ready    master   18m     v1.15.7
master-australia-southeast1-c-0ndl   Ready    master   18m     v1.15.7
nodes-6htd                           Ready    node     18m     v1.15.7
nodes-71x0                           Ready    node     18m     v1.15.7
nodes-wjth                           Ready    node     18m     v1.15.7
```

Figure 18.22: Checking whether the master components on the node have been upgraded

You can see that the first master node is on the **1.15.10** version.

9. Verify that the pods are running on the newly upgraded node:

```
kubectl describe node master-australia-southeast1-a-q2pw
```

Use the name of the node that you upgraded in the previous steps. This will give a long output. Look for the **Non-terminated Pod** section, as shown in the following screenshot:

```
ProviderID:                          gce://kube-test-258704/australia-southeast1-a/master-aust
ralia-southeast1-a-q2pw
Non-terminated Pods:                 (6 in total)
  Namespace                          Name
     CPU Requests  CPU Limits  Memory Requests  Memory Limits  AGE
  ---------                          ----
     ------------  ----------  ---------------  -------------  ---
  kube-system                        etcd-manager-events-master-australia-southeast1-a-q2pw
     100m (10%)    0 (0%)        100Mi (2%)       0 (0%)         3m17s
  kube-system                        etcd-manager-main-master-australia-southeast1-a-q2pw
     200m (20%)    0 (0%)        100Mi (2%)       0 (0%)         3m18s
  kube-system                        kube-apiserver-master-australia-southeast1-a-q2pw
     150m (15%)    0 (0%)        0 (0%)           0 (0%)         3m8s
  kube-system                        kube-controller-manager-master-australia-southeast1-a-q2p
w    100m (10%)    0 (0%)        0 (0%)           0 (0%)         3m32s
  kube-system                        kube-proxy-master-australia-southeast1-a-q2pw
     100m (10%)    0 (0%)        0 (0%)           0 (0%)         2m55s
  kube-system                        kube-scheduler-master-australia-southeast1-a-q2pw
     100m (10%)    0 (0%)        0 (0%)           0 (0%)         3m24s
Allocated resources:
  (Total limits may be over 100 percent, i.e., overcommitted.)
  Resource                           Requests    Limits
```

Figure 18.23: Checking whether our upgraded node is running pods

> **NOTE**
>
> Repeat *steps 7* to *9* for all additional master nodes, using the appropriate names of the corresponding instance groups while updating and verifying.

10. Verify that kops has successfully updated the master nodes:

```
kops rolling-update cluster ${NAME}
```

You should see the following output:

```
I0315 01:41:31.625893    4386 gce_cloud.go:273] Scanning zones: [australia-southeast1-b australia-southeas
t1-c australia-southeast1-a]
NAME                            STATUS          NEEDUPDATE      READY   MIN     MAX     NODES
master-australia-southeast1-a   Ready           0               1       1       1       1
master-australia-southeast1-b   Ready           0               1       1       1       1
master-australia-southeast1-c   Ready           0               1       1       1       1
nodes                           NeedsUpdate     1               0       1       1       1
nodes                           NeedsUpdate     1               0       1       1       1
nodes                           NeedsUpdate     1               0       1       1       1
```

Figure 18.24: Checking whether all the master nodes have been upgraded

As mentioned earlier, this is a dry run, and the output shows which nodes require an update. Since all of them show **STATUS** as **Ready**, we know that they have been updated. By contrast, you can see that **nodes** (the worker nodes) return **NeedsUpdate**, since we have not updated them yet.

11. Verify that all the master nodes have been upgraded to the desired version:

```
kubectl get nodes
```

You should see a response similar to the following:

```
NAME                                  STATUS   ROLES    AGE    VERSION
master-australia-southeast1-a-q2pw    Ready    master   23m    v1.15.10
master-australia-southeast1-b-4jll    Ready    master   10m    v1.15.10
master-australia-southeast1-c-0ndl    Ready    master   2m1s   v1.15.10
nodes-6htd                            Ready    node     39m    v1.15.7
nodes-71x0                            Ready    node     39m    v1.15.7
nodes-wjth                            Ready    node     39m    v1.15.7
```

Figure 18.25: Checking the version of Kubernetes on all the master nodes

As you can see, all the master nodes are running version **1.15.10**, which is the desired version.

In this exercise, you have seen how to upgrade the master nodes of the Kubernetes cluster without any downtime for users. One node update at a time will make sure that enough master servers are available (a minimum of three are required for this to work) and the users and the cluster are not getting impacted during the update.

> **NOTE**
>
> When you apply a rolling update to an instance group, kops will roll out the update through the nodes within the instance group by taking only one node offline at a time. On top of that, in this exercise, we applied a rolling update to only one instance group at a time. Eventually, what you should achieve is a situation where only one node from your cluster is taken offline at a time. Remember this if you choose to automate this process.

UPGRADING KUBERNETES WORKER NODES

Although Kubernetes supports compatibility between master (API server) and worker nodes (kubelet) within one minor version, it is highly recommended that you upgrade the master and worker nodes in one go. Using kops, upgrading worker nodes is similar to upgrading master nodes. Due to the backward compatibility within one minor version, the worker nodes may still work if they are not version-matched by the master nodes, but it is strongly discouraged to run different versions of Kubernetes on worker and master nodes since this may create problems for the cluster.

However, the following considerations are of extreme importance if you want to keep your application online during the upgrade:

- Make sure that your applications are configured to be highly available. This means that you should have at least two pods, each on different nodes, for each of your applications. If this is not the case, your applications may experience downtime once you evict the pods from the nodes.
- If you are running stateful components, make sure that the state of these components is backed up, or that your applications are designed to be able to withstand partial unavailability of the stateful components.

  For example, let's say that you are running a database with a single master node and multiple read replicas. Once the node that is running the master replica of your database evicts the database pod, if your applications are not correctly configured to handle this scenario, they will suffer a downtime. This has nothing to do with the upgrade of the Kubernetes cluster, but it is important to understand how your applications behave during an upgrade and to ensure that they are properly configured to be fault-tolerant.

Now that we have understood the requirements to ensure the uptime of your application, let's see how we can upgrade the worker nodes in the following exercise.

EXERCISE 18.04: UPGRADING THE WORKER NODES

In this exercise, we will upgrade all the worker nodes of the Kubernetes cluster. Worker nodes are the host of your applications:

1. Get the list of instance groups for your worker nodes:

```
kops get instancegroups
```

   You should see a response similar to the following:

```
Using cluster from kubectl context: myfirstcluster.k8s.local

NAME                            ROLE    MACHINETYPE     MIN     MAX     ZONES
master-australia-southeast1-a   Master  n1-standard-1   1       1       australia-southeast1
-a
master-australia-southeast1-b   Master  n1-standard-1   1       1       australia-southeast1
-b
master-australia-southeast1-c   Master  n1-standard-1   1       1       australia-southeast1
-c
nodes                           Node    n1-standard-2   3       3       australia-southeast1
-a,australia-southeast1-b,australia-southeast1-c
```

Figure 18.26: Getting a list of the instance groups

From this image, we can see that the name of the instance group for our worker nodes is **nodes**.

2. Verify that the nodes are ready:

```
kubectl get nodes
```

You should see a response similar to this:

```
NAME                                  STATUS   ROLES    AGE   VERSION
master-australia-southeast1-a-q2pw    Ready    master   40m   v1.15.10
master-australia-southeast1-b-4jll    Ready    master   26m   v1.15.10
master-australia-southeast1-c-0ndl    Ready    master   18m   v1.15.10
nodes-6htd                            Ready    node     55m   v1.15.7
nodes-71x0                            Ready    node     55m   v1.15.7
nodes-wjth                            Ready    node     55m   v1.15.7
```

Figure 18.27: Checking node status

If we had multiple instance groups, we would be upgrading each instance group one by one. However, our task here is simple since we have just one – that is, **nodes**.

3. Run the kops rolling update for the **nodes** instance group **without** the **--yes** flag. This will provide you with a summary of what will be updated with the **kops rolling-update** command:

```
kops rolling-update cluster ${NAME} --node-interval 3m --instance-group nodes --post-drain-delay 3m --logtostderr --v 9
```

Note that we have changed the verbosity value in the preceding command to get more detailed logs.

Let's break down this command:

– The **node-interval** flag sets the minimum delay between different node restarts.

– The **instance-group** flag states which instance group the rolling update should be applied to.

– The **post-drain-delay** flag sets the delay after draining the node before it can be restarted. Remember from earlier in this chapter that the drain operation will wait for the graceful termination of pods. This delay will be applied after that.

The **node-interval** and **post-drain-delay** flags provide an option to control the rate of change in the cluster. The value of these options partially depends on the type of application you are running. For example, if you are running a log agent DaemonSet on the nodes, you may want to give enough time for the pod to flush the content to a central logging server.

> **NOTE**
>
> We did not use these delays when we performed a rolling update in the previous case since in that case, the instance groups each had just one node in them. Here, we have three nodes in this instance group.

- The **logtosterr** flag outputs all the logs to the **stderr** stream so that we can see them in our terminal output.

- The **v** flag sets the verbosity of the logs that we will see.

This command will show the following output:

```
I0315 03:04:31.740608     5159 gce_cloud.go:273] Scanning zones: [australia-southeast1-b australia-southeas
t1-c australia-southeast1-a]
NAME    STATUS          NEEDUPDATE      READY   MIN     MAX     NODES
nodes   NeedsUpdate     1               0       1       1       1
nodes   NeedsUpdate     1               0       1       1       1
nodes   NeedsUpdate     1               0       1       1       1
```

Figure 18.28: Performing a dry run of the rolling update

4. Now, run the upgrade. Use the same command as the previous step with the addition of the **--yes** flag. This tells kops to perform the upgrade:

```
kops rolling-update cluster ${NAME} --node-interval 3m --instance-
group nodes --post-drain-delay 3m --logtostderr --v 9 --yes
```

Kops will drain a node, wait for the post drain delay time, and then upgrade and restart the node. This will be repeated for each node, one by one. You will see a long log in the terminal, and this process may take up to half an hour to complete. In your terminal, you should start seeing the logs, as follows:

```
I0315 03:04:56.809786     5169 factory.go:68] state store gs://faisal-kube
I0315 03:04:56.814808     5169 gsfs.go:231] Reading file "gs://faisal-kube/myfirstcluster.k8s.local/config"
I0315 03:04:57.142717     5169 loader.go:359] Config loaded from file:  /home/masood_faisal/.kube/config
I0315 03:04:57.143909     5169 round_trippers.go:419] curl -k -v -XGET  -H "Accept: application/json, */*"
-H "User-Agent: kops/v0.0.0 (linux/amd64) kubernetes/$Format" -H "Authorization: Basic YWRtaW46QU95ckM2QWh
```

Figure 18.29: Starting the rolling update process

After a while, you will see that the cluster upgrade is finished with a success message, as shown:

```
I0315 03:25:03.482733    5169 rollingupdate.go:184] Rolling update completed for cluster "myfirstcluster.k8s.local"!
```

Figure 18.30: Rolling update completion message

Keen readers will notice, in *Figure 18.29*, that in the author's logs, the cluster upgrade started at around 3:05 and finished, as can be seen in *Figure 18.29*, at around 3:25. The total time is around 20 minutes for three nodes. We had set a delay of 3 minutes for each node after stopping it and 3 minutes for each node after draining all the pods. So, the waiting time for each node adds up to 6 minutes. With three nodes in the instance group, the total wait time is 6 × 3 = 18 minutes.

5. Verify that the worker nodes are updated to the target version – that is, **1.15.10**:

```
kubectl get nodes
```

You should see the following response:

```
NAME                                   STATUS   ROLES    AGE     VERSION
master-australia-southeast1-a-q2pw     Ready    master   9h      v1.15.10
master-australia-southeast1-b-4jll     Ready    master   9h      v1.15.10
master-australia-southeast1-c-0ndl     Ready    master   9h      v1.15.10
nodes-6htd                             Ready    node     7h34m   v1.15.10
nodes-7lx0                             Ready    node     7h20m   v1.15.10
nodes-wjth                             Ready    node     7h27m   v1.15.10
```

Figure 18.31: Checking the version of Kubernetes on worker nodes

6. Verify that the pods are in a running state:

```
kubectl get pods -n upgrade-demo
```

You should see all pods with **STATUS** set to **Running**, as in this screenshot:

```
NAME                         READY   STATUS    RESTARTS   AGE
sleep-8689c746f4-8cjw5       1/1     Running   0          7h35m
sleep-8689c746f4-brdjh       1/1     Running   0          7h28m
sleep-8689c746f4-fb7cv       1/1     Running   0          7h35m
sleep-8689c746f4-l5fkh       1/1     Running   0          7h28m
```

Figure 18.32: Checking the status of our pods

In this exercise, you have seen how easy it is to upgrade the worker nodes through kops. However, we do not recommend upgrading all worker nodes in one go for production clusters and strongly recommend creating instance groups for worker nodes. The following are some strategies that can be used for production-grade clusters:

- Don't keep all of your worker nodes in a single instance group. Create multiple instance groups for different sets of worker nodes. By default, kops creates only one instance group, but you can change this behavior to create many instance groups for worker nodes. We recommend having different worker instance groups for infrastructure components (such as monitoring and logging), ingress, critical applications, non-critical applications, and static applications. This will help you apply the upgrade to less critical parts of your cluster first. This strategy would help limit any issues in the upgrade process, keeping them to a minimum while isolating the affected nodes from the rest of the cluster.
- If you are running the cluster in the cloud, you can provision new nodes on demand. Thus, it may be a good idea to create a sister instance group for upgrades. This new instance group should be running the upgraded version of Kubernetes. Now, cordon and drain all the pods from the old instance group. The Kubernetes scheduler will see that the new nodes are available and will automatically move all your pods to the new nodes. Once this is complete, you can just delete the old instance group and your upgrade is complete.

  This strategy needs a bit of planning, especially if you are running stateful applications on the cluster. This strategy also assumes that you are able to provision new nodes on demand, since creating a sister instance group may require temporary additional hardware, which may be a challenge for an on-premises data center.

Notice that these are advanced strategies and are beyond the scope of this book. However, you can find more information about it at https://kops.sigs.k8s.io/tutorial/working-with-instancegroups/.

Now that you have seen all the steps required to upgrade your cluster, you can bring it all together in the following activity.

ACTIVITY 18.01: UPGRADING THE KUBERNETES PLATFORM FROM VERSION 1.15.7 TO 1.15.10

In this activity, you will upgrade the Kubernetes platform from version **1.15.7** to version **1.15.10**. Here, we will bring together everything that we have learned in this chapter. These guidelines should help you to complete the activity:

> **NOTE**
>
> In this activity, we are showcasing the upgrade from Kubernetes version **1.15.7** to **1.15.10**. You can apply the same steps to upgrade to the version of Kubernetes supported by kops at the time when you perform this activity.

1. Using *Exercise 11.01*, *Setting Up Our Kubernetes Cluster*, set up a fresh cluster running Kubernetes version **1.15.7**. If you are using the cloud to spin up machines, you can take a snapshot of the machines (your cloud vendor may charge you for this) before the upgrade to quickly rerun the upgrade again.
2. Upgrade kops to the version you want to upgrade on the master or bastion node. For this activity, we need to have version **1.15**.
3. Upgrade one of the master nodes to Kubernetes version **1.15.10**.
4. Verify that the master node is back in service and in the **Ready** state.
5. Similarly, upgrade all the other master nodes.
6. Verify that all the master nodes are upgraded to the desired version, as in the following screenshot:

```
NAME                                 STATUS   ROLES    AGE   VERSION
master-australia-southeast1-a-q2pw   Ready    master   40m   v1.15.10
master-australia-southeast1-b-4jll   Ready    master   26m   v1.15.10
master-australia-southeast1-c-0ndl   Ready    master   18m   v1.15.10
nodes-6htd                           Ready    node     55m   v1.15.7
nodes-71x0                           Ready    node     55m   v1.15.7
nodes-wjth                           Ready    node     55m   v1.15.7
```

Figure 18.33: Upgraded version of Kubernetes on master nodes

7. Now, upgrade the worker nodes.
8. Verify that the pods are running successfully on the newly upgraded nodes. Finally, you should be able to verify that your pods are running on the new node, as follows:

```
NAME                       READY   STATUS    RESTARTS   AGE
sleep-8689c746f4-8cjw5     1/1     Running   0          7h35m
sleep-8689c746f4-brdjh     1/1     Running   0          7h28m
sleep-8689c746f4-fb7cv     1/1     Running   0          7h35m
sleep-8689c746f4-15fkh     1/1     Running   0          7h28m
```

Figure 18.34: Pods running on upgraded worker nodes

> **NOTE**
>
> The solution to this activity can be found at the following address: https://packt.live/304PEoD.

SUMMARY

In this chapter, you have learned that keeping your Kubernetes platform up to date is very important when it comes to providing a secure and reliable foundation for running your applications. In this fast-moving digital world, many businesses rely on critical applications and keeping them available, even though upgrading the underlying platform is important.

You have seen that a no-downtime upgrade of the platform is possible if you have set up the cluster in a high availability configuration to start with. However, the platform does not guarantee the availability of your applications unless you have designed and deployed your application in a fault-tolerant manner. One factor is to make sure that you have multiple instances of your application running and that the application is designed to handle the termination of these instances gracefully.

With that taken into account, we have seen the important considerations for upgrading your cluster in a way that the platform itself does not cause downtime for your application. We looked at the upgrade process for the master nodes as well as worker nodes separately. The key takeaway from this chapter is the principles underlined at various instances that you can apply for different kinds of Kubernetes clusters managed by different tools.

As mentioned at the beginning of the chapter, keeping your platform up to date is important to keep up with the latest developments in DevOps and enable your application development team to continue delivering new features to your end customers. With the skills acquired from this chapter, you should be able to handle the upgrade of your platform without causing disruption to your customers.

In the next chapter, we will discuss how to extend your Kubernetes platform with custom resources. Custom resources allow you to offer a Kubernetes native API experience for your own projects.

19

CUSTOM RESOURCE DEFINITIONS IN KUBERNETES

OVERVIEW

In this chapter, we will show how you can use **Custom Resource Definitions** (**CRDs**) to extend Kubernetes and add new functionality to your Kubernetes cluster. You will also learn how to define, configure, and implement a complete CRD. We will also describe various example scenarios where CRDs can be very helpful. By the end of this chapter, you will be able to define and configure a CRD and a **Custom Resource** (**CR**). You will also learn how to deploy a basic custom controller to implement the required functionality of the CR in your cluster.

INTRODUCTION

In previous chapters, we learned about different Kubernetes objects, such as Pods, Deployments, and ConfigMaps. These objects are defined and managed by the Kubernetes API (that is, for these objects, the API server manages their creation and destruction, among other operations). However, you may want to extend the functions provided by Kubernetes to provide a feature that is not shipped with standard Kubernetes, and that cannot be enabled by the built-in objects provided by Kubernetes.

To build these functionalities on top of Kubernetes, we use **Custom Resources** (**CRs**). **Custom Resource Definitions** (**CRDs**) allow us to add a capability through which users can add custom objects to the Kubernetes server and use those CRs like any other native Kubernetes object. A CRD helps us to introduce our custom objects to the Kubernetes system. Once our CRD is created, it can be used like any other object in the Kubernetes server. Not only that, but we can also use the Kubernetes API, **Role-Based Access Control** (**RBAC**) policies, and other Kubernetes features for the CRs we have introduced.

When you define a CRD, it is stored in the Kubernetes configuration database (etcd). Think of CRDs as the definition of the structure of your custom object. Once a CRD is defined, Kubernetes creates objects that abide by the definition of the CRD. We call these objects CRs. If we were to compare this to the analogy of programming languages, CRD is the class and the CR is the instance of the class. In short, a CRD defines the schema of a custom object and a CR defines the desired state of an object that you would like to achieve.

CRs are implemented via a custom controller. We will take a closer look at custom controllers in the first topic of this chapter.

WHAT IS A CUSTOM CONTROLLER?

CRDs and CRs help you define the desired state for your CRs. There is a need for a component that makes sure that the state of the Kubernetes system matches the desired state as defined by the CR. As you have seen in earlier chapters, the Kubernetes components that do this are called controllers. Kubernetes comes up with many of these controllers whose job is to make sure that the desired state (for example, the number of replicas of Pods defined in a Deployment) is equal to the value defined in the Deployment object. In summary, a controller is a component that watches the state of resources through the Kubernetes API server and attempts to match the current state with the desired state.

The built-in controllers that are included in a standard setup of Kubernetes are meant to work with built-in objects such as Deployments. For our CRDs and their CRs, we need to write our own custom controllers.

THE RELATIONSHIP BETWEEN A CRD, A CR, AND A CONTROLLER

The CRD provides a way to define a CR, and custom controllers provide the logic to act on the CR objects. The following diagram summarizes the CRD, CR, and controller:

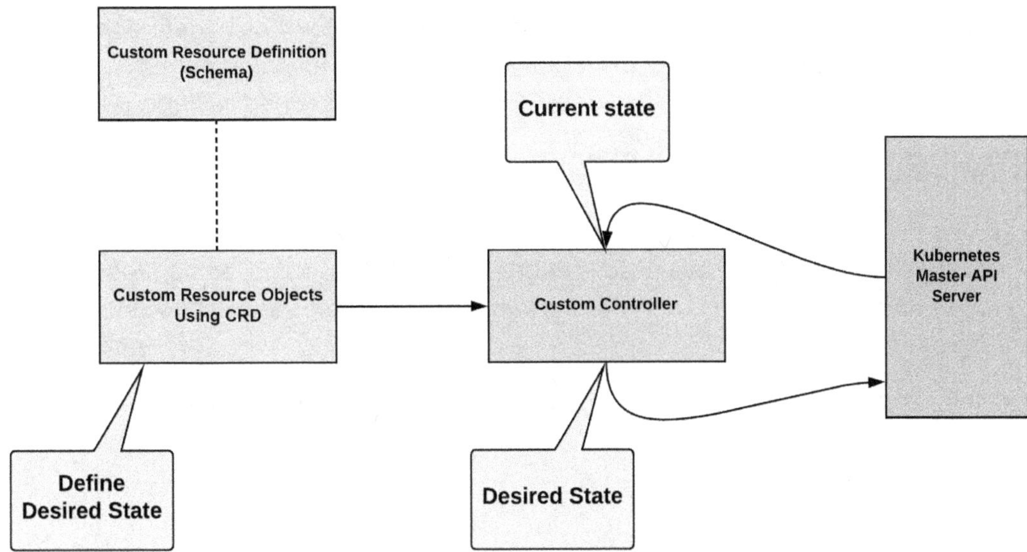

Figure 19.1: How CRD, CR, and controllers are tied together

As illustrated in the preceding diagram, we have a CRD, a custom controller, and the CR object that defines the desired state as per the CRD. There are three things to note here:

- The CRD is the schema that defines how the object will look. Every resource has a defined schema that tells the Kubernetes engine what to expect in a definition. Core objects such as **PodSpec** have schemas that are baked into the Kubernetes project.

> **NOTE**
>
> You can find the source code for PodSpec at this link: https://github.com/kubernetes/kubernetes/blob/master/pkg/apis/core/types.go#L2627

- The CR object, which is created based on the schema (the CRD), defines the desired state of the resource.
- The custom controller is the application that provides the functionality to bring the current state to the desired state.

Remember, the CRD is a way through which Kubernetes allows us to define the schema or definition for our CRs declaratively. Once our CRD (the schema) is registered with the Kubernetes server, a CR (the object) is defined as per our CRD.

STANDARD KUBERNETES API RESOURCES

Let's list all the resources and APIs that are available in the Kubernetes cluster. Recall that everything we have used is defined as an API resource, and an API is a gateway through which we communicate with the Kubernetes server to work with that resource.

Get a list of all the current Kubernetes resources by using the following command:

```
kubectl api-resources
```

You should see the following response:

```
$kubectl api-resources
NAME                              SHORTNAMES   APIGROUP                       NAMESPACED   KIND
bindings                                                                      true         Binding
componentstatuses                 cs                                          false        ComponentStatus
configmaps                        cm                                          true         ConfigMap
endpoints                         ep                                          true         Endpoints
events                            ev                                          true         Event
limitranges                       limits                                      true         LimitRange
namespaces                        ns                                          false        Namespace
nodes                             no                                          false        Node
persistentvolumeclaims            pvc                                         true         PersistentVolumeClaim
persistentvolumes                 pv                                          false        PersistentVolume
pods                              po                                          true         Pod
podtemplates                                                                  true         PodTemplate
replicationcontrollers            rc                                          true         ReplicationController
resourcequotas                    quota                                       true         ResourceQuota
secrets                                                                       true         Secret
serviceaccounts                   sa                                          true         ServiceAccount
services                          svc                                         true         Service
mutatingwebhookconfigurations                  admissionregistration.k8s.io   false        MutatingWebhookConfiguration
validatingwebhookconfigurations                admissionregistration.k8s.io   false        ValidatingWebhookConfiguration
customresourcedefinitions         crd,crds     apiextensions.k8s.io           false        CustomResourceDefinition
apiservices                                    apiregistration.k8s.io         false        APIService
controllerrevisions                            apps                           true         ControllerRevision
daemonsets                        ds           apps                           true         DaemonSet
deployments                       deploy       apps                           true         Deployment
replicasets                       rs           apps                           true         ReplicaSet
statefulsets                      sts          apps                           true         StatefulSet
tokenreviews                                   authentication.k8s.io          false        TokenReview
localsubjectaccessreviews                      authorization.k8s.io           true         LocalSubjectAccessReview
selfsubjectaccessreviews                       authorization.k8s.io           false        SelfSubjectAccessReview
selfsubjectrulesreviews                        authorization.k8s.io           false        SelfSubjectRulesReview
subjectaccessreviews                           authorization.k8s.io           false        SubjectAccessReview
horizontalpodautoscalers          hpa          autoscaling                    true         HorizontalPodAutoscaler
cronjobs                          cj           batch                          true         CronJob
jobs                                           batch                          true         Job
certificatesigningrequests        csr          certificates.k8s.io            false        CertificateSigningRequest
leases                                         coordination.k8s.io            true         Lease
events                            ev           events.k8s.io                  true         Event
daemonsets                        ds           extensions                     true         DaemonSet
deployments                       deploy       extensions                     true         Deployment
ingresses                         ing          extensions                     true         Ingress
networkpolicies                   netpol       extensions                     true         NetworkPolicy
podsecuritypolicies               psp          extensions                     false        PodSecurityPolicy
replicasets                       rs           extensions                     true         ReplicaSet
ingresses                         ing          networking.k8s.io              true         Ingress
networkpolicies                   netpol       networking.k8s.io              true         NetworkPolicy
runtimeclasses                                 node.k8s.io                    false        RuntimeClass
poddisruptionbudgets              pdb          policy                         true         PodDisruptionBudget
podsecuritypolicies               psp          policy                         false        PodSecurityPolicy
clusterrolebindings                            rbac.authorization.k8s.io      false        ClusterRoleBinding
clusterroles                                   rbac.authorization.k8s.io      false        ClusterRole
rolebindings                                   rbac.authorization.k8s.io      true         RoleBinding
roles                                          rbac.authorization.k8s.io      true         Role
priorityclasses                   pc           scheduling.k8s.io              false        PriorityClass
csidrivers                                     storage.k8s.io                 false        CSIDriver
csinodes                                       storage.k8s.io                 false        CSINode
storageclasses                    sc           storage.k8s.io                 false        StorageClass
volumeattachments                              storage.k8s.io                 false        VolumeAttachment
```

Figure 19.2: Standard Kubernetes API resources

In the preceding screenshot, you can see that the resources defined in Kubernetes have an **`APIGroup`** property, which defines what internal API is responsible for managing this resource. The **`Kind`** column lists the name of the resources. As we have seen earlier in this topic, for standard Kubernetes objects such as Pods, the schema or definition of a Pod object is built into Kubernetes. When you define a Pod specification to run a Pod, this could be said to be analogous to a CR.

For every resource, there is some code that can take action against the resource. This is defined as a group of APIs (**`APIGroup`**). Note that multiple API groups can exist; for example, a stable version and an experimental version. Issue the following command to see what API versions are available in your Kubernetes cluster:

```
kubectl api-versions
```

You should see the following response:

```
$kubectl api-versions
admissionregistration.k8s.io/v1beta1
apiextensions.k8s.io/v1beta1
apiregistration.k8s.io/v1
apiregistration.k8s.io/v1beta1
apps/v1
apps/v1beta1
apps/v1beta2
authentication.k8s.io/v1
authentication.k8s.io/v1beta1
authorization.k8s.io/v1
authorization.k8s.io/v1beta1
autoscaling/v1
autoscaling/v2beta1
autoscaling/v2beta2
batch/v1
batch/v1beta1
certificates.k8s.io/v1beta1
coordination.k8s.io/v1
coordination.k8s.io/v1beta1
events.k8s.io/v1beta1
extensions/v1beta1
networking.k8s.io/v1
networking.k8s.io/v1beta1
node.k8s.io/v1beta1
policy/v1beta1
rbac.authorization.k8s.io/v1
rbac.authorization.k8s.io/v1beta1
scheduling.k8s.io/v1
scheduling.k8s.io/v1beta1
storage.k8s.io/v1
storage.k8s.io/v1beta1
v1
```

Figure 19.3: Various API groups and their versions

In the preceding screenshot, note that the **apps** API group has multiple versions available. Each of these versions may have a different set of features that is not available in other groups.

WHY WE NEED CUSTOM RESOURCES?

As stated earlier, CRs provide a way through which we can extend the Kubernetes platform to provide functionalities that are specific to certain use cases. Here are a few use cases where you will encounter the use of CRs.

EXAMPLE USE CASE 1

Consider a use case in which you want to automate the provisioning of a business application or a database onto the Kubernetes cluster automatically. Abstracting away the technical details, such as configuring and deploying the application, allows teams to manage them without having an in-depth knowledge of Kubernetes. For example, you can create a CR to abstract the creation of a database. Thus, users can create a database Pod by just defining the name and size of the database in a CRD, and the controller will provision the rest.

EXAMPLE USE CASE 2

Consider a scenario where you have self-serving teams. Your Kubernetes platform is used by multiple teams and you would like the teams to provision namespaces and other resources by themselves. In this case, you want teams to define the total CPU and memory they need for the workloads, as well as default limits for a Pod. You can create a CRD and teams can create a CR with the namespace name and other parameters. Your custom controllers would create the resources they need and associate the correct RBAC policies for each team. You can also add additional functionality, such as a team being restricted to three environments. The controller can also generate audit events and record all the activities.

EXAMPLE USE CASE 3

Let's say you are an administrator of a development Kubernetes cluster where developers come and test their application. The problem you are facing is that the developers left the Pods running and have moved on to new projects. This may create a resource issue for your cluster.

In this chapter, we will build a CRD and a custom controller around this scenario. A solution that we can implement is to delete the Pod after a certain amount of time has passed following their creation. Let's call this time **podLiveForThisMinutes**. A further requirement is to have a configurable way of defining **podLiveForThisMinutes** for each namespace, as different teams may have different priorities and requirements.

We can define a time limit per namespace and that would provide the flexibility to apply controls on different namespaces. To implement the requirements defined in this example use case, we will define a CRD that allows two fields – a namespace name and the amount of time to allow the Pods to run (**podLiveForThisMinutes**). In the rest of this chapter, we will build a CRD and a controller that will allow us to achieve the functionality mentioned here.

> **NOTE**
>
> There are other (better) ways to implement the preceding scenario. In the real world, a Kubernetes **Deployment** object would recreate the Pod if the Pod had been created using the **Deployment** resource. We have chosen this scenario to keep the example simple and easy to implement.

HOW OUR CUSTOM RESOURCES ARE DEFINED

To come up with a solution for *Example Use Case 3* in the previous section, we have decided that our CRD will define two fields, as mentioned in the preceding example. To accomplish this, our CR object will look as follows.

```
apiVersion: "controllers.kube.book.au/v1"
kind: PodLifecycleConfig
metadata:
  name: demo-pod-lifecycle
spec:
  namespaceName: crddemo
  podLiveForThisMinutes: 1
```

The preceding specification defines our target object. As you can see, it looks just like normal Kubernetes objects, but the specifications (the **spec** section) are defined as per our requirements. Let's dig a bit deeper into the details.

APIVERSION

This is the field required by Kubernetes to group objects. Note that we put the version (**v1**) as part of the group key. This grouping technique helps us keep multiple versions of our object. Consider whether you want to add a new property without affecting existing users. You can just create a new group with **v2**, and an object definition with both versions — **v1** and **v2** — can exist at the same time. Because they are separated, it allows different versions of different groups to evolve at a different rate.

This approach also helps if we want to test new features. Say we want to add a new field to the same object. Then, we could just change the API version and add the new field. Thus, we can keep the stable version separate from the new, experimental version.

KIND

This field mentions a specific type of object in a group defined by **apiVersion**. Think of **kind** as the name of the CR object, such as **Pod**.

> **NOTE**
>
> Do not confuse this with the name of the object that you create using this specification, which is defined in the **metadata** section.

Through this, we can have multiple objects under one API group. Imagine you are about to create an awesome functionality that would require multiple different types of objects to be created. You can have multiple objects using the **Kind** field under the same API group.

SPEC

This field defines the information needed to define the specification of the object. The specification contains information that defines the desired state of our resource. All the fields that describe the characteristics of our resource go inside the **spec** section. For our use case, the **spec** section contains the two fields that we need for our CR - **podLiveForThisMinutes** and **namespaceName**.

NAMESPACENAME AND PODLIVEFORTHISMINUTES

These are the custom fields that we want to define. **`namespaceName`** will contain the name of the target namespace, and **`podLiveForThisMinutes`** will contain the time (in minutes) that we want the Pod to be active for.

THE DEFINITION OF A CRD

In the previous section, we showed the different components of a CR. However, before we define our CR, we need to define a schema, which governs how the CR would be defined. In the following exercise, you will define the schema or the CRD for the resource mentioned in the *How Our Custom Resources Are Defined* section.

Consider this example CRD, which we will use in the following exercise. Let's understand the important bits of the CRD by observing the following definition:

`pod-normaliser-crd.yaml`

```
apiVersion: apiextensions.k8s.io/v1beta1
kind: CustomResourceDefinition
metadata:
  name: podlifecycleconfigs.controllers.kube.book.au
spec:
  group: controllers.kube.book.au
  version: v1
  scope: Namespaced
  names:
    kind: PodLifecycleConfig
    plural: podlifecycleconfigs
    singular: podlifecycleconfig
 #1.15 preserveUnknownFields: false
  validation:
    openAPIV3Schema:
      type: object
      properties:
        spec:
          type: object
          properties:
            namespaceName:
              type: string
            podLiveForThisMinutes:
              type: integer
```

Now, let's look at various components of this CRD:

- **apiVersion** and **kind**: These are the API and the resource for the CRD itself and are provided by Kubernetes for the CRD definition.
- **group** and **version**: Think of an API group as a set of objects that are logically related to one another. These two fields define the API group and the version of our CR, which will then be translated into the **apiVersion** field of our CR, defined earlier in the previous section.
- **kind**: This field defines the **kind** of our CR, defined earlier in the *How Our Custom Resources Are Defined* section.
- **metadata/name**: The name must match the **spec** fields, and the format is a combination of two fields – that is, **<plural>.<group>**.
- **scope**: This field defines whether the CR will be namespace-scoped or cluster-scoped. By default, the CR is cluster-scoped. We have defined it as namespace-scoped here.
- **plurals**: These are plural names to be used in the Kubernetes API server URL.
- **openAPIV3Schema**: This is the schema that is defined based on the OpenAPI v3 standards. It refers to the actual fields/schema of our CR. A schema is something that defines what fields are available in our CR, the names of the fields, and the data types for them. It basically defines the structure of the **spec** field in our CR. We have used the **namespaceName** and **podLiveForMinutes** fields in our CR. You can see this in *step 2* of the following exercise.

It is interesting to know that the component of the API server that serves the CRs is called **apiextensions-apiserver**. When kubectl requests reach the API server, it first checks whether the resource is a standard Kubernetes resource, such as a Pod or a Deployment. If the resource is not a standard resource, then **apiextensions-apiserver** is invoked.

EXERCISE 19.01: DEFINING A CRD

In this exercise, we will define a CRD, and in the next exercise, we will create a CR for the defined CRD. The definition of the CRD is stored in the Kubernetes etcd server. Remember that the CRD and CR are just definitions, and until you deploy a controller that is associated with your CRs, there is no functionality attached to the CRD/CR. By defining a CRD, you are registering a new type of object with the Kubernetes cluster. After you define the CRD, it will be accessible via the normal Kubernetes API and you can access it via Kubectl:

1. Create a new namespace called **crddemo**:

    ```
    kubectl create ns crddemo
    ```

    This should give the following response:

    ```
    namespace/crddemo created
    ```

2. Now, we need to define a CRD. Create a file named **pod-normaliser-crd.yaml** using the following content:

    ```
    apiVersion: apiextensions.k8s.io/v1beta1
    kind: CustomResourceDefinition
    metadata:
      name: podlifecycleconfigs.controllers.kube.book.au
    spec:
      group: controllers.kube.book.au
      version: v1
      scope: Namespaced
      names:
        kind: PodLifecycleConfig
        plural: podlifecycleconfigs
        singular: podlifecycleconfig
      #1.15 preserveUnknownFields: false
      validation:
        openAPIV3Schema:
          type: object
          properties:
            spec:
              type: object
              properties:
                namespaceName:
                  type: string
    ```

```
          podLiveForThisMinutes:
            type: integer
```

3. Using the definition from the previous step, create the CRD using the following command:

```
kubectl create -f pod-normaliser-crd.yaml -n crddemo
```

You should see the following response:

```
$kubectl create -f pod-normaliser-crd.yaml -n crddemo
customresourcedefinition.apiextensions.k8s.io/podlifecycleconfigs.controllers.kube.book.au created
```

Figure 19.4: Creating our CRD

4. Verify that the CR is registered with Kubernetes using the following command:

```
kubectl api-resources | grep podlifecycleconfig
```

You should see the following list of resources:

```
podlifecycleconfigs  controllers.kube.book.au    true  PodLifecycleConfig
```

Figure 19.5: Verifying whether the CR has been registered with Kubernetes

5. Verify that the API is available in the Kubernetes API server by using the following command:

```
kubectl api-versions | grep controller
```

You should see the following response:

```
controllers.kube.book.au/v1
```

In this exercise, we have defined a CRD, and now, Kubernetes will be able to know what our CR should look like.

Now, in the following exercise, let's create a resource object as per the CRD we defined. This exercise will be an extension of the previous exercise. However, we have separated them because CRD objects can exist on their own; you don't have to have a CR paired with a CRD. It may be the case that a CRD is provided by some third-party software vendor, and you are only required to create the CR. For example, a database controller provided by a vendor may already have a CRD and the controller. To use the functionality, you just need to define the CR.

Let's proceed to make a CR out of our CRD in the following exercise.

EXERCISE 19.02: DEFINING A CR USING A CRD

In this exercise, we will create a CR as per the CRD defined in the previous exercise. The CR will be stored in the etcd datastore as a normal Kubernetes object, and it is served by the Kubernetes API server – that is, when you try to access it via Kubectl, it will be handled by the Kubernetes API server:

> **NOTE**
>
> You will only be able to perform this exercise after successfully completing the previous exercise in this chapter.

1. First, make sure that there is no CR for the **podlifecycleconfigs** type. Use the following command to check:

```
kubectl get podlifecycleconfigs -n crddemo
```

   If there is no CR, you should see the following response:

```
No resources found.
```

   If there is a resource defined, you can delete it using the following command:

```
kubectl delete podlifecycleconfig <RESOURCE_NAME> -n crddemo
```

2. Now, we have to create a CR. Create a file named **pod-normaliser.yaml** using the following content:

```
apiVersion: "controllers.kube.book.au/v1"
kind: PodLifecycleConfig
metadata:
  name: demo-pod-lifecycle
  # namespace: "crddemo"
spec:
  namespaceName: crddemo
  podLiveForThisMinutes: 1
```

3. Issue the following command to create the resource from the file created in the previous step:

```
kubectl create -f pod-normaliser.yaml -n crddemo
```

You should see the following response:

```
$kubectl create -f pod-normaliser.yaml -n crddemo
podlifecycleconfig.controllers.kube.book.au/demo-pod-lifecycle created
$
```

Figure 19.6: Creating our CR

4. Verify that it is registered by Kubernetes by using the following command:

```
kubectl get podlifecycleconfigs -n crddemo
```

You should see the following response:

```
NAME                  AGE
demo-pod-lifecycle    48s
```

Note that we are using normal kubectl commands now. This is a pretty awesome way to extend the Kubernetes platform.

We have defined our own CRD and have created a CR against it. The next step is to add the required functionality for our CR.

WRITING THE CUSTOM CONTROLLER

Now that we have a CR in our cluster, we will proceed to write some code that *acts* upon it to achieve the purpose of the scenario we set out in the *Why We Need Custom Resources* section.

> **NOTE**
>
> We will not teach the actual programming for writing the Go code for our controller since that is beyond the scope of this book. However, we will provide you with the programming logic required for *Example Use Case 3*.

Let's imagine that our custom controller code is running as a Pod. What would it need to do to respond to a CR?

1. First, the controller has to be aware that a new CR has been defined/removed in the cluster to get the desired state.
2. Second, the code needs a way to interact with the Kubernetes API server to request the current state and then ask for the desired state. In our case, our controller has to be aware of all the pods in a namespace and the time when the Pods have been created. The code can then ask Kubernetes to delete the Pods if the allowed time is up for them, as per the CRD. Please refer to the *Example Use Case 3* section to refresh your memory on what our controller would be doing.

The logic for our code can be visualized using the following diagram:

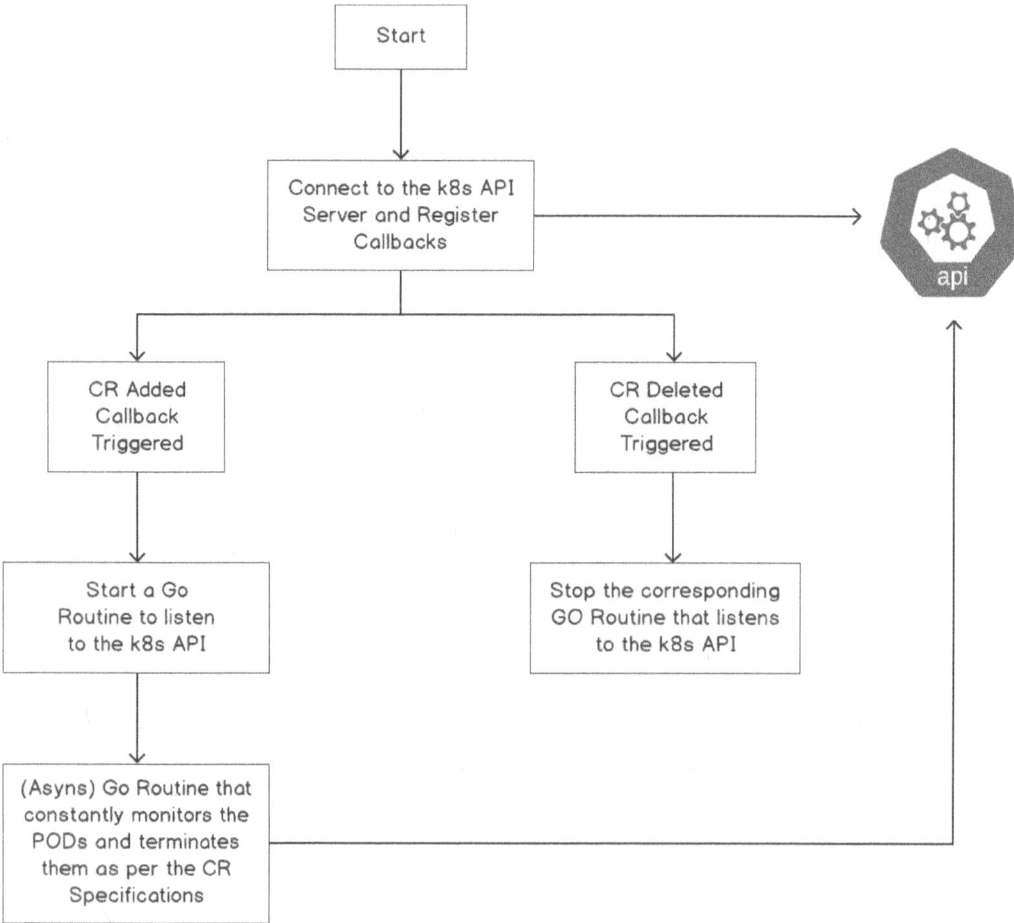

Figure 19.7: Flowchart describing the logic for a custom controller

If we were to describe the logic as simple pseudocode, it would be as follows:

1. Fetch all the new CRs that have been created for our custom CRD from the Kubernetes API server.
2. Register callbacks in case CRs are added or deleted. The callbacks would be triggered each time a new CR is added or deleted in our Kubernetes cluster.
3. If the CR is added to the cluster, the callback will create a sub-routine that continuously fetches the list of Pods in the namespace defined by the CR. If the Pod has been running for more than the time specified, it will be terminated. Otherwise, it will sleep for a few seconds.
4. If the CR is deleted, the callback will stop the sub-routine.

THE COMPONENTS OF THE CUSTOM CONTROLLER

As mentioned earlier, explaining in detail how custom controllers are built is beyond the scope of this book, and we have provided a fully working custom controller to suit the needs of *Example Use Case 3*. Our focus is to make sure that you can build and execute the controller to understand its behavior and that you are comfortable with all the components involved.

Custom controllers are components that provide functionality against a CR. To provide this, a custom controller would need to understand what a CR is meant for and its different parameters, or the *structural schema*. To make our controller aware of the schema, we provide the details about our schema to the controller through a code file.

Here is an excerpt of the code for the controller that we have provided:

types.go

```
type PodLifecycleConfig struct {

    // TypeMeta is the metadata for the resource, like kind and apiversion
    meta_v1.TypeMeta `json:",inline"`

    // ObjectMeta contains the metadata for the particular object like labels
    meta_v1.ObjectMeta `json:"metadata,omitempty"`

    Spec PodLifecycleConfigSpec `json:"spec"`
}

type PodLifecycleConfigSpec struct{
    NamespaceName   string `json:"namespaceName"`
    PodLiveForMinutes int `json:"podLiveForThisMinutes"`
}
...
type PodLifecycleConfigList struct {
    meta_v1.TypeMeta `json:",inline"`
    meta_v1.ListMeta `json:"metadata"`

    Items []PodLifecycleConfig `json:"items"`
}
```

You can find the complete code at this link: https://packt.live/3jXky9G.

As you can see, we have defined the **`PodLifecycleConfig`** structure as per our example of the CR provided in the *How Our Custom Resources Are Defined* section. It is repeated here for easier reference:

```
apiVersion: "controllers.kube.book.au/v1"
kind: PodLifecycleConfig
metadata:
  name: demo-pod-lifecycle
  # namespace: "crddemo"
spec:
  namespaceName: crddemo
  podLiveForThisMinutes: 1
```

Note that in **types.go**, we have defined objects that can hold the full definition of this example spec. Also, notice in **types.go** that **namespaceName** is defined as **string** and **podLiveForThisMinuets** is defined as **int**. This is because we are using strings and integers for these fields, as you can see in the CR.

The next important function of the controller is to listen to events from the Kubernetes system that are related to the CR. We are using the **Kubernetes Go** client library to connect to the Kubernetes API server. This library makes it easier to connect to the Kubernetes API server (for example, for authentication) and have predefined request and response types to communicate with the Kubernetes API server.

> **NOTE**
>
> You can find more details about the Kubernetes Go client library at this link: https://github.com/kubernetes/client-go.

However, you are free to use any other library or any other programming language to communicate with the API server over HTTPS.

You can see how we have implemented it by checking the code at this link: https://packt.live/3ieFtVm. First, we need to connect to the Kubernetes cluster. This code is running inside a Pod in the cluster, and it will need to connect to the Kubernetes API server. We need to give sufficient rights to our Pod to connect to the master server, which will be covered in the activity later in this chapter. We will use RBAC policies to achieve this. Please refer to *Chapter 13, Runtime and Network Security in Kubernetes*, to get a refresher on how Kubernetes implements RBAC functionality.

Once we are connected, we use the **SharedInformerFactory** object to listen to Kubernetes events for the controller. Think of the event as a way for us to be notified by Kubernetes when a new CR is created or deleted. **SharedInformerFactory** is a way provided by the Kubernetes Go client library to listen to events generated by the Kubernetes API server. A detailed explanation of **SharedInformerFactory** is beyond the scope of this book.

The following snippet is an excerpt from our Go code to create **SharedInformerFactory**:

main.go

```
// create the kubernetes client configuration
    config, err := clientcmd.BuildConfigFromFlags("", "")
    if err != nil {
        log.Fatal(err)
    }
    // create the kubernetes client
    podlifecyelconfgiclient, err := clientset.NewForConfig(config)
    // create the shared informer factory and use the client
       to connect to kubernetes
    podlifecycleconfigfactory :=
      informers.NewSharedInformerFactoryWithOptions
        (podlifecyelconfgiclient, Second*30,
    informers.WithNamespace(os.Getenv(NAMESPACE_TO_WATCH)))
```

You can find the complete code at this link: https://packt.live/3lXe3FM.

Once we have connected to the Kubernetes API server, we need to register to be notified whether our CR has been created or deleted. The following code performs this action:

main.go

```
// fetch the informer for the PodLifecycleConfig
podlifecycleconfiginformer :=
  podlifecycleconfigfactory.Controllers().V1().
  PodLifecycleConfigs().Informer()
// register with the informer for the events
podlifecycleconfiginformer.AddEventHandler(
...
//define what to do in case if a new custom resource is created
        AddFunc: func(obj interface{}) {
...
// start the subroutine to check and kill the pods for this namespace
            go checkAndRemovePodsPeriodically(signal, podclientset, x)
        },
//define what to do in case if a  custom resource is removed
        DeleteFunc: func(obj interface{}) {
```

You can find the complete code at this link: https://packt.live/2ZjtQoy.

Note that the preceding code is an extract from the full code, and the snippet here is modified slightly for better presentation in this book. This code is registering callbacks to the Kubernetes server. Notice that we have registered for **AddFunc** and **DeleteFunc**. These will be called once the CR has been created or deleted, and we can write custom logic against that. You can see that for **AddFunc**, a Go subroutine is being called. For every new CR, we have a separate subroutine to keep on watching for the Pods created in the namespace. Also, note that **AddFunc** will print out **A Custom Resource has been Added** to the logs. You may also have noticed that in **DeleteFunc**, we have closed the **signal** channel, which will flag the Go subroutine to stop itself.

ACTIVITY 19.01: CRD AND CUSTOM CONTROLLER IN ACTION

In this activity, we will build and deploy custom controllers, CRs, and CRDs. Note that the coding required for building the custom controller is beyond the scope of this book and a ready-made code is provided in the code repository to facilitate the Deployment of a working controller.

We will create a new CRD that can take two fields - a **podLiveForThisMinutes** field, which defines the time (in minutes) for a Pod to be allowed to run before it is killed, and the **namespaceName** field, which defines which namespace these rules will be applied to.

We will create a new CR as per the CRD. Also, we will create a new Kubernetes role that allows this new CRD to be queried from the Kubernetes API server. We will then show you how to associate the newly created role with the ServiceAccount named **default**, which is the default ServiceAccount that a Pod will use when we run it in the namespace named **default**.

Generally, we build a custom controller that provides logic against the CRD we created. We will just use the code packaged as a container and deploy it as a Pod. The controller will be deployed as a normal Pod.

At the end of the activity, to test our controller, you will create a simple Pod and verify whether our custom controller can delete the Pod.

Activity Guidelines:

1. Delete the existing **crddemo** namespace and create a new one with the same name.
2. Get the code and the **Dockerfile** for creating the controller using the following command:

```
git clone  https://github.com/PacktWorkshops/Kubernetes-Workshop.git

cd Chapter19/Activity19.01/controller
```

3. Create a CRD with the following fields.

   The metadata should contain the following:

```
name: podlifecycleconfigs.controllers.kube.book.au
```

   The **OpenAPIV3Schema** section should contain the following **properties** settings:

```
openAPIV3Schema:
  type: object
  properties:
    spec:
      type: object
      properties:
        namespaceName:
          type: string
        podLiveForThisMinutes:
          type: integer
```

4. Create a CR that allows Pods to live for 1 minute in the **crddemo** namespace.
5. Create a Role that allows the following permissions for the specified API resources:

```
rules:
- apiGroups: ["controllers.kube.book.au"]
  resources: ["podlifecycleconfigs"]
  verbs: ["get", "list", "watch"]
- apiGroups: [""]
  resources: ["pods"]
  verbs: ["get", "watch", "list", "delete"]
```

6. Using a RoleBinding object, associate this new Role with the **`default`** ServiceAccount in the **`crddemo`** namespace.
7. Build and deploy the controller Pod using the **`Dockerfile`** provided in *step 2*.
8. Create a Pod that runs for a long time using the **`k8s.gcr.io/busybox`** image in the **`crddemo`** namespace.

   Watch the Pod created in the previous step and observe whether it is being terminated by our controller. The expected result is that the Pod should be created, and then it should be automatically terminated after about a minute, as in the following screenshot:

```
$kubectl get pods -w -n crddemo
NAME                           READY   STATUS      RESTARTS   AGE
crd-server-77ffcff74b-wdk9j    1/1     Running     0          3m19s
long-running-pod-example       0/1     Pending     0          0s
long-running-pod-example       0/1     Pending     0          0s
long-running-pod-example       0/1     ContainerCreating   0          0s
long-running-pod-example       1/1     Running             0          4s
long-running-pod-example       1/1     Terminating         0          61s
long-running-pod-example       1/1     Terminating         0          61s
```

Figure 19.8: The expected output of Activity 19.01

> **NOTE**
>
> The solution to this activity can be found at the following address: https://packt.live/304PEoD.

ADDING DATA TO OUR CUSTOM RESOURCE

In the previous activity, you created a CRD and CR. We mentioned earlier that once we define our CR, we can query them using standard kubectl commands. For example, if you would like to see how many CRs of the **`PodLifecycleConfig`** type have been defined, you can use the following command:

```
kubectl get PodLifecycleConfig -n crddemo
```

You will see the following response

```
NAME                   AGE
demo-pod-lifecycle     8h
```

Note that it only shows the name and age of the object. However, if you issue a command for a native Kubernetes object, you will see a lot more columns. Let's try that for Deployments:

```
kubectl get deployment -n crddemo
```

You should see a response similar to this:

```
NAME          READY    UP-TO-DATE    AVAILABLE    AGE
crd-server    1/1      1             1            166m
```

Notice the additional columns that Kubernetes has added, which provide way more information about the objects.

What if we want to add more columns so that the output of the preceding command shows more details for our CRs? You are in luck, as Kubernetes provides a way to add additional information columns for the CRs. This is useful for displaying the critical values of each type of custom object. This can be done using additional data defined in the CRD. Let's see how we can do that in the following exercise.

EXERCISE 19.03: ADDING CUSTOM INFORMATION TO THE CR LIST COMMAND

In this exercise, you will learn how to add custom information to the CR list obtained by means of the **kubectl get** command:

> **NOTE**
>
> You will only be able to perform this exercise after successfully completing *Activity 19.01, CRD and Custom Controller in Action*.

1. Let's define another CRD with additional columns. Create a file named **pod-normaliser-crd-adv.yaml** with the following content:

```
apiVersion: apiextensions.k8s.io/v1beta1
kind: CustomResourceDefinition
metadata:
  name: podlifecycleconfigsadv.controllers.kube.book.au
spec:
  group: controllers.kube.book.au
  version: v1
  scope: Namespaced
  names:
    kind: PodLifecycleConfigAdv
```

```
    plural: podlifecycleconfigsadv
    singular: podlifecycleconfigadv
  #1.15 preserveUnknownFields: false
  validation:
    openAPIV3Schema:
      type: object
      properties:
        spec:
          type: object
          properties:
            namespaceName:
              type: string
            podLiveForThisMinutes:
              type: integer
  additionalPrinterColumns:
  - name: NamespaceName
    type: string
    description: The name of the namespace this CRD is applied
      to.
    JSONPath: .spec.namespaceName
  - name: PodLiveForMinutes
    type: integer
    description: Allowed number of minutes for the Pod to
      survive
    JSONPath: .spec.podLiveForThisMinutes
  - name: Age
    type: date
    JSONPath: .metadata.creationTimestamp
```

Notice how we have a new section named **additionalPrinterColumns**. As the name suggests, this defines additional information for your resource. The two important fields of the **additionalPrinterColumns** sections are as follows:

- **name**: This defines the name of the column to be printed.

- **JSONPath**: This defines the location of the field. Through this path, the information is fetched from the resources and is displayed in the corresponding column.

2. Now, let's create this new CRD using the following command:

```
kubectl create -f pod-normaliser-crd-adv.yaml -n crddemo
```

You will see the following output:

```
$kubectl create -f pod-normaliser-crd-adv.yaml -n crddemo
customresourcedefinition.apiextensions.k8s.io/podlifecycleconfigsadv.controllers.kube.book.au created
```

Figure 19.9: Creating our modified CRD

3. Once we have created the CRD, let's create the object for the CRD. Create a file named **pod-normaliser-adv.yaml** with the following content:

```
apiVersion: "controllers.kube.book.au/v1"
kind: PodLifecycleConfigAdv
metadata:
  name: demo-pod-lifecycle-adv
  # namespace: "crddemo"
spec:
  namespaceName: crddemo
  podLiveForThisMinutes: 20
```

Now, the fields in the **spec** section should be visible in the list obtained by the **kubectl get** command, similar to native Kubernetes objects.

4. Let's create the CR defined in the previous step using the following command:

```
kubectl create -f pod-normaliser-adv.yaml -n crddemo
```

This should give the following response:

```
$kubectl create -f pod-normaliser-adv.yaml -n crddemo
podlifecycleconfigadv.controllers.kube.book.au/demo-pod-lifecycle-adv created
```

Figure 19.10: Creating our CR

5. Now, let's issue the **`kubectl get`** command to see whether additional fields are displayed:

```
kubectl get PodLifecycleConfigAdv -n crddemo
```

You should see the following information displayed for our object:

```
NAME                       NAMESPACENAME   PODLIVEFORMINUTES   AGE
demo-pod-lifecycle-adv     crddemo         20                  27m
```

You can see that the additional fields are displayed and we now have more information about our CRs.

In this exercise, you have seen that we can associate additional data for our CR while querying it via the Kubernetes API server. We can define the field names and the path for the data for the fields. This resource-specific information becomes important when you have many resources of the same type, and it is also useful for the operations team to better understand the resources defined.

SUMMARY

In this chapter, you learned about custom controllers. As per the Kubernetes glossary, a controller implements a control loop to watch the state of the cluster through the API server and makes changes in an attempt to move the current state toward the desired state.

Controllers can not only watch and manage user-defined CRs, but they can also act on resources such as Deployments or services, which are typically part of the Kubernetes controller manager. Controllers provide a way to write your own code to suit your business needs.

CRDs are the central mechanism used in the Kubernetes system to extend its capability. CRDs provide a native way to implement custom logic for the Kubernetes API server that satisfies your business requirements.

You have learned about how CRDs and controllers help provide an extension mechanism for the Kubernetes platform. You have also seen the process through which you can configure and deploy custom controllers on the Kubernetes platform.

As we come to the end of our journey, let's reflect on what we have achieved. We started with the basic concepts of Kubernetes, how it is architected, and how to interact with it. We were introduced to Kubectl, the command-line tool to interact with Kubernetes, and then later, we saw how the Kubernetes API server works and how to communicate with it using **`curl`** commands.

The first two chapters established the fundamentals of containerization and Kubernetes. Thereafter, we learned the basics of kubectl – the Kubernetes command center. In *Chapter 04, How to Communicate with Kubernetes (API Server)*, we looked at how kubectl and other HTTP clients communicate with the Kubernetes API server. We consolidated our learning by creating a Deployment at the end of the chapter.

From *Chapter 5, Pods*, through to *Chapter 10, ConfigMaps and Secrets*, we dug into concepts that are critical to understanding the platform and to start designing applications to run on Kubernetes. Concepts such as Pods, Deployments, Services, and PersistentVolumes enable us to use the platform to write fault-tolerant applications.

In the next series of chapters, stretching from *Chapter 11, Build Your Own HA Cluster*, to *Chapter 15, Monitoring and Autoscaling in Kubernetes*, we learned about installing and running Kubernetes on a cloud platform. This covered the installation of the Kubernetes platform in high availability (HA) configuration and how to manage network security in the platform. In this part of the book, you also looked at stateful components and how applications can use these features of the platform. Lastly, this section talked about monitoring your cluster and setting up autoscaling.

Finally, in this last part, starting from *Chapter 16, Kubernetes Admission Controllers*, we began learning about advanced concepts such as how you can apply custom policies using admission controllers. You have also been introduced to the Kubernetes scheduler, a component that decides where your application will be running in the cluster. You learned how to change the default behavior of the scheduler. You have also seen how CRDs provide a way to extend Kubernetes, which can be useful not only to build custom enhancements but also as a way for third-party providers to add functionality to Kubernetes.

This book serves as a good launchpad to get started with Kubernetes. You are now equipped to design and build systems on top of Kubernetes that can bring cloud-native experience to your organization. Although this is the end of this book, it is only the beginning of your journey as a Kubernetes professional.

INDEX

H

I

J

K

L

M

N

O

P

R

S

T

U

V

W

www.ingramcontent.com/pod-product-compliance
Lightning Source LLC
LaVergne TN
LVHW081326050326
832903LV00024B/1048

* 9 7 8 1 8 3 8 8 2 0 7 5 6 *